INTERNATIONALE VEREINIGUNG
FÜR THEORETISCHE UND ANGEWANDTE LIMNOLOGIE

INTERNATIONAL ASSOCIATION
OF THEORETICAL AND APPLIED LIMNOLOGY

ASSOCIATION INTERNATIONALE
DE LIMNOLOGIE THÉORIQUE ET APPLIQUÉE

Mitteilungen · Communicat

No. 24

David Dudgeon and Paul K. S. Lam

Inland waters of tropical Asia and Australia: Conservation and management

With 83 figures and 101 tables in the text

Edited for the Association by A. Sládečková

World List Abbreviation: *Mitt. int. Ver. Limnol.*
DIN-Norm-Abkürzung: *Mitt. Internat. Verein. Limnol.*

E. Schweizerbart'sche Verlagsbuchhandlung
(Nägele u. Obermiller) · Stuttgart 1994

ISSN: 0538-4680
ISBN: 3 510 52024 6

Printed in Germany

Contents

Mitt. Internat. Verein. Limnol.	24	1–3	Stuttgart, Februar 1994

Inland waters of tropical Asia and Australia: Conservation and management

David Dudgeon and Paul K. S. Lam

Introduction

The rate of degradation of tropical inland-water habitats cannot fail to alarm limnologists everywhere. The search for economic advancement in less developed countries in general, and several Southeast Asian cities in particular, is putting a severe strain on many habitats which are threatened already. Traditionally, research efforts aimed at addressing these problems have tended to concentrate on the effects of various types of pollutants on streams, rivers and lakes, but more recently inland water systems are increasingly subject to unprecedented, large-scale habitat alterations or degradation (e.g. deforestation of upland watersheds, and impoundment of streams and rivers to form reservoirs). Over and above this, the introduction of exotic species into inland waterways has posed significant problems for native flora and fauna. These activities are proceeding at astonishingly high rates although – in many cases – the potential impacts have not been assessed thoroughly.

On the political front, many policy makers are of the view that the environment can be sacrificed 'temporarily' for economic growth and that the environment can be restored once extra financial resources become available as a result of a strong economy. Such a philosophy towards conservation is evident in many tropical Asian countries and, to a lesser degree, in Australia. This approach to environmental management contains at least three important assumptions. Firstly, that there is an inevitable trade-off between economic success and environmental conservation; secondly, that environmental degradation is not an irreversible process; and thirdly, that when we want to restore the environment we will be able to accomplish it. On the question of possible conflicts between economics and conservation, it seems that such problems will be resolved successfully only by the combined effort of natural and social scientists, the participation of local people, and the cooperation of decision-makers. In most cases, when decisions are made on environmental matters, participation by interested parties falls far short of this ideal level of consultation.

Our need to explore the above issues and the necessity to protect threatened habitats are hampered by our lack of knowledge of tropical systems. Like almost all other areas of scientific research, work on tropical inland waters lags behind investigations of their temperate counterparts. Obviously, such a phenomenon cannot be attributed to a paucity of research material in the tropics, but rather to historical reasons, a shortage of money, barriers to communication and the free flow of information, and – in a few cases – a lack of expertise. Judging by the outcome of the 1992 Earth Summit in Brazil, this shortage of research funding is likely to continue in the foreseeable future, and hence tropical ecologists must try even harder to make use of their limited resources to attain maximum useful output. Of course, this may be achieved through careful planning of one's own research, but we believe that it is also important to increase communication and cooperation amongst researchers in different research areas and geographic zones. By doing so, we can tackle timely problems with the most appropriate methods, and appreciate the wider implications of our research findings in the context of protection and management of tropical inland waters. In particular, we need to examine more closely the structure and function of tropical systems and focus on approaches which will shed light on both the similarities and dissimilarities in patterns and processes operating in tropical and temperate latitudes.

We often expected ecological principles useful in explaining temperate processes to work equally well in the tropical environment. Although some phenomena may be universal, there is no *a priori* reason why tropical systems in general, and tropical inland waters in particular, should behave in the same way as their temperate counterparts. Instead of treating the study of tropical inland waters as merely an extension of temperate limnology, we should view tropical systems with fresh eyes, appreciate their uniqueness, and try not to squeeze them into ecological frameworks (such as the River Continuum Concept) adopted by temperate limnologists. Our requirement for limnological theories and concepts

0538-4680/94/0024-0001 $ 0.75

relevant to the tropics is made even more urgent by the need for management and protection of tropical inland waters. Perhaps due to the general lack of information, tropical limnologists have not been forthcoming in formulating broad-based theories that may help in our understanding of the workings of tropical inland waters. Even if such theories lack an underpinning of extensive, long-term data sets, they will be valuable if they generate testable predictions and especially if they can be used to inform habitat management strategies.

Despite the need to study tropical inland waters in their geographical context, developments in temperate freshwater studies have undoubtedly provided us with indications as to the possible directions in which we should be heading. For example, the recent application of experimental field manipulations to hypothesis testing by temperate freshwater investigators is a powerful approach, but this has yet to be taken up widely by workers in the tropics. The strength of aquatic microcosm technology as a research tool in environmental toxicology in the tropics also deserves detailed examination. In addition, an appreciation of the powers and limitations of both reductionist and holistic approaches in ecology is necessary. The systems approach has been useful in unravelling some of the important patterns and processes in complex lotic and lentic systems. The large-scale, multidisciplinary and long-term investigation on the forest ecosystem at Hubbard Brook, U.S.A., provides an excellent example of an integrative study of aquatic ecology and habitat management, but no studies of tropical drainage basins have been undertaken in comparable scope and depth.

Another research approach to temperate limnologists has concerned the impact of environmental stressors, such as toxic chemicals, on the biochemistry and physiology of individual organisms, and the extent to which such influences affect population dynamics and community processes. In particular, there have been recent attempts to quantify key life-history components and determine the quantitative relationships and interactions among these parameters in individual organisms exposed to environmental stresses under the general framework of evolutionary-ecological theories and resource-allocation principles. Conceivably, such information on the basic processes through which individual organisms function can be successfully translated into population or ecosystem levels through the building of predictive models. It is likely that a combination of approaches involving sub-organismic and organismic systems, as well as population and ecosystem processes, would be helpful in formulating better management strategies for large-scale problems in the tropics such as habitat degradation, environmental pollution and so on.

This book arose from contributions to a conference on 'Conservation and Management of Tropical Inland Waters' held at the University of Hong Kong in September 1991. After submitted papers had gone through a process of refereeing, revisions and editing, the contents of the resulting volume had evolved towards a focus upon tropical Asia and Australia. We hope that this publication will provide insight into some of the work done or being carried out in relation to the conservation and management of inland water systems in the above regions, and function as a catalyst for future cooperation and collaboration. In particular we hope that recommendations for future action and/or new approaches to conservation and management considered in these papers and the ensuing discussions (summarized in the final chapter) will provide a basis for formulation or re-evaluation of policies and practises relating to tropical inland waters.

Acknowledgements

The preparation and planning for this volume began in July 1990 and continued through 1991, when the conference on 'Conservation and Management of Tropical Inland Waters' was held in September at The University of Hong Kong. Work continued into 1992 when manuscripts arising from the conference were refereed, revised and edited, and then collated for publication. During this extended period, a considerable amount of assistance was requested from – and given by – individuals and organizations.

Financial support for travel and subsistence allowances for conference delegates were received from the Asian Wetland Bureau (AWB), the Beijing-Hong Kong Academic Exchange Centre, the International Lake Environment Committee (ILEC), Societas Internationalis Limnologiae (S.I.L.), UNESCO and UNESCO (ROSTSEA), The University of Hong Kong (Academic Staff Interchange Scheme), the Wei Lun Foundation Ltd, and the K.C. Wong Education Foundation Ltd. We are particularly grateful to R. Jaensch and D. Parish of AWB, M. Ando of ILEC, F. Fournier and K. Kartawinata of UNESCO, R.C. Petersen Jr. and Boonyajiat Seangwan of the Mekong Committee, and especially R.G. Wetzel of SIL for their interest in and support of the conference and proceedings.

In the Zoology Department of The University of Hong Kong, which was host to the conference, essential logistical assistance was given by Cecilia Chan, Sylvia Chan, Y.P. Lee, D.W. Kwan, Shirley Yu, Bonnie To, Tong Ming So and especially Rebecca Fung. Professor D.K.O. Chan placed the resources of the department at our disposal and thus facilitated conference planning and organization. Undergraduate and postgraduate students of the Department of Zoology who provided particular help were Gary Ades, Anjali Chandrasekar-Rao, Michael Lau, Tony Miu, Alice Ng, Graham Reels, Eve Wong and Lew Young. The University of Hong Kong Estates Office, the Finance Office, Robert Black College hall of residence, and the Information Office provided assistance with numerous matters, and the Vice Chancellor of the University, Professor Wang Gungwu, hosted a welcoming reception for conference delegates. The World Wide Fund for Nature Hong Kong was instrumental in arranging a visit to the Mai Po Nature

Reserve for conference delegates, and the Hong Kong Tourist Association provided valuable documentation and advice.

All papers included in this volume were refereed; ANGELA ARTHINGTON, DONALD BAIRD, MALCOLM BEVERIDGE, STEVEN BIGGER, W.Y.B. CHANG, SATISH CHOY, H.H. COSTA, K.H.G.M. DE SILVA, WIM GIESEN, S.-C. HO, CHRIS HUMPHREY, RO LOWE-MCCONNELL, MIKE O'CONNOR, RICHARD PEARSON and BILL WILLIAMS are thanked particularly for their efforts in this regard. Dr. A. SLÁDEČKOVÁ of S.I.L., served as executive editor for this volume and is thanked for her efforts in this regard.

Finally, we are grateful to our spouses – May and Lydia – for their forebearance and support during the conference planning and its aftermath.

The Editors:

DAVID DUDGEON, Department of Zoology, Hui Oi Chow Science Building, The University of Hong Kong, Pokfulam Road, Hong Kong.

Paul K.S. Lam, Department of Environmental Management, Victoria University of Technology, St. Albans, Victoria 3021, Australia.

Mitt. Internat. Verein. Limnol.	24	5–10	Stuttgart, Februar 1994

The role of ecological science in addressing wetland conservation and management in the tropics

Patrick J. Dugan

Abstract

With growing understanding of the importance of wetland ecosystems, has come increasing support for their conservation and sustainable utilization. Yet with the growing demand for wetland management has come greater appreciation of our limited understanding of the functioning of these ecosystems. This has in turn led to an upsurge of interest in wetlands research. Nevertheless, in a time of limited economic resources, the conservation community is increasingly asked to focus upon priorities and to channel funding towards these alone. This has led to more careful analyses of the pressures leading to wetland loss and the approaches that are needed to address these. This paper reviews these pressures and the mechanisms giving rise to them, and on the basis of this analysis examines research priorities in the 1990s.

Introduction

For much of recorded history many human societies on all continents have been closely dependent upon wetland ecosystems for the agricultural base of their economy and culture. Many of these have exploited these resources without altering substantially the natural characteristics of the ecosystems. For example, in many African floodplains integrated systems of agriculture, fisheries, pastoral production, and harvesting of wild products, often involving many different ethnic groups, were pursued under a complex set of access rules agreed by local tribal leaders (e. g. Skinner 1987). Others, such as the intensive rice production systems upon which the empires of Angkor and the Indus Valley were built, altered the natural ecosystem, but replaced this with a sustainable system of agricultural production while still providing an important habitat for wildlife (McNeely & Wachtel 1991).

Large-scale conversion of wetlands to irrigated agriculture, pasture, and aquaculture, and reclamation for urban and industrial development, is a comparatively recent phenomenon, growing in Europe and the United States over the 18th and 19th centuries to reach its peak in the second half of the 20th century. Since the end of the Second World War, a period of unprecedented economic growth, billions of dollars have been spent in altering river systems, building dams, and converting wetlands over much of the world. The development of this 'conversion culture' is reflected in the 1982 publication *Polders of the World* (van Dam & van Diepen 1982). In mapping the potential polder lands across the globe, this analysis neatly mapped the world's major wetland systems more effectively than any conservation study had yet managed to do.

Yet even as *Polders of the World* was published, awareness of the environmental and social costs of wetland loss had grown sufficiently for wetlands to be ranked second only to tropical forests amongst the international priorities for ecosystem conservation. And already in 1971, the Ramsar Convention was adopted in Iran. As the first of the global conventions concerned with the conservation of natural resources the Ramsar Convention has done much to draw the attention of governments worldwide to the importance of wetlands, the need for their conservation and sustainable use, and the importance of international collaboration in achieving this.

With this growing awareness of the importance of wetland resources has also come greater appreciation of the constraints in their utilization. Wetland conservation efforts today must confront higher population densities than at any time in the past, and substantially increased demands upon these resources, many of which are degraded. At the same time the decision-making process is frequently centralized in national capitals, and unable to take account of the understanding of people that have used their resources sustainably. There is therefore a major, and ever-increasing, demand for information which can provide the basis for wetland management.

This modern demand for improved information on wetlands throws into sharp focus the evolution that has occurred in the information used to manage wetlands as human society's relationship with wetlands has changed. For much of the past, management was based upon empirical knowledge applied through a gradual process which tested new ideas slowly. Subsequently, in the age of large scale wetland conversion, wetlands were dominated by engineering technology which was generally applied in the pursuit of single purpose goals. Today, the focus has shifted once more to centre upon the need for well structured arguments against sectoral use, based upon a sound scientific understanding of ecosystems, and the multiple benefits which can be generated through integrated use. In the face of this demand there

0538-4680/94/0024-0005 $ 1.50

is an urgent need to identify clear priorities for investment of available resources in scientific study of wetlands. The purpose of this paper is to examine these priorities in the light of the need for integrated management of wetlands.

Wetlands: managing complex ecosystems

Wetlands are complex ecosystems which result from the interaction of four biological and physical components: soils, water, plants and animals. The central principle of an integrated approach to wetland management is that this should recognize the interrelationships between these biological and physical components and seek to maximize the benefits that can be obtained from sustainable multiple use. However, only rarely are these components managed in an effectively-integrated manner. Rather emphasis tends to be upon maximizing benefit from a single product obtained from one resource. Today there is growing recognition that much of this investment in single purpose use of wetlands has led to the destruction of these natural ecosystems and deprived the rural poor of natural resources which could have served a broad-based development process, rather than one slanted for the urban centres. For example, dams to provide power for domestic needs and development of industry have often disrupted floodplain agriculture, reduced the area of floodplain pastures, and devastated fisheries (Scudder 1989). Similarly, intensive investment in coastal agriculture and aquaculture has in many areas destroyed the potential for low-input agriculture, while reducing the catch of coastal fisheries (Burbridge et al. 1988). Such development policies are now widely criticized as having neglected the millions of small-farm and fishing families whose rising disposable income could drive development. To rectify this neglect, small-scale development approaches building on the productivity of the natural ecosystem are now being developed.

The critical need today is to recognize the interlinkages and benefits to be obtained from integrated management of fish, trees, water, and wildlife. This will however require integration of management institutions such as departments of forestry, fisheries, and agriculture, while developing a perspective which looks beyond individual wetland sites, to take account of the hydrological basin and coastal zone within which the wetlands lie and which maintain the flow of nutrients and water upon which the wetlands depend for their productivity. Such an approach should also consider the downstream benefits of wetland conservation such as flood control, and maintenance of water quality, thus emphasizing further the central role that wetlands can play in regulating the hydrological cycle. While this requires major institutional change, it also needs to be accompanied by substantial policy change.

To add to this complexity we need to recognize that management of wetland systems also requires us to address factors whose interaction with the biological and physical resources governs the pressures upon wetlands and thus lie at the heart of successful long-term management. The first of these factors is economics. National economic and agricultural policies frequently determine the rate at which wetlands are converted. Thus in Europe wetland drainage has been stimulated by the artificially high prices paid for a number of crops under the EEC's Common Agricultural Policy. For example EEC wheat prices were 40% to 60% above world market prices over the period 1978–80. As a result, the conversion of lowland wet-grazing meadows for growing winter wheat became a very profitable financial investment for individual farmers. In the USA price supports for sugar, together with strategic economic considerations, have favoured agricultural conversion of the Everglades marsh in Florida.

A more complex example is provided by northern Nigeria where, despite efforts by the states of Borno, Kano, and Bauchi to conserve the natural floodplain of the Hadejia River system, agricultural and economic policies are spurring conversion. In response to falling oil prices and the need to save hard currency, the federal government banned all wheat imports as of January 1987. At the same time a 50% subsidy on inputs and equipment for wheat cultivation was made available while, as a result of the import ban, the producer price for domestic wheat rose by 1,000% between 1986 and 1989. By the 1988–89 growing season in Kano State alone, some 30,000 ha had been converted for wheat cultivation. While this wheat boom will generate a profit for individual farmers, the benefits will be short-lived. The sandy soils are predicted to degrade rapidly under irrigated wheat cultivation, thus compromising long-term options for rural development in the region (Kimmage 1991).

In much of South-East Asia, where in some countries economic growth has risen above 10% per annum in recent years, wetland loss is frequently the direct consequence of this rapidly expanding economy. For example, the rapid rise in demand for land for urban and industrial development generates an economic momentum which renders invalid many conservation arguments based upon the multiple values of these natural systems. Thus, even when it can be shown that development of aquaculture in coastal wetland systems will yield little long-term economic value, private developers continue to invest in drainage and conversion in expectation that even if aquaculture fails, the land is worth more as wasteland upon which one can build houses, than as wetland. While such calculus ignores the public benefits of these systems, it is nevertheless a central force and one that needs to be addressed by any comprehensive wetland conservation programme. Specifically it argues for an aggressive conservation policy, based upon establishment of exclusive protected areas in priority sites, in those countries where the economic pressures have favoured the rise of a group of wealthy entrepreneurs who have no interest in sustainable use and are concerned only with short-term personal profit.

The second major system which determines how best to manage wetland resources is formed by the social, cultural, and institutional context within which wetland management is carried forward. As discussed previously, many traditional societies have developed complex systems to regulate access to resources. These can in many instances provide the basis for multiple use under present conditions, yet where control over all natural resources is vested in agencies of central government which are often based hundreds of kilometers away from the resources concerned, such locally-based management of natural resources is severely hampered. In addition, many of the technical staff responsible for administering government policy often have little knowledge of the ecosystems for which they are responsible. In designing and establishing planning and management frameworks for long-term conservation and use of wetland resources, special care needs to be taken in order to ensure that these are pursued within an appropriate institutional arrangement. This must combine the central role of government and the necessary supporting legislation with the capacity to vest power in the local resource users and draw upon traditional knowledge as appropriate.

Identifying research priorities

The message of the preceding paragraphs is that the wetland conservation challenge is certainly complex. It requires action at many levels. However, in a time of limited economic resources, the conservation community is increasingly asked to focus upon priorities, and to channel funding towards these alone. This has led to more careful analysis of the pressures leading to wetland loss and the approaches needed to address these. Within this context, wetland research needs to be focused upon those areas where detailed research will make a significant contribution to wetland conservation. There are two major fields where such a contribution is especially important: Policy and management.

Policy

The principal forces driving government policies such as those on land use, on agricultural subsidies, and on water pricing, are economic. There is therefore an urgent need to effect detailed analyses which can demonstrate the multiple public benefits of wetland conservation, as opposed to the public cost and more limited private benefits of wetland conversion. Such research can be carried out independently from management projects, but it should be focused upon clear priorities. These include functional and economic analyses, and studies of ecological coupling and biological diversity.

a) Functional analyses

The multiple ecological and hydrological functions performed by wetlands are well documented (Dugan 1990). However, the majority of the detailed examples available come from a limited number of industrialized, temperate countries, and are therefore of only limited value in discussion with governments in other regions which are convinced of the economic potential of conversion. This is especially important in developing nations, where many governments see exploitation of their rich natural resources, including wetlands, as providing the basis for rapid economic development. There is therefore a major need to increase substantially the quantity of high quality research documenting the ecological and hydrological functions of these tropical wetlands, and the dependence of rural people upon them. Special priority needs to be given to those systems which are under greatest pressure, such as coastal wetlands and floodplains. In addition, the critical role of wetland conservation in management of the water cycle merits increasing attention. Wherever possible, such research should be linked to specific policy initiatives. For example, in Uganda analysis of the role played by Papyrus in absorbing excess nutrients and other pollutants, and of the fisheries potential of freshwater swamps, were carried out in support of the National Wetland Policy being prepared by the Ministry of Environment Protection. In this way the research had a direct and immediate impact upon policy.

b) Economic analysis

More cooperative research between ecologists, hydrologists, geographers, social scientists and economists needs to be carried out in order to provide information on the full economic value of integrated multiple use of wetlands. As is the case for functional analysis, these investigations should be designed to feed into the appropriate decision-making process. Special attention should be given to quantifying the combined economic value of the diverse functions of individual wetlands, and increasing the quality of information on high-value functions such as fisheries support. The latter is especially important in many developing nations where coastal fisheries are an important source of foreign exchange earnings and both coastal and inland fisheries provide the principal source of animal protein for many rural societies.

c) Ecological coupling

Many wetlands are lost through a gradual process of degradation and conversion of the component habitats, rather than large scale, rapid, conversion. For example, fringing mangroves or salt marsh are often the first targets for coastal reclamation because of their relative proximity to existing infrastructure and due to a widespread perception that these fringing habitats are less valuable than the core of the wetland. However, detailed studies of the specific ecological linkages between different parts of the ecosystem have demonstrated that these fringing areas can play a central role in the life cycle of many wetland species of conservation concern. For example, studies in the Laguna de Terminos (Mexico) have shown that a range of mangrove habitats are important for supporting both rare and commercially important nektonic species, and that the use of different habitats coincides with the periods of highest productivity of each (Yáñez-Arancibia et al. 1980).

d) Biological diversity

While wetlands do not typically support exceptionally high species diversity, many do support large concentrations of individual species at specific times of year. The large flocks of waterfowl which frequent most major wetland systems are amongst the most important groups and have been the major driving force behind wetland conservation in the industrialized world. However, as pressures upon wetlands have increased, so the intensity of the debate between developers and waterfowl conservationists has intensified, and the need for detailed information on the carrying capacity and interdependence of many wetlands used by migratory waterfowl has increased. Detailed understanding of the foraging ecology of the bird species concerned is frequently required to underpin such debates.

Management

On the basis of experience in designing and implementing wetland management projects in many countries in Africa, Asia and Latin America, IUCN has identified four management stepts (Dugan 1990). Research is an integral component of all of these.

a) Ecological study

Following general identification of problems such as floodplain degradation, or mangrove clearance, thorough ecological research should wherever possible be carried out in order to provide a detailed understanding of the extent, severity, and precise character of the environmental problems. By accumulation of quantitative data, such research can lay the basis for a monitoring programme.

b) Socioeconomic study

Many of the ecological studies described reveal that wetland resources are being degraded as a result of a series of human factors such as overgrazing, over-fishing, and unsustainable agricultural practice. In some cases this is a result of limited understanding of the resource and its capacity to absorb certain levels of use. More often however, wetland degradation occurs at the hands of rural communities who are perfectly aware of many of the consequences of their actions, but through poverty, poor social status, or other factors are obliged to pursue practices which are not sustainable. In order to influence these processes, such wetland management efforts need to be based upon detailed socioeconomic studies that can provide an understanding of the changing rural economy and thus provide an insight into the precise reasons why people degrade their resource base. Such research may take many months and ideally should be carried over a minimum of a full annual cycle. Similar studies of how resource use is administered provide insights into the ways in which changes in institutional structures and legislation can provide incentives to people to manage resources more effectively: e.g. legalization of community-managed forests, or local harvesting of wildlife. Wetland management will not be successful in the long-term without this institutional support.

c) Management measures and institutional support

While many rural communities have managed wetland resources sustainably based upon empirical knowledge, most modern societies no longer possesses this. Thus although the ecological and socioeconomic studies described provide the basis upon which management measures can be designed, these will be experimental and require both a cautious approach to application and careful evaluation of the results. This experimental management is an integral part of most wetland conservation projects. Such experiments could be designed to improve resource management by determining the levels at which exploitation will be sustainable. For example in Zambia, where community-based harvesting of wildlife forms one component of an integrated management plan for the Kafue floodplain, detailed understanding of the carrying capacity and population dynamics of the Lechwe antelope (*Kobus leche*) population is essential to determine safe levels of harvest. Other studies may involve attempts to design and apply new or improved techniques of resource use. Thus in Central America, where intensive harvesting of mangroves is leading to degradation, an integrated silviculture scheme for the resources requires better understanding of the precise growth characteristics of the species concerned.

In all situations, the ecological research needs to be complemented by research into post-harvest technologies designed to improve the market value of the resource. For example, research into fish processing techniques such as smoking or drying are required in many situations. Similarly, research into the most efficient techniques for production of tannins from mangrove bark is required if this is to lead to an increased economic output from, and thus help decrease pressure upon, the mangroves of Central America. In Uganda, detailed studies of the growth potential of Papyrus and the impact of regular harvesting have been required in designing a sustainable harvest scheme for this important wetland resource. Other studies, including review of locally-adapted agricultural practices, can assist rural producers to diversify their economy, thus relieving pressure upon wetland ecosystems.

In advocating an increase in research on wetland management, a word of caution is appropriate. Pursuit of this approach must avoid the assumption that such research is the only source of guidance on management solutions. Often, the scientific community advocates an academic approach to management, emphasizing the role of modern science with the customary urban confidence in the ability of technology and science to provide all the answers. Such an approach isolates the scientist from the other experts – the farmers, fishermen and herders – who possess a wealth of knowledge of the ecosystems which they use. Care must be taken to interact and learn from these wetland experts who have not received conventional scientific training, but have the benefit of years of experience in using wetland ecosystems.

d) Monitoring

The experimental nature of most management underlines the need for all these activities to be accompanied by careful monitoring designed to determine the impact of the approaches developed upon the natural resource base, as well as the communities dependent upon these, and to modify the management as appropriate. If the project can be adjusted in the light of experience and changing conditions, a truly-effective system of sustainable use can be designed. Such programmes should monitor both socioeconomic as well as biological and physical parameters, and be designed to allow data to be collected on a long-term basis.

In the absence of appropriate information, it is not always possible to ask for detailed research before management must begin. Accordingly management will frequently need to be based upon elementary biological, physical, social and economic principles and pursued conservatively. In conjunction with this conservative approach, a careful baseline survey of the resource base and the principal uses, combined with an experimental and therefore adjustable approach to resource management, can lay the basis for effective long-term management.

Concluding remarks

There is clearly much to do if wetland science is to meet the growing needs of wetland conservation. However to have a lasting impact, investment in scientific research will need to be targeted at priorities. This requires careful consideration of the factors leading to wetland loss, and the courage to identify those issues which are likely to have the biggest impact upon the policy and management processes, rather than those which are of the most fundamental interest to science. By bringing together the findings of a diverse group of researchers and managers from many countries in the Asian and Australian tropics, this volume – *Inland Waters of Tropical Asia and Australia: Conservation and Management* – may play an important role in building better understanding of priorities – and, above all, of the integrated approach that is needed – in the science of wetland conservation. The challenge now is to move beyond the papers and to apply this philosophy in the research activities of our institutions.

Acknowledgements

I am indebted to Peter Burbridge for numerous discussions on the requirements for integrated management of wetland systems and to Jean-Yves Pirot for comments on a draft of the paper.

References

Burbridge, P. R., Koesoebiono, H., Dirchl, I. & Patton, B. 1988: Coastal Zone Management in the strait of Malacca. – *Proceedings of a Symposium on Environmental Research and Coastal Zone Management in the Strait of Malacca, 11–13 November, 1985. Medan, Indonesia:* 317 pp. – Dalhousie University, Canada.

Dugan, P. J., 1990: Wetlands Conservation: a Review of Current Issues and Required Action: 96 pp. – IUCN, Gland, Switzerland.

Kimmage, K. (1991): Small scale irrigation initiatives in Nigeria: the problems of equity and sustainability. – *Applied Geography* **11**: 5–20.

McNelly, J. A. & Wachtel, P. S., 1991: The Soul of the Tiger. Searching for Nature's Answers in Southeast Asia: 390 pp. – Oxford University Press, Oxford.

Scudder, T., 1989: River basin projects in Africa. – *Environment* **31**: 4–32.

Skinner, J., 1987: Rapport d'activités, projet de création d'une "Forêt villageoise" à Bouna, arrondissement de Kona, 5ème Région, Mali: 15 pp. – IUCN, Gland, Switzerland.

van Dam, A. J. & Van Diepen, C. A., 1982: Polders of the World: the Soils of the Flat Wetlands of the World – their Distribution and their Agricultural Potential: 47 pp. – International Soil Museum, Wageningen, The Netherlands.

Yanez-Arancibia, A. F., Amezcua Linares & Day, J. W., 1980: Fish community structure and function in Terminos Lagoon, a tropical estuary in the Southern Gulf of Mexico. – In: Kennedy, V. (ed.): Estuarine Perspectives: 465–482. – Academic Press, New York.

Author's addresses:

Director of Regional Affaires, IUCN – The World Conservation Union, Ave du Mt Blanc, CH-1196 Gland, Switzerland.

present address: IUCN, Rue Mauverney 28, CH-1196 Gland, Switzerland.

Mitt. Internat. Verein. Limnol.	24	11–16	Stuttgart, Februar 1994

The need for multi-scale approaches to the conservation and management of tropical inland waters

David Dudgeon

Abstract

Many problems faced by those who have to conserve or manage the biota of tropical inland waters arise from the different scales at which problems have to be addressed. Conservation of migratory wetland birds, for example, must take account of geographic distribution, the incidence of habitable wetlands within a species' range, the extent of usable habitat within each wetland, and seasonal changes in bird distribution. In other cases, an aquatic-centred approach to conservation will not maintain ecosystem integrity if we ignore terrestrial linkages which, in any case, are poorly understood. For example, we need to know more about the importance of adult aquatic insects in terrestrial food chains, and the effect that insectivorous birds and bats have on aquatic productivity.

Multi-scale approaches are essential for effective conservation of tropical rivers. These habitats have well-defined longitudinal and lateral dimensions, and the results of investigations are sensitive to the spatial and temporal scales addressed. Seasonal inundation of floodplains and migrations of potadromous fish which are characteristic of Southeast Asian rivers are used as examples of the need for multi-scale approaches to conservation and management of tropical inland waters. Limnologists must now consider how best to undertake the research needed to underpin appropriate management strategies.

Introduction

Recent environmental concerns have compelled scientists to consider problems of ever-increasing scale. The global spectres of acid rain, climatic warming and ozone depletion remind us that political boundaries offer no protection from the consequences of environmental misuse. Limnologists have long been aware of this fact. (It should be added that limnology is used herein to refer to the study of inland water habitats – ponds, streams, salt lakes, etc. – and their associated biota.) The extent of tropical latitudes and the wide range of sizes of tropical inland water habitats must influence the thinking of those charged with their conservation and management. Large rivers such as the Mekong and water bodies as vast as Lake Victoria do not respect international borders; they oblige us to think of ecological processes on a scale large enough to understand how changes to all parts of their expansive terrestrial drainage basins affect the aquatic biota. The hydrologic cycle also ensures that air pollution in one place can have serious consequences on rainwater chemistry and freshwater biota in distant localities. At the other extreme of scale, limnologists or conservationists may be concerned with endemic species in small springs or seeps or with unique populations that are confined to a few rocky outcrops within a larger lacustrine environment, as exemplified by colour varieties of cichlid fishes in Lake Malawi (Lowe-McConnell 1987). In the latter case we must work on more than one scale: at the microhabitat (rock outcrop) scale and at a larger scale relevant to the whole lake. Thus the architecture of an individual outcrop might determine how many breeding pairs can be supported at a given site, but the water chemistry of that part of the lake could affect the outcrop's suitability as a spawning site.

The challenges of scale that we face are magnified by the especially bewildering array of habitats found in the tropics. For example, the discharge regime of a stream in a humid equatorial forest differs from one in the seasonal monsoonal tropics and is quite unlike that of an intermittent stream in the arid tropics. The timing and predictability of rain filling a temporary pool will likewise vary among regions, as will the extent of water-level fluctuations in a lake. Herein, examples of the biota of freshwater systems in Hong Kong and elsewhere in tropical Asia are used to exemplify the management difficulties associated with the extent of their spatial and temporal dimensions. The general points made about scale here are not new (see Minshall 1988, Ward 1989, Farmer & Adams 1991, Fisher 1991) but their repetition in the specific context of tropical limnology is important given the wide variety and distribution of tropical habitats. It must be emphasized that the diversity of tropical inland waters and the proportion of the Earth's surface over which they are dispersed is much greater than that of their temperate counterparts.

The need for multi-scale approaches

The interaction of small and large scales, and the need for multi-scale approaches, is exemplified by species distributions. A species with a wide geographic range may not be prevalent over the

0538-4680/94/0024-0011 $ 1.50

whole of its distribution, and individuals might be confined to a few sites within their range. Where the geographic range covers several countries, it is important to ensure that uncoordinated activity does not eliminate species through destruction of suitable habitats, such destruction proceeding under the assumption that local elimination will not affect adversely a species with a wide geographic range.

Wetland birds present a clear example of this problem. The Spoonbill sandpiper (*Eurynorhynchus pygmaeus*) breeds in northeast Asia, but winters in Southeast Asia. Passage migrants ringed at Mai Po Marshes – Hong Kong's only wetland of international significance – have been recaptured in Australia. It is likely that destruction or drainage of wetlands at critical points along this route would reduce the number of migrants significantly. Elsewhere, the lateral lakes of the Yangtze floodplain (Dongting Lake and especially Poyang Lake) are important wintering grounds of waterfowl such as White-fronted geese (*Anser albifrons*), the rare White and Black storks (*Ciconia ciconia* and *C. nigra*), the Japanese crane (*Grus japonensis*), and 98% of the world population of the endangered Siberian white crane (*G. leucogeranus*) (ZHAO et al. 1990). However, siltation, diking and land reclamation in recent years have reduced the size and depth of Dongting and Poyang Lakes. Almost 1.3 million acres of farmland have been created around Dongting Lake over the last century (VAN SLYKE 1988) and there have been associated problems of eutrophication (LIU 1984). Correlated with these changes has been a recent increase in the number of Oriental white storks (*Ciconia boyciana*, often considered a distinctive subspecies of *C. ciconia*) wintering in Hong Kong: 121 individuals overwintered at Mai Po Marshes in 1990 while only two birds had been recorded prior to that time. These observations suggest that there are few habitable sites for this endangered species within its extensive range. Similar considerations apply to Swinhoe's egret (*Egretta eulophotes*) – one of the rarest birds in the world – which may have its last stronghold in Southern China (COLLAR & ANDREW 1988).

Even within a potentially habitable site, considerations of scale are important: for example, the extent of reed beds may determine the availability of feeding or breeding sites for wetland birds and hence affect the conservation value of that area. Here a multi-scale approach to conservation will be appropriate, involving consideration of geographic distribution, wetland patches within geographic ranges, and the extent of reed beds or open water within these wetland patches.

Bats provide another example of the importance of scale in relation to tropical inland waters. Insectivorous bats – such as Daubenton's bat (*Myotis daubentonii*) – forage for aquatic-insect imagines over the surface of streams in Hong Kong and elsewhere (SWIFT et al. 1985, ADES 1990). One local bat (*Myotis ricketti*) has a diet comprised mainly of fish. The effect that bats have on energy flow in aquatic systems and the linkage between land and water is not known. Without such knowledge, our best option is to preserve the connection between bats and their aquatic prey. Conservation strategies must therefore include maintenance of the terrestrial roosting sites of bats, and take cognisance of the fact that these animals may undertake seasonal migrations. In this instance, an aquatic-centred approach to conservation will not maintain ecosystem integrity if we ignore terrestrial linkages and the importance that aquatic insects can play in terrestrial food chains (JACKSON & FISHER 1986, JACKSON & RESH 1989). Similar considerations apply to the use of aquatic insects as food by terrestrial birds such as warblers (BUSBY & SEALY 1979). Reversing our focus, it is also clear that an understanding of secondary production of aquatic insects must take account of the interactions and habitat conditions experienced by the terrestrial adults.

These examples suggest that a fragmented approach to conservation and management of inland waters – treating aquatic habitats as islands in a terrestrial environment – is myopic. Nor can we disregard the importance of large-scale processes, such as migrations and movement between feeding and breeding habitats which may traverse international boundaries. While it is fitting to expand our scale of attention and adopt multi-scale approaches to conservation and management, it is inappropriate to abandon small-scale work. Scientific understanding is often achieved by reductionist methods that involve dissecting a phenomenon down to finer levels of biological resolution. For example, pollution biologists or toxicologists may compare patterns of energy allocation by organisms experiencing different levels of stress. Because of the principle of compensation, higher expenditure in routine maintenance and metabolism will result in lower allocation to reproduction, scaling up ultimately to population- and community-level effects by way of a decline in recruitment and a change in the magnitude of interspecific interactions (e.g. decreased predation exerted upon prey by the affected population). We should continue to work at small scales in order to explain many phenomena, but in order to appreciate their consequences we must also look to higher levels of biological integration.

Multi-scale approaches: running waters

Running waters epitomize habitats which require the application of large- and multi-scale approaches to conservation and management. This is a result of the strong environmental gradients or axes that run downstream, from headwaters to mouth, and laterally (or transversally) from midstream to banks across riparian zones and flood plains (Ward 1989). Selection of the size of the sampling unit relative to the total sampling area of interest can influence profoundly perceptions of pattern and process in streams (Minshall 1988). The results of examining the factors affecting diversity of stream insects will vary depending upon whether one's approach is to take Surber samples from the centre of a single riffle only, or to include areas upstream, or to expand attention downwards to the hyporheic zone and laterally to encompass the riparian zone and soil water. As the extent of sampling scale increases, so we move towards a multifactor explanation for biological phenomena which requires formulation of more complex (but perhaps more viable) conservation and management strategies.

Multi-scale approaches are critical in understanding ecology of stream animals because of the range of factors influencing their community structure. Research in Hong Kong streams has shown that preference for different types of detrital food, periphyton biomass, substrate type, predation by fish, and riparian vegetation can all affect invertebrate distribution and abundance (Dudgeon 1982, 1988, 1990, 1991, Dudgeon & Chan 1992). These effects are unlikely to be additive in a simple manner. At a larger scale, drainage basin geology will influence water chemistry and the distribution of aquatic organisms.

The duration (temporal scale) of an investigation may also determine the conclusions that can be drawn from it. For example, declining stream flows during the dry season in Hong Kong alter the magnitude of predator effects (Dudgeon 1991) and may have other repercussions. This is significant because, with the possible exception of certain small equatorial streams, all rivers show a marked seasonality dominated by flow regime and/or temperature. With decreasing latitude the significance of temperature as a limiting factor declines generally and the role of discharge regime (determined largely by monsoonal rains) increases. The predictability of discharge regime and amplitude of fluctuations varies from place to place, reflecting local climate, the influence of typhoons or cyclones, and local landscape morphometry. On a broader temporal scale, the intensity of the monsoon will fluctuate from year to year causing variation in the intensity of disruption brought about by spates and modifying the extent and duration of floodplain inundation. Succession in the terrestrial environment following fire or logging will also affect allochthonous inputs to streams on a greater-than-annual time scale. It is the importance of these influences rather than convenience, the calendar year, or the duration of research grants which should set the time scales for our sampling strategies. Again, a mixed scale taking account of seasonal and longer-term changes will probably produce the most useful types of data. Directional changes – of the kind associated with gradual changes in temperature or acidification of precipitation – can be investigated only by long-term (large-scale) investigations. These environmental changes may bring about evolutionary changes in the biota of affected environments.

Investigations of longitudinal zonation along temperate rivers led to formation of the River Continuum Concept (RCC; Vannote et al. 1980) which makes predictions about production and community organization on a broad scale from headwaters to mouth in relation to watershed vegetation and geomorphological conditions. It incorporates different levels of biological integration including rates of community respiration and primary production, abundance of feeding groups, characteristics of detritus, and so on. Reservations have been expressed about the applicability of the RCC to different regions (e.g. Winterbourn et al. 1981), but it remains a useful and testable predictive model which could inform management strategies. At present, we have no complete studies of any tropical river of any size which would allow us to test the predictions of the RCC against nature, nor has there been any attempt to interpret the Concept in terms of river metabolism and fisheries. In almost no cases do we know what type of organisms occur in which habitat type, nor how much each habitat contributes to the productivity of the river as a whole.

The floodplains of many tropical rivers experience seasonal inundation which has important implications for aquatic productivity. We need a better understanding of this phenomenon – termed the flood-pulse system by JUNK et al. (1989) – because it typifies large tropical rivers. Year-to-year variations in the intensity of monsoonal rains affect the extent of floodplain inundation and hence the magnitude of land-water interactions and allochthonous inputs. Long-term studies are needed in this regard. Without a knowledge of the consequences of ecological 'crunch' times – for example, a year when the monsoonal rains are insufficient to inundate the floodplain – we will be in no position to predict the effect of management plans (such as controlling water flow) on river productivity.

Application of the RCC to tropical rivers, and decisions about the scale of investigation, are complicated by the fact that certain fish and shrimps use various habitats at different times in their lives and some of these habitats are inundated only for part of the year. In Southeast Asia, potamodromous fishes migrate upstream during the rainy season to spawn in flooded areas; the downstream migration occurs as river discharge falls upon the onset of the dry season and fishes gather in the river channel. Pelagic fishes that are generally planktivorous or piscivorous ('white fishes') cover a greater distance when migrating than bottom-dwelling 'black fishes'. The former swim upstream, while the latter – which feed on benthic organisms – are confined largely to the floodplain, making lateral movements between the main channel and fringes (SHIRAISHI 1970, WELCOMME 1979, PANTULU 1986).

One of the most impressive river migrants is the giant 3-m Mekong catfish, *Pangasianodon gigas*. It performs spectacular long-range journeys for spawning, travelling from the lower Mekong far upstream to Yunnan Province in China. Declining populations of this catfish have been attributed to overfishing and gradual environmental changes within the Mekong Basin during the last 50 years (SMITH 1945, PANTULU 1986). Attempts to manage or conserve the species face the difficulty of coordinating activities in different countries. In addition, little is known about the species' biology or habitat requirements during breeding or at other times. Another long-distance migrant, the giant cyprinid *Probarbus jullieni* is now endangered in Malaysia. There, population decline resulted from overfishing gravid individuals during upstream spawning migrations, and obstruction of migration routes by the construction of a large dam (the Chenderoh Dam on the Perak River) on one of the only two rivers that the species inhabits (ALFRED 1968, TAN 1980).

The importance of dams is not only that they are a barrier to fish migration but that they introduce serial discontinuity into the longitudinal gradients along rivers (WARD & STANFORD 1983). As well as the small-scale local effects of the barrier, larger-scale changes in flow and temperature regime downstream may remove important directive factors which stimulate breeding migrations. Once a migratory run has been eliminated, it is difficult to re-establish the fishery from other stocks, because local races are adapted to the specific suite of environmental characteristics unique to each river (in the same way that salmon return to spawn in the river where they hatched). Important changes occur also in the relationship between the temporal and spatial axes of river systems. Dams reduce the magnitude and extent of floodplain inundation, and change its frequency. They thereby diminish the extent of land-water interactions and change the trophic base of production. We do not have a good understanding of the consequences of these alterations, but we need the knowledge quickly. In most situations, this goal will not be attained by isolated individuals but by large (sometimes multi-national) teams. The Mekong Commission provides a model of the type of structure and organization that is required for a large river (CHOMCHAI 1987, PETERSEN & SKOGLUND 1990).

One thing is clear: if we wish to understand the ecology of lotic habitats we must not focus our efforts on one element of the system at the expense of others. The importance of lateral and longitudinal dimensions of river systems emphasizes the necessity for large-scale approaches (in time and space) to conservation and management of certain elements of the biota, while a multi-scale approach will be required in other cases.

There are no easy answers as to how multi-scale research can be undertaken or funded. Scientific kudos and rewards are generally received by workers exhibiting great individual effort and productivity; glory is less often dispensed to members of a team who combine to solve a difficult multi-scale problem. We might say that rewards are more likely to accrue to those who work successfully and rapidly on a small-scale problem for a short time, rather than on a large- or multi-scale problem for a long time. Limnologists are likely to agree that greater collaboration among individuals within and between countries is needed, but while this is easy to write it is hard to bring about and thus represents one of the major obstacles to the effective management and conservation of inland waters.

Acknowledgements

The ideas presented in this paper are not new. Similar suggestions have been made in other contexts by a variety of scientists. Sources have been acknowledged in the text as far as possible, and apologies are offered to those whose ideas have been adopted and not credited. Professor W. D. Williams is thanked for his constructive comments on a draft manuscript.

References

Ades, G., 1990: Bats of Hong Kong: 40 pp. – World Wide Fund For Nature, Hong Kong.

Alfred, E. R., 1968: Rare and endangered fresh-water fishes of Malaya and Singapore. – In: Talbot, L. M. & Talbot M. H. (eds.): Conservation in Tropical South East Asia: 325–331. – IUCN Publications New Series No. 10, Morges, Switzerland.

Busby, D. G. & Sealy, S. G., 1979: Feeding ecology of a population of nesting yellow warblers. – *Can. J. Zool.* **57**: 1670–1681.

Chomchai, P., 1987: The Mekong project: an exercise in regional cooperation to develop the lower Mekong basin. – In: Ali, M., Radosevich, G. E. & Ali Khan, A. (eds.): Water Resources Policy for Asia: 497–508. – A. A. Balkema Publishers, Boston.

Collar, N. J. & Andrew, P., 1988: *Birds to Watch.* ICBP Technical Publications Nr. 8., International Council for Bird Preservation, Cambridge, 304 pp.

Dudgeon, D., 1982: An investigation of physical and biological processing of two species of leaf litter in Tai Po Kau Forest Stream, New Territories, Hong Kong. – *Arch. Hydrobiol.* **96**: 1–32.

– 1988: The influence of riparian vegetation on macroinvertebrate community structure in four Hong Kong streams. – *J. Zool., Lond.* **216**: 609–627.

– 1990: Determinants of the distribution and abundance of larval Ephemeroptera (Insecta) in Hong Kong running waters. – In: Campbell, I. C. (ed.): Mayflies and Stoneflies: 221–232. – Kluwer Academic Publishers, Dordrecht.

– 1991: An experimental study of the effects of predatory fish on macroinvertebrates in an Hong Kong stream. – *Freshwat. Biol.* **25**: 321–330.

Dudgeon, D. & Chan, I. K. K., 1992: An experimental study of the influence of periphytic algae on invertebrate abundance in a Hong Kong stream. – *Freshwater Biol.* **27**: 53–63.

Farmer, A. M. & Adams, M. S., 1991: The nature of scale and the use of hierarchy theory in understanding ecology of aquatic macrophytes. – *Aquat. Bot.* **41**: 253–261.

Fisher, S. G., 1991: Presidential Address: emerging global issues in freshwater ecology. – *Bull. N. Amer. Benthol. Soc.* **8**: 235–245.

Jackson, J. K. & Fisher, S. G., 1986: Secondary production, emergence, and export of aquatic insects of a Sonoran Desert stream. – *Ecology* **67**: 629–638.

Jackson, J. K. & Resh, V. H., 1989: Distribution and abundance of adult aquatic insects in the forest adjacent to a northern California stream. – *Environ. Entomol.* **18**: 278–283.

Junk, W. J., Bayley, P. B. & Sparks, R. E., 1989: The flood pulse concept in river-floodplain systems. – *Can. Spec. Publ. Fish. Aquat. Sci.* **106**: 110–127.

Liu, J., 1984: Lakes of the middle and lower basins of the Chang Jiang (China). – In: Taub, F. B., (ed.): Ecosystems of the World 23: Lakes and Reservoirs: 331–355. – Elsevier, Amsterdam

Lowe-McConnell, R. H., 1987: Ecological Studies of Tropical Fish Communities: 382 pp. – Cambridge University Press, Cambridge.

Minshall, G. W., 1988: Stream ecosystem theory: a global perspective. – *J. N. Amer. Benthol. Soc.* **7**:263–288.

Pantulu, V. R., 1989: Fish of the lower Mekong basin: – In: Davies, B. R. & Walker, K. F. (eds.): The Ecology of River Systems: 721–741. – Dr. W. Junk Publishers, The Hague.

Petersen, R. C. & Skoglund, E., 1990: Wetlands Management Programme – Study to Formulate Plans for the Management of the Wetlands in the Lower Mekong Basin (1.3.13/88/SWE): 245 pp. – The Mekong Secretariat, Bangkok, Thailand.

Shiraishi, Y., 1970: The migration of fishes in the Mekong River. – In: Regional Meeting of Inland Water Biologists in Southeast Asia, Proceedings. – Unesco Field Science Office for Southeast Asia, Djakarta, Indonesia, 135–140.

Smith, H. M., 1945: The freshwater fishes of Siam, or Thailand. – *Bull. U.S. Natn. Mus.* **188**: 1–622.

Swift, S. M., Racey, P. A. & Avery, M. I., 1985: Feeding ecology of *Pipistrellus pipistrellus* (Chiroptera: Vespertilionidae) during pregnancy and lactation. II. Diet. – *J. Anim. Ecol.* **54**: 217–225.

Tan, S. P., 1980: Ecological aspects of some Malaysian riverine cyprinids in relation to their aquaculture potential. – In: Furtado, J. I. (ed.): Tropical Ecology and Development. – Proceedings of the Vth International Symposium of Tropical Ecology: 757–762. – International Society of Tropical Ecology, Kuala Lumpur.

Vannote, R. L., Minshall, G. W., Cummins, K. W., Sedell, J. R. & Cushing, C. E., 1980: The River Continuum Concept. – *Can. J. Fish. Aquat. Sci.* **37**: 130–137.

Van Slyke, L. P., 1988: Yangtze: Nature, History and the River: 211 pp. – Addison-Wesley Publishing Company. Inc., Reading, Massachusetts.

Ward, J. V., 1989: The four-dimensional nature of lotic ecosystems. – *J. N. Amer. Benthol. Soc.* **8**: 2–8.

Ward, J V. & Stanford, J. A., 1983: The serial discontinuity concept of lotic ecosystems. – In: Fontaine III T. O. & Bartell, S. M. (eds.): Dynamics of Lotic Ecosystems: 29–42. – Ann Arbor Science, Ann Arbour, Michigan

Welcomme, R. L., 1979: Fisheries Ecology of Floodplain Rivers: 317 pp. – Longman, London.

Winterbourn, M. J., Rounick, J. S. & Cowie, B., 1981: Are New Zealand stream ecosystems really different? – *N.Z. J. Mar. Freshwat. Res.* **15**: 321–328.

Zhao, J., Zheng, G., Wang, H. & Xu, J., 1990: The Natural History of China: 224 pp. – McGraw-Hill Publishing Co., New York.

Author's address:

Department of Zoology, Hui Oi Chow Science Building, The University of Hong Kong, Pokfulam Road, Hong Kong.

Mitt. Internat. Verein. Limnol.	24	17–25	Stuttgart, Februar 1994

The role of ecotones (transition zones) in the conservation and management of tropical inland waters

Brij Gopal

Abstract

All inland water bodies are an integral part of their drainage basins. Most tropical water bodies are shallow and experience large water-level changes. The marginal zones of lentic waters and the floodplains and banks of rivers and streams therefore represent a wide transition zone (or ecotone) between uplands and open water. Since most of the water, silt, nutrients and organic inputs from the catchment must pass through this transition zone before reaching the water body, the biota of this zone and the ecosystem processes operating therein play a significant role in regulating the water quality, biodiversity and productivity of inland waters. During the past few decades, shoreline modification of inland waters for different reasons (flood control, flow regulation, land reclamation, etc.) have reduced greatly the extent of transition zones (= ecotonal area) between land and water, with consequent degradation of water quality. This paper discusses the ecotone concept as applied to land-water interfaces, and highlights important characteristics and functions of ecotones. Attention is drawn to the relevance and importance of ecotones to the conservation and managenent of tropical inland waters, under-scoring the need for investigations of ecosystem processes in these zones.

Introduction

Inland waters derive most of their water as runoff from the surrounding landscape. The water brings with it nutrients and organic matter, and also a variety of organisms or their propagules and resting stages. However, for many decades – indeed, since Forbes (1887) described the lake as "a little world within itself – a microcosm" – lakes remained just lakes without concern for their watershed. The importance of terrestrial inputs to the functioning of inland waterbodies was not realized until the late 1950s when the pioneering studies of H. T. Odum (1957) and Teal (1957) demonstrated the role of allochthonous organic matter in the secondary production of certain flowing waters. Subsequently, Kaushik & Hynes (1968) documented the contribution of terrestrial leaf litter to streams and, in his *Baldi Memorial Lecture,* Hynes (1975) highlighted the dependence of streams on their surrounding landscape. Recent research has emphasized repeatedly the fact that inland water bodies are an integral part of their watersheds (Likens 1984) with which they interact constantly (see Hasler, 1975, Lauga et al. 1988). Diverse natural processes and anthropogenic activities in the catchment basins are thus directly mirrored in the quality of water.

The majority of lentic waterbodies is shallow and exhibits periodic water-level changes so that they have a wide transition or marginal zone between the surrounding uplands and deep water (Fig. 1). Similar transition zones between river channels and uplands are represented by riparian fringes and floodplains. The interactions between waterbodies and their drainage basins take place through these transition zones and, therefore, the biota and the ecosystem processes operating therein influence both of the adjacent systems (McArthur 1989). Marginal zones and floodplains are viewed generally as wetlands (Cowardin et al. 1979, Gopal et al. 1990) and have been investigated in some detail (e.g. Pieczynska 1976, Dykyjová & Květ 1978, Heeg & Breen 1982, Penka et al. 1985, Ellenbroek 1987, Junk & Welcomme 1990), particularly with regard to their importance for open-water habitats (Howard-Williams & Lenton 1975, Wetzel 1979, Welcomme 1979, Whigham et al.

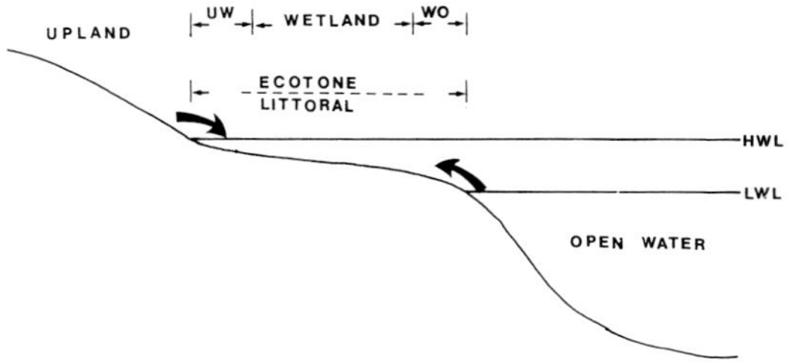

Fig. 1. A conceptual diagram of the wetland transition zone or ecotone between the upland and open water. The transition zone lies between the highest (HWL) and lowest (LWL) mean water levels, and is referred to as the marginal or littoral-zone in lakes and the floodplain or riparian zone along rivers). According to Holland et al. (1991), this wetland has a transition zone or ecotone on either side (UW – upland-wetland ecotone, and WO – wetland-open water ecotone); the arrows mark interactions with the uplands and open water.

0538-4680/94/0024-0017 $ 2.25

1988). However, in most tropical regions and especially in Asia, these transition zones are not well investigated nor is their significance appreciated. In this paper, the important characteristics of the land-water interface are highlighted and its role in the conservation and management of tropical inland waters is stressed.

During the past few years, efforts have been initiated to examine the ecological attributes of land-water transition zones in terms of the ecotone concept (PATTEN et al. 1985, DI CASTRI et al. 1988, NAIMAN et al. 1989). Since the author has been associated with some of these efforts, this emerging approach will be elaborated first.

The ecotone concept

The term ecotone was first coined by CLEMENTS (1905) who defined it as the "tension zone where principal species from adjacent communities meet their limits". It has since been much employed extensively in ecology although few attempts have been made to refine or clarify the term (DAUBENMIRE 1968, ODUM 1971). E. P. ODUM (1971) described the ecotone as "a transition zone between two or more diverse communities as, for example, between forest and grassland or between a soft bottom and hard bottom marine community". He wrote further that it is "a junction zone or tension belt" ... and ... "contains many of the organisms of each of the overlapping communities and, in addition, organisms which are characteristic of and often restricted to the ecotone". DAUBENMIRE (1968), however, considered the ecotone as a zone of intergradation between contiguous communities and recognized three types of ecotones:

1. the transition may be abrupt as a result of abrupt discontinuity in environmental conditions;
2. the transition may be abrupt as a result of plant interactions, especially competition even though the extrinsic factors exhibit a continuous gradient; and
3. the ecotone may be a zone of gradual blending of two vegetation types that reflect a gradual blending of two distinct factor complexes.

The ecotone concept is rooted in the recognition of communities as discrete units, homogeneous in species composition (Fig. 2) and therefore with definite boundaries (CLEMENTS 1916). However, such a view of the community had been challenged right from the beginning (GLEASON 1926). Indeed, some consider that it has been demolished by the continuum concept (MCINTOSH 1967), which seeks to ordinate the communities along environmental gradients (WHITTAKER 1967, 1978) as facilitated by the recent development of powerful numerical techniques (see OKLAND 1990). It now seems clear that discrete communities on the landscape may be envisaged only if there is a distinct heterogeneity of the habitat or there is a disturbance resulting in such heterogeneity. It is interesting to note that, with reference to the ecotone between land and water, DAUBENMIRE (1968) recognized a continuous gradient "progressing from deep water toward the surrounding upland", while nevertheless considering that the vegetation exhibited "steplike discontinuities along the same gradient".

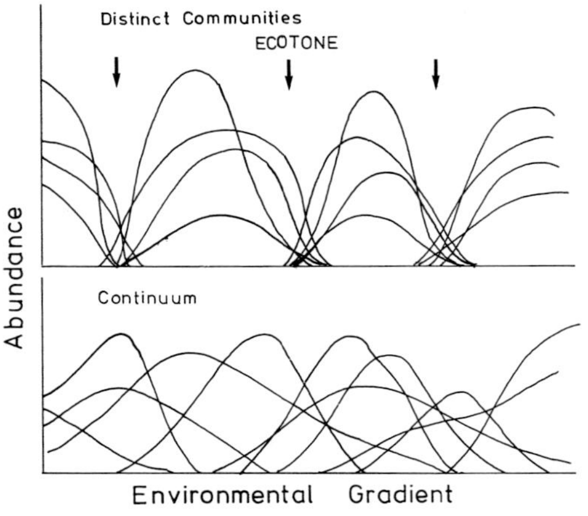

Fig. 2. Diagrammatic representation of species distribution along an environmental gradient. They may form distinct communities and the ecotone or a continuum with no distinct transition zone.

Although there have been several studies of transition zones and of the edges of different communities (CARPENTER 1935, PICKETT & WHITE 1985, TURNER 1987), the resurgence of interest in the ecotone concept can be traced to the proposal for a new programme made to the SCOPE (Special Committee on the Problems of Environment) of the International Council of Scientific Unions (ICSU) by the Scientific Advisory Committee for Wetlands and Shallow Continental Waterbodies (PATTEN et al. 1985). The proposal was followed by a UNESCO/MAB workshop which defined ecotones as the "zone of transition between adjacent ecological systems, having a set of characteristics uniquely defined by space and time scales and by the strength of the interactions between adjacent ecological systems" (HOLLAND 1988). Consequently, both SCOPE and UNESCO have formulated their own programmes focused on ecotone research and management (HANSEN et al. 1988, NAIMAN et al. 1988). The ecotone programme of UNESCO under the Man and the Biosphere (MAB) Project 5 deals specifically with the land-inland water ecotones. Their ecology, management, and role in landscape restoration were the subject of an international workshop in May 1988 (NAIMAN et al. 1989, NAIMAN & DECAMPS 1990).

The key to our understanding of ecotones lies in the emphasis on "the strength of the interactions between adjacent ecological systems" in the SCOPE/MAB definition of ecotones (HOLLAND 1988). All ecosystems interact with adjacent systems to some extent, and these interactions will be more intense at the interface. In case of the land-water interface, the interactions are controlled primarily by hydrological factors and to some extent by biotic exchanges (for details see LOUCKS 1975, 1990). In such environments, the ecotone concept includes the interactions between surface water and groundwater (GILBERT et al. 1990).

Ecotones versus wetlands

The emerging interest in ecotones leads to the discussion of another issue: are all wetlands ecotones? Or, can all land-water ecotones be treated as wetlands? Wetlands have long been considered as transitional systems because most of them lie at the interface between land and water. Thus, it appears that wetlands can be interpreted as ecotones and, by implication, the reverse should be true also. However, the apparent similarities are probably only spatial. Recent syntheses of our knowledge (Mitsch & Gosselink 1986, Patten et al. 1990) show that the wetlands are not just transitional habitats, seral in nature, but are highly productive and stable ecosystems whose stability and diversity are governed primarily by hydrology. Whereas the marginal zones of lakes and reservoirs have been described both as wetlands and ecotones without any distinction (Pieczynska 1972, 1990, Dykyjová & Květ 1978), they can be treated also as wetlands with an ecotone on either side; i.e. an upland-wetland ecotone and a wetland-open water ecotone (Holland et al. 1990). Recently, Tiner (1991) pleaded in favour of recognition of wetlands "as distinct ecosystems along the wetter end of the soil moisture gradient" on the basis of distinctive characteristics of microflora, invertebrate fauna and soils. Floodplains, recognized generally as wetlands, comprise a far more complex and highly dynamic mosaic of systems (Mitsch & Gosselink 1986) which cannot be easily bounded within a simple definition of 'ecotone'. It is therefore doubtful if wetlands are the same as ecotones which have yet to be characterized adequately.

Note that whether the transition zone between the land and water is termed an ecotone or wetland, its characteristics and values are not affected. In this paper, the terms ecotone and transition zone are used synonymously for the entire area between upland and openwater; i.e. the zone between the highest and lowest mean water levels (Fig. 1), which is often referred to as wetland.

Ecological characteristics of transition zones

All ecological characteristics of the transition zone are directly regulated or indirectly influenced by hydrological factors. Thus, the periodicity, duration, amplitude and timing of flooding primarily determine the species composition and various processes in the area. Depending upon the breadth, physiography, and nature of the substratum, the transition zone may be more or less homogeneous (e.g. margins of a pond) or a mosaic of microhabitats (e.g. river floodplains).

The transition zone offers a rich array of niches and, correspondingly, supports high biotic diversity. While the area may be dominated by one or few plant species (for example, species of *Typha, Phragmites, Spartina* and *Taxodium*) or may have a large number of them, the fauna is typically diverse. A large number of planktonic and periphytic species contribute also to the high biodiversity. Further, the periodic flooding and exposure allows many species to colonise the transition zones during one or the other phase, and additional species from adjacent upland and open water systems utilise the transition zones during a part of their lives (Fredrickson 1979). This is especially true for the avifauna which make use of the physical habitat and its biotic resources at different times of the year for feeding, breeding and nesting (cf. Dobrowolski 1973, Kushlan 1990).

Primary productivity in transition zones is generally higher than that in adjacent systems (Wetzel 1990 a). However, the fate of this organic matter depends upon several factors of which climate and hydrology are most important. The organic matter may be transported to the open water where it contributes to increased secondary production, or it may accumulate in situ. The decay processes in the transition zone differ considerably from those in the uplands and in open water. For example, Pieczynska (1990) observed fastest decomposition of both *Salix* leaves and macrophytes (*Potamogeton perfoliatus* and *Elodea canadensis*) on swampy lake shores compared to rates on the exposed shores or in deep water.

Other important characteristics of the transition zone concern the dynamics of nutrients and other elements. The influence of anoxic soil conditions on nitrogen, phosphorus and other chemical transformations are well known (Ponnamperuma 1984, Howard-Williams 1985). Periodic changes in the hydrologic regime result in both spatial and temporal variability in the dynamics of different nutrients as the processes of release and uptake, nitrification and denitrification, immobilisation and remobilisation can occur at different times at the same place within the transition zone.

Wetland plants in the transition zone play an important role in nutrient dynamics. Not only do they absorb larger amounts of nutrients due to higher production, but several species are known to take up nutrients far in excess of their growth requirements (often referred to as 'luxury consumption'; KLOPATEK 1978, REDDY & DEBUSK 1987). In addition, many plants absorb and accumulate a number of organic and inorganic toxic compounds (SIMPSON et al. 1981, BEST 1987). These and related matters have been discussed recently by WETZEL (1990 b) and need not be elaborated here.

Finally, transition zones differ from adjacent systems with respect to microbial communities and their importance. Besides their contribution to element cycling, the microbes play a significant role in energy flow along the detritus pathway which is usually dominant in ecotonal communities (see GOPAL 1990).

Ecological role of transition zones

The transition zone is distinguished from its adjacent upland and open water systems by the regularly changing hydrological regimes, greater floristic and faunal diversity, high organic productivity, the dominant role of microbial communities in energy flow and cycling of materials, and the relative importance of different processes related to the dynamics of nutrients and toxic substances. These characteristics confer upon the transition zones a number of ecological, socioeconomic and aesthetic values (Table 1) which have been discussed in several recent publications (LUGO & BRINSON 1978, BRINSON et al. 1981, ADAMUS & STOCKWELL 1983; PIECZYNSKA 1990, SLATHER et al. 1990, PETTS 1990). Only those values which are related to and are important for the conservation and management of inland waters are examined here.

Table 1. Functions and values of transition zones (ecotones) at the land-water interface (adapted from LUGO & BRINSON 1978, BRINSON et al. 1981, PETTS 1990).

Hydrologic values
Store flood waters and ameliorate downstream flooding
Serve as areas of aquifer recharge or discharge
Organic productivity values
Higher primary productivity than in adjacent systems
High secondary productivity supports fisheries
Export organic matter to open-water systems
Biotic values
Serve as habitat for endangered, rare and seasonally-migrating species
Provide spawning areas for fishes
Provide valuable grazing grounds during dry periods
Biogeochemical values
High capacity to recycle nutrient; usually accumulate nitrogen, phosphorus and other elements
Sequester heavy metals and some poisonous chemicals in anaerobic soil zones, clays, and humic matter
Regulate inputs of nutrients and organic matter to open waters
Geomorphic values
Provide areas of sedimentation for building soils
Contribute to landscape diversity
Other values
Provide valuable natural resources for local people
Provide sites for recreation and relaxation
Natural laboratories for teaching and research

Regulation of water quality

The amounts of silt, nutrients and dissolved or particulate organic compounds entering a water body are a prime determinant of the water quality. The transition zone acts as a filter (LOWRANCE et al. 1984) and contributes to improved water quality by trapping and/or gradually releasing these substances. The resistance to water flow offered by vegetation causes suspended material to settle out, leading to a reduction in silt load (BOTO & PATRICK 1979, BROWN 1984). Further, transition zones allow for the storage of peak water flows and gradual release. This reduces run-off from the uplands and inputs of suspended material. The aquatic vegetation contributes to reduced sediment inputs by dissipating the erosive forces associated with waves, currents and water-level fluctuations.

Nutrients and other substances passing through the transition zone are either retained or removed by various physicochemical and biological processes. The anaerobic conditions caused by periodic flooding help in the removal of nutrients from the water column by denitrification and microbial immobilization. Heavy metals and some poisonous chemicals are sequestered in the anaerobic soils, clays and humic matter. Plants accumulate nutrients, particularly nitrogen and phosphorus, and a variety of toxic substances in large amounts which can then be removed by harvesting the plant biomass. The below-ground organs of many perennial species (e.g. *Typha* and *Phrag-*

mites) serve as storehouses of nutrients over long periods. Food chains in transition zones also support further direct or indirect use of nutrients. The litter accumulating in the transition zone under certain hydrological conditions may act also as a sink for nutrients and toxic substances (RICHARDSON 1990).

Contribution to secondary production

Transition zones provide important feeding and nursery grounds for young fish and many other aquatic animals such as crocodiles (see several papers in SHARITZ & GIBBONS 1990). The detritus produced and processed in the transition zone has generally high nutritive value (DE LA CRUZ 1975, 1979), and therefore contributes significantly to secondary production both within the transition zone and, upon export, in the open-water habitat. The transport of dissolved organic matter and nutrients in a phased manner contributes also to increased secondary production without causing the adverse effects of eutrophication.

Conservation of biodiversity and gene pools

Species diversity is generally higher in transition zones than in adjacent systems. Ecotones not only provide food and cover for a variety of fauna, but are often the only habitats for many rare or endemic species which are adapted to the periodic water-level changes (KUSHLAN 1990). For example, the endangered Unicorned rhino (*Rhinoceros unicornis*) in northeast India depends entirely on *Phragmites* marshes. In Sri Lanka, the otter (*Lutra lutra*) is confined to the land-freshwater interface, whereas endemic fish (*Malpulutta kretseri*) and shrews (*Feroculus feroculus*) are confined to swampy areas (DE SILVA 1991, DESILVA & DE SILVA 1991). Juveniles of some invertebrates, including certain mayflies, develop into adults in isolated pockets of water away from the main stream in which the eggs are laid (HAYDEN & CLIFFORD 1974); their survival depends upon the migration of larvae through the transition zone during a high-water phase. A large number of waterfowl species depend for food on transition zones, and may visit several such habitats during their annual migrations. Some of these species are the subject of international conservation efforts (ANONYMOUS 1985, SCOTT & POOLE 1989). Thus, transition zones have significance for the conservation of biodiversity in general, and endangered and rare species in particular.

The tropical perspective

The importance of transition zones is greater in the tropics than in other regions for several reasons. Firstly, land-water interfaces in the tropics are far more productive than either their temperate counterparts or tropical terrestrial ecosystems (GOPAL 1990). Higher productivity is not only due to conditions favourable for growth throughout the year, but also a reflection of rapid nutrient turnover (high decomposition rates) and efficient nutrient utilization. This has been demonstrated in several studies of floodplain ecosystems in tropical Africa and South America (BREEN et al. 1988, FISHER et al. 1991, LOPEZ-HERNANDEZ 1991).

Secondly, higher productivity implies a greater potential for nutrient regulation as well as for more inputs of organic matter and, consequently, increased secondary production in open waters. Thirdly, species diversity is higher in the tropics due largely to the fact that hydrological regimes are more varied than in temperate regions. Water-level changes and their year-to-year variability are considerably greater in the tropics, particularly in the monsoonal regions of Asia and Africa where a prolonged dry season often causes even large waterbodies to dry up completely. The impact of seasonality in the tropics, therefore, lies not in the extremes of temperature as experienced in the temperate regions, but in the extremes of water regimes. Rapid growth of vegetation and the presence of a large variety of fauna soon after the rains, with subsequent flooding of periodically-exposed transition zones, typify tropical land-water ecotones (e.g. ELLENBROEK 1987, SCOTT & POOLE 1989, FINLAYSON et al. 1990).

Human use of both aquatic and terrestrial systems is much more intense in the tropics than elsewhere. The transitional zones at the land-water interface have been exploited variously for millenia, and are still utilised for harvesting plants for fiber and forage. Throughout the tropics, reeds, sedges and cattails are used for thatching; rhizomes, tubers and tender shoots of many species are harvested for food (see LÖFFLER 1990). Floodplains are important grazing grounds during the dry season (e.g. SHEPPE & OSBORNE 1971). The transition zones thus have great socioeconomic importance in tropical regions. They bear the impact of human activities directly, especially when they are used for recreation or waste disposal, and also play a role in buffering the impacts of these activities both on land and in water.

Conclusions

Considerable emphasis has been laid on research, conservation and management of wetlands and land-water transition zones during recent years. In the tropics, however, neither the ecosystem processes nor the ecological value of ecotones are appreciated. At the same time, these transition zones are being degraded and modified by human activities. Extensive erosion of uplands is causing rapid siltation of shallow water bodies, whereas flood-control measures, construction of reservoirs and dykes (levees), flow regulation, river diversion, and channelisation, as well as land reclamation by drainage and landfills, have reduced or eliminated land-water transition zones and especially floodplains. Unfortunately there are no estimates of the extent of such losses. The land and open-water systems now interact directly without the buffering effect of transition zones. Consequently, inland waters and their living resources are threatened by land-based human activities. To facilitate the conservation and management of inland waters we must pay urgent attention to the processes occurring in transition zones or ecotones at the land-water interface, and take steps to ensure that their contribution to ecosystem functioning is maintained.

References

Adamus, P. R. & Stockwell, L. T., 1983: A Method for Wetland Functional Assessment. Vol. I. Critical Review and Evaluation of Concepts: 176 pp. – U.S. Department of Transportation, Federal Highway Administration, Report FHWA-IP-82-23, Washington, D.C.

Anonymous, 1985: Convention on the Conservation of Migratory Species of Wild Animals (CMS): Proceedings of the First Meeting of the Conference of the Parties. Vols. I & II: 160 + 128 pp. – Secretariat of the Convention Bonn, Nairobi.

Best, G. R., 1987: Natural wetlands – southern environment: wastewater to wetlands, where do we go from here? – In: Reddy, K. R. & Smith, W. H. (eds.): Aquatic Plants for Water Treatment and Resource Recovery: 99–120. – Magnolia Publishing, Orlando, Florida.

Boto, K. G. & Patrick, W. H., 1979: Role of wetlands in the removal of suspended sediments. – In: Greeson, P. E., Clark, J. R. & Clark, J. E. (eds.): Wetland Functions and Values: The State of our Understanding: 479–489. – American Water Resources Association, Minneapolis.

Breen, C. M., Rogers, K. H. & Ashton, P. J., 1988: Vegetation processes in swamps and flooded plains. – In: Symoens, J. J. (ed.): Vegetation of Inland Waters: 223–248. – Kluwer Academic Publishers, Dordrecht.

Brinson, M. M., Swift, B. L., Plantico, R. C. & Barclay, J. S., 1981: Riparian Ecosystems: Their Ecology and Status: 155 pp. – FWS/OBS-81/17. U.S. Fish & Wildlife Service, Washington, D.C.

Brown, R. G., 1984: Effects of an urban wetland on sediment and nutrient loads in runoff. – *Wetlands* **4**: 147–158.

Carpenter, R. J., 1935: Fluctuations in biotic communities. 1. Prairie-forest ecotone of central Illinois. – *Ecology* **16**: 203–212.

Clements, F. E., 1905: Research Methods in Ecology. – University Publishing Co., Lincoln, Nebraska.

– 1916: Plant Succession and Analysis of the Development of Vegetation: 512 pp. – Carnegie Institute, Washington, Publication No. 242.

Cowardin, L. M., Carter, V., Golet, F. C. & Laroe, E. T., 1979: Classification of Wetlands and Deepwater Habitats of the United States: 103 pp. – U.S. Fish and Wildlife Service, Pub. FWS/OBS 79/31, Washington, D. C.

Daubenmire, R. F., 1968: Plant Communities: a Textbook of Plant Synecology: 300 pp. – Harper & Row, New York.

de la Cruz, A. A., 1975: Proximate nutritive value changes during decomposition of salt marsh plants. – *Hydrobiologia* **47**: 475–480.

– 1979: Production and transport of detritus in wetlands. – In: Greeson, P. E., Clark, J. R. & Clark, J. E. (eds.): Wetland Functions and Values: The State of our Understanding: 162–174. – American Water Resources Association, Minneapolis.

De silva, P. K. 1991: The impact of the man's activities on the otter, *Lutra lutra*, a species inhabiting the land-freshwater interface of Sri Lanka. – In: International Conference on Land-Water Interactions. *Abstracts*. 44. – National Institute of Ecology, New Delhi.

De Silva, P. K. & De Silva, K. H. G. M., 1991: The biodiversity and the effect of man's interference on the vertebrate fauna of the freshwater marshy habitats of Sri Lanka. – In: International Conference on Land-Water Interactions. *Abstracts*. 45. – National Institute of Ecology, New Delhi.

Di Castri, F., Hansen, A. J. & Holland, M. M., 1988: A new look at ecotones: emerging international projects on landscape boundaries. – *Biology International, Special Issue* **17**, International Union of Biological Sciences, Paris.

Dobrowolski, K. A., 1973: Role of birds in Polish wetland ecosystems. – *Pol. Arch. Hydrobiol.* **20**: 217–221.

Dykyjová, D. & Květ, J., 1978: Pond Littoral Ecosystem: Structure and Functioning: 464 pp. – Springer Verlag, Berlin.

Ellenbroek, G. A., 1987: Ecology and Productivity of an African Wetland system: The Kafue Flats, Zambia: 267 pp. – Dr. W. Junk Publishers, The Hague.

FINLAYSON, C. M., COWIE, I. & BAILEY, B., 1990: Characteristics of a seasonally flooded freshwater system in monsoonal Australia. – In: WHIGHAM, D. F., GOOD, R. E. KVĚT, J. (eds.): Wetland Ecology and Management: Case studies: 141–162. – Kluwer Academic Publishers, Dordrecht.

FISHER, T. R., LESACK, L. F. W. & SMITH, L. K., 1991: Input, recycling and export of N and P on the Amazon floodplain at Lake Calado. – In: TIESSEN, H., LOPEZ-HERNANDEZ, D. & SALCEDO, I. H. (eds.): Phosphorus Cycles in Terrestrial and Aquatic Ecosystems. Regional Workshop 3: South and Central America: 34–53. – Saskatchewan Institute of Pedology, Saskatoon.

FORBES, S. A., 1887: The lake as a microcosm – *Bull. Peoria Sci. Assoc.* **1887**: 77–87. (Reprinted in *Bull. Illinois Nat. Hist. Surv.* **15**, 537–550, 1925.)

FREDRICKSON, L. H., 1979: Lowland hardwood wetlands: current status and habitat values for wetlands. – In: GREESON, P. E., CLARK, J. R. & CLARK, J. E. (eds.): Wetland functions and Values: The State of our Understanding: 296–306. – American Water Resources Association Minneapolis.

GILBERT, J., DOLE-OLIVIER, M.-J., MARMONIER, P. & VERNIER, P., 1990: Surfaced water-groundwater ecotones. – In: NAIMAN, R. J. & DÉCAMPS, H. (eds.): Ecology and Mangement of Aquatic-Terrestrial Ecotones. – *MAB Book Series* **4**: 199–226. – UNESCO, Paris, and Parthenon Publishing, Carnforth.

GLEASON, H. A., 1926: The individualistic concept of the plant association. – *Bull. Torrey bot. Club* **53**: 7–26.

GOPAL, B., 1990: (with a contribution from V. MASING), Biology and ecology. – In: PATTERN, B. C., JORGENSEN, S. E., DUMONT, H. J., GOPAL, B., KORYAVOV, P., KVĚT, J., LÖFFLER, H., SVERIZHEV, Y. & TUNDISI, J. G. (eds.): Wetlands and Continental Shallow Water Bodies: 91–239. – SPB Academic Publishing, The Hague.

GOPAL, B., KVET, J., LÖFFLER, H., MASING, V. & PATTERN, B. C. 1990: Definition and classification. – In: PATTEN, B. C., JORGENSEN, S. E., DUMONT, H. J., GOPAL, B., KORYAVOV, P., KVĚT, J., LÖFFLER, H., SVERIZEHV, Y. & TUNDISI, J. G. (eds.): Wetlands and Continental Shallow Water Bodies: 9–15. – SPB Academic Publishing, The Hague.

HANSEN, A. J., DI CASTRI, F. & RISSER, P. G., 1988: A new SCOPE project. Ecotones in a changing environment: the theory and management of landscape boundaries. – *Biology International, Special Issue* **17**: 137–161, International Union of Biological Sciences, Paris.

HASLER, A. D., 1975: Coupling of Land and Water Systems. – *Ecological Studies* **10**, Springer Verlag, Berlin.

HAYDEN, W. & CLIFFORD, H. F., 1974: Seasonal movements of the mayfly – *Leptophlebia cupida* (SAY) in a brown-water stream of Alberta, Canada. – *Amer. Midl. Nat.* **91**: 90–102.

HEEG, J. & BREEN, C. M., 1982: Man and the Pongolo floodplain. – S. Africa National Sciences Program, Rept **56**: 113 pp.

HOLLAND, M. M., 1988: SCOPE/MAB technical consultations on landscape boundaries. Report of a SCOPE/MAB workshop on ecotones. – *Biology International, Special Issue* **17**: 47–106, International Union of Biological Sciences, Paris.

HOLLAND, M. M., WHIGHAM, D. F. & GOPAL, B., 1990: The characteristics of wetland ecotones. – In: NAIMAN, R. J. & DÉCAMPS, H. (eds.): Ecology and Management of Aquatic-Terrestrial Ecotones. – *MAB Book Series* **4**: 171–198. – UNESCO, Paris, and Parthenon Publishing, Carnforth.

HOWARD-WILLIAMS, C., 1985: Cycling and retention of nitrogen and phosphorus in wetlands: A theoretical and applied perspective. – *Freshwat. Biol.* **15**: 391–431.

HOWARD-WILLIAMS, C. & LENTON, C. M., 1975: The role of the littoral zone in the functioning of a shallow tropical lake ecosystem. – *Freshwat. Biol.* **5**: 445–459.

HYNES, H. B. N., 1975: The stream and its valley. – *Verh. Internat. Verein. Limnol.* **19**: 1–15.

JUNK, W. & WELCOMME, R. L., 1990: Floodplains. – In: PATTEN, B. C., JORGENSEN, S. E., DUMONT, H. J., GOPAL, B., KORYAVOV, P., KVĚT, J., LÖFFLER, H., SVERIZHEV, Y. & TUNDISI, J. G. (eds.): Wetlands and Continental Shallow Water Bodies: 491–524. – SPB Academic Publishing, The Hague.

KAUSHIK, N. K. & HYNES, H. B. N., 1968: Experimental study on the role of autumn shed leaves in aquatic environments. – *J. Ecol.* **52**: 229–243.

KLOPATEK, J. M., 1978: Nutrient dynamics of freshwater riverine marshes and the role of emergent macrophytes. – In: GOOD, R. E., WHIGHAM, D. F. & SIMPSON, R. L. (eds.): Freshwater Wetlands: Ecological Processes and Management Potential: 195–216. – Academic Press, N.Y.

KUSHLAN, J. A., 1990: Avian use of fluctuating wetlands. – In: SHARITZ, R. R. & GIBBONS, J. W. (eds.): Freshwater Wetlands and Wildlife: 593–604. – U.S. Department of Energy, Office of Health and Environmental Research, Washington, D.C.

LAUGA, J., DECAMPS, H. & HOLLAND, M. M., 1988: Landuse Impacts on Aquatic Ecosystems: The Use of Scientific Information. – Academic de Toulouse, Toulouse, France.

LIKENS, G. E., 1984: Beyond the shoreline: A watershed ecosystem approach. – *Verh. Internat. Verein Limnol.* **22**: 1–22.

LÖFFLER, H., 1990: Human uses. – In: PATTEN, B. C., JORGENSEN, S. E., DUMONT, H. J., GOPAL, B., KORYAVOV, P., KVĚT, J., LÖFFLER, H., SVERIZHEV, Y. & TUNDISI, J. G. (eds.): Wetland and Continental Shallow Water Bodies: 17–27. – SPB Academic Publishing, The Hague.

LOPEZ-HERNANDEZ, D., 1991: Phosphorus dynamics in a flooded savanna. – In TIESSEN, H., LOPEZ-HER-

NANDEZ, D. & SALCEDO, I. H. (eds.): Phosphorus cycles in Terrestrial and Aquatic Ecosystems. Regional workshop 3: South and Central America: 95–105. – Saskatchewan Institute of Pedology, Saskatoon.

LOUCKS, O., 1975: Models linking land-water interactions around Lake Wingra, Wisconsin. – In: HASLER, A. D. (ed.): Coupling of Land and Water Systems: 53–63. – Springer Verlag, Berlin.

– 1990: Land-water interactions. – In: PATTEN, B. C., JORGENSEN, S. E., DUMONT, H. J., GOPAL, B., KORYAVOV, P., KVĚT, J. LÖFFLER, H., SVERIZHEV, Y. & TUNDISI, J. G. (eds.): Wetlands and Continental Shallow Water Bodies: 243–258. – SPB Academic Publishing, The Hague.

LOWRANCE, R., TODD, R., FAIL, J., HENDRICKSON, O., LEONARD, R. & ASMUSSEN, L., 1984: Riparian forests as nutrient filters in agricultural watersheds. – *Bioscience* **34**: 374–377.

LUGO, A. E. & BRINSON, M. M., 1979. – Calculations of the value of salt water wetlands. – In: GREESON, P. E., CLARK, J. R. & CLARK, J. E. (eds.): Wetland Functions and Values: The State of our Understanding: 120–130. – American Water Resources Association, Minneapolis.

MCARTHUR, J. V. (1989): Aquatic and terrestrial linkages: floodplain functions. – In: HOOK, D. D. & LEA, R. (eds.): Symposium Proceedings: The Forested Wetlands of the Southern United States: 107–116. – USDA Southeastern Forest Experimental Station, Asheville, N.C.

MCINTOSH, R. P., 1967: The continuum concept of vegetation. – *Bot. Rev.* **33**: 130–187.

MITSCH, W. J. & GOSSELINK, J. G., 1986: Wetlands: 539 pp. – Van Nostrand-Reinhold, New York.

NAIMAN, R. J. & DECAMPS, H. 1990: Ecology and Management of Aquatic-Terrestrial Ecotones: 316 pp. – MAB Book Series 4, UNESCO, Paris & Parthenon Publishing, Carnforth.

NAIMAN, R. J., HOLLAND, M. M., DÉCAMPS, H. & RISSER, P. G., 1988: A new UNESCO programme: research and management of land/inland water ecotones. – *Biology International. Special Issue* **17**: 197–136. – International Union of Biological Sciences, Paris.

NAIMAN, R. J., DÉCAMPS, H. & FOURNIER, F., 1989: The role of land/inland water ecotones in landscape management and restoration. A proposal for collaborative research. – MAB Digest 4, UNESCO, Paris.

ODUM, E. P., 1971: Fundamentals of Ecology: 574 pp. – Third Edition. – Saunders, Philadelphia.

ODUM, H. T., 1957: Trophic structure and productivity of Silver Springs, Florida. – *Ecol. Monogr.* **27**: 55–112.

OKLAND, R. H., 1990: Vegetation ecology: theory, methods and applications with reference to Fennoscandia. – *Sommerfeltia, Suppl.* **1**: 1–233.

PATTEN, B. C., JORGENSEN, S. E., GOPAL, B., KORYAVOV, P., KVĚT, J., LÖFFLER, H., SVERIZHEV, Y. & TUNDISI, J. G., 1985: Ecotones: An Edge Approach to Gene Pool Preservation and Management in the Biosphere. Prospectus for a New SCOPE Programme from the Scientific Advisory Committee for Wetlands and Shallow Continental Water Bodies. – University of Georgia, Athens.

PATTEN, B. C., JORGENSEN, S. E., DUMONT, H. J., GOPAL, B., KORYAVOV, P., KVĚT, J., LÖFFLER, H., SVERIZHEV, Y. & TUNDISI, J. G. (1990): Wetlands and Continental Shallow Water Bodies: 759 pp. – SPB Academic Publishing, The Hague.

PENKA, M., VYSKOT, M., KLIMO, E. & VASICEK, F., 1985: Floodplain Forest Ecosystem. I. Before Water Management Measures: 466 pp. – Elsevier Science Publishers, Amsterdam.

PETTS, G., 1990: The role of ecotones in aquatic landscape management. – In: NAIMAM, R. J. & DÉCAMPS, H. (eds.): Ecology and Management of Aquatic-Terrestrial Ecotones. – MAB Book Series **4**, UNESCO, Paris & Parthenon Publishing, Carnforth, U.K.

PICKETT, S. T. A. & WHITE, P. S., 1985: The Ecology of Natural Disturbance and Patch Dynamics: 472 pp. – Academic Press, N.Y.

PIECZYNSKA, E., 1972. Ecology of the eulittoral zone of lakes. – *Ekol. Pol.* **20**: 637–732.

– 1976: Lake Littoral Ecology: 238 pp. – Polish Science Publishers, Warsaw.

– 1990: Lentic aquatic-terrestrial ecotones: their structure, function and importance. – In: NAIMAN, R. J. & DÉCAMPS, H. (eds.): Ecology and Management of Aquatic-Terrestrial Ecotones. MAB Book Series 4. 103–140. – UNESCO, Paris & Parthenon Publishing, Carnforth.

PONNAMPERUMA, F. N., 1984: Effects of flooding on soils. – In: KOZLOWSKI, T. T. (ed.): Flooding and Plant Growth: 10–45. – Academic Press, N.Y.

REDDY, K. R. & DEBUSK, T. A., 1987: Plant nutrient storage capabilities. – In: REDDY, K. R. & SMITH, W. H. (eds.): Aquatic Plants for Water Treatment and Resource Recovery: 337–358. – Magnolia Publishing, Orlando, Florida.

RICHARDSON, C. J., 1990. Freshwater wetlands: transformers, filters or sinks? – In: SHARITZ, R. R. & GIBBONS, J. W. (eds.): Freshwater Wetlands and Wildlife: 25–46. – U.S. Department of Energy, Office of Health and Environmental Research, Washington, D.C.

SATHER, J. H., SMITH, R. D. & LARSON, J. S. (1990): Natural values of wetlands. – In: PATTEN, B. C., JORGENSEN, S. E., DUMONT, H. J., GOPAL, B., KORYAVOV, P., KVĚT, J. LÖFFLER, H., SVERIZHEV, Y. & TUNDISI, J. G. (eds.): Wetlands and Continental Shallow Water Bodies: 373–387. – SPB Academic Publishing, The Hague.

SCOTT, D. A. & POOLE, C. M., 1989: A Status Overview of Asian Wetlands: 140 pp. – Asian Wetland Bureau, Kuala Lumpur.

SHARITZ, R. R. & GIBBONS, J.W., 1990: Freshwater Wetlands and Wildlife: 1265 pp. – U.S. Department of

Energy, Office of Health and Environmental Research, Washington, D.C.

SHEPPE, W. & OSBORNE, T., 1971: Patterns of use of a floodplain by Zambian mammals. – *Ecol. Monogr.* **41**: 179–205.

SIMPSON, R. L., GOOD, R. E., WALKER, R. & FRASCO, B. R., 1981: Dynamics of nitrogen, phosphorus and heavy metals in Delaware River freshwater tidal wetland: 192 pp. – Final Technical Completion Report, Corvallis Environmental Research Laboratory, Environmental Protection Agency, Corvallis, Oregon.

TEAL, J. M., 1957: Community metabolism in a temperate cold spring. – *Ecol. Monogr.* **27**: 283–302.

TINER, R W., 1991: Wetlands are ecotones – reality or myth? – In: International conference on land-water interactions, Abstracts: 3. – National Institute of Ecology, New Dehli.

TURNER, M. G., 1987: Landscape Heterogeneity and Disturbance: 536 pp. – Springer Verlag, N.Y.

WELCOMME, R. L., 1979: Fisheries Ecology of Floodplain Rivers: 317 pp. – Longman, London.

WETZEL, R. G., 1979: The role of the littoral zone and detritus in the lake metabolism. – *Arch. Hydrobiol. Beih. Ergebn. Limnol.* **13**: 145–161.

WETZEL, R.G., 1990 a: Wetland and littoral interfaces of lakes: productivity and nutrient regulation in the Lawrence Lake ecosystem. – In: SHARITZ, R. R. & GIBBONS, J. W. (eds.): Freshwater Wetlands and Wildlife: 283–302. – U.S. Department of Energy, Office of Health and Environmental Research, Washington, D.C.

– 1990 b: Land-water interfaces: metabolic and limnological regulators. – *Verh. Internat. Verein Limnol.* **24**, 6–24.

WHIGHAM, D. F., CHITTERLING, C. & PALMER, B., 1988: Impacts of freshwater wetlands on water quality: a landscape perspective – *Environment Management* **12**: 663–671.

WHITTAKER, R. H., 1967: Gradient analysis of vegetation. *Biol. Rev.* **42**: 207–264.

– 1978: Classification of Plant Communities. – Dr. W. Junk Publishers, The Hague.

Author's address:

School of Environmental Sciences, Jawaharlal Nehru University, New Delhi 10067, India.

Mitt. Internat. Verein. Limnol.	24	27–39	Stuttgart, Februar 1994

Towards a methodology for identifying tropical freshwater wetlands for protection

Jon Davies and Wim Giesen

Abstract

A methodology to assess the ecological value and viability for protection of tropical freshwater wetlands is presented. A major feature of the methodology is the use of two sets of criteria – one ecological, the other concerned with viability. The viability set of criteria aims to answer two questions. How long is the site likely to retain its conservation value? How feasible is management of the site? This approach enables scarce resources to be focused on sites of high ecological value which have the potential to be managed successfully.

An account of application of the methodology in two situations is given. Firstly, it has been employed to identify wetlands of potential importance – which are worthy of, or in need of, further study – in Sumatra (Indonesia) by using a set of preliminary ecological criteria. Secondly, it has been employed to identify freshwater wetlands in the Philippines for inclusion in a protected-areas system by using a set of detailed ecological criteria.

It is hoped that the adoption of the methodology described here will result in a more systematic approach to the identification of tropical freshwater wetlands of ecological importance. The approach could be used also as a training tool through practical use of the method in the field. However, the methodology must not be regarded as an end-point in itself, but rather as a stage in the evolution of more sophisticated methods as the data-base becomes more comprehensive.

Introduction

If tropical inland waters are to be conserved for their ecological value, there must be a methodology in place which can assess objectively, as far as possible, the ecological value of a range of wetlands and their suitability for subsequent management. In many tropical and developing countries, a systematic methodology to identify wetlands of ecological value has been lacking, with the result that many valuable sites are left out of protected-areas systems.

An important factor to build into any methodology is the viability of the potential protected area; i.e. how long is the area likely to retain its conservation value, and how feasible is management of the area? In developing countries, where financial resources are scarce, conservation is often regarded as a low priority in the overall context of development. Thus, we have to accept that certain areas, even those of high ecological value, may not be conserved if there are strong pressures favouring an alternative land use which brings in direct financial returns. The use of a methodology which evaluates this problem and other factors involved in the viability of a site is a pragmatic response which ensures that scarce time, trained personnel, and funds are channelled to those areas of high ecological value which are likely to retain that ecological value in the near future. One of the objectives of this methodology then, is not only to evaluate the ecological value of a range of sites in terms of habitat- and species diversity and rarity, but also to assess the future conservation potential of those sites.

The methodology employs a multicriteria evaluation of tropical wetlands to achieve four major objectives:

i) Development of a rapid, objective methodology to assess wetlands of importance in countries where data on habitat- and species diversity and rarity are scarce.
ii) Adoption of a pragmatic approach to evaluation of ecologically-important sites by incorporating into the assessment process a set of viability criteria which ascertain the management feasibility of the stites.
iii) Adoption of a relatively simple approach which can be understood and applied by personnel concerned with protected areas and which can be used with a minimum of training and equipment.
iv) Adoption of an approach which can be applied in training through practical use of the method in the field.

Recently, the use of multicriteria techniques to identify areas of ecological value has been criticised as being too subjective, and for masking specific attributes by ranking sites according to one summed score (e.g. Smith & Theberge 1987, Margules 1989). The use of a computerised data base and an algorithmic approach, as in the work of Pressey & Nicholls (1989a) and Margules et al. (1988), is more efficient in terms of objectivity and identification of the minimum number of sites needed to conserve all features of ecological value (Pressey & Nicholls 1989b). If multicriteria techniques are to be used, one has to bear in mind their limitations. One of the assumptions often made in their use is that the criteria are independent of each other. This is untrue in most cases. For example, the diversity of

0538-4680/94/0024-0027 $ 3.25

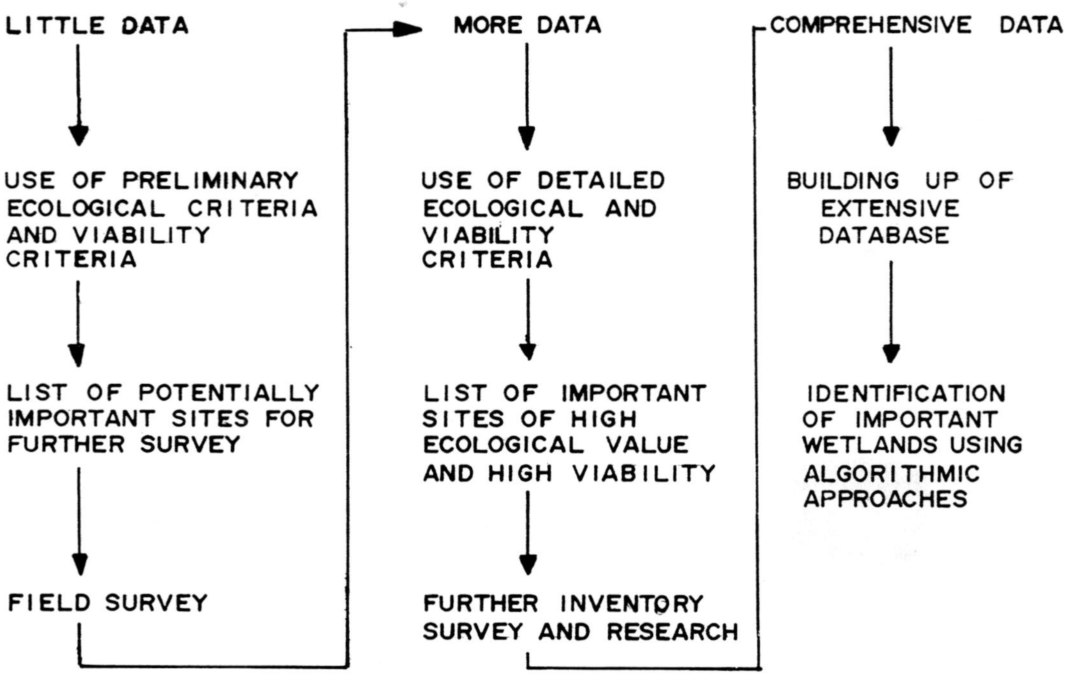

Fig. 1. The evolution of methods for ecological and viability assessment of freshwater wetland sites.

birds, fishes and so on depends – to a large extent – on habitat diversity; thus the criteria of habitat diversity and species diversity are correlated and tend to reinforce each other. Similarly, a criterion for rare wetland vegetation will be strongly linked to a criterion for rare habitats. The bias or weighting induced by such correlations must be borne in mind.

In addition, there is a large degree of subjectivity in assigning scores to criteria. Certain value judgements have to be made; for example, is a species of fish endemic to only one site equivalent in value to ten species widely distributed throughout the country? Is one fish species endemic to a single site equivalent in value to a species of amphibian endemic to only one site? In other words, to what extent do we consider diversity more or less important then rarity, and how do we consider the relative importance of different animal and plant taxa?

Nonetheless, one must also consider what evaluation method is compatible to the objectives (i–iv) outlined above. It is doubtful whether algorithmic approaches are much more efficient when data are scanty. Because of inadequate data for assessment, and a lack of funds for collecting such data, developing countries may temporarily have to adopt an evaluation system which is simple and straightforward, which uses the minimum of equipment, and which can be used also as a training tool. Moreover, tropical and/or developing countries do not have the luxury of waiting until they have a comprehensive database on which to base their choices. In the present situation it is felt that the methodology outlined below, admittedly with limitations, is appropriate for situations where resources and trained personnel are lacking, but where there is an urgency to identify areas for protection. The methodology should not be considered as an end point in itself, but rather as a stage in the evolution of the data-gathering exercise where more sophisticated methods can be used as the database becomes more comprehensive (Fig. 1).

The methodology

The steps below show the process of data collection and assessment for wetlands of any given country, and indicate where the ecological and viability criteria may be applied.

Step 1. Inventory of wetland sites for the country, including collation of all available data on these wetlands on standard data sheets for ease of access to information.

Step 2. Short field surveys for rapid assessment of sites for which there is little previous data.

Step 3. Publication of an initial national wetland inventory which can be continuously updated.

Step 4. Application of the set of preliminary ecological criteria and viability criteria in order to draw up a list of potentially important sites to be studied further in detailed field surveys.

Step 5. More detailed surveys of those wetlands identified as being of potential importance by the application of preliminary criteria in *Step 4*.

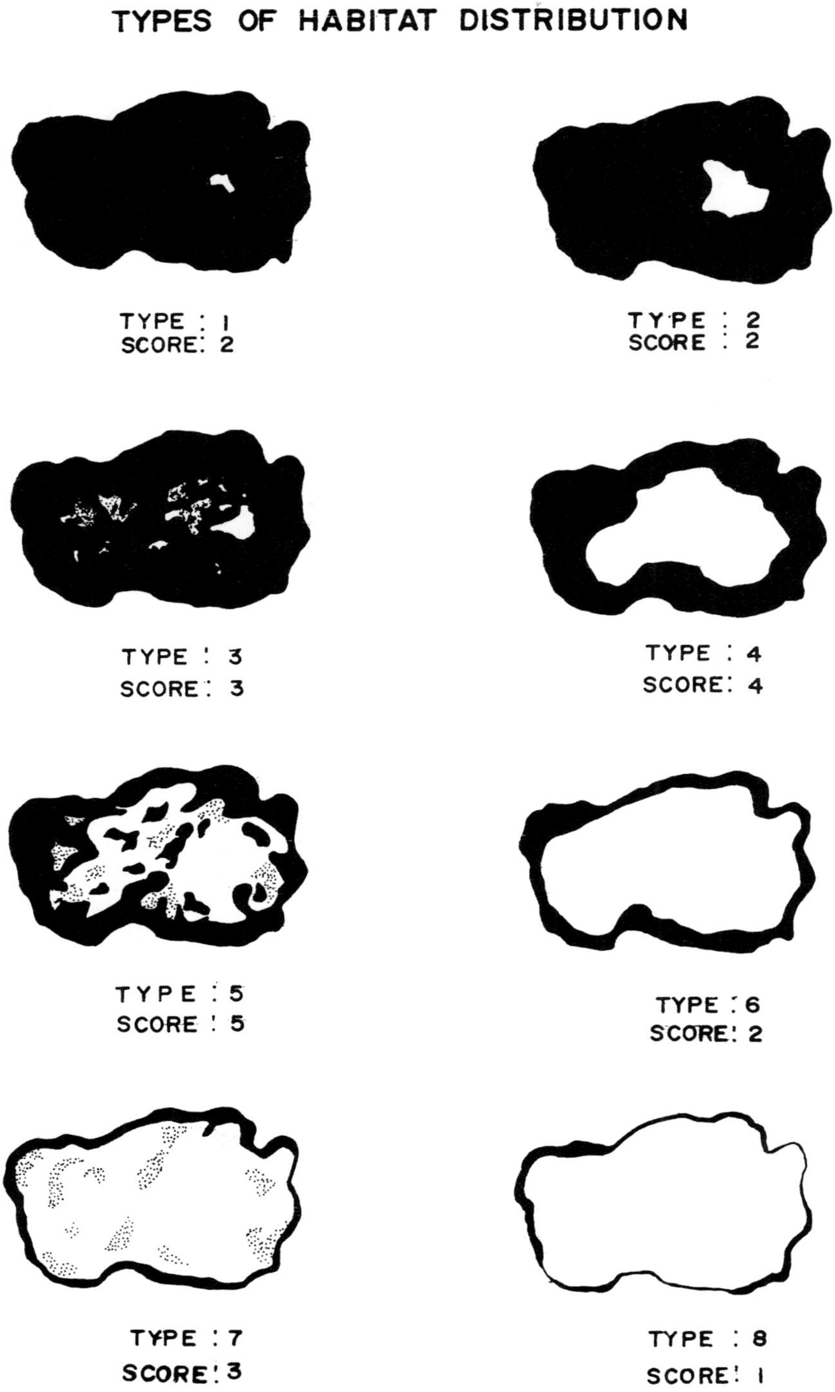

Fig. 2. Types of habitat distribution. White areas indicate open water or herbaceous swamp; black areas indicate scrub, swamp forest or herbaceous swamp. Modified from GOLET (1976).

Step 6. Application of detailed ecological criteria and viability criteria to take full advantage of the data gathered in order to make final selection more precise.
Step 7. Output: a list of wetlands of high ecological value and high viability suitable for protection.

The proposed methodology involves the use of two sets of ecological criteria: a preliminary set when data are scarce which aims to identify wetlands of potential importance that are to be subjected to further field survey; and a detailed set of ecological criteria to be used when additional data have been gathered from field survey. Both sets of ecological criteria are applied together with the viability criteria (Table 1).

The preliminary set of criteria is relatively simple and is based on habitat- and species diversity and rarity. Information to apply these criteria can be gleaned from national inventories, but much useful material (especially for the habitat diversity criterion) can be obtained from aerial photos, remote-sensing data and land-use maps (for example, see Fig. 2). In cases where there is a lack of information, species diversity may have to be inferred from habitat diversity. It must be remembered that only recent photos and maps should be used because of rapid rates of land-use change in most developing countries.

The preliminary set of criteria is applied together with the set of viability criteria, which are composed of factors which evaluate how long the area is likely to retain its conservation value (which depend, for example, upon the size of the area and level of disturbance), and factors which aim to evaluate management feasibility (e.g. land tenure status and the peace and order situation). Almost all of the viability criteria can be assessed, in the first instance, from photos, maps and government statistics, and refined later on the basis of socioeconomic information gathered during later field surveys. The set of detailed ecological criteria are based upon habitat diversity and distribution, as well as species richness, abundance and rarity of selected organisms. Although the method uses these criteria to select wetlands of ecological importance, they could be used for other types of ecosystem.

The methodology has been applied in two situations to assess its usefulness and practicality of use. Firstly, it has been employed to identify wetlands in Sumatra (Indonesia) worthy of further survey by using preliminary ecological criteria. Important wetland sites in Sumatra were identified on the basis of the Indonesian Wetland Inventory (Silvius et al. 1987), the Review of Sumatra for Transmigration (RePPProT 1988), and 1988 1:250,000 scale SLAR images. In all, 68 potential sites were reviewed according to this methodology. The aim of the project was to select Sumatra's most important wetlands for conservation so that conservation resources can be allocated to these sites effectively.

Secondly, the methodology has been used to identify freshwater wetlands in the Philippines to be incorporated into a protected-areas system using both preliminary and detailed ecological criteria. The set of preliminary ecological criteria was applied to freshwater sites listed in the Directory of Philippine Wetlands (Davies et al. 1991) to produce a list of those to be subjected to

Table 1. List of preliminary and detailed ecological criteria and viability criteria used in the wetlands evaluation methodology.

Preliminary Ecological Criteria
Habitat diversity
Unique/rare habitats
Species diversity
Occurrence of rare/endemic/endangered species
Detailed Ecological Criteria
Habitat diversity
Habitat distribution
Wetland vegetation species richness
Rare Wetland Plants
Wetland bird species richness
Wetland bird numbers
Presence of rare/endemic/endangered birds
Fish species richness
Fish endemism
Special considerations (e.g. top predators)
Viability Criteria
Size
Shape
Site condition
Catchment condition
Land tenure status
Peace and order situation
Development plans for site
Population within site
Population in adjacent area

Table 2. Scoring used for preliminary ecological criteria.

Habitat Diversity	
Score 1 point for each wetland type (categorized in Table 3)	
Unique or Rare Habitats	
Add 1 extra point for each unique or rare habitat (e.g. in the Philippines freshwater swamp forest and peat swamp forest would be considered rare).	
Species Diversity	
4	very diverse
3	diverse
2	relatively diverse
1	poor
Rare/Endemic/Threatened Species occurrence	
4	> 3 spp.
3	2–3 spp.
1	1 species
0	none

Table 3. Scoring used for detailed ecological criteria in evaluation of freshwater wetlands for inclusion in the Philippines protected-areas system.

Habitat Diversity

Riverine (rivers/streams)
- i) montane/torrential (> 1,000 ml ASL)
- ii) upland (100–1,000 m ASL)
- iii) lowland/slow-flowing (< 1,000 m ASL)

Lacustrine (lakes and ponds)
- i) permanent
  - a) lakes (>8 ha)
  - b) ponds (<8 ha)
- ii) temporary (seasonal ponds and lakes including floodplain lakes)

Palustrine (swamps and marshes)
- i) herbaceous (surface below water table for most or all of year)
  - a) permanent
  - b) seasonal or temporary (flooded meadows, sedge marshes etc.)
  - c) peat-based
- ii) shrubby
  - a) permanent
  - b) temporary
  - c) peat-based
- iii) trees
  - a) permanent freshwater swamp forest
  - b) seasonally-inundated freshwater swamp
  - c) peat swamp forest

For each wetland habitat type within the site score 1 point, except for rare habitats which have a premium; for peat-based herbaceous swamp and peat-based scrub swamp score 2 points; for permanent freshwater swamp forest, seasonally inundated freshwater swamp forest, and peat swamp forest score 3 points each.

Habitat Distribution (cover type from GOLET [1976]; see Fig. 2)

5	cover type 5
4	cover type 4
3	cover types 3 & 7
2	cover types 1, 2 & 6
1	cover type 8

Wetland Vegetation Species Richness

	Lake		Marsh
8	>15 spp.	very high	>30 spp.
6	10–15 spp.	high	20–30 spp.
4	5–10 spp.	medium	10–20 spp.
1	<5 spp.	low	<10 spp.

Rare Wetland Plants

3	endemic to the site alone
2	endemic to the country
1	restricted distribution in the country

Score appropriate number of points for each rare plant species.

Wetland Bird Species Richness

8	very high (>30 spp.)
6	high (20–30 spp.)
3	medium (10–20 spp.)
1	low (5–10 spp.)

Wetland Bird Abundance

8	very high (>20,000)
6	high (10,000–20,000)
4	medium (5,000–10,000)
1	low (1,000–5,000)
0	very low (<1,000)

Table 3. (Continued).

Presence of Rare/Endangered/Endemic Birds	
4	Red Data Book inclusion
3	species endemic to site alone
2	species endemic to island
1	species endemic to Philippines
0.5	distinct race
Fish Species Richness	
8	very high (>50 spp.)
6	high (30–50 spp.)
4	medium (10–30 spp.)
1	low (<10 spp.)
Fish Endemism	
3	endemic to site alone
2	endemic to island or restricted area
1	endemic to the Philippines
0.5	subspecies or race confined to the Philippines
0.25	subspecies or race with restricted distribution in the Philippines
Special Considerations	
Species for faunal groups to be given special consideration which will vary from country to country: e.g. top predators in the site (mammals, crocodiles, etc.). In the Philippines, crocodiles and crocodilian habitat are accorded special conservation priority.	
8	*Crocodylus mindorensis* present
6	*Crocodylus porosus* present
3	*C. mindorensis* present until recently, habitat still intact
2	*C. porosus* present until recently, habitat still intact.

further survey. The detailed ecological criteria were then applied to these sites of potential ecological importance.

Each criterion has a range of conditions from high conservation value to low. Tables 2, 3 and 4 show the scores assigned to each criterion. The appropriate condition is selected for each wetland and the sum of the scores found for each set of criteria. High values indicate significant ecological value and high viability. The scores for ecological value and viability must not be added together to avoid masking the separate values because each gives a different type of information about a site. Interpretation of the scores obtained is facilitated by presenting them on a scatter diagram of ecological value (X axis) against viability (Y axis).

The set of detailed ecological criteria can be modified according to the situation in the country or area. The set shown here has been modified for the Philippine situation. For example, only those faunal groups for which there is sufficient data have been considered; e.g. amphibians have not been included because to date data on their status are scarce. Also, the numbers used in the species richness criteria will vary from country to country. The fish species richness numbers may need to be much higher in the countries of continental Southeast Asia. A special feature of the Philippines is the urgency to conserve rapidly dwindling crocodile populations, and that special criterion was added to the evaluation criteria. A summary of the specific attributes which contributed most to the ecological value and viability of each of the Philippine sites was employed to supplement the evaluation scores.

Results

The scores for preliminary ecological value and viability of the 68 Sumatran sites are plotted in Fig. 3, Figs 4 & 5 show the plots of preliminary ecological value and viability, and detailed ecological criteria and viability (respectively) for the Philippines wetlands.

In many cases little or no data were available on species diversity in the Sumatran sites, and this information had to be inferred from habitat diversity. A total of 24 sites that scored high on both ecological value and viability were identified as target sites for field surveys. Care was taken in the selection to avoid excessive replication of habitats and to ensure inclusion of as many habitat types as possible. Accordingly, all eight first-choice sites (Fig. 3) were selected for inclusion in detailed surveys, along with sixteen second-choice sites which were added to ensure inclusion of all major habitat types.

Table 4. Scoring for viability criteria in wetland evaluation.

Size (ha)		
	Lake	Marsh
8	> 10,000	> 50,000
6	1,000–10,000	30,000–50,000
4	100–1,000	10,000–30,000
2	10–100	5,000–10,000
1	< 10	< 5,000
Shape		
6	roughly circular	
4	elongated	
0	outline irregular	
Site Condition		
8	unpolluted/undisturbed	
6	slightly/degraded/disturbed	
2	moderately degraded/disturbed	
0	very degraded/disturbed	
Catchment Condition		
8	fully forested or in natural condition	
6	partly forested or partly in natural condition	
4	converted but stable tree cover or perennial crops	
0	denuded, or annual cropping or slash and burn	
Land Tenure Status		
6	already gazetted for protection	
4	gazetting under consideration	
3	government land	
1	for disposal	
0	privately titled/owned	
Peace and Order Situation		
6	no problems	
4	minor problems	
2	military/insurgents in the area but no conflict	
0	serious problem; regular conflict in the area	
Development Plans for Site		
6	no conflicting plans for site	
2	conflicting development plans for catchment	
0	conflicting development plans for site	
Population in Site		
6	low density	
3	medium density	
0	high density	
Population in Adjacent Area		
3	low density	
1	medium density	
0	high density	

Among the Philippine wetlands, it is apparent that few sites combined high ecological value with high viability. This is not surprising considering the high population pressures and over-exploitation of inland waters in the country, and the reduced diversity and abundance of many animal groups because of disturbance and habitat loss. Many sites are not suitable for inclusion in a protected-areas system due to low viability arising from conflicting development plans (e.g. industrial development and hydroelectric power schemes) or due to the peace and order situation.

The interpretation of the scatter diagrams can be aided by dividing them into quadrants according to the degree of ecological value and viability. hese lines have to be drawn subjectively, based on experience of the local situation, by judging the 'bottom line' of minimal importance of ecological value and viability for protection. This will give a quadrant which includes all those sites of high ecological value and high viability which should be considered for protection (Fig. 5). Using this scheme, it is clear that by far the most important Philippines wetlands sites, both ecologically and in terms of viability, are Agusan Marsh in Mindanao, Lake Manguao in Palawan, and Naujan Lake in Mindoro. These sites should have priority for protection. Summary information on the Philippines wetlands of conservation importance is given below; their locations are shown in Figs 6 & 7.

Agusan Marsh, Mindanao

This was by far the most important Philippines wetland identified by the multicriteria method. Its ecological importance was mainly due to habitat diversity and the rarity of some of the habitats. In particular, there are extensive areas of freshwater swamp forest which occur nowhere else in the Philippines. Agusan Marsh is also considered to hold the largest remaining crocodile population in the Philippines. The high viability of this wetland is due to its size and low population pressure compared to many other wetlands.

Lake Manguao, Palawan

Lake Manguao is the least-disturbed lowland lake in the Philippines with a high ecological value due to endemics confined to the site and the presence of species with a restricted distribution. High viability reflects the low population pressure and the undisturbed nature of the lake and its catchment.

Naujan Lake, Oriental Mindoro

Although several sites were more important in terms of ecological value, Naujan Lake had high viability due to its declaration as a national park

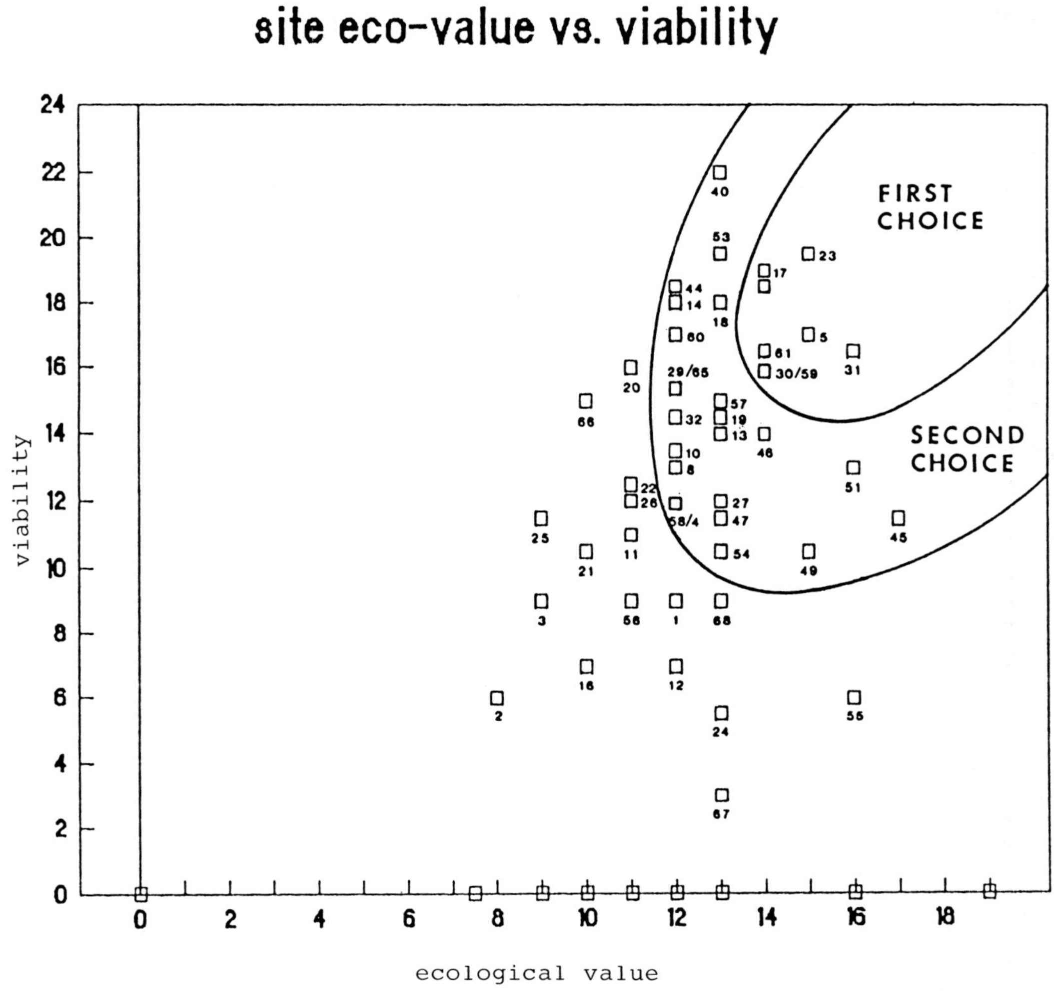

Fig. 3. Scatter diagram to identify Sumatran wetlands requiring further field surveys based on preliminary ecological and viability criteria.

and the presence of stable conditions in the catchment. Although the catchment has been cleared of primary forest, it is under tree cover which has led to the maintenance of good water quality. The diversity of fishes (mostly migratory forms), wetland vegetation, and the presence of migratory waterbirds at the site are the main contributors to its ecological importance.

Leyte-Sab-a Basin

The ecological value of this site was high due to the presence of rare peat-based habitats. The viability was relatively high also as there was little disturbance at the site. However, there are little data for this site compared to most of the others and it has been recommended as a priority area for further work.

Lake Lanao, Mindanao

This lake has extremely high ecological value, and would have been ranked higher if some of the endemic cyprinid flock had not become extinct. Unfortunately, the bad peace and order situation at the site has greatly diminished its viability for protection. It has been recommended that the situation be closely monitored to ascertain whether

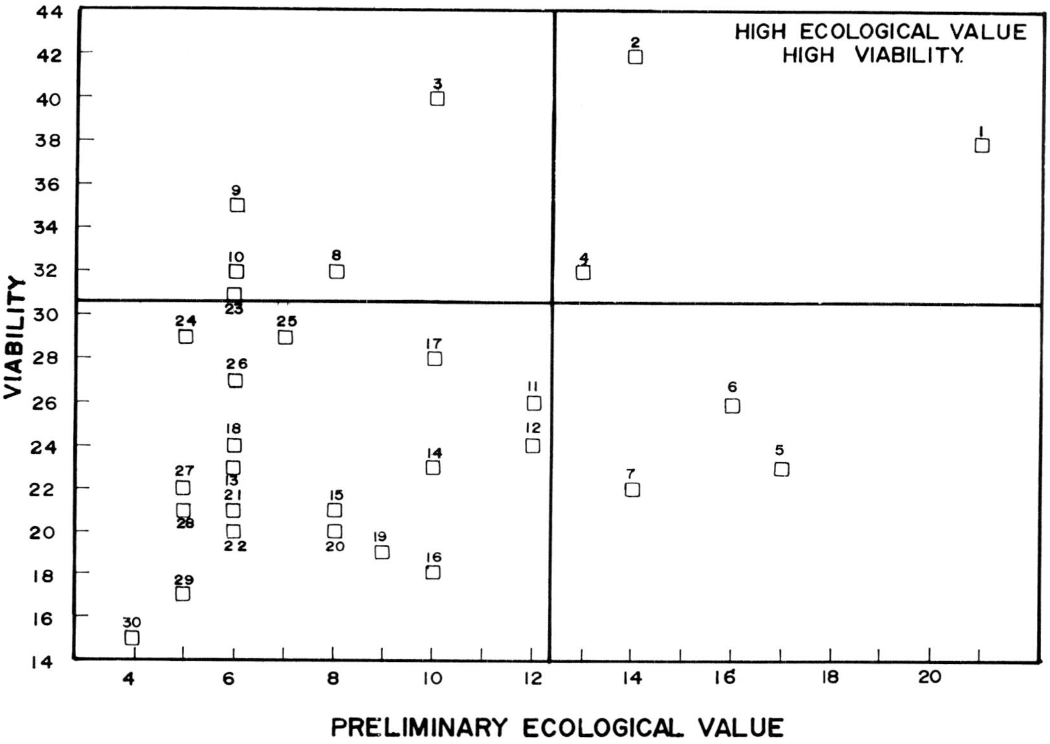

Fig. 4. Scatter diagram to assess the importance of Philippine freshwater wetlands for requiring further study and survey based on preliminary ecological and viability criteria. Sites are numbered as follows: 1) Agusan Marsh, Mindanao; 2) Lake Manguao, Palawan; 3) Naujan Lake, Oriental Mindoro; 4) Leyte Sab-a Basin, Leyte; 5) Liguasan Marsh, Mindanao; 6) Lake Lanao, Mindanao; 7) Candaba Swamp, Central Luzon; 8) Lake Taal, Luzon; 9) Lake Maughan, Mindanao; 10) Lake Danao, Camotes Islands, Cebu; 11) Lake Bato, Bicol Luzon; 12) Lake Baao, Bicol, Luzon; 13) Lake Leonard, Mindanao; 14) Lake Buhi, Bicol, Luzon; 15) Lake Mainit, Mindanao; 16) Lalaguna Marsh, Luzon; 17) Lake Dapao, Mindanao; 18) Ajuy, Dionisio and Sara Wetlands, Panay; 19) Manlubas Swamp, Luzon; 20) Laguna de Bay, Luzon; 21) Lake Buluan, Mindanao; 22) Lake Wood, Mindanao; 23) Lake Balanan, Negros; 24) Twin Lakes, Negros; 25) Lake Imelda, Leyte; 26) Paoay Lake, Luzon; 27) Lake Sebu, Mindanao; 28) Panimaloy Lake, Mindanao; 29) Hinunungan Rice Paddies, Leyte; 30) San Pablo Lakes, Luzon (see also Fig. 5).

conservation measures would be worthwhile in the future. Whilst not suitable at the moment for protection, there are several activities which could be carried out. Priorities include an up-to-date evaluation of the status of the species flock of endemic fishes, an investigation on the taxonomy of these cyprinids, and captive breeding of the endemics which have not yet become extinct.

Lake Taal, Luzon

Lake Taal is a borderline case; although fish diversity is high, this is the only factor contributing strongly to its ecological value. Its viability is fairly high, but development plans for the surrounding area are very extensive. The lake is more suitable for a fisheries management plan rather than for protection in a protected areas system.

Liguasan Marsh, Mindanao and Candaba Swamp, Luzon

There is no doubt that these two large sites are of high ecological value. However, the bad peace and order situation around the Liguasan Marsh and conversion and development plans for the Candaba Swamp render management of both sites non-viable. As with Lake Lanao, the future viability should be monitored. Attention should be given to the establishment of smaller reserves within

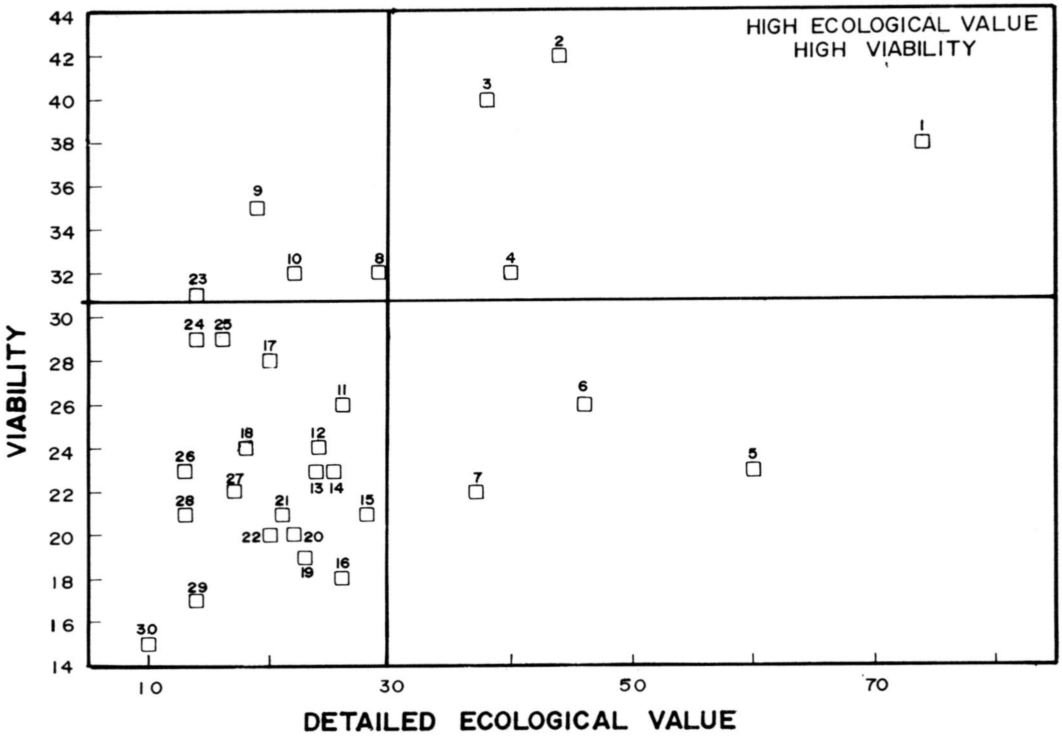

Fig. 5. Scatter diagram to identify Philippine freshwater wetlands for protection based on detailed ecological criteria and viability criteria. For identification of numbered sites, see legend for Fig. 4.

both sites, especially in the Candaba Swamp where there are areas of importance for migratory waterfowl.

Discussion

The methodology outlined above has been used to identify wetlands of ecological importance in Sumatra and in the Philippines, and should be suitable for use in other regions where data are scarce. Some of the drawbacks in the use of multi-criteria techniques can be minimized by recognition of their limitations and by methods to supplement the information gained. When a large amount of information on ecology and viability is condensed into a single score, there is a danger that data will be lost or masked. To reduce this problem, the scores should be supplemented by a concise description of the site, as shown in the results concerning Philippines wetlands, explaining the most important ecological and viability attributes of significant sites. In addition, there may be sufficient information to develop recommendations as to the management of the sites, or to re-rank sites should factors – such as the peace and order situation – alter and make future management of particular areas more viable.

Some small sites may be missed using the present method because they tend to score low on diversity and viability, even though they may have great value for rare or endemic species. Moreover, some small sites have an importance out of all proportion to their size, if they are used as roosting, breeding, feeding or nursery areas where large numbers of a widely-distributed species become concentrated during certain periods. Special attention should be given to identification of such areas and the most important of these should also be considered for protection. The result of such a two-tier selection procedure could be establishment of a main network of relatively large sites (that are especially important for conservation of diversity and maintenance of populations) combined with an array of smaller sites that are important for threatened and endemic species or used by animals at certain times in their life cycles.

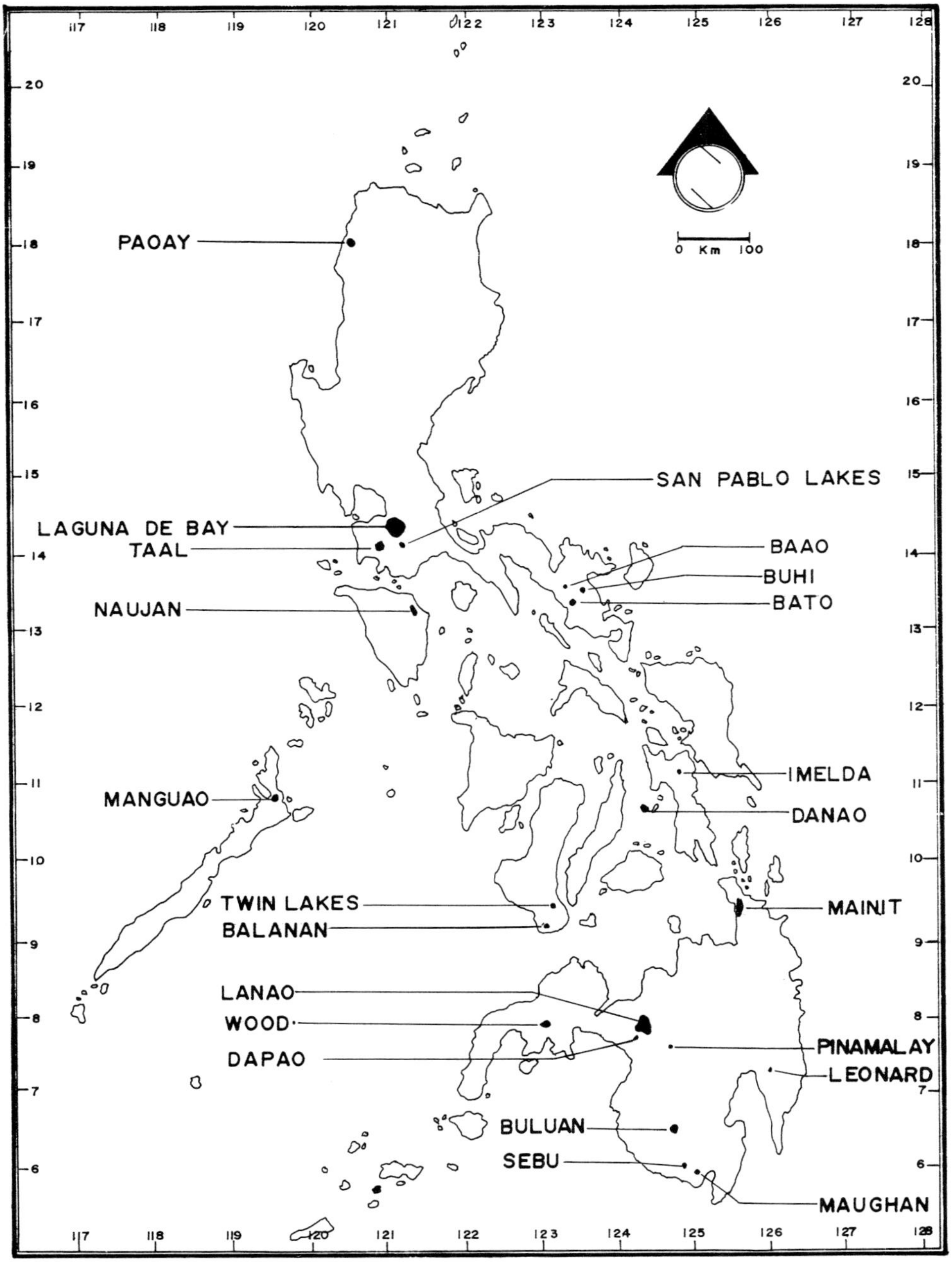

Fig. 6. Location map for Philippine lakes of conservation significance mentioned in the text.

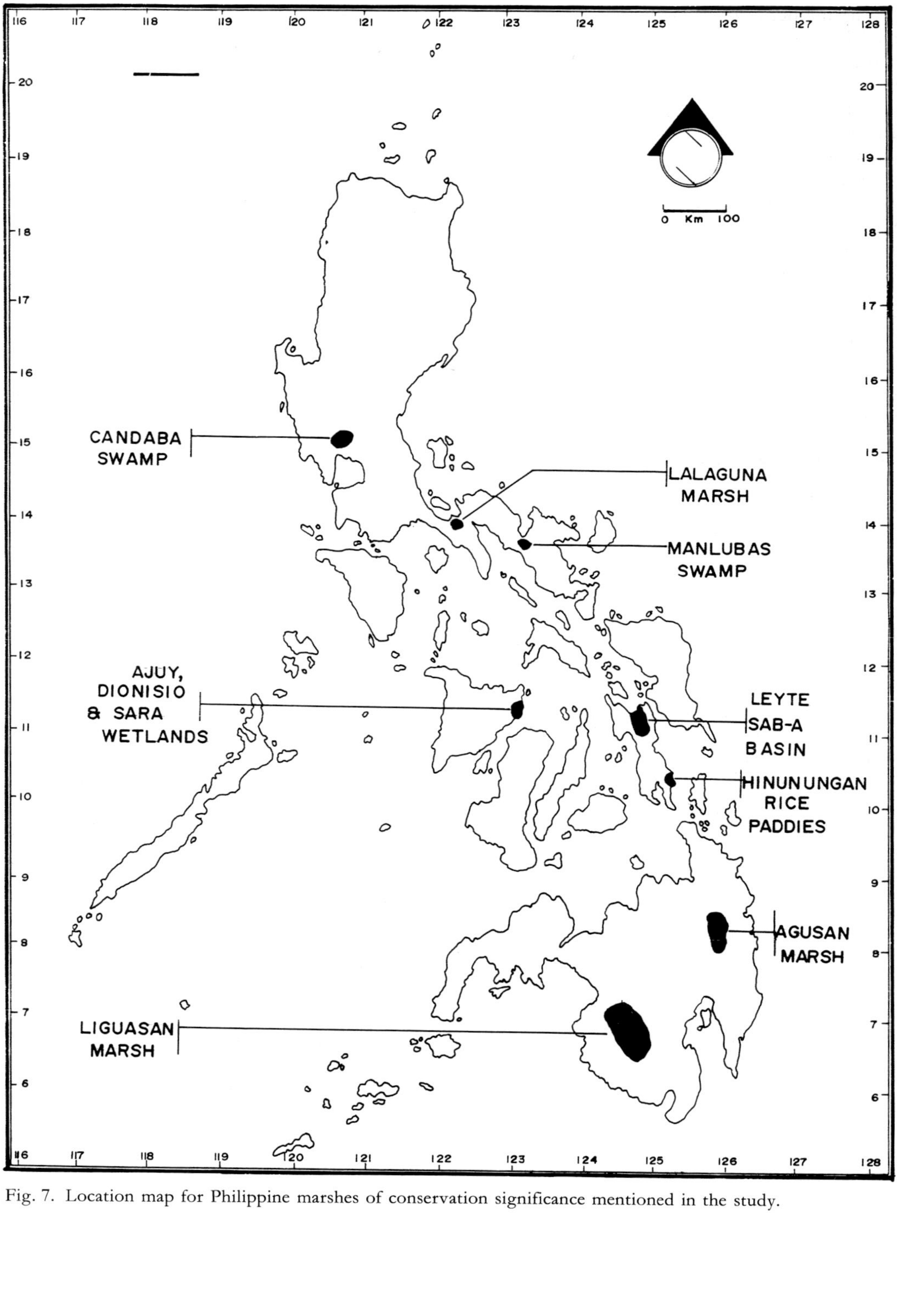

Fig. 7. Location map for Philippine marshes of conservation significance mentioned in the study.

The multicriteria methodology should also be useful as a training tool. The different criteria serve as a checklist, guiding the user to the important features that have to be established regarding ecological value and viability. It should be simple enough to be applied using the minimum of equipment and/or training; moreover, experience gained in using the 'checklist approach' will provide personnel with a systematic basis to build up experience with site evaluation and habitat assessment. The step-by-step method is easy to follow and should result in more involvement of protected area personnel at the local rather than at the national level. All too often, data gathering, processing and interpretation are performed far away from the site to be managed, leaving on-site personnel who will actually have to carry out management work with little responsibility or sense of involvement. The methodology described here can be seen as a means of increasing the involvement of local personnel, and boosting their commitment to their areas which could lead to greater efficiency of on-site management.

References

DAVIES, J., MAGSALAY, P. M., RIGOR, R., MAPALO, A. & GONZALES, H., 1991: A Directory of Philippine Wetlands. A Preliminary Compilation of Information on Wetlands of the Philippines: 444 pp. – Asian Wetland Bureau/Haribon Foundation, Cebu, Philippines.

GOLET, F. C., 1976: Wildlife wetland evaluation model. – In: LARSON, J. S. (ed.): A Guide to Important Characteristics of Freshwater Wetlands in the Northeast. Models for Assessment of Freshwater Wetlands: 13–34. – Water Resources Research Center, University of Massachusetts at Amherst.

MARGULES, C. R., 1989: Introduction to some Australian developments in conservation evaluation. – *Biological Conservation* **50**: 1–11.

MARGULES, C. R., NICHOLLS, A. O. & PRESSEY, R. L., 1988: Selecting networks of reserves to maximise biological diversity. – *Biological Conservation* **43**: 63–76.

PRESSEY, R. L. & NICHOLLS, A. O., 1989 a: Application of a numerical algorithm to the selection of reserves in semi-arid New South Wales. – *Biological Conservation* **50**: 263–278.

– 1989 b: Efficiency in conservation evaluation: scoring versus iterative approaches. – *Biological Conservation* **50:** 199–218.

RePPProT., 1988: Review of Phase I Results, Sumatra. – Regional Physical Planning Programme for Transmigration, ODA for Government of Indonesia, Ministry of Transmigration: Two volumes & three series of 1:250,000 scale maps.

SILVIUS, M. J., STEEMAN, A. P. J. M., BERCZY, E. T., DJUHARSA, E. & TAUFIK, A. W., 1987: The Indonesian Wetland Inventory. A Preliminary Compilation of Existing Information on Wetlands of Indonesia. – PHPA, AWB/INTERWADER, EDWIN, Bogor, Indonesia: Two volumes.

SMITH, P. G. R. & THEBERGE, J. B., 1987: Evaluating natural areas using multiple criteria: theory and practice. – *Environmental Management* **11**: 447–460.

Authors' addresses:

JON DAVIES, Asian Wetland Bureau, Institute of Advanced Studies, University of Malaya, Lembah Pantai, 59100 Kuala Lumpur, Malaysia.
WIM GIESEN, Asian Wetland Bureau-Indonesia, P.O. Box 254/BOO, Bogor 16002, Indonesia.

Mitt. Internat. Verein. Limnol.	24	41–46	Stuttgart, Februar 1994

The socioeconomic conditions in the vicinity of Huai Nam Un Wetland, Songkhram River, Lower Mekong Basin, Thailand

Sansanee Choowaew, Wanchai Chandrachai and Robert C. Petersen Jr

Abstract

The socioeconomic conditions of five villages in the vicinity of the Huai Nam Un Wetland, Songkhram River, in the Lower Mekong Basin (Thailand) are presented. Average population density was 5.8 persons per household, with an average household income of 20,379 Baht/yr (approximately US $ 815) which is below average for northeast Thailand. More than 90% of the households were involved in agriculture, with approximately 5 ha of cultivated land each. Over 85% of household heads had completed primary education.

Analysis of food consumption revealed that sticky (glutinous) rice was the staple food; 577.5 g/person/day were eaten. Lack of protein was a significant problem in the study area, and only 142.0 g/person/day was consumed. The major protein source (61% of the total) came from capture fisheries. Wetland wildlife such as paddy rats, frogs, snakes, insects, molluscs and birds were an important protein source, providing 34.8 g/person/day. Daily intake of vegetables was 105.4 g/person. Domestic fuel comprised firewood (200 kg/household/month) collected from farmlands, and charcoal (84 kg/household/month). Differences in food and fuel consumption among villages depended upon distance from the Songkhram River, and the lowest rate of protein consumption was recorded in the village farthest from the river. Such observations indicate the importance of wetlands in augmenting the diet and, through the harvest and sale of wetland produce, the income of rural inhabitants in northeast Thailand.

Introduction

One important wetland function is providing a source of water and products, such as food and fuel, for human consumption. Wetlands thus have a significant effect on the welfare of people who live in their vicinity. An important part of wetland management programmes should comprise identification of the value of wetlands as a source of produce so as to maintain their traditional use in accordance with local socioeconomic traditions. At present, however, detailed information regarding such practises in many tropical wetlands is scant or inadequate.

The present study was undertaken as part of the Wetland Management Programme of the Mekong Secretariat for the Lower Mekong Basin. Its aim was a preliminary identification of the types of food and fuel products generated by the Huai Nam Un Wetland, including an estimate of their consumption rates, so as to assess the contribution of the Wetland to the socioeconomy of nearby regions.

Study area

The Huai Nam Un is a branch of the Songkhram River which is a main tributary of the Mekong River (Fig. 1). The study area was a riparian wetland situated within 50 km west of the Mekong (between 17° 20′ and 17° 40′ N and 104° OO′ and 104° 30′ E) in the Nakhonphanom Province in upper northeast Thailand. The survey was conducted at five villages in the vicinity of the wetland (Fig. 1).

Methodology

The primary data were obtained from in-depth interviews of a random selection of households from five villages. The villages were visited twice: the first intensive visit was between May 2 – 20, 1988, and the second was during the same period in 1991. The households sampled for interview comprised between five and 25% of the total number of households in each village. Observations and measurements were undertaken on site to obtain data on the utilization or consumption rates of wetland produce. Additional data were derived from government documents and Mahidol University research reports (see References).

Results

General characteristics of the population

There was a total of 809 households and 4,603 persons in the five villages surveyed. All were Buddhists. Average household size was 5.8 persons, and the average age of the head of the household was 46 years. More than 85% of household heads had completed primary education.

0538-4680/94/0024-0041 $ 1.50

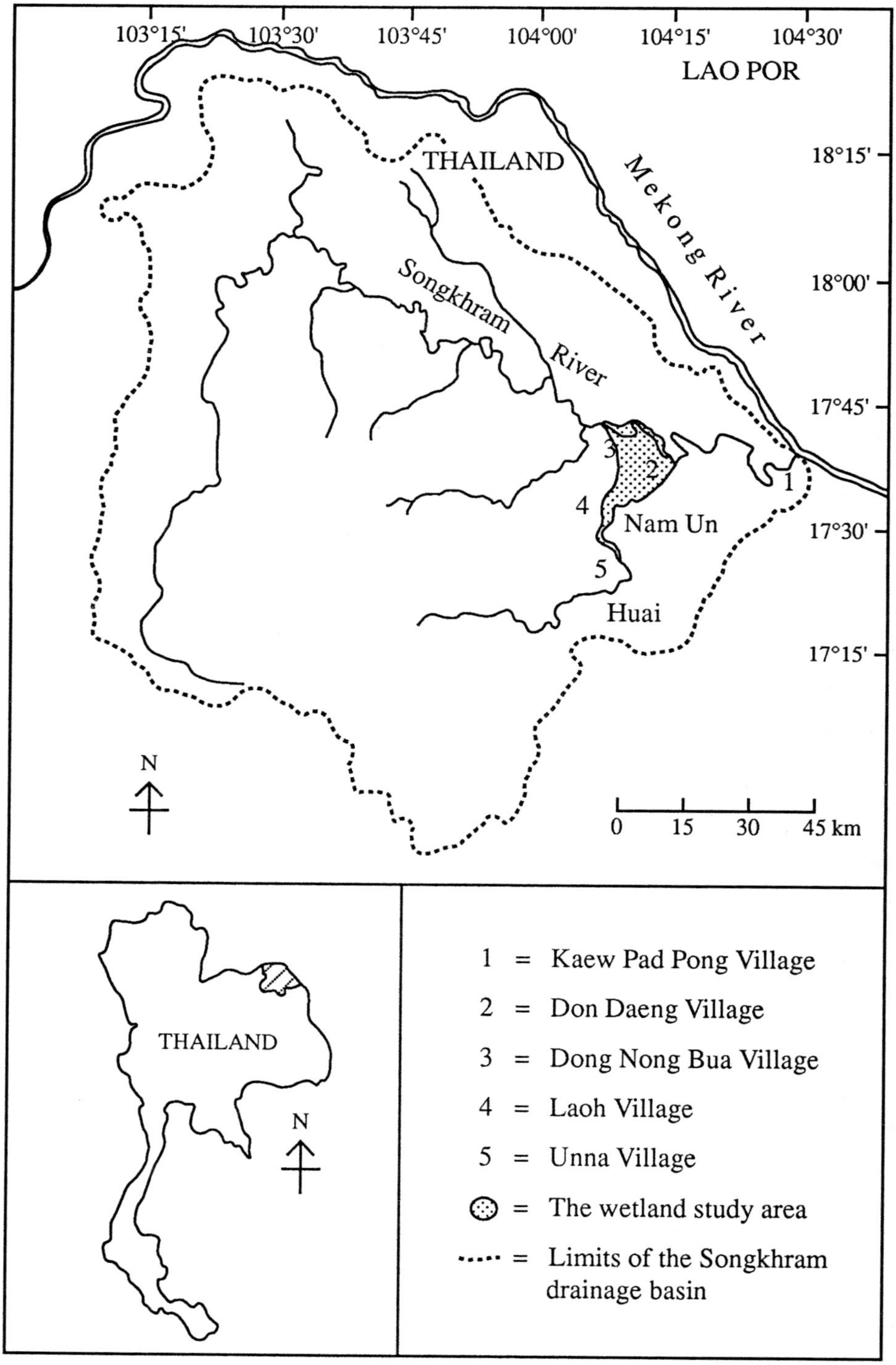

Fig. 1. The Huai Nam Un Wetland, Songkhram River, Lower Mekong Basin, Thailand. The study area is stippled.

Basic socioeconomic status

Over 90% of the households were engaged in farming, with an average of 5 ha farmland/household. From this source, the average income per household was 20,379 Baht/yr (approximately US $ 815). Besides field cropping, sticky rice was grown and cattle rearing and small-scale fisheries were undertaken. In addition, some vegetables were grown seasonally in the wetland. Approximately 93% of household consumption was derived from 'in house' activities; the remainder was purchased.

Food consumption

Sticky (glutinous) rice was the staple food of almost all households. Only three percent consumed both white rice and glutinous rice. Protein was derived from three sources: animal flesh, eggs, and vegetables. The major source of animal protein is fish comprising 61.0% of the total. Beef ranks second (22.1%), above poultry (13.1%) and pork (3.9%). All of the beef and pork consumed was bought, while more than 98% of fish protein was obtained from capture fisheries. Eighty percent of poultry consumption was derived from animals raised by the household. Although some eggs were purchased, most were a byproduct of chicken and duck rearing.

Certain wetland wildlife was eaten, the amounts and type depending upon such factors as the number of household members, educational level of the household head, household occupation and economic status, season, and local preference. In essence, the greater the number of household members, the lower was per capita consumption of protein. Lower-income households were especially dependent on wetland wildlife as protein sources, whereas higher-income households consumed more animal protein and vegetables. The education level of the household affected the intake of protein, with greater education being associated with higher intake of animal protein and a corresponding decline in the use of wetland wildlife as a food source. In a few cases, marked local preference led to high consumption of particular types of wetland wildlife, overriding the socioeconomic trends described above.

Table 1. The major food products derived from the Huai Nam Un Wetland, northeast Thailand.

Common name	Scientific name
Rice	
White rice	*Oryza sativa*
Sticky or Glutinous rice	*Oryza glutinosa*
Animal protein	
Freshwater catfish	*Clarias batrachus*
Snake-head, Murrel	*Channa striatus, Ophiocephalus striatus*
Catfish	*Pangasius sutchi*
Sipat siam	*Trichogaster trichopterus, T. pectoralis*
Climbing perch	*Anabas testudineus*
Nil	*Tilapia nilotica*
Carp	*Cyprinus carpio*
Field eel	*Fluta alba*
Croaker	*Pseudosciaena* sp.
Tarpon, Lady fish	*Cirrhinus micropeltes*
Featherback	*Notopterus notopterus*
Barb	*Puntius gonionotus*
Wildlife	
Frog	*Rana tigrina, Rana vittigera*
Kiad	*Rana limnocharis*
Ueng	*Kaloula pulchra*
Paddy rat	*Rattus rattus*
Pond snail	*Filopaludina doliaris, Vicisara doliaris*
Yae	*Leiolepis belliana*
Pom, Kapom	*Calotes mystaceus*
Jing Rheed	*Gryllus testaceus*
Mang Da Na	*Lethocerus indicus*
Jak Jan	*Dundubia intermerata*
Sparrow	*Passer montanus*

Table 2. Food and fuel consumption rates.

Product	Consumption rate
Rice	577.5 g/person/day
Animal protein	142.0 g/person/day
Wildlife	34.8 g/person/day
Vegetables	105.4 g/per/day
Drinking water	5.4 l/person/day
Domestically-used water	50.3 l/person/day
Firewood	200.0 kg/household/month
Charcoal	84.0 kg/household/month

Products of the Huai Nam Un Wetland

Food products generated by the Huai Nam Un Wetland could be classified into five major types: rice, animal protein (fish), wildlife, vegetables, wetland plants, and water. Both white and sticky rice were grown in the wetland, although sticky rice was more important. Fish comprised the bulk of animal protein, but shrimp, crabs and ant eggs from the wetland were consumed regularly. Salt-

Table 3. Basic composition (per 100 g of foodstuff) of food products consumed around the Huai Nam Un Wetland.

Name of foods	Moisture g	Calories Unit	Fat g	Carbohydrate g	Fibre g	Protein g
Rice						
White rice	13.7	341	2.3	73.4	10.4	5.8
Sticky rice	11.3	355	0.3	81.1	0	7.0
Animal protein						
Chicken	55.9	302	25.0	0	0	18.0
Duck	54.4	326	28.6	0	0	16.0
Hen egg, whole	73.7	163	11.5	0.8	0	12.9
Duck egg, whole	70.6	188	14.2	0.7	0	13.2
Pork	42.5	457	45.0	0	0	11.9
Beef	59.8	273	22.1	0	0	17.2
Buffalo	76.5	120	4.9	0	tr.	17.7
Freshwater catfish	78.1	98	2.2	0	0	18.2
Snake-head fish	79.6	78	0.1	0.1	0	19.1
Catfish	54.0	321	28.2	2.5	0	14.4
Sipat siam, fresh	80.9	76	0.8	0	0.1	17.2
Sipat siam, dry	27.3	318	17.4	0	0	40.3
Climbing perch	74.7	137	7.1	0	0	17.2
Carp	75.4	118	3.9	0	0	19.4
Field eel	82.0	77	0.7	0	0	16.5
Croaker	77.3	102	2.2	0	0	19.2
Tarpon, Lady fish	77.3	102	2.2	0	0	19.6
Featherback	78.5	83	0.2	2.0	0	18.0
Barb	74.1	112	2.6	0.2	0	22.0
River shrimp	78.7	78	1.2	1.0	0	15.8
Small crab	68.1	151	3.8	14.1	–	13.8
Salt fermented fish	55.7	134	4.7	8.9	0	13.9
Wildlife						
Frog	77.5	95	0.6	0	–	20.9
Yae, dry	10.0	317	5.4	0	0	67.0
Ueng, dry	9.3	458	21.5	10.4	0	55.6
Pond snail	79.3	73	0.7	4.5	0.4	12.1
Sparrow	72.5	124	4.6	0	0	19.4
Ant eggs	71.0	129	3.8	5.0	–	17.4

fermented fish was a major source of protein and minerals in the region, and is eaten widely throughout northeast Thailand (Table 1). However, other elements of the wildlife from the Huai Nam Un Wetland which were sold regularly in local markets are eaten only in the immediate vicinity of the wetland. A wide range of wetland plants was used as food and building material, among them edible bamboo (*Bambusa arundinacea*), the sedge *Cyperus corymbosus*, and certain Dipterocarpaceae. During the dry season (from December to March), cabbage, chili, pumpkin and tomatoes were planted in wetland areas along the Songkhram River and its branch (i.e. Huai Nam Un).

The wetland supplies water to underground aquifers from where water is drawn for drinking and domestic use. More than 75% of the water consumed by households was obtained from shallow wells, the remaining 20% was derived from rain water.

The total consumption of wetland products by villagers in the vicinity of the Huai Nam Un Wetland is shown in Table 2. The significance of wetland wildlife is apparent in that it amounted to 25% of animal protein derived from other sources (i.e. capture fish, beef, poultry and pork).

Nutritional and economic value of major food products

By using analytical data from reports of the Department of Health (Ministry of Public Health 1978), a comparison of the nutritive value of foods

Table 4. Comparison of the nutrient and vitamins content (per 100 g of foodstuff) of foods consumed around the Huai Nam Un wetland.

	Ca	P	Fe	Vitamins				
				A	B1	B2	Niacin	C
	mg	mg	mg	I.U.	mg	mg	mg	mg
Rice								
White rice	24	236	1.4	–	0.33	0.06	5.6	–
Sticky rice	12	46	1.3	0	0.06	0.03	–	0
Animal protein								
Chicken, meat	14	200	1.5	809	0.08	0.16	8.0	–
Duck, meat	15	188	1.8	–	0.10	0.24	5.6	–
Hen egg, whole	61	222	3.2	1,950	0.10	0.40	0.1	0
Duck egg, whole	64	220	3.6	1,541	0.16	0.40	0.2	0
Pork	7	117	1.8	–	0.58	0.14	3.1	–
Beef	8	130	2.3	67	0.06	0.36	4.5	0
Buffalo	14	221	3.3	19	0.06	0.16	3.5	0
Freshwater catfish	34	116	0.2	283	0.10	0.04	2.2	–
Snake-head fish	14	114	0.4	–	0.01	0.01	–	0
Catfish	19	104	0.9	–	0.01	0.10	–	2
Sipat siam, fresh	70	170	2.3	1,092	1.00	0.19	2.0	–
Sipat siam, dry	500	1,000	2,7	–	0.06	0.14	–	0
Climbing perch	98	160	1,6	1,117	0.02	0.27	3.2	–
Carp	57	189	1.4	133	0.03	0.07	2.6	–
Field eel	50	158	2.2	255	0.13	0.07	2.6	0
Croaker	41	162	1.0	75	0.04	0.15	3.7	0
Tarpon, Lady fish	54	263	0.7	–	0.02	0.06	5.1	–
Featherback	49	26	0.3	–	–	–	–	–
Barb	32	102	0.4	–	–	–	–	–
River shrimp	9,200	2,690	1.8	–	–	–	–	–
Small crab	210	–	1.1	–	–	–	–	–
Salt fermented fish	581	336	–	–	–	–	–	–
Wildlife								
Frog	46	168	1.8	–	0.06	0.12	5.0	–
Yae, dry	5,250	1,129	4.1	–	0.16	0.45	–	0
Ueng, dry	2,150	616	26.3	–	0.13	2.90	–	0
Pond snail	1	114	25.2	1,350	0.01	0.49	0.6	–
Sparrow	470	590	–	50	0.30	0.25	5.0	–
Ant eggs	73	217	2.0	–	0.43	0.74		

consumed by villagers in the vicinity of the Huai Nam Un Wetland was undertaken (Tables 3 & 4). The nutritional value of wetland products was equitable to or even higher than that of other foods. Besides rice – which is the main source of calories – and fish – which is the major protein source – wetland wildlife such as *Leiolepis belliana* and *Kaloula pulchra* provided significant calories and were rich in protein. In addition, *Passer montanus, L. belliana, K. pulchra, Trichogaster pectoralis,* river shrimp, crabs and salt-fermented fish were good sources of calcium and phosphorus. *Kaloula pulchra* and *Filopaludina doliaris* were rich in iron, while *Anabas testudineus* and *F. doliaris* had a high vitamin A content. *Trichogaster pectoralis* and *K. pulchra* were rich in vitamins B1 and B2 respectively.

Table 5 presents the prices of some wetland food products as recorded from village markets, and gives an indication of their relative values.

Discussion

Because of the low average household income, products derived from the Huai Nam Un Wetland played an important role in the sustenance of villagers in the vicinity of the wetland. This is indi-

Table 5. Local sale price of some wetland food products. Note: 25 Baht = US $ 1.

Product	Sale price (1985–1988) Baht/kg
Freshwater catfish	30–35
Snake-head	30–35
Climbing perch	20
Barb	20–30
Nil	20–25
Carp	20–25
Sipat siam	20
Catfish	15–16
Field eel	20–25
River shrimp	40
Frog	40 Baht/bag of 6 frogs
Ueng, dry and grilled	20 Baht/Row of 5–6 *Ueng*
Mang Da Na, fried, crisp	1 Baht each
Yae, grilled	200 Baht/10 rows of 2–*3 Yae*

cated by the fact that the distance of each of the five study villages from the Songkhram River draining the wetland was a significant factor affecting the rate of protein consumption. The nearer the village, the higher the rate. Wetland products were not only domestically consumed, but were also sold in local markets, providing additional income for households as well as creating jobs for household labour.

Of particular significance was the finding that the size of the household affected per capita protein consumption rate; the more family members, the less animal protein was consumed and – in economically-disadvantaged households – wetland wildlife was an important nutrition item. Future increases in population projected for the area will therefore place additional pressure on the wetland to provide wildlife protein to meet escalating demands. This may lead, in the longer term, to over-exploitation of the wetland. Developments – such as the replacement of small-scale capture fisheries by culture fisheries, the intrusion of intensive farmlands into wetland, and the conversion of wetland to other uses – are taking place already. Moreover, local residents report that the species diversity and abundance of wildlife resources from the wetland seem to be diminishing. Unless ways of meeting the needs of the increasing population and their greater demands upon wetland resources can be met through management and maintenance of the ecosystem, or through diversification, of the rural economy, then pressures on the wetland and concomitant loss of habitat will continue. To prevent such losses, both socioeconomic and ecological considerations must be built in to proposed wetland-management programmes.

References

Department of Health, 1978: Nutritional Table. – Nutrition Division, Ministry of Public Health, Bangkok, Thailand. 48 pp. (In Thai).

Faculty of Environment and Resources Studies 1988: Report on Study of Resource Utilization Planning, A case Study of Songkhram Watershed, Upper Northeast of Thailand: 340 pp. – Mahidol University, Nakornpathom, Thailand. (In Thai).

Authors' addresses:

Sansanee Choowaew, Faculty of Environmental and Resource Studies, Mahidol University, Salaya, Nakornpathom 73170 Thailand.

Wanchai Chandrachai, Land Use Planning Division, Department of Land Development, Bangkok 10900, Thailand.

Robert C. Petersen Jr, U.S. Geological Survey, Water Resources Division, Box 25046 MS 406, Denver, CO 80225, USA.

Mitt. Internat. Verein. Limnol.	24	47–52	Stuttgart, Februar 1994

Threats to, and conservation of, tropical freshwater fishes

Rosemary Lowe-McConnell

Abstract

Threats to fishes in tropical inland waters, arising mainly from expanding human populations, include habitat changes in rivers due to deforestation, the creation of hydroelectric barrages which block fish migrations and alter flow-regimes, pollution, and wetland drainage. Threats to lake fishes, in particular, originate from overfishing and introductions of exotic species. The unique endemic faunas of the African Lakes Tanganyika and Malawi need special protection.

Taxonomic and basic biological research on the diverse tropical fish faunas is needed if we are to provide or maintain the long-term catch statistics which would give an early warning of population decline and potential species loss. Methods to combat increasing fragmentation of riverine fish populations by new hydroelectric barrages, and identifying species that will exploit conditions in new reservoirs without the damaging effects of some exotic species are highlighted as urgent topics requiring research.

Overview

Threats to freshwater fishes have been considered in three recent international symposia: on 'Rare Fish' by the Fisheries Society of British Isles 1990 (Lowe-McConnell 1990); on 'Biodiversity' by ASIH New York, 1991; and 'The Threatened World of Fishes' at the Ichthyological Congress, the Hague, 1991. These all emphasized that biodiversity in aquatic systems is declining rapidly, mainly due to environmental changes that result from expanding human populations.

This brief review aims to draw attention to work on tropical inland waters which has relevance for conditions in Southeast Asia. However, examples of threats to these fishes come mainly from Africa and South America, reflecting the relative paucity of information from tropical Asia and the Author's own research experience.

Taxonomic diversity in tropical freshwaters is so great, and so many species have yet to be described, that it is impossible to say how many species have vanished or are endangered. One can only look at what is happening to the most well-studied species, mainly fishes of commercial importance as food or those exported as ornamental fishes.

A range of habitat changes threaten freshwater fishes. Among them, deforestation around headwater streams leads to sedimentation affecting fish spawning and feeding grounds. Deforestation is also a problem in lateral swamp forests which are important fish-feeding grounds along (for example) Amazon blackwater rivers (Goulding et al. 1988). Hydroelectric barrages block fish migrations and alter river flowregimes downstream. The man-made lakes created behind barrages lead to faunal changes; however, these lakes can, if well managed support valuable fisheries although yields are often not in excess of those on the original floodplains downstream of the dam.

Pollution threats include eutrophication by organic wastes and fertilizers (which can often be remedied), sedimentation, and poisoning. Among the latter are toxins from mining – such as the use of mercury for gold extraction in Brazil – agrochemical runoff, and industrial wastes. Wetland drainage for agriculture, combined with use of fertilizers and pesticides, poses an additional threat. Overfishing, especially of fish on spawning runs, is a further danger. Although overfishing can be rectified if a series of reliable catch-effort records are available, much taxonomic work on tropical fish faunas is needed to enable these statistics to be kept. Introductions of exotic species and escapes from fish culture, which can engender extinctions through predation, competition, habitat alteration, or spread of disease, are yet another threat. Introductions of piscivorous sport fish are particularly damaging. A problem is the likelihood that many of these threats will act synergistically.

Seasonally-migrating otophysan fishes predominate in the riverine faunas of the three tropical landmasses of Asia, Africa, South America; east of Wallace's line, in Papua New Guinea and the Australian tropics, most fishes are representatives of marine families. In Southeast Asia, cyprinids (carps) are the dominant group (comprising over 40% of the species; Rainboth 1991), but siluroids (catfishes of various families, 18%) are also important. Southeast Asia has few large natural lakes, but the reservoir areas, totalling an estimated 3×10^6 ha (compared with 3.5×10^6 ha of natural and floodplain lakes, as well as 12.5×10^6 ha of freshwater swamps), are expected to increase to 20×10^6 ha by 2000 AD (Fernando 1984). As the freshwater fish fauna is mainly riverine in origin, and riverine fishes colonising lakes tend to stay near banks and inflows, lacustrine fishes are needed to exploit open-water niches (Fernando & Holčík 1987).

Southeast Asia has few truly lacustrine fish species. What fish should be stocked in these reservoirs? Data on ASEAN reservoirs (Baluyut 1983) indicate that introduced gouramies, carps, and exotic African cichlids

0538-4680/94/0024-0047 $ 1.50

(tilapia) – all non-piscivores – have in many cases boosted yields. Tilapias have been stocked in many reservoirs (for example, in Sri Lanka and Malaysia) and also support a fishery in the Sepik River (Papua New Guinea) which lacks indigenous primary freshwater fish (COATES 1985).

South American studies

The South American fish fauna is, like that of Southeast Asia, mainly riverine, otophysan-dominated; cyprinids are absent but characoids fill many of their ecological roles. They are riverine fishes undertaking seasonal spawning and feeding migrations. There are many siluriform families, also indigenous cichlids, though here, too, African tilapias are often stocked in reservoirs. The Amazon has an estimated 2000 plus fish species, of which over 100 may be found in Manaus (Brazil) fish markets at one time. Many studies have centred on Manaus where the nutrient-rich whitewaters of the main Amazon are joined by nutrient-poor acid blackwaters of the Rio Negro, in which fish are dependent on the flooded forest for allochthonous foods (fruits and invertebrates; GOULDING 1980). Many characoids and catfishes migrate long distances, both up and down tributaries and the main river. Indeed, large catfishes appear to travel from estuary to headwater streams over 3000 km upriver. The creation of hydroelectric barrages and large man-made lakes block these migrations and present an increasing threat even greater than that posed by large-scale forest clearance (BAYLEY & PETRERE 1989, PETRERE 1989, BARTHEM et al. 1991). Particular concern derives from the fact that many other barrages are planned for the Amazon region.

Brazil has created over 15,000 multipurpose reservoirs in the dry Northeast (PETRERE 1989). Post-impoundment fish yields have been augmented (to ca 125 kg/ha/yr) by introduced fish from other river systems and African tilapias *Oreochromis niloticus* (LINN.) and *Tilapia rendalli* (BOULENGER). For successful stocking, the abundant predatory piranhas (*Serrasalmus*) which increase following impoundment (as seen in the Tucuruí dam on the Tocantins River, Brazil; LEITE 1991) have first to be controlled; to aid this the piscivorous *Cichla ocellaris* SCHNEIDER has been introduced into some impoundments. However, *C. ocellaris*, which was introduced as a sport fish into an inflowing river, descended to Gatun Lake in the Panama Canal where it ravaged indigenous fishes and altered the lake's whole ecology (ZARET & PAINE 1973).

Estimates of fish production and yield from floodplains – with management options – have been assessed (BAYLEY 1989, BAYLEY & PETRERE 1989, MERONA 1990). Commercial and artisanal fisheries tend to take different species, but migratory fishes are important elements of both fisheries. Overfishing occurs near large towns. The big new hydroelectric barrages lack fish passes; the Tucuruí dam has decreased commercial catches by 60 per cent, and affected fishing both upstream and downstream of the dam (LEITE 1991). An effective fish pass has, however, existed on the Mogi Guassu (Brazil) since the 1930s. Tagging studies over ten years have shown the regularity of seasonal migrations of the large fishes between spawning and feeding areas, a 1200-km round trip, with fish moving upriver at rates of between five and eight km day (GODOY 1967; see also WELCOME 1985, PETRERE 1989). Tagging in the Paraná (Argentina) has also shown the long distances moved (over 1,000 km), at speeds of around seven km/day or faster.

African studies

Africa has many large lakes, and the African fauna is particularly rich in cichlids. In the rivers, otophysans include both cyprinids (such as the genus *Labeo*, also found in Asia) and characoids (absent from Asia). Siluriform families include four which also occur in Asia (Ariidae, Bagridae, Clariidae and Schilbeidae). Africa also has many endemic fish families. The large lakes of eastern Africa are inhabited by spectacular flocks of endemic cichlid species which breed in the lakes, generally throughout the year.

Much work has been concentrated on the African Great Lakes. The effects of introduced fishes, such as exotic tilapias and the predatory Nile perch *Lates niloticus* (LINN.) (Centropomidae), into the huge (68,800 km^2) Lake Victoria has provided a spectacular example of recent faunal change, leading to the loss of an estimated 200 taxa of endemic cichlids (BAREL et al. 1991). These cichlids had formed the basis of classic evolutionary studies by Greenwood (1981). Fishery biologists are, however, at present pleased that fish yields from Lake Victoria have increased fourfold since the Nile Perch became abundant. But how long will this last? In a small lake (Kyoga) into which Victoria flows, where Nile perch were established earlier than in the main lake, the predator-dominated catches which followed *Lates* introduction have since declined (OGUTO-OHWAYO 1990). Fur-

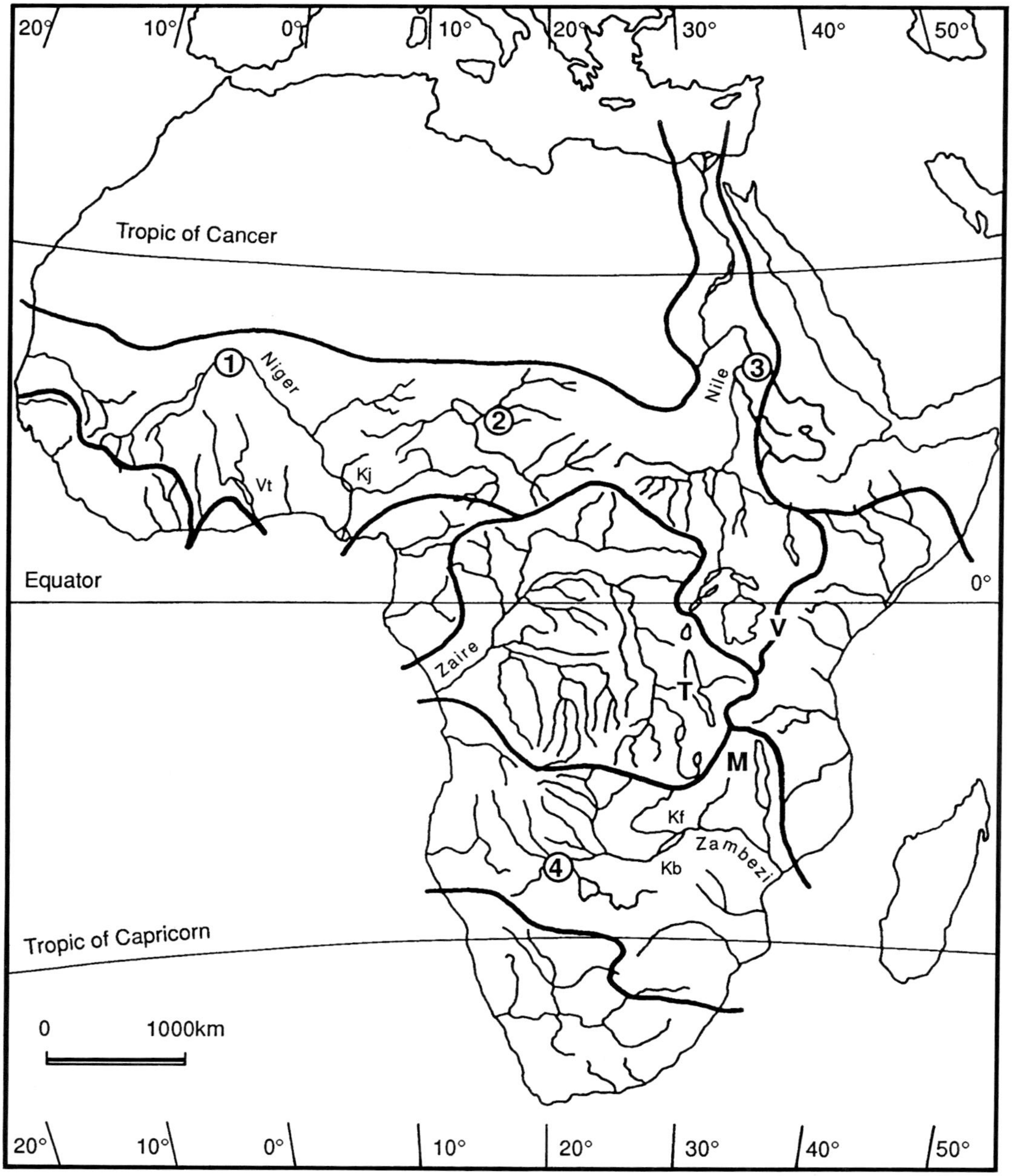

Fig. 1. Sites of African studies mentioned in the text. Great Lakes: V = Victoria (Nile drainage); T = Tanganyika (Zaire drainage); M = Malawi (Zambezi drainage). Man-made lakes: Kb = Kariba; Kf = Kafue; Vt = Volta; Kj = Kainji. Floodplain areas: 1 = Middle Niger delta; 2 = Lake Chad affluents; 3 = Nile Sudd; 4 = Okavango.

thermore, Lake Victoria is now undergoing limnological changes, with increased eutrophication and fish kills. Future trends cannot be predicted with certainty.

Numerous ecological studies of riverine and floodplain fishes (references in Beadle 1981, Lowe-McConnell 1975, 1987, Welcomme 1985) have included basic studies of the central Niger delta, and inflowing rivers of Lake Chad, in the Nile Sudd area, and Okavango swamps (Fig. 1). The creation of large man-made lakes behind hydroelectric barrages in the nineteen-fifties and sixties stimulated pre- and post-impoundment investigations. Examples include the Zambezi River behind the Kariba dam (closed 1958); the Kafue tributary and further downriver at Cabora Bassa; the Volta River in Ghana (dam closed 1964); the River Niger at Kainji (1968); and at Kossou, Ivory Coast, among many others. These studies all demonstrated how otophysan-dominated riverine faunas undergo a transition to lacustrine cichlid-dominated ones, with an initial loss of species. Fish production tends to show initially high yields, when allochthonous inputs from drowned vegetation are plentiful, followed by a decline, before a gradual increase to a new stable level based on autochthonous food sources.

At Kariba (4,300 km^2, 300 km × 30 km, 30 m deep) on the Zambezi River, exotic (South American) *Salvinia molesta* (D.S. Mitchell) ferns covered 20% of the lake surface, proving an initial nuisance. The middle-Zambezi had 31 fish species prior to dam closure; another nine species colonized later from the upper Zambezi and became established in the new impoundment (Balon & Coche 1974). The Tilapia *Oreochromis macrochir* (Boulenger) from upper Zambezi was artifically stocked, as it was thought the indigenous *Oreochromis mortimeri* (Trewavas) would not adapt quickly; however, *O. mortimeri* became the more important species. The clupeid *Limnothrissa miodon* (Boulenger) was introduced from Lake Tanganyika in 1965 to utilise the open-water zooplanktivore niche. A commercial fishery which started six years after introduction produced 12,000 t in 1981, then decreased, but the fish feeding on *Limnothrissa* increased (Marshall 1984). *Limnothrissa* subsequently spread downriver where they colonized the new Cahora Bassa Lake.

Volta Lake is the largest artifical lake in Africa (8,500 km^2). Little terrestrial vegetation was cleared and decomposition of this material caused temporary deoxygenation of the water column after filling. No artificial stocking was undertaken here or in Kainji Lake (Fig. 1), but indigenous riverine tilapias and small pelagic fishes became abundant. Volta's peak catch (61,700 t) was made five years after dam closure but has now stabilized at around 40,000 t/yr (Petr 1986). Kainji's peak catch (28,000 t/yr) was recorded between two and three years after dam closure, then stabilized at around 4500 t, equivalent to 35 kg/ha/yr, approximately equal to the original yield of the floodplain (Welcomme 1986). A fall in catches on the river below the dam has been attributed to changes in flow regime and flood-plain inundation.

Discussion

Tropical inland fish faunas are diverse in all three land masses – South Asia, Africa and South America – and much taxonomic and basic biological research into life histories and fish movements is still needed. To correct overfishing, it is essential to have good catch-effort statistics. These are lacking in many places, but in all three tropical areas there are numerous examples of fisheries declining due to human activities. For example, populations of endemic cichlids in Madagascar which are of great scientific interest have been much reduced by deforestation and introduced fish species (Reinthal & Stiassny 1991). Fish populations have been affected by draining or modifying floodplains for rice cultivation, as in West Africa and around Lake Chad. In the Benue River (Nigeria), the impact of damming, drought and overexploitation has led to simplification of the fauna, with an increase in 'weed' species (Neiland et al. 1990). Cyprinid (*Labeo*) fisheries have disappeared due to overfishing during upriver spawning migrations (Skelton et al. 1991). In South America, pollution of the Mogi Guassu (Brazil) has caused population declines: the catch of migrating fishes 20 years ago was 400–1000 kg/man/day and is now only 80–100 kg/man/day (Petrere 1989). Pantanal fisheries have been reduced by drainage for soybean cultivation. Flood-forest clearance in the Amazon has removed important fish-feeding areas (Goulding et al. 1988), and the new lakes behind hydroelectric dams have much reduced faunas. Introductions of exotic species have decimated endemic faunas: for example, the Nile Perch (*Lates*) in Lake Victoria, the sport-fish *Cichla ocellaris* in Gatun Lake (Zaret & Paine 1973), and tilapias in Madagascar.

Which of these issues can we tackle? One possible remedy to blockage of migration routes by hydroelectric barrages is provision of fish passes.

However, many of the new dams are very high. Moreover, it is now clear that research into the habits and behaviour of individual fish species is needed for the design of suitable passes, and studies of characoid and catfish migrations are being intensified in the Amazon (e.g. RIBEIRO & PETRERE 1990; BARTHEM et al. 1991). WELCOMME (1985) pointed out that fish passes have not been very successful with warm-water fish, the Mogi Gaussu pass which has special tunnels for catfishes, being an exception. Another approach is artificial spawning and stocking, as is usual in the USA and is now being explored in Thailand for the potamodromous Mekong giant catfish *Pangasianodon gigas* CHEVEY (PHOLPRASITH et al. 1990; pers. comm.).

Introductions cause declines of native fishes but can lead to higher yields of marketable fish. Are they then justifiable? Here the choice must be to decide on priorities at the particular locality: diversity or fish yield? There are many socioeconomic and political issues involved in fish introductions. Commercial versus artisanal fisheries is a concern in some places. From Brazil come reports that, because farmers carry more political weight than itinerant fishermen, fisheries have been halted when controversies have arisen over pesticides, etc. In at least one state artisanal fisheries have been forbidden (PETRERE 1989).

When considering introductions, it has to be kept in mind that introduced fish will escape, and once established are virtually impossible to eradicate. Accordingly, the whole drainage basin – and not just the locality of introduction – is likely to be affected. The two African Great lakes, Tanganyika and Malawi, with their spectacular endemic fish faunas of worldwide interest for scientific studies (see COULTER 1991), need priority protection – more so as in the third great cichlid lake, Victoria, the endemic fauna has been decimated in recent years. Introductions can be a useful management tool (WELCOMME 1988), but should only be made after the most thorough investigations (see Papua New Guinea Sepik River symposium on this subject in Pollard 1989). Piscivores (most sport fish) are likely to be particularly destructive. Detritivore/algivores, like many tilapias, may not be so dangerous, but they ousted indigenous cichlids in Madagascar (REINTHAL & STIASSNY 1991). Even tilapias compete with one another, as the elimination of Lake Victoria's two endemic tilapia species following the introduction of exotic *Oreochromis niloticus* and other tilapias has shown (LOWE-MCCONNELL 1982, 1987). Furthermore, it is now realised that *Oreochromis mossambicus* (PETERS, which is stocked widely throughout the tropics does not grow as well as do strains of *O. niloticus*, and substitution is difficult (PULLIN 1988). Better-growing genetic strains of *O. niloticus* are now being produced by ICLARM (MACLEAN & DIZON 1991). A possible role for introduced fish is seen in cases where the zooplankton-feeding niche becomes enlarged by creation of man-made lakes, as the development of the clupeid *Limnothrissa* fishery in Lake Kariba has shown. Even here the introduced clupeids colonized habitats downriver, and would thus spread any possible deleterious influence on the indigenous aquatic communities.

One thing is certain, for the sake of future management and conservation options, records should be kept of fish transfers and introductions; in Brazil anyone can move fish around (PETRERE 1989). Stocking has also been rather haphazard in waters of the ASEAN region (BALUYUT 1983), where fish are chosen for their popularity as food rather than to fit a particular vacant niche. For such niche-fitting, however, more biological research is needed.

References

BALON, E. K. & COCHE, A. G., 1974: Lake Kariba: a Man-made Tropical Ecosystem in Central Africa: 767 pp. – Dr W. Junk Publishers, The Hague.

BALUYUT, E. A., 1983: Stocking and introduction of fish in lakes and reservoirs in the ASEAN countries. – *FAO Fish. Tech. Pap.* (**236**). 82 pp.

BAREL, C. D. N., LIGTVOET, W., GOLDSCHMIDT, T., WITTE, F. GOUDSWAARD, P. C., 1991: The haplochromine cichlids in L. Victoria: an assessment of biological and fisheries interests. – In: KEENLEYSIDE, M. H. A. (ed.): Cichlid Fishes: Behaviour, Ecology and Evolution: 258–279. – Chapman & Hall, London.

BARTHEM, R. B., RIBEIRO, M. C. L. DE & PETRERE Jr., M., 1991: Life strategies of some long-distance migratory catfish in relation to hydroelectric dams in the Amazon basin. – *Biol. Conserv.* **55**: 339–345.

BAYLEY, P. B., 1989: Aquatic environments in the Amazon basin, with an analysis of carbon sources, fish production and yield. – *Can. Spec. Publ Fish. Aquat. Sci.* **106**: 399–408.

BAYLEY, P. B. & PETRERE Jr., M., 1989: Amazon fisheries: assessment methods, current status and management options. – *Can. Spec. Publ. Fish. Aquat. Sci.* **106**: 385–398.

BEADLE, L. C., 1981: The Inland Waters of Tropical Africa. 2nd Ed.: 475 pp. – Longman, London.

BONETTO, A. A., 1986: Fish of the Paraná River system. – In: DAVIES, B. R. & WALKER, K. F. (eds.): The

Ecology of River Systems: 573–588. – Dr W. Junk Publishers, Dordrecht.

COATES, D., 1985: Fish yield estimates for the Sepik River, Papua New Guinea, a large floodplain system east of 'Wallace's line'. – *J. Fish. Biol.* **27**: 431–443.

COULTER, G. W., 1991: Lake Tanganyika and its Life: 354 pp. – Natural History Museum & Oxford University Press, London, Oxford, New York.

FERNANDO, C. H., 1984: Reservoirs and lakes of Southeast Asia (Oriental Region). – In: TAUB, F. B. (ed.): Lakes and Reservoirs. Ecosystems of the World **23**: 411–446. – Elsevier, Amsterdam.

FERNANDO, C. F. & HOLČIK, J., 1987: The nature of fish communities: a factor influencing the fishery potential and yields of tropical lakes and reservoirs. – *Hydrobiologia* **97**: 127–140.

GODOY, M. P. DE, 1967: Ten years of observations on the periodicity of fish migrations in the Mogi Guassu River. – *Rev. Bras. Biol.* **27**: 1–12. (In Portuguese).

GOULDING, M., 1980: The Fishes and the Forest: 280 pp. – University of California Press, Los Angeles.

GOULDING, M., CARVALHO, M. L. & FERREIRA, E. G., 1988: Rio Negro: Rich Life in Poor Water: 200 pp. – SPB Acad. Publ. The Hague.

GREENWOOD, P. H., 1981: The Haplochromine fishes of the East African Lakes: 839 pp. – Brit. Mus. (Nat. Hist.), London & Kraus International Publishers, Munich.

LEITE, R. A. N. de, 1991: The effects of the Tucurui hydroelectric dam on the fish fauna of the lower Tocantins River (Para, Brazilian Amazon). – *Abstract, ASIH 71st Annual Meeting*, New York.

LOWE-MCCONNELL, R. H., 1975: Fish Communities in Tropical Freshwaters. Longman, London. 337 pp.

– 1982: Tilapias in fish communities. – In: PULLIN, R. S. V. & LOWE-MCCONNELL, R. H. (eds.): The Biology and Culture of Tilapias. – *ICLARM Conf. Proc.* **7**: 83–113 International Centre for Living Aquatic Resources Management, Metro Manila, Philippines.

– 1987: Ecological Studies in Tropical Fish Communities: 382 pp. – Cambridge University Press, Cambridge.

– 1990: Summary address: rare fish, problems, progress and prospects for conservation. – *J. Fish Biology* **37**, Suppl. A: 263–269.

MACLEAN, J. L. & DIZON, L. B., 1991: *ICLARM Report 1990:* 152 pp. – International Centre for Living Aquatic Resources Management, Manila, Philippines.

MARSHALL, B. E., 1984: Small pelagic fishes and fisheries in African inland waters. – *FAO CIFA Techn. Pap.* (**14**): 25 pp.

MERONA, B. DE, 1990: Amazon fisheries: general characteristics based on two case-studies. – *Interciencia* **15**: 461–468.

NEILAND, A. E., GODDARD, J. P. & REID, G. MCG., 1990: The impact of damming, drought and overexploitation on the conservation of marketable fish stocks of the River Benue, Nigeria. – *J. Fish. Biol.* **37**, Suppl. A: 203–5.

OGUTU-OHWAYO, R. (1990): The decline of the native fishes of lakes Victoria and Kyoga (East Africa) and the impact of introduced species, especially the Nile perch (*Lates niloticus*) and Nile tilapia *Oreochromis niloticus*. – *Envir. Biol. Fish.* **27**: 81–96.

PETRERE, Jr. M., 1989: River fisheries in Brazil: a review. – *Regulated Rivers: Research and Management* **4**: 1–16.

PETR, T., 1986: The Volta River system. – In: DAVIES, B. R. & WALKER, K. F. (eds.): The Ecology of River Systems: 163–183. – Dr. W. Junk Publishers, Dordrecht.

PHOLPRASITH, S., PHURAKKIAT, C., PONGSRI, C. & LEELAPATRA, W., 1990: The Mekong giant catfish: conservation through induced spawning (Title only). – *J. Fish. Biol.* **37**, Suppl. A: viii.

POLLARD, D. A., 1989: Introduced and translocated fishes and their ecological effects: 181 pp. – *Proc. No.* **8**, Australian Society of Fish Biology, Bureau of Rural Resources, Canberra.

PULLIN, R., 1988: Tilapia genetic resources for aquaculture: 108 pp. – ICLARM Conf. Proc. No. **16**, International Centre for Living Aquatic Resources Management, Metro Manila, Philippines.

RAINBOTH, W. J., 1991: Cyprinids of South East Asia. – In: WINFIELD, I. J. & NELSON, J. S. (eds.): Cyprinid Fishes: Systematics, Biology and Exploitation: 156–210. – Chapman & Hall, London.

REINTHAL, P. N. & STIASSNY, M. L. J., 1991: The freshwater fishes of Madagascar: a study of an endangered fauna with recommendations for a conservation strategy. – *Conserv. Biol.* **5**: 231–243.

RIBEIRO, M. C. L. B. & PETRERE, Jr. M., 1990: Fisheries ecology and management of the Jaraqui (*Semaprochilodus taeniurus, S. insignis*) in Central Amazonia. – *Regulated Rivers: Research & Management* **5**: 195–215.

SKELTON, P. H., TWEDDLE, D. & JACKSON, P. B. N., 1991: Cyprinids of Africa. – In: WINFIELD, I. J. & NELSON, J. S. (eds.): Cyprinid Fishes: Systematics, Biology and Exploitation: 211–239. – Chapman & Hall, London.

WELCOMME, R. L., 1985: River fisheries. – *FAO Fish. Tech. Pap.,* (**262**). 330 p.

– 1986: Fish of the Niger system. – In: DAVIES, B. R. & WALKER, K. F. (eds.): The Ecology of River Systems: 61–74. – Dr W. Junk, Publishers, Dordrecht.

– 1988: International introductions of inland aquatic species. – *FAO Fish Tech. Pap.* **294**. 318 pp.

ZARET, T. M. & PAINE, R. T., 1973: Species introduction in a tropical lake. – *Science* **182**: 449–455.

Author's address:

Stratwick, Streat nr. Hassocks, Sussex BN6 8RT, United Kingdom.

Mitt. Internat. Verein. Limnol.	24	53–62	Stuttgart, Februar 1994

Distribution, genetics, ecology and status of the introduced cichlid, *Oreochromis mossambicus*, in Australia

Angela H. Arthington and David R. Blühdorn

Abstract

The African cichlid, *Oreochromis mossambicus* (PETERS), has established breeding populations in a variety of water bodies in Queensland and in one Western Australian river system. The origin of all stocks is the aquarium trade. This paper reviews the distribution, genetic differentiation, somatic characteristics and ecological relationships of *O. mossambicus* (Tilapia) in Australia and the evidence of adverse ecological effects in terms of competition for food and space, predation, and the importation of parasites and diseases. We also discuss the implications of there being two different genetic strains of Tilapia in Australia, one relatively pure form of *O. mossambicus* and one based on this species but with hybrid introgression from one or more of *O. niloticus, O. hornorum* and *O. aureus*. The paper describes Federal and State legal and informal prohibitions on the importation and translocation of Tilapias, existing management policies and practices, and options for the management of Tilapias in different habitats and circumstances. Finally, we examine the ways in which research directed towards understanding the ecology of *O. mossambicus* in Australia could be of benefit to other countries as well as to the needs of Australian management agencies.

Introduction

The African cichlid, *Oreochromis mossambicus* (PETERS), also known as Tilapia and Mozambique mouthbrooder, has established breeding populations in inland waterbodies at several locations in Queensland and in the Gascoyne-Lyons river system in Western Australia (Fig. 1). The origin of all stocks is the aquarium trade (MCKAY 1978, 1984). Several mechanisms of establishment have been invoked, including disposal of aquarium fish into impoundments and riverine pools, escape of fish from outdoor ornamental ponds during flooding (ARTHINGTON et al. 1984), and possibly also deliberate but unauthorised releases to enhance indigenous recreational fisheries and to control phytoplankton blooms.

The existence of feral introduced fishes has long been of concern to fisheries scientists and conservation authorities in Australia, who generally share the view that Australia's unique but species-poor fish fauna may be particularly vulnerable to biological invasions (e.g. MCKAY 1984). Only some 180 fish species spend most of their life cycle in freshwater (ALLEN 1989). Australians are also acutely aware of the environmental problems associated with introduced biota, and millions of dollars have been spent annually in efforts to control pest species such as Prickly pear cactus (*Opuntia stricta* [HAW.] HAW. var. *stricta*), the rabbit (*Oryctolagus cuniculus L.*), various shrubs (e.g. *Lantana camara L.*), Water hyacinth (*Eichhornia crassipes [Mart.] Solms*) and European carp (*Cyprinus carpio L.*).

A series of review papers has summarised the origins and distributions of introduced fishes, including cichlids, in Australia, their known and possible effects on aquatic ecosystems, and management and policy issues (e.g. POLLARD et al. 1980, MCKAY 1984, ARTHINGTON 1986, FLETCHER 1986, ARTHINGTON & MITCHELL 1986, ARTHINGTON 1989 MCKAY 1989). Papers on these themes have most recently been published in the Proceedings of the Australian Society for Fish Biology's workshop on "Introduced and Translocated Fishes and their Ecological Effects" (POLLARD 1990, ARTHINGTON et al. 1990, BLÜHDORN et al. 1990), and in the special publication arising from a similar meeting held in Canada in 1990 (see BILLINGTON & HEBERT 1991; ARTHINGTON 1991).

The objectives of this paper are to provide an overview of the distribution, genetic differentiation and characteristics of Australian populations of *O. mossambicus*, and the evidence of adverse ecological effects in different habitats. We then discuss existing management policies and practices, legal and informal prohibitions, and the possibilities for management of Tilapias within Australia. Finally, we examine the ways in which research directed towards understanding the ecology of *O. mossambicus* in Australia could be of benefit to other countries as well as to the needs of Australian management agencies.

Distribution

The distribution of *O. mossambicus* was carefully documented in 1989 (BLÜHDORN et al. 1990) but reports of new sightings and captures since then are relatively common. Without exception, all confirmed reports have come from sub-tropical and tropical Queensland and the Gascoyne-Lyons river system in Western Australia; *O. mossambicus*

0538-4680/94/0024-0053 $ 2.50

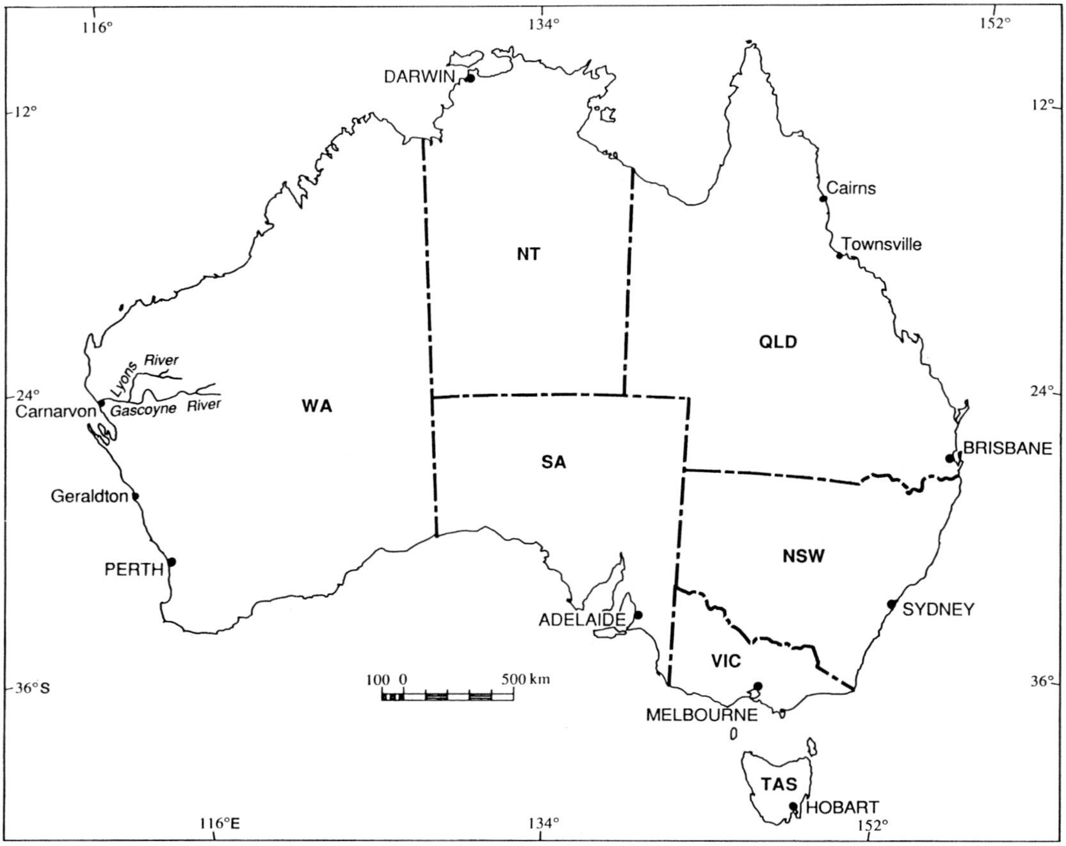

Fig. 1. Map of Australia showing state boundaries, major cities and towns and localities mentioned in the text as supporting *Oreochromis mossambicus* in Queensland and Western Australia.

has not become established in the wild in other Australian states. Currently, the known populations of *O. mossambicus* in Queensland are centred on three urban areas, Brisbane, Townsville and Cairns (Fig. 1). The Black mangrove or Niger cichlid, *Tilapia mariae* Boulenger, has also become established in the Cairns area.

Although there is presently no systematic monitoring of most feral Tilapia populations, there is increasing evidence that existing populations are spreading into new habitats in areas where they already occur, and into new areas where previously they were absent (R. McKay, pers. comm.). Natural dispersal occurs primarily during flooding when infested waterbodies (impoundments, ponds and drains) overflow, flushing adult Tilapia downstream. The subsequent survival of such fish depends in part on the habitat disruption caused by flooding. In Townsville (Fig. 1), a newly constructed artificial lake appears to have been colonised initially by the migration of juvenile Tilapia (adult fish were unable to bypass mesh screens), facilitating range expansion of *O. mossambicus* in this area.

Human translocation is probably responsible for a high proportion of the new infestations, and all of the original ones. Although there are prohibitions on moving live fish between waterbodies, and heavy penalties with respect to *O. mossambicus* (see below), there is no practical way to prevent clandestine translocations. There is insufficient agency support for surveillance even in urban areas and prosecutions are almost impossible to secure. These difficulties, coupled with the environmental tolerances (Philippart & Ruwet 1982) and invasive abilities of *O. mossambicus* (Arthington & Mitchell 1986, Bruton & van As 1986, Bruton 1989), mean that feral populations will continue to expand and new ones will establish in many types of freshwater habitat, and possibly also in estuarine and marine environments, as in other countries (e.g. WHITFIELD & BLABER 1979, LOBELL 1980).

Genetic relationships

Feral Tilapia in Australia are believed to have resulted from the introduction of a small number of progenitors from aquarium stocks, probably originating in Singapore or Indonesia. Feral populations were assumed to belong to one common Tilapia species, *O. mossambicus*, although other closely-related cichlids were brought to Australia during the same period by aquarists (MCKAY 1978, CALDWALLADER et al. 1980). Cichlids will often freely hybridize in the wild and in captivity (TREWAVAS 1980). In some instances, interspecies hybrids have proved to be greater pests than 'pure' species because of hybrid vigour and enhanced reproductive potential. This is certainly the case with European carp (*C. carpio*) in Australia, where of the three genetically distinct strains originally established in the wild, only the hybrid 'Boolara' strain has become a widespread pest, requiring control measures in the south-eastern states (SHEARER & MULLEY 1978).

An electrophoretic analysis of *O. mossambicus* populations in Australia has identified two distinct genetic strains, a common southern strain found in Brisbane, Townsville and the Gascoyne-Lyons system (Fig. 1), and a northern strain found only in the Cairns area. The southern strain is a relatively pure form of *O. mossambicus*, the only real distinction among populations from the three geographic areas being the lower level of genetic variability in fish from the Gascoyne-Lyons system, presumed to be a consequence of the small number of individuals originally released near Carnarvon (R. MCKAY, pers. comm.) and the 'founder effect' (MATHER & ARTHINGTON 1991). The northern strain from Cairns is polymorphic at three enzyme loci that are monomorphic in the southern populations. This finding is significant because *O. mossambicus* has relatively low levels of genetic variability compared to other Tilapia species (MCANDREW & MAJUMDAR 1983, 1984). Comparisons of the two strains with reference tissues from pure cultures held at Stirling University (Scotland) indicate that the polymorphic strain of Tilapia in Australia is an interspecies hybrid based on *O. mossambicus* but with genes from at least one or more of *O. niloticus* (L.), *O. hornorum* and *O. aureus* (STEINDACHNER) (MATHER & ARTHINGTON 1991). Hybrid introgression may have occurred among Australian aquarium stocks, but is more likely to have taken place in captivity prior to the importation of *O. mossambicus* into Australia.

Experiences with hybrid Tilapias in other countries, and Australia's problems with hybrid European carp, demonstrate the importance of genetic studies in the overall effort to understand the processes leading to successful biological invasions. However idealistic this may seem when resources for such work are extremely limited, we should know the physiological tolerances, ecological characteristics and hence possibly the potential for spread and adverse impacts of all imported strains, rather than focusing simply on the assessment of each species. Similarities and differences among the Australian strains of *O. mossambicus* are almost entirely unknown, although to date only the hybrid strain inhabits both freshwater and tidal habitats (MATHER & ARTHINGTON 1991).

There is also the possibility of further hybridization among Australian stocks of *O. mossambicus*. At present the wide geographic separation of most Tilapia populations makes population mixing most unlikely, but not impossible, since illegal translocations have occurred within Queensland and between Queensland and New South Wales (Fig. 1), irrespective of the official 'noxious' status of this species. To date there is no genetic evidence of hybridization between *O. mossambicus* and *T. mariae* in the Cairns area (MATHER & ARTHINGTON 1991).

Characteristics and habitats of Tilapia populations

Both the 'pure' strain of *O. mossambicus* and the hybrid strain from Cairns exist as normal-sized and under-sized ('stunted') populations, but there are no genetic differences between the two growth forms of the individual strains (BLUHDORN & ARTHINGTON 1990a). In the various situations and habitats in which they occur, the two strains inhabit environments that range from severely disturbed (e.g. man-made lakes in Brisbane, shallow drains in Townsville, impounded rivers in Brisbane and Townsville, and isolated tidal pools enriched with septage and bird wastes in Cairns) to relatively pristine conditions (*Melaleuca* swamps and tidal estuaries in Cairns, and riverine habitats in the Gascoyne-Lyons river system). Detailed information on the somatic characteristics of the *O.*

mossambicus populations from these sites is provided by Blühdorn & Arthington (1990a, 1990b, 1992) and Blühdorn et al. (1990), and summarized below.

Briefly, the North Pine Dam population from Brisbane can be described as normal-sized, growing to 35 cm standard length and 2 kg weight (Blühdorn et al. 1990), as do many populations established in other countries (see Blühdorn & Arthington 1990a), whereas the population from Tingalpa Reservoir, Brisbane, shows early signs of 'stunting' (Blühdorn & Arthington 1990a). We do not wish to elaborate here on the strict definition of 'stunting' as opposed to 'dwarfism' but note that these terms are frequently confused in the literature and need to be defined (M. Bruton, pers. comm.). In Townsville, Tilapia captured from an extensive swampy drainage system grow to 30 cm standard length and fish from most locations in the Cairns area (i.e. *Melaleuca* swamps and tidal estuaries of short coastal streams) grow to full size. The only stunted Cairns fish originate from a small isolated pool with high turbidity and nutrient levels.

Habitat modifications are believed to have facilitated the establishment of introduced warm-water fishes in Australia, especially hardy, opportunistic species such as *O. mossambicus* and various poeciliids, e.g. *Gambusia holbrooki* (Girard). This topic has been reviewed in terms of both its theoretical and practical significance (Arthington et al. 1990) but, nevertheless, in less than 10 years *O. mossambicus* has invaded almost the entire length of a near-pristine river system in the arid zone of Western Australia (Fig. 1). This population is highly 'stunted', and sexual maturity is reached at a mean standard length of 9 cm compared to 18+ cm in Tilapia from other Australian locations. We have suggested that breeding at early age and small size is advantageous in a harsh environment characterised by intermittent and often localised flow events (Blühdorn & Arthington, 1992). Further investigation of the factors regulating growth rates and body size of the various Australian Tilapia populations may shed considerable light on the initiation of stunting (and/or dwarfism) and the adaptive significance of flexible life history strategies in this invasive species (see Bruton 1989).

It has been argued that the establishment of introduced fishes in highly disturbed systems (e.g. polluted urban drains) is of little consequence given the poor condition of these habitats and their limited capacity to support indigenous biota. In addition, it has been suggested that the natural herbivory of Tilapia may assist in suppressing algal and macrophyte blooms in enriched streams and impoundments, thereby enhancing their environmental quality, and even that streams with introduced fishes are somehow better than streams with no fish at all. Such reasoning misses several important points.

The first is that the establishment of an introduced species in any habitat, however severely disturbed, represents a potential source of propagules to other aquatic systems. This is especially a danger in flood-prone areas of Australia. Secondly, indigenous fishes may be able to survive intermittently or in low numbers in disturbed habitats, with the possibility of population recovery and breeding or dispersal under improved environmental conditions, whereas the presence of an introduced species may further stress indigenous species to the point where individuals are unable to compete for the available resources or are prevented from breeding by environmental or aggression-induced stress (Arthington et al. 1990). The third (and perhaps most important) point is that if habitat disturbance is a significant factor in the establishment of introduced fishes, then one of the most obvious avenues for inhibiting invasions is habitat protection, restoration and enhancement. Li & Moyle (1989) have remarked that introductions of tolerant species or hatchery-reared fishes are frequently made in the USA to provide better fishing because reversing environmental degradation is so difficult. This appears to be a case of letting a situation go from 'bad' to 'worse'. Authorities responsible for water resource management, and the general public, must recognise that habitat protection benefits the entire biotic community as well as its dominant fishes, and that 'healthy' systems have the capacity to recover from perturbations and pollution events. Finally, the maintenance of indigenous biotic diversity is fundamental to all environmental management and nature conservation, and species introduced from other biogeographic regions have no role to play in this context.

Ecological impacts of Tilapia in Australia

The major impacts of introduced fishes may involve: genetic effects, such as hybridization with indigenous fish species and among introduced species or strains; habitat and water-quality alterations; competition for space and food; predation;

and the importation of parasites and diseases (COURTENAY & STAUFFER 1984, MOYLE et al. 1986). To date there is little evidence that *O. mossambicus* has had any such impacts in Australia (see MCKAY 1984, ARTHINGTON 1991), perhaps because of the relative recency of the introductions. It is not uncommon for several decades to elapse before introduced biota show any adverse impacts (COURTENAY 1990 a), and Tilapia has been feral in Australia for less than 20 years. The history of European carp in Australia illustrates this point (POLLARD et al. 1980). Furthermore, the precise impacts of introduced biota are often hard to establish because the prior condition of the system that has been invaded has usually not been recorded. This is certainly the case with Tilapia in Australia, where none of the environments now supporting *O. mossambicus* had been studied prior to invasion. Finally, it is often impossible to identify the independent but coincident impacts of introduced fishes and habitat disturbance, and the experimental studies which could assist in this regard have not attracted funding support except in the most tangential ways.

Competition

Field studies have made a contribution to understanding the possible mechanisms of ecological impact of Tilapia in Australia. The diet of *O. mossambicus* and two common indigenous fishes has been investigated in a eutrophic sub-tropical impoundment (North Pine Dam, Brisbane) under two different resource states: i.e. at low water levels, when the marginal zone supports dense stands of *Hydrilla verticillata* (L.f.) ROYLE and other submerged macrophytes, and at high water levels, when terrestrial vegetation is inundated and aquatic macrophytes are 'drowned'. At low water levels in North Pine Dam, *O. mossambicus* derived 94% of its mean diet (across all seasons) from *H. verticillata*, phytoplankton and filamentous algae (ARTHINGTON et al. 1992), whereas at higher water levels there was a massive increase in the consumption of algae. Under both resource states, there was very little dietary overlap among *O. mossambicus* and the two indigenous species, a bottom feeding eel-tailed catfish (*Tandanus tandanus* MITCHELL) and an opportunistic omnivorous teraponid (*Leiopotherapon unicolor* GÜNTHER). Moreover, distinct partitioning of food resources occurred in all seasons. It therefore appears that maturing and adult Tilapia probably do not compete with these indigenous species for food, largely as a consequence of their different foraging strategies and the natural herbivory of Tilapia. However, we do not know how the juveniles of these species and others interact in any type of water body in Australia, and competition for food may be more important at the recruitment stage than in later life.

It is worthwhile considering the possible environmental impacts, and also the benefits of herbivory. Species of Tilapia have been introduced in various countries specifically to control aquatic plants, but *Tilapia zilli* (GERVAIS) reduced the abundance of indigenous macrophytes in Californian systems to such a serious extent that its release for plant control was abandoned. *Oreochromis mossambicus* has also been used in other countries to control aquatic weeds and algae in irrigation canals and rice fields (ERDMAN 1984; SHIREMAN 1984), and in an integrated algae-mosquito control programme where fish grazing reduced the filamentous algae sheltering mosquito larvae from predators. Environmental impacts associated with such uses, if any, have not been documented.

The case for the use of *O. mossambicus* biological control programmes in Australia is raised occasionally, but has been rejected by management authorities. The use of fish in biological control should not be undertaken lightly, as world experience with *Gambusia* in mosquito control has demonstrated amply (LLOYD 1986). Fish are rarely monophagous and even the essentially herbivorous/detritivorous Tilapias are omnivorous in some situations and may therefore have an impact on non-target organisms. The use of triploid Grass carp, *Ctenopharyngodon idella* VALENCIENNES, is one of the few successes in the biological control of aquatic plants in ponds, lakes and impoundments (MCDOWALL 1990), but it has not been useful in flowing waters (COURTENAY 1990 a).

Competition among Tilapia and indigenous fishes for other resources, such as habitat, remains unstudied in Australia. We have suggested that there may be some interaction over breeding territories between *O. mossambicus* and the nest-building eel-tailed catfish (*T. tandanus*) (BLÜHDORN & ARTHINGTON 1992) and have attempted unsuccessfully to find the funds for experimental investigation of such interactions.

Predation

There is no relevant information on the importance of *O. mossambicus* as a predator in Australia. However, the analysis of fish diets provides some evidence that *O. mossambicus* consumes small forage fish (Melanotaeniidae, Eleotriidae) in subtropical impoundments, and that the consumption of fish and aquatic invertebrates may be higher in waterbodies with low primary productivity (ARTHINGTON & MILTON, unpubl. data).

Parasites and diseases

Australia is taking a hard line on the importation of aquarium fishes, partly because exotic diseases and parasites may be introduced together with the fish and the water used during their transport (see MCKAY 1984, LANGDON 1990). There is good evidence that disease organisms have entered Australia via the aquarium trade. LANGDON (1990) has summarised the major pathogens of fish in Australia. Concern over imported fish diseases has led to the establishment of quarantine facilities at major ports handling aquarium stocks (McKay 1984), and some states have banned translocations of introduced fishes because of the threat of disease. For example, Victoria has banned translocation of Redfin (*Perca fluviatilis* L.) and Tasmania now requires that imported Goldfish (*Carassius auratus* L.) be certified free of goldfish ulcer disease (LANGDON 1990).

There has been no investigation of the parasites and pathogens associated with *O. mossambicus* in Australia, although we should be forewarned by experiences with other introduced fishes (see summaries in LANGDON 1990, ARTHINGTON 1991). MOYLE (1986) noted that indigenous Californian fishes seemed to be more heavily parasitized by introduced parasites such as *Lernaea cyprinacea* than did the exotic carrier fishes; the same tendency has been observed with diseases. In several instances infectious agents are more pathogenetic, or only cause clinical disease, in atypical hosts, and so become a problem when the typical host species come into contact with unusual hosts (LANGDON 1990). Examples are whirling disease in Rainbow trout, proliferative kidney disease of salmonids, and the North American crayfish plague fungus which has devastated European astacids.

Management policies and practises

The importation of Tilapias (*Tilapia, Sarotherodon* and *Oreochromis*) is prohibited throughout Australia under Commonwealth legislation (Quarantine Act and the Wildlife Protection Act: Regulation of Exports and Imports), enforced by the Australian Quarantine and Inspection Service. The Advisory Committee on Live Fish (ACOLF) makes recommendations to the Standing Committee on Fisheries as to the fish species which may be imported into Australia, using several criteria (summarised by MICHAELIS 1989). Under the present criteria, tilapiine species would not be listed as species permitted importation, and their import has, in fact, been prohibited since 1963.

Fisheries management in Australia is the responsibility of individual state and territorial governments which set their own policies for the management of introduced species. In most states there is a policy of prohibiting or otherwise discouraging the importation, possession and translocation of Tilapias, and there are penalties for various offences, ranging from substantial fines to imprisonment for two years (see BLÜHDORN & ARTHINGTON 1992). Offenders can also be required to pay for the costs of eradication or removal of feral Tilapia populations. Some states have set up public-education programmes aimed at preventing the spread of *O. mossambicus*, whereas Western Australia has avoided publicising the issue; this strategy seems to have been successful to date. Several additional measures have prevented commercial exploitation of extant feral Tilapia stocks, such as fish-farm licensing provisions and State Stock Acts directed at the containment of diseases.

The current management strategy in Queensland is to eradicate the smaller, more accessible populations of *O. mossambicus* using fish poisons. However, most existing Tilapia populations present intractable management problems, as was also the case with European carp in southern Australia (MORISON & HUME 1990). A number of practical suggestions for Tilapia management have been aired (BLÜHDORN et al. 1990), including manipulation of water levels to interfere with food and habitat resources, appropriately timed water releases from impoundments, habitat enhancement for indigenous species, the use of the sterile male technique, and encouragement of predators such as indigenous Silver barramundi (*Lates calcarifer* BLOCH). There has been little reaction to these suggestions and none have been researched or implemented. The situation in Australia at present is that many important issues remain to be investigated before it will be possible to understand the process of invasion by *O. mossambicus*, to predict where it is likely to succeed, and to decide how best to approach its management in each situation.

Tilapia as a resource

Tilapias have contributed to food supplies, employment and regional economies in many Asian countries. There, fish contribute on average 35% of animal protein (CHUA 1986), and much higher levels in some cultures: e.g. 70–80% in Sri Lanka and Bangladesh (SUBASINGHE & GODAKANDA 1986, AGUERO 1986). However, the use of Tilapias has not been without problems and several countries now regard *O. mossambicus* in particular as unsuitable for culture (China and Malaysia) or as a pest (Taiwan and to some extent in brackish-water Milkfish ponds in the Philippines [GUERRERO 1988] (see details in DESILVA 1989 a). Tilapias have interfered with the development of aquaculture in several South Pacific islands (NELSON & ELDREDGE 1991), and are believed to have replaced more highly-valued species in shallow nearshore habitats in Micronesia (LOBELL 1980).

The attitude to Tilapias in Australia is essentially a conservative one, but it must be appreciated that this country has struggled for decades with problems resulting from the unwise introduction of plants and animals. Fisheries scientists and managers are also well aware of the substantial body of theoretical and empirical evidence that additions to indigenous fish faunas are seldom entirely successful and more often than not have unanticipated and undesirable consequences (WELCOMME 1984, 1988, COURTENAY 1990 a, 1990 b). There is no economic rationale for the exploitation of Tilapias for animal protein in Australia, where commercial fisheries are based almost entirely on marine and estuarine resources. Commercial freshwater fishing contributes less than 2% of Australia's annual fisheries production and most of this is used for bait rather than for food (MACKINNON 1987).

Can any use be made of feral Tilapia populations in Australia? We have suggested elsewhere (BLÜHDORN & ARTHINGTON 1992) that there are two potential avenues for their utilization which would not compromise Australian policies regarding Tilapias. Firstly, *O. mossambicus* from the southern Australian strain could serve as brood stock to re-introduce a pure strain with good growth characteristics into countries which are beginning to experience declining catches due to over-fishing, inbreeding and hybridization of stocks (see DESILVA 1985, DE SILVA & AMARASINGHE 1989). Secondly, Australian populations could be investigated to explore phenomena of particular relevance to tropical inland fisheries (e.g. the factors and physiological mechanisms which govern growth, reproductive mode and 'stunting'), under varying environmental conditions, without the confounding influences of inbreeding, uncontrolled hybridization and exploitation of stocks. Australian research on these topics could have valuable outcomes for countries which are dependent on exotic *O. mossambicus* for significant subsistence fisheries, such as Papua New Guinea (COATES 1985, 1987), Sri Lanka (DE SILVA 1989 b), Indonesia (COSTA-PIERCE et al. 1988) and India (SHETTY et al. 1989). An appropriate programme of research would contribute simultaneously to the development of practical management strategies for feral Tilapia populations in Australia.

Conclusions

A number of conferences and international meetings have elaborated the problems arising from biological invasions (e.g. DE SILVA 1989 a, POLLARD 1990, BILLINGTON & HEBERT 1991). The common themes can be summarised in terms of four major issues:

i) The need for more research on the processes governing successful biological invasions and hence a sound basis for preventing them;
ii) National strategies to ensure full consideration of the probable consequences of biological introductions (e.g. following the model of entomologists working with entomophagous and parasitic insects introduced for biological control);
iii) Greater regulatory control over biological introductions and stronger legislation to discourage the spread of extant feral organisms (both national and international agreements will be needed here);
iv) Monitoring and research aimed at developing effective control measures for particular species.

In Australia, the greatest need is for research on the biology and ecology of introduced fishes and measures for their control, but funding for such studies is limited, even though major national initiatives are pressuring scientists and managers for strategies to achieve the conservation and sustainable use of natural resources. We believe that Australia can offer expertise and assistance in several fields of Tilapia research that could be of benefit internationally, especially in countries with extensive culture or subsistence fisheries based on *O. mossambicus*.

Acknowledgements

We acknowledge research grants from the Australian National Parks and Wildlife Service, the former Australian Water Research Advisory Council, the Australian Research Council and Griffith University for the study on introduced fishes in Queensland and Western Australia. Dr P. B. Mather, Mr R. J. McKay, Mr D. A. Milton, Ms K. Hedstrom and two AWRAC Summer Research Scholars are thanked for their contributions to these studies.

References

Aguero, M., 1986: Bangladesh fisheries: a challenge to resource managers. – *NAGA* **9:** 11–12.

Allen, G. R., 1989: *Freshwater Fishes of Australia:* 240 pp. – T.F.H. Publications, Inc., Neptune City, New Jersey.

Arthington, A. H., 1986: Introduced cichlid fishes in Australian inland waters. – In: De Deckker, P. & Williams, W. D. (eds.): Limnology in Australia 239–248. – CSIRO, Melbourne & Dr W. Junk Publishers, Dordrecht.

– 1989: Impacts of introduced and translocated freshwater fishes in Australia. In: De Silva, S. S. (ed): Exotic Aquatic Organisms in Asia. Proceedings of the Workshop on Introduction of Exotic Aquatic Organisms in Asia. – *Asian Fish. Soc. Spec. Publ.* **3**: 7–20.

– 1991: Ecological and genetic impacts of introduced and translocated freshwater fishes in Australia. – *Can. J. Fish. Aquatic Sci.* **48**: (Suppl. 1): 33–43.

Arthington, A. H., Blühdorn, D. R. & Delaney, K. J., 1992: *Hydrilla verticillata* – the basis of aquatic food chains in North Pine Dam, Queensland. – In: Yezdani, H. (ed.): Proceedings of a Workshop held at Queensland University of Technology on Water Weeds Management in Queensland: 142–162. – Centre for Biological Population Management, Queensland University of Technology, Brisbane.

Arthington, A. H., Hamlet, S. & Blühdorn, D.R., 1990: The role of habitat disturbance in the establishment of introduced warm-water fishes in Australia. – In: Pollard, D. A. (ed.): Proceedings of the Australian Society for Fish Biology's Workshop on Introduced and Translocated Fishes and their Ecological Effects. – *Bureau of Rural Resources Proceedings No.* **8**, 61–66. Australian Government Publishing Service, Canberra.

Arthington, A. H. & Lloyd, L. N., 1989: Introduced Poeciliidae in Australia and New Zealand. – In: Meffe, G. K. & Snelson, F. F. (ed.): Evolution and Ecology of Livebearing Fishes (Poeciliidae): 333–348. Prenctice-Hall, New York.

Arthington, A. H., McKay, R. J., Russel, D. J. & Milton, D. A., 1984: Occurrence of the introduced cichlid, *Oreochromis mossambicus* (Peters) in Queensland. – *Aust. J. Mar. Freshwat. Res.* **35**: 267–272.

Arthington, A. H. & Mitchell, D. S., 1986: Aquatic invading species. – In: Grooves, R. H. & Burdon, J. J. (eds.): Ecology of Biological Invasions: An Australian Perspective: 34–52. – Australian Academy of Science, Canberra.

Billington, N. & Hebert, P. D. N., 1991: International Symposium on "The Ecological and Genetic Implications of Fish Introductions (FIN)." – *Can. J. Fish. Aquatic Sci.* **48** (Suppl. 1): 181 pp.

Blühdorn, D. R. & Arthington, A. H., 1990a: The incidence of stunting in Australian populations of the introduced cichlid *Oreochromis mossambicus* (Peters). – In: Hirano, R. & Hanyu, I. (eds.): The Second Asian Fisheries Forum: 41–44. – Asian Fisheries Society, Manila, Philippines.

– – 1990b: Somatic characteristics of an Australian population of *Oreochromis mossambicus* Peters (Pisces: Cichlidae). – *Env. Biol. Fishes* **29**: 277–291.

– – 1992: Tilapia in Australia and small Pacific islands: unwanted pest or unappreciated resource? In: Papers contributed to the Workshop on Tilapia in Capture and Culture-based Fisheries and Country Reports presented at the Fifth Session of the Indo-Pacific Fishery Commission Working Party of Experts on Inland Fisheries, Bogor, Indonesia 24–29 June 1991. – *FAO Fisheries Report No.* **458** (Supplement): 120–138. FAO, Rome.

Blühdorn, D. R., Arthington, A. H. & Mather, P. B., 1990: The introduced cichlid, *Oreochromis mossambicus*, in Australia: a review of distribution, population genetics, ecology, management issues and research priorities. – In: Pollard, D. A. (ed.): Proceedings of the Australian Society for Fish Biology's Workshop on Introduced and Translocated Fishes and their Ecological Effects. – *Bureau of Rural Resources Proceedings* No. **8**: 83–92. Australian Government Publishing Service, Canberra.

Bruton, M. N., 1989: The ecological significance of alternative life-history styles. – In: Bruton, M. N. (ed): *Alternative Life-History Styles of Animals*: 503–553. – Kluwer Academic Publishers, Dordrecht.

Bruton, M. N. & Van As, J. G. 1986: Faunal invasions of aquatic ecosystems in southern Africa, with suggestions for their management. – In: Macdonald, I. A. W., Kruger, F. J. & Ferrar, A. A. (eds.): The Ecology and Management of Biological Invasions in Southern Africa: 47–61. – Oxford University Press, Cape Town.

Cadwallader, P. L., Backhouse, G. N. & Fallu, R., 1980: Occurrence of tropical fish in the cooling pondage of a power station in temperate south-eastern Australia. – *Aust. J. Mar. Freshwat. Res.* **31**: 541–546.

Chua, T.-E., 1986: An overview of the fisheries and aquaculture industries in Asia. – In: MacLean, J. L., Dizon, L. B. & Hosillos, L. V. (ed.): The First Asian Fisheries Forum: 1–8. – Asian Fisheries Society, Manila, Philippines.

COATES, D., 1985: Fish yield estimates for the Sepik River, Papua New Guinea, a large floodplain system east of "Wallace's Line'. – *J. Fish. Biol.* **27**: 431–443.

– 1987: Consideration of fish introductions in the Sepik River, Papua New Guinea. – *Aquacult. Fish. Manag.* **18**: 231–241.

COSTA-PIERCE, B. A., ZAINAL, S. & EFFENDI, P., 1988: ICLARM and South-South technology transfer: Philippine aquaculture technology and Indonesia. Part 1. – *NAGA* **11**: 10–11.

COURTENAY, W. R., 1990a: Fish conservation and the enigma of introduced species. – In: POLLARD, D. A. (ed.): Proceedings of the Australian Society for Fish Biology's Workshop on Introduced and Translocated Fishes and their Ecological Effects. Bureau of Rural Resources Proceedings No. **8**: 11–20. Australian Government Publishing Service, Canberra.

– 1990b: Fish introductions and translocations, and their impacts in Australia. – In: POLLARD, D. A. (ed.): Proceedings of the Australian Society for Fish Biology's Workshop on Introduced and Translocated Fishes and their Ecological Effects. – Bureau of Rural Resources Proceedings No. **8**: 171–179. Australian Government Publishing Service, Canberra.

COURTENAY, W. R. & STAUFFER, J. R., 1984: Distribution, Biology and Management of Exotic Fishes: 430 pp. – Johns Hopkins University Press, Baltimore.

DE SILVA, S. S., 1985: Status of the introduced cichlid *Sarotherodon mossambicus* (PETERS) in the reservoir fishery of Sri Lanka: a management strategy and ecological implications. – *Aquacult. Fish. Manag.* **1**: 91–102.

– 1989a: Exotic Aquatic Organisms in Asia. Proceedings of the Workshop on Introduction of Exotic Aquatic Organisms in Asia. – *Asian Fish. Soc. Spec. Publ.* **3**: 154 pp.

– 1989b: Exotics – A global perspective with reference to finfish introductions in Asia. – In: DE SILVA, S. S. (ed.): Exotic Aquatic Organisms in Asia. Proceedings of the Workshop on Introduction of Exotic Aquatic Organisms in Asia. – *Asian Fish. Soc. Spec. Publ.* **3**: 1–6.

DE SILVA, S. S. & AMARASHINGHE, U. S., 1989: Stunting in *Oreochromis mossambicus* (PETERS) (Pisces: Cichlidae): An evaluation of past and recent data from Sri Lankan reservoir populations. – *J. Ichthyol.* **5**: 203–210.

ERDMAN, D. S., 1984: Exotic fishes in Puerto Rico. In: COURTENAY, W. R. & STAUFFER, J. R. (eds.): *Distribution, Biology and Management of Exotic Fishes*: 162–176. – Johns Hopkins University Press, Baltimore.

FLETCHER, A. R., 1986: Effects of introduced fish in Australia. – In: DE DECKKER, P. & WILLIAMS, W. D. (eds.): Limnology in Australia: 231–238. – CSIRO, Melbourne & Dr W Junk Publishers, Dordrecht.

GUERRERO, R. D. III (1988): Philippines. – In: PULLIN, R. S. V. (ed.): Tilapia Genetic Resources for Aquaculture. – *ICLARM Conference Proceedings No.* **16**, Makati, Metro Manila: 42–45.

LANGDON, J. S., 1990: Disease risks of fish introductions and translocations. – In: POLLARD, D. A. (ed.): Proceedings of the Australian Society for Fish Biology's Workshop on Introduced and Translocated Fishes and their Ecological Effects. – *Bureau of Rural Resources Proceedings No.* **8**: 98–107. Australian Government Publishing Service, Canberra.

LI, H. W. & MOYLE, P. B., 1989: Management of introduced fishes. – In: KOHLER, C. & HURLBERT, W. (eds.): Inland Fisheries Management in North America: 15 pp. – American Fisheries Society, Bethesda, Md.

LLOYD, L. N., 1986: An alternative to insect control by "Mosquitofish", *Gambusia affinis*. – In: St. GEORGE, T. D., KAY, B. H. & BLOK, J. (eds.): Arbovirus Research in Australia. – *Proceedings of the Fourth Symposium on Arbovirus Research*: 156–163. – Queens- land Institute of Medical Research, Brisbane.

LOBELL, P. S., 1980: Invasion by the Mozambique tilapia (*Sarotherodon mossambicus*; Pisces; Cichlidae) of a Pacific marine ecosystem. – *Micronesica* **16**: 349–355 (cited in NELSON & ELDREDGE 1991).

MACKINNON, M., 1987: Review of inland fisheries – Australia. – In: PETR, T. (ed.): Reports and papers presented at the Indo-Pacific Fishery Commission Expert Consultation on inland fisheries of the large Indo-Pacific islands: 258 pp. – *FAO Fisheries Report* **371** Supplement, FAO, Rome.

MCANDREW, B. J. & MAJUMDAR, K. C., 1983: Tilapia stock identification using electrophoretic markers. – *Aquaculture* **30**: 249–261.

– 1984: Evolutionary relationships within three tilapiine genera (Pisces: Cichlidae). – *Zool. J. Linn. Soc.* **80**: 421–435.

MCDOWALL, R., 1990: Filling in the gaps – the introduction of exotic fishes into New Zealand. – In: POLLARD, D. A. (ed.): Proceedings of the Australian Society for Fish Biology's Workshop on Introduced and Translocated Fishes and their Ecological Effects. – Bureau of Rural Resources Proceedings No. **8**: 69–82. Australian Government Publishing Service, Canberra.

MCKAY, R. J., 1978: The exotic freshwater fishes of Queensland: 103 pp. – Report to the Australian National Parks and Wildlife Service, Canberra.

– 1984: Introductions of exotic fishes in Australia. – In: COURTENAY, W. R. & STAUFFER, J. R. (eds.): Distribution, Biology and Management of Fishes: 177–199. – Johns Hopkins University Press, Baltimore.

– 1989: Exotic and translocated freshwater fishes in Australia. – In: DE SILVA, S. S. (ed.): Exotic

Aquatic Organisms in Asia. Proceedings of the Workshop on Introduction of Exotic Aquatic Organisms in Asia. – *Asian Fish. Soc. Spec. Publ.* **3**: 21–34.

MATHER, P. B. & ARTHINGTON, A. H., 1991: An assessment of genetic differentiation among feral Australian Tilapia populations. – *Aust. J. Mar. Freshwat. Res.* **42**: 721–728.

MICHAELIS, F. B., 1989: Australian Government position: introduction of exotic aquatic species. – In: DE SILVA, S. S. (ed.): Exotic Aquatic Organisms in Asia. Proceedings of the Workshop on Introduction of Exotic Aquatic Organisms in Asia. – *Asian Fish. Soc. Spec. Publ.* **3**: 125–132.

MORISON, A. & HUME, D., 1990: Carp (*Cyrpinus carpio L.*) in Australia. – In: POLLARD, D. A. (ed.), Proceedings of the Australian Society for Fish Biology's Workshop on Introduced and Translocated Fishes and their Ecological Effects. – Bureau of Rural Resources Proceedings No. **8**: 110–113. Australian Government Publishing Service, Canberra.

MOYLE, P. B., 1986: Fish introductions in California: history and impact on native fishes. – *Biol. Conserv.* **9**: 101–118.

MOYLE, P. B., LI, H. W. & BARTON, B. A., 1986: The Frankenstein Effect: Impact of introduced fishes on native fishes in North America. – In: STROUD, R. H. (ed.): Fish Culture in Fisheries Management: 415–426. – American Fisheries Society, Bethesda, Md.

NELSON, S. G. & ELDREDGE, L. G., 1991: Distribution and status of introduced cichlid fishes of the genera *Oreochromis* and *Tilapia* in the islands of the South Pacific and Micronesia. – *Asian Fish. Sci.* **4**: 11–22.

PHILIPPART, J. & RUWET, J., 1982: Ecology and distribution of Tilapias. – In: PULLIN, R. S. V. & LOWE-MCCONNELL, R. H. (eds.): The Biology and Culture of Tilapias: 15–59. – International Center for Living Aquatic Resources Management.

POLLARD, D. A., LLEWELLYN, L. C. & TILZEY, R. D. J., 1980: Management of freshwater fish and fisheries. – In: Williams, W. D. (ed.): An Ecological Basis for Water Resource Management: 227–270. – Australian National University Press, Canberra.

POLLARD, D. A., 1990: Proceedings of the Australian Society for Fish Biology's Workshop on Introduced and Translocated Fishes and their Ecological Effects. – *Bureau of Rural Resources Proceedings No.* **8**. Australian Government Publishing Service, Canberra. 181 pp.

SHEARER, K. D. & MULLEY, J. C., 1978: The introduction and distribution of the carp, *Cyprinus carpio Linnaeus*, in Australia. – *Aust. J. Mar. Freshwat. Res.* **29**: 551–564.

SHETTY, H. P. C., NANDEESHA, M. C. & JHINGRAN, A.G., 1989: Impact of exotic aquatic species in Indian waters. – In: DE SILVA, S.S. (ed.): Exotic Aquatic Organisms in Asia. Proceedings of the Workshop on Introduction of Exotic Aquatic Organisms in Asia. – *Asian Fish. Soc. Spec. Publ.* **3**: 45–55.

SHIREMAN, J. V., 1984: Control of aquatic weeds with exotic fishes. – In: COURTENAY, W. R. & STAUFFER, J. R. (eds.): Distribution, Biology and Management of Exotic Fishes: 302–312. – Johns Hopkins University Press, Baltimore.

SUBASINGHE, S. & GODANKANDA, J. C., 1986: Quality loss and wastage in the processing and preparation of fresh fish in Sri Lanka. – In: MACLEAN, J. L. DIZON, L. B. & HOSILLOS, L. V. (eds.): The First Asian Fisheries Forum: 459–462. – Asian Fisheries Society, Manila, Philippines.

TREWAVAS, E., 1980: *Tilapia* and *Sarotherodon*. – *Buntbarsche Bulletin* **81**: 1–6.

WELCOMME, R. L., 1984: International transfer of inland fish species. – In: COURTENAY, W. R. & STAUFFER, J. R. (eds.): Distribution, Biology and Management of Exotic Fishes: 22–40. – Johns Hopkins University Press, Baltimore.

WELCOMME, R. L., 1988: International introductions of inland aquatic species. – *FAO Fisheries Technical Paper* **294**, FAO, Rome. 318 pp.

WHITFIELD, A. K. & BLABER, S. J. M., 1979: The distribution of the freshwater cichlid *Sarotherodon mossambicus* in estuarine systems. – *Env. Biol. Fish.* **4**: 77–81.

Authors' address:

Centre for Catchment and In-stream Research, Griffith University, Nathan, Old 4111, Australia.

Mitt. Internat. Verein. Limnol.	24	63–71	Stuttgart, Februar 1994

Diversity and endemism of three major freshwater groups in Sri Lanka: Atyidae (Decapoda), Gastropoda and Teleostei

K.H.G.M. de Silva

Abstract

Eleven species of atyid shrimps (including ten *Caridina* species), 30 species of freshwater gastropods (including 12 *Paludomus* species), and 72 indigenous and endemic fishes (including 32 cyprinids of which 16 are *Barbus* species) have been recorded from fresh and slightly-brackish waters in Sri Lanka. Of these, six *Caridina* species, at least 11 gastropods (including 10 *Paludomus* species) and 30 fishes (including 17 cyprinids of which 9 are *Barbus* species) are endemic. The diversity and endemism of all three groups in Sri Lanka is greater in lotic than lentic waters, and greater in the Wet Zone than in the Dry Zone. Most of the indigenous aquatic fauna is related to that of southern India, but Southeast Asian and African affinities are present also, especially among the atyids. The hypotheses that have been proposed to account for the affinities of the Sri Lankan fauna are reviewed briefly.

Faunal diversity decreases with increasing elevation. Nine species of atyids, 28 species of gastropods and all but one species of fish are found below 500 m, but only two atyids, six gastropods and seven indigenous fishes are found above 1000 m. Of the endemics, three atyids, four gastropods and 11 fishes – all lotic forms – have restricted ranges. Increasing human modification of their habitats could lead to extinctions.

Introduction

Sri Lanka is situated at the southern tip of the Indian sub-continent and is isolated by vast stretches of the Indian ocean on three sides. The island has an area of 65,525 km², and is rich in lotic and lentic waters. There are 103 river basins, 18 of them with catchments larger than 1,000 km². Although significant natural lakes are absent, more than 12,000 man-made irrigation reservoirs – ranging in size from <10 ha to >7,000 ha – are present (Baldwin 1991).

There have been several faunal surveys of Sri Lankan freshwaters during the past three decades (Deraniyagala 1952, Costa & Starmühlner 1972, Starmühlner 1974, Senanayake 1980, De Silva 1983 and unpublished data, Pethiyagoda 1991). The results of these surveys indicate that teleosts, gastropods and atyids are major elements of the freshwater fauna, and the distribution of some taxa is now well established. Although aquatic insects are a diverse and important group, they have yet to be the subject of an island-wide study.

The present review is based mainly on the author's own unpublished faunal surveys of Sri Lankan freshwaters as well as those of Deraniyagala (1952), Starmühlner (1974), Senanayake (1980), de Silva (1983) and Pethiyagoda (1991). In the data base used, localities of occurrence for each species of the three major faunal groups reported in various surveys were marked on one-inch (1:63,360) maps of the island. The elevation and river systems were also recorded. Note that, unless otherwise specified, the term "indigenous" is used herein to indicate only those indigenous species that are non-endemic.

Topography, climate, vegetation and water chemistry

Sri Lanka was formed by the vertical uplift of land in three stages, and is therefore composed of three erosion surfaces or peneplains. The lowest rises to approximately 125 m, the middle portion reaches between 305 and 760 m, and the highest attains an elevation of 1,525–1,830 m with peaks of 2,200 m or more (Cooray 1984; Fig. 1). The highest peneplain is more in the nature of a complex of plateaux, mountain chains, massifs and basins, and appears to be geologically the youngest. The landmass of Sri Lanka dates back to Gondwanaland, but the second and third peneplains were block faulted during the Permian and the Cretaceous respectively (Cooray 1984).

The climate in different parts of the island depends upon elevation and rainfall. The temperature varies from about 30 °C at sea level to about 15 °C at 1,800 m elevation. Annual variation is generally less than 5 °C. Depending on the pattern of precipitation, two major climatic zones can be recognized. The Dry Zone which receives a mean annual rainfall of 1,450 mm between October to March and has a distinct dry period, extends over about three-quarters of the island encompassing the north-western, northern and the eastern parts (Fig. 2). The Wet Zone, which receives a mean annual precipitation of 2,400 mm (especially during the two monsoons) and lacks a marked dry season, extends over the south-western sector of the island and the central massif. A

0538-4680/94/0024-0063 $ 2.25

Fig. 1. The topography and major river systems of Sri Lanka.

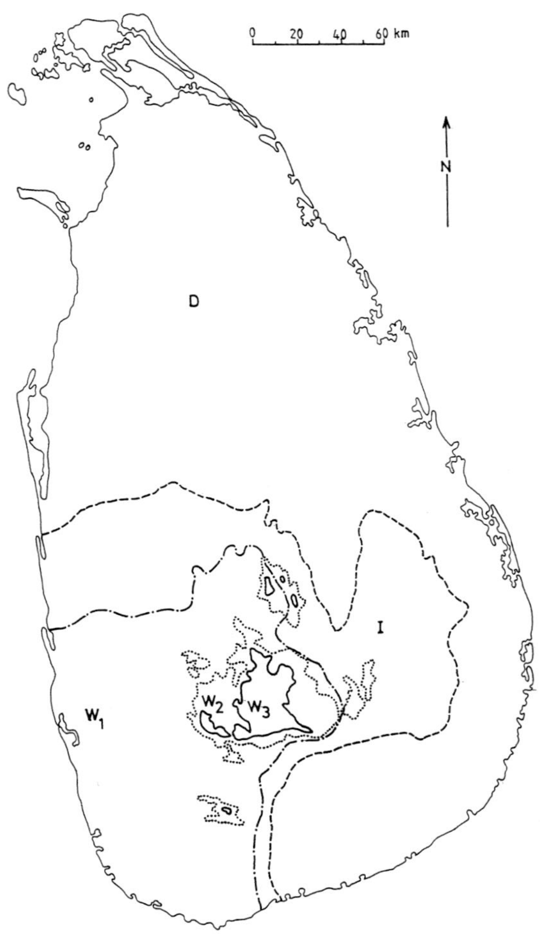

Fig. 2. Major climatic and vegetational zones of Sri Lanka: D – Dry Zone; I – Intermediate Zone; W_1 – lowland Wet Zone; W_2 – submontane Wet Zone; W_3 – montane Wet Zone.

narrow belt – the Intermediate Zone – between the two major zones can be recognized also. The Dry Zone and the Intermediate Zone support monsoon scrub forest and grasslands whereas the Wet Zone contains tropical rain forest. Three major forest types can be recognized in the Wet Zone (Fig. 2): lowland forest (lowland Wet Zone - W_1) extends up to about 900 m, and montane rain forest or cloud forest (montane Wet Zone – W_3) occurs above an elevation of about 1500 m; submontane rain forest (submontane wet zone – W_2) grows between 900 and 1,500 m. The montane forest is confined largely to the highest peneplain, whereas the submontane forest and the upper part of the lowland rain forest are on the mountain slopes and basins between the second and third peneplains.

The temperature, pH, alkalinity, conductivity and calcium levels of streams and rivers increase with decreasing elevation, and can be very low in the montane zone (Table 1). Reservoir waters have generally higher conductivity and alkalinity than running waters.

Faunal distribution

Sri Lanka supports 72 species of freshwater teleosts, 30 species of aquatic gastropods, and 11 species of atyid shrimps (Table 2). Although 30 of the freshwater fishes are endemic, there are only two endemic genera, both monotypic: the belontiid *Malpulutta kretseri* DERANIYAGALA and the cyprinid *Horadandia atukorali* DERANIYAGALA. Of the 32 cyprinids, 16 are *Barbus* species – a genus which includes 9 endemic species. There are 16

Table 1. Physicochemical characteristics of lotic and lentic waters at different elevations;* indicates hydroelectric reservoirs created by impounding the main river. Sources: WENINGER 1972, AMARASINGHE et al. 1983, K.H.G.M. DE SILVA, unpublished data.

	Alt. m	Temp. °C	pH	Cond. μS^{20-25}	Alk. meq/l	Ca^{++} mg/l
Kelani River System						
	2,200		6.0	22	0.38	1.81
	1,850	16.6	5.5	9	0.08	0.24
	1,500	16.9	5.8	10	0.13	0.56
	1,500	17.0	6.1	24	0.45	1.94
	1,300	19.7	5.7	25	0.40	1.86
	1,200	19.7	6.0	37	0.60	2.98
	1,200	19.1	6.3	11	0.15	0.65
	1,000		6.7	20	0.40	1.15
Mahaweli River system						
	2,000	15.1	5.8	26	0.65	1.94
	1,700	18.0	5.4	25		
	1,400	21.0	5.7	32		
	1,300	22.5	6.3	40		
	1,100	21.0	5.3	22		
	1,000	21.0	5.7	45		
	800	24.5	6.1	46		
Kotmale*	700	25.6	6.6	51	0.65	1.27
	600	25.0	6.9	67		
	500	25.6	7.2	75		
Victoria*	430	26.9	7.1	77	0.86	3.02
	300	26.5	6.9	64		
Randenigala*	230	28.3	7.4	90	0.94	4.04
	100	28.5	7.0	80		
Irrigation Reservoirs						
Hurulu wewa		29.5	7.9	220	2.24	
Kala wewa		29.1	8.0	241	1.70	
Mahakandarawa		29.8	8.2	665	2.96	
Mahavilachchiya		30.9	8.2	600	2.56	
Nachchaduwa		30.8	8.0	460	1.86	
Parakrama Samudra		28.1	8.5	195	1.75	4.55

species of thiarid snails including 12 *Paludomus* species, of which 10 species and one subspecies are endemic; a single species of Bulliminidae is also endemic. The atyid shrimps comprise ten *Caridina* species, of which 6 species (one with two subspecies) are endemic (Table 2).

Distribution at different elevations

The number of indigenous and endemic species of fishes, snails and shrimps declines dramatically with increasing altitude. Less than 50 % of the species in all three faunal groups are present above an elevation of 500 m; 82 % of atyids, 90 % of gastropods, and 99% of fish species are found below 500 m. Only about 10 % of fishes, 19 % of snails, and 17 % of atyids are found above 1000 m. In the freshwaters above 1,500 m (i.e. on the third peneplain or montane Wet Zone), only one indigenous fish species (the carplet *Danio malabaricus* [JERDON]) one endemic gastropod (*Paludomus nigricans* REEVE) and a single endemic atyid (*Caridina singhalensis* ORTMANN, which is confined to the region) have been recorded (K.H.G.M. DE SILVA, unpubl. observations). However, there are records of three endemic fish species – the carplets *Barbus bimaculatus* (BLEEKER) and *Garra ceylonensis* BLEEKER, and the hill stream loach *Schistura notostigma* (BLEEKER) – from the region (SENANAYAKE 1980). Three exotic fish species – the common carp *Cyprinus carpio* L., the rainbow trout *Oncorhynchus mykiss* (WALBAUM) and the swordtail

Table 2. Indigenous and endemic species of freshwater teleosts, gastropods and atyids in Sri Lanka.

Family	Non-endemic	Endemic	Total
Teleostei			
Cyprinidae	15	17	32
Balitoridae		2	2
Cobitidae	1	1	2
Bagridae	3		3
Siluridae	2		2
Clariidae		1	1
Heteropneustidae	1	1	2
Oryziidae	1		1
Aplocheilidae	1	2	3
Cichlidae	2		2
Anabantidae	1		1
Belontiidae	1	2	3
Channidae	4	1	5
Mastacembelidae	2		2
Anguillidae [1]	2		2
Gobiidae [1]	3	3	6
Kuhliidae [1]	1		1
Belonidae [1]	1		1
Syngnathidae [1]	1		1
Total	42	30	72
Gastropoda			
Neritidae	2		2
Viviparidae	1		1
Ampullariidae	1		1
Hydrobiidae	1		1
Stenothyridae	1		1
Bulliminidae	2	1	3
Synceridae	2		2
Thiaridae [2]	5 + 1	10 + 1	17
Lymnaeidae	1		1
Planorbidae	2		2
Total	19	11	31
Decapoda			
Atyidae [3]	5	5 + 2	12

[1] May enter or breed in salt water but has resident freshwater populations.
[2] Subspecies of *Paludomus tanschauricus*, one endemic and one non-endemic, are treated as two taxa.
[3] Two subspecies of *Caridina pristis* are treated as two endemic taxa.

Xiphophorus helleri HECKEL – occur in the montane Wet Zone; the rainbow trout is confined to this region.

The fish species recorded in the montane Wet Zone (three endemic and one indigenous species) have been observed also in the submontane region (i.e. between 900 and 1,500 m), which spreads over the erosion slopes and basins of the third peneplain. All endemic fish species occur in the lowland Wet Zone, except *Barbus srilankensis* SENANAYAKE which is represented by a small population in the type locality; a tributary of the Mahaweli River in the Intermediate Zone. The lowland Wet Zone also contains all indigenous species except *Barbus ticto* (HAMILTON), a species that is confined to the Dry and Intermediate Zones. Twenty of the 30 endemic fish species are confined to the lowland Wet Zone. The indigenous *Kuhlia marginata* (CUVIER), which enters salt water, has been recorded only from this zone.

Most (77 %) indigenous gastropod species and all endemic species except *Paludomus palustris* (LAYARD), which is known only from a single location in the Dry Zone, are present in the lowland Wet Zone. All atyid species except endemic *Caridina kumariae* and *Caridina singhalensis* are found there. The endemic *Caridina pristis pristis* DE SILVA is distributed in slow-flowing streams at elevations between 300 and 1,000 m; the other subspecies, *Caridina pristis cruszi* DE SILVA, which is also endemic, has been recorded only from the streams of Sinharaja Forest at 425 m.

The Intermediate Zone is similar to the lowland Wet Zone with respect to the distribution of the three faunal groups, except that *Barbus srilankensis* is confined to that region. The endemic gastropod *Paludomus decussatus* has been recorded from only a single locality in the Intermediate Zone, but further surveys may reveal its presence in the lowland Wet Zone. Fishes such as *Microphis ocellatus* (DUNCKER) and *Xenentodon cancila* HAMILTON, which enter salt water, have not been recorded from the Intermediate Zone but, given their presence in several rivers in the Dry Zone and lowland Wet Zones, it is possible that these species may be present in the Intermediate Zone as well. The Dry Zone contains 95 % of the indigenous fish species (all except *Kuhlia marginata*) but only 13 % of the endemic fish species. The same general pattern (i.e. a paucity of endemics) is observed among snails and shrimps.

Distribution in different habitats

The aquatic fauna of Sri Lanka is mainly lotic; 96 % of fish species (95 % indigenous and 97 % endemic), 74 % of snail species (63 % indigenous and 92 % endemic) and 75 % of atyids (60 % indigenous and 86 % endemic) are found in lotic habitats. The major lentic habitats are irrigation reservoirs, which are man-made and no older than 2,500 years. The 38 indigenous species found in these habitats occur also in lotic waters and many of them (but not all) have been recorded from marshes. All endemic fishes except *Horadandia atukorali* have been recorded from lotic waters, and 22 of them are confined to streams and rivers. Only four endemic species, *Barbus bimaculatus, Esomus thermoicos* (VALENCIENNES), *Clarias brachysoma* GÜNTHER and *Belontia signata* (GÜNTHER), are found in reservoirs. Eight endemic fishes (*Horadandia atukorali, Heteropneustes microps* [GÜNTHER], *Aplocheilus dayi* [STEINDACHNER], *Channa orientalis* BLOCH & SCHNEIDER and the four species present in reservoirs) occur in swamps and marshes; *Horadandia atukorali* is confined to these habitats.

Of the 19 indigenous gastropods, only two (*Mysorella costigera* [KÜSTER] and *Faunus ater* [L.]) are not found in lotic habitats; they are confined to coastal freshwater or brackish habitats at elevations below 50 m. All endemic snails occur in lotic waters except *Paludomus palustris*, which has been recorded from a Dry-zone reservoir (STARMÜHLNER, 1974). Most (15 of 19) indigenous snails are recorded from lentic waters. Of these *Indoplanorbis exustus* (DESHAYES), *Melanoides tuberculata* (MÜLLER) and *Radix luteola* (LAMARCK) are widespread and found also in marshes. Of the endemic species, only *Bellamya dissimilis* (O. F. MÜLLER) and *P. palustris* have been recorded from irrigation reservoirs; *B. dissimilis* is common also in marshes and swamps.

Among the atyids, *Caridina gracilirostris* DE MAN and *Caridina propinqua* DE MAN are found only in estuaries, while *Caridina zeylanica* ARUD & COSTA occurs in brackish marshes. *Atyoides spinipes* (NEWPORT) has been recorded only from fast-flowing waters. Although *Atyoides spinipes* is reported to breed in brackish water (JOHNSON 1966), females with mature eggs (containing embryos with well-developed eyes) in brood pouches occur in waters more than 70 km from river estuaries (K. H. G. M. DE SILVA, unpubl. observations). The indigenous *Caridina simoni* BOUVIER has been recorded from both reservoirs and marshes but, of the endemic atyids, only *Caridina fernandoi* ARUD & COSTA has been recorded from reservoirs.

Distribution in river systems

Most of the indigenous fish species are widely distributed among the 20 major river systems (i.e. those with basins areas >900 km^2) in Sri Lanka. The exceptions are given in Table 3. Among gastropods, indigenous *Bellamya dissimilis*, *Pila globosa* (SWAINSON), *Melanoides tuberculata, Radix luteola* and *Indoplanorbis exustus* are widespread in both Wet and Dry Zones, as are the endemics *Bulimus inconspicus* (DOHRN) and *Paludomus chilinoides* (REEVE). *Caridina fernandoi* and *Caridina simoni* are likewise widely distributed in both Wet and Dry Zone river basins while three *Caridina* species are known from only one locality each (Table 3).

Origins and history of the Sri Lanka freshwater fauna

The presence of any species in a particular water body depends on the physicochemical characteristics of the water body, its accessibility, and the past evolutionary history of the species concerned. For instance, the present geographic distribution of aquatic fauna within Sri Lanka appears to be partly a result of barriers such as rapids and waterfalls and physical complexity arising from the formation of different erosion surfaces (peneplains), and partly a result of different species colonizing the island at different times.

The Sri Lankan aquatic fauna, as can be expected, shows strong affinities to that of India, especially South India. In general, however, the Sri Lankan fishes, shrimps and snails show far less diversity than their Indian counterparts. Among freshwater fishes, the family Sisoridae (46 species in India), Schilbeidae (14 species in India) and Nandidae (5 species in India), which are distributed also in South Asia and further afield, are absent in Sri Lanka. Even the family Cyprinidae, represented by 32 genera and 178 species in India, has only 10 genera and 32 species in Sri Lanka. Cyprinid genera such as *Barilius* (13 species in India) and *Salmostroma* (9 species in India), which are distributed widely in southern India, are not found in Sri Lanka. Similarly, there are 30 species of *Schistura* (Family Balitoridae) in India, but only the endemic *Schistura notostigma* BLEEKER in Sri Lanka. However, all freshwater fish families and all genera except three (non-endemic *Belontia* and endemic *Horadandia* and *Malpulutta*) that are present in Sri Lanka occur also in India. While there are likely to have been barriers to the migration of Indian freshwater fish species to Sri Lanka, the latter is a small area when compared to India although it does contain a wide range of aquatic habitats. When species richness is expressed per unit area, Sri Lanka comes a close second to Bangladesh in the southern Asian region in terms of the number of species and genera (Table 4).

Table 3. Distribution of rare freshwater species in Sri Lanka. All species are endemic except where indicated (*). Status: E – endangered; V – vulnerable; U – unknown.

Taxon	River system	Status	Remarks
Teleostei			
Cyprinidae			
Barbus asoka	Kelani, Kalu	V	3 tributaries, localized
B. bandula	Kelani	E	type locality only
B. martenstyni	Mahaweli	V	1 tributary, localized
B. srilankensis	Mahaweli	E	type locality only
Danio pathirana	Nilwala	V	1 stream, localized
Garra phillipsi	Mahaweli	V	2 tributaries, localized
Labeo fisheri	Mahaweli	E	2 tributaries, localized, range decreasing
Rasbora wilpita	Nilwala, Kelani	E	2 localities, 2 river systems
Heteropneustidae			
Heteropneustes microps	Attanagalu oya	E	1 locality
Cobitidae			
Lepidocephalichchys jonklaasi	Kalu, Gin, Nilwala	V	1 locality in each river system
Cobiidae			
Schismatogobius deraniyagalai	Kelani, Gin	V	1 locality in each river system
*Sicyopterus griseus**	Kelani	V	1 locality
Gastropoda			
Thiaridae			
Paludomus palustris	Aruvi?	U	1 locality
P. decussatus	Gal	U	1 locality
P. regalis	Gin	U	1 locality
P. solidus	Kirindi	U	1 locality
Atyidae			
Caridina costai	Kalu	U	1 locality
C. kumariae	Mahaweli	E	1 locality
C. singhalensis	Walawe	E	1 locality

Table 4. Abundance of freshwater fish species per unit land area in Sri Lanka, India, Pakistan, Bangladesh and Burma. The number of species, except those inhabiting Sri Lanka, are according to JAYARAM (1981).

	Bangladesh	Sri Lanka	Burma	Pakistan	India
Species/1,000 km^2 of land area	0.95	0.92	0.26	0.18	0.12
Genera/1,000 km^2 of land area	4.86	4.12	1.11	0.78	0.32

Although several workers (SENANAYAKE 1980, CRUSZ 1986, ERDELEN 1989) have assumed that Sri Lanka broke away from the Indian sub-continent in the Miocene (COORAY 1984), the geological evidence indicates that the Sri Lankan mini-plate separated from the Indian major plate 130 million years ago in the Cretaceous (VITANAGE 1986) before the Indian plate collided with Laurasia in the Palaeocene (THOMPSON 1976). However, there would have been intermittent land connections between Sri Lanka and India until the Miocene, during which period down-warping in the north-west and the south-eastern coastal areas of the island reached a maximum (VITANAGE 1986).

Many zoogeographers (DARLINGTON 1957, BRIGGS 1979, BANARESCU & NALBANT 1982, MENON 1987) consider that the Indian freshwater fish fauna originated in Indochina and migrated to India. Recently, however, this hypothesis has been questioned by KOTTELAT (1989), who supports the alternative hypothesis of NOVACEK & MARSHALL (1976), according to which the Ostariophysi, which later gave rise to primitive Cypriniformes and Siluriformes, originated in South America and then spread through West Africa to Europe and Asia. According to this hypothesis, southern Indian Ostariophysi would have arrived through west India. In any event, the Ostariophysi fauna of peninsular India could not be older than 55 million years, since this is the time at which the Indian plate collided with Laurasia. The migration of freshwater fish from India to Sri Lanka must therefore have taken place only after the separation of Sri Lankan mini-plate from the Indian major plate. Since there were only intermittent land connections between the two land masses after separation, there could not have been extensive migrations of freshwater fishes to Sri Lanka. This would probably account for the low diversity of Sri Lankan fish relative in India. It is noteworthy that the Indian families that are absent in Sri Lanka are mostly bottom-living, slow-moving fishes, such as the catfishes (Sisoridae and Schilbeidae) and mud-loaches (Nandidae). Similarly the paucity of the fish fauna in the middle and highest peneplains may reflect difficulties in reaching montane areas. Significantly, shrimps and almost all fish species are absent at elevations above 1200 m in Malaysia (Johnson 1966) where high-altitude streams are separated from lower ones by steep rapids and waterfalls, a situation similar to that in Sri Lanka.

The highest peneplain of Sri Lanka is separated from the middle peneplain by a 1000 m escarpment, where there are high waterfalls and steep rapids. The second peneplain is separated from the first peneplain by a 200 m escarpment, but this escarpment is eroded in many places where streams and rivers have enlarged their drainage basins by cutting into the rock wall (COORAY 1984). As a result, it constitutes a less significant barrier to dispersal than the upper escarpment, as is reflected in the similarity of the faunas of the first and second peneplains. It is interesting to note that those fish species that have been recorded from the third peneplain (*Barbus bimaculatus*, *Danio malabaricus*, *Garra ceylonensis* and *Schistura notostigma*) are all widely-distributed, pioneering species that are capable of ascending steep slopes.

Some of the Sri Lankan fish taxa show an affinity to Malaysian fish fauna. Several Sri Lankan cyprinids have perforations missing from the lateral line, a feature shown by Malaysian – but not Indian – cyprinids (DERANIYAGALA 1952). In the only cyprinid genus endemic to the island, the monotypic *Horadandia atukorali*, the lateral line perforations are entirely absent. The anabantoid genus *Belontia* is represented world-wide by only two species, *Belontia signata* in Sri Lanka and *Belontia hasselti* (CUVIER) in Sumatra, Java and Borneo. The absence of this genus in the Indian sub-continent is significant since other anabantoids are common in the region. Fossils similar to *Macropodus* spp. have been found in Eocene strata in India (SILAS 1952) and Sri Lankan *Pseudosphromenus cupanus* was earlier considered to be *Macropodus cupanus*. The occurrence of an endemic anabantoid genus *Malpulutta* (with a single species *Malpulutta kretseri* DERANIYAGAL) shows that the family has been in Sri Lanka for a long time.

Three hypotheses have been advanced to expain the affinities of the Sri Lankan fish fauna. The Land Bridge Hypothesis visualizes faunal migrations over land bridges between land masses separated by the sea. Islands are postulated as stepping stones during the periods when the sea levels were lower. In order to explain the affinities between the Sri Lankan and Indo-Malayan fauna, DERANIYAGALA (1946) postulated (among other things) intermittent island bridges between Sri Lanka and the Malayan Archipelago and the Sunda islands. However, the geological evidence does not support such land or island bridges.

The Satpura Hypothesis was postulated by HORA (1949) to explain the discontinuous distribution of some hill stream fishes between India and Sri Lanka on the one hand and those of Indochina on the other. The hill stream fishes were thought to have evolved in Yunnan and migrated westwards during the Pleistocene along the mountain ranges of Khasi, Garo, Rajmahal, Maika, Satpura and Vindya, and then southwards along the western Ghats. However, how the montane fishes crossed the lowland gap between the Garo and Rajmahal ranges in Bangladesh has not been satisfactorily explained.

NANI (1974) considers the discontinuous distribution observed in fish taxa as being secondary developments of recent origin derived from previously continuous patterns. He argues that the taxa of Indochinese derivation, when taken as a whole, show a continuous distribution in South East Asia, India and Sri Lanka. Therefore, taxa showing discontinuous distribution could be considered as geographic relicts isolated owing to events of recent occurrence. For example, *Belontia* may have been widely distributed in the Indo-Malayan region until the Miocene when eruptions in the late Miocene may have caused the extinction of the genus in southern India (SENANAYAKE 1980). Other puzzling features, such as the tendency towards the loss of lateral-line perforations may be a parallel evolutionary feature in Sri Lankan and Malayan cyprinids.

The aquatic gastropod fauna shows a close affinity to South Indian species, and all 16 Sri Lankan genera occur there (STARMÜHLNER 1974). The species found in river mouths, such as *Faunus ater* and *Syncera* cf. *hidalgoi* GASSIES have a wide Indo-Malayan or Indo-Pacific distribution. The thiarids *Thiara scabra* (MÜLLER), *Melanoides tuberculata* and *M. torulosa* (BRUGUIERE), and the two planorbids *Indoplanorbis exustus* and *Gyraulus convexiusculus*, are likewise distributed widely. The genus *Paludomus*, which shows the highest number of endemic species, occurs throughout the Indo-Malayan region. The sub-genus *Paludomus*, which contains six Sri Lankan species (including four endemics), is found in India, but the sub-genus *Philopotamis* with three Sri Lankan endemics is confined to Sri Lanka and Sumatra. The sub-genus *Tanalia* contains three species (including *Paludomus nigricans* that inhabits the montane Wet Zone) and is endemic to Sri Lanka (STARMÜHLNER 1974). It should be noted that, unlike fishes, aquatic snails can be passively distributed over long distances and mountain ranges by wading birds and other disperal agents. The paucity of aquatic snails in the montane and submontane regions could be due to factors other than accessibility. STARMÜHLNER (1974) points out that molluscs do not occur in streams where concentrations of Calcium are less than 0.7 mg/l and pH is below 5.8. These factors could limit snail establishment in the montane and submontane stream areas of Sri Lanka (Table 1).

Sri Lankan atyids show affinities to Indian as well as to Indo-Malayan and African atyids. The only *Atyoides* species found in Sri Lanka, *Atyoides spinipes*, is widespread in Southeast Asia and the western Pacific. It has been recorded also from southern India (JOHNSON 1966) as has *Caridina propinqua*. *Caridina simoni* and *Cardinia gracilirostris* are also distributed widely in the Indo-Pacific region, while *Caridina typus* has not been recorded from India to date, but is widespread in West Africa, Madagascar, southeast Asia and the western Pacific.

Electrophoretic data on protein variation are available for most Sri Lankan atyids (BENZIE & DE SILVA 1984). The cladistic analysis of these data indicates two lineages, *fernandoi-pristis* stock containing only *Caridina fernandoi* and *C. pristis*, and *simoni-typus* stock containing *C. simoni, C. zeylanica, C. gracilirostris, C. typus* and *C. singhalensis* (Fig. 3). *Simoni-typus* stock appears to be older

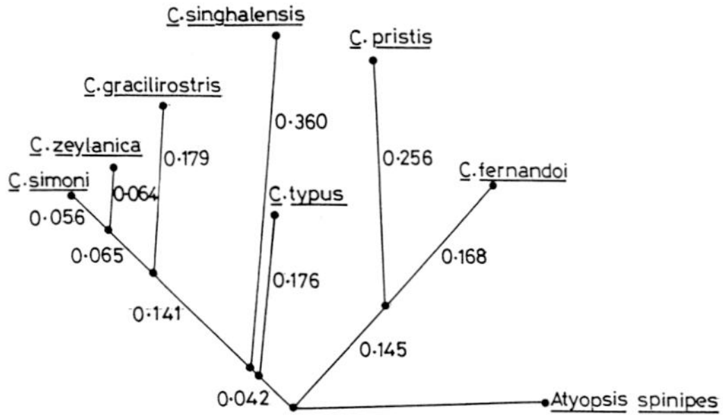

Fig. 3. A Wagner tree based on protein electrophoretic variation at 29 loci showing the phylogenetic relationship between Sri Lankan Atyidae (modified after BENZIE & DE SILVA 1984).

since it includes species that are distributed widely in the Indo-Pacific, and because *fernandoi-pristis* stock contains endemic species only. BENZIE & DE SILVA (1984) suggest that there have been two invasions corresponding to the two lineages, that of *simoni-typus* being older, with a possibility of a third invasion represented by *C. typus* and *C. singhalensis* only.

Given the paucity of freshwater shrimps in montane and submontane zones, the occurrence of *Caridina kumariae* in the submontane zone and *C. singhalensis* in the montane zone is important. *Caridina singhalensis* has declined in recent years (DE SILVA 1982), but it has never been recorded outside the montane zone (third peneplain) at any time. However, this montane species shows closer affinities with coastal *C. typus* (Fig. 3) than with other *Caridina* spp. that occur on the first and second peneplains. *Caridina typus* has a discontinuous distribution in the Pacific, southeast Asia (including Sri Lanka), Madagascar and West Africa which may reflect its presence in these areas before Gondwanaland broke up. It is possible that *C. singhalensis* was derived from *C. typus* stock which migrated to the central part of Sri Lanka prior to the peneplanation of the island. The electrophoretic work of BENZIE & DE SILVA (1984) was carried out before endemic *C. kumariae* was described. As that species is morphologically similar to *C. singhalensis*, it is possible that both shrimps are evolutionary and geographic relicts.

Acknowledgements

I am greatly indebted to the Asian Wetland Bureau, especially to Dr. ROGER JAENSCH, and to the organizers of the conference for financial support.

References

AMARASINHE, U. S., COSTA, H. H. & WIJEYARATNE, M. J. S., 1983: Limnology and fish production potential of some reservoirs in Anuradhapura district, Sri Lanka. – *J. Inland Fish.* **2**: 14–29.

BALDWIN, M. F., 1991: Natural resources of Sri Lanka – Conditions and Trends: 280 pp. – Natural Resources, Energy and Science Authority of Sri Lanka, Colombo.

BANARESCU, P. & NALBANT, T. T., 1982: New data about the Malayan-Indochinese affinities of the aquatic fauna of the Western Ghat, South India. – *Rev. Roum. Biol., Biol. Anim.* **27**: 23–27.

BENZIE, J. A. H. & DE SILVA, P. K., 1984: The taxonomic relations of the Atyidae (Decapda: Caridea) of Sri Lanka determined by electrophoretically detectable protein variation. – *J. Crust. Biol.* **4**: 632–644.

BRIGGS, J. C., 1979: Ostariophysan zoogeography: an alternative hypothesis. – *Copeia* **1979**: 111–118.

COORAY, P. G., 1984: An Introduction to the Geology of Ceylon (2nd edition): 324 pp. – National Museum of Sri Lanka, Colombo.

COSTA, H. H. & STARMÜHLNER, F., 1972: Results of the Austrian-Ceylonese-Hydrobiological Mission 1970. I. Preliminary report. – *Bull. Fish. Res. Stn. Ceylon* **23**: 43–76.

DARLINGTON, P. J., 1957: Zoogeography: the Geographical Distribution of Animals: 675 pp. – Wiley, New York.

DERANIYAGALA, P. E. P. 1952: A colored Atlas of some Vertebrates from Ceylon. 1. Fishes: 149 pp. – National Museum of Ceylon, Colombo.

– 1946: Some phases in the evolution of Ceylon. – *Proc. Ceylon Assoc. Adv. Sci.* (D) **1947**: 1–26.

DE SILVA, K. H. G. M., 1982: Aspects of the ecology and conservation of Sri Lanka's endemic freshwater shrimp *Caridina singhalensis*. – *Biol. Conserv.* **24**: 219–231.

– 1983: Studies on Atyidae (Decapoda, Caridea) of Sri Lanka. II. Distribution of atyid shrimps in Sri Lanka. – *Crustaceana* **44**: 205–215.

ERDELEN, W. 1989: Aspects of the biogeography of Sri Lanka. – In: SCHWEINFURTH, U. (ed.): Forschungen auf Ceylon. **III**: 73–100. – Franz-Steiner-Verlag, Stuttgart.

HORA, S. L. 1949: Satpura hypothesis of the distribution of the Malayan fauna and flora to peninsular India. – *Proc. Natn. Inst. Sci. India* **15**: 309–314.

JAYARAM, K. C. 1981: The Freshwater Fishes of India, Pakistan, Bangladesh, Burma and Sri Lanka – a Handbook: 475 pp. – Zoological Survey of India, Calcutta.

JOHNSON, D. S., 1966: Some factors influencing the distribution of freshwater prawns in Malaya. – *Proc. Symp. Crustacea, Erunaakulam* (India): 418–433.

KOTTELAT, M., 1989: Zoogeography of the fishes from Indochinese inland waters with an annotated check-list. – *Bull. zool. Mus. Univ. Amsterdam* **12**: 1–54.

MANI, M. S., 1974: Biogeographical evolution in India. – In: MANI, M. S. (ed.): Ecology and Biogeography in India: 698–724. – Dr. W. Junk Publishers, The Hague.

MENON, A. G. K., 1987: *The fauna of India and adjacent countries. Pisces IV. Teleostei – Cobitoidea. Part I. Homalopteridae:* 259 pp. – Zoological Survey of India, Calcutta.

NOVACEK, M. J. & MARSHALL, L. G., 1976. Early biogeographic history of Ostariophysan fishes. – *Copeia* **1976**: 1–12.

PETHIYAGODA, R. 1991: Freshwater Fishes of Sri Lanka: 362 pp. – Wildlife Heritage Trust, Colombo.

SENANAYAKE, F. R., 1980: The Biogeography and Ecology of the Inland Fishes of Sri Lanka: 421 pp. – Unpublished Ph. D. dissertation, University of California, Davis.

SILAS, E. G., 1952: Further studies regarding Hora's Satpura hypothesis. 2. Taxonomic assessments and levels of evolutionary divergences of the fishes with the so-called Malayan affinities in Peninsular India. – *Proc. Natn. Inst. Sci. India* **18**: 423–448.

STARMÜHLNER, F., 1974: Results of the Austrian-Ceylonese-Hydrobiological Mission 1970. XVII. The freshwater Gastropoda of Ceylon – *Bull. Fish. Res. Stn. Ceylon* **25**: 97–181.

THOMPSON, T. L., 1976: Plate tectonics and oil and gas exploration of continental margins: *Bull. AAPG* **60**: 1463–1501.

VITANAGE, P. W., 1986: The geology structure and tectonics of Sri Lanka and South India. – In: Recent Advances in the Geology of Sri Lanka. – *CIFEG Occasional Publ. No.* **6** (Paris): 5–15.

WENINGER, G., 1972: Results of the Austrian-Ceylonese-Hydrobiological Mission 1970. II: Hydrochemical studies on montane rivers in Ceylon. – *Bull. Fish. Res. Stn. Ceylon* **23**: 77–100.

Author's address:

Department of Zoology, University of Peradeniya, Peradeniya, Sri Lanka.

Note added in proof:

After the manuscript was received, *Barbus bimaculatus* and *Horadandia atukorali* have been recorded from S. India. Also, *B. srilankensis* is now considered as a subspecies of the S. Indian *B. arulius*.

Mitt. Internat. Verein. Limnol.	24	73–85	Stuttgart, Februar 1994

The status of limnology in Sri Lanka

H. H. Costa

Abstract

The island of Sri Lanka (area 65,525 km²) is drained by 103 river systems. There are no natural lakes, but a multitude of man-made lakes, both ancient and recent, is present. For many years, limnological research in Sri Lanka was confined to taxonomic studies of flora and fauna. It was only during the late nineteen-sixties that adequate attention was paid to functional relationships of the flora and fauna of the inland waters and to the dynamics of their environment. Remarkable progress in understanding the physical, chemical and biological processes of Sri Lankan inland waters has been achieved in the last two decades through the combined efforts of local and foreign scientists. This progress reflects interest in the maintenance of water quality and the need to develop fisheries resources, especially in lentic environments.

Major limnological investigations that have been undertaken in Sri Lanka are reviewed. These include taxonomic and ecological studies of organisms in lentic and lotic environments, physico-chemical studies of inland water bodies, estimates of primary productivity, and analysis of problems related to fish production. However, there are still significant gaps in our understanding of inland waters, especially with reference to the effects of human activities on water quality. The major constraints upon limnological teaching and research in universities and research institutes in Sri Lanka are the lack of qualified limnologists, the scarcity of analytical and experimental equipment, and inadequate funds.

Introduction

The island of Sri Lanka (6–10° N; 80–82° E), which is separated from the Indian Subcontinent by the narrow Palk Strait, covers an area of 65,525 km² and has a maximum north-south length of 432 km. A major feature of the landscape is the abundance of perennial rivers. There are no natural lakes. Nevertheless a multitude of ancient man-made lakes of varying sizes are present; they are situated mainly in the Dry Zone in the north and east of the island.

Geologically Sri Lanka is an extension of Peninsular India, and thus part of the Gondawana Shield. The island is a detached part of the continental Deccan Plateau made up of ancient crystalline rocks (Cooray 1984). These Precambrian rocks cover about 90% of the surface area of the island; the Highland Series and the South-western Group falls within the Wet- and Intermediate Zones and the Vijayan Series falls entirely within the Dry Zone (Cooray 1984). The ecology of these areas is determined mainly by the climatic conditions of the different zones.

Sri Lanka experiences slight seasonal variations in temperature, humidity and day length. Mean annual temperatures in the lowlands are approximately 27 °C with a daily range of 6 °C. In the Central Highlands (altitudes up to 2,400 m), cooler conditions prevail: at Nuwara Eliya (altitude 1,800 m) the mean annual temperature is 15 °C and the mean daily range is 10 °C. Rainfall is the most seasonal climatic factor in Sri Lanka. Depending on the pattern of precipitation, two major climatic zones can be recognized. The Dry Zone receives a mean annual precipitation of 1,450 mm from October to March and is characterized by a distinct dry period. The Dry Zone extends over three-quarters of the island encompassing the north-western, northern and eastern parts (see Fig. 2; de Silva, this volume). The Wet Zone receives a mean annual precipitation of 2,400 mm in two monsoons and two inter-monsoons, and therefore has a more evenly-distributed rainfall over the year. The Wet Zone extends over the south-west sector of Sri Lanka and the central massif. A narrow Intermediate Zone in between the two major zones can be recognised also.

Much of the natural vegetation of Sri Lanka has been cleared, and only about 36.5% of the island retains the original cover. The pattern of vegetation can be related to climatic zones (Muller-Dombois 1968). The Dry Zone contains mainly monsoon scrub-forest and grassland but, in unmodified parts of the Wet Zone in the south and south-west, tropical lowland rain forest is present (Perera 1975). Between 600 and 1,500 m the lowland forest gives way to tropical submontane rain forest; this is replaced by tropical montane rain forest between 1,500 and 2,500 m.

Inland water resources

Sri Lanka has considerable inland water resources including river systems, ancient man-made reservoirs (both seasonal and perennial), recent man-made irrigation reservoirs, perennial minor reservoirs, and marshes. The major rivers arise in the Central Highlands in the south, and flow more-or-less in a radial fashion through the low country. Some of these rivers inundate flood

0538-4680/94/0024-0073 $ 3.25

Table 1. Principal features of the main rivers of Sri Lanka. Data from various sources including ARUMUGAM (1969).

River	Length (km)	Catchment area (km^2)	Precipitation ($m^3 \times 10^6$)	Annual discharge ($m^3 \times 10^6$)	Discharge as % of precipitation
Mahaweli Ganga	329	10,327	26,804	11,016	40
Aruvi Aru	166	3,246	4,592	568	12
Kala Oya	155	2,772	4,424	587	13
Kelani Ganga	144	2,278	8,692	5,474	62
Yan Oya	150	1,520	2,269	300	19
Deduru Oya	139	2,616	4,794	1,608	34
Maduru Oya	138	1,541	2,476	805	32
Walawe Ganga	133	2,442	9,483	2,165	22
Menik Ganga	130	1,272	1,472	486	33
Maha Oya	125	1,510	4,132	1,608	39
Kirindi Oya	117	1,165	1,606	476	30
Kalu Ganga	112	2,628	10,122	7,862	77
Gin Ganga	112	922	3,039	1,903	62
Kumbukkan Oya	112	1,218	2,140	774	36
Mi Oya	107	1,516	2,176	338	16
Gal Oya	99	1,792	4,031	1,250	31

Table 2. The estimated surface area of lentic water bodies in Sri Lanka including the recently-constructed Mahaveli Reservoirs; data from SREENIVASAN & THAYPARAN (1983).

Type	Number	Combined area (ha)
Major irrigation reservoirs (ancient)	73	70,850
Medium scale reservoirs (ancient)	160	17,004
Minor irrigation reservoirs (ancient)	10,000	39,271
Flood plain lakes	–	4,049
Upland hydroelectric reservoirs (recent)	7	8,097
Mahaweli multipurpose system of reservoirs (recent)		
Maduru Oya		6,280
Victoria		2,270
Kotmale		970
Randenigala		2,750
Ulhitiya-Ratkinda		2,270
Total		153,811

plains along their lower reaches. The inundation may be temporary, lasting only during the floods, or it may be permanent as in the lower reaches of the Mahaweli River. During severe drought conditions, rivers in the Dry Zone may be reduced to a series of pools.

The rivers of Sri Lanka are remarkable for their number rather than their size. There are 103 perennial rivers (Table 1, Fig. 1), and they have flow characteristics dependent on their geographical position, physical characteristics of the terrain, and the regional climatic parameters (ERB 1984). The total annual discharge from all of the rivers to the sea is approximately 38,868 million m^3 which is 31% of the estimated precipitation in their drainage basins (ARUMUGAM 1969; Table 1).

Ancient civilization in Sri Lanka was centred in the Dry Zone where the rainfall is seasonal. This necessitated the conservation of rain water that fell during the wet season (November to February). For this reason, a system of man-made lakes was developed that was unsurpassed for engineering sophistication anywhere in the ancient world. The system comprised a variety of reservoirs (up to 3,000 ha area) and an associated irrigation system for rice cultivation. Over time, and with shifts in human settlements, most of these reservoirs fell into disuse until the end of the nineteenth century. Then, as a result of resettlement and revitalization of agriculture in the Dry Zone, a large number of the irrigation reservoirs were rehabilitated and made functional. Though primarily serving an irrigation requirement, they are also utilized for fish production. The combined surface area of lentic water bodies (i.e. man-made reservoirs and marshes) in Sri Lanka has been estimated at approximately 153,811 ha (SREENIVASAN & THAYAPARAN 1983) (Table 2; Fig. 1).

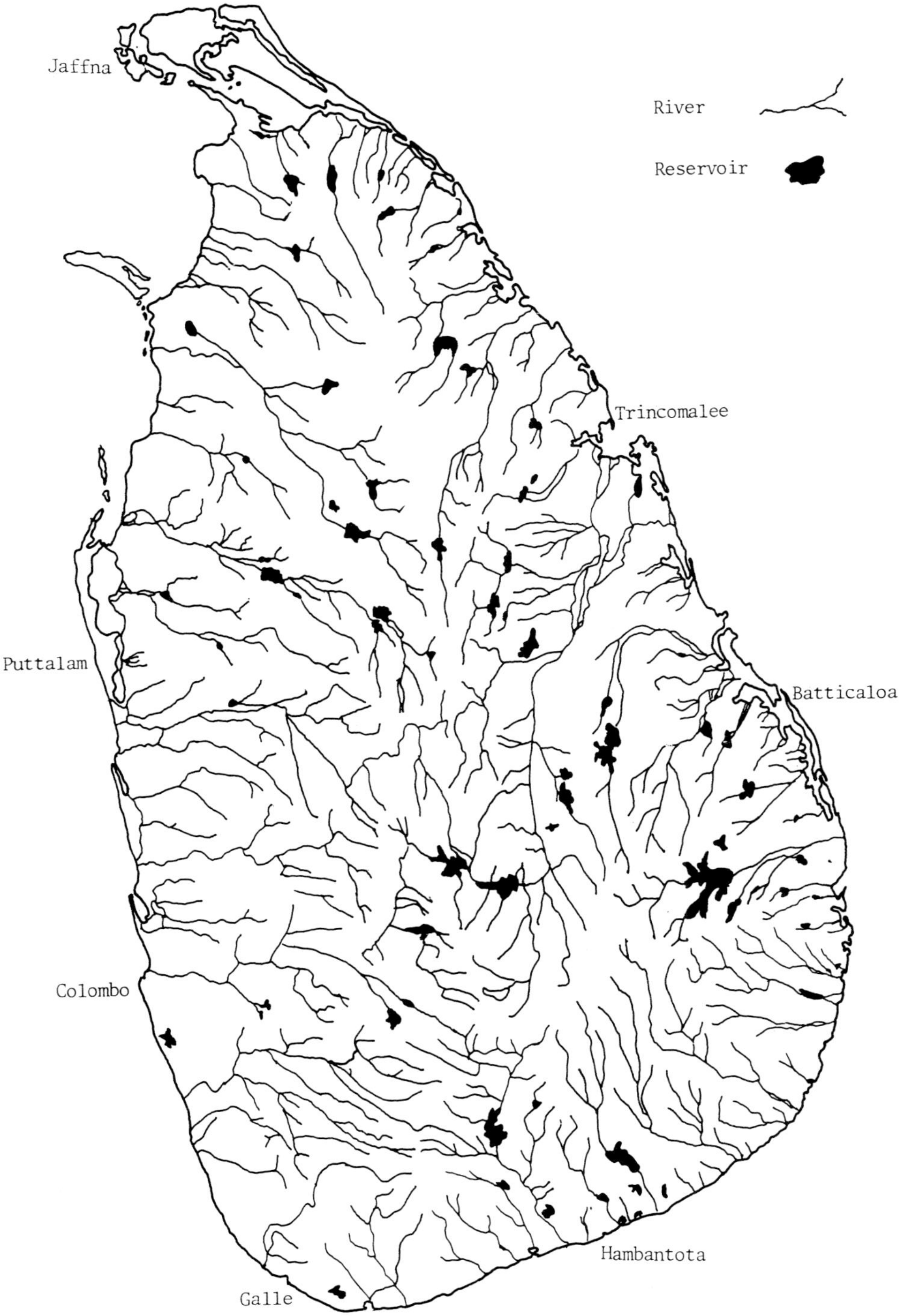

Fig. 1. Rivers and major reservoirs of Sri Lanka.

Table 3. Physicochemical characteristics of perennial reservoirs in Sri Lanka.

Site	Author	Temp. °C	*p*H	Total alkalinity (mg/l)	Conductivity (µmhos/cm)	Secchi disc depth (cm)	Phosphates (mg/l)	Nitrates (mg/l)
Dry Zone								
Parakrama Samudra (2,262 ha)	Gunatilaka 1983	28–34	8.1–9.1	1.76–3.18 (meq/l)	155–354	–	2.3–18.4 (µg/l)	–
Hurulu Wewa (2,195 ha)	Amarasinghe et al. 1983	20–34	7.0–8.5	59–164	140–300	40–111	–	–
Kala Wewa (2,598 ha)	Amarasinghe et al. 1983; Gunawardhana & Adikari 1981	27–32	7.4–8.4	50–119	82–400	41–94	8.38–15.72	–
Mahakandara Wewa (1,457 ha)	Amarasinghe et al. 1983	23–32	7.9–8.45	107–189	402–910	40–95	–	–
Mahavilichchiya Wewa (1,784 ha)	Amarasinghe et al. 1983	28–34	7.5–8.48	81–147	400–800	42–78	–	–
Nachaduwa Wewa (1,748 ha)	Amarasinghe et al. 1983	28.6–32.9	7.5–8.5	5.3–150	350–570	40–90	–	–
Nuwara Wewa (1,196 ha)	Amarasinghe et al. 1983	28–31.3	8.2–8.6	7.47–133.3	300–850	22–54	–	–
Rajangana Wewa (1,199 ha)	Amarasinghe et al. 1983	26–32	7.47–8.57	124–191	455–650	65–151	–	–
Badagiriya Wewa (482 ha)	Wijeyaratne & Costa 1983; de Silva & Sirisena 1987; Daniel et al. 1988	26–34	7.9–8.8	–	360–1110	20–75	–	–
Ridiyagama Wewa (888 ha)	Wijeyaratne & Costa 1981; de Silva & Sirisena 1987; Daniel et al. 1988	26–32.9	7.6–8.6	4.4 (meq/l)	400–1050	50–100	–	–
Wirawila Wewa (567 ha)	Wijeyaratne & Costa 1981; Daniel et al. 1988	28–34	7.5–9.5	–	400–1050	20–100	–	–
Tissa Wewa (233 ha)	Wijeyaratne & Costa 1981; de Silva & Sirisena 1987; Daniel et al. 1989	27–31	7.6–9.5	–	360–830	100–300	–	–
Udawalawe Wewa (3282)	Chandrasoma et al. 1986	28–36	7.1–9.1	53–105	112–260	–	–	–
Yodakandiya Wewa (488 ha)	Wijeyaratne & Costa 1981; de Silva & Sirisena 1987; Daniel et al. 1988	29–32	7.8–8.7	–	400–1050	25–100	–	–
Pimburattewa Wewa (834 ha)	Amarasinghe 1987; Costa, pers. observations	28–32	7.5–8.3	8.4– (meq/l)	450–	7.5–650	–	–
Wet Zone								
Colombo Lake (65 ha)	Costa & de Silva 1978a; Costa & Liyanage 1978	26–34	7.5–9.1	50–155	2200	20–60	0.0–2.0	0.01–1.25
Kandy Lake (18 ha)	de Silva & de Silva 1984	28–31	7.0–7.3	0.18–1.9 (meq/l)	–	–	16.2 (µg/l)	–

Table 4. Physicochemical characteristics of some seasonal reservoirs in the Dry Zone of Sri Lanka; data from CHANDRASOMA (1986).

Reservoir	Area (ha)	*p*H	Secchi disc depth (cm)	Calcium hardness (mg/l)	Conductivity (μmhos/cm)	Oxygen (mg/l)
Tunkama	4.0	4.2–8.7	40–75	130–220	530–750	2.5–6.4
Mahawewa	6.0	7.1–7.8	33–75	55–120	640–950	3.0–6.4
Epitagoda	3.5	7.1–7.9	22–40	20–31	90–120	4.2–5.2
Maduranwela	3.5	7.0–7.7	70–110	52–67	135–250	5.0–8.7
Benthis Wewa	2.0	7.3–8.1	40–70	50–65	210–390	3.7–10
Nika Wewa	0.6	7.2–8.3	30–70	40–70	155–540	4.1–4.7
Welapahale	2.5	6.9–7.4	80–100	58–64	110–125	4.4–5.8
Komaligama	3.0	5.0–7.5	80–110	50–72	200–240	4.3–5.8
Angunakolapelassa	4.0	7.1–7.6	30–35	30–60	80–105	4.6–10.2
Kalwegala	4.0	7.0–8.0	30–70	28–40	50–92	4.6–10.3

Table 5. Some physicochemical characteristics of irrigation reservoirs of the Mahaweli River system.

	Temp. °C	*p*H	Total alkalinity (meq/l)	Conductivity (μmhos/cm)	Secchi disc depth (cm)	Oxygen (mg/l)
Kotmale (DE SILVA 1991, PIYASIRI 1991)	23–27	6.8–7.19	0.23–0.43	30–90	200–230	7.47–8.09
Victoria (DE SILVA 1991, PIYASIRI 1991)	25–29	6.7–7.8	0.45–0.82	100–140	120–161	6.0–8.0
Randenigala (DE SILVA 1991, PIYASIRI 1991)	26–30	7.0–7.2	0.68–0.97	110–180	251–301	6.4–8.8

Physicochemical features of lentic waters

Lentic water bodies in Sri Lanka vary in their characteristics according to whether or not they retain water throughout the dry season. Investigations of the physicochemical parameters of perennial reservoirs in the Dry Zone, and their seasonal dynamics, have been carried out by MENDIS (1965), GUNAWARDHANA & ADIKARI (1981), GUNATILAKA & SENARATNE, (1981) AMARASINGHE et al. (1983), WIJEYARATNE & AMARASINGHE (1984) and DANIEL et al. (1988). Similar studies in the Wet Zone have been undertaken by COSTA & DE SILVA (1969, 1978a), DE SILVA & DE SILVA (1984), and COSTA et al. (in press) (Table 3). The high dissolved phosphate content (15.1 mg/l) in the waters of Kala Wewa has been attributed to the extraction of apatite from the reservoir banks, but levels had declined to 1.2 mg/l in 1991 (GUNAWARDHANA, pers. comm.).

Seasonal reservoirs are relatively small and shallow. Most are located in the Dry Zone and receive rain during the north-east monsoon. Filling occurs in January or February, and they are completely dry by June, July or August. Although these reservoirs have recently become more important because of their use in fish culture, only a few studies have been carried out on their physicochemical characteristics (CHANDRASOMA 1986, WIJEYARATNE & WANNINAYAKE 1993; Table 4). The development of new irrigation works in Sri Lanka will create a large number of reservoirs. For example, ongoing developments along the Mahaweli River system include seven major reservoirs which, when completed, will cover a surface area of over 20,000 ha. The physicochemical characteristics are known only for a few of these reservoirs (DE SILVA 1991, PIYASIRI 1991; Table 5). Their water levels fluctuate markedly during different seasons making them unsuitable for large-scale fisheries development.

Physicochemical features of lotic waters

In contrast to lentic waters bodies, little information is available on the physicochemical characteristics of running waters. What is available is scattered and fragmentary, and most data concern running waters of the mountains and coastal areas of south-west Sri Lanka (Table 6; see also Geisler 1967, Weninger 1972, Costa 1974, 1984).

Physiography, geology, geochemistry and climate have a great influence on the hydrochemistry of Sri Lankan rivers (Weninger 1972). The rivers of the Wet Zone have low concentrations of dissolved minerals, the headwaters being slightly acidic. In their lower courses the electrolyte concentrations and humic-acid levels increase. Sodium predominates over calcium, while calcium predominates over magnesium in the upper and middle courses. Conductivity, total hardness and alkalinity generally increase with decreasing altitude. In the lower reaches there is often evidence of eutrophication, and total nitrogen levels are elevated when rivers flow through densely-populated areas. There are also distinct longitudinal trends in water temperature, and temperatures can increase from 15 °C to greater than 28 °C over a distance 100 to 150 km (Costa & Starmühlner 1972). Temperatures at the lower elevations vary greatly, and can reach >30 °C in river mouths.

Table 6. Physicochemical characteristics of three Sri Lankan rivers; data from Weninger (1972) and Costa (unpubl. observations).

	Kelani River (upper course)	Gin River (middle course)	Mahaweli River (lower course)
Temperature °C	19	26	29
Conductivity (µS cm)	11	36	280
*p*H	5.1–6.1	5.5–6.6	6.5–7.3
Total hardness	0.5	3.2	22
Ca^{2+} mg/l	0.65	5.3	2.01
Mg^{2+} mg/l	0.26	3.3	5.41
Na mg/l	0.70	2.0	3.81
Fe^{2+} mg/l	0.005	–	–
Al^{3+} mg/l	0.03	–	–
NH_4 mg/l	0.04	–	–
Cl mg/l	1.70	2.41	0.38
PO_4 mg/l	0.00	0.1	1.15
SiO_2 mg/l	3.15	10.3	3.50
NO_3 mg/l	0.05	0.01	1.25

Phytoplankton, macrophytes and primary productivity

The species composition of freshwater phytoplankton is fairly well known. Interest in phytoplankton arose because of its importance as a source of food for aquatic fauna, specially *Oreochromis mossambicus* (Peters) which constitutes about 90% of the fish caught from Sri Lankan reservoirs. Cyanophyceae is the dominant phytoplankton group in lentic water bodies in Sri Lanka. Their dominance reflects eutrophication, which has been attributed mainly to sewage pollution leading to proliferation of *Microcystis* sp. and *Oscillataria* sp. (De Alwis 1990).

Investigations on seasonal variation, species composition, biomass, distribution and ecology of the major phytoplankton groups have now been carried out for a reasonable number of large and small lentic water bodies in the Wet Zone (Holsinger 1965, Costa & De Silva 1978 b, De Silva 1991), and for perennial and seasonal water bodies in the Dry Zone (Amarasinghe et al. 1988, Dokulil et al. 1983, Silva & Davies 1986, Daniel et al. 1988, Wijeyaratne & Wanninayake 1993). Phytoplankton densities range from 50–5,100,000/l in major and medium-sized reservoirs, but densities and community composition vary seasonally and even among days of the year (Costa & De Silva 1978 b), as well as with the location of the reservoirs.

The primary productivity for major and medium-sized lentic water bodies in the Dry Zone varies from 0.03–5.63 g C/m²/day (Amarasinghe et al. 1983, Daniel et al. 1988) and for minor seasonal waterbodies from 2.82–6.15 g C/m²/day (Chandrasona 1986, Wijeyaratne & Wanninayake 1993). The gross primary productivity of minor perennial reservoirs in the Wet Zone ranges from 2.32–5.32 g C/m²/day (Costa & De Silva 1978 d). Community respiration resulting from primary production is high during the rainy season (Costa & De Silva 1978 d).

A rich array of aquatic macrophytes is present in the reservoirs, streams and marshes of Sri Lanka. A brief account of these aquatic plants has been given by Abeywickrema (1956). In the past few years, the rapid invasion of the reservoirs, ponds and channels by two exotic aquatic plants, *Eichhornia crassipes* (Mart.) Solms and *Salvinia molesta* (Mitchell), has given cause for concern. *E. crassipes* and *S. molesta* cover about 5,000 and 20,000 ha of water surface respectively (Costa 1986). In the past few years, success has been achieved in controlling *S. molesta* with an exotic beetle, *Cryptobagous salviniae* (Calder & Sands) (I. V. S. Fenando, pers. comm.).

Table 7. Studies conducted on Sri Lankan zooplankton.

Reservoir	Author/s	Topics studied
Lake Gregory	CHENGALATH & FERNANDO (1973)	Composition
Lake Gregory	CMENGALATH et al. (1984)	Composition and distribution
Lake Gregory	FENANDO (1980)	Composition and distribution
Beira Lake	COSTA & DE SILVA (1969)	Diurnal variation
Kalawewa	JAYATUNGA (1982)	Composition, distribution and seasonal variation
Parakrama Samudra	RAJAPAKSE & FERNANDO (1984)	Seasonal changes
Parakrama Samudra	DUNCAN (1983)	Composition, density and distribution
Parakrama Samudra	DUNCAN & GULATI (1983)	Dynamics of zooplankton groups
Seven reservoirs in Hambantota District	DANIEL et al. (1988)	Seasonal variation

Table 8. Aquatic invertebrate fauna described from Sri Lanka.

Taxon	Author	Year
Platyhelminthes	BEAUCHAMP	1973
Annelida		
Oligochaeta	COSTA	1967
Hirudinea	COSTA	1978
Arthropoda		
Crustacea		
Ostracoda	NEALE	1984
Atyidae	ARUDPRAGASAM & COSTA	1962
	DE SILVA	1983
Palaemonidae	COSTA	1979
Potamonidae	BOTT	1970
Insecta		
Coleoptera	BERTRAND	1972
	WEWALKA	1973
	JAECH	1982
Diptera	DAVIS	1984
Ephemeroptera	HUBBARD & PETER	1984
Heteroptera	POLHEMUS	1979
Plecoptera	ZWICK	1980
Trichoptera	SCHMIDT	1985
	MALICKY	1973
Mollusca		
Gastropoda	STARMÜHLNER	1974

Zooplankton and zoobenthos

Recent studies of zooplankton have contributed immensely to our knowledge of this group in Sri Lankan reservoirs. The systematics of the zooplanktonic groups Rotifera, Cladocera and Copepoda are better known for Sri Lanka than for any other tropical country (CHENGALATH & FERNANDO 1973, FERNANDO 1980); 138 species of Rotifera, 58 species of Cladocera and 23 species of free-living Cyclopoida and Calanoida have been recorded from the island. A list of relevant investigations is given in Table 7. The zooplankton species found in Sri Lanka are either cosmopolitan or pantropical (RAJAPAKSE & FERNANDO 1984). Uniform high temperatures, flushing rates and fish predation are the major factors that determine the densities of zooplankton. Unfortunately, data on the ecology and production of zooplankton are lacking almost entirely.

The benthic fauna of streams and large rivers has yet to be studied in great detail, although some information is available for molluscs and shrimps (STARMÜHLNER 1974; see also DE SILVA, this volume). Data from lentic habitats are a little more plentiful. There has been a single study of the invertebrates associated with aquatic plants (COSTA & DE SILVA 1978c), and one investigation of benthic standing stocks (MENDIS 1965). The latter included 18 reservoirs in the Dry and Wet Zones and yielded zoobenthos biomass figures ranging from 4.5 to 41.0 kg/ha. Other investigations of lentic zoobenthos have concentrated on the marginal-zone fauna (FERNANDO 1965, FERNANDO & ELLEPOLA 1969, COSTA & DE SILVA 1978c). Despite this research, however, hardly anything is known of seasonality or the factors controlling the abundance of Sri Lankan zoobenthos. Nevertheless, many elements of the zoobenthos have been well served by taxonomic studies (Table 8), so that a good foundation has been provided for future research.

Fish and fisheries management

About 55 species of fish are native to Sri Lankan freshwaters (COSTA 1980, DE SILVA 1988; see also DE SILVA 1994). Since 1892; 17 species of exotic fish have been introduced into Sri Lanka. Of these exotic fish, only the tilapia, *Oreochromis mossambi-*

Table 9. Water quality and pollution studies conducted in Sri Lanka.

Waterbodies	Subjects studied	Author
Kelani river	Industrial effluents	Gunatilaka (1975, unpublished)
Kelani river	Industrial effluents	de Silva et al. (1984)
Colombo Lake	Bacterial ecology	Costa & Gunatilaka (1978e)
Nuwara Eliya Lake	Agricultural chemicals	Dissanayake et al. (1990)
Colombo Lake	Sewage discharge	de Alwis (1990)
Katunayake Streams	BOD	de Alwis et al. (1988)
Coastal domestic sewers	BOD	Costa (1970)
	Effects of insecticides on shrimps	Costa (1970)
	Effects of pesticides on fish	Shafiei & Costa (1990)

cus, has established itself in reservoirs where it forms the most important component of reservoir fisheries. This success is due mostly to its food habits (Costa & Abeyasiri 1978). Because of the importance of *O. mossambicus* in fisheries, much biological work has been devoted to this fish (e.g. Wijeyaratne & Costa 1981, Wijeyaratne & Amarasinghe 1984), while relatively little research has been undertaken on the biology of indigenous food fishes and other introduced species (De Silva 1988).

The relevance of limnological studies to the development of fisheries in Sri Lanka has been documented recently by Costa (1980) Fernando & De Silva (1984) and De Silva (1988). The freshwater fishery of Sri Lanka is mainly a capture fishery confined to large and medium-sized reservoirs, although a culture fishery is centred upon minor reservoirs. The total annual fish yield from these smaller reservoirs is about 30,000 kg which is about 20% of the total fish production. Studies on physicochemical characteristics of water bodies, plankton, primary productivity, benthic productivity, rates of nutrient flux, food habits of fish and so on, have contributed considerably to the developmental and management aspects of reservoir fisheries.

Pollution

In recent years there has been an upsurge of interest in Sri Lanka regarding the quality of freshwaters, partly because of global concern about the threat of widespread pollution of the aquatic environment and also because of the economic value of freshwaters for fisheries, aquaculture and domestic use. Few studies have been conducted on the effects of human activities on water quality in lentic and lotic waterbodies of Sri Lanka, and much of the work which has been undertaken is unpublished. Investigations that have been carried out are listed in Table 9.

External assistance provided for the development of aquatic resources

The development of limnological studies has a great bearing on the development of inland fisheries in Sri Lanka. A concerted effort to develop reservoir fisheries through research and experimental work began in 1978. In addition to the Inland Fisheries Division of the Ministry of Fisheries, a new organization called the National Aquatic Resources Research and Developmental Agency (NARA) was created in 1981 for the purpose of conducting and coordinating research on the aquatic resources of Sri Lanka. Most of the projects carried out by this agency and the Ministry of Fisheries are funded by external organizations.

External assistance for developmental programmes received so far is summarized in Table 10. This amounts to approximately US $ 23 million. However, these programmes lack funding components for fundamental limnological research, although the donor agencies have recognized that such research is vital for a better understanding of the biological basis of production in reservoirs.

Future research needs of Sri Lankan limnology

The present state of limnological knowledge of Sri Lankan waters, although not impressive when compared with that of the temperate regions, is nevertheless quite substantial. However, there are still significant gaps in our understanding of the

Table 10. External grants provided for the development of freshwater fisheries from international organizations.

Name of project/ Activity	Source	Year	Amount (US$ million)
Inland fisheries development	FAO/TCP	1962	0.0415
Training of limnologists/fishery biologists/ aquaculturists	FAO/UNDP	1975	0.0756
Fish breeding stations for training (at Udawalawe)	China	1975/6	1.2000
Training of Sri Lankans in aquatic sciences	FAO/UNDP	1977	0.0078
Development of fisheries in man-made lakes and reservoirs	FAO/TCN	1970/80	0.040
Technical equipment	UNICEP	1981/84	0.255
Aquaculture development projects and training	FAO/UNDP/ADB	1981/84	1.700
Cage culture	IDRC	1982/85	0.200
Aquaculture development (seasonal reservoirs)	ADB	1984/87	17.27
Inland fisheries development	CIDA	1985/89	2.00
Fish nutrition	IDRC	1985/87	0.11
Total			22.89

dynamics of Sri Lankan freshwaters, especially lotic environments. The entire ecological spectrum of rivers and reservoirs has to be studied to evaluate productivity. Topics such as land-water interactions, watershed management, and conservation have not yet been sutdied properly, and more effort should be put into understanding the ecology of lotic habitats and their drainage basins. Much work is still needed in lentic environments to increase knowledge of seasonal, vertical and diurnal variations of thermal features, oxygen regimes, nutrient cycling, organic inputs and dissolved solids. No work has been undertaken on microbial ecology and decomposition processes, the relationship of detritus to fish production, or the metabolic activities of the marginal zone and sediments.

More research on planktonic and benthic organisms is essential to guide fish-stocking programmes in reservoirs. Basic biological research on indigenous fish and aquatic organisms has to be undertaken to provide a good understanding of the ecological energetics of aquatic habitats. Work must be initiated to develop predictive models, based on limnological data, so as to permit effective managment of the diverse reservoirs and water bodies of Sri Lanka. Large gaps in knowledge exist as to the quantities of domestic sewage, agricultural chemicals and industrial effluents that are discharged into waterbodies, and their effect on aquatic organisms and human health. Detailed studies involving biological monitoring have yet to be carried out.

Constraints

The lack of trained limnologists and technical personnel has been the biggest constraint in the development of limnological studies in Sri Lanka (Table 11). In the past, this deficiency was to some extent overcome by joint investigations on prearranged projects by Sri Lankan scientists in association with foreign workers from limnological institutes in developed countries. (Brink et al. 1971, Costa & Starmühlner 1972, Schiemer 1983).

Research on limnology has been limited also by lack of funds. Out of approximately US $ 23 million given to the government of Sri Lanka as assistance for development of aquatic resources by foreign agencies and organizations (Table 10), no specific component has been assigned for pure limnological research. Meagre funds are sometimes available to universities for study of waterbodies through national funding authorities and from international agencies such as International Foundation for Science (Sweden).

Modern analytical and sampling equipment used in limnological research, and infrastructure such as specialized laboratories, are lacking in most universities and government research institutes. Lack of technicians to repair equipment, most of which is imported, is another factor which is limiting research work. Scarcity of literature and pertinent reference works, inability to obtain scientific information in particular fields, restricted import of limnological journals, and lack of expe-

Table 11. Universities and research institutes engaged in limnological research in Sri Lanka.

Organization	Number of scientists trained to postgraduate level engaged in limnology fisheries or aquaculture	Scientists trained at Ph.D. level in limnology	Institutes offering courses or course units in limnology
University of Colombo	2	1	+
University of Peradeniya	3	1	+
University of Kelaniya	5	1	+
University of Jayawardanepura	3	1	+
University of Ruhuna	2	1	+
Eastern University Sri Lanka	1	+	
University of Jaffna	1	–	+
National Aquatic Resources Agency (NARA)	14	1	–
Ministry of Fisheries			
Division of Inland Fisheries *	1	–	
Total	72	8	

* abolished 31 December, 1991.

rienced senior limnologists for guidance and advice are the other major constraints. The greatest obstacle to future development of limnological studies is the recent decision by the Government of Sri Lanka to abolish the Inland Fisheries Division of the Ministry of Fisheries (effective 31 December 1991). This will terminate government subsidies and aid programmes to freshwater fisheries and aquaculture projects in Sri Lanka.

Strategies for enhancement of limnological research and training

The development of Sri Lankan limnology – both in terms of manpower and infrastructure – should be combined with the identification of national research programmes which will form a basis for strengthening limnological research. These objectives could be achieved, directly or indirectly, by a variety of strategies as listed below.

i) Establish or strengthen university infrastructure to allow undergraduate and postgraduate training in limnology so as to provide the expertise needed to conduct specific research programmes.
ii) Establish or strengthen limnological research laboratories with specialized scientific equipment and personnel.
iii) Establish short-term training and long-term fellowships in foreign limnological institutes to upgrade individual scientific capabilities.
iv) Strengthen and upgrade library facilities with essential reference works and monographs in limnology.
v) Provide mechanisms for collaborative research with internationally-known limnologists at the research level.
vi) Provide travel grants to young Sri Lankan limnologists which will permit them to attend international conferences and workshops.

Acknowledgements

I am very grateful to *Societas Internationalis Limnologiae* for providing a travel and subsistence grant to attend the Hong Kong conference. Mr. G. A. Weerasundara is thanked for typing the original manuscript.

References

Abeywickrama, B. A., 1956: The origin and the affinities of the flora of Ceylon. – *Proc. Ceylon Assoc. Adv. Sci.* **XX** 99–121.

Amarasinghe, U. S., 1987: Status of the fishery of Pimburettewa wewa, a man-made lake in Sri Lanka. – *Aquacult. Fish. Manag.* **18**: 375–385.

Amarasinghe, U. S., Costa, H. H. & Wijeyaratne, M. J. S., 1983: Limnology and fish production potential of some reservoirs in Anuradapura district, Sri Lanka. – *J. Inland Fish. Sri Lanka* **2**: 14–29.

Arudpragasam, K. D. & Costa, H. H., 1962: The Atyidae of Ceylon I. – *Crustaceana* **4**: 7–24.

BEAUCHAMP, P. de, 1973: Freshwater triclads (Turbellaria, Tricladida) from Ceylon. – *Bull. Fish. Res. Stn. Sri Lanka* **24**: 95–112.

BERTRAND, H. P. I., 1973: Results of the Austrian-Ceylonese hydrobiological Mission 1970 Part-XI. Larvae and pupae of water beetles collected in the island of Ceylon. – *Bull. Fish. Res. Stn. Sri Lanka* **24**: 95–112.

BOTT, R., 1970: Die Süsswasser Krabben von Ceylon (Crustacea Decapoda). – *Ark. Zool.* **22**: 627–640.

BRINCK, P., ANDERSON, H. & CEDERHOLM, L. 1971: Report No. 1 from the Lund University, Ceylon expedition in 1962, Introduction. – *Ent. Scand., Suppl.* **1**: 1–36.

CHANDRASOMA, J., 1986: Primary productivity and fish yields in ten seasonal tanks in Sri Lanka. – *J. Inland Fish. Sri Lanka* **3**: 56–63.

CHANDRASOMA, J., MUTHUKUMARAN, G., PUSPAKUMARA, U. & SREENIVASAN, A., 1986: Limnology and fish production in Udawalawe Reservoir. – *J. Inland Fish. Sri Lanka* **3**: 69–88.

CHENGALATH, R. & FERNANDO, C. H., 1973: Rotifers from Sri Lanka including the description of two new species. – *Bull. Fish. Res. Stn. Sri Lanka* **24**: 13–27.

CHENGALATH, R., FERNANDO, C. H. & KOSTE, W., 1984: The Rotifera of Sri Lanka 3. Descriptions of new species and new records with a list of species in Sri Lanka and discussion and distribution. – *Bull. Fish. Res. Stn. Sri Lanka* **25**: 83–96.

COORAY, P. G., 1984: An Introduction to the Geology of Ceylon (2nd Edition): 324 pp. – Ceylon National Museum Publication.

COSTA, H. H., 1967: A taxonomic study of the freshwater Oligochaeta of Sri Lanka. – *Ceylon J. Sci. (Biol. Sci.)* **7**: 37–51.

COSTA, H. H., 1970: Effects of some common insecticides and other environmental factors on the heart beat of *Caridina pristis*. – *Hydrobiologia* **35**: 469–480.

– 1974: Limnology and fishery biology of the streams at Horton Plains, Sri Lanka. – *Bull. Fish. Res. Stn. Sri Lanka* **25**: 15–26.

– 1978: The freshwater Hirudinea of Sri Lanka. – *Bull. Fish. Res. Stn. Sri Lanka* **32**: 326–341.

– 1979: The Palaemonidae of the inland waters of Sri Lanka. – *Ceylon J. Sci. (Biol. Sci.)* **13**: 39–64.

– 1980: The physical, chemical and biological characteristics of freshwater bodies of the lowlands of Sri Lanka. – *Spol. Zeylan.* **35**: 43–99.

– 1986: Freshwater as a Natural Resource in Sri Lanka: 58 pp. – Science Educational Series, No 18. NARESA, Colombo.

– 1989: Land Based Marine Pollution in Sri Lanka. – Paper presented at workshop on Land based Marine Pollution, Bangkok, Thailand (unpublished).

COSTA, H. H. & ABEYASIRI, R., 1978: The hydrobiology of Colombo Lake VII. The food and feeding ecology of *Tilapia mossambica*. – *Spol. Zeylan.* **32**: 94–100.

COSTA, H. H. & DE SILVA, S. S., 1969: Hydrobiology of Columbo Lake 1. Diurnal variations in temperature, hydrochemical factors and zooplankton. – *Bull. Fish. Stn. Sri Lanka* **20**: 141–149.

– – 1978a: Hydrobiology of Colombo Lake II. Seasonal variation in physico-chemical factors. – *Spol. Zeylan.* **32**: 26–41.

– – 1978b: Hydrobiology of Colombo Lake III. Seasonal fluctuations of plankton. – *Spol. Zeylan.* **32**: 35–72.

– – 1978c: Hydrobiology of Colombo Lake IV. Seasonal fluctuations in aquatic fauna living on water plants. – *Spol. Zeylan.* **32**: 60–75.

– – 1978d: Hydrobiology of Colombo Lake VI. Seasonal variations in primary productivity. – *Spol. Zeylan.* **32**: 84–94.

COSTA, H. H. & GUNATILAKA, W. D. A., 1978: Hydrobiology of Colombo Lake VIII. Bacterial ecology. – *Spol. Zeylan.* **32**: 115–132.

COSTA, H. H. & LIYANAGE, H., 1978: Hydrobiology of Colombo Lake IX. Productivity of *Tilapia mossambica*. – *Spol. Zeylan.* **32**: 115–132.

COSTA, H. H. & STARMÜHLNER, F., 1972: Results of the Austrian-Ceylonese hydrobiological mission 1970 of the 1st Zoological Institute of University of Vienna Austria and the Department of Zoology of Vidyalankara University of Ceylon, Kelaniya Part 1. Introduction and description of the stations. – *Bull. Fish. Res. Stn. Sri Lanka* **23**: 43–76.

COSTA, H. H., WANNINAYAKE, T. B. & WIJEYARATNE, M. J. S., in press: The hydrobiology of Ihalagama wewa, Ragama. – *Spol. Zeylan.*

DANIEL, D. J., COSTA, H. H. & WIJEYARATNE, M. J. S., 1988: The hydrobiology and fish production potential of major freshwater reservoirs in Hambantota District. – *J. Inland Fish. Sri Lanka* **4**: 95–121.

DAVIES, D. M., 1984: Notes on the Simulidae (Diptera) in Sri Lanka. – In: FERNANDO, C. H. (ed.): Ecology and Biogeography of Sri Lanka: 275–381. – Dr. W. Junk Publishers, The Hague.

DE ALWIS, P.; 1990: Investigation of a Reported Mass Fish Mortality in Beira Lake: 12 pp. – National Aquatic Research Agency, Colombo, Sri Lanka (unpublished).

DE ALWIS, P., YATAPANA, H., DISSANAYAKE, W. H. & PEREIRA, R., 1988. Monitoring of Industrial Effluents with a View to Pollution Control. – Paper presented at the 43rd annual session of the Sri Lankan Association for the Advancement of Science (unpublished).

DE SILVA, M. K. W., NANDANI, C. & JAYAWEERA, V. 1984: Mass Mortality of Fish in Kelani River: 11 pp. – National Aquatic Research Agency, Colombo, Sri Lanka (unpublished).

DE SILVA, K. H. G. M., 1983: Studies on Atyidae (Decapoda, Caridea) of Sri Lanka II. Distribution of atyid shrimps. – *Crustaceana* **44**: 205–215.

DE SILVA, P. K., in press: Physico-chemical characteristics, phytoplankton and fishery of Victoria Reservoir. *Ceylon J. Sci. (Biol. Sci.)*.

De Silva, P. K. & De Silva, K. H. G. M., 1984: An ecological study of the meso- and macrofauna of the littoral region of the Lake Kandy in Sri Lanka. – *Arch. Hydrobiol.* **102**: 53–72.

De Silva, S. S., 1988: Reservoirs of Sri Lanka and their fisheries. – *FAO Fish Tech. Pap.* **298**: 1–128.

De Silva, S. S. & Sirisena, H. K. G., 1987: New fish resources of reservoirs of Sri Lanka: feasibility of introduction of a subsidiary gillnet fishery. – *Fish. Res.* **6**: 17–34.

Dissanayake, N. H., De Alwis, P. & Perera, R., 1990: Preliminary Results of an Environmental Survey: 16 pp. – National Aquatic Research Agency (NARA), Colombo, Sri Lanka (unpublished).

Dokulil, M., Bauer, K. & Silva, I., 1983: An assessment of the phytoplankton biomass and primary productivity of Parakrama Samudra, a shallow man-made lake in Sri Lanka. – In: Schiemer, F. (ed.): Limnology of Parakrama Samudra, Sri Lanka: 49–76. – Dr. W. Junk Publishers, The Hague.

Duncan, A., 1983: The composition, density and distribution of the zooplankton in Parakrama Samudra, Sri Lanka. – In: Schiemer, F. (ed.): Limnology of Parakrama Samudra, Sri Lanka: 85–94. – Dr. W. Junk Publishers, The Hague.

Duncan, A. & Gulati, R. D., 1983: A diurnal study of the rotifer populations in Parakrama Samudra Reservoir, Sri Lanka. – In: Schiemer, F. (ed.) Limnology of Parakrama Samudra, Sri Lanka: 95–104. Dr. W. Junk Publishers, The Hague.

Erb, D. K., 1984: Land forms and drainage. – In: Fernando, C. H. (ed.): Ecology and Biogeography of Sri Lanka: 35–63. – Dr. W. Junk Publishers, The Hague.

Fernando, C. H., 1980: The freshwater zooplankton of Sri Lanka with discussion of tropical zooplankton composition. – *Int. Rev. Ges. Hydrobiol.* **65**: 85–125.

Fernando, C. H. & De Silva, S. S., 1984: Man-made lakes, ancient heritage and modern biological reservoirs. – In: Fernando, C. H. (ed.): Ecology and Biogeography of Sri Lanka: 431–451. – Dr. W. Junk Publishers, The Hague.

Fernando, C. H. & Ellepola, W. B., 1969: A preliminary study of two village tanks in the Polonnaruwa area with biological notes on these reservoirs in Ceylon. – *Bull. Fish. Res. Stn. Sri Lanka* **20**: 3–13.

Geisler, R., 1967: Limnologisch-ichthyogische Beobachtungen in S. W. Ceylon. – *Int. Rev. ges. Hydrobiol.* **5**: 559–572.

Gunatilaka, A., 1983: Phosphorus and phosphate dynamics in Parakrama Samudra based on diurnal observations. – In: Schiemer, F. (ed.): Limnology of Parakrama Samudra, Sri Lanka: 35–47. – Dr. W. Junk Publishers, The Hague.

Gunawardhana, H. D. & Adikari, A. M. K. R., 1981: Studies on the quality of irrigation waters in Kalawewa area. – *J. Nat. Sci. Counc. Sri Lanka* **9**: 121–148.

Holsinger, E. C. T., 1955: The planktonic algae of three Ceylon lakes. – *Hydrobiologia* **7**: 8–24.

Hubbard, M. D. & Peters, W. L., 1984: Ephemeroptera of Sri Lanka. – In: Fernando, C. H. (ed.): Ecology and Biogeography of Sri Lanka: 257–273. – Dr. W. Junk Publishers, The Hague.

Jaech, M., 1982: Neue Dryopidae und Hydracaenidae aus Ceylon Nepal, New-Guinea und der Turkei (Coleoptera). – *Koleopt. Rundschau.* **56**: 89–114.

Jayatunga, Y. N. A, 1982: Studies on the Hydrobiology and Zooplankton in the Kalawewa Area. – Unpublished M. Phil. Thesis, University of Colombo, Sri Lanka.

Malicky, H., 1973: The Ceylonese Trichoptera. – *Bull. Fish. Res. Stn. Sri Lanka.* **24**: 153–157.

Mendis, A. S., 1965: A preliminary study of twenty one Ceylon lakes 2. Limnology and fish production. – *Bull. Fish. Res. Stn. Sri Lanka.* **18**: 7–16.

Mueller-Dombois, D., 1968: *Climatic Maps of Ceylon.* – Survey Department, Sri Lanka.

Neale, J. W., 1984: The freshwater Ostracoda. – In: Fernando, C. H. (ed.): Ecology and Biogeography of Sri Lanka: 171–194. – Dr. W. Junk Publishers, The Hague.

Perera, N. P., 1975: A physiognomic vegetation of Sri Lanka. – *J. Biogeog.* **2**: 185–203.

Piyasiri, S., 1991: Limnology project of Mahaweli reservoirs 1. Some physical properties of Kotmale, Victoria and Randenigala Reservoirs. – *Vidyodaya J. Sci.* **3**: 44–63.

Polhemus, J. J., 1979: Aquatic and semiaquatic Hemiptera of Sri Lanka. – *Bull. Fish. Res. Stn. Sri Lanka* **29**: 89–113.

Rajapakse, R. & Fernando, C. H., 1984: Freshwater zooplankton. – In: Fernando, C. H. (ed.): Ecology and Biogeography of Sri Lanka: 155–166. – Dr. W. Junk Publishers, The Hague

Schafiei, T. M. & Costa, H. H., 1990: The susceptibility and resistance of fry and fingerlings of *Oreochromis mossambicus* Peters to some pesticides commonly used in Sri Lanka. – *J. Appl. Ichthyol.* **6**: 73–80.

Schiemer, F., 1983: The Limnology of Parakrama Samudra, Sri Lanka: 192 pp. – Dr. W. Junk Publishers, The Hague.

Schmidt, F., 1958: Trichopteres de Ceylon. – *Arch. Hydrobiol.* **54**: 1–173.

Silva, E. I. L. & Davies, R. W., 1986: Primary productivity and related parameters in three different types of inland waters in Sri Lanka. – *Hydrobiologia* **137**: 239–249.

Sreenivasan, A. & Thayparan, K., 1983: Fisheries development in the Mahaweli system. – *J. Inland Fish. Sri Lanka* **1**: 89–96.

Starmühlner, F. 1974: The freshwater gastropods of Ceylon. – *Bull. Fish. Res. Stn. Sri Lanka* **25**: 97–181.

WENINGER, G., 1972: Hydrochemical studies on mountain rivers in Ceylon. – *Bull. Fish. Res. Stn. Sri Lanka* **23**: 77–100.

WEWALKA, G., 1973: Results of the Austrian-Ceylonese Hydrobiological Mission Part 9. Dytiscidae (Coleoptera). – *Bull. Fish. Res. Stn. Sri Lanka* **24**: 83–87.

WIJEYARATNE, M. J. S. & AMARASINGHE, U. S., 1984: Estimations of maximum sustainable fish yields and stocking densities of inland reservoirs of Sri Lanka. – *J. Nat. Aquat. Resources Agency, Sri Lanka* **31**: 65–72.

WIJEYARATNE, M. J. Z. & COSTA, H. H.; 1981: Stocking rate estimations of *Tilapia mossambica* fingerlings for some reservoirs of Sri Lanka. – *Int. Rev. ges. Hydrobiol.* **66**: 327–333.

WIJEYARATNE, M. J. S. & WANNINAYAKE, T. B., 1993: Limnology and fish production potential of Anamaduwa Wewa. – *Int. Rev. ges. Hydrobiol.* (in press).

ZWICK, P., 1980: The genus *Neoperla* (Plecoptera, Perlidae) from Sri Lanka. – *Orient. Ins.* **14**: 263–269.

Author's address:

Department of Zoology, University of Kelaniya, Kelaniya, Sri Lanka.

Mitt. Internat. Verein. Limnol.	24	87–94	Stuttgart, Februar 1994

The effects of human modification of lotic habitats on the freshwater fauna of Sri Lanka

K.H.G.M. de Silva and P.K. de Silva

Abstract

The island of Sri Lanka (65,525 km^2) has no significant natural lakes but contains 103 river basins. Accordingly, the indigenous aquatic fauna are mainly lotic. Man has been modifying the freshwaters in the Dry Zone of Sri Lanka for more than 2,000 years. Over 12,000 irrigation reservoirs, which vary in size from <10 ha to >7000 ha and cover an area of over 175,000 ha, have been created. More recently, human interference with lotic habitats of the Wet Zone has increased. This is a matter for concern as the Wet Zone supports most of the biodiversity and endemism of Sri Lanka. The paucity of indigenous lentic fauna allows exotic lentic species to spread rapidly, as has been observed in the recent success of Java tilapia (*Oreochromis mossambicus*). Exotic species introductions may be detrimental to the indigenous aquatic fauna and should be undertaken with extreme caution.

An array of human activities affect lotic habitats and their fauna. Deforestation, river impoundment and diversion, gem and sand mining, as well as the establishment of settlements, crop plantations and industries followed by urbanization and water pollution, lead to habitat changes and affect the fauna indirectly. Direct effects include over-exploitation of indigenous species, species introductions and translocations. As a result of these activities, several endemic aquatic animals are on the brink of extinction.

In the face of the need to develop natural resources to maintain a viable economy, a problem compounded by the rapidly-increasing human population (presently 17 million with an annual growth rate of 1.7%), an integrated master plan for development, management and conservation of natural and wildlife resources – including inland waters – is needed urgently.

Introduction

The island of Sri Lanka (65,525 km^2 in area) is composed of a large lowland plateau and a central massif which rises to more than 2,000 m. Based on the rainfall pattern, two major climatic zones can be recognized: a Wet Zone (which receives a mean annual precipitation of 2,400 mm distributed rather evenly throughout the year) extending over about a quarter of the island in the south-western sector and the central massif, and a Dry Zone (which receives a highly-seasonal mean annual rainfall of 1,450 mm) comprising the rest of the island. A narrow intermediate zone may be recognized between the two major zones (Fig. 1).

Sri Lanka contains a large number of freshwater bodies, both lotic and lentic. Almost all lentic water bodies are man-made and most are irrigation reservoirs, the number and the extent of which has been estimated at over 12,000 (BALDWIN 1991) covering an area of 175,000 ha (Table 1). The major lotic habitats are 103 river basins, which have a total area of 59,233 km^2 (SOMASEKARAM 1988). Their combined mean annual discharge is $56,281 \times 10^6$ m^3. Of the 103 rivers, 19 are in the Wet Zone, 82 in the Dry Zone, and two arise in the Hills of the Wet Zone but flow through the Dry Zone. Only 36 rivers have basins larger than 250 km^2, of which 18 are larger than 1,000 km^2.

The rivers radiate out from the centre of the island. The four largest rivers arise in the central massif, while others originate either from the foothills or within the lowland plateau itself. Most of the streams and small rivers in the Dry Zone are seasonal whereas those in the Wet Zone are perennial. The river headwaters and streams in the central massif and foothills flow through forests or tea and rubber plantations.

Human modification of lentic waters

Sri Lanka had few lentic water bodies prior to the creation of man-made lakes. The country has a recorded history of more than 2,500 years and, from the early days of colonization, rice cultivation was well developed. Apparently, the extensive Dry Zone plains were either scrub-forest or marshy areas prior to human settlement, and it would not have been difficult to convert these marshes into paddy fields. However, since the Dry Zone rains are seasonal, it was important to store water for year-round cultivation. By the eighth century, a well-organized irrigation system had been developed, including a large number of reservoirs which ranged in size from <10 ha to $>2,500$ ha. Once this stored water was available, it was possible to transform low-lying areas from scrub-forest to paddy fields. Thus, early settle-

0538-4680/94/0024-0087 $ 2.00

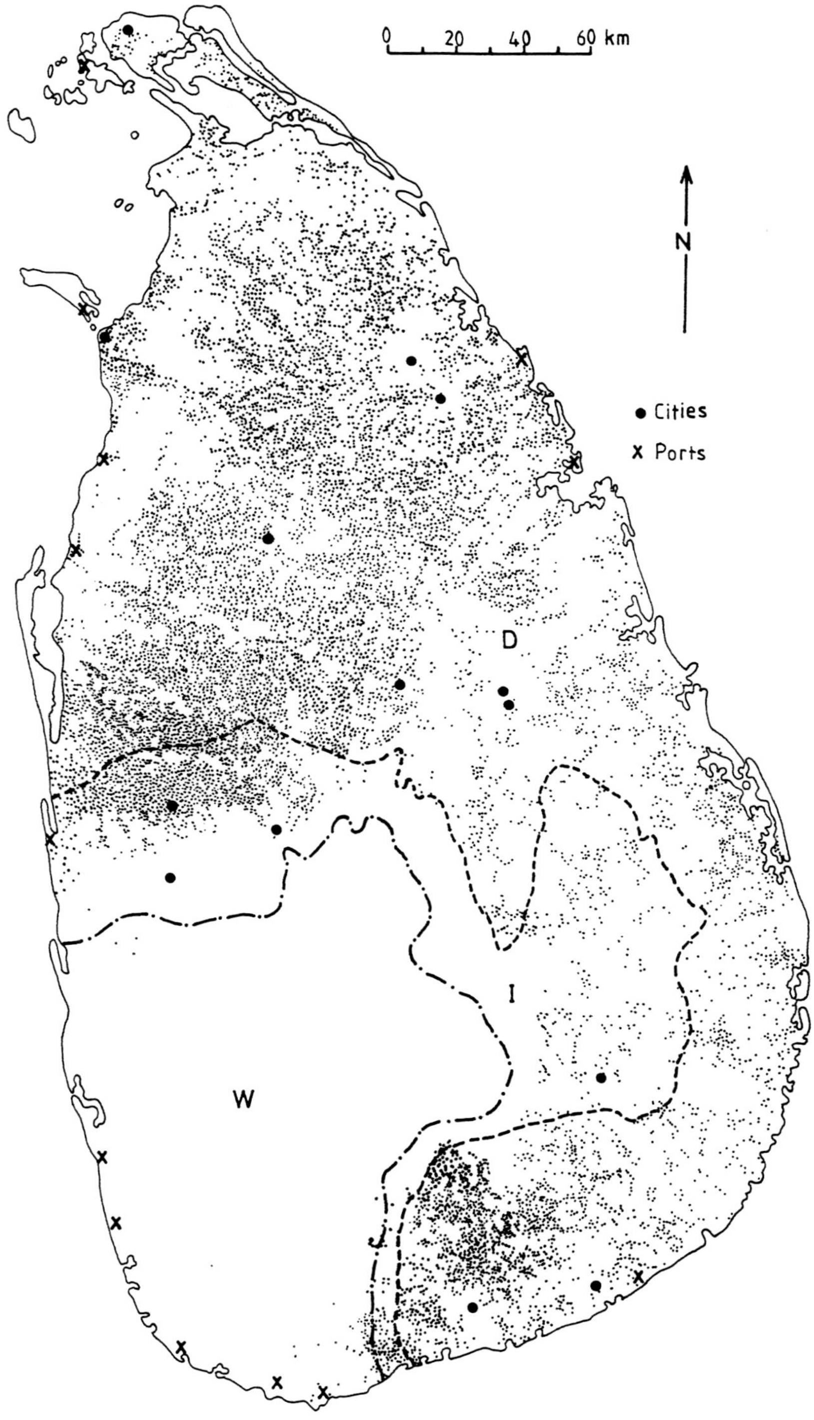

Fig. 1. Ancient settlements in Sri Lanka; D, Dry Zone; I, Intermediate Zone; W, Wet Zone.

Table 1. Lentic water resources in Sri Lanka.

Type	Area (ha)
Lowland Reservoirs (<300 m MSL)	
Large reservoirs (>300 ha)	124,000
Medium-sized reservoirs (10–300 ha)	19,000
Small-reservoirs (<10 ha) (mostly seasonal)	39,000
Upland Reservoirs (>300 m MSL)	11,000
Flood-plain lakes (mostly seasonal)	20,000
Paddy fields (seasonal)	900,000
Lagoons, estuaries and marshes	122,000
Total lentic freshwaters	1,113,000
Total lentic inland waters	1,235,000

ments were concentrated in the Dry Zone (Fig. 1), and human modification of freshwaters at the time took the form of a great increase in the extent of lakes and associated wet agricultural habitats (paddy fields).

The seasonal drying of rice fields causes the aquatic fauna to take refuge in the irrigation canals and reservoirs of present-day Sri Lanka, many of which also dry up during prolonged droughts. As a result, these habitats must be recolonized periodically. At present, at least 30 non-endemic indigenous freshwater fish species (out of a total of 42 for the island) and eight endemic species (out of 30) inhabit marshes in the Wet Zone. All 30 non-endemic freshwater fish species and two of the endemic species present in the Wet Zone marshes are also found in the Dry Zone. Whether the conversion of marshes to paddy fields during historic times caused extinction of any marshland species will never be known. However, there is no evidence of such a change from the present faunal composition of the marshes.

Early modification of lotic waters

With the advent of international trade, especially with European countries, the lowland Wet Zone assumed a greater importance and more settlements were established there. However, the uplands (300–1,000 m elevation) and highlands (>1,000 m elevation) remained relatively undisturbed until the early 19th century. From the latter half of the 19th century until the middle of the present century, large-scale deforestation took place in the uplands and highlands. This resulted initially from the development of coffee plantations and, subsequently, the establishment of tea and rubber plantations. Clearly, therefore, the lotic waters of the Wet Zone (especially those at higher elevations), which are biodiverse and support most of the endemic freshwater fauna of Sri Lanka, were not affected by man to any significant extent until about 150 years ago.

Recent modification of lotic waters

Recent human interference has been confined mainly to lotic habitats and takes two forms: activities that affect the fauna directly, and those that cause habitat changes. Activities that affect the fauna directly are fishing, the introduction of exotic species, and translocation of local species. Important changes in lotic habitats are caused by river impoundment and diversion, deforestation, gem and sand mining, and pollution. These effects can best be demonstrated with reference to the abundance and distribution of fishes.

Fishing

Capture fisheries are limited largely to reservoirs in the Dry Zone. The effect on endemic species, which are confined mainly to the lotic waters of the Wet Zone, is therefore not great. However, the exploitation of natural populations for export as part of the aquarium trade may influence endemic fishes significantly. Of the 30 endemic species, at least 24 are exported including those that have restricted ranges. Four of these – *Barbus nigrofasciatus* Günther, *Barbus titteya* (Deraniyagala), *Belontia signata* (Günther) and *Rasbora vaterifloris* Deraniyagala – are heavily exploited, and their populations are dwindling and/or the mean length of captured individuals is decreasing. Of the endemic species, only *Garra phillipsi* Deraniyagala, *Heteropneustes microps* (Günther) and *Labeo fisheri* Jordan & Starks are not exported. The first two are not usually recognized as separate species, and are confused with *Garra ceylonensis* Bleeker and *Heteropneustes fossilis* (Bloch) respectively, while the juveniles of *Labeo fisheri* are extremely difficult to find. Three endemic species – *Barbus bandula* Kottelat & Pethiyagoda, *Barbus martenstyni* Kottelat & Pethiyagoda and *Rasbora wilpita* Kottelat & Pethiyagoda – were described in 1991, and the first two are so far known only from their respective type localities. *Rasbora wilpita* has been collected from the Kelani River in addition to its type locality in Nilwala River (R. Pethiyagoda, pers. comm.).

The Sri Lankan government departments with responsibility for regulating exports for the aquarium trade keep no record of the numbers of fish of

Table 2. Exotic species that have been introduced into Sri Lankan waters and their present status: – breeding populations not established; ± a few instances of breeding reported; + small scattered breeding populations present; + + breeding populations established in some parts of the country; + + + breeding populations common in most parts of the country.

Species	Time of Introduction	Purpose	Present status	Likely fate of population
Aristichthys nobilis	1948/75	food	–	extinction
Barbus gonionotus gonionotus	1951?	food	–	extinction
Carassius auratus	1915	food	–	extinction
Catla catla	1942/82	food	–	extinction
Cirrhinus mrigala	1981	food	–	extinction
Ctenopharyngodon idella	1948/75	food	–	extinction
Cyprinus carpio	1915	food	±	reduction
Hypophthalmichthys molitrix	1948/81	food	–	extinction
Labeo rohita	1981	food	–	extinction
Osphronemus gorami	1939	food	+	reduction
Helostoma temmincki	1951	food	+	reduction
Trichogaster pectoralis	1951	food	+ +	stabilization
T. trichopterus	1951?	accidental	±	extinction
Oreochromis mossambicus	1952	food	+ + +	stabilization
O. niloticus	1956/75	food	+ +	stabilization
O. urolepis	1969/75	food	–	extinction
Tilapia rendalli	1969	food	+	stabilization
T. zillii	1969	food	–	estinction
Oncorhynchus mykiss	1889–93	recreation	±	stabilization
Salmo trutta	1882-93	recreation	–	extinction
Gambusia affinis	1980?	mosquito control	±	extinction
Poecilia reticulata	1928/45	mosquito control	+	expansion
Yiphophorus	1958	accidental	+	expansion
X. maculatus	1965?	accidental?	+	expansion

each species exported, and there has been no attempt to regulate this fishery. Although some collectors and exporters may voluntarily refrain from exploiting threatened population, such actions are left to the individual and depend upon the attitudes of those involved. So far, there have been no studies of the effects of the aquarium-trade fishery on endemic Sri Lankan fishes. SENANAYAKE (1980), however, observed that the abundance of endemic *Barbus pleurotaenia* (BLEEKER) was reduced from 3 to 1 (on a scale of abundance of 1 to 5) in a stream after a single group of collectors had completed their harvesting. He also recorded that as many as 40% of the fish collected died during handling and transport. PETHIYAGODA (1991) observed that less than 10% of *Rasbora vaterifloris*, a rare endemic captured from the wild, reached the aquarium trader alive.

Fish introductions

Twenty four exotic species – mostly food fish – have been introduced to Sri Lankan waters (Table 2). Of these only the Java tilapia – *Oreochromis mossambicus* (PETERS) – has been a resounding success. Three other species – *Oreochromis niloticus* (L.) *Tilapia rendalli* BOULENGER and *Trichogaster pectoralis* (REGAN) – now occur in significant breeding populations. A few other species persist in small, isolated populations, but most have dwindled recently and may die out in the near future. At least five exotic species – *Carassius auratus* (L.)., *Barbus gonionotus* BLEEKER, *Oreochromis urolepis* (NORMAN) (= *Tilapia hornorum* TREWAVAS), *Tilapia zillii* (GERVAIS) and *Salmo trutta* (L.) – may have already died out as they were not found during recent surveys. However, *Poecilia reticulata* PETERS, *Xiphophorus helleri* HECKEL and *Xiphophorus maculatus* (GÜNTHER) occur in substantial populations and may spread in the future.

It is probable that exotic species exert pressure on the native fauna and may, in many instances, result in a decrease in the size and geographic range of indigenous populations. For instance, *Labeo dussumieri* (VALENCIENNES), a non-endemic indigenous species which formed a major portion of the food fishery in the 1950s, is now scarce; *Labeo porcellus* (HECKEL), another non-endemic indigenous species, which was once common, has now become so rare that some authors (see PETHIYAGODA 1991) consider it to be endangered in Sri Lanka. Both *Labeo* species were abundant in irrigation reservoirs, and their decline may have been due to the introduction of exotic species. In this instance, exotic major carps – *Cyprinus carpio* L., *Labeo rohita* (HAMILTON) and *Cirrhinus mrigala* (HAMILTON) – may have been the cause of declines of native fishes, although Java tilapia are usually blamed for the loss of native fish populations. The stocking of major carp species has now been stopped and, since they do not breed in Sri Lanka (except *Cyprinus carpio*, which seems to have established breeding populations in montane streams), it is hoped that the populations of *Labeo dussumieri* and *Labeo porcellus* will recover.

Translocations

Chanos chanos (FORSKAL), *Etroplus suratensis* (BLOCH) and *Mugil cephalus L.* have been translocated from estuaries to irrigation reservoirs to boost fisheries yields. Although *Etrophus suratensis* is now well-established in lowland reservoirs, the other two species cannot sustain breeding populations in freshwater since both spawn in the sea. *Barbus cumingi* (GÜNTHER), *Barbus nigrofasciatus*, *Barbus titteya* and *Rasbora vaterifloris* have been translocated from the Kelani basin to the Mahaweli basin (WICKRAMANAYAKE 1990), and all four species are now well-established in that area. So far there appears to be no detrimental effect of this translocation. However, it is clear that inter-basin translocations should only be attempted after careful study of the fauna and flora of the area to which the translocation will be made.

River impoundment and diversion

Habitat modification is the main threat to the endemic freshwater fauna of Sri Lanka at present. Particular dangers are river impoundment and diversion, which causes loss of lentic habitats, and deforestation of the catchment areas. There is good evidence that the impoundment of Mahaweli River, for purposes of hydroelectric power generation, and creation of the deep Victoria Reservoir (full supply level at 438 m MSL and maximum depth 102 m) has endangered the endemic *Labeo fisheri*. This fish has been recorded only from the Victoria Reservoir area of Mahaweli River (Fig. 2), where it inhabits river rapids among the bedrock and boulder substratum. *Labeo fisheri* had been caught regularly by fishermen prior to river impoundment, but it is now captured rarely and has become restricted to a few larger streams within a small area (Fig. 2). Subsequent to the impoundment, individuals were observed in deep pools along a partially dewatered stretch of the former river which was diverted through a tunnel to the power house of the Victoria Reservoir dam; however, breeding has not been recorded in such pools (K. H. G. M. DE SILVA, pers. observations). *Labeo fisheri* feeds on algae scraped from the submerged rocks (R. PETHIYAGODA, pers. comm.), but the creation of a deep reservoir with steep banks and frequent water-level fluctuations is likely to hinder algal growth.

Many other hydroelectric reservoirs which involve impoundment of Sri Lankan hill streams and rivers are at the planning stage. A critical area in relation to freshwater fauna would be the Knuckles Hill Region (Fig. 2), in which seven impoundments are planned. Many endemic plants as well as six endemic fish species – four of them rare – have been recorded in this region: in addition to *Labeo fisheri*, this is the only area in which *Barbus martenstyni, Barbus srilankensis* SENANAYAKE and *Garra phillipsi* are found. *Barbus srilankensis*, an endangered species, is found only in a small population in the type locality (Fig. 2). If plans for the impoundment of the tributaries go ahead, there is a strong possibility that these species will disappear.

Deforestation

The natural forest cover is fast disappearing in Sri Lanka, especially from the Wet Zone. In 1991, forest covered only 1.58 million ha – about 24% of the total land area – compared to 44% of the land area in 1961 (BALDWIN 1991). Although vast areas of natural forest were cleared during the latter part of the 18th century for plantations, logging (much of it illegal) for timber and firewood is the major present-day threat. Once a forest area is degraded, squatters move in and ultimately the area is transformed into a human settlement with associated cropland. All forest areas in Sri Lanka are government-owned, and the political pressures tend to favour human settlements rather than reforestation. In an attempt to provide housing in rural areas, the government has recently established many villages in logged forest; at least some of these areas could have been restored by reforestation.

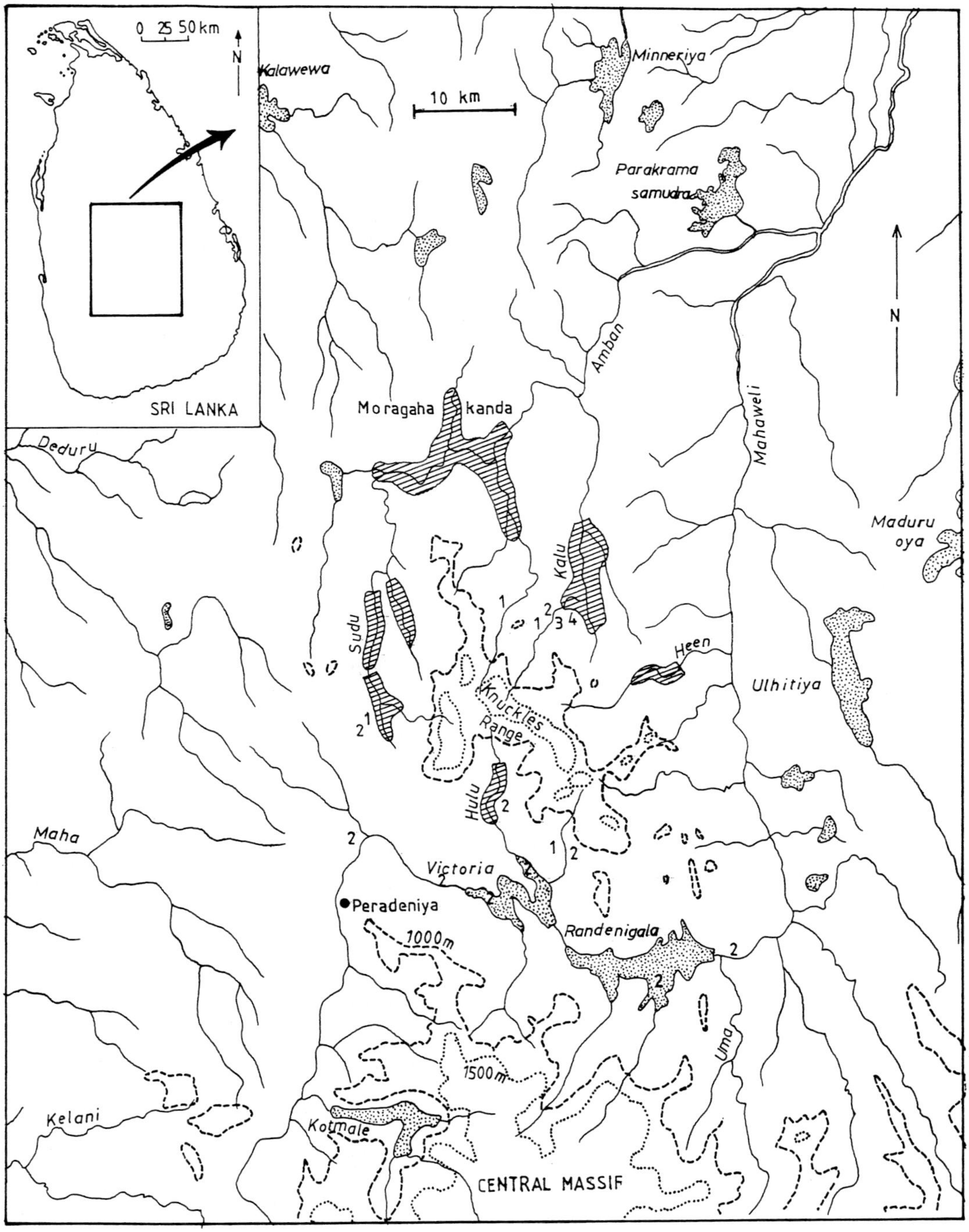

Fig. 2. The Knuckles Hill Region: the stippled areas show the existing reservoirs while the striped area indicate the planned reservoirs; the 1000 m and 1500 m contours are also shown. Numbers 1–4 indicate the localities of endemic fish species: 1, *Garra phillipsi*; 2, *Labeo fisheri*; 3, *Barbus martenstyni*; 4, *Barbus srilankensis*.

Deforestation is perhaps the most important cause of stream degradation in Sri Lanka. The main consequence of deforestation is the siltation of river headwaters, streams and marshes. Knock-on effects can include a lower water table, reduction of precipitation, changes in flow regime, and undermining of river and stream banks. Many fishes that inhabit forest streams are habitat specialists; environmental degradation will reduce their populations drastically. Moreover, many fishes – even some found in reservoirs – breed in small streams, and siltation can cause a loss of spawning grounds. Reductions in the extent of shading is another detrimental factor, as most forest stream fishes appear to have a requirement for shaded habitat. It will never be known whether any endemic species were lost from the Wet Zone when the primeval forests were cleared during the establishment of tea and rubber plantations, which today extend over 200,000 and 170,000 ha respectively.

Mining

Lotic habitats in Sri Lanka are affected mainly by gem mining (a high foreign-exchange earner for the country), although sand mining is important also in some localities. Most impacted habitats are in the Wet Zone. Once the earth containing gems is mined, it is washed in wicker baskets in rivers and streams and the gemstones are hand-picked from material retained. This process causes an increase in turbidity and deposition of sediment on the stream bed. Sand is mined from streams and rivers for house-building purposes, and the process disrupts bottom sediments and degrades the habitat.

Pollution

The rivers and streams of Sri Lanka have long been used as a general dumping ground for both domestic and urban wastes and sewage, agricultural and industrial effluents, and toxic materials. These can cause eutrophication and/or poisoning of waterways. The impacts of these changes on the aquatic fauna are well known from research undertaken in Asia and elsewhere, and will not be considered further here.

Synergistic effects

The combined effects of habitat changes on aquatic animals is apparent not only with reference to fishes. Indeed, they are exemplified by the status of the endemic atyid shrimp *Caridina singhalensis* ORTMANN. This is the only atyid in the world that occurs at such altitudes. It was once distributed over a wide area at high elevations, but is now confined to a 10-km stretch of a single stream within the Horton Plains National Park at 2,200 m elevation (DE SILVA 1982). Stream catchments over most of its former range are now under potato and vegetable cultivation. Intensive agriculture has resulted in siltation and pollution of streams and this may have caused the disappearance of the shrimp from its former habitats. During the period 1961 to 1979, potatoes were cultivated (by the Sri Lankan government Agriculture Department) within the Horton Plains National Park and Nature Reserve close to the last *Caridina singhalensis* habitat; the distribution range of the shrimp along the stream appeared to contract during that time.

Effective conservation

It is unlikely, and in fact unrealistic, to expect that all remaining natural forest and wetland areas in Sri Lanka could be conserved effectively. Developing countries tend to exploit their natural resources in order to stimulate their economies. Sri Lanka is no exception, and has a large, fast-growing population. Given the importance of managing natural resources for human use, while at the same time recognizing the need to conserve as many of the endangered species as possible, it is of the utmost importance to have an integrated master plan for development, management and conservation of all natural and wildlife resources. Unfortunately, such plans (for example, the recent Forestry Master Plan of Sri Lanka) are usually prepared without consultation with informed ecologists, conservationists and environmentalists.

The Knuckles Hill Region of Sri Lanka (Fig. 2) is a good example of an area which needs urgent conservation of both the forest and the streams draining. The area rises to about 1,900 m and is separated from the central massif to the north-east. Despite a high degree of biodiversity and endemism of plants and fish (much of the invertebrate fauna of the area is still to be surveyed), large tracts of the higher slopes between 750–1,300 m are given over to tea and cardamom (*Elettara cardamomum* L.) cultivation while illegal gem mining takes place in stream beds.

Efforts to conserve the Sri Lankan flora and fauna have so far been concentrated in the Dry

Zone, mainly because of the importance laid on the large mammals which at present are found mostly in the Dry-Zone monsoon forest. Of the 11 National Parks (total area of 466,070 ha), and five Nature Reserves with a (total area of 64,124 ha), only one National Park (Horton Plains; with an area of 3,160 ha) and a single Nature Reserve (Hakgala; 1,142 ha) have been established in the Wet Zone. Forty wildlife sanctuaries (total area 221,432 ha) are located in the Dry Zone, whereas there are only nine (total area 23,268 ha) in the lowland Wet Zone. In view of the high biodiversity and endemism in the Wet Zone, and the endangered status of several fish species, demarcation of critical Wet-zone areas for strict conservation is required urgently.

Acknowledgements

The authors are grateful to the conference organizers and the Asian Wetland Bureau, Kuala Lumpur, for providing necessary funds for the first author to attend the conference and present this paper.

References

Baldwin, M. F., 1991: Natural resources of Sri Lanka: conditions and trends: 280 pp. – Natural Resources, Energy and Science Authority of Sri Lanka, Colombo.

De Silva, K. H. G. M., 1982: Aspects of the ecology and conservation of Sri Lanka's endemic freshwater shrimp *Caridina singhalensis*. – *Biol. Conserv.* **24**: 219–231.

Pethiyagoda, R., 1991: Freshwater fishes of Sri Lanka: 362 pp. – Wildlife Heritage Trust, Colombo.

Senanayake, F. R., 1980: The biogeography and ecology of the inland fishes of Sri Lanka: 421 pp. – Ph. D. Dissertation, Univ. of California, Davis.

Somasekaram, T., 1988: The Natural Atlas of Sri Lanka: 141 pp. – Survey Department, Colombo.

Wickramanayake, E. D. 1990: Conservation of endemic rain forest fishes of Sri Lanka: results of a translocation experiment. – *Conserv. Biol.* **4**: 32–37.

Authors' address:

Department of Zoology, University of Peradeniya, Peradeniya, Sri Lanka.

Note added in proof:

After the manuscript was received, *Barbus srilankensis* has been revised as a subspecies of the South Indian *Barbus arulius*.

Mitt. Internat. Verein. Limnol.	24	95–113	Stuttgart, Februar 1994

The status of limnology in Indonesia

Anugerah Nontji

Abstract

A brief inventory of the inland-water resources of Indonesia (lakes, reservoirs, rivers and swamps) is presented, and the water-supply situation is reviewed. The development of limnology in Indonesia may be divided into three periods: prior to 1950; between 1950–1970; and after 1970. The most significant early contribution during the first period was made by the 'Sunda Expedition' in 1928–1929 (led by FRANZ RUTTNER) which involved intensive investigation of the islands of Sumatra, Java and Bali. Little limnology was undertaken subsequently until the second period (1950–1970), when the Inland Fisheries Research Institute began several limnological investigations to support fisheries development. Growing concern over environmental matters since the 1970s distinguished the third period of limnology, when the science began to grow to support fisheries and to provide solutions to various environmental problems. Basic and applied limnological work is carried out by government institutions such as the Inland Fisheries Research Institute, the Department of Public Works, and the Research and Development Centre for Limnology, as well as by universities, and environmental consultants contribute to limnological studies in relation to environmental impacts. In early 1991, the National Committee on Hydrological Programme and the Indonesian Society of Limnology were established to promote the growth of limnology in Indonesia. Among the main obstacles to the further development of limnology in Indonesia are a general lack of relevant education, facilities and research funds, as well as obstacles to communication and difficulty in accessing publications.

Introduction

Indonesia is a vast tropical archipelago between 6°N–11°S and 95°–141°E. It stretches, 5,110 km east-west and 1,888 km north-south. The total area of the Republic of Indonesia is about 5 million km², comprising about 1.9 million km² of land; the remainder is territorial waters. The land area consists of more than 17,000 islands with a total coastline of approximately 81,000 km. The physical structure is varied including high mountain chains, rows of volcanoes, vast alluvial plains, lakes, swamps, and so on.

The Indonesian climate is governed mostly by the monsoons; i.e. the wet northeast monsoon from December to February, and the dry southeast monsoon from June to August. Annual rainfall depends on the location. For example, inland parts of Kalimantan receive over 6,000 mm/annum, but Palu Bay in central Sulawesi receives only one tenth of that amount. The air temperature varies generally between 27–32°C, although temperatures are lower (10–17 °C) in montane regions.

The total populations of Indonesia is approximately 180 million (1990 census) with an annual growth rate of 1.98 %. The population will increase to 216 million by the year 2000. About 60 % of the total populations is concentrated on Java, an island of only 7 % of the total land area, where the population density may reach 755/km². In the provinces of Irian Jaya and Maluku, by contrast, the population is sparse with a density of only 6/km².

Limited land area and high population growth rates (especially on the densely populated islands), coupled with the increasing demands for better living standards, have given rise to significant environmental problems relating to inland-water resources. The demand for water, in terms of quantity and quality, has kept increasing although the supply is limited. Indeed, in many instances the quality of water is deteriorating. It is clear that effective and wise management of water resources will depend upon greater development of limnological knowledge in Indonesia.

Water resources

According to the Department of Agriculture (DEPARTEMEN PERTANIAN 1990) the total area of inland waters in Indonesia is about 53 million ha, consisting of natural and man-made lakes (2.1 million ha), rivers and their flood plains (11.95 million ha), and swamps (39.4 million ha).

Lakes

A detailed inventory of all Indonesian lakes has yet to be drawn up (but see GIESEN 1994). Inventories for restricted regions have, however, been attempted. For example, 173 lakes have been recorded from the Botabek area (in the vicinity of Jakarta) ranging in size from < 3 ha to 30 ha; the lakes are distributed across the districts of Bogor (122), Tangerang (42) and Bekasi (9) (BAPPEDA JABAR 1986). Inventories such as this reveal that

0538-4680/94/0024-0095 $ 4.75

Table 1. Major lakes in Indonesia.

Province/Island	Lake	Max. area (ha)	Max. depth (m)	Elevation (m)	Source*
Aceh/Sumatra	1. Laut Tawar	7,000	80	1,100	A
North Sumatra	2. Toba	112,970	529	905	B
West Sumatra	3. Maninjau	9,790	169	465	C
	4. Singkarak	10,780	269	362	C
	5. Dibawah	1,120	309	1,462	H
	6. Diatas	1,230	44	1,531	H
Jambi/Sumatra	7. Kerinci	4,600	97	787	G
South Sumatra	8. Ranau	12,590	229	540	C
West Kalimantan	9. Sentarum	27,500	8	35	I
Central Kalimantan	10. Sembuluh	7,500	?	30	D
East Kalimantan	11. Semayang	12,000	6	?	A
	12. Jempang	15,000	6	?	A
North Sulawesi	13. Tondano	5,000	20	600	E
	14. Limboto	5,600	2.5	25	E
Central Sulawesi	15. Poso	32,320	450	500	E
	16. Lindu	3,200	100	1,000	E
South Sulawesi	17. Matano	16,408	590	382	E
	18. Mahalona	2,440	73	310	E
	19. Towuti	56,108	203	293	E
	20. Tempe (+Sidenreng & Buaya)	35,000	2	5	E
Bali	21. Batur	1,590	88	1,031	C
Irian Jaya	22. Ayamaru	2,200	20	250	F
	23. Anggi (Gita + Gigi)	4,500	?	1,780	F
	24. Yamur	3,750	?	90	F
	25. Tigi	3,000	?	1,650	F
	26. Paniai (+Tage & Tigi)	19,550	50	1,742	F
	27. Rombebai	14,000	?	?	D
	28. Sentani	9,360	52	70	F

* A: Saanin (1981), B: Ruttner (1952), C: Ruttner (1931), D: Silvius et al. (1987), E: Whitten et al. (1987), F: FAO (1972), G: DPU & Yaramaya (1983), H: Nakano et al. (1987), I: Giesen (1987).

many former lakes have now dried up or have been reclaimed for agricultural, housing, and industrial purposes.

A list of major lakes in Indonesia larger than 1,000 ha is presented in Table 1; their distribution is shown in Fig. 1. Our knowledge on these lakes is still meagre or nonexistent in many cases. The lakes of Irian Jaya Province, in particular, are poorly known. The largest Indonesian lake is Lake Toba (112,970 ha) in Sumatra with a maximum depth of 529 m (Ruttner 1952). The second largest is Lake Towuti (56,108 ha), while the deepest is Lake Matano (590 m); both are in Sulawesi (Whitten et al. 1987). The latter is one of the deepest lakes in the world and, with a surface altitude of only 382 m, the bottom is actually below sea level.

Most of the natural Indonesian lakes were created by volcanic or tectonic forces, or a combination of both. The remainder were formed by processes such as land slides, river action, or solution in karstic regions. For example, in the lowlands of Sumatra, Kalimantan and Irian Jaya shallow lakes develop where adjacent rivers flood seasonally; such lakes reach their maximum size during the wet season but may become dry or almost dry at other times. Because of such seasonal changes and the diverse types and origins of Indonesian lakes, their physical and chemical characteristics vary greatly (Table 2). As a result, it is not possible to make general statements that can be applied to a 'typical' Indonesian lake.

Reservoirs

Traditional irrigation has a long history in Indonesia, as demonstrated by the discovery of an eighth-century AD stone inscription found near the River Brantas (East Java) describing the opening of an irrigation and flood control system (Duarsa &

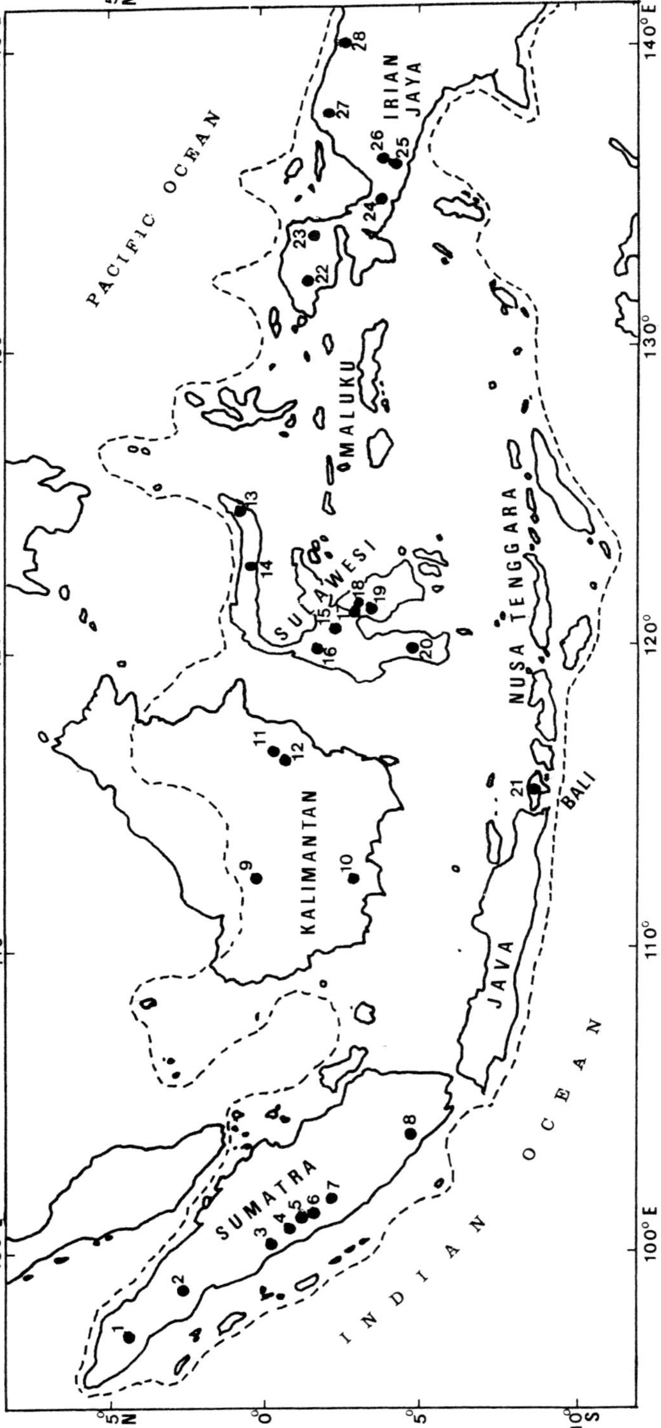

Fig. 1. Major lakes in Indonesia: 1) Laut Tawar; 2) Toba; 3) Maninjau; 4) Singkarak; 5) Dibawah (=Dibaruh); 6) Diatas; 7) Kerinci; 8) Ranau; 9) Sentarum; 10) Sembuluh; 11) Semayang; 12) Jempang; 13) Tondano; 14) Limboto; 15) Poso; 16) Lindu; 17) Matano; 18) Mahalona; 19) Towuti; 20) Tempe; 21) Batur; 22) Ayamaru; 23) Anggi; 24) Yamur; 25) Tigi; 26) Paniai; 27) Rombebai; 28) Sentani.

SASONGKO 1986). The first big dam in Indonesia was constructed at Kali Badak, one of the tributaries of the River Brantas near the city of Blitar, during the Dutch colonial period but it was destroyed by the eruption of Mount Kelud in 1919.

The Jatiluhur Reservoir (completed in 1967) on the River Citarum was the first large multipurpose reservoir constructed in Indonesia. The reservoir has an area of 8,300 ha, a volume of 2,970 million m^3, and serves the functions of irrigation, electricity generation, fisheries, tourism, and provision of municipal water supplies. Two more reservoirs built on the upper course of the river, Saguling Reservoir (5,606 ha) and Cirata Reservoir (6,200 ha), were completed in 1985 and 1988 respectively (BRUTUISWORO 1989). More reservoirs have been built or are planned elsewhere in Indonesia to meet the increasing demand for irrigation water, electricity, flood control, etc. The total area of reservoirs in Indonesia is estimated at approximately 53,000 ha (HARDJAMULIA & SUWIGNYO 1988), and the major reservoirs are concentrated in Java (Fig. 2).

Elsewhere, Riam Kanan Reservoir (south Kalimantan) is notable, with an area of 9,200 ha and a volume of $1,200 \times 10^6$ m^3. Bakaru Reservoir in south Sulawesi, which was completed in 1990, is the newest reservoir and the greatest generator of hydroelectric power in eastern Indonesia. The characteristics of some of Indonesia's major reservoirs are presented in Tables 3 & 4.

Table 2. Physical and chemical characteristics of several Indonesian natural lakes (source: SARNITA 1986).

Parameter	Toba [1]	Klakah [2]	Batur [2]	Bratan [2]	Buyan [2]	Poso [3]	Lindu [3]	Matano [4]	Mahalona [4]	Towuti [4]
Area, ha	112,970	34	1,590	380	390	32,320	3,150	16,480	2,440	56,108
Depth, m	529	28,5	88	22	30	450	100	590	73	203
Altitude, m	905	240	1,031	1,231	1,214	500	1,000	382	310	293
Transparency, m	1.8–13	1.5	2.4	4.0	2.25	0.8–1.0	1.6–2.4	11–16	11	15–22
Temperature, °C	25–26	25–30	20–23	20–23	20–22	28–30	26–29	28–29	29–30	29–301
pH	6–8.5	7–8.5	8–8.7	6–7.2	6–7.7	6.2–6.5	5.6–6	–	8.1–8.4	–
Total alkalinity (mg/l $CaCO_3$)	65–85	195–240	250–300	5–7	140	120–139	75–115	–	125–235	–
Dissolved oxygen, mg/l	1–7.5	0–9.5	0.3–6.5	6–7	1–4	4.5–5.5	4.6–5.6	–	11–14.5	–
Free CO_2, mg/l	2.8–60.8	4–39	–	–	–	3.5–5.3	3.5–8.8	–	1.7–3.6	–
Total phosphorus, µg/l	–	20–450	–	–	–	–	–	–	30–40	–
N-NH_3, µg/l	–	70–4,700	–	–	–	–	–	–	–	–
Year of observation	1968	1928	1974	1974	1974	1973	1973	1966	1966	1966

[1] North Sumatra; [2] Bali; [3] Central Sulawesi; [4] South Sulawesi.

Rivers

There are a great number of rivers in Indonesia. The largest are located on the bigger islands of Sumatra, Kalimantan, and Irian Jaya; the total length of these major rivers is about 18,000 km (KATILI 1983). They are important means of transportation particularly where road systems are poor. River Kapuas on West Kalimantan is the longest (1,143 km) and navigable upstream to Putussibau – 900 km from the coast – where the altitude is only 50 m above sea level (GIESEN 1987). Other major rivers in Kalimantan are the Mahakam, Kahayan and Barito; those in Sumatra are the Musi, Rokan, Batanghari and Indragiri Rivers; in Irian Jaya, the Mamberamo and Digul Rivers are notable.

Swamps

SILVIUS et al. (1986) have listed the total area of wetland habitats per province in Indonesia, from

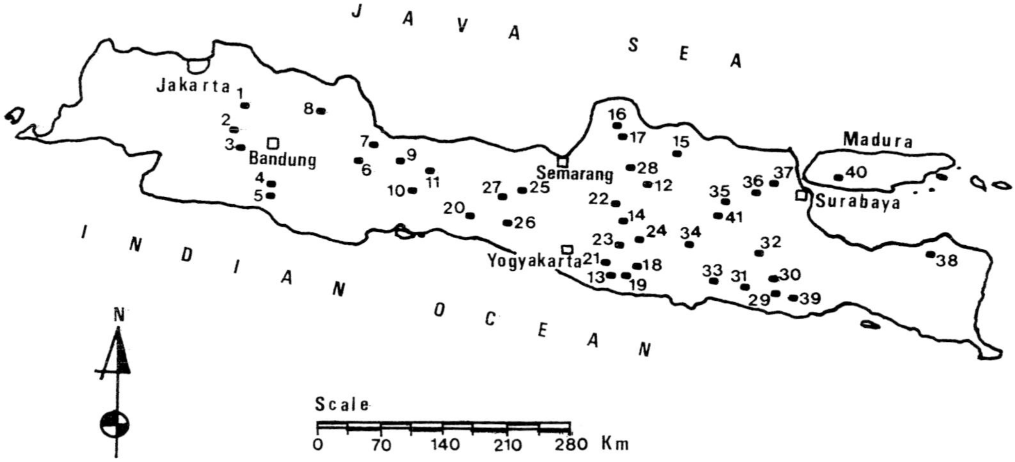

Fig. 2. Major reservoirs in Java: 1) Jatiluhur (Ir. H. Juanda); 2) Cirata; 3) Saguling; 4) Cileunca; 5) Cipanunjang; 6) Darma; 7) Situpatok; 8) Cipancuh; 9) Malahayu; 10) Penjalin; 11) Cacaban; 12) Nglangon; 13) Plumbon; 14) Delingan; 15) Tempuran; 16) Gembong; 17) Gunung Rowo; 18 Ngancar; 19) Nawangan; 20) Sempor; 21) Parangjoho; 22) Ketro; 23) Wonogiri; 24) Songputri; 25) Garung; 26) Wadaslintang; 27) Mrica; 28) Kedung Ombo; 29) Karangkates (Sutami); 30) Lahor; 31) Wlingi; 32) Selorejo; 33) Wonorejo; 34) Tlogo Ngebel; 35) Pacal; 36) Prijetan; 37) Gondang; 38) Sampean Baru; 39) Sengguruh; 40) Klampis (Madura); 41) Bening.

which the area of swamp (freshwater swamp and peat swamp) can be derived. According to their figures, the original swamp area comprised about 32,241,000 ha, but only 22,158,500 remains (Table 5). The main areas are in Sumatra, Kalimantan, and Iran Jaya. Swamp reclamation has been undertaken in many areas, mainly as a means of extending agricultural lands. It is estimated that 5,600,000 ha of the remaining Indonesian swamps are suitable for agriculture, and reclamation of 600,000 ha of these will be undertaken during the fifth Five-Year Development Plan (1989–1994) (Triwasono 1987).

Water supply and demand

An increasing population has led to a rising demand for water which has reached critical proportions in many places. Surface water supplies, in terms of potential water available for human use and the projected demand for the year 2000, have been estimated recently by the Directorate General of Irrigation (Directorat Jenderal Pengairan 1986). Although total demand over the whole of Indonesia will be only 23% of supply, the actual values vary greatly with location. For example, the high demand : supply ratios for Java and Madura (189%) and Bali (113%) indicate that supplies will be unable to meet needs in the near future. However, Irian Jaya, Kalimantan and Maluku have projected demand: supply ratios of less than 5%. Nation-wide, the demand for water is mainly agricultural (irrigation making up 63%), although the requirement for hydroelectric-power generation is also substantial (31%). Domestic (5%) and industrial (1%) needs are relatively low.

History of Indonesian limnology

The history of limnology in Indonesia may be divided into three periods: prior to 1950; between 1950–1970; and after 1970. The first period is characterized by the visit of scientists or expeditions from Europe that were attracted to the rich biological diversity of the tropics. The most significant contribution of all was made by the German 'Sunda Expedition' in 1928–1929. During their 10-month expedition, thorough studies were undertaken on 15 lakes in Sumatra, Java, and Bali. The results, comprising the joint effors of over 100 experts, were published in *Archiv für Hydrobiologie (Supplement)* between 1931 and 1958. Most of the papers were taxonomic, and over 1,100 new species were described providing an important basis for ecological studies. The hydrographical and hydrochemical data recorded by Ruttner (1931) are still used as important references. Very little limnological work was conducted in Indonesia between the expedition and the end of the 1940s.

Table 3. The major reservoirs of Indonesia and their characteristics (source: HARDJAMULIA & SUWIGNYO 1988).

Reservoir	Purpose (a)	Volume ($\times 10^6$ m^3)	Area (km^2)	Drawdown (m)	Annual fish (kg/ha)	Fish species (b)
West Java						
Darma	I	40	4.0		270	T, C, L
Lido	I		0.3			T, C, L
Jatiluhur	F, E, I	2,970	83.0	32.0	15	T, C, L, H, S, P, M
Saguling	E	982	53.4	20.0		T, C, L, J, S, M
Cirata	E	2,165	62.0	20.0		
Central Java						
Cacaban	I	86				
Sempor	E, I	52		29.0		
Wonogiri	F, E, I	736	90.0	9.0		T, C, L, H, S, P
Wadaslintang	E, I	443	14.6	61.0		
Kedung Ombo	E, I	723	46.0	25.0		
East Java						
Prijetan	I	10	2.2		50	
Pacal	I	41	4.5		380	
Selorejo	F, E, I	62	4.0	24.0	250	T, C, L, P, S
Karangkates	F, E, I	343	15.0	26.0	50	T, C, L, H, M, S
Lahor	E, I	37	2.6	19.0	50	T, C, L, H, M, S
Wlingi	E, I	24	3.8	1.5	25	
Bening	E, I	37	5.7	12.0	150	T, L, S
Wonorejo	E, I	122	3.8	42.0		
Lampung (Sumatra)						
Way Jepara	I	50				
Way Rarem	I	72		6.8		
South Kalimantan						
Riam Kanan	F, E, I	1,200	92	8.0		T, C, L, H, S, M
West Nusa Tenggara						
Batujai	I	17	8.9	5.0		

(a) I) irrigation; F) flood control; E) electricity.
(b) T) *Oreochromis mossambicus* and *O. niloticus*; C) Common carp (*Cyprinus carpio*); L) *Puntius gonionotus*; H) *Hampala macrolepidota*; S) snakehead (*Ophicephalus seriatus*); P) *Pangasius pangasius*; M) *Macrones nemurus*.

In the second period (1950–1970), limnology was revived and became based firmly in Indonesia when the Inland Fisheries Research Institute in Bogor began limnological work to support freshwater fisheries. Among the results of these efforts, were reports on the ecology and fisheries of some Javanese freshwaters (VAAS & SACHLAN 1949, 1952, VAAS & SCHUURMAN 1949); in particular, the Ogan and Komering Rivers in South Sumatra (VAAS et al. 1953), and Rawa Aopa River in southeast Sulawesi (VAAS 1956). Collections of algae (especially desmids) by M. SACHLAN during the 1950s were the basis of a publication by SCOTT & PRESCOTT (1961). During this period SCHUSTER & DJAJADIREDJA (1952) listed the Indonesian fishes giving local, English and scientific names. Unfortunately, political and economic turmoil in the 1960s did not favour the growth of research work and little progress was made in limnology.

The third period (after 1970) started with the commencement of the first Indonesian Five-Year Development Plan. This period was characterized also by growing public concern with the environment. As a result, limnology began to develop on a broader front, not only to support fisheries but also to promote better understanding and management of the environment. Limnological activities were no longer undertaken solely by fisheries institutes, but also by various centres and universities. A review of these limnological activites and research in Indonesia prior to 1980 is given by WIDJAJA (1980).

Table 4. Physical and chemical properties of seven major reservoirs in Indonesia (sources: Hardjamulia & Suwignyo 1988, Sarnita 1986).

	Saguling[1]	Jatiluhur[1]	Karangkates[2]	Selorejo[2]	Pacal[2]	Wonogiri[3]	Riam Kanan[4]
Temperature (°C)	23.0–29.0	28.2–30.5	27.0–34.0	27.0–34.0	27.0–34.0	26.0–29.0	28.0–29.5
Secchi disk transparency (cm)	80–240	26–230	–	90	129	–	220–300
Turbidity	11–62	3–300	–	–	–	68–350	–
Conductivity (μmhos/cm)	110–500	108–155	–	–	–	269–364	–
Total dissolved solids (mg/l)	–	–	–	–	–	81–345	–
Morphoedaphic index	6.3–28.6	3.0–4.3	–	–	–	31.6–42.8	–
Dissolved oxygen (mg/l)	2.0–6.5	4.7–7.1	–	9–11	8.0–9.0	3.8–4.6	6.9–7.2
CO_2 (mg/l)	0.5–4.5	1.7–4.1	0–12	0–11	–	–	4.7–7.5
pH	4.5–9.5	7.2–8.0	7.8–9.2	5–9	6.0–8.4	6.2–8.2	6.0–8.4
Alkalinity (mg/l $CaCO_3$)	5–60	45–67	78–85	–	–	44–259	56–65
Phosphate (mg/l)	0.07–0.85	0.04–0.06	0.48	0.06	–	0.28–0.90	–
Nitrite (mg/l)	0–0.09	0.01–0.15	–	–	–	–	–
Nitrate (mg/l)	0.09–3.57	0.28–0.64	–	–	–	0.11–0.92	–
Ammonium (mg/l)	0.07–0.53	0.01–0.25	0.53	0.2–0.3	–	–	–
Sulphate (mg/l)	0.39–1.47	0.87–1.63	–	–	–	–	–
Calcium (mg/l)	33–79	40–47	–	–	–	34.5–42.0	–
Hardness (mg/l $CaCO_3$)	48–135	59–72	–	–	–	91.5–157.0	–

[1] West Java; [2] East Java; [3] Central Java; [4] South Kalimantan.

Table 5. Total area of swamps in Indonesia (source: Silvius et al. 1986)

Island/Province	Original area (ha)	Remaining area (ha)
Sumatra	(12,172,000)	(5,703,000)
Freshwater swamp	4,890,000	1,090,000
Peat swamp	7,282,000	4,613,000
Java & Bali	(72,000)	(4,500)
Freshwater swamp	72,000	4,500
Kalimantan	(8,308,000)	(5,248,000)
Freshwater swamp	3,895,000	1,717,000
Peat swamp	4,413,000	3,531,000
Sulawesi	(326,000)	(100,000)
Freshwater swamp	282,000	66,000
Peat swamp	44,000	34,000
Maluku	(94,000)	(63,000)
Freshwater swamp	48,000	42,000
Peat swamp	46,000	21,000
Nusa Tenggara	(4,000)	(2,000)
Freshwater swamp	4,000	2,000
Irian Jaya	(11,265,000)	(11,038,000)
Freshwater swamp	2,336,000	2,266,000
Seasonal freshw. swamp	19,000	19,000
Peat swamp	8,530,000	8,398,000
Seasonal peat swamp	380,000	355,000
Total	32,241,000	22,158,000

Biotrop (Regional Centre for Tropical Biology) under SEAMEO (Southeast Asian Ministers of Education Organization), which was established in 1968, has been involved in various short-term training and research activities in aquatic biology. Undergraduate courses in limnology are offered by many state universities and some limited research is carried out also. With growing concern for the environment, many Centres for Environmental Studies have been established within state and private universities. Some of these centres have undertaken limnological studies involving water-quality monitoring and environmental impact assessment. The Research and Development Centre for Water Resources (Department of Public Works) has also conducted pollution studies and water-quality monitoring in lakes, reservoirs, and rivers. Most recently, a Research and Development Centre for Limnology (Indonesian Institute of Sciences) was established (1986) to promote limnology. A National Committee on Hydrological Programme has just been established (1991) to coordinate hydrological activites in Indonesia. The need for environmental impact assessments as a prerequsite for the construction of major projects has stimulated private consultants to initiate research on certain aspects of limnology.

Despite the growing interest in limnology, formal publication and scientific journals having wide distribution are rather scarce. Many of the study reports are written in Indonesian and produced for limited distribution or as internal reports. Seminars are other sources of valuable information. Several national seminars and symposia discussing freshwater problems have been held, such as the Seminar on Management of Water Resources in Bandung (1974), Seminar on Water Quality in Cisarua (1980), Workshop on Water Quality Management in Bandung (1984), Seminar an Open Water Fisheries I and II in Jakarta (1981 and 1986), and the Seminar on Limnology and Development in Bogor (1986). The Indonesian Biological Society holds national seminars every two years in which aquatic biology has always been an important component. Most recently an International Symposium on Lake Toba was held in Jakarta (1990) where the unusual circumstances of the fall in lake water levels and resulting environmental impacts were discussed.

Limnological studies

Most limnological research undertaken on Indonesian inland waters has been based on surveys or short-term visits. Seasonal studies are lacking, despite significant monsoons governing the wet and dry seasons and the environmental effects that these must have. Long-term observations which may reveal gradual changes have not been made.

Sumatra

Five lakes in Sumatra (Toba, Diatas, Maninjau, Singkarak and Ranau) were studied thoroughly by the German Sunda Expedition in 1928–1929, and their hydrochemistry was reported by RUTTNER (1931). Lake Toba (north Sumatra) was oligotrophic with transparency reaching more than 12 m and a small vertical-temperature gradient. Subsequently, MIZUNO (1980) found that the water column was thermally homogenous to 300 m. Work in Lake Toba has been complemented by ONDARA (1969), UI & DPU (1979), EYANUER et al. (1981), SARNITA (1986) and KARTAMIHARDJA (1987) who have investigated the water chemistry, biology and fisheries of the lake. A summary of general information on Lake Toba was presented recently by ILEC & UNEP (1989). The recent lowering of lake levels following the commissioning of a large hydroelectric power generator (which supports a heavy aluminium-smelting plant) downstream of Lake Toba stimulated an International Conference on the lake Toba in May 1990 sponsored by the Indonesian Agency for Technological Study and Application. Proceedings of the conference have not yet been published, but a critical analysis of the cause of the declining water levels has been made by LOEBIS & PUTUHENA (1990).

Lakes Kawar and Mardingding on the slopes of Mount Sinabung have been studied briefly by a team from the University of North Sumatra and the results are described by WHITTEN et al. (1987). Lakes Maninjau and Singkarak in West Sumatra were studied by UI & DPU (1978), who concluded that both lakes are mesotrophic although the primary productivity of Lake Maninjau is the higher of the two. The hydrology, fisheries, molluscs and aquatic weed problems of the lakes were documented also. PUSLITBANG PENGAIRAN (1986 a) carried out water-quality and hydrolobiological studies on Lakes Maninjau, Singkarak, Diatas and Dibawah (Dibaruh), and again noted relatively high productivity in Lake Maninjau.

Environmental problems affecting smaller lakes in west Sumatra (Lakes Diatas, Dibaruh and Talang) were studied by NAKANO et al. (1987); WATANABE & USMAN (1987) have reported upon their epilithic diatom flora. The ecology of Lake Kerinci has been investigated by UI & DPU (1979 b), SOERJANI (1981) and DPU & YARAMAYA (1983). The geological origin of the lake – which is located in an enclave within the Kerinci-Seblat National Park – has been discussed by VERSTAPPEN (1961) and PARDEDE (1982). Little is known about Lake Ranau and, apart from a study by the Sunda Expedition, only PULN & JICA (1988) have surveyed the lake in relation to a planned hydroelectric power plant.

The ecology and fisheries of the shallow, seasonal flood lakes (= lebak) along the Ogan and Komering Rivers of south Sumatra were investigated by VAAS et al. (1953) who found the areas to be highly productive due to regular inundation by river water. More recently, however, the fisheries of the lebak have declined (GIESEN 1990 b). The limnological characteristics of the River Komering itself have been studied by GAFFAR et al. (1988) who found that the pH decreased from the upper to the lower course. The only other study of a Sumatran river documents pollution and water quality of the River Musi (SAENI et al. (1980).

Java

The natural lakes of Java are generally small. Lakes Lamongan, Bedali, Klindungan, Pakis,

Telaga Pasir, Telaga Ngebel, and Cigombong were studied by the Sunda Expedition (RUTTNER 1931), and ecological and fisheries investigations of other lakes have been undertaken also. Among them were studies of some small lakes near Bogor (then Buitenzorg) by VAAS & SACHLAN (1949), Lake Ciburuy in west Java by VAAS & SACHLAN (1952), and Rawa Pening and Bonorowo Marsh of central Java by VAAS & SCHUURMAN (1949). The results of recent work on the limnology of Lake Bojongsari (west Java) have been compiled by NONTJI & HARTOTO (1989).

After the Sunda Expedition, Lake Lamongan was revisited by GREEN et al. (1976) who recorded no discernible change in the phytoplankton composition after almost 45 years. They were able to study the re-establishement of stratification after overturn, and constructed a food web for the faunal community associated with *Eichhornia crassipes* (water hyacinth) in the lake.

The water quality and hydrobiology of several Javan lakes and reservoirs were reported by PUSLITBANG PENGAIRAN (1986 c, 1986 d), and limnological and fisheries investigations of Javan reservoirs have been summarized by HARDJAMULIA & SUWIGNYO (1988). The Jatiluhur, Cirata, and Saguling Reservoirs on the River Citarum (West Java) have attracted most attention, including recent work by KRISMONO & HARDJAMULIA (1986 a, 1986 b), TJAHJO (1986), KARTAMIHARDJA et al. (1987) and TJAHJO et al. (1987). The environmental problems that resulted from the construction of these reservoirs are described by BRUTUISWORO (1988), and in a number of articles included in a recently-published book (COSTA-PIERCE & SOEMARWOTO 1990).

There is little information on the limnology of Javan rivers, apart from reports of pollution and water-quality status. However, NEAME (1988) has documented the hydrochemistry of the Solo River, and SABAR (1990) presents information on the hydrobiology of some rivers in the vicinity of Bogor.

Bali

The limnology of the volcanic Lake Batur was investigated by RUTTNER (1931) and later by GREEN et al. (1978) The latter also studied some smaller Balinese lakes: Lakes Bratan, Buyan, and Tamblingan. Lake Batur showed little change during the 45 years since the Sunda Expedition, but Lake Bratan exhibited some signs of cultural eutrophication. A more recent hydrological study of Lake Batur (DPU & EXSA INTERNATIONAL 1981) concluded that elevated pH (8.9) and a high total salt content made the lake waters unsuitable for irrigation and household purposes.

Kalimantan

Little research has been undertaken on the extensive freshwater bodies of Kalimantan. Riverine limnology is practically unknown, apart from a brief account of water temperatures, pH and transparency along the River Mahakam, East Kalimantan (Mizuno 1980). A recent study of the ecology of the Lake Sentarum complex on the upper Kapuas River (West Kalimantan) was undertaken by GIESEN (1987), while ROBERTS (1989) has inventoried the freshwater fishes of West Kalimantan. The water quality, hydrobiology and aquatic weed problems of Riam Kanan (Ir. P. M. Noor) Reservoir has been documented by PUSLITBANG PENGAIRAN (1986 b) and HISBI (1990).

Sulawesi

Brief accounts of Lake Matano, Mahalona and Towuti are given by FERNANDO (1984), WHITTEN et al. (1987) and GIESEN (1990 a). These old tectonic lakes harbour a considerable number of endemic aquatic species which are endangered by recent environmental changes. A short account of the limnology and fisheries of Lake Poso and Lake Lindu in central Sulawesi is available also (AHMAD 1973). The ecology of Lake Tempe and the adjacent Lake Sidenreng and Lake Buaya were studied by BIOTROP & DPU (1977, 1978), while an 'improvement plan' for the lake was formulated by DPU & Indah Karya (1981); GIESEN (1990 a) has also reported upon Lake Buaya.

Other limnological work includes investigations on Lake Limboto (north Sulawesi) with emphasis on the factors underlying the recent decline in water levels (DPU & Geojaya Tehnik 1985, PUSLITBANG Pengairan 1990) and concomitant effects on the fisheries (RONDO 1990). The fisheries ecology and hydrotechnology of Lake Tondano (north Sulawesi) has been studied by UI & DPU (1979 c), SOEROTO (1989) and DPU & Rayakonsult (1981, 1983). Among other habitat types, the Aopa peat swamp of southeast Sulawesi was first investigated by VAAS (1956) and aspects of its ecology were described by WHITTEN et al. (1987). Information on riverine limnology is conspicuously absent.

Irian Jaya

Little is known of the limnology of Irian Jaya. Lake Sentani is the best-studied water body (FAO 1972, SUKARWO 1990). There is a plan to use the lake water for hydroelectric power generation, and the relevant environmental impact assessment was conducted by UNCEN (1984). The current general situation at Lake Sentani has been described by LUKMAN & FAUZI (1991). Other major lakes of Irian Jaya include Paniai Lakes (Paniai, Tigi, and Tage) Ayamaru Lakes (Jow, Semitu, Jate), Anggi Lakes (Anggi and Gita) and Lake Yamur (FAO 1972). Of special limnological interest is the occurrence of freshwater sawfish (*Pristis microdon* LATHAM) in Lake Sentani (BOESEMAN 1955) and the freshwater shark (*Carcharinus leucas* MÜLLER & HENLE) in Lake Yamur (BOESEMAN 1964).

Water pollution

Reports on the pollution of inland waters have been increasing throughout Indonesia, especially during the last decade. In numerous cases, the adverse effects on the environment have become serious. The direct menace to human health is significant because many people still draw upon untreated natural waters for household use. A national household health survey in 1986 indicated that 48.6% of respondents used well waters and 20.7% used river water for drinking (HARTONO 1988).

Siltation

Forest cutting, shifting cultivation and improper land-use practices give rise to soil erosion and siltation of inland waters. As a consequence, Lake Tempe (south Sulawesi) has become shallower and the high siltation rate, estimated at 10–20 cm/year, has been associated with declining fish production (BIOTROP & DPU 1978). This conclusion contrasts with a recent study by GIESEN (1990a) who refers to the very high productivity of this lake system. However, GIESEN (1990a) documents an annual siltation rate of 1–3 cm which, if maintained, would result in the diasappearence of Lake Tempe within the next 100 years. High siltation rates prevail also in Lake Tondano and Lake Limboto in north Sulawesi. The area and depth of Lake Tondano has decreased from 5,600 ha and 40 m in 1934, to 4,278 ha and 18 m in 1987. More serious is the case of Lake Limboto, which has diminished from 7,000 ha and 28.5 m in 1934, to 1,500 ha and 1.5 m in 1987 (RONDO 1990). In both lakes, a decline in fish production has been associated with siltation (SOEROTO 1989, RONDO 1990).

Reservoirs, too, are adversely impacted by siltation arising from soil erosion in the drainage basin, as exemplified by changes in the upper Citarum basin of Saguling Reservoir, west Java (BRUTUISWORO 1988). Similarly, Wonogiri Reservoir (central Java), commissioned in 1981, was originally designed for a 100-year effective life, but a recent study by PANGESTI & ISNUGROHO (1989) suggests that the high sedimentation rates (6.6 million m^3/year) will reduce the reservoir's effective life to only 18 years. In response to such problems, plans for 'regreening' and reforestation of critical watersheds are under development.

Domestic wastes

Water pollution due to domestic wastes is generally associated with high population concentrations near rivers or other water bodies. River systems traversing large cities such as Jakarta, Bandung, Semarang and Surabaya receive heavy loads of domestic wastes. Municipal sewerage systems do not exist in Indonesia, and rivers or streams are used as defaecation sites. As a result, the population of Jakarta and its vicinity (known as Jabotabek), comprising approximately 12 million persons, discharge wastes into receiving waters equivalent to 120 t BOD/day (PUSLITBANG PENGAIRAN 1986e). Almost all the river and shallow wells in Jakarta are highly polluted by faecal coliforms, especially during the dry season. The situation in many regions of Indonesia is similar and has been well reviewed by HARTONO (1988).

Detergents from human dwellings contaminate river waters and shallow wells in and around Jakarta (SUCOFINDO-ITB-DKI 1977; BADRUDDIN 1986). The foam produced may be seen sometimes in rivers and raises cleansing problems for municipal drinking-water plants. In addition, the phosphorus present in the detergents may contribute to eutrophication. Garbage is a further problem in cities. Jakarta produces 17,000 m^3 garbage each day, a great proportion of which consists of undegradable plastic materials; only 12,000 m^3 of this can be handled by the municipal services. The outstanding 5,000 m^3/day is left unattended and much of it is washed into rivers where it blocks flows and contributes to flooding during the wet season.

Industrial wastes

A great number of Indonesian factories discharge their wastes into freshwaters with little or no treatment, causing a significant pollution problem. Even large factories which own waste treatment plants do not treat their wastes fully. The problem is exacerbated by the quality and diversity of wastes and the attitude and behaviour of industrial management to waste disposal. Small-scale or cottage industries which are generally abundant in Indonesia do not treat their wastes at all and their contribution to water pollution is often overlooked. The extent of the problem is indicated by a study by Puslitbang Pengairan (1986) which showed that there were more than 250 factories which could be classified as potential water polluters in the Jabotabek area. These included textile, paper, and leather factories which together discharged 42 t BOD/day, equivalent to 35 % of the total domestic waste load.

Toxic and dangerous substances may be discharged into water bodies and degrade water quality. THAMZIL et al. (1980) reported high concentrations of heavy metals, especially mercury and lead, in the River Sunter, Jakarta. Moreover, HUTAGALUNG & SUWIRMA (1987) found heavy-metal contamination of several aquatic organisms from the coastal water near Jakarta. In east Java, Amsyari (in HARTONO 1988) found contamination of fishes in the Surabaya River by mercury, copper and cadmium.

Cases of water pollution or potential pollution from various kinds of factories have been reported from many regions in Indonesia and have been reviewed by HARTONO (1988). These included factories manufacturing gold-plated accessories in Gersik (east Java), batik-printing factories in Yogyakarta, a paper factory in Bekasi (west Java), food additive (monosodium glutamate) factories in Mojokerto and Probolinggo (east Java), sugar and spirit factories in Madukismo (central Java), fertilizer and rubber factories along the River Musi (south Sumatra), a tapioca factory in Lampung (Sumatra), and tofu (soya cake) factories in Jakarta. Although the Indonesian government Environmental Act, established in 1982, was aimed at regulating pollution control, implementation and law enforcement are still inadequate. To cope with pollution problems in rivers, the Clean River Programme (Prokasih) was launched in 1989. It involved government and industries in a coordinated effort to clean up 20 rivers in eight provinces regarded as seriously polluted (KLH 1990). They include the Rivers Deli, Asahan and Musi in Sumatra; Citarum, Cisadane, Ciliwung, Kali Garang, Bengawan Solo, and Brantas in Java; and the River Mahakam in Kalimantan. An account of pilot schemes to treat industrial wastes from factories and industrial estates is given by BADRUDDIN (1986). Most research into treatment of industrial effluents in Indonesia has been undertaken by the Research and Development Centre for Water Resources.

Pesticides

Intensive and extensive agricultural activities have brought Indonesia from being the biggest rice importer in the world to a position where it is self-sufficient with respect to food needs. This has been made possible by modern agricultural practices including the application of pesticides which has been increasing steadily. Most of the pesticides used are insecticides, followed by herbicides and fungicides. Among the insecticides, organophosphate is employed widely. Use of DDT (organochlorine) is restricted by law to malaria control only, but it is applied to crops ocassionally by farmers (Sumatra 1982). Organochlorines are notorious for their persistence and potential for biomagnification.

Pesticide residues have been measured in several places in Indonesia (Sumatra 1982, 1990). DDT residues and their metabolites have been detected in water, sediments, benthos, fish, and agricultural land in Java. Other organochlorines found in some of the same samples were endosulfan, aldrin, dieldrin and lindane. KOESOEMADINATA (1982) employed Common carp (*Cyprinus carpio*) and Tawes (*Puntius gonionotus*) to test the toxicity of insecticides, and determined that 64% of those employed in irrigated fields were highly toxic to fish, 20 % moderately toxic, and only 16 % of low toxicity. HARDJAMULIA & RABEGNATAR (1991) have listed those pesticides compatible with fish culture in rice fields.

Eutrophication and aquatic weeds

Eutrophication of water bodies degrades water quality and enhances the growth of nuisance phytoplankton and aquatic weeds. The nutrient sources contributing to eutrophication are derived from domestic wastes, fertilizers, and erosion of the drainage basin.

PANCHO & SOERJANI (1978) have listed 112 species of aquatic weeds in Southeast Asia. Not all of these plants are indigenous. Water hyacinth (*Eichhornia crassipes*) was introduced to Indonesia in

1894 through the Bogor Botanical Garden, and *Salvinia molesta* was first recorded in 1951 (Tjitrosoepomo et al. 1974). A short time after their introduction, these aquatic weeds had spread widely and seemed to supress the growth of native aquatic plants. The importance of such aquatic weeds is determined by the extent of their distribution in Indonesia, the significance of nuisance effects, difficulties of control, and poor or negligible utilization value. The top four on a list of 20 aquatic weeds are *Eichhornia crassipes, Salvinia molesta, Pistia stratiotes* and *Hydrilla verticillata* (Soerjani & Widyanto 1977). Heavy infestations of aquatic weeds in many lakes and reservoirs reflect rapid vegetative growth rates. Soerjani & Widyanto (1977) showed that, in optimum conditions, the leaf addition rates of *Eichhornia, Salvinia,* and *Pistia* varied between 7.5–12.5% /day; fresh weights could increase by 13.8–27.9%/day. The area covered by *Salvinia* in Indonesian water bodies can double every 2.2 days under optimum growth conditions (Whitten et al. 1987).

Excessive growth of aquatic weeds may have harmful or disadvantageous effects on fisheries, irrigation, water transportation, electricity generation, aesthetics, and human health. Moreover, these plants also play important roles in enhancing evapotranspiration, and silting of lakes, waterways, swamps, pools and other wetlands. Serious aquatic weed problems have been reported from many places, among them Lake Rawapening in central Java (Tjitrosoepomo et al. 1974), and Lake Kerinci in Sumatra (Soerjani 1981). Almost 60% of the 8 million ha of open waters in Kalimantan is densely covered with Water hyacinth and *Salvinia* (Tjitrosoepomo et al. 1974).

Phytoplankton may also cause a nuisance under certain conditions. Blooms of planktonic blue-green algae, *Microcystis*, have been reported in Jatiluhur Reservoir, west Java. (Karyono & Pandi 1977, Kabinawa 1987) but the occurence diminished after two more reservoirs (Saguling and Cirata) were built in the upper reaches of the same river (Kartamihardja, pers. comm.). Blooms of *Microcystis* occur also in many other lakes, for instance in Lake Maninjau in Sumatra (Puslitbang Pengairan 1986a) and Lake Sentani in Irian Jaya (FAO 1972, Lukman & Fauzi 1991).

Control of aquatic weeds in Indonesia has been attempted using mechanical, chemical, and biological methods but success has been partial only. Mechanical control involves removal of plants from the water, but the rate of proliferation and growth has overcome most of these efforts. Chemical control using herbicides, has also been attempted (Vaas 1951) but there has been concern over possible side effects. Biological control using herbivorous Grass carp (*Ctenopharyngodon idella*) and Tawes (*Puntius gonionotus*) have been attempted to a limited extent. Schuster (1952) reported that stocking of *Puntius gonionotus* in the reservoirs of east Java could free the surface from aquatic weeds within a trial area of 284 ha in less than eight months. Other alternatives under consideration include utilizing the plant biomass for animal feed, compost, and bio-gas or paper production (Soerjani 1981). To date, no method is available that combines the need to control the nuisance weeds in a manner that is ecologically safe, effective, feasible, and economically viable.

Applied limnology

Fisheries

The application of limnological concepts to the development of freshwater capture fisheries and aquaculture has long been acknowledged. Early studies in Java (Vaas & Sachlan 1949, 1952, Vaas & Schuurman 1949), Sumatra (Vaas et al. 1953) and Sulawesi (Vaas 1956) showed the importance of, and need for, limnological support in promoting fisheries development (see also review by Hardjamulia & Rabegnater 1986). More recently, estimates of potential fisheries production in lakes and reservoirs, based on measurements of primary producitivity, plankton and physicochemical parameters, have been undertaken at Jatiluhur Reservoir (Sarnita 1981), Lake Toba (Kartamihardja 1987) and Saguling Reservoir.

Aquaculture production has increased significantly in Indonesia during recent years, with yields rising from 117,000 t in 1968 to 464,000 t in 1989 (Table 6). This remarkable increase is due to the development of aquaculture in brackish and freshwater ponds and ricefields. Fish culture has also been practised in many reservoirs and lakes using pens, cages and floating nets (Hardjamulia & Suwignyo 1988). Indeed, development of cage culture in the newly-constructed reservoirs of Saguling and Cirata has provided some job opportunities for families displaced from the inundated areas (Brutuisworo 1988, Costa-Pierce et al. 1988). However rapid expansion and over-crowding of floating nets and cages in a localised areas can lead to eutrophication (E. S. Kartamihardja, pers. comm.). The general environmental problems arising from reservoir construction, and the

Table 6. Inland fisheries production, 1968–1989 (× 1,000 t) (source: President of the Republic of Indonesia 1990).

Type of fisheries	1968	1973	1978	1983	1988	1989
Open Water	320	250	249	266	285	290
Aquaculture	117	139	171	267	426	464
Brackish pond	45	60	88	134	233	258
Freshwater pond	53	52	58	80	104	113
Rice field	19	27	25	53	89	93
Total	437	389	420	533	711	754

importance of developing fisheries and aquaculture, are described in a volume edited by COSTA-PIERCE & SOEMARWOTO (1990) which draws upon research on Jatiluhur, Saguling, and Cirata Reservoirs. BRUTUISWORO (1988) has also researched Saguling Reservoir with the aim of reducing population pressure on the surrounding land by making full use of the new water resources through a programme of aquaculture and fisheries development (see also COSTA-PIERCE & SOEMARWOTO 1990). Related problems of lake restoration are being studied by the Research and Development Centre of Limnology. Restoration of eutrophic lakes through aeration of the hypolimnion has yielded promising results (HARTOTO & SULASTRI 1990).

Conservation

There is an urgent need for effective conservation of Indonesian inland waters and their biota. For example, increasing popoulation pressure, forest clearance and improper agricultural practices have led to changes in drainage basins and hydrology; water pollution from various sources is widespread and increasing; over-exploitation of aquatic resources and the introduction of exotic species can change ecosystem structure and function and threaten indigenous species; fishing by using poisons and explosives is still practised widely; and, the construction of major dams and artificially-induced water-level functuations in natural lakes may have a variety of far-reaching consequences.

Several important legal measures have been undertaken recently with the goal of protection and conservation of living resources and the environment. They include the following: Act of the Republic of Indonesia No. 4 (1982) which concerns the basic provision for the management of the living environment; Government Decree No. 29 (1986) requiring environmental impact assessments on major projects; decree of the Minister of Population and Environment No. Kep-02/MEN-KLH/I/1988 giving guidelines for the determination of environmental quality criteria; and, Act of the Republic of Indonesia No. 5 (1990) relating to conservation of living resources and ecosystems.

The basic strategy for the conservation of living resources (as stated in the Act No. 5, 1990) is to guarantee the continuation of ecological processes; to maintain genetic diversity; and, to direct methods of utilizing living natural resources to assure their sustainability. MANAN et al. (1986) have prepared a list of 63 terrestrial conservation areas or reserves in 20 Indonesian provinces which contain freshwater lakes and other wetlands. The wetlands of Indonesia (231 sites) have been inventoried by SILVIUS et al. (1987), so strengthening the basic information needed for an effective conservation strategy.

Some elements of Indonesia's freshwater fauna have become threatened, endangered, or perhaps even extinct in recent years. The occurrence of the freshwater sawfish (*Pristis microdon*) in Lake Sentani (Irian Jaya), for instance, was first reported in 1955 (BOESEMAN 1955). Although the species has been legally protected since 1980, there have been no recent records of this fish. SUWELO et al. (1986) listed those freshwater species which are legally protected in Indonesia. They comprise six fishes, 20 reptiles and 26 waterfowl. A number of endangered species are not yet protected (SUWELO et al. 1986), and the need for legal protection of many species is likely to increase once detailed evaluation of their status in Indonesia has been made. Recent changes in some areas may mean also that their conservation status should be reevaluated. When Lake Matano was gazetted as recreation park, for instance, the exceptional significance of the unique endemic fish fauna was not realized. The existence of a nickel-mining industry on the shores of the lake, the introduction of exotic species, and the use of the lake water to generate hydroelectric power is likely to have affected the endemic species deleteriously, and the legal status of the lake should now be reconsidered.

Although legal aspects of conservation have been addressed, and Indonesia is a signatory to CITES, much depends on the participation of the local populace and the extent to which the law can be enforced. Information and environmental education is needed at formal and informal levels in Indonesia to increase public awareness. Law enforcement must be strengthened in areas where it is still inadequate.

Institutional structures

The oldest institution in Indonesia working on limnology is the Inland Fisheries Research Institute under the Department of Agriculture. The central offices are located in Bogor, and there are two field laboratories at Jatiluhur Reservoir (west Java) and at Palembang on the banks of the Musi River (south Sumatra). The institute publishes a journal, *Bulletin Penelitian Perikanan Darat*. BIOTROP or the ASEAN Regional Centre for Tropical Biology, established in 1968, is also located in Bogor. Under its Tropical Aquatic Programme, the Centre regularly conducts short-term training and research programmes concerning freshwater environments and fisheries for ASEAN participants. For some time, aquatic weeds were the main research area. The Centre publishes the *BIOTROP Newsletter*, but numerous survey or research reports have been issued separately.

Many state and private universities are involved in limnological training and research, usually as part of fisheries, biology, geography or environmental studies. They include IPB (Bogor Agricultural University, Bogor), UNPAD (University of Padjadjaran, Bandung), UI (University of Indonesia, Jakarta), USU (University of North Sumatra, Medan), UGM (Gajah Mada University, Yogyakarta), UNHAS (Hasanuddin University, Ujung Pandang), UNRI (University of Riau, Pekanbaru), UNAND (University of Andalas, Padang), and UNSRAT (Sam Ratulangi University, Manado). Graduate study leading to a doctoral degree in aquatic science is now available at IPB. Some universities produce periodicals concerning fisheries and related areas: *Terubuk* is published by UNRI, and *Jurnal Fakultas Perikanan Unsrat* by UNSRAT. To cope with widespread environmental problems, Centres for Environmental Studies have been established within many state and private universities. ROMIMOHTARTO (1990) listed 49 such Centres distributed in all provinces of Indonesia except East Timor. Many of them are involved in pollution and environmental impact studies.

The Research and Development Centre for Water Resources (Department of Public Works) in Bandung has undertaken numerous studies of water quality, pollution monitoring and hydrotechnical engineering. The Centre is well equipped, and publishes a regular publication: *Jurnal Penelitian dan Pengembangan Pengairan*; survey reports are issued irregularly. The Research and Development Centre for Geotechnology (Indonesian Institute of Science) in Bandung studies the hydrology of surface and ground waters in various parts of Indonesia. The Centre has facilities for remote sensing. The Research and Development Centre for Limnology (Indonesian Institute of Sciences) in Bogor, established in 1986, has focused on lake eutrophication as a major topic of research, and results are issued as special publications (e.g. *Limnologi Situ Bojongsari*) as well as in other formats.

To a limit extent, the Forest Research and Development Centre (Department of Forestry) conducts hydrological studies and with emphasis on the role of forests in the hydrological cycle. The Directorate General for Forest Protection and Nature Conservation (PHPA), also under the Department of Forestry, has the mandate to manage Indonesian Protection Forests (30 million ha) and the Conservation Area System (17 million ha). The latter system comprises 24 National Parks, 179 Nature Reserves, 72 Wildlife Sanctuaries, 55 Recreation Parks, 11 Hunting Parks and 16 Marine Reserves. About 70 of these conservation areas contain wetlands. PHPA collaborate with AWB (Asian Wetland Bureau) and WWF/IUCN on studies of Indonesian wetlands with the objective of evaluating conservation needs and strategies.

In 1991, a National Committee on Hydrological Programme was established to promote and coordinate hydrological studies in Indonesia, and to foster cooperation with international organizations, particularly the International Hydrological Programme of UNESCO. The Secretariat has been placed under the aegis of the Indonesian Institute of Sciences.

Scientific societies

There are few scientific societies in Indonesia concerned with general or specific freshwater problems. None of them publishs regular scientific journals, but some produce newsletters. Symposia or seminars and their proceedings are useful sources of information. PBI (Perhimpunan Biologi Indonesia – Biological Society of Indonesia) holds regular national seminars every two years; aquatic biology is a major subject area at these meetings. Formerly, the society sponsored the journal *Berita Biologi*. HATHI (Himpunan Ahli Teknik Hidrologi Indonesia – Indonesian Society for Hydrological Engineers) holds regular seminars and publishes a newsletter; PALI (Perhimpunan Ahli Limnologi Indonesia – Indonesian Society for Limnology) was established in 1991 to promote limnology in the country.

Conclusions

In the last two decades limnology in Indonesia has progressed from a science that was concerned largely with support of fisheries, to a discipline including many aspects of science especially those concerning the environment. The vast area of inland waters in Indonesia, and the great challenges they offer, have given rise to the need for a considerable number of well-trained limnologists. Training and research in limnology must be encouraged and supported with adequate facilities. Basic inventories of Indonesian inland waters are required as a basis for resource management and conservation. Current knowledge of Indonesian inland waters is generally based on brief or sporadic field observations. Long-term studies are required to understand seasonality and gradual changes.

Lack of research funds is the most significant obstacle to the growth of Indonesian limnology. Most research funds come from the government, but the allocation of money to limnology has a low priority. Attempts to draw financial support from the private sector have been encouraged. This may be enhanced by recent government legislation that will require Environmental Impact Assessments of proposed projects which may alter natural environments significantly (e.g. UNCEN 1984). Close cooperation between private consultants and Centres for Environmental Studies should result from this legislation. A further obstacle is that many survey or research reports are not easily accessible. Often, they are scattered among the libraries of various institutes and/or cannot be published due to financial restrictions. For the same reason, international scientific journals on relevant subjects are scarce. Some, but not all, of these constraints could be reduced by closer cooperation among scientists and institutions in Indonesia.

Acknowledgements

The author expresses his gratitude to UNESCO, the Indonesian National MAB Committee, and the conference organizers for financial support that enabled him to attend the meeting on Conservation and Management of Tropical Inland Waters.

References

AHMAD, S., 1973: Fishery Survey Report of Lake Lindu and Lake Poso (Laporan Survey Perikanan Danau Lindu dan Poso). – *Lembaga Penelitian Perikanan Darat, Bogor, Laporan* No. **58**. (In Indonesian).

BADRUDDIN, M., 1986: Limnology and pollution (Limnologi dan pencemaran). – Prosiding Ekspose Limnologi dan Pencemaran, Bogor 28–29 Oktober 1986, *Pusat Penelitian dan Pemgembangan Limnologi-LIPI*: 61–79. (In Indonesian).

BADRUDDIN, M., SUYATNA, U., IBRAHIM, S., ARMAITA, S., RAHMADI & ISKANDAR, J., 1988: Pollution of Surabaya River and proposal for its mitigation (Pencemaran air Sungai Surabaya dan usulan penanggulangannya). – *Jurnal Penelitian dan Pengembangan Pengairan* **9**: 3–11. (In Indonesian).

BAPPEDA, JABAR, 1986: Inventory of lake data of Botabek Area (Inventarisasi data situ-situ di wilayah Botabek): 94 pp. – Bappeda Propinssi Daerah Tingkat I Jawa Barat. (In Indonesian).

BEMMELEN, R. W. VAN, 1939: The volcano-tectonic origin of Lake Toba (North Sumatra). – *De Ingenieur in Nederlandsch-Indie. IV. Mijnbou en Geologie. De Mijningenieur* **6**: 126–140.

BIOTROP & DPU 1977: Biological survey of Lake Tempe and its Vicinity, September 1976 (Survei biologi Danau Tempe dan sekitarnya, September 1976). – Regional Centre for Tropical Biology, Departmen Pekerjaan Umum. (In Indonesian).

–– 1978: Final Report of Ecological Survey of Lake Tempe in the Year 1977–1978 (Laporan akhir survai ekologi Danau Tempe tahun 1977–1978). – Regional Centre for Tropical Biology, Departemen Pekerjaan Umum. (In Indonesian).

BOESEMAN, M., 1955: Sawfishes in Lake Sentani. – *Science* **121**: 759.

– 1964: Notes on the fishes of western New Guinea. III. The freshwater shark of Jamoer Lake. – *Zool. Med., Leiden* **40**: 9–22.

BRUTUISWORO, E., 1988: Environmental management of the Saguling Dam. – In: JORGENSEN, S. E. & VOLLENWEIDER, R. A. (eds.): Guidelines of Lake Management. Vol. 1. Principles of Lake Management: 171–189. – International Lake Environment Committee – United Nations Environment Programme, Otsu.

COSTA-PIERCE, B. A., ATMADJA, G. W., EFFENDI, P. & ZAINAL, S., 1988: Integrated aquaculture systems in the Saguling Reservoir, West Java, Indonesia. – In: DE SILVA, S. S. (ed.): Reservoir Fishery Management and Development in Asia: 224–233. – International Development Centre, Ottawa.

COSTA-PIERCE, B. A. & SOEMARWOTO, O., 1990: Reservoir Fisheries and Aquaculture Development for Resettlement in Indonesia: 378 pp. – Perusahan Listrik Negara, Institute of Ecology Padjadjaran University, International Centre for Living Aquatic Resources Management.

Departmen Pertanian, 1990: Technical Guidelines for the Management of Open Waters for Fisheries Development (Petunjuk Teknis Pegelolaan Perairan umum bagi Pembangunan Perikanan): 80 pp. – Seri Pengembangan Hasil Penelitian Perikanan No. PIP/KAN/09/1990. (In Indonesian).

Direktorat Jenderal Kehutanan, 1980: Study on the Habitat and Population of Sentani Sawfish in Lake Sentani Jayapura – Irian Jaya (Studi Pembinaan Habitat dan Populasi hiu Gergaji [Ikan pari Sentani] di Danau Sentani Jayapura – Irian Jaya). – Direktorat Jenderal Kehutanan. (In Indonesian).

Direktorat Jenderal Kehutanan, 1986: Long term development plan (year 2000) (Rencana pembangunan jangka panjang [tahun 2000]. – Direktorat Jenderal Pengairan, Departemen Pekerjaan Umum. (In Indonesian).

DPMA, 1983: Control of Heavy Metal Pollution in Jabotabek Area and the Bay of Jakarta (Pengendalian pencemaran logam berat daerah Jabotabek dan Teluk Jakarta). – Direktorat Jenderal Pengairan, Departemen Pekerjaan Umum. (In Indonesian).

DPU & Exsa international, 1981: Summary of Preliminary Survey on the Flood Control Regulation of Lake Batur (Ringkasan Survey Pendahuluan Pengaturan Pengamanan Banjir Danau Batur). – Draft Final Report Juni 1981, Departemen Pekerjaan Umum. (In Indonesian).

DPU & Geojaya Technik, 1985: Study on the Development Plan of Lake Limboto (Studi Perencanaan Pengembangan Danau Limboto). – Departemen Pekerjaan Umum. (In Indonesian).

DPU & Indah Karya, 1981: Final Report on the Study of the Planning of Lake Tempe, South Sulawesi Province (Laporan Akhir Pekerjaan Studi Perencanaan Keadaan Danau Tempe Propinsi Sulawesi Selatan). – Direktorat Jenderal Pengairan, Departemen Pekerjaan Umum. (In Indonesian).

DPU & Rayakonsult, 1981: Study on the Planning of the Development of Water Resources in the Area of Tondano River, North Sulawesi (Perkerjaan Studi Perencanaan Pembangunan Sumber-sumber air Wilayah Sungai Tondano, Propinsi Sulawesi Utara). – Departemen Pekerjaan Umum. (In Indonesian).

– – 1983: Draft Final Report on the Study of the Water Balance of Lake Tondano (Pekerjaan Pengukuran dan Studi Perimbangan Tata air Danau Tondano). – Departemen Pekerjaan Umum. (In Indonesian).

DPU & Yaramaya, 1983: Draft Final Report on the Water Balance of Lake Kerinci (Studi Perimbangan Tata air Danau Kerinci). – Departemen Pekerjaan Umum. (In Indonesian).

Duarsa, P., & Sasongko, D., 1986. Irrigation and its Problems Related with Limnology (Pengairan dan Masalah-masalahnya yang Berkaitan Dengan Limnologi). – *Prosiding Ekspose Limnologi dan Pembangunan. Pusat Penelitian dan Pengembangan Limnologi, LIPI, Bogor*: 80–86 (In Indonesian).

Eyanuer, H. F., Sembiring, N., Madjnu, M., Damanik, S. J. & Anwar, J., 1981: Community, aquatic environment and biology of Lake Toba (Komunitas, lingkungan perairan dan kehidupan biologi Danau Toba di Sumatra Utara). – *Lingkungan dan Pembangunan* **1**: 89–121. (In Indonesian).

FAO 1972: Inland Fisheries Development in West Irian. – Food and Agriculture Organization of the United Nations.

Fernando, C. H., 1984: Reservoirs and lakes of Southeast Asia (Oriental Region). – In: Taub, F. B. (ed.): Lakes and Reservoirs. Ecosystems of the World series: 411–446. – Elsevier, Amsterdam.

Gaffar, A. K., Rifai, S. A, Utomo, A. D. & Adjie, S., 1989: Limnological characteristics of River Komering, South Sumatra (Karakteristik limnologi Sungai Komering, Sumatra Selatan). – *Bull. Penelitian Perikanan Darat* **7**: 66–74. (In Indonesian).

Giesen, W., 1987: Danau Sentarum Wildlife Reserve: Inventory, Ecology and Management Guidelines: 284 pp. – A World Wildlife Report for the Directorate General of Forest Protection and Nature Conservation (PHPA). Bogor, Indonesia.

– 1990 a: Wetland conservation in South Sulawesi. – *Asian Wetland News* **3**: 16–18.

– 1990 b: The Ogan-Komering lebaks of South Sumatra, Indonesia. – *Asian Wetland News* **3**: 20–21.

– 1994: Indonesia's major freshwater lakes: a review of current knowledge, development processes and treats. – *Mitt. Internat. Verein Limnol.* **24**: 115–118.

Green, J., Corbet, S. A., Watts, E. & Oey Biauw Lan 1976: Ecological studies on Indonesian lakes: overturn and restratification of Ranu Lamongan. – *J. Zool., Lond.* **180**: 315–354.

– – – – 1978: Ecological studies on Indonesian lakes: The montane lakes of Bali. – *J. Zool., Lond.* **186**: 15–38.

Hardjamulia, A. & Rabegnatar, I. N. S., 1986: Status of the open water fisheries of Indonesia. – Paper presented at the third session of the IPFC Working Party of Experts on Inland Fisheries, Bangkok, 19–27 June 1986.

Hardjamulia, A. & Rabegnatar, I. N. S., 1991: Freshwater fisheries research, its results and its impact on artisanal fisheries (Penelitian perikanan air tawar, hasil dan dampaknya bagi perkembangan perikanan rakyat). – Prosiding Temu Karya Ilmiah Perikanan Rakyat, Jakarta 18–19. Desember 1989, *Pusat Penelitian dan Pengembangan Perikanan:* 63–77. (In Indonesian).

Hardjamulia, A. & Suwignyo, P., 1988: The present status of the reservoir fishery in Indonesia. In: De Silva, S. S. (ed.): *Reservoir Fishery Management and development in Asia.* 8–13. International Development Research Centre, Ottawa.

Hartono, B., 1988: Review on water pollution studies in Indonesia. – *Bulletin Penelitian Kesehatan* **16**: 1–14.

Hartoto, D. I. & Sulastri, 1990: Preliminary Ecological Response of Lake Bojongsari to Aeration with Limnotek 3.0: 65 pp. – Research and Development Centre for Limnology, Bogor.

Hehuwat, F., 1982: Tao Toba: Batak tumor, Toba tuff, volcano-tectonic depression, the history of the formation Lake Toba (Tao Toba: Tumor Batak, tufa Toba, depressi vulkanotektonik. Sejarah terjadinya Danau Toba). – *Suara Alam* **16**: 18–20. (In Indonesian).

Hisbi, D., 1990: Weed *Polygonum barbatum* problem and its control in Ir. P. M. Noor Reservoir, South Kalimantan, Indonesia. – *Symposium on Aquatic Weed Management,* Bogor 15–17 May 1990.

Hutagalung, H. P. & Suwirma, S. 1987: Heavy metal content in some seafood collected from Muara

Angke fish auction place, Jakarta. – *Marine Research in Indonesia* **26**: 51–52.

ILEC & UNEP, 1989: Danau Toba (Lake Toba). In: Lake Biwa Research Institute and International Lake Environment Committee (eds), Data Book of World Lake Environments: A survey of the World Lakes. – International Lake Environment Committee, United Nations Environment Programme. Otsu, ASI-10: 1–7.

Kabinawa, I. N. K., 1987: Analyses on several physical and chemical features of the water in the occurrence of *Microcystis aeruginosa* Kütz, bloom in the central part of Jatiluhur Reservoir (Analisa beberapa sifat fisika kimia air terhadap adanya blooming *Microcystis aeruginosa* Kütz, di bagian tengah Waduk Jatiluhur). – *Berita Biologi* **3**: 321–325. (In Indonesian).

Kartamihardja, E. S., 1987: Production potential and fisheries management of Lake Toba, North Sumatra (Potensi produksi dan pengelolaan perikanan di Danau Toba, Sumatra Utara). – *Bulletin Penelitian Perikanan Darat* **6**: 65–77. (In Indonesian).

Kartamihardja, E. S., Nastiti, A. S., Krismono, Purnomo, K. & Ardjamulia, A., 1987: Limnobiological investigation of Saguling Reservoir during the pre-inundation stage (Penelitian limnobiologis Waduk Saguling Pada tahap pra-inundasi). – *Bulletin Penelitian Perikanan Darat* **6**: 32–62. (In Indonesian).

Katili, J., 1983: Natural Resources for National Development (Sumberdaya Alam untuk Pembangunan Nasional). – 192 pp. Ghalia Indonesia, Jakarta. (In Indonesian).

KLH, 1990: Prokasih, the Clean River Programme (Prokasih, Program Kali Bersih). 30 pp. – Kantor Menteri Negara Kependudukan dan Lingkungan Hidup. (In Indonesian).

Krismono, A. & Hardjamulia, A., 1986 a: Vertical distribution of dissolved oxygen, water temperature and organic content in Jatiluhur Reservoir (Distribusi vertikal oksigen terlarut, suhu air dan kandungan bahan organik di Waduk Jatiluhur, Jawa Barat). – *Bull. Penelitian Perikanan Darat* **5**: 83–89. (In Indonesian).

– – 1986 b: Limnology: physical and chemical condition of the water of Jatiluhur Reservoir, West Java, in 1983 (Limnologi: kondisi fisika dan kimiawi air di Waduk Jatiluhur, Jawa Barat, dalam tahun 1983). – *Bull. Penelitian Perikanan Darat* **5**: 100–110. (In Indonesian).

Loebis, Y. & Putuhena, W., 1990: Comments on the lowering of the surface of Lake Toba (Ulasan mengenai menurunnya muka air Danau Toba). – *Jurnal Penelitian dan Pengembangan Pengairan* **5**: 27–33. (In Indonesian).

Lukman & Fauzi, H., 1991: Report on the Presurvey of Lake Sentani (Laporan Prasurvai Danau Sentani, Irian Jaya, dan Wilayah Sekitarnya). – Pusat Penelitian dan Pengembangan Limnologi – LIPI: 64 pp. (In Indonesian).

Manan, S., Taufik, A. W. & Djuharsa, E., 1986: Limnology and forestry (Limnologi dan kehutanan). – Prosiding Ekspose Limnologi dan Pembangunan, Bogor 28–29 Oktober 1986, Pusat Penelitian dan Pembangunan Limnologi – LIPI: 61–79. (In Indonesian).

Manggabarani, H., 1981: Status of open water fisheries in South Sulawesi (Status perikanan perairan umum di Sulawesi Selatan). – Prosiding Seminar Perikanan Perairan Umum, Jakarta 19–21 Agustus 1981. *Pusat Penelitian dan Pengembangan Perikanan*: 131–134. (In Indonesian).

Mizuno, T., 1980. Some limnological features of Southeast Asian inland waters and growth rates of freshwater shrimp and *Chironomus* in the black water swamps of West Malaysia. – In: Mori, S. & Ikusima, I. (eds): *Proceedings of the First Workshop for the Promotion of Limnology in the Developing countries*. 13–23. – Societas Internationalis Limnologiae, Kyoto.

Nakano, K., Watanabe, T., Usman, R. & Syahbuddin 1987: A fundamental study of overall conservation of terrestrial and freshwater ecosystems in montane region of western Sumatra: vegetation, land use, and water quality. – *Memoirs of the Kagoshima University Research Centre for the Pacific* **8**: 87–124.

Neame, P. A., 1988: Hydrochemistry of the lower Solo River, Indonesia. – *Verh. Internat. Verein. Limnol.* **23**: 1327–1379.

Nontji, A. & Hartoto, D. I., 1989: Limnology of Lake Bojongsari (Limnologi Situ Bonjongsari). – Pusat Penelitian dan Pengembangan Limnologi – LIPI: 159 pp. (In Indonesian).

Ondara, 1969: Survey Report of Lake Toba (North Sumatra) (Laporan Survai di Danau Toba [Sumatra Utara]). – Lembaga Penelitian Perikanan Darat Cabang Palembang No. 3. (In Indonesian).

Pancho, J. V. & Soerjani, M., 1978. – *Aquatic weeds of Southeast Asia*. – 130 pp. National Publishing Corporation Incorporated, Quezon City, Philippines.

Pangesti, D. R. & Isnugroho, 1989: Observation on the erosion of the Wonogiri watershed and its impact on reservoir sedimentation (Pengamatan erosi pada DPS Wonogiri serta pengaruhnya terhadap sedimentasi waduk). – *Jurnal Penelitian dan Pengembangan Pengairan* **15**: 106–111. (In Indonesian).

Pardede, R., 1982: The formation of the old Lake Kerinci, its relation with Pengasih Formation in Sumatra (Terbentuknya Danau Kerinci purba, kaitannya dengan Formasi Pengasih di Sumatra). – Prosiding PIT XI Ikatan Ahli Geologi Indonesia, Jakarta 8–9 Desember 1982 (In Indonesian).

President of the Republic of Indonesia, 1990: The Execution of the Fifth Five-Year Plan, the Second year. Annex to the Presidential State Address to the Indonesian Parliament, 16 August 1990. (Pelaksanaan Repelita V, Tahun Kedua. Lampiran Pidato Kenegaraan Presiden Republik Indonesia di depan sidang Dewan Perwakilan Rakyat, 16 Agustus 1990). (In Indonesian).

PULN & JICA 1988: Feasibility Study Report on Ranu Hydrolelectric Power Development Project. – Perusahaan Umum Listrik Negara.

Puslitbang Pengairan, 1986 a: Studies on the Water Quality and Hydrobiology of the Lakes of West Sumatra (Penelitian Kualitas Air dan Hidrobiologi Danau-danau di Sumatra Barat). – Badan Penelitian dan Pengembangan Pekerjaan Umum, Departemen Pekerjaan Umum. (In Indonesian).

– 1986 b: Studies on the Water Quality and Biology of Riam Kanan Reservoir (Penelitian Kualitas Air dan biologi Waduk Riam Kanan). – Badan Penelitian dan Pengembangan Pekerjaan Umum, Departemen Pekerjaan Umum. (In Indonesian).

– 1986 c: Studies on the Water Quality and Hydrobiology of Lakes and Reservoirs of West Java (Penelitian Kualitas Air dan Hidrobiologi Danau dan Waduk Di Jawa Barat). – Badan Penelitian dan Pengembangan Pekerjaan Umum, Departemen Pekerjaan Umum. (In Indonesian).

– 1986 d: Studies on the Water Quality and Hydrobiology of Central Java (Penelitian Kualitas Air dan Hidrobiologi Danau dan Waduk di Jawa Tengah). – Badan Penelitian dan Pekerjaan Umum, Departemen Pekerjaan Umum. (In Indonesian).

– 1986 e: Water Pollution in the Area of Jabotabek and in the Bay of Jakarta (Pencemaran Air di Daerah Jabotabek dan Teluk Jakarta). – Badan Penelitian dan Pengembangan Pekeriaan Umum, Departemen Pekerjaan Umum. (In Indonesian).

– 1990: Several Hydrological Aspects Causing the Shallowing of Lake Limboto and Flooding of the City of Gorontalo (Beberapa Aspek Pengairan yang Menyebabkan Pendangkalan Danau Limboto Dan Banjir Kotamadya Gorontalo). – Badan Penelitian dan Pengembangan Pekerjaan Umum, Departemen Pekerjaan Umum. (In Indonesian).

Roberts, T. R., 1989: The freshwater fishes of Western Borneo (Kalimantan Barat, Indonesia). – *Memoirs of the California Academy of Sciences* **14**: 1–210.

Romimohtarto, K., 1990: Introduction to Marine Pollution Monitoring (Pengantar pemantauan pencemaran laut). – Paper presented in the Course on Marine Pollution Monitoring II, Jakarta, 13–23 March 1990. (In Indonesian).

Rondo, M., 1990: Status of the inland water quality in North Sulawesi. – Symposium on the Inland Aquatic Environmental Stress Monitoring, BIOTROP, Bogor, 25–27 July 1990.

Ruttner, F., 1931: Hydrographische und hydrochemische Beobachtungen auf Java, Sumatra und Bali. *Arch. Hydrobiol. Suppl.* **8**: 197–454.

Ruttner, F., 1952: Planktonstudien der deutschen limnologischen Sunda-Expedition. – *Arch. Hydrobiol. Suppl.* **21**: 1–274.

Saanin, H. H., 1981: Types of open waters in Indonesia with special reference on the important factors governing fisheries potential (Jenis-jenis perairan umum di Indonesia dengan penekanan khusus pada faktor-faktor yang menpengaruhi potensi perikanan dari jenis-jenis terpenting). – *Prosiding Seminar Perairan Perikanan Umum, Jakarta 19–21 Agustus 1981, Pusat Penelitian dan Pengembangan Perikanan*: 1–12. (In Indonesian).

Sabar, F., 1990: Aquatic Biology in the Vicinity of Bogor (Biologi Perairan Sekitar Bogor). – Pusat Penelitian dan Pengembangan Limnologi-LIPI. (In Indonesian).

Saeni, M., Sutamihardja, R. T. M. & Sukra, J., 1980: Water quality of the Musi River in the city area of Palembang. – *Tropical Ecology and Development*: 712–714.

Sarnita, A., 1981: Fisheries management of Jatiluhur Reservoir (Pengelolaan perikanan Waduk Jatiluhur). – *Prosiding Seminar Perikanan Perairan Umum, Jakarta 19–21 Agustus 1981, Buku II. Pusat Penelitian dan Pengembangan Perikanan*: 211–215. (In Indonesian).

– 1986: Open waters in Indonesia as natural resources (Perairan umum di Indonesia sebagai salah satu sumberdaya alam). – *Prosiding Seminar Perikanan Umum, Jakarta, 1 September 1986, Pusat Penelitian dan Pengembangan Perikanan:* 17–31. (In Indonesian).

Schuster, W. H., 1952: Fish culture as a means of controlling aquatic weeds in inland waters. – *FAO Fish. Bull.* **5**: 15–24.

Schuster, W. H. & Djajadiredja, R. R., 1952: Local Common Names of Indonesian fishes: 276 pp. – W. van Hoeve, Bandung.

Scott, A. M. & Prescott, G. W. 1961: Indonesian desmids. – *Hydrobiologia* **17**: 1–132.

Silvus, M. J., Steeman, A. P. J. M, Berczy, E. T., Djuharsa, E. & Taufik, A. W., 1987: The Indonesian Wetland Inventory: a Preliminary Compilation on Wetlands of Indonesia. – PHPA, AWB/INTERWADER, EDWIN, Bogor.

Soerjani, M.; 1981: Utilization of Aquatic Weeds as Part of the Management of Lake Kerinci (Pemanfaatan Gulma Air Sebagai Bagian dalam Pengelolaan Danau Kerinci). – PSLM – Ul dan Ditjen Pengairan, Departemen Pekerjaan Umum. (In Indonesian).

Soerjani, M. & Widyanto, L., 1977: Mass growth of aquatic weeds and its effects on the water quantity and water quality (Pertumbuhan massal tumbuhan air dan pengaruhnya terhadap kuantitas dan kualitas air). – *Ekologi dan Pembangunan* **5**: 121–142. (In Indonesian).

Soeroto, B., 1989: Several problems of Lake Tondano and attempts for their solution (Beberapa masalah di Danau Tondano dan usaha penanggulangannya). – *Jurnal Fakultas Perikanan Unsrat* **1**: 45–52. (In Indonesian).

SUCOFINDO-ITB-DKI, 1977: The Jakarta River System. An Environmental Study with Particular Reference to Synthetic Detergents: vols 1, 2 & 3.

Sukarwo, P., 1990: Vegetation analysis of the aquatic weeds of Lake Sentani, Jayapura, Irian Jaya (Analisis Vegetasi Gulma Air di Daunau Sentani Jayapuran Irian Jaya). – Fakultas Pertanian, Universitas Cendrawasih, Manokwari. (In Indonesian).

SUMATRA, M., 1982: Insecticide residue monitoring in sediment, water, fish and mangroves at the Cimanuk Delta. – *Majalah BATAN* **15**: 18–30.

– 1990: Pesticide Residue Analysis (Analisis residu Pestisida). Course on Marine Pollution Monitoring II. Jakarta 13–23 March 1990. – Pusat Penelitian dan Pengembangan Oseanologi, LIPI. (In Indonesian).

SUWELO, I. S., SUPANGKAT & YUNIA, C. 1986: Limnology and conservation of living environment: conservation of swamps, lakes and rivers as habitat of rare species (Limnologi dan konservasi lingkungan hidup: Pelestarian rawa, danau dan sungai habitat biota langka). – *Prosiding Ekspose Limnologi dan Pembangunan, Bogor 28–29 Oktober 1986, Pusat Penelitian dan Pengembangan Limnologi-LIPI*: 87–95. (In Indonesian).

THAMZIL, L., SUWIRMA & SURTIPANTI, S., 1980: Study on the heavy metal content of the River Sunter (Studi kandungan logam berat pada aliran Sungai Sunter). – *Majalah BATAN* **13**: 41–58. (In Indonesian).

TJAHJO, D. W. H., 1986: Morphological characteristics and fisheries development potential of Saguling, Jatiluhur and Wonogiri Reservoir (Ciri-ciri morfologi dan potensi pengembangan perikanan Waduk Saguling, Jatiluhur dan Wonogiri). – *Bull. Penelitian Perikanan Darat* **5**: 47–55. (In Indonesian).

TJAHJO, D. W. H., HARDJAMULIA, A., NURONIAH, S. & UMAR, C., 1987: Limno-biological investigation of Saguling reservoir in the post inundation stage (Penelitian limno-biologis Waduk Saguling pada tahap post-inundasi). – *Bull. Penelitian Perikanan Darat* **6**: 1–31. (In Indonesian).

TJITROSOEPOMO, G., WIRJAHARDJA, S. & SOERJANI, M., 1974: Important aquatic weeds and their problems in Indonesia. – Paper presented at the Southeast Asian Workshop on Aquatic Weeds, Malang, 25–29 June 1974.

TRIWASONO, 1987: Conversion of swamp land into agricultural land and its impact on mangrove (Konversi lahanrawa menjadi tanah berproduksi dan dampaknya terhadap mangrove. – *Prosiding Seminar III Ekosistem Mangrove*: 55–62. (In Indonesian).

UI & DPU 1978: Final Report of Ecological Survey of Lake Singkarak and Lake Maninjau, 1977–1978. (Laporan Akhir Survai Ekologi Danau Singkarak dan Danau Maninjau, tahun 1977–1978). Universitas Indonesia, Departemen Pekerjaan Umum. (In Indonesian).

– – 1979 a: Final Report of Ecological Survey of Lake Toba, 1978–1979 (Laporan Akhir Survai Ekologi Danau Toba Tahun 1978–1979). – Universitas Indonesia, Departemen Pekerjaan Umum. (In Indonesian).

– – 1979 b: Preliminary report on the Ecology of Lake Kerinci, 1978–1979 (Laporan pendahuluan survaiekologi Danau Kerinci tahun 1978–1979). – Universitas Indonesia, Departemen Pekerjaan Umum. (In Indonesian).

– – 1979 c: Ecology of Lake Tondano (Ekologi Danau Tondano). – Universitas Indonesia, Departemen Pekerjaan Umum. (In Indonesian).

UNCEN 1984: Environmental Impact Analysis of Sentani Lake Hydroelectric Power Project, Irian Jaya. – Environmental Study Centre, Cendrawasih University, Jayapura.

VAAS, K. F., 1951: Notes on the water hyacinth in Indonesia and its eradication by spraying with 2,4-D – *Contributions of the General Agricultural Research Station (Bogor, Indonesia)* **120**: 1–55.

– 1956: Report on the Study of Rawa Aopa (Laporan Pemeriksaan Rawa Aopa [Sulawesi Tenggara]). – *Balai Penjelidikan Perikanan Darat,* No. **8**. (In Indonesian).

VAAS, K. F. & SACHLAN, M., 1949: On the ecology of some small lakes near Buitenzorg, Java. – Hydrobiologia **1**: 238–250.

– – – 1952: Notes on fisheries exploitation of the artificial Lake Tjiburuj in West Java. – *Contribution of the General Agricultural Research Station, Bogor* **128**: 1–122

VAAS, K. F., SACHLAN, M. & WIRAATMADJA, G., 1953: On the ecology and fisheries of some inland waters along the rivers Ogan and Komering in South-east Sumatra. – *Contribution of the Inland Fisheries Research Station, Bogor* **3**: 1–32.

VAAS, K. F. & SCHUURMAN, J. J., 1949: On the ecology and fisheries of some Javanese freshwaters. – *Communications of the General Agricultural Research Station, Buitenzorg* **97**, 1–61.

VERSTAPPEN, V. T., 1961: Some "volcano-tectonic" depressions of Sumatra, their origin and mode of development. – *Koninklijke Nederlandse Akademie van Wetenschappen, Proceedings Series B Physical Science* **64**: 428–443.

WATANABE, T. & USMAN, R., 1987: Epilithic freshwater diatoms in Central Sumatra. – *Diatom* **3**: 33–87.

WHITTEN, A. J., DAMANIK, S. J., ANWAR, J. & HISYAM, N., 1987: *The Ecology of Sumatra* (2nd Edition). – 537 pp. Gajah Mada University Press, Yogyakarta.

WHITTEN, A. J., MUSTAFA, M. & HENDERSEN, G., 1987: The Ecology of Sulawesi: 777 pp. – Gajah Mada University Press, Yogyakarta.

WIDJAJA, F., 1980: A review of activities and research on limnology in Indonesia. – In: MORI, S. & IKUSIMA, I. (eds.): Proceedings of the First Workshop on the Promotion of Limnology in the Developing Countries: 75–80. – Societas Internationalis Limnologiae, Kyoto.

Author's address:

Puslitbang Limnologi, Jl. Juanda 3, P.O. Box 355, Bogor 16122, Indonesia.

Mitt. Internat. Verein. Limnol.	**24**	115–128	Stuttgart, Februar 1994

Indonesia's major freshwater lakes: A review of current knowledge, development processes and threats

Wim Giesen

Abstract

Indonesia has over 500 lakes, varying from deep tectonic basins to volcanic, glacial and ephemeral floodplain types, but the paucity of data is striking. Hydrological data, for example, are scarce, and information on aquatic fauna mostly consists of lists of commercial fish, many of which have been introduced. Indonesia's lakes are valuable assets. Flood-plain lakes such as those of the Ogan-Komering (Sumatra), Upper Kapuas (Kalimantan) and Lake Tempe (Sulawesi) form the basis of important fisheries which in the case of Lake Tempe are at least as productive as artificial fishponds. Tectonic and volcanic lakes such as Lake Toba (Sumatra) and Lake Batur (Bali) are popular tourist destinations, and lake water resources are important for potable water, irrigation and hydropower. Large and ancient lakes often harbour endemics. Those of the Matano-Towuti lake system in Sulawesi, for instance, include more than 20 fish, 12 molluscs and 7 plant species.

A review of 35 large lakes throughout the archipelago shows that many have undergone major changes over the past decades, often resulting in degradation, and development plans threaten to disturb those relatively unaffected up to now. Dams occur in one third of all lakes and have been planned in another five. Siltation is a major problem in at least three lakes, while the introduction of water hyacinth and exotic fishes has been ubiquitous. Although poorly documented, losses of fishery production and fish extinctions are apparent. A combination of surveying, data evaluation and the formulation of a national strategy for the wise use of Indonesia's lakes and lake resources is urgently required to curb further loss of natural assets.

Introduction

The total area of natural lakes in Indonesia measures more than 5,000 square kilometres, or about 0.25 per cent of the country's land surface. In all there are over 500 lakes, the majority of which are still *limna incognita* for limnologists. These waters are unevenly distributed throughout the archipelago, as numerous small lakes occur in tecto-volcanically active regions, while relatively few are found on stable land masses and the smaller islands (Table 1). In terms of lake surface area, two-thirds of Indonesia's permanent lake area is found in

Table 1. Natural lakes in Indonesia.

Island (-group)	Number of lakes per size category			Total area[2] (ha)	Max. area[3] (ha)
	1–99[1] ha	100–999 ha	> 999 ha		
Sumatra	88	69	13	190,043	370,043
Kalimantan	61	61	17	84,231	114,231
Java + Bali	19	10	2	6,270	6,270
Lesser Sunda's	7	4	3	6,041	6,041
Sulawesi	11	10	9	141,871	159,871
Maluku	5	3	2	3,438	3,438
Irian Jaya	39	76	12	59,830	unknown
Total	230	233	58	491,724	719,724*

Notes:
1. Small lakes are under-represented because of the scale of maps used.
2. Calculated from 1:250,000 scale *RePPProT* (1986–89) maps; these do not include maximum extensions of floodplain lakes.
3. Where known, maximum sizes of floodplain lakes are included.

* In this total, 59,830 hectares is taken as the lake area of Irian Jaya; this is expected to be much greater but no reliable figures are known.

0538-4680/94/0024-0115 $ 3.50

Table 2. Location and general features of the 35 selected lakes.

No. lake (-system)	lat./long.[1]	island/province	altitude (m)	size[2] (ha)	depth[3] max.	pH[4]	Secchi (m)	type[5]	nutr.[6]
1. L. Laut Tawar	4°37′N/96°56′E	Aceh	1,126	5,500	na	na	na	7/8	na
2. L. Toba	2°30′N/99°00′E	North Sumatra	906	112,970	450	8.3	8.6	16	olig.
3. Siak Kecil lakes	0°12′N/101°40′E	Riau	10	9,000*	<5	3.5	<1	70	olig.
4. Ogan-Komering lakes	3°35′S/104°45′E	South Sumatra	20	200,000	5	4–6	0.6	52, 56	vari.
5. L. Maninjau	0°20′S/100°10′E	West Sumatra	463	9,950	169	7.5	10.7	13	olig.
6. L. Singkarak	0°36′S/100°30′E	West Sumatra	364	13,011	268	8.0	3.8	9	meso.
7. L. Di-atas	1°04′S/100°45′E	West Sumatra	1,531	1,230	44	7.3	8.3	9	eutr.
8. L. Di-bawah	1°01′S/100°43′E	West Sumatra	1,462	1,120	309	7.3	11.1	9	eutr.
9. L. Kerinci	2°08′S/101°30′E	Jambi	783	4,200	110	6.8	2.2	9, 19a	eutr.
10. L. Ranau	4°50′S/103°48′E	Lumpung/S. Sumatra	540	12,500	229	8.4	na	9/13	na
11. Upper Kapuas lakes	0°45′N/112°09′E	West Kalimantan	35	27,500	8	5.3	2	52, 56	olig.
12. Bangkau lakes	2°39′S/115°12′E	South Kalimantan	10	2,000	4.5	5	0.5	52	meso.
13. Middle Mahakam lakes	0°25′S/116°15′E	East Kalimantan	50?	45,000	4	6.7	0.35	52, 56	eutr.
14. L. Rawa	6°11′S/105°59′E	West Java	115	250	13	6.9	low	13	eutr.
15. L. Pening	7°17′S/110°26′E	Central Java	463	2,500	4.4	7.3	0.75	73	eutr.
16. L. Lamongan	7°59′S/113°23′E	East Java	240	35	32	8.4	1.0	10	eutr.
17. L. Tondano	1°13′N/124°57′E	North Sulawesi	600	5,000	20	8	1.5	10	eutr.
18. L. Limboto	0°35′N/123°00′E	North Sulawesi	25	5,600*	2.5	8.2	0.28	52	eutr.
19. L. Poso	2°01′S/120°40′E	Central Sulawesi	300?	32,320	450	7.5	9.3	4/7	olig.
20. L. Lindu	1°19′S/120°09′E	Central Sulawesi	1,000	3,200	100	5	2.0	4/7	meso.
21. Tempe lakes	4°06′S/119°52′E	South Sulawesi	6	35,000*	9.5	5.5	0.20	52	eutr.
22. Matano-Towuti lakes	2°39′S/120°20′E	South Sulawesi	350	74,956	600	6.5	18.5	9	olig.
23. L. Rawa Aopa	4°05′S/122°02′E	Southeast Sulawesi	50	38,000*	6	5	0.29	52/70	eutr.
24. L. Batur	8°15′S/115°25′E	Bali	1,031	1,590	91	8.5	2.4	13	olig.
25. L. Buyan	8°15′S/115°07′E	Bali	1,214	390	30	7.6	2.3	13	olig.
26. L. Bratan	8°17′S/115°10′E	Bali	1,231	380	23	7.0	4.0	13	olig.
27. L. Segara-anak	8°26′S/116°24′E	Lombok	2,030	1,125	160	7.4	clear	13	na
28. L. Kelimutu	8°45′S/121°47′E	Flores	1,410	40	60	acid	na	12/13	na
29. L. Surubel #	8°27′S/127°08′E	East Timor	na	2,200	na	na	na	na	na
30. L. Sentani	2°35′S/140°31′E	Irian Jaya	70	9,360	52	7.4	na	20?	eutr.
31. Enarotali lakes # #	3°50′S/136°20′E	Irian Jaya	1,742	19,550	na	na	na	52/43?	na
32. Ayamaru lakes	1°16′S/132°15′E	Irian Jaya	250	2,200	20	na	na	43	na
33. Anggi lakes	1°21′S/133°55′E	Irian Jaya	1,780	4,687	na	na	na	43?	na
34. L. Jamur	3°41′S/135°56′E	Irian Jaya	107	3,187	na	na	na	43	na
35. Triton lakes	3°40′S/134°17′E	Irian Jaya	300–1000	6,210	50?	8.0	na	43	na

Sumatra and Sulawesi, which together comprise only one third of the total land mass. The largest permanent lake is Lake Toba, Sumatra, which measures 112,970 hectares (BEMMELEN 1949); floodplain lake systems such as those of the Ogan-Komering in South Sumatra are regularly even larger, reportedly attaining a size of 200,000 hectares (VAAS et al. 1953). Indonesia's deepest lake is Lake Matano, Sulawesi, which reaches a depth of 600 m (GIESEN et al. 1990); it is the deepest lake in Southeast Asia and the eighth deepest in the world (HUTCHINSON 1975).

Tecto-volcanic lakes dominate in terms of numbers, but the area covered by floodplain lakes is greater than 55 percent of the total. Less common, though well represented lake types are dystrophic lakes in peat dome areas (especially in Riau Province, Sumatra), and solution lakes in karst regions (especially Java and Irian Jaya). Floodplain lakes such as those of the Ogan-Komering (Sumatra), Upper Kapuas (Kalimantan) and Lake Tempe (Sulawesi) form the basis of very important fisheries (VAAS 1952, VAAS et al. 1953, HICKLING 1961, GIESEN 1987, GIESEN et al. 1990, GIESEN & SOEKOTJO 1991 b) which in the case of Lake Tempe are at least as productive as artifical fishponds in terms of kilograms of fish per hectare per year (GIESEN et al. 1990). Tectonic and volcanic lakes such as Toba (Sumatra), Kelimutu (Flores) and Batur (Bali) are popular tourist destinations, and lake water resources are important for potable water, irrigation and hydropower. Large and ancient lakes often harbour endemic species. Endemics of the Matano-Towuti lake system in Sulawesi, for instance, include more than 20 fish, 12 molluscs and 7 plant species (WHITTEN et al. 1988; GIESEN et al. 1990).

Current knowledge

Further discussion will centre on 35 lakes and lake systems (further referred to as "the 35 lakes"), distributed throughout the archipelago, which were selected on the basis of size (for those in Sumatra, Kalimantan, Sulawesi, Timor and Irian Jaya), or on the basis of fame (for those in Java, Bali, Lombok and Flores). Together these comprise 85 percent of the total permanent lake area of Indonesia. Locations and general features are given in Table 2, while Table 3 lists basic inventories and endemism of flora, molluscs, fish and birds. Table 3 further indicates availability of data on lake fisheries. Approximate locations of these 35 lakes are given in Fig. 1.

General physical data is available for all lakes of this group, apart for those in the eastern part of the archipelago (Timor, Irian Jaya). In terms of area, the largest lakes are seasonally inundated floodplain lakes (Hutchinson's types 52 and 56; see Table 2), which alto-

Notes for Table 2.

na = not available

1. Latitude and longitude are given for centre of lake (-system).
2. Given is the average lake size, in hectares. Exceptions are made for floodplain lakes, for which maximum sizes are given (marked by an asterix *).
3. Maximum (wet season) depths are indicated in metres.
4. pH = (average) surface value
5. Lakes types are according to HUTCHINSON (1975).
   - 4 – (tectonic) lakes formed by upwarping around a basin
   - 7 – (tectonic) lakes on old peneplain surfaces in intermontane basin
   - 8 – (tectonic) lakes in basin on tilted fault blocks
   - 9 – (tectonic) lakes in grabens between faults
   - 10 – (volcanic) lakes in relatively unmodified craters
   - 12 – (volcanic) crater lakes in stratovolcanoes modified in terminal phase of eruption
   - 13 – (volcanic) caldera lakes, in large basins due to collapse of central part of a volcano
   - 16 – (volcanic) lakes in volcano-tectonic basins comparable to calderas, but in line with pre-existing faults
   - 19 a – (volcanic) lakes formed by damming of a valley by lava/ash
   - 20 – lakes held by landslide dams
   - 43 – (solution) lakes formed in limestone areas
   - 52 – (fluvial/floodplain) lakes, lateral to rivers, formed when the sediments deposited as levees back up tributary waters
   - 56 – (fluvial/floodplain) lakes in floodplain depressions, caused by uneven aggradation during floods
   - 70 – (dystrophic) lakes in closed phytogenic basins
   - 73 – man-made dams
6. Nutrient status: oligotrophy, mesotrophy and eutrophy as given by authors, or as defined for N and P by WETZEL (1975), with status defined by the limiting nutrient, and with the limits defined as 7.5 μg/l < mesotrophic P > 20 μg/l, and 300 μg/l < mesotrophic N > 475 μg/l. Variable nutrient status occurs in some lake systems, where one lake may be oligotrophic, and another meso- or eutrophic (e.g. Ogan-Komering lakes).

Formerly known as Lagoa Ira Lalaro.

Formerly known as the Wissel lakes.

Table 3. Basic inventories of flora, molluscs, birds, fish and fisheries.

No. lake (-system)	Flora		Molluscs		Fish		Fish-eries	Bird data
	data	end.	data	end.	data	end.		
1. L. Laut Tawar	na	na	na	na	+/−	2	na	na
2. L. Toba	+/−	−	na	na	+	1	+	+/−
3. Siak Kecil lakes	+/−	−	na	na	na	na	+/−	+
4. Ogan-Komering lakes	+	−	+/−	−	+	−	+	+
5. L. Maninjau	+	−	+	−	+	1	+	+/−
6. L. Singkarak	+	−	+	−	+	1	+	+/−
7. L. Di-atas	+	−	+	−	+	1	+	−
8. L. Di-bawah	+	−	+	−	+	na	+	−
9. L. Kerinci	+	−	+	−	+	na	+	−
10. L. Ranau	+/−	na	na	na	+/−	na	+/−	na
11. Upper Kapuas lakes	+	−	+	−	+	na	+	+
12. Bangkau lakes	+	−	na	na	+	−	+	+
13. Middle Mahakam lakes	+	−	na	na	+	na	+	+/−
14. L. Rawa	+	−	na	na	na	na	na	+
15. L. Pening	+	−	+	−	+	−	+	+
16. L. Lamongan	+	−	+	−	+	−	+	+
17. L. Tondano	+/−	−	+	2	+	−	+	na
18. L. Limboto	+/−	−	+	−	+	−	+	na
19. L. Poso	na	na	+	8	+	4	+	na
20. L. Lindu	na	na	+	4	+	1	+	+
21. Tempe lakes	+	−	+	1	+	1 (?)	+	+
22. Matano-Towuti lakes	+	7	+	12	+	20+	+	+
23. L. Rawa Aopa	+/−	−	na	na	+	na	+	+
24. L. Batur	+/−	−	+	−	+	1	+	+
25. L. Buyan	+/−	−	+	−	+	1	+	na
26. L. Brantan	+/−	−	+	−	+	1	+	na
27. L. Segara-anak	+/−	na	na	na	na	na	na	na
28. L. Kelimutu	+/−	na	na	na	na	na	na	na
29. L. Surubel	na	na	na	na	na	na	na	na
30. L. Sentani	+	−	na	na	+/−	5	+/−	na
31. Enarotali lakes	+/−	na	na	na	+/−	1	+/−	na
32. Ayamaru lakes	na	na	na	na	+	3	+/−	na
33. Anggi lakes	na	na	na	na	na	na	+/−	na
34. L. Jamur	na	na	na	na	+	4	+/−	na
35. Triton lakes	na	na	na	na	+	3	na	na

data: na = data not available; + = data available; +/− = only partially recorded
endemics: na = data not available; − = no endemics known. Figures denote the number of endemics

gether comprise just over half of this group of largest lakes. Tecto-volcanic lakes (types 1–19a) are next in terms of size, comprising 40 percent of total area. Many of Irian Jaya's major lakes are calcareous solution lakes (type 43), accounting for five percent of the total area of this group of largest lakes. The remainder are dystrophic lakes of peat domes (type 70), here represented by the Siak Kecil lakes which comprise 1.3 percent of the total area. Ten of the 35 lakes recorded here are deeper than 100 metres, and six are deeper than 200 metres.

Some basic inventory information is available for most lakes, except those in the eastern part of the archipelago (Irian Jaya, Timor, Flores), and a few less accessible lakes elsewhere (Laut Tawar, Siak Kecil, Ranau, Rawa). Molluscs and birds have generally been poorly studied.

In summary, at least 14 out of the 35 lakes have been studied relatively comprehensively, while 13 are virtually undocumented and still poorly understood.

Human-induced changes in Indonesian lakes

Human-induced changes recorded for this group of 35 lakes are listed in Table 4. These changes have been placed in two categories, those affecting hydrology and water quality (e.g. dam construc-

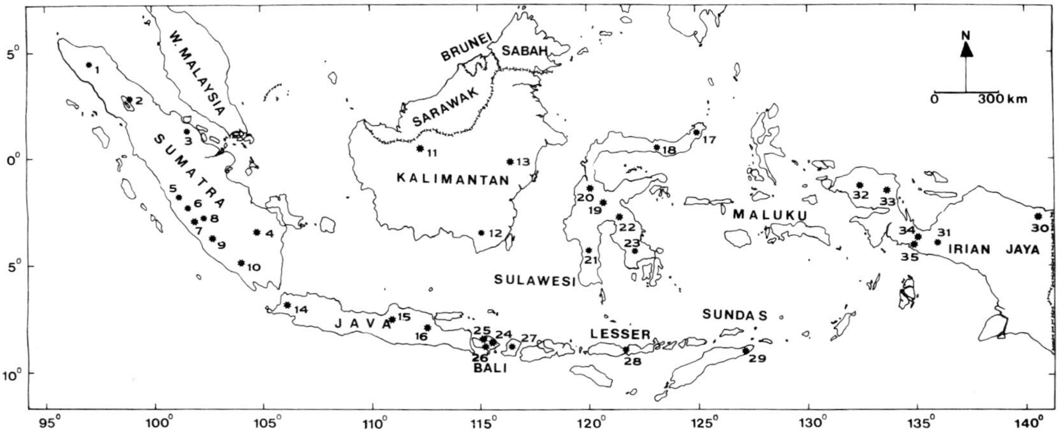

1. L.Laut Tawar
2. L.Toba
3. Siak Kecil lakes
4. Ogan-Komering lakes
5. L.Maninjau
6. L.Singkarak
7. L.Diatas
8. L.Dibawah
9. L.Kerinci
10. L.Ranau
11. Upper Kapuas lakes
12. Bangkau lakes
13. Middle Mahakam lakes
14. L.Rawa
15. L.Pening
16. L.Lamongan
17. L.Tondano
18. L.Limboto
19. L.Poso
20. L.Lindu
21. Tempe lakes
22. Matano-Towuti lakes
23. L.Rawa Aopa
24. L.Batur
25. L.Buyan
26. L.Bratan
27. L.Segara-anak
28. L.Kelimutu
29. L.Surubel
30. L.Sentani
31. Enarotali lakes
32. Ayamaru lakes
33. Anggi lakes
34. L.Jamur
35. Triton lakes

Fig. 1. Thirty-five Indonesian lake (-system).

tion and siltation), and those affecting biological aspects (e.g. weed infestation and loss of species).

Control dams have been constructed at 12 lakes and are planned for another five, while for eight lakes no information is available about possible dam construction. In eight cases dams have been constructed or planned in combination with a hydropower plant, though flood control and water resources for dry season irrigation and drinking water are ubiquitously mentioned as additional benefits. Major changes, usually widespread deforestation or conversion of forests, have occurred in the watersheds of over one-third of the lakes for which information is available, and have led to significant changes in lake hydrology. In many instances this has also led to siltation, which has become a significant problem in 25 percent of lakes for which information is available. Other forms of pollution have apparently not yet caused major problems in any of these lakes, though signs of pollution are conspicuous in about half.

In 14 lakes changes have occurred in lake flora and vegatation, and in nine cases this has been significant. For instance, clearing and burning of swamp forest has removed most of the original vegetation of the Mahakam and Ogan-Komering lakes, and similar clearing is ongoing at the Siak Kecil lakes. For 11 lakes no information is available.

Changes in hydrology and water quality are known to have led to changes in the fish fauna of 11 lakes, but in 15 cases no data is available. Exotic plants are known to have been (unwittingly) introduced in 20 lakes, or 77 percent of those sites for which information is available. In 40 percent of the cases with introduced species, weed infestation (usually of water hyacinth *Eichhornia crassipes* Solms.) has become a significant problem. In the case of fish, introducion of exotic species (see below) has been even more general a phenomenon, as this has occurred in 25 lakes, or 90 percent of all documented lakes. Loss of endemic species is rarely recorded, but is suspected in the case of fish species in four lakes. Overfishing occurs in ten out of 23 documented lakes, and in six instances this over-utilization is reportedly significant.

Apparent neglect of eastern Indonesia

Throughout its development, limnology in Indonesia has primarily focused on the western half of the archipelago. This began with the German

Table 4. Human-induced changes in 35 Indonesian lakes, and inclusion in the Indonesian Protected Areas System (PAS).

No. lake (-system)	Hydrology/Water quality[1]					Biology[2]						Inclusion[3] in PAS
	CD	HP	WA	SD	PL	FL	FN	EP	EF	LE	OF	
1. L. Laut Tawar	na	na	na	na	na	na	na	na	na	na	na	–
2. L. Toba	+	+	++	–	–	na	na	+	+	na	na	–
3. Siak Kecil lakes	–	–	++	–	–	++	na	–	–	na	+	SM
4. Ogan-Komering lakes	–	–	++	++	–	++	+	++	+	–	++	–
5. L. Maninjau	+	+	–	–	–	–	–	++	+	–	–	–*
6. L. Singkarak	+p	+p	+	+	+	+	na	+	+	na	–	–
7. L. Di-atas	+	–	–	–	+	–	–	+	+	na	–	–
8. L. Di-bawah	–	–	–	–	+	–	–	–	+	na	–	–
9. L. Kerinci	+	–	++	+	+	++	++	++	+	na	+	–
10. L. Ranau	+p	+p	na	na	na	na	na	na	na	na	na	–
11. Upper Kapuas lakes	+p	–	+	–	+	+	+	+	+	–	++	SM
12. Bangkau lakes	+	–	+	+	+	++	++	++	+	–	++	P/SM
13. Middle Mahakam lakes	–	–	++	++	+	++	++	++	+	na	++	P/CA
14. L. Rawa	+	–	++	++	na	++	+	++	na	na	–	CA
15. L. Pening	+	–	++	+	+	++	++	++	+	–	++	–
16. L. Lamongan	+	na	+	–	–	–	–	++	+	–	–	–
17. L. Tondano	na	na	+	++	na	+	na	+	+	na	+	–
18. L. Limboto	–	–	++	++	+	++	++	+	+	na	na	–
19. L. Poso	+	+	na	–	–	–	+	+	+	s	+	–
20. L. Lindu	+	+p	–	–	–	–	+	–	+	s	–	TN
21. Tempe lakes	+p	–	++	++	++	++	++	+	+	s	++	P/SM
22. Matano-Towuti lakes	+	+	+	–	+	+	–	+	+	s	–	TW**
23. L. Rawa Aopa	+	–	+	–	–	+	na	+	+	na	–	TN
24. L. Batur	–	–	–	–	–	–	–	–	+	–	–	P/TW +SM
25. L. Buyan	–	–	+	–	–	–	–	+	+	–	–	CA
26. L. Bratan	–	–	na	–	+	–	–	+	–	–	–	CA
27. L. Segara-anak	–	–	na	na	na	na	na	na	na	na	na	–
28. L. Kelimutu	–	–	–	–	–	–	–	–	–	–	–	P/TW
29. L. Surubel	na	na	na	na	na	na	na	na	na	na	na	–
30. L. Sentani	+p	+p	na	–	–	+?	na	++	+	na	na	–
31. Enarotali lakes	na	na	+	na	na	+	+	–	+	na	na	CA
32. Ayamaru lakes	na	na	+?	na	na	na	na	na	+	na	+	–
33. Anggi lakes	na	na	na	na	na	na	na	na	+	na	na	HL
34. L. Jamur	na	na	na	na	na	na	na	na	na	na	na	HL
35. Triton lakes	na	na	na	na	na	na	na	na	na	na	na	–

na = not available

1. Hydrology and water quality:
   - CD = control dam at outlet or major inlet (p = planned)
   - HP = hydropower plant at or near outlet (p = planned)
   - WA = changes in water regime due to deforestation (+ = occurred; ++ = significant)
   - SD = siltation lake (+ = occurred; ++ = significant)
   - PL = eutrophication (+ = evident; ++ = significant)
   - ? = possible
2. Biological changes:
   - FL = changes in the original flora/vegetation (+ = occurred; ++ = significant)
   - FN = changes in the fauna (+ = occurred; ++ = significant)
   - EP = exotic plants introduced (+ = occurred; ++ = weed problem)
   - EF = exotic fish introduced (+ = occurred; ++ = problem)
   - LE = loss of endemic species (s = suspected; + = occurred)
   - OF = overfishing (+ = occurred; ++ = significant)
   - ? = possible

Sunda Expedition in 1928–1929, which concentrated on the lakes of Sumatra, Java and Bali (RUTTNER 1932, STEENIS et al. 1933, FILARSZKY 1934, THIENEMANN 1957). Later emphasis was on supporting fisheries (WIDJAJA 1980) in Sumatra, Kalimantan, Java and Sulawesi, and this work was chiefly carried out by the Inland Fisheries Research Institute (BIJLEVELD et al. 1940, HOEKS 1941, VAAS & SCHUURMAN 1949, EELAART 1950, VAAS 1952, 1956, VAAS et al. 1953; SANITA 1973, 1974, ARIFIN 1978, WARDOYO 1978, WARDOYO & THANA 1978, THANA & WARDOYO 1980, THANA et al. 1980, SIMANJUNTAK 1981, SUNYATA 1981, ARIFIN et al. 1982). By the late 1970s a number of institutes were involved with limnological investigations, most notably BIOTROP (Bogor), and the Faculty of Fisheries of the Agricultural University (IPB, Bogor). In spite of this, the need for further promotion of limnology persisted as more concerted efforts covering broader fields were considered necessary (WIDJAJA 1980). The Institute of Limnology was established in Bogor in 1986, and its further development will be dealt with in another paper in this volume (NONTJI 1993).

The focus in the development of limnology on western Indonesia partly explains the paucity of data from the eastern half of Indonesia. These areas were and still are less populated and less important for fisheries, which has been a major force in initiating studies in other locations. Many studies have also been carried out by the Ministry of Public Works (PU), to obtain data pertaining to water resources for irrigation, hydro-electicity or potable water (e.g. PPPP-PU 1986). Obviously, their studies are also limited to areas with higher population pressure, and thus appear to avoid the eastern part of the country.

Threats

The human-induced changes listed in Table 4 indicate that major changes have occurred in most of the selected lakes, and that in many instances this has affected water quality and lake biota. Ten of the 19 tecto-volcanic lakes (53 %) already have dams (existing or under construction) at their outlet river. These affect lake hydrology and fish migration, as water levels are often raised and usually no allowances are made to facilitate fish movements. A second dam under construction in the Matano-Towuti lake system in South Sulawesi, for instance, is expected to raise waterlevels and seriously reduce the area of littoral habitat that harbours the many endemic fish, molluscs and plants (GIESEN et al. 1990). Siltation caused by enhanced erosion in lake drainage basins has affected five out of eight floodplain lakes (63 %), and is known to be causing significant problems in four cases. In at least three lakes (Tempe, Ogan-Komering, Limboto) siltation has altered lake vegetation, hampers lake transport, and is affecting important fisheries. Several solutions under consideration to alleviate these problems are likely to cause even more disruption; these include dredging and diversion-dam construction in L. Tempe; (JICA 1979, 1980 b, MUSTAFA 1980), and outright reclamation in Lake Ogan-Komering (GIESEN & SOEKOTJO 1991 b).

Lake biota has been much affected in most of the 35 lakes, and the most common agents of change are burning or clearing of lake-edge vegetation, the unwitting introduction of exotic weeds, and the deliberate introduction of exotic fish species. Lake-edge clearing is a common feature of floodplain lakes, where annual deposits of silt often result in fertile lake banks. Very little remains of the original vegetation on the perimeter of the Mahakam, Ogan-Komering, Tempe, Enarotali and Bangkau lakes. An exception in this group of floodplain lakes are the Upper Kapuas lakes in West Kalimantan, where a combination of deep annual flooding and poor soil fertility has discouraged clearing. The most commonly introduced exotic weeds that significantly affect lake ecology are *Eichhornia crassipes* (Water hyacinth), *Salvinia molesta* D. S. MITCHELL (Kariba weed) and *Mimosa*

Continuation notes to Table 4.

3. PAS = Protected Areas System of the Indonesian Directorate General of Forest Protection and Nature Conservation (PHPA). Status abbreviations are:

HW = Tourist Reserve	SM = Wildlife Reserve	CA = Strict Nature Reserve
TN = National Park	HB = Hunting Reserve	P = Proposed
HL = Protection Forest		

* surrounding forest is SM and HL

** surrounding forest is HL

pigra L. (Giant mimosa). Water hyacinth and Kariba weed shade out submerged vegetation, deplete oxygen levels and compete with indigenous plant species, while Giant mimosa creates impenetrable thickets.

The introduction of exotic fish species has a long history in Indonesia and is, for instance, considered to date back centuries ago in Sulawesi (Whitten et al. 1988), Java and Lombok (Lowe-McConnell 1987). Fish introduction has been a part of the programme of the Indonesian Fisheries Service (Dinas Perikanan) at least since the 1920s (Vaas & Schuurman 1949, Vaas 1952, 1956, Vaas et al. 1953, Hickling 1961), and has greatly boosted fisheries production in some lakes, such as Lake Tempe (Hickling 1961). Simultaneously, however, this practise has resulted in the occurrence of exotics in 90 percent of all documented lakes, and the ousting of indigenous species (Whitten et al. 1988, Giesen et al. 1990). Initially the main introduced species were *Cyprinus carpio* C. V. (common carp.), *Helostoma temmincki* C. V. (an anabantid), *Puntius gonionotus* (Blkr) (silver carp) and *Trichogaster pectoralis* (Regan) (an anabantid) (Schuurman 1949; Vaas 1952, 1956, Vaas et al. 1953, Hickling 1961, Vaas & Giesen 1987, Whitten et al. 1988, Giesen et al. 1990) while in the last two decades tilapia (*Oreochromis mossambicus* (Peters) and *O. niloticus* (Linn) have become more widespread (Whitten et al. 1987, 1988). This policy has resulted in the possible extinction of a number of endemic fish species in Lake Poso and Lake Lindu, and will soon perhaps have similar effects in the Matano-Towuti lakes (Whitten et al. 1987).

Overfishing is significant in a quarter of the documented lakes, and has resulted in a decline of production and possible local extinction of economically important species. The latter has been documented for the Ogan-Komering lakes in South Sumatra (Danielsen & Verheugt 1990, Giesen 1991), the Upper Kapuas lakes in West Kalimantan (Giesen 1987), the Bangkau lakes in South Kalimantan (Chairuddin 1990), and for the valuable and endangered ornamental species *Scleropages formosus* (Müller & Schlegel), the Asian Bonytongue or Asian Arowana (Matsumura & Millikan 1984, Giesen 1987). The usual cause of overfishing is population pressure, but specific practices, such as the annual auctioning of fishing rights in the Ogan-Komering lakes (Danielsen & Verheugt 1990, Giesen & Soekotjo 1991 b), occasionally aggravate the situation. Part of the overfishing problem may be attributed to a dual approach by the Fisheries Service. At a local level, for instance, overfishing may be acknowledged and fishing reserves established by district Fisheries Service staff to preserve stocks (Chairuddin 1990, Giesen et al. 1990; Giesen & Soekotjo 1991 a, 1991 b), while at the same time five-year-plans (REPELITAs) formulated by provincial Fisheries Service target large annual increases in fishery production of the same waters.

Mitigation of the impacts of development

It is unlikely that the present trends of human-induced changes will alter in the near future, although positive shifts are occurring. Legislation concerning environment has been made available since the early 1980s, entitled Basic Provisions for the Management of the Living Environment. This states, among other things, that: 1) protection shall be based on environmental standards; 2) Environmental Impact Assessments (EIAs) will be required for new developments, and 3) there should be overall and sectoral prevention and abatement of pollution (Alabaster 1986). However, these regulations still await effective implementation. For example, a number of dams at lake outlets are under construction without any prior assessment of their environmental impact (notably Lake Ranau and L. Matano). Pollution abatement is also slowly being enforced. For instance, in June 1989, 403 polluting companies throughout Indonesia pledged to abide by government requirements, and were given one year for implementation. By August 1991 only 33 percent had taken any effective action, while 22 percent had ignored the government's call altogether (Jakarta Post 1991). Solutions considered for mitigating environmental problems may bring new dilemmas. For instance, desktop solutions to siltation problems generally involve high-tech engineering work, and often concentrate only marginally on de-forestation, which is almost always the root of the problem (Jica 1979, 1980 a, 1980 b, Mustafa 1980). Reportedly, about 1.3 percent of Indonesia's land surface is heavily eroded, and the figure for densely populated Java may even be as high as six percent (Alabaster 1986).

The inclusion of lakes in the Indonesian Protected Areas System (Table 4) does not appear to have had any beneficial effect on their management. Partly, this is because numerous human-induced changes occurred before areas were gazetted by the Indonesian Directorate General of Forest Protection and Nature Conservation (PHPA) (e.g. Enarotali; PETOCZ 1989), though part of the problem is undoubtedly the lack of staff and funding, which has led to low staffing levels in the field. Further complications are that traditional fishing is allowed under certain protection categories; in some instances none of the watershed is included in the gazetted area; and, lastly, lake areas are often disputed by the Fisheries Service. Under present definitions, fish are not considered "wildlife", and only receive PHPA protection if they are listed as vulnerable or endangered.

To prevent further loss of lake resources, their importance to fisheries, tourism, biodiversity and as sources of potable and irrigation water should be more widely recognized, and taken into consideration when designing development projects. Lake resources are recognized by individual departments and other government bodies, but an overview of these assets is apparently lost in regional planning processes, where decisions often reflect the current limitations of cross-sectoral planning. Two examples illustrate this. Firstly, an irrigation project designed for the Komering river region in South Sumatra is expected to divert almost 80 percent of river water in the dry season. This is likely to affect the livelihood of thousands of families in the Ogan-Komering lake system who are dependent on these waters for fisheries, drinking water and transport. Apparently in an attempt to mitigate negative impacts, draining and converting the lake area to agriculture is being considered, but as potential acid sulphate soils occur throughout the region this would likely cause new problems (GIESEN & SOEKOTJO 1991 b).

A second example is Lake Tempe, South Sulawesi, where recent plans have been made to construct barriers around the lake to prevent flooding of lake-edge agricultural fields (pers. comm. Public Works, Ujung Pandang, 1991). Agriculture is only of marginal importance, as most villagers are dependent on fisheries from this highly productive lake. Fisheries are dependent on lake-edge vegetation to maintain productivity (GIESEN 1990, GIESEN et al. 1990), and this is bound to be disrupted. Furthermore, the lake is becoming increasingly important to tourism (GIESEN 1990, GIESEN et al. 1990), and is of international importance to conservation as it is visited annually by more than 20,000 migratory waterfowl (BALTZER 1990). Conservation, tourism and fisheries are incompatible with the construction under consideration. Furthermore, Tempe's lake-edge agriculture is highly productive at present because of the annual deposition of silt, which will no longer continue if barriers are constructed. Obviously, more cross-sectoral planning and functional and resource-economic evaluation is required to avoid further resource depletion.

In the short term, basic inventories and ecological studies are required so that baseline data is sufficiently available to assess the regional importance of lakes and their biota, and provide some framework for EIAs. These studies should primarily cover lakes in Indonesia's eastern region and certain neglected taxa such as molluscs and birds. Such studies should be complemented with increasing the accessibility of existing data, much of which was published some time ago in journals with limited availability, and often in languages such as Dutch or German. Simultaneously, data should be evaluated, and a national strategy for a wise use of Indonesia's lakes and lake resources formulated, in order to curb further loss of natural assets.

References

ALABASTER, J. S., 1986: Review of the state of water pollution affecting inland fisheries in Southeast Asia. – *FAO Fisheries Technical Paper No.* **260**, Rome: 25 pp.

ALLEN, G. R., 1991: Personal communication.

ALLEN, G. R. & BOESEMAN, M. 1982: A collection of freshwater fishes from Western New Guinea with descriptions of two new species (Gobiidae and Eleotridae). – *Rec. West. Aust. Mus.* **10**: 67–103.

Anonymous, 1981: Lore Lindu National Park management plan 1981–1986. – World Wildlife Fund, Bogor, Indonesia.

ARIFIN, Z., 1978: Several aspects about fish trapping in the waters of Lubuk Lampan (Beberapa aspek tentang penangkapan ikan di perairan Lubuk Lampam). – Lembaga Penelitian Perikanan Air Tawar, Palembang (Inland Fisheries Res. Inst.), internal report: 36 pp. (In Indonesian).

ARIFIN, Z. & ONDARA, 1982: Results of fisheries in the waters of Lubuk Lampam (Pengelolaan perikanan di perairan Lubuk Lampam). – *Pros. S. Perikanan Perairan Umum, Bogor* **1**: 171–185. (In Indonesian).

BALEN, S. VAN, 1991: Draft report on the avifauna of Siak Kecil, Sungai Rokan and Sungai Bangkung, Riau, Sumatra. – Project to improve wetland management and conservation in Indonesia, part I, Sumatra. PHPA/Asian Wetland Bureau Sumatra Wetland Project Interim Publication No. 22.

BALGOOIJ, M. M. J. VAN & TANTRA, I. G. M., 1986: The vegetation in two areas in Sulawesi, Indonesia: 61 pp. – Bulletin Penelitian Hutan (Forest Research Bulletin), of the Pusat Penelitan dan Pengembangan Hutan (Foresty Research and Development Center), Bogor, Indonesia. Special edition.

BALTZER, M. C., 1990: A report on the wetland avifauna of South Sulawesi. – *Kukila* **5**: 27–55.

BEMMELEN, R. W. VAN, 1949: The geology of Indonesia, Vol. **1A**. Geology of Indonesia and adjacent archipelagoes: 732 pp. – Government Printing Office, the Hague.

BIJLEVELD, R. & MARTOATMODJO, R. S. 1940: Fishstocks and fisheries in West Koetai (East Borneo) (Vischstand en visserij in West Koetai (Oost Borneo)). – Landbouw (Landbouwkundig Tijdschrift voor Nederlandsch-Indie), Buitenzorg, Java **16**: 516–549. (In Dutch).

BOESEMAN, M., 1963: Notes on the fishes of Western New Guinea I. – *Zool. Meded.* 38: 221–242.

– 1964: Notes on the fishes of Western New Guinea III. The freshwater shark of Jamoer Lake. – *Zool. Meded.* **40**: 9–22.

BOULENGER, G. A. 1897: An account of the freshwater fishes collected by Drs. P. and F. Sarasin. – *Proc. zool. Soc. Lond.* **13**: 426–429.

CARLANDER, K. D., 1980: Water Hyacinth and overfishing problems on an Indonesian Lake. – *Proc. Iowa Acad. Sci.* **87**: 20–22.

CHAIRUDDIN, G. T., 1990: Fisheries of the Sungai Negara Wetlands: 173–199. – Proc. Workshop on Conservation of Sungai Negara wetlands, Barito basin, South Kalimantan, Banjarbaru, 6–8 March 1989. PHPA/AWB-Indonesia, Bogor, Indonesia.

CHRISTENSEN, M. S., MULU, A. & AKBAR, A., 1986: Technical report. Investigations into the fisheries of the Middle Mahakam Area, 1986. – Technical Cooperation for Area Development Kutasi District, East Kalimantan. Samarinda, Indonesia, Report No. **86**: 161 pp.

COERT, J. H., 1934: Excursions in east Java, 2. The Rawah Bening (Kediri) (Excursies in Oost-Java 2. De Rawah Bening (Kediri)). – *De Tropische Natuur* **23**: 6–14, 26–31. (In Dutch).

DANIELSEN, F. & VERHEUGT, W. J. M., 1990: Integrating conservation and land-use planning. Coastal region of South Sumatra: 210 pp. – PHPA/AWB-Indonesia, Bogor, Indonesia.

Direktorat Perlindungan Dan Pengawetan Alam, 1977: Survey report for measuring the forest unit Lake Matano – Lake Towuti in South Sulawesi Province. (Laporan survai penjajagan areal kelompok hutan Danau Matano – Danau Towuti di Propinsi Sulawesi Selatan): 42 pp. – PPA, Bogor, Indonesia. (In Indonesian).

– 1981: A detailed survey of the proposed Wildlife Reserve Lake Tempe and Environs, including Lake Lapongpakka (Survai detail areal Cadangan Suaka Margasatwa Danau Tempe dan sekitarnya, termasuk didalamnya Danau Lapongpakka, 18,297 ha): 40 pp. – Bogor, Indonesia. (In Indonesian).

DJADJASASMITA, M., 1972: A list of the freshwater molluscs of Sulawesi (= Celebes). Unpubl. ms.

– 1975: On the species of the genus *Corbicula* from Celebes, Indonesian (Mollusca, Corbiculidae). – *Bull. Zool. Mus.* **4**: 83–88.

EELAART, A. VAN DEN, 1950: The Tempe lakes area. Lakes and swamps in the Wadjo, Soppeng, Sidenreng and Bone area, South Sulawesi (Daereh danau-danau Tempe. Danau-danau dan rawa-rawa didaerah Wadjo, Soppeng, Sidenreng dan Bone, Sulawesi Selatan). – *Berita Perikanan* (*Visserijnieuws*) **2**: 3–4 + 26–27. (In Indonesian).

ENDERT, F. H., 1927: Floristic report of the Mid-east Borneo Expedition, 1925 (Floristisch verslag van de Midden Oost Borneo Expeditie, 1925). – *Indisch Comite voor Wetenschappelijke Onderzoekingen, Batavia, Java*: 200–312. (In Dutch).

– 1932: The Nature Reserve Danau in Bantam. (Het natuurmonument Danau in Bantam). – *Tectona* **25**: 963–986. (In Dutch).

FILARSZKY, F., 1934: The Characeae of the German Limnological Sunda Expedition (Die Characeen der Deutschen Limnologischen Sunda-Expedition). – *Arch. Hydrobiol. Suppl.* **12**: 705–726.

GAFFER, A. K., RIFAI, S. A., UTOMO, A. D. & ADJIE, S., 1988: Limnological characteristics of the Komering river, South Sumatra (Karakteristik limnologi S. Komering, Sumatera Selatan). – *Bull. Penel. Perik. Darat* **7**: 66–74. (In Indonesian, with English summary).

GERLACH, L. W. C. 1881: Travels to the lake region of the Kapoeas in Borneo's western regency (Reis naar het meerengebied van den Kapoeas in Borneo's Westerafdeeling). – *Bijdragen tot de Land-, Taal- en Volkenkunde van Nederlandsch-Indie* **5**: 285–322.

GIESEN, W., 1987: Danau Sentarum Wildlife Reserve. Inventory, ecology and management guidelines: 284 pp. – World Wildlife Fund/PHPA, Bogor, Indonesia.

– 1990: Vegetation of the Negara River Basin. – Proc. Workshop on Conservation of Sungai Negara wetlands, Barito Basin, South Kalimantan, Banjarbaru, 6–8 March 1989: 1–51. – PHPA/AWB-Indonesia, Bogor, Indonesia.

– 1990: The importance of wetlands in South Sulawesi. – *Prosiding Seminar "Keterpaduan antara konservasi dan tata guna lahan basah di Sulawesi Selatan"*, Ujung Pandang, 1–2 March 1990: 15–45.

GIESEN, W., BALTZER, M. & BARUADI, R., 1990: Integrating conservation with land-use development in wetlands of South Sulawesi, Indonesia: 240 pp. – AWB-Indonesia/PHPA, Bogor, Indonesia.

GIESEN, W. & SOEKOTJO, 1991 a: Draft report of Lake Kerinci and the wetlands of Kerinci Seblat N.P., Sumatra. – Project to improve wetland management and conservation in Indonesia, part I, Sumatra. *PHPA/Asian Wetland Bureau Sumatra Wetland Project Interim. Publication No.* **6**: 84 pp.

– – 1991 b: Draft report of the Ogan-Komering Lebaks, South Sumatra. – Project to improve wetland management and conservation in Indonesia, part I, Sumatra. *PHPA/Asian Wetland Bureau Sumatra Wetland Project Interim Publication No.* **8:** 75 pp.

– – 1991 c: Draft report on the Lakes of West Sumatra. – Project to improve wetland management and conservation in Indonesia, part I, Sumatra. *PHPA/Asian Wetland Bureau Sumatra Wetland Project Interim Publication No.* **16**: 46 pp.

GOELTENBOTH, F., 1978: The Rawa Pening Lake – Background information, facts and problems. – *Proc. First Seminar Aquat. Biol. & Aquat. Managm. of Rawa Pening Lake, Salatiga, Indonesia:* 4–19.

GOELTENBOTH, F. & BELSCHNER, D., 1978: The ecology of the Rawa Pening Lake I. Contribution to the knowledge of some physical properties. – *Proc. First Seminar Aquat. Biol. & Aquat. Managm. of Rawa Pening Lake, Salatiga, Indonesia:* 4–19.

GREEN, J., CORBET, S. A., WATTS, E. OEY, B. L., 1976: Ecological studies on Indonesian lakes. Over-turn and restratification of Ranu Lamongan. – *J. Zool., Lond.* **180**: 315–354.

GREEN, J., CORBET, S. A., WATTS, E. & OEY, B. L., 1978: Ecological studies on Indonesian lakes. The montane lakes of Bali. – *J. Zool., Lond.* **186**: 15–38.

HARDENBERG, J. D. F., 1935/36: On a collection of freshwater fishes from the estuary and the lower and middle courses of the river Kapuas (W. Borneo). – *Treubia* **15**: 225–254.

HICKLING, C. F., 1961: Tropical Inland Fisheries: 287 pp. – Wiley, New York.

HISBI, D., 1990: Water quality of the Sungai Negara Wetlands. – Proc. Workshop on Conservation of Sungai Negara wetlands, Barito basin, South Kalimantan, Banjarbaru, 6–8 March 1989. 255–270. PHPA/AWB-Indonesia, Bogor, Indonesia.

HOEKS, B. M., 1941: Causes of the rise in fisheries production in Lake Tempe (South Celebes) (Oorzaken van de stijging van de vischproductie in het Tempemeer (Zuid Celebes)). – *Landbouw (Landbouwkundig Tijdschrift voor Nederlandsch-Indie)* **17**: 1–12. (In Dutch).

HUTCHINSON, G. E., 1975: A treatise on limnology. Vol. I. Geography, physics, and chemistry. Part 1. Geography and physics of lakes: 540 pp. – Wiley Interscience, New York.

IMAKI, A., KAWAMOTO, A. & SUZUKI, A., 1978. A collection of freshwater fishes collected from the Kapuas river, West Kalimantan, Indonesia. – The Institute for Breeding Research, Tokyo Agricultural University, Japan.

IUCN, 1985: The Corbett Action Plan for Protected Areas of the Indomalayan Realm: 23 pp. – IUCN Commission on National Parks and Protected Areas. Prepared during 25th Working Session, 4–8 Feb. 1985, Corbett National Park, India.

JAKARTA POST, 1991: Anti-pollution drive gets little support. – Vol. **9** (88), 9 August 1991: p. 1.

JICA, 1979: Draft final report on master plan study for the Central South Sulawesi water resources development project. Supporting Report (Volume 3), Part 3, Flood Control. – 126 pp. Japan International Cooperation Agency, Tokyo.

– 1980 a: Master Plan for the Central South Sulawesiwater resources development project. Main Report: 261 pp. – Japan International Cooperation Agency, Tokyo.

– 1980 b: Master Plan study for the Central South Sulawesi water resources development project. Supporting Report (Volume 1), Part 1, Hydrology. – 108 pp. Japan International Cooperation Agency, Tokyo.

KLEPPER, O., 1990: An overview of the hydrology of the Sungai Negara Wetlands in relation to their ecology. – *Proc. Workshop on Conservation of Sungai Negara wetlands. Barito Basin, South Kalimantan, Banjarbaru, 6–8 March 1989. PHPAS/AWB-Indonesia, Bogor, Indonesia*: 229–254.

KOTTELAT, M., 1990: Synopsis of the endangered Buntingi (Osteoichthyses: Adrianichthyidae and Oryziidae) of Lake Poso, Central Sulawesi, Indonesia, with a new reproductive guild and descriptions of three new species. – *Ichthyol. Explor. Freshwaters* **1**: 49–67.

– 1990: The ricefishes (Oryziidae) of the Malili Lakes, Sulawesi, Indonesia, with description of a new species. – *Ichthyol. Explor. Freshwaters* **1**: 151–166.

– 1990: Sailfin silversides (Pisces: Telmatherinidae) of Lakes Towuti, Mahalona and Wawontoa (Sulawesi, Indonesia) with descriptions of two new genera and two new species. – *Ichtyhol. Explor. Freshwaters.* **1**: 227–246.

KRAKATAU, STEEL, P. T. & SEAMEO-BIOTROP, 1986: Final report of the study on the protection of the water source Rawa Danau, Serang Regency (Laporan akhir penelitian usaha pelestarian sumber air Rawa Danau Kabupaten Serang). – South-East Asian Regional Center for Tropical Biology, Bogor, Indonesia, report no. BIOTROP/TAgP/86/611. 157 pp. (In Indonesian).

KSDA, 1985: Assessment of inventory and problems in the Rawa Danau Nature Reserve (Penilaian potensi dan permasalahan di Cagar Alam Rawa Danau): 22 pp. – Balai Konservasi Sumber Daya Alam III, Ditjen Perlindungan Hutan dan Pelestarian Alam, Departemen Kehutanan, Bandung, Indonesia. (In Indonesian).

LOWE-MCCONNELL, R. H., 1987: Ecological studies in tropical fish communities: 382 pp. – Cambridge Tropical Biology Series, Cambridge Univ. Press, Cambridge.

MATSUMURA, S. & MILLIKAN, T., 1984: The Japanese trade in bonytongue and CITES-listed fish. – *Traffic Bull.* **6**: 42–50.

MEIJERINK, A. M. J., et al., 1988: Downstream damage caused by upstream land degradation in the Komering river basin. – *ITC Journal, (Enschede, The Netherlands)* **7**: 96–108.

MORLEY, R. J., FLENLEY, J. R. & KARDIN, M. K. 1973: Preliminary notes on the stratigraphy and vegetation of the swamps and small lakes of the central Sumatran highlands. – *Sumatra Res. Bull.* **2**: 51–61.

Mustafa, M., 1980: Observations on the shallowing of Lake Tempe and several alternatives for countering this (Tinjauan pendangkalan Danau Tempe dan beberapa alternatif penanggulang-annya): 24 pp. – Pusat Penelitian dan Pengembangan Sumberdaya Alam dan Lingkungan Hidup Universitas Hasanuddin (PSL-UNHAS). (In Indonesian).

Nakano, K., Watanabe, T., Usman R. & Syabuddin, 1987: A fundamental study of overall conservation of terrestrial and freshwater ecosystems in a montane region of Western Sumatra: vegetation, land-use and water quality. *Mem. Kagoshima Univ. Res. Center S. Pac.* **8**: 87–124.

NIPPON KOEI CO. LTD., 1986: Upper Komering Irrigation Project Design Report Volume 1, Main Report. Ministry of Public Works, Jakarta.

Nontji, A, 1994: Status of limnology in Indonesia. – *Mitt. Internat. Verein Limnol.* **24**: 95–113.

Ondara, 1969: Report of fisheries survey of lake Toba (Laporan survey perikanan di Danau Toba). Research Report No. 3, Lembaga Penelitian Perikanan Darat (Inland Fisheries Research Institute), Palembang, Indonesia: 18 pp. Also printed at the Lembaga Penelitan Perikanan Darat, Bogor, as report no. 6/1974. (In Indonesian).

Ondara & Samuel, 1987: Preliminary study of aquatic plants at Lubuk Lampam, South Sumatra (Penelitian pendahulanan tumbuh-tumbuhan di Lubuk Lampam, Sumatra Selatan). – *Bull. Penelit. Perik. Darat* **6**: 48–52. (In Indonesian, with English summary).

Petocz, R. G., 1989: Conservation and development in Irian Jaya. A strategy for rational resource utilization. 218 pp. E. J. Brill Publ., Leiden, New York.

Polak, B., 1949: Report of a visit to the Kapuas and the Kapuas lakes, 18 September – 30 October 1949 (Verslag ener tournee naar de Kapuas en Kapuasmeren, 18 September – 30 October 1949): 32 pp. – Internal report, Soils Institute, Agricultural Research Station, Bogor, Indonesia (Bodemkundig Instituut, Algemeen Proefstation voor de Landbouw, Bogor). (In Dutch).

PPPP-PU, 1986: Water quality and hydrobiological study of lakes in West Sumatra (Penelitian kualitas air dan hidrobiologi danau-danau di Sumatera Barat). Pusat Penelitian dan Pengembangan Pengairan, Departemen Pekerjaan Umum (Public Works Dept.), Bandung, Indonesia: 32 pp. (In Indonesian).

PSL UNIVERSITAS ANDALAS, 1984: Study of water and aquatic biota in Lake Singkarak, Lake Maninjau, Lake Diatas and Lake Dibwah, West Sumatra Province (Penelitian air dan biota akuatik Danau Singkarak, Danau Maninjau, Danau Diatas dan Danau Dibawah Propinsi Sumatera Barat). – Pusat Studi Lingkungan (Environmental Study Center), Universitas Andalas, Padang, Indonesia: 122 pp. (In Indonesian).

PSL UNIVERSITAS HASANUDDIN? 1981: Quality of the Lake Tempe ecosystem, and it's development (Mutu ekosistem Danau Tempe dan pengembangannya). – Pusat Studi Lingkungan, University of Hasanuddin, Ujung Pandang, South Sulawesi, Indonesia. 85 pp. (In Indonesian).

REPPPROT, 1986: Review of phase 1 results Irian Jaya. – Regional Physical Planning Programme for Transmigration, ODA, for Gov. Indonesia, Min. Transmigration, 2 volumes + 3 series of 1:250,000 scale maps. 502 pp.

– 1988: Review of phase 1 results Sumatra. – Regional Physical Planning Programme for Transmigration, ODA, for Gov. Indonesia, Min. Transmigration, 2 volumes + 3 series of 1:250,000 scale maps: 359 & 482 pp, respectively.

– 1987: Review of phase 1 results East and South Kalimantan. – Regional Physical Planning Programme for Transmigration, ODA, for Gov. Indonesia. Min. Transmigration, 2 volumes + 3 series of 1:250,000 scale maps.

– 1988: Review of phase 1 results Sulawesi. – Regional Physical Planning Programme for Transmigration, ODA, for Gov. Indonesia, Min. Transmigration, 2 volumes + 3 series of 1:250,000 scale maps.

– 1989: Review of phase 1 results Java & Bali. Regional Physical Planning Programme for Transmigration, ODA, for Gov. Indonesia, Min. Transmigration, 2 volumes + 3 series of 1:250,000 scale maps.

Rudin, W. F. 1935: About wildlife stocks in the Ranau area (Over den wildstand in het Ranaugebied). – *De Tropische Natuur* **24**: 125–130 + 151–156. (In Dutch).

Ruttner, F., 1931: Hydrographic and hydrochemical observations on Java, Sumatra and Bali. (Hydrographische und hydrochemische Beobachtungen auf Java, Sumatra und Bali.) – *Arch. Hydrobiol. Suppl.* **VIII**, *Tropische Binnengewässer*: 197–454.

– 1932: Lake studies in the Netherlands-Indies. Some results of the German Limnological Sunda Expedition (Merenonderzoek in Nederlandsch Indie. Eenige resultaten der Duitsche Limnologische Soenda-Expeditie). – *De Tropische Natuur* **21**: 151–157 + 178–184. (In Dutch).

Sanita, A. S. 1973: Survey report of the fisheries of Lake Lindu and Lake Poso (Laporan survey perikanan Danau Lindu dan Poso). – Lembaga Penelitian Perikanan Darat (Inland Fisheries Research Institute), Bogor. (In Indonesian).

– 1974: Several limnological aspects about Lake Towuti, Lake Matana and Lake Mahalona (South Sulawesi) (Beberapa aspek limnologi tentang Danau Towuti, Danau Matana dan Danau Mahalona (Sulawesi Selatan)). – *Lembaga Penelitian Perikanan Darat (Inland Fisheries Research Insti-*

tute), Bogor, Indonesia, Report no. **27**: 21 pp. (In Indonesian).

SCHOPHUYS, H. J., 1936: The Barito Basin. Agricultural overview and extension. (Het stroomgebied van de Barito. Landbouwkundige kenschets en landbouwvoorlichting): 150 pp. – PhD thesis, Veenman Publ., Wageningen, The Netherlands: (In Dutch).

SCHUILING, R., 1903: The Upper Kapoeas lake basin (De Boven Kapoeas meervlakte). – *Tijdschrift voor Geschiedenis, Land- en Volkenkunde* **18**: 42–55. (In Dutch).

SILVIUS, M. J. et al. 1987: The Indonesian wetland inventory. A preliminary complication of information on wetlands of Indonesia, 2 volumes. – PHPA, AWB/INTERWADER, EDWIN, Bogor, Indonesia: 121 & 268 pp., respectively.

SIMANJUNTAK, B. T. H., 1981: Present status of open water fisheries in Central Sulawesi (Status perikanan perairan umum di Sulawesi Tengah). – *Prosiding seminar perikanan perairan umum, Jakarta, 19–21 August 1981, Badan Penelitian dan Pengembanan Pertanian, Pusat Penelitian dan Pengembanan Perikanen:* 135–139 (In Indonesian, with English abstract).

SOERJANI, M., 1976: Results of a study on problems and control of weeds in the waters of Rawa Pening, Final Report 1975–1976. (Hasil penelitian masalah dan pengendalian tumbuhan pengganggu air Rawa Pening, Laporan akhir 1975–1976). – SEAMEO-BIOTROP Regional Centre for Tropical Biology & Departemen PUTL, No. Doc. BIOTROP/TP/76/208: 20 pp. (In Indonesian).

– 1981: Utilizing aquatic weeds for different purposes in Lake Kerinci (Pemanfaatan gulma air sebagai bagian dalam pengelolaan Danau Kerinci): 33 pp. – Pusat Studi Lingkungan Univ. Indonesia & Ditjen Pengairan Dep. PU. (In Indonesian).

SOETIKNO, 1981: Present status of open water fisheries in West Kalimantan (Status perikanan perairan umum Kalimantan Barat). – *Prosiding seminar perikanan perairan umum, Jakarta, 19–21 August 1981, Badan Penelitian dan Pengembanan Pertanian, Pusat Penelitian dan Pengembanan Perikanan:* 107–114. (In Indonesian, with English abstract).

STEENIS, C. G. G. J., VAN, 1933–38: Lake Danoe. Report on a survey of the nature reserve Lake Danone or the Danoe swamp in Bantam (Het Danoe-meer. Rapport van een dienstreis naar het natuurmonument Danoe-meer of Danoe-moeras in Bantam). – *Drie Jaren Indisch Natuurleven, Buitenzorg, Nederlandsch-Indie:* 214–233. (In Dutch).

STEENIS, C. G. G. J. VAN & RUTTNER, F., 1933: The Pteridophytes and Phanerogams of the German Limnological Sunda Expedition (Die Pteridophyten und Phanerogamen der Deutschen Limnologischen Sunda-Expedition). *Arch. Hydrobiol. Suppl.* **11**: 231–387.

STEHN, C. E., 1939: The new bathymetric map of lake Toba (North Sumatra) of Drost and Bekkering (De nieuwe dieptekaart van het Tobameer (Noord-Sumatra – van Drost & Bekking). *De Ingenieur in Nederlandsch-Indie, IV. Mijnbouw en geologie, "De Mijningenieur"* **6**: 121–126. (In Dutch, with English summary).

SUKARWO, P., 1991: Analysis of vegetation of aquatic weeds in Sentani Lake, Irian Jaya. – *Proc. Symp. Aquatic Weed Managm., Bogor, Indonesia, 15–17 May 1990:* 79–85

SUNYATA, B., 1981: Present status of open water fisheries in Irian Jaya (Status perikanan perairan umum die Irian Jaya). – *Prosiding seminar perikanan perairan umum, Jakarta, 19–21 August 1981. Badan Penelitian dan Pengembanan Pertanian, Pusat Penelitian dan Pengembanan Perikanan:* 147–151. (In Indonesian, with English abstract).

SUWIGNYO, P., 1978: Development planning of Lake Tempe, and the biological/ecological aspects of its waters. (Kasus perencanaan Danau Tempe ditinjau dari aspek biologi/ekologi perairannya). – BIOTROP-SEAMEO Regional Center for Tropical Biology, Bogor, Indonesia, Report No. BIOTROP/TA/78/310: 21 pp (In Indonesian).

– 1979: Lake Tempe, the fish bowl of Indonesia. – *BIOTROP Newsletter* **17**: 19.

TAUFIK, A. G., YACOB, J. & ABAS, R., 1980: Preliminary study Waya Massapi influence to silver eel during spawning migration from and to Poso lake (Penelitian pendahuluan pengaruh waya massapi terhadap ruaya sidat dari dan ke Danau Poso). – *Prosiding seminar perikanan perairan umum, Jakarta 19–21 August 1981, Badan Penelitian dan Pengembanan Pertanian, Pusat Penelitian dan Pengembanan Perikanan: 291–296.* (In Indonesian, with English abstract).

THANA, D., ABBAS, R. & WARDOYO, S. E., 1980: Study of the fisheries of Rawa Aopa from the point of increasing utilization efforts (Penelitian Perikanan Rawa Aopa dalam rangka usaha peningkatan daya gunanya). – Badan Penelitian dan Pengembangan Pertanian, Lembaga Penelitian Perikanan Darat Cabang Ujung Pandang, Indonesia, report no. 6–IV: 20 pp. (In Indonesian).

THANA, D. & WARDOYO, S. E., 1980: Study of the fisheries of Lake Tondano, North Sulawesi (Penelitian Perikanan Danau Tondano Sulawesi Utara). – Departemen Pertanian, adan Penelitian dan Pengembangan Pertanian, Lembaga Penelitian Perikanan Darat Cabang Ujung Pandang, Indonesia, report no. 3-III: 20 pp. (In Indonesian).

THIENEMANN, A., 1957: Die Fische der Deutschen Limnologischen Sunda-Expedition. – *Arch. Hydrobiol. Suppl.* **23**: 471–477.

TJITROSOEDIRDJO, S. S., & WIDJAJA, F., 1991: Aquatic weed management in Indonesia. – *Proc. Symp. Aquatic Weed Managm., Bogor, Indonesia, 15–17 May* 1990: 25–35.

TRICON JAYA, P. T., 1980: Preliminary report of a study of plans to improve conditions in Lake Kerinci, Jambi Province (Laporan pendahuluan, study perencanaan perbaikan keadaan Danau Kerinci, Propinsi Jambi): 45 pp. – Departemen Pekerjaan Umum, Dirjen Pengairan, Jakarta. (In Indonesian).

UI/PU, 1979: Preliminary report on an ecological survey of Lake Kerinci 1978–79 (Laporan pendahuluan Survai Ekologi Danau Kerinci): 36 pp. – Universitas Indonesia/Pekerjaan Umum, Jakarta. (In Indonesian).

Uttley, J., 1987: Survey of Sulawesi Selatan to assess the status of wetlands and to identify key sites for breeding and migratory waterbirds. – 28 pp. PHPA/INTERWADER Report No. 2, INTERWADER Publ. No. 11, Kuala Lumpur.

Vaas, K. F., 1952: Fisheries in the lake district along the river Kapuas in West Borneo. – *Proc. Indo-Pacific Fisheries Council Madras, India, Sect.* **II**: 1–10.

– 1956: Survey report of Rawa Aopa, (South east Sulawesi) (Lapuran Pemeriksaan Rawa Aopa, Sulawesi Tenggara). – Balai Penjelidikan Perikanan Darat Laboratorium Perikanan Darat Bogor, Indonesia, Report No. **8**: 16 pp. (In Indonesian).

Vaas, K. F., Sachlan, M. & Wiraatmadja, G., 1953: On the ecology and fisheries of some inland waters along the rivers Ogan and Komering in South-east Sumatra. – *Contr. Inland Fish. Res. Stat. Jakarta-Bogor* **3**: 1–32.

Vaas, K. F. & Schuurman, J. J., 1949: On the ecology and fisheries of some Javanese freshwaters. – *Mededelingen van het Algemeen Proefstation voor de Landbouw (Communications of the General Agricultural Research Station), Buitenzorg, Java* **97**: 3–61.

Veen, R. van der, 1937: The Segara Anak in the Rindjani mountains (De Segara Anak in het Rindjanigebergte). *De Tropische Natuur* **26**: 195–201. (In Dutch).

Verstappen, H. T., 1973: *A geomorphological reconnaissance of Sumatra and adjacent islands (Indonesia)*. – International Institute for Aerial Survey and Earth Sciences (ITC), Enschede. Wolters-Noordhoff Publ., Groningen, The Netherlands: 182 pp + 1 map.

Voogd, C. N. A., de, 1941: Botanical notes of the Lesser Sunda Islands (VI). The coloured lakes of the Keli Moetoe on Flores. (Botanische aantekeningen van de Kleine Sunda Eilanden (VI). Naar de gekleurde meren van den Keli Moetoe op Flores). – *De Tropische Natuur* **30**: 119–125 (In Dutch).

Wardoyo, S. E., 1978. Survey of the fisheries of Lake Matano and Lake Towuti, South Sulawesi (Penelitian perikanan Danau Matano dan Danau Towuti, Sulawesi Selatan). – Lembaga Penelitian Perikanan Darat (Inland Fisheries Research Institute), Ujung Pandang, Indonesia, Report No. 17. (In Indonesian).

Wardoyo, S. E. & Thana, D., 1978: Survey of the fisheries of Lake Limboto, North Sulawesi (Penelitian perikanan Danau Limboto, Sulawesi Utara). – Lembaga Penelitian Perikanan Darat (Inland Fisheries Research Institute), Ujung Pandang, Indonesia, Report No. 20. (In Indonesian).

Wargasasmita, S., 1982: The fish community of several lakes in Sumatra and Sulawesi (Komunitas ikan di berberapa danau di Sumatera dan Sulawesi). – *Lingkungan & Pembangunan* **2**: 119–130. (In Indonesian, with English abstract).

Weber, M. & Beaufort, C. F. de, 1911–22: *Fishes of the Indo-Australian Archipelago*. – E. J. Brill. Publ., Leiden: 8 volumes.

Wetzel, R. G., 1975: Limnology: 743 pp. – Saunders, Philadelphia.

Whitten, A. J., Damanik, S. J., Anwar, J. & Hisyam, N., 1984: The Ecology of Sumatra: 583 pp. – Gadjah Mada University Press, Yogyakarta, Indonesia.

Whitten, A. J., Mustafa, M. & Henderson, G., 1987: One or more extinctions from Sulawesi, Indonesia? – *Conservation Biology* **1**: 42–48.

– – – 1988: The Ecology of Sulawesi. – 777 pp. Gadjah Mada University Press, Yogyakarta, Indonesia.

Widjaja, F. T., 1980: A review of activities and research on limnology in Indonesia. – Proc. First Workshop for Promotion of Limnology in Dev. Countries, Kyoto: 75–80.

Wulf, R. de, Supomo, D. & Rauf, K., 1981: Kerinci-Seblat Proposed National Park Preliminary Management Plan 1982–1987. – UNDP/FAO National Parks Development Project INS/78/061.

Yaramaya, P. T., 1983: Draft final report, hydrological study of Lake Kerinci, Main Report (Studi Perimbangan Tat Air Danau Kerinci, Laporan Utama). – 75 pp. Departemen Pekerjaan, Umum, Dirjen Pengairan, Jakarta. (In Indonesian).

Zain, I. H., 1981: Present status of open water fishery in South Sumatra (Status perikanan perairan umum di Sumatera Selatan). – Prosiding seminar perikanan perairairan umum, Jakarta, 19–21 August 1981, Badan Penelitian dan Pengembangan Pertanian, Pusat Penelitian dan Pengembangan Perikanan: 81–85. (In Indonesian, with English abstract).

Zehrfeld, E. H., 1985: The production and marketing of fish harvested both from open waters and culture operations in the Middle Mahakam and it's surroundings. (An analysis of the past and present situation, with projections for the future). – 146 pp. Technical Cooperation for Area Development Project, Samarinda, Indonesia.

Zwahlen, R., 1989: Pers. comm., Public Works office, Kendari.

Author's address:

Asian Wetland Bureau, P. O. Box 254 BOO, Bogor 16002, Indonesia.

Mitt. Internat. Verein. Limnol.	24	129–145	Stuttgart, Februar 1994

Status of limnological research and training in Malaysia

Sinn-Chye Ho

Abstract

Limnological research and training in Malaysia have progressed steadily in the last 15 years due to the efforts of an increasing number of trained limnologists and scientists from related fields based in universities, government departments (e.g. Department of Environment, Government Chemistry Department, Drainage and Irrigation Department, State Water Authorities), and research centres (e.g. Freshwater Fish Research Centre). Non-governmental organizations (e.g. Malayan Nature Society, Asian Wetland Bureau) and the private sector (e.g. hydro-engineering firms) play an active supporting role in this respect. The main driving force has been the pace of implementation of Malaysia's long-term socio-economic and urban development plans, which require a thorough inventorying and optimal utilization of its limited freshwater resources. Malaysian limnologists have been involved in the search for solutions related to water-resource protection and formulation of environmental conservation strategies and assessment methods. The latter has been promoted by Malaysia's Environmental Quality Act (1974) with its inherent Environmental Impact Assessment Regulation (1985).

The current trend is towards organized, multidisciplinary, applied studies at the drainage basin or ecosystem level. This has been made possible by the enhancement of research and training infrastructure at universities and research institutions which still serve as the main repositories and source of trained aquatic biologists in general, and limnologists in particular. There has been regular review and introduction of new courses to the teaching curricula to reflect prevailing man-power needs and changing perspectives of the importance of the country's finite aquatic resources and its fragile environment.

Funding opportunities both from the government and private sector have been encouraging in recent years. Local intiatives have made possible extra financial, technological and human resource inputs from collaborating countries including Japan (JSPS, JICA), Canada (IDRC), Europe (ASEAN-EEC), Australia (ASEAN-AUSTRALIA) United Kingdom (Royal Society of United Kingdom), WHO and UNESCO. There is as yet no national body for coordinating limnological research and training. A national journal of limnology likewise does not exist. Regional institutional linkages through post-graduate studies, exchange of research or academic staff, inter-library loan services, and fellowship offers amongst developing countries would be beneficial and timely; as such they should be promoted and sustained.

Introduction

In the first *Societas Internationalis Limnologiae* (S.I.L.) workshop for the promotion of limnology in developing countries held during August 1980 in Kyoto (Japan), Furtado (1980), Ho (1980 a) and Lim (1980 a) presented a composite picture of the status of limnological research and training in Malaysia with reference to natural and man-made aquatic ecosystems. This paper appraises the state of limnological development in Malaysia with particular emphasis on the last 15 years. It is based on a survey of available literature, information from colleagues in various Malaysian institutions involved with limnological research and/or training, and also on the personal experiences and observations of the author.

Geoclimatic features of Malaysia

Geographic location

Malaysia lies just above the equator (lat. 0°60′–6°40′N, long. 99°35′–119°25′E). The country is a federation of 13 states. Eleven of them are located on Southeast Asia's southernmost peninsula, south of the Kra Isthmus, and occupy a land area of 131,235 km^2. The remaining two states of Sabah (76,115 km^2) and Sarawak (124,499 km^2) are situated on the north and north-western parts of the island of Borneo. Thus 11 states of West or Peninsular Malaysia are separated geographically from the two states of East Malaysia by approximately 500 km of the South China Sea.

Climate and rainfall

Proximity to the equator has given Malaysia a climate of high humidity (mean 80%), high temperature (annual mean 26.7 °C) and abundant rainfall (2000–5000 mm). There is little variation in day length which averages at least 8 hours of intense sunshine per day. The diurnal temperature range is 8.9 °C. For every 100-m increase in altitude, the air temperature drops by roughly 0.6 °C. Freezing point is reached rarely, and only on the highest peak in Malaysia (Mount Kinabalu in Sabah: 4,102 m).

0538-4680/94/0024-0129 $ 4.25

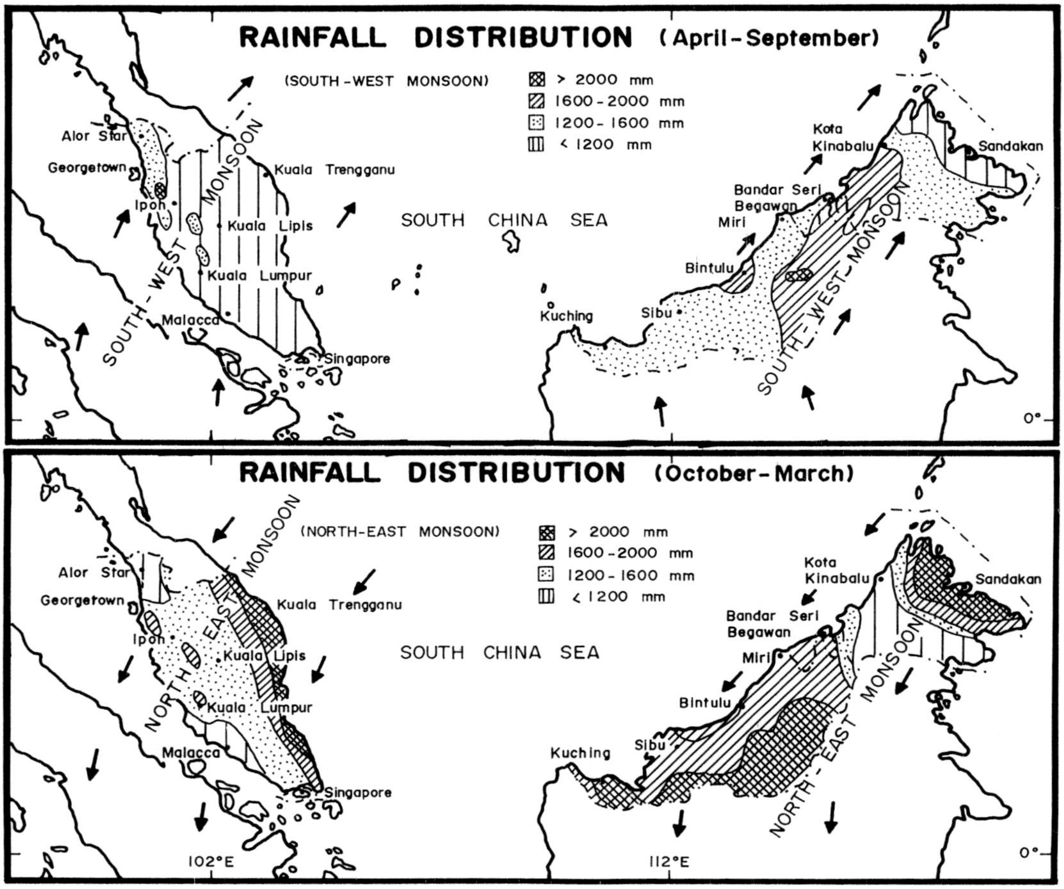

Fig. 1. Rainfall distribution in Malaysia.

The equatorial climate is modified by the region's insularity and exposure to a monsoonal wind system that originates in the Indian Ocean and the South China Sea. Malaysia lies outside the tropical cyclone (typhoon) belt, and precipitation cycles are linked to the two monsoon seasons (Fig. 1). The northeast monsoon begins in October/November and ends by February/March. The southwest monsoon blows from mid-April/May to September/mid-October. In between these are the two intermonsoon periods, each lasting generally about eight weeks. There are no prevailing winds during the intermonosoonal periods but daily convectional rain is abundant. The country experiences between 150–200 raindays per year. The most intense rainfall occurs during the inter-monsoonal periods, but the northeast monsoon period brings the greatest amount of rain as a whole. The average rainfall in Peninsular Malaysia is about 2,500 mm a year; the east coast receives an average of 4,000 mm per year. Maxwell Hills near Taiping receives 5,000 mm while the Jelebu district, which is sheltered from both monsoons, receives only 1,650 mm per year. A large area of Sarawak experiences 3,000–5,000 mm of rain per year while Sabah receives about 1,600–4,500 mm. In spite of the high average rainfall, the total water resources of Malaysia are only moderate due to the high potential evaporation. Droughts occur in certain areas of the country owing to wide spatial and temporal variations in rainfall.

Relief and drainage

The topography of Peninsular Malaysia is dominated by two mountain ranges, the Main or Central Range and the Bintang Range which are mostly granitic. The Central Range extends from near the Thai border in the north to Tampin in Negri Sembilan in the south; it is just out of alignment with the longitutinal axis of the peninsula. North-west of the Central Range is the Bintang Range which extends from the Thai border to the Taiping area. East of the Main Range are the highland areas of

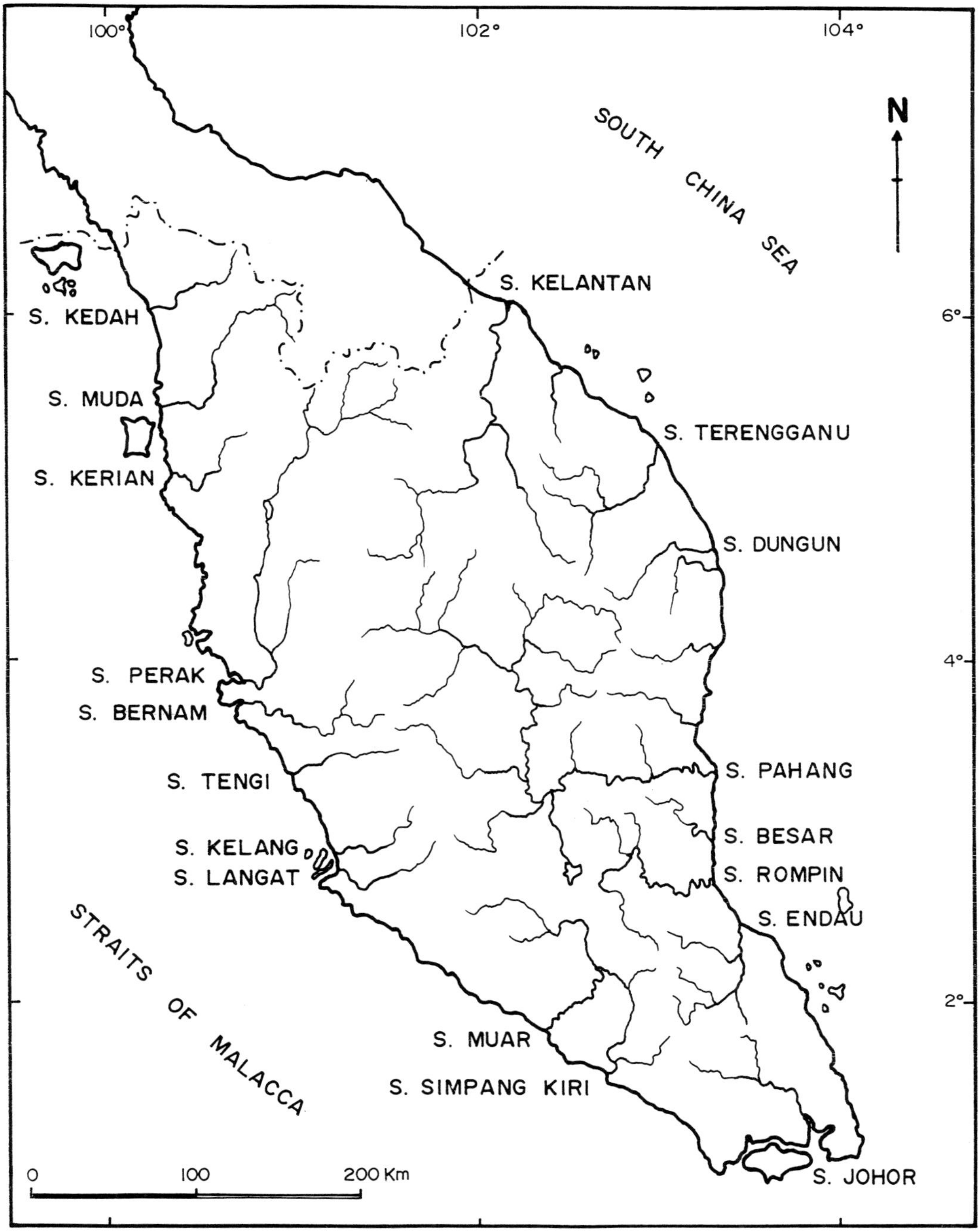

Fig. 2. Main rivers of Peninsular Malaysia.

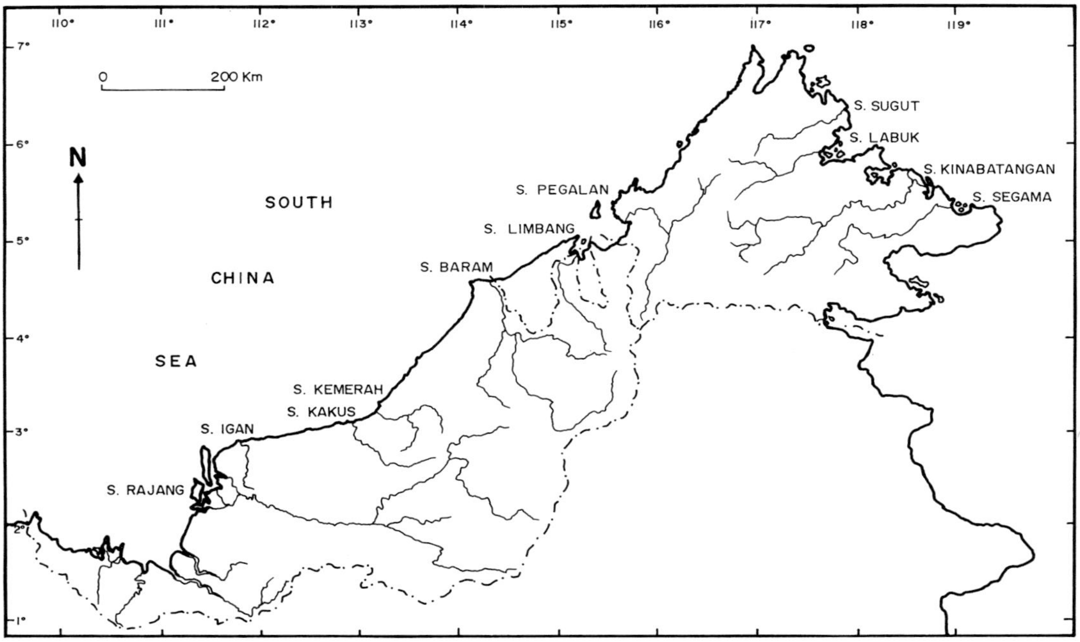

Fig. 3. Main rivers of Sabah and Sarawak.

Table 1. The main Malaysian rivers and their catchment areas.

River	Catchment area (km²)
Sungai Pahang	29,137
Sungai Perak	15,151
Sungai Kelantan	12,691
Sungai Muar	6,062
Sungai Muda	4,273
Sungai Johor	2,720
Sungai Linggi	1,306
Sungai Kelang	1,212

Kelantan and Terengganu. The highest peak found on the peninsular is Gunung Tahan (2,188 m). Narrow stretches of lowland lie on either side of the mountain series, and limestone outcrops occur in some areas. Most of the non-urban lowlands are dominated by ricefields, oil-palm, rubber and fruit plantations.

The juxtaposition of the mountain masses demarcates the major drainage basins on the peninsula. Three large river basins stand out distinctly on the map (Fig. 2): the Sg. (= Sungai or river) Perak, Sg. Kelantan and Sg. Pahang (Table 1). The Sg. Perak (drainage area 15,151 km²) flows from between the Bintang and Central Ranges westward into the Straits of Malacca. From between the Central Range and the Terengganu Highlands, the Sg. Kelantan (drainage area 12,691 km²) flows northward to discharge into the South China Sea. The Sg. Pahang (drainage area: 29,137 km²), flows first south and then eastward to the South China Sea.

High rainfall contributes greatly to the flows in most fluvial systems in Malaysia. The rivers are generally narrow and swift in their upper courses with many waterfalls (114 documented to date; ANON 1990), and carry a high silt load in their lower reaches. However, their descent to the coastal plain in the lower reaches in gradual. On the west coast, the lower courses of the rivers may flow through swamps while on the east coast, discharge into the sea is sometimes impeded by coastal sand bars. Moreover, while abundant rainfall ensures perennial river flow, discharge volumes fluctuate widely. As a result, water resources use often involves construction of dams to regulate river flows and control floods (LEIGH & LOW 1973). Rivers and streams – especially those on the east coast – flood regularly during the northeast monsoon. Sg. Pahang, for example, floods annually. The tendency for floods is aggravated by human activities such as logging and mining which disrupt the natural hydrological regimes of rivers and their drainage basins.

East Malaysia is traversed by relatively dissected highlands, with peaks generally less than 1,800 m in height. An exception is Mount Kinabalu which is part of the Crocker Range in Sabah. Mount Murud (2,438 m) is the highest mountain in Sarawak. Much of the interior of Sarawak is forested and relatively undeveloped. Lowlands are interspersed among the mountain ranges. An alluvial plain runs northeast-southwest along the coasts

Table 2. A partial list of dams and impoundments in Malaysia. * New dams which have been proposed or are under construction.

State	Dam	Surface area (ha)
Perlis	* Timah Tasuh Dam	1,330
Penang	Air Itam Dam	–
Perak	Bukit Merah Dam	3,500
	Cenderoh Dam	2,500
	Jor Dam	20
	Kenering Dam	–
	Mahang Dam	10
	* Taiping Dam	70
	Temenggor Dam	15,200
Federal Territory	Klang Gates Dam	–
Selangor	Semenyih Dam	350
	Subang Dam	10,455
Johore	* Linggiu Dam	5,600
	Macap Dam	800
	Sembrong Dam	820
Negri Sembilan	Pedas Dam	–
	* Ulu Mular	7,605
Malacca	Air Keroh Dam	–
	Durian Tunggal Dam	–
Pahang	Ringlet Dam	55
Kedah	Pedu Dam	6,400
	Muda Dam	–
Kelantan	* Pergau Dam	430
Terengganu	Kenyir Dam	37,000
Sabah	Lahad Datu Dam	–
	Semporna Dam	–
	Sook Dam	–
Sarawak	Batang Ai Dam	–
	Matang Dam	–

of Sarawak and western Sabah. This low-lying coastal land varies in width from less than one to tens of kilometers. It is interrupted in a few areas by encroaching cliffs of low mountains. Coastal swamps are more recent, but less extensive, in Sabah than in Sarawak. The Sabah coastline is transected by 37 rivers, many of which are swift flowing and laden with silt. Sarawak is drained by about 20 rivers of various sizes, most of which flow north-west into the South China Sea (Fig. 3).

Malaysia has few natural lakes. The two most-studied freshwater swamp lakes – Tasek Bera and Tasek Cini – have drainage links with the Sg. Pahang. Tasek Bera was the subject of extensive limnological study under the IBP/PF Programme (Furtado & Mori 1982), but some data on the Ulu Lepar River-Lake wetland ecosystem in Pahang are available also (Nather Khan 1990a.).

There are 51 impoundments in Malaysia, of which 46 are located in Peninsular Malaysia, three in Sabah, and two in Sarawak (Fig. 1). Their surface areas range from 10 ha (Mahang Dam, Pahang) to 37,000 ha (Kenyir Dam, Terengganu) (Table 2). The oldest is the Bukit Merah Reservoir (3,500 ha) in Perak which was built in 1906. More dams are due to be completed over the next few years. Among the roles intended for them are hydroelectric power generation, irrigation, drinking water supply, river regulation, flood mitigation, inland fisheries development and, of late, the added roles of recreation and tourism. The total reservoir area in Peninsular Malaysia has been estimated to be about 80,000 ha. It is estimated that by the year 2000 this figure could increase to 206,000 ha owing to the demand for irrigation and hydropower dams.

Natural vegetation

About 18.5 million ha (56.3%) of Malaysia's 32.9 million ha land area is covered by forest. The natural vegetation is tropical rainforest: lowland dipterocarp forest occupies areas below 300 m, hill dipterocarp forest dominates between 300 m and 1300 m, and montane forest at higher altitudes. Many of the hill forests are located in water catchments. Peat swamps and freshwater swamp forests occupy some lowlying areas. Mangrove forests fringe estuaries and coastal mudflats. Forests play an important role in the hydrologic cycle and in maintaining the water belance of drainage basins. In Malaysia, forested land has 38% water retainability, whereas rubber estate has 27%, and oil-palm estate only 16%.

Freshwater resources

Freshwater supply and demand

Malaysia's average annual rainfall is 990×10^9 megalitres (Ml). of this, 360×10^9 Ml return to the atmosphere as evapotranspiration, 64×10^3 Ml recharge ground water, and the remaining 566×10^3 Ml appear as surface runoff. Rivers and other forms of surface water supply about 97% of the country's total water needs while ground water accounts for the rest, although in some states (Perlis and Kelantan) ground water contributes significantly (30–70%) to the water budget. A study conducted in 1989 found that 43% of treated water is lost through leakage caused by factors including water pipe deterioration, inferior materials and workmanship, earth movement, excessive pressure, irresponsible public usage and water theft.

The present annual domestic, industrial and irrigation water demand is about 11.6×10^9 Ml and is projected to increase to 15.2×10^9 Ml by the year 2000. The total daily water demand is approximately 4,979 Ml while production capacity is 6,513 Ml (Table 3). Despite the excess capacity, there are still some areas (Muda and Malacca, for example) experiencing water shortage owing to geographical barriers and disruption of the hydrologic cycle in degraded drainage basins. The State Government of Malacca has even resorted to a multi-million dollar cloud-seeding venture involving foreign expertise to try

Table 3. The water-supply situation in Malaysia; units in Ml/day.

	Peninsular Malaysia	Sabah	Sarawah
Storage Capacity			
1990	5,758	367	388
1995	9,417	–	709
Water Demand			
1990	4,334	363	282
1995	7,254	–	433

to overcome an acute water shortage problem. Attempts are now being made to promote inter-basin and inter-state water transfers. This approach to water-resource development is likely to become widespread in the future, with the Malaysian central government playing an increasing role. At present, water supply comes under the jurisdiction of the States in accordance with provisions stipulated in the Federal Constitution.

A national water resource study was carried out in 1982 by a team of consultants from Japan International Cooperation Agency (JICA) who produced a master plan up to the year 2000. The Malaysian Government updates this plan from time to time to meet the anticipated demand for water beyond that date.

Water use and misuse

Water use in Malaysia can be categorised as domestic water supply, industrial water supply, agricultural irrigation, supply to lifestock and wildlife, recreation and aesthetics, hydro-power generation, navigation (transportation), waste disposal, flood mitigation, and prevention of seawater intrusion.

Development is proceeding apace in Malaysia in order to achieve targeted socioeconomic objectives. This has resulted, inevitably, in adverse changes in the natural environment. Foremost among these are the impacts on the hydrology and ecology of Malaysian rivers. The Department of Environment (DOE) has ascertained that a total of 42 rivers in the country is biologically dead. Among them are Sg. Cuping (Perlis), Sg. Pinang and Juru (Penang), Sg. Raja Hitam, Sg. Sepetang, Perak, Sg. Kinta, Semagagah and Sg. Tumboh (Perak), Sg. Klang (Kuala Lumpur), Sg. Sepang (Selangor), Sg. Batang Benar (N. Sembilan), Sg. Malacca (Malacca), Sg. Seriong (Johor), and Sg. Sarawak (Sarawak). The main pollutants are domestic garbage, livestock and farm wastes, raw sewage and limestone quarry sludge, as well as untreated or poorly-treated chemical and organic wastes from palm-oil, rubber and wood-based industries. About 65,000 kg of garbage is estimated to be dumped daily into the Sg. Kelang and 45 polluntants are known to enter the Sg. Pinang.

According to the Ministry of Agriculture, Malaysia has 52 freshwater fish species which are of commercial importance. Over the last 20 years, the Sg. Gombak (Selangor) has lost about 60% of its indigenous fish fauna which once totalled 27 species. This reflects excessive land clearance in the drainage basin resulting in river bank erosion and severe silt pollution. The Sg. Perak has lost six out of the nine commercially important riverine fishes during the last 15 years (Khoo et al. 1987). According to farmers and breeders of the giant prawn (*Macrobrachium rosenbergii*) in the Tanjung Tualang area, pollution of the Sg. Kinta (Perak) and its tributaries by suspended solids (>300 mg/l) has reduced the cultured prawn harvest by 50% over the past ten years.

The level of many riverbeds in Malaysia has been raised by siltation caused by improper drainage-basin development for large-scale projects including urban housing schemes. The consequences, which can be translated into economic terms, include poor water quality, reduced drainage and flash floods. A flood mitigation plan proposed by the JICA for Penang island – estimated cost 260 million ringgit (MYR$ m where US$ 1.00 = MYR$ 2.78) – will involve extensive improvement and diversion work on the Sg. Penang drainage system and the construction of dual-purpose retention ponds and water-pumping stations. The frequent occurrence of flash floods has also prompted the Federal and Peak State Governments to allocate MYR$ 5 million to alleviate flood problems in the Taiping (Perak) district.

Sediment pollution of reservoirs is a major cause for concern in Malaysia as it leads to silting of dams. This problem occurred at the 50-ha Ringlet Reservoir in Cameron Highlands (Pahang) and has prompted the National Electricity Board (Tenaga Nasional) to construct a desander across the Sg. Telom at a cost of MYR$ 3 million. This reservoir was also plagued by water hyacinth (*Eichhornia crassipes*) infestation in mid-1989; clearing this weed cost MYR$ 200,000.

Flooded ricefield habitats receive pollutants, and excessive use of pesticides (e.g. gramaxone, thiodan, malathion, gramma-BHC and sevin) has resulted in declining fish yields from ricefields. The problem is compounded by the double-cropping practice which shortens the rice growing season and limits the production of fish in the culture system.

Sound planning and proper management of water resources at the scale of entire drainage basins is essential if pollution problems are to be overcome and if continuing economic development and social advancement are to be ensured. Malaysian limnologists can and do play an important role in these matters.

Development of limnology in Malaysia

Historical development

An account of the historical development of limnology in Malaysia up to the late 1970s has been given by Furtado (1980). The limnological studies undertaken on natural and man-made ecosystems in Malaysia during the same period have been elaborated by LIM (1980a) and HO (1980a) respectively. Briefly, limnology in Malaysia had its beginnings in the early 1950s. Several key scientists played important roles during the formative years, including M.W.F. TWEEDIE, D.S. JOHNSON, G. A. PROWSE, M. K. SOONG, C. H. FERNANDO and J. I. FURTADO. The period 1965–75 saw the gradual establishment of a pool of researchers, lecturers and graduate students trained in aquatic ecology at the Universiti Malaya (Kuala Lumpur) which subsequently enabled Malaysia to host and participate actively in the joint Malaysian/Japanese IBF/PF Tasek Bera Project in the early 1970s (FURTADO & MORI 1982). Well-known Japanese limnologists including S. MORI, I. IKUSIMA, T. MIZUNO, S. KUMANO and several others contributed significantly to the Tasek Bera project. In the ensuing years, more specialists in aquatic biology have been recruited at Universiti Kebangsaan Malaysia (UKM), Universiti Pertanian Malaysia (UPM) and Universiti Sains Malaysia (USM). Undergraduate and postgraduate programmes in aquatic biology were introduced which invariably included a limnology component.

Present trends

Interdisciplinary research and training in Malaysia are being pursued actively by universities and government research institutions (e.g. fisheries, medical and health departments) in relation to water-resource development and management, as well as water-pollution studies. This is due partly to the rapid pace of socioeconomic development which necessitates, among other things, a thorough inventorying and optimal utilization of limited aquatic resources. Such tasks require a holistic approach with multidisciplinary inputs. Advances in analytical techniques, computer technology, and availability of remote-sensing techniques have contributed to this research. Several Image Processing Systems (e.g. DRAGON, MERIDIAN, ERDAS) and at least ten different Geographical Information Service (GIS) software packages (e.g. ARC/INFO, RAISON, SPANS, TERRASOFT, etc.) are currently in use for various purposes (see MACRES 1991). These include river-basin planning and management as well as environmental protection studies.

Another recent change is an increase in the number of Malaysian scientists, whether trained locally or overseas. This has been made possible through long-term human resource development planning, and improved training and research facilities now available in Malaysia. Malaysian limnologists are often involved jointly in water-resource development programmes and the formulation of environmental conservation strategies and assessment methodologies. Some participate in environmental impact assessment (EIA) studies, while others lend their expertise towards the evaluation of EIA reports upon the request of the Department of Environment (DOE). An EIA is mandatory for approval of proposed development projects in accordance with the requirements of the Environmental Quality (Amendment) Act (1985) and the Environmental Quality (Prescribed Activities) (Environmental Impact Assessment) Order (1987).

Research funding, especially when limited, seems to favour applied research. While studies on plant and animal systematics may have been overshadowed by applied biological studies, the academic community remains aware of the fundamental importance of a sound knowledge of systematics in limnological research. Courses imparting this information still form the core of university curricula. Fortunately, basic research in these areas is still very much alive owing to the efforts of researchers who are attracted to the rich diversity of Malaysia's aquatic flora and fauna, but who recognise that gaps still exist in our knowledge of the aquatic biota.

Major fields of limnological research

Rivers and streams

Much of the earlier limnological work on rivers and streams could be attributed to ALFRED (1964), JOHNSON (1957, 1967), CHENG (1965, 1966), CHENG & FERNANDO (1969) and FURTADO (1969). However, the first comprehensive study of the limnology of a lowland Malaysian river, the Sg. Gombak, was undertaken by BISHOP (1973). This was followed by the work of HO (1973, 1975, 1976a, 1976b) who investigated the impacts of water pollution on the ecology of Sg. Renggam at Shah Alam industrial estate (Selangor). An account of the general ecology of lowland rivers and streams in West Malaysia has been given by HO & FURTADO (1982).

Considerable research on the ecological impacts of changes in river water quality as a result of drainage-basin development has been undertaken by Malaysian limnologists. For example, PEH (1981) studied the sediment loads of small forested drainage basins in Peninsular Malaysia, while LAI & SAMSUDDIN (1985) compared the suspended and dissolved loads in two disturbed lowland drainage basins in the Air Itam Forest Reserve (Selangor). An environmental study on the Sg. Klang, which examined especially impacts on the fish fauna, was carried out by MOHSIN & LAW (1980), and fishes of rivers in Taman Negara and Ulu Endau have been studied by ZAKARIA-ISMAIL (1984, 1987). Riverine fisheries potential in Malaysia has been discussed by TAN (1980) and KHOO et al. (1987), and CHIANG & LEONG (1979) have investigated fish parasites in two rivers in Penang. LIM (1989) examined the water quality and faunal composition in the streams and rivers of the Ulu Endau area (Johor) and, more recently, NATHER KHAN (1990 b, 1990 c) undertook separate studies on the pollution status of the Sg. Sedili Kecil and Sg. Linggi. Even tourism seems to have exerted some influence on limnological study, as exemplified by LAI & LIM's (1988) quantitative assessment of the riverscape (cf. landscape) of the Sg. Endau to evaluate its recreational potential.

The Department of Environment (DOE) plays a key coordinating role in river water-quality monitoring and management. The approach adopted is one of integrated multidisciplinary study at the river basin level (Ho 1976 c). In 1978, DOE initiated a national water-quality monitoring programme (NWQMP). The programme commenced with establishment of study sites on 33 rivers in 13 river basins, but the numbers have grown since then. Many of these rivers were polluted, in particular by discharges from palm-oil and rubber factories. Phase I of the programme, which involved an extensive water-quality standards study, was by carried out by UNIVERSITI MALAYA (1986). Phase II dealt with the development of criteria and waterquality standards for Malaysia. A study team comprising a private consultancy firm in association with the Universiti Pertanian Malaysia (UPM), the Universiti Teknologi Malaysia (UTM) and the Universiti Malaya (UM), was commissioned by DOE to undertake the Phase II study (see DOE-SHB 1989). Six river basins were studied in detail: Sg. Muda, Sg. Perak, Sg. Kelang, Sg. Linggi, Sg. Muar and Sg. Pahang. A computerised integrated river-basin information system (IRBIS) was developed subsequently for DOE. The user-friendly IRBIS system provides a rationalised database, including catchment data, pollution sources and river water quality, which can be used for GIS applications. Phase III of the programme was concerned with data collection and classification of river basins on the basis of beneficial use. The resultant database facilitated the establishment of interim water-quality criteria (based on human health, aquatic life protection, livestock drinking, irrigation and recreation) and a water-quality index system to improve drainage basin management (see NORHAYATI 1981). Under Phase IV, which is to begin soon, another ten river basins will be included in the classification. Five Malaysian universities (UM, UKM, UPM, USM, UTM) will be involved.

Lakes and freshwater swamps

Owing to the scarcity of natural lakes in Malaysia, limnological work on such habitats has been limited, although Tasek Bera swamp lake is an exception to this generalization (FURTADO et al. 1980, MIZUNO & MORI 1982). FATIMAH et al. (1986) studied the zooplankton fauna in another freshwater swamp while, with the support of the Asian Wetland Bureau, NATHER KHAN (1990 a) made a preliminary assessment of the water quality and pollution threat to the Ulu Lepar wetland in Pahang. This shallow wetland (ca. 18,000 ha), comprising Tasek Beringin, Tasek Bungor and 12 other permanent or semi-permanent lakes, was one of the major wetlands identified and included in the Malaysian Wetlands Directory (DWNP 1987). In recent years, some research has been directed towards developing the aquaculture potential of ox-bow lakes. An economic feasibility study on one such lake, isolated from Sg. Perak at Teluk Intan, has been carried out by YAP et al. (1989).

Reservoirs and disused mining pools

Although there are at least 50 reservoirs of various sizes in Malaysia (Fig. 4), the amount of published work on the limnology of these reservoirs is scarce. However, in the case of small man-made lakes, reference is made to the work of FATIMAH et al. (1984) and FATIMAH & SHARR (1982, 1987, see also ANTON 1994). Scarcer still is work on disused tin-mining pools (JOTHY 1968, but see ARUMUGAM 1994). The investigations of HO (1976 a) on Ampang Reservoir, LAI & CHUA (1976) on Pedu and Muda Reservoirs, and that of ARUMUGAM & FURTADO (1980 a, 1980 b) on Subang Reservoir, are three examples of early studies on man-made lakes. Data on the water quality of reservoirs are collected routinely by the relevant

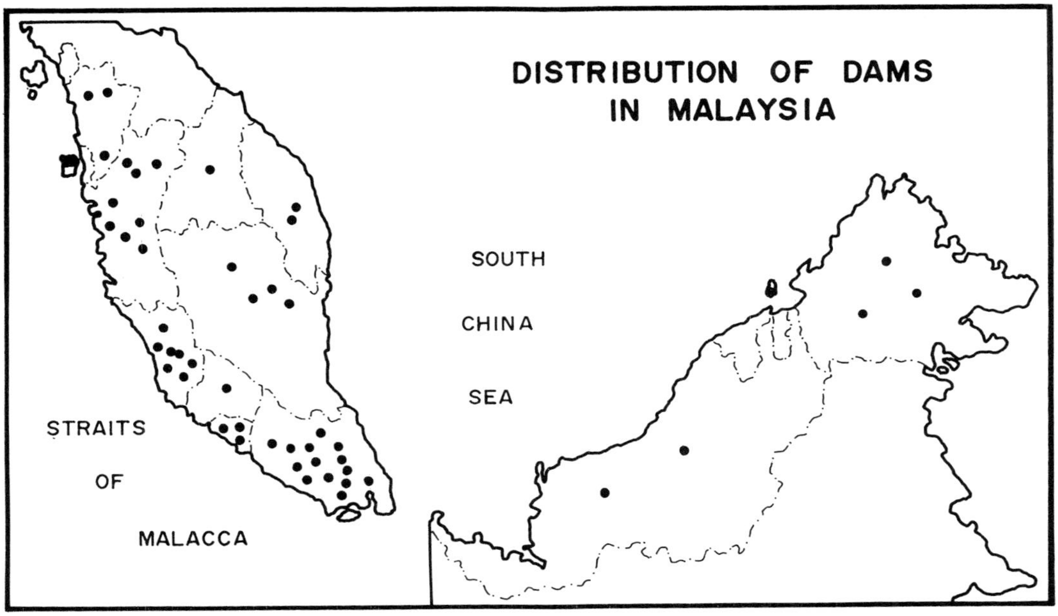

Fig. 4. Distribution of dams and impoundments in Malaysia.

state water authorities, but these are seldom published. An attempt at establishing water-quality criteria for the protection of aquatic life in tropical Asian reservoirs has been made by YAP (1988 a).

The fisheries and aquaculture potential of reservoirs in Malaysia have not yet been exploited fully. Studies carried out on fish species composition in Muda and Pedu Reservoirs (LAI & CHUA 1976), Temengor Reservoir (KHOO et al. 1982), Bukit Merah Reservoir (YAP 1988 b) and Cenderuh Reservoir (LEE 1989, LEE & AHYAUDIN 1989) indicate that, with proper planning and management, reservoirs can contribute to increased fish production in Malaysia. Such findings have been reaffirmed by feasibility studies carried out by the Freshwater Fish Research Centre (FFRC) at Batu Berendam (Malacca) between 1984 and 1987. These investigations involved determination of the physicochemical characteristics and plankton composition of six reservoirs in Peninsular Malaysia: Bukit Merah Reservoir (Taiping, Perak), Ringlet Reservoir, Jor Reservoir and Mahang Reservoir (Cameron Highlands, Pahang), Sembrong Reservoir (Batu Pahat, Johor) and Macap Reservoir (Kluang, Johor) (FFRC Report 1987). The FFRC proposed subsequently that both open-water stocking as well as cage-culture techniques be attempted using indigenous lacustrine and riverine fishes. Other studies on the feeding ecology (YAP & FURTADO 1981) and food-resource utilization of reservoir fishes have been undertaken also (YAP 1987, 1988 b), while LEONG et al. (1987) reported upon the parasite fauna of fishes at Temengor Dam.

Ricefield and irrigation canals

Limnological interest in ricefields has been focused mainly on water quality, phyto- and zooplankton composition, and fish culture potential. FERNANDO et al. (1980) considered the ecological importance of the aquatic fauna of ricefields, and NIRYATI (1981) gave an account of algal diversity in the ricefields of Balik Pulau, Penang. The aquaculture potential of ricefields and sump-ponds for integrated rice-fish farming has long been recognised (Tan 1973), and the Malaysian government is making efforts to develop this potential using modern technology. In this regard ALI & AHMAD (1988) studied the water quality of ricefields and sump ponds in relation to phytoplankton growth in the ricefield fish-culture system. YUNUS & LIM (1971) and LIM et al. (1984) investigated the problem of insecticide usage in ricefields in West Malaysia, while freshwater molluscs were studied by BERRY (1963, 1974 a, 1974 b) with reference to their parasitological significance. LIM (1980 b) documented changes in aquatic invertebrate populations while MOHAMAD (1982) surveyed the freshwater Protozoa of ricefields. Studies upon ricefield fish populations (ALI 1988, 1990a) as well as microcrustaceans and rotifers (ALI 1990b) have been undertaken also. ZAMAN & LEONG (1987, 1988) studied the seasonal occurrences of cestode and nematode parasites in the catfishes *Clarias batrachus* and *Clarias macropcephalus* in the Krian rice growing district. MASHHOR et al. (1989) worked on the problem of aquatic weed infestation in the same area.

Irrigation canals have been the subject of fewer investigations, but HO (1980b) studied the water chemistry and algal-growth potential of the Muda Rice Irrigation System. Elsewhere, LEONG (1986) documented the seasonal occurrence of metazoan parasites of *Puntius binotatus* in the irrigation canal system of Sg. Pinang West (Penang).

Systematic study

Rather few groups of freshwater organisms have been investigated from a taxonomic perspective. PROWSE (1957, 1958, 1962) studied the desmids, flagellates and diatom flora of Malaysian freshwater. In addition, members of a few genera of red algae such as *Batrachospermum* and *Ballia* have been described (KUMANO 1978, KUMANO & PHANG 1987, RATNASABAPATHY & KUMANO 1982, KUMANO & RATNASABAPATHY 1984). Our knowledge of the taxonomy and biology of freshwater crabs and shrimps are due mainly to the efforts of Ng (1988, 1990), NG & CHOY (1989) and NG & STEUBING (1989). The cyclopoid Copepoda and Cladocera have been studied by FERNANDO & PONYI (1981), IDRIS & FERNANDO (1981) and LIM & FERNANDO (1985). Accounts of the rotifers have been given by FERNANDO & ZANKAI (1981) and KARUNAKARAN & JOHNSON (1978). TWEEDIE (1952, 1953a, 1953b), SONG (1948, 1949, 1950). ALFRED (1964, 1969, 1971), MOHSIN (1980), MOHSIN & AMBAK (1982a, 1982b), CHIN (1989), ZAKARIA-ISMAIL (1989) and LIM et al. (1989) have contributed significantly to our knowledge of the fishes of the rivers, streams and freshwater swamps of Peninsular Malaysia. JONES & LEONG (1986) researched the parasitic trematodes (amphistomes) of Malaysian freshwater fishes.

Training in limnology

Educational role of Malaysian universities

Universities train the majority of limnologists and other aquatic biologists in Malaysia, and provide facilities that are unavailable elsewhere. The teaching curricula have evolved and expanded in scope to meet the demands of a rapidly-developing nation. Of the seven established universities in Malaysia, four have both basic and applied biology programmes at the undergraduate and postgraduate levels: Universiti Malaya (UM), Universiti Kebangsaan Malaysia (UKM), Universiti Pertanian Malaysia (UPM) and Universiti Sains Malaysia (USM).

Taking Universiti Sains Malaysia (USM) – established in 1969 – as an example, there has always been a strong aquatic biology component in the teaching programme of the School of Biological Sciences. The school established an undergraduate 'thrust area' in Aquatic Biology in the early 1970s. Third and final-year courses offered include 'Physico-chemical Limnology and Oceanography', 'Plankton and Productivity', 'Tropical Aquatic Ecosystems', 'Malaysian Fisheries', 'Fisheries Management', 'Aquaculture', and 'Water Pollution and Conservation'. Postgraduate research degrees in limnology are offered also. Short courses dealing with GIS applications to environmental studies and inland fisheries management are conducted, as is a diploma-level programme aimed at producing qualified field and laboratory technologists. In the case of UM, courses related to freshwater biology are offered by the Departments of Zoology, Ecology and Botany. The Institute for Advanced Studies, UM, also conducts short-term courses for graduate students. At UPM, the Faculty of Fisheries & Marine Sciences and the Faculty of Science and Environmental Studies offer undergraduate courses in aquatic botany, ecology, limnology and pollution biology. Similar courses are also offered by the Faculty of Life Sciences at UKM.

Research role of Malaysian universities

Universities in Malaysia have evolved gradually from teaching institutions to institutions with an increasing emphasis on research. Each of the four major universities now has at least five faculty members involved in limnological or freshwater biological research. This pool of expertise is called upon in various ways by government and quasi-government authorities and also the private sector. The DOE and the private sector often invite university staff to undertake studies, advise, or sit on committees such as State Pollution Committees, Watershed Management Committee, EIA Review Panels and so on.

Malaysian universities often initiate and host national and international scientific seminars and symposia. Three such examples are:
i) National Seminar on Water Resources Modelling and Management held on 26–27 August 1991 at the Universiti Sains Malaysia, Penang;
ii) Regional Seminar on the Ecology and Conservation of South East Asian Marine and Freshwaters held in 4–6 November 1991 at the Universiti Malaya, Kuala Lumpur; and
iii) National Biology Symposium held 26–27 November 1991 at Universiti Kebangsaan Malaysia, Bangi.

Role of the Freshwater Fish Research Centre

The Freshwater Fish Research Centre (FFRC) at Batu Berendam (Malacca) was established in 1957. It is a branch of the research division of the Department of Fisheries, Ministry of Agriculture, and is charged with carrying out research in the field of aquaculture and inland fisheries. The current research programme of the FFRC includes breeding indigenous and exotic fish in captivity, studies on fish nutrition, fish diseases, live-feed culture, experimental culture of fish and shrimps in ponds and in suspended cages, water quality in aquaculture, and reservoir limnology. Besides research activites, the FFRC also provides technical advice to fish farmers, carries out training programmes for field staff and farm managers, provides practical training facilities to university students, and supplies fish fry to farmers.

In 1989 the FFRC established a bilateral link with the Department of Fish Culture and Fisheries (DFCF) of the Wageningen Agricultural University in the Netherlands, under the framework of the ASEAN-EEC Aquaculture Development and Coordination Programme (AADCP 1990). A joint project entitled the Development of Lakes and Reservoirs for Fish Production in Malaysia was initiated in 1990 and will continue until December 1994. The project was formulated in response to the rapid development of reservoirs in Malaysia, and their immense potential for fisheries development. The study will focus on two Malaysian reservoirs: Kenyir Reservoir (Terengganu) and Semenyih Reservoir (Selangor). Subjects studied will include physiochemical characteristics, plankton diversity and productivity, feeding biology and stock assessment of native fishes, and cage-culture feasibility using introduced fishes.

The workplan of the AADCP includes also an exchange programme for the staff of the FFRC and DFCF, three training courses for ASEAN participants, two workshops and two M. Sc. fellowships for FFRC staff. The proposed themes of the training courses are 'Modelling and Management of Reservoir Fisheries'. 'Fish Ecology in ASEAN Lakes and Reservoirs' and 'Dynamic Simulation Modelling in Aquatic Production'.

Regional and institutional links

Various forms of technical cooperation exist among Southeast Asian countries which involve some participation from institutions of higher learning. One example is the training programmes and institutions of the Southeast Asian Members of Education Organisations (SEAMEO). The Tropical Biological Programme (SEAMEO/BIOTROP) in Bogor (Indonesia) organises aquatic biology workshops, where limnologists from Malaysian universities have participated as instructors, resource persons, or as trainees. However, this link is maintained through the Ministry of Education rather than through direct institutional connections between BIOTROP and the universities.

Limnologists have contributed also to the coastal study programmes implemented in ASEAN countries under the framework and guidance of the ASEAN Committee on Science and Technology (COST) and involving three ASEAN dialogue partners: Australia, Canada and USA. An example is the technical study (Task 200-M) of the ASEAN/US Coastal Resources Management Project (CRMP) which developed a water-quality management scheme for South Johor, Malaysia. Both the coastal waters and rivers were included in the study. These programmes provide opportunities for aquatic biologists from ASEAN countries to meet to exchange information and research findings. However, such programmes are again coordinated by the Ministry of Science, Technology and Environment, and formal links between participating institutions are not established.

Regional institutional links through jointly-developed postgraduate limnological study programmes, research and academic staff exchange, inter-library loans services and fellowship offers amongst developing countries themselves are lacking currently. A concerted move in this direction would be timely and beneficial and as such should be encouraged.

Funding opportunities and agencies

Under the Sixth Malaysian Plan (1991–1995), a total sum of MYR $ 1.16 billion has been allocated for research and development. About MYR $ 560.3 million will be allocated to research institutions and universities to finance research projects approved under the Intensification in Research and Priority Areas (IRPA) Programme. As far as limnological research is concerned, funding for projects related to aquaculture, fisheries and water-pollution research, is available under IRPA's R & D Programmes for Agriculture and Strategic Development. Limnologists involved in government-funded projects, such as the DOE's own National Water Quality Monitoring Project (see above), are provided with financial support also.

Funds from the private sector are usually channelled through short-term donor-defined projects orientated to solve a particular problem. Some of these may involve limnologists; for example, aquaculture feasibility studies, water pollution studies, and EIAs dealing with flood mitigation and reservoir/dam construction.

The integration of limnology in Malaysia has to some extent been reinforced by financial, technical and human resource inputs through international agencies like the Japan Society for the Promotion of Sciences (JSPS), Japan International Cooperation Agency (JICA), Royal Society of the United Kingdom (RSUK), International Development Research Centre of Canada (IDRC), Gesellschaft für Technische Zusammenarbeit (GTZ) of Germany, and the United Nations Educational, Scientific and Cultural Organization (UNESCO). Scholarships and fellowships are offered by organizations such as the Canadian International Development Agency (CIDA), the European Community and Association of South-East Asian Nations (EC-ASEAN) and the European Environmental Research Organization (ERRO).

Scientific societies and publications

Of the few scientific societies existing in Malaysia, there is not one that deals specifically with limnological work or even freshwater studies. The Ecological Association of Malaysia (EAM) was established in July 1990 to serve as a platform for its members to help ensure a high quality of life for present and future generations through activities designed to curb environmental degradation. Besides organising seminars, workshops and conferences from time to time, the EAM produces its own *Journal of Ecological Science* and the *Malaysian Ecology Bulletin*.

A more established scientific society is the Malayan Nature Society (MNS) which produces a quarterly scientific journal, the *Malayan Nature Journal*, and a quarterly magazine, the *Malayan Naturalist*. The *Malayan Nature Journal* publishes refereed scientific articles on the natural history, biology and conservation of Malaysia and the surrounding region. The *Malayan Naturalist* publishes articles, directed at the layman, on natural history, environmental and conservation issues. Periodically, the Malayan Nature Society also organises national workshops, seminars and international conferences, and publishes the proceedings of such meetings.

Limnological research in Malaysia has increased significantly over the years. Certain areas have received well-merited attention, while others have not, as reflected in the literature. The published works are scattered in a variety of journals. A national journal of limnology has yet to be established. Much of the limnological papers are submitted to international journals for publication, but less-technical research papers are submitted to the *Malayan Nature Journal* or to journals published by the government and local universities: e.g. *Malaysian Agricultural Journal, Journal of Bioscience* (USM), *Journal of Science* (UM), *Pertanika* (UPM), *Journal of Ecological Science* (UPM), and *Science Malaysiana* (UKM).

Role of NGOs in promoting limnology

Non-governmental organisations (NGOs) contribute significantly toward raising public awareness of environmental issues and problems. They play an active role in promoting environmental issues at state, national and international levels. These NGOs include the World Wide Fund for Nature (WWF), Asian Wetland Bureau (AWB), the Sahabat Alam Malaysia (SAM), the Environmental Protection Society of Malaysia (EPSM) and the Consumer's Association of Penang (CAP), with their associated networks such as the Tropical Rainforest Network and the Asian and Pacific Environmental Network (APPEN). The International Organisation of Consumer Unions (IOCU) has a base in Malaysia, but their involvement in environmental issues is focused at the regional and international level rather than at national level. The long-established (51 years) Malayan Nature Society is also an active NGO.

The issues taken up by NGOs are broad in scope. From its office at the Institute for Advanced Studies, Universiti Malaya, AWB sponsors and coordinates projects in the fields of biodiversity and water resources and assists in strengthening of local institutions' efforts in wetland management. AWB also undertakes certain activities in collaboration with other international NGOs such as WWF and IUCN. National NGOs (e.g. SAM, EPSM and MNS), though not directly involved in any form of limnological work, have been pivotal in raising issues such as the impacts of water pollution on Malaysian rivers (e.g. Juru estuary) and the impacts of deforestation in ecologically-sensitive water catchments.

In some cases, the NGOs have been able to mobilize considerable public support which has led to the reconsideration of certain development projects. The Malayan Nature Society too has played an important role in controversies over logging in the proposed Endau-Rompin National Park, the planned construction of a hydro-power dam in Taman Negara and, in conjunction with CAP and SAM, the proposed 'mega development' of Penang Hill. The Malayan Nature Society Malaysian Heritage and Scientific Expedition to Rompin-Endau (1985–1986) resulted in 36 scientific papers in a special issue of the *Malayan Nature Journal* (Davison 1989). A few of these papers concern work on the Sg. Kinchin in Pahang.

Concluding remarks

As the pace of socio-economic development accelerates in Malaysia, there will be greater demands imposed upon its limited water resources. Wise use and careful management of all such resources are imperative to prevent their scarcity from limiting the nation's socioeconomic growth. In this respect, Malaysian limnologists must continue to play an active role in conducting basic and applied studies, and in the formulation of water-resource management policies and future development plans.

There are still gaps in our knowledge of Malaysian limnology. An in-depth understandings of nutrient budgets and trophic relationships in almost all reservoirs in the country is lacking. The aquaculture potential of these water bodies cannot be realised fully without such quantitative data. There is a dearth of basic limnological information on many systems, especially the rivers of Sabah and Sarawak. Large tropical rivers such as Sg. Kinabatangan (Sabah) and Sg. Rajang (Sarawak) warrant close investigation which should go beyond physicochemical and water-quality considerations. The aquarium or hobby potential of fishes in Malaysia's abundant streams and soft-water, acid swamps has yet to be tapped (but see Tweedie 1953a, 1953b, 1953c). Long-term integrated multidisciplinary study programmes are needed and, given sufficient financial support, Malaysian limnologists and other local scientists are capable of formulating as well as implementing such programmes.

On a regional basis, ASEAN member countries should explore and make concerted efforts to formulate limnological research and training programmes for their mutual benefit. This could be undertaken among themselves or with potential international dialogue partners such as Australia, Canada, EEC countries, Japan and USA. It is unfortunate that following the successful completion of the Malaysian/Japanese IBP/PF Tasek Bera Project in the late 1970s, no limnological study of a similar scale and nature has been organised. Besides the large rivers of East Malaysia, some major reservoirs in Peninsular Malaysia (for example, the 37,000 ha Kenyir Reservoir in Terengganu) are suitable candidates for a multinational limnological research venture.

Acknowledgements

The Vice-Chancellor and the Dean of the School of Biological Sciences, Universiti Sains Malaysia are thanked for their support. The financial support provided by USM, S. I. L. and UNESCO is gratefully acknowledged.

References

AADCP, 1990: Research Programme for the Development of Lakes and Reservoirs for Fish Production in Malaysia. – Freshwater Fish Research Centre (FFRC), Batu Berendam, Malaysia and Department of Fish Culture and Fisheries (DFCF), Wageningen, The Netherlands.

Alfred, E. R., 1964: Notes on a collection of freshwater fishes from Penang. – *Bull. Singapore Nat. Mus.* **32**: 143–154.

–– 1969: The Malayan cyprinid fishes of the subfamily Rasborinae. – *Fed. Mus. J.* **16**: 99–122.

– 1971: The Malayan cyprinid fishes of the subfamily Garrinae. – *Fed. Mus. J.* **16**: 97–103.

Ali, A. B., 1988: Some ecological aspects of snakeskin goramy, *Trichogaster pectorailis* (Regan) populations harvested from ricefield-fish culture system. – *Indo-Malayan Zoology* **5**: 101–110.

– 1990a: Some ecological aspects of fish populations in tropical ricefields. – *Hydrobiologia* **190**: 215–222.

– 1990b: Seasonal dynamics of microcrustacean and rotifer communities in Malaysian rice fields used for rice-fish farming. – *Hydrobiologia* **206**: 139–148.

Ali, A. B. & Ahmad, M., 1988: Water quality in ricefields and sump ponds and its relationship to phytoplankton growth in ricefield fish culture system. – *Trop. Ecol.* **29**: 63–70.

ANON, 1990: Waterfalls of Malaysia. – 181 pp. Design Dimension Sdn. Bhd., Petaling Jaya, in collaboration with Department of Irrigation and Drainage,

Ministry of Agriculture and Tourist Development Corporation Malaysia.

Anton, A., 1994: Long-term phytoplankton changes in a tropical reservoir. – *Mitt. Internat. Verein. Limnol.* **24**: 243–249.

Arumugam, P. T., 1994: Present utilisation and recommendations for management of Tin-mine lakes in Malaysia. – *Mitt. Internat. Verein. Limnol.* **24**: 265–272.

Arumugam, P. T. & Furtado, J. I., 1980a: Physicochemistry, destratification and nutrient budget of a lowland eutrophicated Malaysian reservoir and its limnological implications. – *Hydrobiologia* **70**: 11–24.

– 1980b: Eutrophication of a Malaysian reservoir: Effects of agroindustrial effluents. – *J. Trop. Ecol.* **22**: 272–275.

ASEAN-USAID, 1989: Final Report on Task 220-M: Water Quality Management Scheme, South Johore, Malaysia. – Coastal Resources Management Project, Asean/US Cooperative Programme on Marine Sciences.

Berry, A. J., 1963: An introduction to the non-marine molluscs of Malaya. – *Malay. Nat. J.* **17**: 1–18.

– 1974a: Freshwater bivalves of Peninsular Malaysia with special reference to sex and breeding. – *Malay. Nat. J.* **27**: 99–100.

– 1974b: The anatomy of West Malaysian snails of parasitological significance. – *Malay. Nat. J.* **27**: 131–165.

Bishop, J. E., 1973: Limnology of a Small Malayan River Sungai Gombak: 485 pp. – Dr. W. Junk Publishers, The Hague.

Cheng, L. 1965: The Malayan pond skaters. – *Malay. Nat. J.* **19**: 115–123.

– 1966: Three new species of *Esakia Lundblad* (Heteroptera: Gerridae) from Malaya. – *Proc. Roy. ent. Soc. Lond. (B)* **35**: 16–22.

Cheng, L. & Fernando, C.H., 1969: Taxonomy of Malayan Gerridae (Hemiptera: Heteroptera), with notes on biology and distribution. – *Oriental Insects* **3**: 97–160.

Chee Phaik Ean, 1975: Some Dissolved Nutrient Salts and Their Availability from Submerged Leaf Litter in a Tropical Hill-Country Stream. – Unpublished B. Sc. (Hons.) dissertation, Universiti Sains Malaysia, Penang, Malaysia.

Chiang, G. L. & Leong, T. S., 1979: Parasites of fishes from Sungai Pinang and Sungai Teluk Behang, Pulau Pinang, Malaysia. – *Malay. Nat. J.* **32**: 247–251.

Chin, P. K., 1989: A new Bornean species of loach, *Elxis sabanus* (Cobitidae), from Mendolong, Sabah. – *Malay. Nat. J.* **43**: 72–76.

Davison, G. W. H., 1990: The Malayan Nature Society Rompin-Endau Expedition: 1989. – *Malay. Nat. J.* **43**: 212–219.

DOE-SHB, 1989: Development of Criteria and Standards for Air Quality and Water Quality (Phase II). Draft Final Report. – Department of Environment, Malaysia, Syed Muhammed, Hooi and Binnie Sdn. Bhd.

DWNP, 1987: Malaysian Wetland Directory. – Department of Wildlife and National Parks (DWNP), Kuala Lumpur, Malaysia.

Fatimah, M. Y., Mohsin, A. K. M. & Mustafa Kamal, A. S., 1984: Phytoplankton composition and productivity of a shallow lake. – *Pertanika* **7**: 101–113.

– 1986: Zooplankton in a tropical freshwater swamp in Malaysia. – *Malays. Appl. Biol.* **15**: 1–6.

Fatimah, M. Y. & Sharr, H. A. 1982: Siltation in Zoo Negara Lake. – *Pertanika* **5**: 240–245.

– 1987: Physico-chemical limnology of Zoo Negara Lake, Malaysia. – *Arch. Hydrobiol. Beih. Ergebn. Limnol.* **28**: 435–446.

Fernando, C. H., Furtado, J. I. & Lim, P. R., 1980: The ecology of ricefields with special reference to the aquatic fauna. – In: Furtado, J. I. (ed.), Tropical Ecology and Development. *Proc. 5th Int. Symp. Trop. Ecol., 16–21 April 1979. – Kuala Lumpur, Malaysia*: 943–951.

Fernando, C. H. & Ponyi, J. E., 1981: The free living freshwater cyclopoid Copepoda (Crustacea) of Malaysia and Singapore. – *Hydrobiologia* **78**: 113–123.

Fernando, C. H. & Zankai, 1981: The Rotifera of Malaysia and Singapore, with remarks on some species. – *Hydrobiologia* **78**: 205–219.

FFRC Report, 1987: Report on the Limnological Study of Reservoirs in Malaysia for Inland Fisheries Development. 75 pp. – Freshwater Fish Research Centre, Batu Berendam, Melaka, Malaysia.

Furtado, J. I., 1969: Ecology of Malaysian odonates: biotope and association of species. – *Verh. Internat. Verein. Limnol.* **17**: 863–887.

– 1980a: Limnological research and training in developing countries with reference to Malaysia. – In: Mori, S. & Ikusima, I. (eds.): Proceedings of the First Workshop for Promotion of Limnology in the Developing Countries, 29–30 August 1980: 53–56. – Societas Internationalis Internationalis Limnologiae, Kyoto.

– 1980b: Freshwater swamp and lake resources: a synthesis. – In: Furtado, J. I. (ed.): Tropical Ecology and Development. Proc. 5th Int. Symp. Trop. Ecol., 16–21 April 1979. – Kuala Lumpur, Malaysia: 797–798.

Furtado, J. I. & Mori, S., 1982: Tasek Bera. The Ecology of a freshwater Swamp: 413 pp. – Dr. Junk Publishers, The Hague.

Furtado, J. I., Verghese, S., Liew, K. S. & T. H., 1980: Litter production in a freshwater swamp forest, Tasek Bera, Malaysia. – In: Furtado, J. I. (ed.): Tropical Ecology and Development. Proc. 5th Int. Symp. Trop. Ecol., 16–21 April 1979. – Kuala Lumpur, Malaysia: 815–822.

Ho, S. C., 1973: The Ecology of a Lowland Stream: Sungai Renggam, with Special Reference to Water Pollution. – Unpublished M. Sc. thesis, Universiti Malaya, Kuala Lumpur.

– 1975: Some aspects of the bacteriological conditions of Sungai Renggam, Shah Alam, Selangor. – *Malay. Nat. J.* **29**: 70–82.

– 1976a: Periphyton production in a tropical lowland stream polluted by inorganic sediments and organic wastes. – *Arch. Hydrobiol.* **77**: 485–494.

– 1976b: The physicochemical limnology of the Ampang Impounding Reservoir, Kuala Lumpur. – *Malays. Agri. J.* **50**: 527–544.

– 1976c: The watershed approach to water pollution studies in Peninsular Malaysia. – Report on the International Workshop on Energy, Resources and the Environment, February, 1975, Penang: 27–38.

– 1980a: Research and training in limnology with respect to man-made system in Malaysia. – In: MORI, S. & IKUSIMA, I. (eds.): Proceedings of the First Workshop for Promotion of Limnology in the Developing Countries, 29–30 August 1980. 67–73. – Societas Internationalis Limnologiae, Kyoto.

– 1980b: On the chemistry and algal growth potential of the surface water of the Muda river irrigation system, West Malaysia. – In: FURTADO, J. I. (ed.): Tropical Ecology and Development. Proc. 5th. Int. Symp. Trop. Ecol., 16–21 April 1979. – Kuala Lumpur, Malaysia: 989–998.

HO, S. C. & FURTADO, J. I., 1982: The limnology of lowland streams in West Malaysia. – *Trop. Ecol.* **23**: 86–97.

IDRIS, B. A. G. & FERNANDO, C. H., 1981: Cladocera of Malaysia and Singapore with new records, rediscriptions and remarks on some species. – *Hydrobiologia* **77**: 223–256.

JOHNSON, D. S. 1957: A survey of Malayan freshwater life. – *Malay. Nat. J.* **12**: 57–65.

– 1967: On the chemistry of freshwaters in southern Malaya and Singapore. – *Arch. Hydrobiol.* **63**: 477–496.

JONES, A. & LEONG, T. S., 1986: Amphistomes from Malaysian fishes, including *Osteochilotrema malayae* gen. nov. sp. nov. (Paramphistomidae: Osteochilotrematinae subfam. nov.). – *J. Nat. Hist.* **20**: 117–129.

JOTHY, A. A., 1968: Preliminary Observations of Disused Mining Pools in Malaysia and their Potentials for Fish Production. 21 pp. – IPFC/C68/Tech. 25, 13th Session, IPFC Brisbane.

KARUNAKARAN, L. & JOHNSON, A., 1978: A contribution to the rotifer fauna of Singapore and Malaysia. – *Malay. Nat. J.* **32**: 173–208.

KHOO, K. H., LEONG, T. S., SOON, F. L., TAN, S. P. & WONG, S. Y., 1987: Riverine fisheries in Malaysia. – *Arch. Hydrobiol. Beih. Ergebn. Limnol.* **28**: 261–268.

KHOO, K. H., LEONG, T. S., TAN, S. P., WONG, S. Y. & SOON, F. L., 1982: Study Plan for Temengor Lake Fisheries Project. – Report No. USM/TF/02, Universiti Sains Malaysia.

KOVAC, D. & YANG, C. M., 1990: A preliminary checklist of the semiaquatic and aquatic Hemiptera (Heteroptera: Gerromorpha and Nepomorpha) of Ulu Kinchin, Pahang, Malaysia. – *Malay. Nat. J.* **43**: 282–288.

KUMANO, S., 1978: Notes on freshwater red algae from West Malaysia. – *Bot. Mag., Tokyo* **91**: 97–107.

KUMANO, S. & PHANG, S. M., 1987: Studies on freshwater red algae of Malaysia VII. *Batrachospermum tapirense* sp. nov. from Sungai Tapir, Johor, Peninsular Malaysia. – *Jap. J. Phycol.* **35**: 259–264.

– 1990: *Ballia prieurii Kuetzing* and the related species (Ceramiaceae, Rhodophyta). – *Jap. J. Phycol.* **38**: 125–134.

KUMANO, S. & RATNASABAPATHY, M., 1984: Studies on freshwater red algae of Malaysia IV. *Batrachospermum bakarense,* sp. nov. from Sungai Bakar, Kelantan, West Malaysia. – *Jap. J. Phycol* **32**: 19–23.

LAI, H. C. & CHUA, T. E., 1970: Limnological features of Muda and Pedu Reservoirs with an observation on their suitability for fish culture. – *Malays. Agric. J.* **50**: 480–501.

LAI, H. C. & FERNANDO, C. H., 1978: The freshwater Calanoida (Crustacea: Copepoda) of Singapore and Peninsular Malaysia. – *Hydrobiologia* **61**: 113–127.

– 1981: Zoogeographical distribution of Southeast Asian freshwater Calanoida. – *Hydrobiologia* **74**: 53–66.

LAI, F. S. & LIM, M. T., 1988: A quantitative assessment of the riverscape of Sg. Endau. – *Malay. Nat.* **42**: 26–36.

LAI, F. S. & SAMSUDDIN, M., 1985: Suspended and dissolved sediment concentrations of two disturbed lowland forested watersheds in Air Hitam Forests Reserve, Selangor. – *Pertanika* **8**: 112–115.

LEE, K. L., 1989: A Survey of Fish Populations in Tasik Cenderoh, Perak. – Unpublished B. Sc. (Hons.) dissertation, Universiti Sains Malaysia, Penang.

LEE, K. L. & AHYAUDIN, A., 1989: The status of reservoir fisheries in Tasik Cenderuh, Perak: a case study. – Proc. 12th Annual Seminar of Malaysian Society of Marine Sciences: 231–239.

LEIGJ, C. H. & LOW, K. S., 1977: An appraisal of the flood situation in West Malaysia. – Proceedings of a Symposium on Biological Research & Development: 57–72.

LEONG, T. S., 1986: Seasonal occurrence of metazoan parasites of *Puntius binotatus* in an irrigation canal, Pulau Pinang, Malaysia. – *J. Fish Biol.* **28**: 9–16.

LEONG, T. S., KHOO, K. H., SOONG, F. L., BAN, E. S. P. & WONG, S. Y., 1987: Parasites of fishes from Tasik Temengor in Perak, Malaysia. – *Malay. Nat. J.* **41**: 75–82.

LIM, K. K. P., KOTTELAT, M. & NG, P. K. L., 1989: Freshwater fish of Ulu Kinchin, Pahang, Malaysia. – *Malay. Nat. J.* **43**: 314–320.

LIM, R. P., 1980a: Limnological research and education with reference to natural ecosystems in Malaysia. – In: MORI, S. & IKUSIMA, I. (eds): Proceedings of the First Workshop for Promotion of Limnology in the Developing Countries, 29–30 August 1980.

57–65. – Societas Internationalis Limnologiae, Kyoto.
– 1980 b: Population changes of some aquatic invertebrates in ricefields – In: FURTADO, J. I. (ed.): Tropical Ecology and Development. Proc. 5th Int. Symp. Trop. Ecol., 16–21 April 1979. – Kuala Lumpur, Malaysia: 971–980.
– 1989: Water quality and faunal composition in the streams and rivers of the Ulu Endau area, Johor, Peninsular Malaysia. – *Malay. Nat. J.* **41**: 337–347.

LIM, R. P., ABUULLAH, M. F. & FERNANDO, C. H., 1984: Ecological studies of Cladocera in the ricefields of Tanjung Karang, Malaysia, subjected to pesticide treatment. – *Hydrobiologia* **113**: 99–103.

LIM, R. P. & FERNANDO, C. H., 1985: A review of Malaysian freshwater Copepoda with notes on new records and little known species. – *Hydrobiologia* **128**: 71–89.

MACRES, 1991: Malaysian Remote Sensing Inventory: 203 pp. – Malaysian Centre for Remote Sensing (MACRES), Ministry of Science, Technology and The Environment, Malaysia.

MASHLOR, M., AZINUDDIN, M. & SAMSUDDIN, Y., 1989: Aquatic weeds of irrigation and drainage canals in Kerian Rice Growing District, Malaysia. – Proc. 12th Conference of the Asian-Pacific Weed Science Society: 761–770.

MOHAMAD, N. A. H., 1982. – A survey of freshwater protozoa in rice-field ecosystem in Penang. – Unpublished B. Sc. (Hons.) dissertation, Universiti Sains Malaysia, Penang. (In Malay).

MOHSIN, A. K. M., 1980: Ecology and morphology of the freshwater fishes of Selangor. Part I. Cyrinoid fishes of the subfamilies Abraminae, Rasborinae and Garrinae and families Homalopteridae and Cobitidae. – *Malay. Nat. J.* **34**: 73–100.

MOHSIN, A. K. M & AMBAK, M. A., 1982 a. Cyprinoid fishes of the subfamily Cyprininae in Selangor. – *Malay. Nat. J.* **35**: 29–35.
–– 1982 b: Freshwater siluroid fishes of Selangor. – *Malay. Nat. J.* **36**: 99–112.

MOHSIN, A. K. M. & LAW, A. T., 1980: Environmental studies of Kelang River 2. Effect on fish. – *Malay. Nat. J.* **33**: 189–199.

MOULTON, T. P., 1973: The effect of various insecticides (especially Thiodan and BHC) on fish in paddy fields in West Malaysia. – *Malays. Agric. J.* **49**: 224–253.

NATHER KHAN, I. S. A., 1990 a: Preliminary Assessment of the Water Quality and Pollution Threat at the Ulu Lepar Wetland System. – *Asian Wetland Bureau Publication No.* **60**: 21 pp
– 1990 b: Water Quality Survey of the Sungai Sedili Kecil, Malaysia. A Study Carried out in Conjunction with ASEAN/USAID Coastal Resources Management Project. – *Asian Wetland Bureau Report No.* **61**: 32 pp.
– 1990 c: Assessment of water pollution using diatom community structure and species distribution – A case study in a tropical river basin. – *Int. Rev. ges. Hydrobiol.* **75**: 1–22.
– 1990 d: Diatom distribution and intersite relationship in the Linggi River Basin, Peninsular Malaysia. – *Malay. Nat. J.* **44**: 85–95.
– 1991: Effect of urban and industrial wastes on species diversity of the diatom community in a tropical river, Malaysia. – *Hydrobiologia* **224**: 175–184.

NATHER KHAN, I. S. A. & H. I. MOHAMED, M., 1985: Freshwater Malaysian Algae 2. The Diatoms. – *Nature Malaysiana* **10**: 28–31.

NATHER KHAN, I. S. A., FURTADO, J. I. & LIM, R. P., 1987: The periphyton on artificial and natural substrates of a tropical river. – *Arch. Hydrobiol. Beih. Ergebn. Limnol.* **28**: 473–484.

NATHER KHAN, I. S. A., LIM, R. P. & RATINASABAPATHY, M., 1986: Changes in river diatom structure due to natural rubber effluent. – *Malay. J. Sci.* **8**: 85–89.

NG, P. K. L., 1988: The Freshwater Crabs of Peninsular Malaysia and Singapore: 156 pp. – Department of Zoology, National University of Singapore.
– 1990: The taxonomy and biology of *Parathelphusa maculata* DE MAN, 1879 (Crustaceae: Decapoda: Brachyura: Parathelphusidae). – *Malay. Nat. J.* **44**: 45–60.

NG, P. K. L. & CHOY, S. C., 1989: The Caridean prawns (Crustacea: Decapoda) of the Endau-Rompin Park, Malaysia. – *Malay. Nat. J.* **43**: 302–312.

NG, P. K. L. & STEUBING, R., 1989: Description of a new species of montane freshwater crab of the genus *Sundathelphusa* BOTT, 1969 (Crustaceae: Decapoda: Brachyura: Gecarcinucoidea). – *Malay. Nat. J.* **43**: 13–19.

NIRYATI, H. M., 1981: A Study of the Diversity of Algal Communities in the Ricefields of Balik Pulau, Pulau Piang. – Unpublished B. Sc. (Hons.) dissertation, Universiti Sains Malaysia, Penang.

NORHAYATI, M., 1981: Indices for Water Quality Assessment in a River. – Unpublished M. E. thesis, Asian Institute of Technology, Bangkok.

OSMAN, R., 1970: Some aspects of the feeding biology of *Puntius bulu* BLEEKER (Cyprinidae), *Channa micropeltes* CUVIER (Ophicephalidae) and *Wallago leerii* (Siluridae). – 19 pp. B. Sc. (Hons) Thesis, Ecology, Division, Science Faculty, University of Malaya, Kuala Lumpur.

PEH, C. H., 1981: The suspended and dissolved sediment loads of three small forested drainage basins in Peninsular Malaysia. – *Malayan Forester* **44**: 438–452.

PROWSE, G. S., 1962: Diatoms of Malayan freshwaters. – *Gard. Bull. Singapore* **19**: 1–104.
– 1957: An introduction to the desmids of Malaya. – *Malay. Nat. J.* **11**: 42–58.
– 1958: The Eugleninae of Malaya. – *Gard. Bull. Singapore* **16**: 136–204.

PROWSE, G. S. & RATNASABAPATHY, M., 1970: A species list of freshwater algae from the Taiping Lake,

Perak Malaysia. – *Gard. Bull. Singapore* **25**: 179–187.

RATNASABAPATHY, M. & KUMANO, S. 1982: Studies on freshwater red algae of Malaysia I. Some taxa of the genus *Batrachospermum, Ballia* and *Caloglossa* from Pulau Tioman, West Malaysia. – *Jap. J. Phycol.* **30**: 15–22.

SOONG, M. K., 1948: Fishes of Malayan paddy fields I: Sepat Siam (*Trichogaster pectoralis*). – *Malay. Nat. J.* **3**: 87–89.

– 1949: Fishes of Malayan paddy fields II: Aruan: Serpent head fishes. – *Malay. Nat. J.* **4**: 29–31

– 1950: Fishes of Malayan paddy fields III: Keli: Catfish: – *Malay. Nat. J.* **5**: 88–91.

TAN, E. S. P., 1973: The significance of sump-ponds in harvesting paddy-field fishes in North Krian, Perak. – *Malay. Nat. J.* **26**: 26–31.

– 1980: Ecological aspects of some Malaysian riverine cyprinids in relation to their aquaculture potential. – In: FURTADO, J. I. (ed.): Tropical Ecology and Development. Proc. 5th Int. Symp. Trop. Ecol., 16–21 April 1979. – Kuala Lumpur, Malaysia: 757–762.

TWEEDIE, M. W. F., 1952. Malayan aquarium fishes. 1: The genus *Rasbora*. – *Malay. Nat. J.* **7**: 121–124.

– 1953a: Malayan aquarium fishes. 2: The carps and loaches. – *Malay. Nat. J.* **7**: 167–172.

– 1953b: Malayan aquarium fishes 3: The anabantoid fishes. – *Malay. Nat. J.* **8**: 47–51.

WONG, W. C. & LIM, H. F., 1990: The non-government organizations and government policy on environmental issues in Malaysia. – *Wallaceana* **59/60**: 10–15.

YAP, S. Y., 1983: A holistic ecosystem approach to investigating tropical multispecies reservoir fisheries. – *ICLARM Newsletter* **6**: 10–11.

– Recent developments in reservoir fisheries research in tropical Asia. – *Arch. Hydrobiol. Beih. Ergebn. Limnol.* **28**: 295–303.

– 1988: Food resource utilization partitioning of fifteen fish species at Bukit Merah Reservoir, Malaysia. – *Hydrobiologia* **157**: 143–160.

– 1988: Water-quality criteria for the protection of aquatic life and its users in tropical Asian reservoirs. – In: DE SILVA, S. (ed.): Reservoir Fishery Management and Development in Asia. – Proceedings of Workshop at Kathmandu, Nepal, 23–28 Nov. 1987: 74–86.

YAP, S. Y. & FURTADO, J. I., 1981: The feeding ecology of *Cyclocheilichthys apogon* V. (Cyprinidae) in Subang Reservoir, Malaysia. – *Trop. Ecol.* **22**: 194–203.

YAP, S. Y., ONG, H. T. & LIM, K. S., 1989: Formulation of aquaculture development at an ox-bow lake in Malaysia: economic feasibility analysis. – *Aquaculture & Fisheries Management* **20**: 427–439.

YUNUS, A. & LIM, G. S., 1971: A problem in the use of insecticides in paddy fields in West Malaysia – A case study. – *Malays. Agric. J.* **48**: 167–178.

ZAKARIA-ISMAIL, M., 1984: Checklist of fishes of Taman Negara. – *Malay. Nat.* **37**: 21–26.

– 1987: The fish fauna of the Ulu Endau river system, Johor, Malaysia. – *Malay. Nat. J.* **41**: 403–411.

– 1989: First record of the loach, *Botia beauforti* (Cobitidae), from Peninsular Malaysia. – *Malay. Nat. J.* **43**: 78–82.

ZAMAN, Z. & LEONG, T. S., 1987: Seasonal occurrence of *Lytocestus lativitellarium Furtado & Tan* 1973 in *Clarias macrocephalus* GUENTHER in Kedah and Perak, Malaysia. – *Aquaculture* **63**: 319–327.

– 1988: Occurrence of *Procamallanus malaccensis* FERNANDO & FURTADO 1963 in *Clarias batrachus* and *C. macrocephalus* from Kedah and Perak, Malaysia. *Asian Fish. Sci.* **2**: 9–16.

Author's address:

School of Biological Sciences, Universiti Sains Malaysia, 11800 Penang, Malaysia.

Mitt. Internat. Verein. Limnol.	24	147–154	Stuttgart, Februar 1994

The status of limnological research in Bangladesh

Moniruzzaman Khondker

Abstract

A review of limnology in Bangladesh, spanning more than 25 years, is presented. The country has a rich array of aquatic resources including streams, rivers, *beels, haors, baors,* reservoirs and ponds. Research work that has been undertaken on physicochemical limnology and phytoplankton ecology (community composition, abundance and seasonality) is summarized, and quantitative and qualitative studies of the limnological factors affecting a wide range of aquatic organisms are discussed. Human influences on inland waters – which have been increasing – are described, and the facilities available for limnological research, training and education are listed. An attempt has been made to identify the major limnological problems facing Bangladesh, and to indicate some possible solutions.

Introduction

Bangladesh is situated in the humid tropics of southern Asia. Except for a part of the southeastern border (Arakan Province bordering Burma) and the Bay of Bengal in the south, the country is bounded on all sides by India (Fig. 1). The land mass of Bangladesh can be divided into three physiographic regions: Pleistocene uplands (highest peak 46 m), Tertiary hills (highest peak 1,004 m), and Recent plains of low elevation which comprise approximately 80% of the total land area. Much of the latter consist of flood plains and deltaic deposits associated with the confluences of the Ganges, Brahmaputra and Meghna River systems. The Sundarbans in the southwestern portion of Bangladesh constitute one of the world's largest mangrove forests. Further information on the geography and topology of Bangladesh are given by Rashid (1977) and Miah (1981).

Bangladesh has a monsoonal climate characterized by hot, wet, humid summers and mild, dry winters (Table 1). Heavy rainfall during the four- to five-month monsoon season, combined with flooding of the major river systems, contribute to the existence of a diverse array of aquatic habitats of varying dimensions and durational stability. Although Bangladesh has extensive aquatic resources (combined area estimated at 36,663 km^2), the country is densely populated and there has been significant degradation of the inland waters. Nevertheless, these habitats have the potential to provide protein for the growing population, and this fact underscores the importance of limnological research in Bangladesh. The present review describes the limnological potential of Bangladesh together with the investigations completed so far and the research yet to be undertaken.

Inland-water resources

The deltaic nature of much of the land mass of Bangladesh has the consequence that perennial and seasonal water bodies are influenced greatly by the flooding activity of major rivers, and the accumulation of monsoonal rain water in shallow tectonic depressions. A brief account of the major types of inland waters is given below; the area occupied by each is shown in Table 2.

Rivers, flood plains and tributaries

The larger rivers of Bangladesh (e.g. the Ganges, Jamuna, Padma and Meghna) tend to be slow-flowing with high silt loads and a tendency to shift their meandering courses within the flood plains. The lowlying areas surrounding these rivers are inundated by rising water levels between June and early November. Deep-water rice (a strain of *Oryza sativa* L.) is widely cultivated in such habitats. The main river courses, which are often braided, are fed by tributaries of varying sizes such that the land is crisscrossed by interconnecting networks of channels. Their density increases towards the estuarine southwest of the country.

Beels

Beels occupy basins between the levees of large rivers. They are generally saucer-like depressions and frequently occupy channels that have been abandoned by meandering rivers. During the monsoon season they are filled with water and resemble lakes, but when water levels recede they become marshy with extensive growths of emergent plants. Some *beels* dry up completely and are cultivated for part of the year, while others retain extensive areas of open water in all seasons (Rashid 1977). *Beel* Mishra (6,475 ha), Chalan

0538-4680/94/0024-0147 $ 2.00

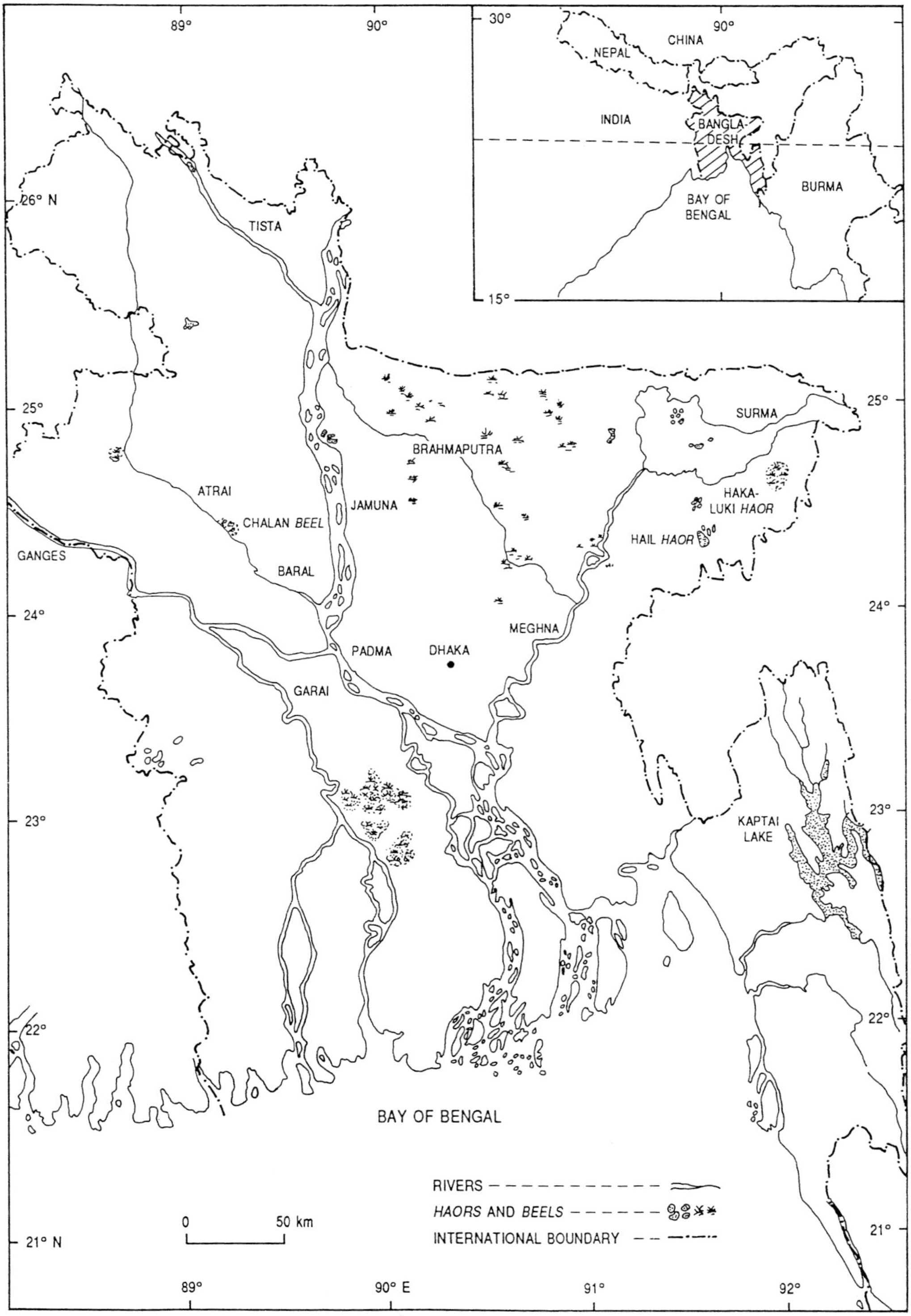

Fig. 1. Map of Bangladesh showing major rivers, *haors, beels* and Kaptai Lake. Inset shows the geographical location of the country in the Indian sub-continent.

Table 1. Geoclimatic condition of Bangladesh. Data from RAHMAN (pers. comm.; Department of Geography, University of Dhaka).

Latitude	20°34′N–26°38′N
Longitude	88°01′E–92°41′E
Area	143,998 km²
Population (1991)*	107,992,140
Rural	90.05%
Urban	9.95%
Population density	782/km²
Literacy	24.8%
Mean air temperature (1983)	11.1–34.8 °C
Total mean annual rainfall (1984)	2,569.5 mm
Mean humidity (1983)	79.6%

* *Preliminary Population Census data,* 1991.

Table 2. The inland waters of Bangladesh; data derived from AMEEN (1987), DUIJVENDIJK (1987) and RAHMAN (1988).

Type	Area (km²)	Per cent of total area
Rivers (excluding estuaries)	2,171	5.9
Tributaries	2,626	7.2
Beels and *haors*	1,148	3.1
Ox-bow lakes	55	0.2
Seasonal flood plains	28,328	77.3
Kaptai Lake	688	1.9
Feni Reservoir	12	0.03
Ponds	1,635	4.5
Total	36,663	

Beel, Kamaladaha, Dakatia and Arial *Beel* are examples of the latter category (AMEEN 1987).

Haors

These characteristic water bodies occur within tectonic depressions or *haor* basins in Sylhet, Netrokona and Kishoreganj Districts. *Haors* are formed in those parts of the basins which are especially deeply depressed. The entire basin is flooded during the monsoon, but the shallower portion dries up during the inter-monsoon period; the deeper parts do not dry out, however, and form perennial water bodies. Examples include Hakaluki *haor* (34,437 ha), Tangua *haor* (25,506 ha) and Hail *haor*.

Baors

Baors are ox-bow lakes formed by when the loop of a meandering river is cut off from the main flow. Typically they are shallow, stagnant water bodies with much rooted aquatic vegetation. Some are perennial. All of the *baors* are located in the moribund delta area of southwest Bangladesh (Jessore District). The main *baors* in this area include Baluhar (282 ha), Makjat (253 ha) and Gabindapur *baor* (217 ha).

Lakes and reservoirs

There are only three natural lakes in Bangladesh: Rainkhyongkine Lake (1.6 km × 0.4 km; Z_{max} = 26 m), which has been formed in a kettle-hole type depression (ISLAM 1969), and Bogakine Lakes – both in the Chittagong Hill-Tracts – and Ashula *beel* in Eastern Barind Tract (ISLAM 1969, RASHID 1977, AMEEN 1987). The country has only two reservoirs. Kaptai Reservoir is an H-shaped water body with a deep-water discharge. It was formed by impounding the River Karnaphuli in the Chittagong Hill-Tracts in 1961 to generate hydroelectric power. Feni Reservoir was commissioned in 1986 for flood control and irrigation by construction of a cross dam and regulator at the mouth of the Feni River (Feni District). It is a surface-release reservoir (AMEEN 1987, DUIJVENDIJK 1987).

Ponds

Village ponds play an important socioeconomic role in the rural communities of Bangladesh. Ponds may be dug for fish culture or domestic water storage; in the lower flood-plain area they arise from the accumulation of water in pits dug to obtain building material. Pond basins which are constructed deliberately are dug sufficiently deep to reach the sub-soil water and thus contain water throughout the year. Large ponds – known as *dighi* – are relics of recreational ponds which tradition dictated were usually present in the grounds of the residential palaces of zamindars (fuedal landlords or collectors of land revenue).

Trends in limnological research

Limnological research in Bangladesh was pioneered by the Phycological Research Group of the Department of Botany, Dhaka University, under the guidance of Professor A. K. M. NURUL ISLAM. ISLAM & KHATUN (1966) published the first limnological research study in Bangladesh dealing with organically-polluted ponds in and around Dhaka University campus. In particular, they recorded the conditions under which blooms of blue-green algae and bacteria occurred in the ponds. Additional research on the same ponds (Islam & Nahar 1967) concentrated on blue-green algae, especially *Microcystis* sp. Other investigations carried out around the same period included the use of algal flora to characterize Lake Rainkhyongkine as a semi-hard water body in the late oligotrophic stage (Islam 1969). Islam & Begum (1970) recorded 110 species of phytoplankton (mainly Chlorococcales) from Dhaka District and made some observations on seasonal changes in water temperature and pH.

Limnological research in Bangladesh began to increase between 1971 and 1980. A study of eight stations along a five-km stretch of the River Buriganga between Parzoar and Postgola, yielded data on water quality including dissolved oxygen, total nitrogen, phosphates and pH, and demonstrated that phytoplankton abundance peaked from March to May and declined during the winter (Islam et al. 1974). The Freshwater Fisheries Research Station at Chandpur conducted a limnological survey between 1969 and 1971; although rather few variables were measured the survey considered rivers, *baors* and *dighis* in different districts throughout Bangladesh (Anonymous 1971, 1973). Other work included studies by Islam & Saha (1975) of Ramna Lake (Dhaka City) and Islam & Mendes (1976) of Sher-e-bangla Nagar *jheel,* and a two-year investigation of biomass and biomass content (protein, lipid, ash, etc.) of *Wolffia arrhiza* (L.) Wimm, in a shallow pond in Faridpur District (Islam & Paul 1977). Details of the physico-chemical limnology and abundance of plankton in three ponds in Dhaka City were reported by Oppenheimer et al. (1978), while surveys of the macrophytes and phytoplankton of Hakaluki *haor* and Dhanmondi Lake were undertaken by Islam & Paul (1978), Islam & Chowdhury and Islam et al. (1979) who provided also some limnological notes on these water bodies.

More recently Chowdhury & Mazumder (1981) studied the seasonal, vertical, horizontal and diurnal fluctuations in water temperature, transparency, pH, dissolved oxygen, carbon dioxide, phosphates and nitrates in Kaptai Reservoir which they characterised as oligotrophic. Diurnal fluctuations in physicochemical factors and the population dynamics of plankton (*Cyclops, Daphnia, Diaphanosoma, Diaptomus* and rotifers) in a holding tank in the grounds of the Freshwater Fisheries Research Station at Chandpur have been described by Ali et al. (1982), and Ali et al. (1985) reported upon an inverse relationship between macroinvertebrate abundance (especially Ceratopogonidae) and water depth in a fish pond. Other work in fish ponds, involving comparative studies of semi-intensive and extensive fish culture ponds in southeastern districts of Bangladesh have been undertaken by Ameen et al. (1986) and Begum & Alam (1987). Research on rivers has been less intensive, but Ittekot et al. (1985) and Safiulah et al. (1985) have documented the aspects of the limnology of the Ganges and Brahmaputra, particularly levels of dissolved oxygen, alkalinity, hardness, suspended solids, and organic loads (sugars, amino acids, etc.).

Data on primary production of inland waters in Bangladesh are meagre. The earliest records are by Mahmood (1986) who quotes a value for Kaptai Lake of 2.39 g $O_2/m^2/day$ (average of one year's data); however, details of measurement technique and areal integration procedure are lacking. Khondker et al. (1988) and Khondker & Parveen (unpublished observations) have carried out detailed studies of the primary productivity (at 0.5 m depth) over one year in Dhanmondi Lake, Dhaka City, arriving at a mean value of 26.19 g $O_2/m^2/day$. Additional data on the comparative limnology of lentic habitats in Bangladesh are given in Table 3.

River flood plains, which are inundated for four to five months each year, account for 77 % of the total aquatic resources of Bangladesh. They are important sites for open-water fisheries and cultivation of deep-water rice. The limnology of the inundated flood-plain under rice cultivation has been researched by B. A. Whitton and co-workers during 1981-83, 1985 and 1986. A wide variety of factors were investigated including water chemistry, biogenic gases, and species composition, biomass and chemical composition of aquatic macrophytes, as well as epiphytic algae on rice stems and the role of heterocystous blue-greens in nitrogen fixation (Rother & Whitton 1988, Rother et al. 1988; Whitton & Rother 1988, Whitton et al. 1988a, 1988b, 1988c).

The development of limnology in Bangladesh during recent years has begun to provide a theoretical base for the science, but many generalizations about inland waters are still based upon the findings of research undertaken in temperate regions where limnology has a relatively long history. Although it is assumed that tropical lakes are generally similar in many (but not all) of their

Table 3. Comparative limnology (mean values) of three lentic habitats around Dhaka, Bangladesh. Kaptai Lake data are from MAHMOOD (1986), Dhanmondi Lake data are from KHONDKER & PARVEEN (unpubl. observ.), and Circuit House Pond data are from OPPENHEIMER et al. (1978).

Parameters	Kaptai Lake ($n = 12$)	Dhanmondi Lake ($n = 22$)	Circuit House Pond ($n = 12$)
PAR input ($\mu E/m^2/s^1$)	–	834	–
Z_{max} (m)	36	4.77	2.54
Z_s (m)	2.03	0.40	–
Water temp. (°C)	27	27.9	25.53
pH	7.20	7.43	6.89
Alkalinity (meq/l)	0.88	3.70	1.30
Conductivity ($\mu S/cm$)	114	579	170
DO (mg/l)	5.3	7.77	3.18
DO (% sat.)	67	99	39
Silicate (mg/l)	7.67	30.55*	–
SRP (mg/l)	0.53	0.88	0.22
NO_3-N (mg/l)	1.63	0.16	0.78
Chl *a* (mg/m^3)	–	265	–

* Data from KHONDKER & RAHIM (unpubl. observ.)

features (FERNANDO 1980), it will be interesting to discover the ways in which the structure and metabolism of aquatic communities are adapted to the particular habitat features and patterns of thermal mixing in the inland waters of Bangladesh.

Human influences upon inland waters of Bangladesh

As in most densely-populated countries, the inland waters of Bangladesh are affected profoundly by human activities. Despite intense human impacts upon small water bodies such as ponds, ditches and roadside canals, these habitats are host to a wide range of organisms including algae, macrophytes, zooplankton, fishes and birds. However, there are signs that environmental degradation is increasing. Studies of organic pollution incorporating measurements of water chemistry, periphytic algae, and the seasonality and diversity of plankton in a number of ponds and in Dhanmondi Lake have been undertaken by ISLAM & KHONDKER (1991) KHONDKER et al. (1990) and KHONDKER & RAHIM (unpublished observations). Organically enriched ponds were often dominated by *Euglena;* profuse growths of *Spirodela polyrhiza* (L.) SCHLEID and *Lemna perpusila* TORREY were frequent also. More generally, high temperatures and high inputs of nutrients in many shallow water bodies favours development of blooms of coccoid cyanobacteria and euglenoid algae. Such habitats become choked with aquatic weeds such as *Eichhornia crassipes* (MART.) SOLMS, *Pistia stratiotes* L., *Lemna perpusila, Spirodela polyrhiza, Salvinia* spp. and *Azolla pinnata* R. BROWN.

Pollution of inland waters by human wastes are a matter for particular concern in areas lacking sewerage systems, where water-borne diseases such as typhoid, cholera, diarrhoea, bacterial dysentery, hepatitis A and polio can occur. Diarrhoea claims many lives in Bangladesh every year through contamination of drinking water, and is especially important in drought years when villagers may be forced to take drinking water from polluted sources. Less serious, but still a matter for some concern, are skin rashes and irritation reported by persons bathing in hypertrophic waters contaminated by algal blooms. Occasional fish kills occur in such waters and at sites where there are high levels of pollution by industrial wastes.

Intensive agriculture in Bangladesh has given rise to a further threat. The 'green revolution' aimed at increasing food production – and which has given rise, in particular, to rice monocultures – intensified the use of urea, potash, phosphate and pesticides on cultivated land by factors of 14, 7, 10 and 44 fold (respectively) between 1970 and 1984 (SAFIULLAH & HUQ 1986). Monsoonal rains wash the residues of these compounds into freshwaters and, as WHITTON et al. (1988a) have shown, may lead to high loads of heavy metals (cobalt, nickel, copper, zinc, cadmium and lead) in deep-water rice fields. Furthermore, nitrate concentrations in a ground-water aquifer in the vicinity of Chalan *beel* have been reported to reach 27 mg/l at times, exceeding the maximum safe level of 11 mg/l recommended by the World Health Organization (Safiullah & Huq 1986). High nitrate levels in drinking water can have detrimental health effects, especially in small children (methaemoglobinemia) but also in adults when nitrosamines – which are known carcinogens – are formed.

Although manufacturing is not well developed in Bangladesh, industries involved in the production of jute, textiles, leather, fertilizers, cane sugar, cement, ceramics, and pulp and paper are present. Most lack any form of pollution-control system and effluents are discharged without treatment. Scant attention has been paid to these polluters, and there is little public awareness of the issues involved. The severity of the problem can be illustrated by two examples. Tannery effluents discharged in Dhaka City into the River Buriganga have BOD levels of 800–3,300 mg/l, COD of 1,870–31,200 mg/l and concentrations of chromium exceeding 5 mg/l. Wastes discharged from a fertilizer factory into the River Sitalakhya contain 50–400 mg/l organic nitrogen, and the receiving water is said to be devoid of fish. It is clear that a coherent policy to protect the aquatic resources of Bangladesh from industrial pollution is needed sooner rather than later.

Among the wide range of human influences upon freshwaters in Bangladesh, the regulation of the flow of the Ganges through water-sharing with India, is especially important. Water is diverted from the Ganges into irrigation systems at the Farakka barrage in India and, in drought years when river discharge is low, relatively small amounts of water flow beyond the barrage into Bangladesh. As a result, negotiations on water sharing are an important feature of international relations between Bangladesh and India.

Fisheries

Fisheries is second to agriculture as a foreign-exchange earner for Bangladesh, contributing approximately 9% to total earnings. Fish also comprise 6 % of the per-capita protein intake and about 80% of the animal protein intake of the population (Rahman 1988). A 40 % decrease in per-capita fish protein consumption has been recorded over the past three decades, and the present intake rate (21 g/person/day) is only 37 % of the value required for healthy nutrition. Clearly, efforts are needed to promote aquaculture and enhance capture fisheries in Bangladesh, but the potential for increasing catches from natural stocks is limited by increasing degradation and pollution of inland waters. Development of aquaculture is likely to become increasingly important, and limnologists can play an important role in this multidisciplinary subject. The potential for progress in aquaculture is highlighted by the observation that maximum fish production in semi-intensively managed ponds in Bangladesh is only 14 % of production rates obtained in Israel and Taiwan (Ameen 1987, Hepher & Pruginin 1981).

Limnological research and education

There is no independent limnological research institute in Bangladesh. The discipline has developed so far as an outgrowth of other aspects of biology, such as zoology, botany and ecology. The Department of Botany at Dhaka University offers undergraduate courses in limnology at the undergraduate and postgraduate levels, and there is a well-organized research team working on hydrobiology and limnology. The Zoology Department, too, has the potential to carry out research on aquatic fauna. Elsewhere in Bangladesh, limnological research (involving, in some cases, doctoral programmes) is being undertaken in the Department of Zoology and the Marine Science Institute at Chittagong University, the Department of Botany at Rajshahi University and in the Life Science Institute at Jahangir Nagar University. Investigations of phytoplankton, zooplankton, zoobenthos and fishes are carried out in the Department of Limnology and Fisheries Biology and in the Department of Aquaculture and Management at the Bangladesh Agriculture University (Mymensingh), while limited limnological research is conducted by the River Research Institute (Faridpur), the Environmental Pollution Control Board (Government of Bangladesh), and the Civil Engineering Department of Bangladesh University of Engineering and Technology (Dhaka). Moreover, a number of government fisheries institutes offer training programmes dealing with fish culture in inland waters.

Conclusions

Despite progress in recent years, limnological research in Bangladesh is still in its infancy. Most of the habitats studied so far were selected for the convenience of sampling which was often dictated by their proximity to research centres. As a result, the vast majority of the country's *haors, baors, beels* and other water bodies have yet to be investigated. While these habitats remain attractive sites for scientific investigation, there are at least three topics in applied limnology where research is needed urgently: nutrient cycling and productivity, pollution and eutrophication, and aquaculture. Data from such studies can be combined with basic information from hydrobiological and limnological surveys, and should be used to develop management and conservation strategies for the inland waters of Bangladesh. Some matters of current concern include the effects of increasing usage of chemical fertilizers and pesticides in agriculture upon the open-water capture fisheries which provide 61 % of the country's total fish catch. Greater use of wetland products is being considered also since, besides fish, the fruits, seeds, rhizomes, peduncles and young shoots of many aquatic plants (e.g. *Nelumbo nucifera* GAERTN., *Euryale ferox* SALISB., *Trapa bispinosa* ROXB., *Nymphaea nouchali* BURM., *Telanthera philoxeroides* MOQ., *Alternanthera philoxeroides* (Mart.) GRISCO. and *Ipomoea aquatica Forsk.)* are consumed in rural areas. Many of these are rich in vitamins and minerals and, if they could be included as aquaculture crops, would contribute to the reduction of malnutrition among young children. Recycling wastes, the production of compost, and cattle- or poultry-feed could also involve the utilization of fast-growing macrophytes.

Bangladesh has already developed some expertise in limnology and new graduates are being added constantly to this 'think tank'. It is now time to establish a well-equipped limnological institute in the country, to assist the government in halting the tide of environmental degradation and to undertake research into all aspects of limnology. A considerable amount of funding will be needed to found an institute capable of meeting all of the current and projected needs of limnology in Bangladesh, and it is unlikely that such a goal can be attained without substantial financial help from abroad.

References

ALI, S., MAJID, A. & CHOWDHURY, A. Q., 1985. Studies on the benthic macroinvertebrates in a freshwater pond, Bangladesh. – *Pakistan J. Zool.* **17**: 301–306.

ALI, S., RAHMAN, A. K. A., PATWARY, A. R. & ISLAM, K. R., 1982: Studies on the diurnal variations in physico-chemical factors and zooplankton in a freshwater pond. – *Bangladesh J. Fish.* **2–5**: 15–24.

AMEEN, M. U., 1987: Fisheries resources and opportunities in freshwater fish culture in Bangladesh. – 244 pp. NRD-II Project/DANIDA, Noakhali, Bangladesh.

AMEEN, M. U., BEGUM, Z N. T., ALI, S., RAHMAN, M. M. & ROY, T. K., 1986: A comparative limnological study of two fish ponds in Raipur. – *Dhaka University Stud. Pt. E* **1**: 25–34.

Anonymous, 1971: Annual report of the Freshwater Fisheries Research Station at Chandpur, Comilla (FFRS), for the 1969–1970 and 1970–1971. – Government of the People's Republic of Bangladesh, Directorate of Fisheries.

– 1973: Annual report of the Freshwater Fisheries Research Station at Chandpur, Comilla (FFRS), for the year ending 30th June, 1969. – Government of the People's Republic of Bangladesh, Directorate of Fisheries.

BEGUM, Z. N. T. & ALAM, M. J., 1987: Plankton abundance in relation to physicochemical variables in two ponds in Maijdee Court, Noakhali. – *J. Asiatic Soc. Bangladesh (Sci.)* **13**: 55–63.

CHOWDHURY, S. H. & MAZUMDER, A., 1981: Limnology of lake Kaptai: I. Physicochemical features. – *Bangladesh J. Zool.* **9**: 59–72.

DUIJVENDIJK, H. V., 1987: They stopped the sea. – *National Geographic* **172**: 92–100.

FERNANDO, C. H., 1980: Some important implications for tropical limnology. – In: MORI, S. & IKUSIMA, I. (eds.). Proceedings of the First Workshop on the Promotion of Limnology in the Developing Countries: 103–107. SIL Kyoto.

HEPHER, B. & PRUGININ, Y., 1981: Commercial fish farming with special reference to fish culture in Israel: 261 pp. – John Wiley & Sons, N.Y.

ISLAM, A. K. M. N., 1969: A preliminary report on the phytoplanktons and other algal flora of Chittagong Hill-Tracts. – *J. Asiatic Soc. Pakistan* **14**: 343–363.

ISLAM, A. K. M. N. & BEGUM, Z. N. T., 1970: Studies on the phytoplankton of Dacca district. – *J. Asiatic Soc. Pakistan* **15**: 227–271.

ISLAM, A. K. M. N. & CHOWDHURY, A. R., 1979: Hydrobiological studies of Dhanmondi Lake, Dacca II. Phytoplankton. – *J. Asiatic. Soc. Bangladesh (Sci.)* **5**: 47–57.

ISLAM, A. K. M. N., HAROON, A K. Y. & ZAMAN, K. M., 1974: Limnological studies of the river Buriganga. – *Dacca Univ. Stud. Pt. B* **22**: 99–111.

ISLAM, A. K. M. N. & KHATUN, M., 1966: Preliminary studies on the phytoplanktons of polluted waters. – *Sci. Res.* **3**: 94–109.

ISLAM, A. K. M. N. & KHONDKER, M. 1991: Preliminary limnological investigations on some polluted waters covered by duckweeds. – *Bangladesh J. Bot.* **20**: 73–75.

ISLAM, A. K. M. N. & MENDES, F., 1976: Limnological studies of a jheel in Sher-e-Bangla Nagar. – *Dacca Univ. Stud. Pt. B* **24**: 63–71.

ISLAM, A. K. M. N. & NAHAR, L., 1967: Preliminary studies on the phytoplanktons of polluted waters. Part II. Blue-green algae. – *Sci. Res.* **4**: 141–149.

ISLAM, A. K. M. N. & PAUL, N., 1978: Hydrobiological study of the Haor Hakaluki in Sylhet. – *J. Asiatic Soc. Bangladesh (Sci.)* **3**: 83–91.

– 1977: Limnological studies on *Wolffia arrhiza* (L.) WIMM. – *J. Asiatic Soc. Bangladesh (Sci.)* **3**: 111–123.

ISLAM, A. K. M. N., RAHMAN, M. & CHOWDHURY, A. R., 1979: Hydrobiological studies of Dhanmondi Lake, Dacca. 1. Macrophytes and benthic flora. – *J. Asiatic Soc. Bangladesh (Sci.)* **5**: 59–75.

ISLAM, A. K. M. N. & SAHA, J. K. 1975: Limnological studies of the Ramna Lake at Dacca. – *Dacca Univ. Stud. Pt. B* **23**: 39–46.

ITTEKOT, V., SAFIULLAH, S., MYCKE, B. & SEIFERT, R., 1985: Seasonal variability and geochemical significance of organic matter in the river Ganges, Bangladesh. – *Nature* **317**: 800–802.

KHONDKER, M., ISLAM, A. K. M. N., BEGUM, Z N. T. & HAQUE, S., 1990: Limnological studies of four polluted ponds in and around Dhaka city with reference to indicator species. – *Bangladesh J. Bot.* **19**: 51–63.

KHONDKER, M., ISLAM, A. K. M. N. & ISLAM, R., 1988: Studies on the primary productivity of Dhanmondi lake. – *Dhaka Univ. Stud. Pt. E* **1**: 15–21.

MAHMOOD, N., 1986: Hydrobiology of the Kaptai Reservoir. Final report on the Kaptai Reservoir studies programme: 190 pp. – FAO/UNDP Aquaculture Development and Coordination Programmes, Rome, Italy. Contract No. DP/BGD/79/615-4/Fl.

MIAH, M. M., 1981: The physical environment: physiography, rivers and flood. – In: ISLAM, M. A. & MIAH, M. M. (eds.): Bangladesh in maps: 77 pp. – University of Dhaka.

OPPENHEIMER, J. R., AHMED, M. G., HUQ, A., HAQUE, K. A., ALAM, A. K. A. U., AZIZ, K. M. S., ALI, S. & HAQUE, A. S. M. M., 1978: Limnological studies of three ponds in Dacca, Bangladesh. – *Bangladesh J. Fish.* **1**: 1–26.

RAHMAN, M. A., 1988: The need for reservoir fishery management in Bangladesh. – In: DE SILVA, S. S. (ed.): Reservoir fishery management and development in Asia: 246 pp. – International Development Research Centre, Ottawa, Ontario, Canada.

RASHID, H. E. R., 1977: Geography of Bangladesh: 579 pp. – University Press Ltd., Dhaka, Bangladesh.

ROTHER, J. A., AZIZ, A., KARIM, N. H. & WHITTON, B. A., 1988: Ecology of deepwater rice-fields in Bangladesh. 4. Nitrogen fixation by blue-green algal communities. – *Hydrobiologia* **169**: 43–56.

ROTHER, J. A. & WHITTON, B. A., 1988: Ecology of deepwater rice-fields in Bangladesh 5. Mineral composition of the rice plant and other aquatic macrophytes. – *Hydrobiologia* **169**: 57–67.

SAFIULLAH, S., CHOWDHURY, M. I., MAFIZUDDIN, M., ALI, I. & KARIM, M., 1985: Monitoring of the Padma (Ganges), the Jamuna (Brahmaputra) and the Baral in Bangladesh. – *Mitt. Geol. Palaeont. Inst. Univ. Hamburg, SCOPE/UNEP Sonderband* **58**: 519–524.

SAFIULLAH, S. & HUQ, S., 1986: Environmental studies in Bangladesh – a perspective for the less developed countries. – *The Science of the Total Environment* **55**: 165–173.

WHITTON, B. A., AZIZ, A., FRANCIS, P., ROTHER, J. A., SIMSON, J. W. & TAHMIDA, Z. N., 1988a: Ecology of deepwater rice-fields in Bangladesh. 1. Physical and chemical environment. – *Hydrobiologia* **169**: 3–22.

WHITTON, B. A., AZIZ, A., KAWECKA, B. & ROTHER, J. A., 1988 b: Ecology of deepwater rice-fields in Bangladesh. 3. Associated algae and macrophytes. – *Hydrobiologia* **169**: 31–42.

WHITTON, B. A. & ROTHER, J. A., 1988: Diel changes in the environment of a deepwater rice-field in Bangladesh. – *Verh. Internat. Verein. Limnol.* **23**: 1074–1079.

WHITTON, B. A., ROTHER, J. A. & PAUL, A. R., 1988 c. Ecology of deepwater rice-fields in Bangladesh. 2. Chemistry of sites at Manikganj and Sonargaon. – *Hydrobiologia* **169**: 23–30

Author's address:

Department of Botany, University of Dhaka, Dhaka 1000, Bangladesh.

Mitt. Internat. Verein. Limnol.	24	155–163	Stuttgart, Februar 1994

Limnology in the northeastern tropics of Australia, the wettest part of the driest continent

R. G. Pearson

Abstract

Until recently, research work dealing with the inland waters of northern Australia was neglected. The current increase in environmental awareness has provided a stimulus for research on the fresh waters of tropical Queensland and the Northern Territory, and – in 1988 – led to the establishment of the Australian Centre for Tropical Freshwater Research (ACTFR) at James Cook University of North Queensland. This review briefly describes the inland water habitats of tropical Queensland, and summarizes previous and ongoing research on these habitats, with emphasis upon work undertaken by the ACTFR which has centred mainly upon streams. These ecosystems are biodiverse, and an important research goal of ACTFR is to understand the biological processes in tropical Australian inland waters, with a view to long-term management and conservation of aquatic resources. A brief account of priorities for future research on these ecosystems is included.

Introduction

Australia is said to be the world's largest island and its smallest continent (area 7,682,300 km^2). Two-fifths of it lie north of the Tropic of Capricorn (Fig. 1), but the majority of the population lives in the large cities to the south. Australia is also said to be the driest inhabited continent, and its perennial freshwater bodies are rather scarce. However, parts of the eastern ranges receive good rainfall, and this contributes to the diversity of vegetation on the continent. In the tropical north the climate is largely governed by rainfall seasonality, with a summer wet season and winter dry season (Fig. 2). On the mountains and coastal plains of north Queensland, tropical rainforest is the natural vegetation; with progression inland this grades through open forest, woodland and savanna to desert, in accordance with the rainfall distribution.

Despite the general dryness of the continent and the need to conserve water supplies and maintain high water quality, ecological studies of fresh waters have only in recent years become a significant portion of the scientific literature for Australia. Governments are now recognising the need for ecological work and are beginning to provide better funding for their environmental departments and agencies. Much of the stimulus for increased research has come from the dire state of some major southern freshwater systems, such as the Murray River, which is a reflection of poor land and water management.

Until recently research into inland waters in the north of Australia was particularly neglected. The majority of biological publications resulted from brief collecting trips by taxonomists and, occasionally, ecologists. This neglect was due partly to there being little perception of problems in water supply and quality because of the low population density, limited industrial development and, in coastal areas, a relatively copious supply of water. It was also due to the absence of scientists with interests in freshwater systems in the north. Growth of population centres and of agricultural and mining based industries has necessitated the construction of large water-storage bodies and the closer monitoring of water quality. Concurrently, there has been a great increase in public environmental awareness. As a result, during recent years there has been a steady output of reports on the ecology of freshwater systems from regions as far-flung as the Alligator Rivers east of Darwin (e.g. Humphrey & Dostine 1994), the Mt. Isa area of western Queensland (e.g. Boland & Imberger 1994), and coastal north Queensland, near Townsville (Fig. 1).

The main problem with the applied mission-based research in the northern region is that there are few reference points in natural systems. The research in the Alligator Rivers region has had to address this problem in order to find solutions to practical problems in relation to uranium mining (e.g. Hart & McGregor 1980, Marchant 1982, Bishop et al. 1986, Outridge 1987, Tait 1988, Finlayson et al. 1990, Humphrey et al. 1990, Humphrey & Dostine 1994). In northern Queensland, research until recently was undertaken on an *ad hoc* basis, depending on small-scale needs of industry and on individual scientists' interests. The Australian Centre for Tropical Freshwater Research (ACTFR) was established in 1988 at James Cook University of North Queensland in Townsville to consolidate and expand research programmes and to increase commercial awareness and inputs to aquatic research in tropical Australia. Two of the long-term aims of the Centre are to provide basic physical and biological inventories of tropical aquatic systems and to understand processes in them, with a view to long-term management and conservation of aquatic resources. These resources include the water itself as a

0538-4680/94/0024-0155 $ 2.25

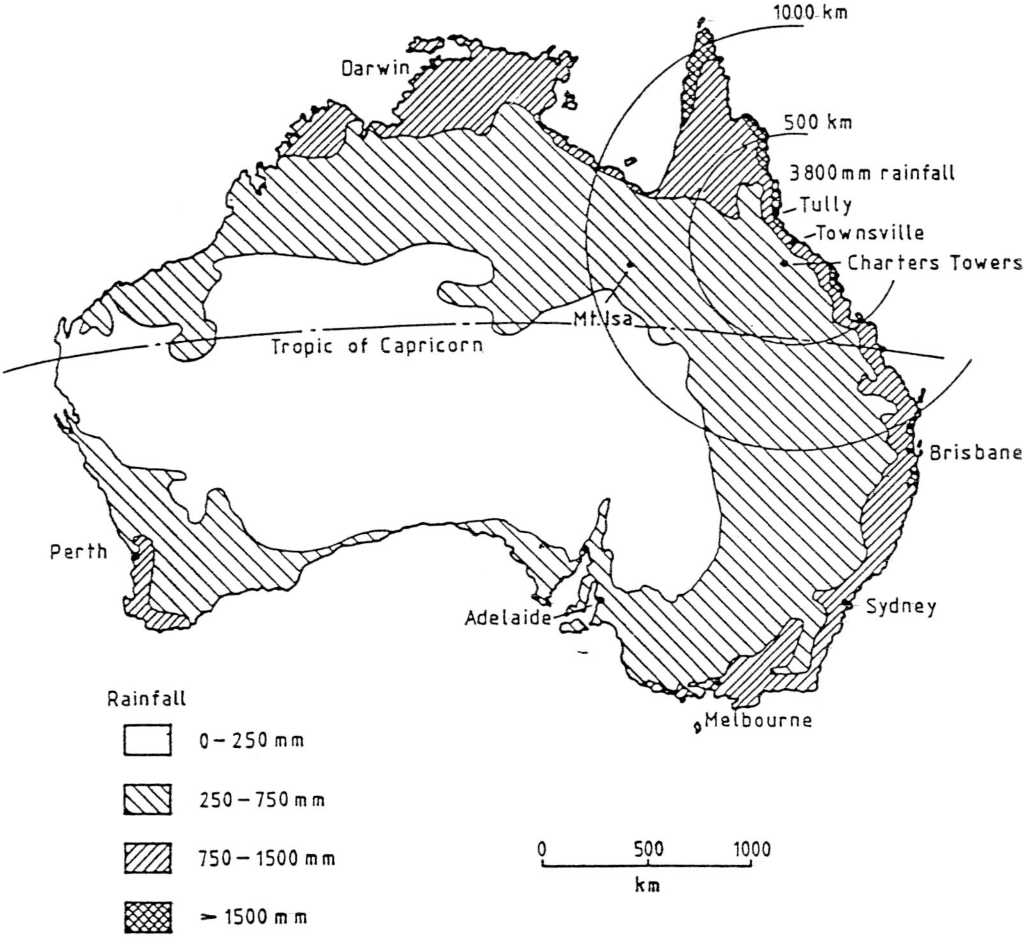

Fig. 1. Map of mainland Australia showing rainfall distribution, location of some cities, and location of places in tropical Queensland mentioned in the text and Fig. 2. The circles show distances of 500 km and 1000 km from Townsville.

usable commodity, the biodiversity dependent on water bodies and the aesthetic values of aquatic environments. This review briefly summarises some of the work of the Centre and its associates.

Characteristics of inland waters of tropical Queensland

Staff and students associated with the Centre have been undertaking a range of studies in tropical Queensland both to address applied problems and, especially, to seek basic understanding of the functioning and interactions of tropical freshwater systems and their individual animal and plant populations. We have undertaken studies in a variety of habitats, from dune lakes to Lake Dalrymple (Burdekin Dam), and from temporary pools to the Burdekin River, and we have extended our interests further afield through contract research in Indonesia and New Guinea. This review deals mainly with work done or in progress in tropical Queensland in the continent's north east, and especially the coastal belt from Townsville to Cooktown. This area includes the Queensland wet tropics which is the only region of the Australian tropics not to experience a water deficit (Body 1979). It is, therefore, relatively well endowed with fresh waters. However, even in the wettest parts of the region precipitation is highly seasonal as are, accordingly, most freshwater systems (Fig. 2).

On much of the coastal plain there are seasonal swamps but other bodies of standing water are scarce: they include several crater lakes on the Atherton Table-

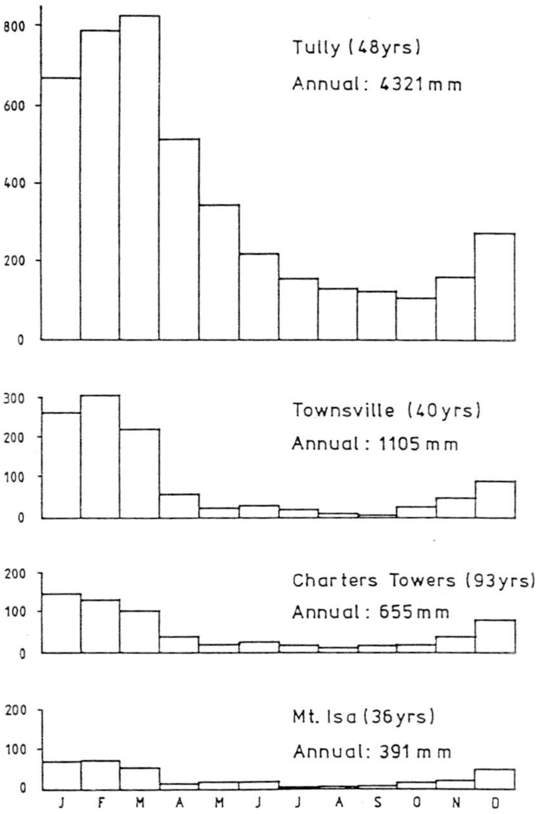

Fig. 2. Mean monthly and annual rainfall (mm) from various locations in tropical Queensland (see Fig. 1 for locations).

lands, north of Tully, and a few other small lakes. The largest lakes in the region are the seasonal and saline Lakes Buchanan and Galilee, south-west of Charters Towers; others are man-made (e.g. Lakes Dalrymple, near Charters Towers, Tinaroo, north of Tully and Julius at Mt. Isa). Natural lakes are not, therefore, a major feature of the region. However, there are many small permanent water bodies, ranging from dune lakes on the far northern coast, through the billabongs and lagoons of the flood plains of major rivers, to the inland permanent pools in otherwise intermittent rivers. Additionally there are numerous farm dams throughout the region. ARTHINGTON & HEGERL (1988) and ARTHINGTON (1988) have reviewed the occurrence and conservation status of wetlands and natural lakes in Queensland.

Freshwater streams and rivers are prominent features of the eastern tropics. Much of the landscape of the coastal ranges is heavily dissected by steeply descending rocky streams in steep-sided forested valleys. The intensity of wet season rainfall leads to highly erosive discharges in these streams; however, for much of the year the discharge is only a small fraction of the peak, in accordance with the seasonal climate. A characteristic of these streams, therefore, is their seasonal hydrograph and, because of the extreme intensity of wet season storms, they are very prone to sudden and frequent spates.

Similarly, the large rivers draining the inland plains are highly seasonal. The Burdekin River, which flows past Charters Towers and meets the coast south of Townsville (Fig. 1), has the highest recorded peak discharge of any Australian river, but is reduced to a sandy stream in the dry season. Thus, at one point in its middle reaches, following a cyclone in early 1991, the river was 800 m wide, 12 m deep and flowing at 4 m/s; a month later it was 15 m wide, <1 m deep and flowing at <0.5 m/s.

Ecological research on inland waters in the wet tropics

Excluding the work done on seasonal coastal swamps (mostly on birds and their habitats – e.g. LAVERY & BLACKMAN 1971), most of the research on bodies of standing water has concentrated on man-made lakes, including short studies on water quality (e.g. FINLAYSON & GILLIES 1982). Current studies on physical and chemical attributes of Lake Tinaroo (P. VALENTINE, pers. comm.) are valuable because they link water quality with agricultural practices in the catchment. Brief surveys have dealt with the limnology of the deep crater lakes by TIMMS (1979), and studies of dune lakes (HAWKINS et al. 1988, TIMMS 1986) and saline lakes (TIMMS 1987) have also been limited to brief surveys of limnological conditions and biota. The only reasonably long-term limnological study of a lake in the region was that undertaken by HAWKINS (1985 *et seq.*) on the Solomon Dam, Palm Island. A long-term study of the man-made Lake Dalrymple by the ACTFR has been ongoing since the lake first filled in 1987. This water body is interesting as it has maintained a high level of turbidity throughout its existence.

Research on the ecology of running waters is now progressing as a result of efforts by a small group working at or in association with the ACTFR. Preliminary work on Yuccabine Creek, a small upland stream 160 km north of Townsville (PEARSON et al. 1986), provided a summary of the community composition over one year. The stream was shown to be highly seasonal, with high and variable flows in the wet season and declining flows in the dry season. In one year (1983), the stream ceased to flow at the surface and was reduced to a series of pools. The invertebrate species diversity in Yuccabine Creek was higher than had been previously recorded for any single stream site anywhere in the world. While it was recognised that streams in many parts of the world had not been adequately sampled or described, it was clear that Yuccabine Creek had a species-rich fauna. About 250 species of invertebrates were recorded from one 50 m stretch of stream, comparing favourably with, for example, streams in north America (Minshall et al. 1985) and Malaysia (Bishop 1973). Many of the species recorded were rare, and the fauna as a whole was not abundant compared with streams elsewhere. Studies on the adults of aquatic insects have complemented this work and have further demonstrated the high diversity: for example, the trichopteran fauna caught in a low-power light trap at Yuccabine Creek included 78 species (Benson & Pearson 1988). Continuing work (Lake et al. 1994) aims to resolve some current, inadequately evidenced arguments about latitudinal diversity gradients in Australian stream invertebrate communities.

Mechanisms for the maintenance of species diversity of invertebrate communities are being studied experimentally. For example, most of the mayfly species have similar diets but nevertheless coexist in the forest streams (Hearnden & Pearson 1991 a, 1991 b). They have specific microhabitat preferences despite the fact that most species occurred in all microhabitats examined. It is likely that these possible habitat refuges are only of any importance when stream discharges decline causing densities of insects to increase to a level which leads to interspecific competition; for most of the time it is probable that densities of insects are too low to result in competitive interactions. However, preliminary observations suggest that other species such as tadpoles may have some impact on browsing insects including mayflies. These ideas are being examined in an experimental stream system at Birthday Creek, 80 km north of Townsville. This system has recently been used to study interactions and habitat preference of dragonfly larvae (Charlton & Pearson, unpubl. data), which like the mayflies, have overlapping diets but definite microhabitat preferences.

Because of the seasonality of discharge and the frequency of spates in rainforest streams, subsequent studies at Yuccabine Creek examined the downstream drift, upstream movements and colonisation capabilities of the invertebrate fauna (Benson & Pearson 1987 a, 1987 b). Invertebrate drift had not previously been documented over a year for any stream in Australia, and thus the study had more than regional significance. Drift in Yuccabine Creek followed much the same cycle as in northern temperate streams, with peaks at dawn and dusk, and with a large proportion of the benthic species involved. Wet-season flows did not cause disproportionate increases in drift, and drift caused redistribution of the fauna rather than depletion. Subsequent monitoring of conditions after cyclonic floods suggested that drift was much more depletive during these rarer events. Nevertheless, the fauna showed a great capacity for recovery from floods, and recolonisation mechanisms included drift and upstream movements. Studies of recovery following large-scale disturbance are continuing in Birthday Creek, as are studies of the role of disturbance in community dynamics (Rosser & Pearson unpubl. data).

The strong seasonality of rainfall leads to some streams being intermittent, particularly outside the wet tropical area. Studies of such streams have examined population and community biology of fishes (Beumer 1980, Orr & Milward 1984) and invertebrates (Smith & Pearson 1987). Even in these intermittent streams, species diversity of insects was high in comparison with streams elsewhere in Australia. Many species were able to recolonise from elsewhere, but at least one, a species of psephenid beetle, withstood drying over several months in the larval state (Smith & Pearson 1984).

A characteristic of forest streams in all latitudes is that much of the organic production within them is detritus-based, depending on the input of terrestrial material. This material consists of plant litter that falls directly into the stream, or which is blown or washed in, and dissolved organic matter leached from the soil and leaves. The level of retention of the litter may be of more significance than input *per se,* in these tropical streams. Retention is dependent both on the discharge and on the occurrence of obstacles such as logs, rocks and pools that arrest the passage of suspended leaves. The riffles appear to have a maximum holding capacity beyond which litter is lost. Virtually all organic material is washed out of the stream after cyclones, and it is likely that the detritus-based food web takes some time to recover.

The availability of litter in Yuccabine Creek, and its decomposition in the stream and in the laboratory has been investigated (Pearson & Tobin 1989, Pearson 1989). Of particular interest were the high diversity of the litter input from the riparian vegetation compared with non-tropical systems; the continuity of input throughout the year (Spain 1984); the occurrence of peak input in the summer (as elsewhere in Australia) which contrasts with the autumn peak in northern temperate forests (BUNN 1986); and the reactions of the leaf-shredding animals to these circumstances.

A small suite of species, mainly caddisfly larvae, was responsible for the primary consumption of leaves, and subsequent release of the fine particulate matter which is consumed by other animals. However, different leaf species were consumed at different rates, and some species were not eaten at all. Presumably the differences in consumption rate were due to differences in the nutritional quality of the leaves and/or the amounts of unpalatable or toxic substances in the leaves. Some leaf species decomposed rapidly in the absence of animals, through leaching and microbial processes. Subsequent work has concentrated on the ecology of individual animal species, their food preferences and the rates at which they consume leaf material. Experimental work has been undertaken on populations of a calamoceratid caddis larva, *Anisocentropus kirramus* (NOLEN & PEARSON 1992, 1993), and a crayfish, *Cherax depressus* (COUGHLAN 1990) at Birthday Creek. Both species are abundant in small headwater forest streams and are major consumers of litter. It was estimated that the crayfish population processed approximately 1% of all the litter entering the stream.

The relative rates of decomposition of different leaf species on the land and in the water at Birthday Creek have been studied by R. W. DAVIES & D. MONITA (unpubl. data); they have also examined colonisation of litter by micro-organisms. Their concurrent studies of community respiration in Birthday Creek will help to quantify the relative contribution to organic production of allochthonous and autochthonous material.

Fish diversity in small forest streams is low. For example, only three species of fish were found in the small tributaries of the Annan River, despite the accessibility of upstream habitats to a more diverse downstream fauna (HORTLE & PEARSON 1993). The eel, *Anguilla reinhardtii* (Anguillidae), is ubiquitous, but the only other species in small streams are the purple-spotted gudgeon, *Mogurnda adspersa* (Eleotridae), and the rainbowfish, *Melanotaenia splendida* (Melanotaeniidae). In Yuccabine Creek, the rainbowfish was absent, and in Birthday Creek only the eel occurs. It is possible that other species are excluded by waterfalls and occasional drying of the streams to form isolated pools. In larger streams, fish diversity increases (ALLEN & HOESE 1980, BEUMER 1980, HORTLE & PEARSON 1993) and the relationship between diversity and catchment area is comparable with elsewhere despite some beliefs that the tropical Australian fauna is depauperate.

The only fish population to have been studied over a period of time in the forest streams is *Mogurnda adspersa* in Yuccabine Creek. WHITEHEAD (1985) examined population dynamics and feeding ecology in this species and showed it to be a generalist predator, feeding on both drifting and benthic organisms. Preliminary experiments suggested that at moderate densities, these fish had measurable impact on the benthos, a result that is not usually recorded in comparable studies (ALLAN 1982).

The use of Birthday Creek and other rainforest streams by adult and larval frogs has been studied in detail over the past few years by R. A. ALFORD, S. RICHARDS & M. TRENERRY (unpubl. data). The activities and densities of tadpoles have been monitored at Birthday Creek since March 1988, and adult frogs have been monitored since March 1989. This information will provide a much clearer picture of the role of frogs in the rainforest stream community. Tadpoles reach high densities in stream pools – for example, $10/m^2$ in Birthday Creek (TRENERRY 1988). Tadpoles of some species consume fallen leaves, which suggests that they, like caddis larvae and crayfish, may be major producers of fine particulate organic matter for other detritivores. Unusual aspects of the natural history of rainforest frogs continue to be discovered. RICHARDS & ALFORD (1991) found that one species of *Litoria* excavates nests similar to those constructed by South American rainforest frogs, the first known incidence of such behaviour in Australian hylid frogs.

The ecology of several crustacean species has been studied in some detail. These include the long-armed prawns (*Macrobrachium* spp.; Palaemonidae), studied by KNEIPP (1979). The prawns varied in their requirements for saline water during development such that some species were restricted to estuaries whereas one (*M. australiense*) could complete its life cycle in fresh water. This species occurs in streams throughout much of eastern Australia. Most other species do not penetrate far upstream; however, a large, colourful species, *M. tolmerum,* is a conspicuous inhabitant of some coastal hill streams, and the large *M. rosenbergii* and *M. lar* are common in many far northern rivers.

The most detailed population study of an invertebrate species in rainforest streams is of the shrimp *Australatya striolata* (Atyidae) (SMITH 1987) which occurs in coastal streams from Cooktown to Victoria. In the wet season, adult females living in forest streams release larvae which are washed downstream. They develop into young shrimp in the estuary and then gradually migrate upstream, arriving in the headwaters as males perhaps two years after their birth. The distance of this migration at Yuccabine Creek is about 160 km. The shrimp breed as males then undergo a growth spurt and change sex. This species feeds mainly by filtering organic material out of the water current, and by sweeping the rocks with brush-like appendages. *Australatya striolata* inhabits all parts of a stream/river during its life cycle and is therefore vulnerable to (even) local changes in water quality, especially because of its filter-feeding habits.

Applied research

Applied work completed or continuing in the region includes water-quality monitoring of several rivers by the Sir George Fisher Centre for Tropical Marine Studies at James Cook University and by the Australian Institute of Marine Science. These studies are concerned with the contribution of nutrients and pesticides from the rivers and their catchments to the Great Barrier Reef province, and not with the ecology of the water bodies and their catchments *per se*. Similarly, the pioneering long-term studies of water movements in catchments near Tully by M. BONELL and colleagues (e.g. GILMOUR 1971, BONELL 1987), have relevance for stream ecology.

Studies of the effects of sugar mill effluents on lowland streams have been undertaken along much of the Queensland coast (PEARSON & PENRIDGE 1979, 1987). The organic effluents from mills have much the same effects as sewage effluents in streams elsewhere in the world (HYNES 1960). The worst effects, in cases where the effluent was not well diluted by the receiving water body, resulted in severe reductions in the diversity of the aquatic fauna, although the biomass of tolerant species increased. A good indicator of the pollution was the relative abundance of a readily recognised *Chironomus* (Diptera) species (expressed as a proportion of all other species of chironomids). Until recently, no work had been undertaken on the effects of non-point discharges on stream biotas in the region. However, a new study funded by CSR Ltd on the effects of sugar cane fertilisers on streams is being carried out in the Mackay region (R. G. PEARSON & P. CLAYTON, unpubl. data).

Current research in the wet tropics

Other recent and continuing research at Birthday Creek includes studies of the ecology of frogs and tadpoles (R. ALFORD & S. RICHARDS, unpubl. data), dragonfly larvae (CHARLTON 1989, R. ROWE, unpubl. data), mayflies (I. C. CAMPBELL, unpubl. data) and caddisflies (R. M. ST. CLAIR, unpubl. data), as well as the affects of cyclonic disturbance on the benthic community (R. G. PEARSON & J. A. NOLEN, unpubl. data). Various aspects of community and population dynamics are being examined *in situ* and in artificial stream channels. Experimental studies include the effect of substrate texture on communities, and the role of disturbance on stone faunas. Studies of nutrient pathways and budgets are continuing (CONGDON & LAMB 1989, R. A. CONGDON, unpubl. data), as are investigations of water accession and movements, while sediment dynamics are being monitored in the catchment (R. A. CONGDON, R. E. VOLKER & A. POMEROY, unpubl. data). These research projects are collaborative and will form a basis for future integrated studies of rainforest catchments and their streams.

A broad-scale study has recently commenced to examine the relationships between stream biotas and physical and chemical attributes of streams (R. G. PEARSON & R. M. ST. CLAIR, unpubl. data). The aim is to produce a classification of rainforest streams based on the biota which can be related to landscape features. The classification will provide the capacity to predict biotas expected in certain types of stream, and will allow rapid assessment of stream quality and normal functioning. As streams are linked closely to their catchments, it is expected that the classification scheme will provide a practical catchment monitoring tool. Allied to this work is a project on waterfall ecology and classification (P. D. CLAYTON, unpubl. data), an area of research that has been surprisingly neglected world-wide, despite the attraction of waterfalls and their frequent focal role in reserves and recreational areas.

Ongoing research on wetlands includes assessment of the effects of developing sugar cane farms on the complex wetland system on the Burdekin Delta (R. A. CONGDON, R. G. PEARSON, G. LUKACS & J. NOLEN, unpubl. data). Developments within the delta include an extensive irrigation scheme from the Burdekin Falls Dam, allowing large-scale expansion of the sugar cane growing area. There is potential for deleterious effects on the wetlands from clearing, from changes in the hydrological regime, and from chemical inputs. The research includes long-term monitoring of water quality and a classification of the wetlands on the basis of physical, chemical and biological attributes.

There is a substantial programme of research being undertaken on aquatic vectors of disease in the Townsville region, with particular focus on mosquito and snail populations (M. R. HEARNDEN, pers. comm.). A number of diseases with aquatic vectors are endemic in the region (e.g. dengue fever, Ross River virus) and there is potential for others to become established. The research includes population studies on vector organisms and studies of their habitat requirements.

A long-term research project has been examining the establishment and spread of several exotic fish species, especially Tilapia (*Oreochromis mossambicus:* Cichlidae), in tropical waterways in north Queensland (A. WEBB and N. MILWARD, pers. comm.; see also ARTHINGTON & BLÜHDORN 1994). The effects of such species on native fish communities are being monitored closely, as is the establishment and spread of recently detected introduced species.

Research needs

This review is intended to show the scope and directions of previous and current research. One thing is clear: despite attempts to develop research programmes in an integrated and coordinated way, the lack of funding for most projects has precluded the continuity of basic research vital for this integration. We are currently at a stage where there are many pieces of a jigsaw puzzle available, but few of them are contiguous. Nevertheless, the picture that is emerging does suggest major areas where research is needed.

The threats to the terrestrial and aquatic ecosystems in northern Queensland have been reduced somewhat since Wet Tropics World Heritage Area (WTWHA) listing of much of the remaining rainforest. However, this represents only a small part of the total land area, and it is only recently that land managers and farmers have begun to take positive steps towards soil and water conservation. Moreover, there are likely to be various types of development in the WTWHA (mostly small-scale, but including large scale enterprises such as hydroelectric schemes) as well as maintenance of current infrastructure such as roads. Moreover, the WTWHA will be affected by activities in adjacent areas, especially where the upper parts of catchments are outside its boundaries. Extensive research is required to understand the extent of these anthropogenic influences and to develop strategies to monitor and ameliorate them. To this end, fundamental research on freshwater systems will be invaluable, and will provide a basis for developing their potential utility for catchment monitoring.

While the monitoring role of fresh waters is expected to be of broad application and great utility, the inherent values of these systems should not be ignored. Fresh waters contribute to the biotic diversity of the region and provide habitat for numerous interesting species, some of which have general appeal as part of the region's wildlife. These species include a wide diversity of invertebrates and vertebrates which are of great scientific interest and some of which are of actual or potential commercial value. For example, the crayfish *Cherax quadricarinatus* is currently the subject of great interest as a species suitable for aquaculture (N. MILWARD, pers. comm.); several species of fish endemic to the region are prized in the aquarium trade; and there are numerous endemic freshwater invertebrate species.

Australia is in the fortunate position of not developing at such a rapid rate that control is impossible. Declaration of the WTWHA, the management model provided by the adjacent Great Barrier Reef World Heritage Area, government-sponsored integrated management plans, and the establishment of rural landcare groups to look after the land, provide grounds for cautious optimism concerning the future integrity of ecosystems in the wet tropics. The research undertaken in some of these systems is of direct application to other tropical regions, but – despite funding problems – does not suffer some of the constraints on research and other activity experienced in some tropical developing countries. Collaboration within the tropics may result in an ability to better manage our environment in the face of global problems.

Acknowledgements

I thank Drs. A. H. ARTHINGTON and C. L. HUMPHREY for helpful comments on the manuscript.

References

Allan, J. D., 1983: Predator-prey relationships in streams. – In: Baranes, J. R. & Minshall, G. W. (eds.): Stream Ecology: Application and Testing of General Ecological Theory: 191–229. – Plenum Press, New York.

Allen, G. R. & Hoese, D. F., 1980: A collection of fishes from the Jardine River, Cape York Peninsula, Australia. – *J. Roy. Soc. West. Aust.* **63:** 53–62.

Arthington, A. H., 1988: The distribution, characteristics and conservation status of lakes in the wet tropics and subtropics of Queensland. – *Proc. Ecol. Soc. Aust.* **15:** 177–189.

Arthington, A. H. & Bluhdorn, D. R., 1993: Distribution, genetics, ecology and status of the introduced cichlid, *Oreochromis mossambicus,* in Australia. – *Mitt. Internat. Verein. Limnol.* **24:** 53–62.

Arhtington, A. H. & Hegerl, E. J., 1989: The distribution, status and management problems of Queensland's athalassic and tidal wetlands. – In: McComb, A. J. & Lake, P. S. (eds.): The Conservation of Australian Wetlands: 59–109. – Surrey Beatty & Sons Ltd, Chipping Norton, Australia.

Benson, L. J. & Pearson, R. G., 1987 a: Drift and upstream movement in Yuccabine Creek, an Australian tropical stream. – *Hydrobiologia* **153:** 225–239

– – 1987 b: The role of drift and effect of season on macroinvertebrate colonisation of implanted substrata in a tropical Australian stream. – *Freshwat. Biol.* **18:** 109–116.

– – 1988: Diversity and seasonality of adult Trichoptera captured in a light-trap at Yuccabine Creek, a tropical Australian rainforest stream. – *Aust. J. Ecol.* **13:** 337–344.

Beumer, J., 1980: Hydrology and fish diversity of a north Queensland tropical stream. – *Aust. J. Ecol.* **5:** 159–186.

Bishop, J. E., 1973: Limnology of a Small Malayan River Sungai Gombak: 485 pp. – Dr W. Junk Publishers. The Hague.

Bishop, K. A., Allen, S. A., Pollard, D. A. & Cook, M. G., 1986: Ecological studies on the freshwater fishes of the Alligator Rivers Region, Northern Territory. Vol. 1. Outline of the study, Summary, Conclusions and Recommendations: 55 pp. – Supervising Scientist for the Alligator Rivers Region, Research Report No. 4, Australian Government Publishing Service, Canberra.

Body, D. N., 1979: Australia's surface water resources. – In: Hallsworth, E. G. & Woodcock, J. T. (eds.): Land and Water Resources of Australia: 59–70. – Australian Academy of Technological Sciences.

Boland, K. & Imberger, J., 1993: An analysis of dynamic stability in two inland lakes of northern Australia. – *Mitt. Internat. Verein. Limnol.* **24:** 337–344.

Bonell, M., 1987: Aspects of the hydrology of the Townsville region. – In: Hopley, D. (ed.): Geographical studies of the Townsville Region. – *James Cook University Monograph Series Occasional Paper* **2:** 18–27.

Bunn, S. E., 1986: Origin and fate of organic matter in Australia upland streams. – In: De Deckker, P. & Williams, W. D. (eds.): Limnology in Australia: 277–291. – CSIRO, Melbourne/Dr W. Junk Publishers, Dordrecht.

Charlton, L., 1989: The Ecology of Dragonflies (Odonata) in a Tropical Australian Stream. – 88 pp. B. Sc. Hons. Thesis, James Cook University.

Congdon, R. A. & Lamb, D., 1989: Essential biogeochemical cycles in Australian tropical rainforests. – In: Walby, B. (ed.): *Australian Tropical Rainforest: Science, Values and Meaning.* – Proceedings, 1987 ANZAAS Symposium, CSIRO, Melbourne.

Coughlan, J., 1990: Population and Trophic Ecology of the Freshwater Crayfish *Cherax depressus* (Crustacea: Parastacidae) in a North Queensland Tropical Rainforest Stream: 74 pp. – B. Sc. Hons. Thesis, James Cook University.

Finlayson, C. M., Cowie, I. D. & Bailey, B. J., 1990: Characteristics of a seasonally flooded freshwater system in monsoonal Australia. – In: Whigham, D. F., Good, R. E. & Květ, J. (eds.): Wetland Ecology and Management: Case Studies: 141–162. – Kluwer Academic Publishers, Dordrecht.

Finlayson, C. M. & Gillies, J. C., 1982: Biological and physico-chemical chararceristics of the Ross River Dam, Townsville. – *Aus. J. Mar. Freshwat. Res.* **33:** 811–827.

Gilmour, D. A., 1971: The effects of logging on streamflow and sedimentation in a north Queensland rainforest catchment. – *Commonwealth Forestry Review* **50:** 39–48.

Hart, B. T. & McGregor, R. J., 1989: Limnological survey of eight billabongs in the Magela Creek catchment, Northern Territory. – *Aust. J. Mar. Freshwat. Res.* **31:** 611–626.

Hawkins, P. R., 1985: Thermal and chemical stratification and mixing in a small tropical reservoir, Solomon Dam, Australia. – *Freshwat. Biol.* **15:** 493–503.

Hawkins, P. R., Taplin, L. E., Duivenvoorden, L. J. & Scott, F., 1988: Limnology of oligotrophic dune lakes at Cape Flattery, North Queensland. – *Aust. J. Mar. Freshwat. Res.* **88:** 535–554.

Hearnden, M. N. & Pearson, R. G., 1991 a: The diets of mayflies (Ephemeroptera) in an Australian tropical rainforest stream. – *Trop. Freshwat. Biol.* **2:** 203–212.

– – 1991 b: Resource use and partitioning by mayflies in an Australian tropical stream. – *Oecologia* **87:** 91–101.

Hortle, K. G. & Pearson, R. G., 1993: The fauna of the Annan River, north Queensland, with reference to the effects of alluvial tin mining. I. Fish. – *Aust. J. Mar. Freshwat. Res.* (in press).

HUMPHREY, C. L., BISHOP, K. A. & BROWN, V. M., 1990: Use of biological monitoring in the assessment of effects of mining wastes on aquatic ecosystems of the Alligator Rivers Region, tropical northern Australia. – *Environmental Monitoring* **14:**139–181.

HUMPHREY, C. L. & DOSTINE, P. L., 1994: Development of biological monitoring programs to detect mining-waste impacts upon aquatic ecosystems of the Alligator Rivers Region, Northern Territory, Australia. – *Mitt. Internat. Verein. Limnol.* **24:**293–314.

HYNES, H. B. N., 1960: The Biology of Polluted Waters: 202 pp. – Liverpool University Press, Liverpool.

KNEIPP, I. J., 1979: The Ecology of *Macrobrachium* species (Decapoda, Palaemonidae) in a coastal stream in north Queensland: 267 pp. – Ph. D. Thesis, James Cook University.

LAKE, P. S., SCHREIBER, E. S. G., MILNE, B. J. & PEARSON, R. G., 1994: Species richness in streams: patterns over time, with stream size and with latitude. – *Verh. Internat. Verein. Limnol.* **25** (in press).

LAVERY, H. J. & BLACKMAN, J. G., 1971: Studies on waterfowl (Anatidae) in north Queensland. 7. Long-term changes in habitat. – *Qld J. Agric. Anim. Sci.* **28:**275–280.

MARCHANT, R., 1982: Seasonal variation in the macroinvertebrate fauna of billabongs along Magela Creek, Northern Territory. – *Aust. J. Mar. Freshwat. Res.* **33:**329–342.

MINSHALL, G. W., PETERSEN, R. C. & NIMZ, C. F., 1985: Species richness in streams of different size from the same drainage basin. – *Amer. Nat.* **125:**16–38.

NOLEN, J. A. & PEARSON, R. G., 1992: Life history studies of *Anisocentropus kirramus* NEBOISS (Trichoptera: Calamoceratidae) in a tropical Australian rainforest stream. – *Aquat. Insects:* **14:**213–221.

– 1993: Factors affecting litter processing by *Anisocentropus kirramus* (Trichoptera: Calamoceratidae) from an Australian tropical rainforest stream. *Freshwater Biology* **29:**469–479.

ORR, T. M. & MILWARD, N. E., 1984: Reproduction and development of *Neosilurus ater* (Perugia) and *Neosilurus hyrtii* STEINDACHNER (Teleostei: Plotosidae) in a tropical Queensland stream. – *Aust. J. Mar. Freshwat. Res.* **35:**187–195.

OUTRIDGE, P. M., 1987: Possible causes of high species diversity in tropical Australian freshwater macrobenthic communities. – *Hydrobiologia* **150:**95–107.

PEARSON, R. G., BENSON, L. J. & SMITH, R. E. W., 1986: Diversity and abundance of the fauna in Yuccabine Creek, a tropical rainforest stream. – In: DE DECKKER, P. & WILLIAMS, W. D. (eds.): *Limnology in Australia* 329–342. – CSIRO, Melbourne/Dr. W. Junk Publishers, Dordrecht.

PEARSON, R. G. & PENRIDGE, L. K., 1979: An Ecological Survey of Selected Rivers in Queensland: 234 pp. – James Cook University of North Queensland, Townsville.

PEARSON, R. G. & PENRIDGE, L. K., 1987: The effects of pollution by organic sugar mill effluent on the macroinvertebrates of a stream in tropical Queensland, Australia. – *J. Env. Management* **24:**205–215.

PEARSON, R. G. & TOBIN, R. K., 1989: Litter consumption by invertebrates from an Australian tropical rainforest stream. – *Arch. Hydrobiol.* **116:**71–80.

PEARSON, R. G., TOBIN, R. K., BENSON, L. J. & SMITH, R. E. W., 1989: Standing crop and processing of rainforest liter in a tropical Australian stream. – *Arch. Hydrobiol.* **115:**481–498.

RICHARDS, S. J. & ALFORD, R. A. (in review): Nest construction and larval development of an Australian rainforest frog (*Litoria leseurii* complex, Anura: Hylidae). – *Copeia.*

SMITH, R. E. W., 1987: The Ecology of *Australatya striolata* (MCCULLOCH & MCNEILL) (Decapoda: Atyidae): 177 pp. – Ph. D. Thesis, James Cook University.

SMITH, R. E. W. & PEARSON, R. G., 1984: Survival of the water penny *Sclerocyphon bicolor* in an intermittent stream in north Queensland. – *J. Aust. Ent. Soc.* **24:**101–102.

– – 1987: The macroinvertebrate communities of temporary pools in an intermittent stream in tropical Queensland. – *Hydrobiologia* **150:**45–61.

SPAIN, A. V., 1984: Litterfall and the standing crop of litter in three tropical Australian rainforests. – *J. Ecol.* **72:**947–961.

TAIT, R. D., 1988: Macroinvertebrate communities of Magela Creek billagongs, Northern Territory, Australia. – *Verh. Internat. Verein. Limnol.* **23:**1080–1084.

TIMMES, B. V., 1979: The benthos of some lakes in northeastern Queensland. *Proc. R. Soc. Qld.* **90:**57–64.

– 1986: Reconnaissance limnology of some coastal dune lakes of Cape York Peninsula, Queensland. – *Aust. J. Mar. Freshwat. Res.* **37:**167–176.

– 1987: Limnology of Lake Buchanan, a tropical saline lake, and associated pools, of north Queensland. – *Aust. J. Mar. Freshwat. Res.* **38:**877–884.

TRENERRY, M., 1988: The Ecology of Tadpoles in a Tropical Rainforest Stream: 65 pp. – B. Sc. Hons. thesis, James Cook University.

WHITEHEAD, M., 1985: Ecology of the Purple-Spotted Gudgeon *Mogurnda adspersa* (CASTELNAU) (Pisces: Eleotridae) in a Tropical Upland Rainforest Stream: 93 pp. – B. Sc. Hons. thesis, James Cook University.

Author's address:

Australian Centre for Tropical Freshwater Research and Department of Zoology, James Cook University of North Queensland, Townsville, Qld 48111, Australia.

Mitt. Internat. Verein. Limnol.	24	165–177	Stuttgart, Februar 1994

A holistic approach to water allocation to maintain the environmental values of Australian streams and rivers: A case history

Angela H. Arthington

Abstract

This paper describes the key features of a holistic approach for assessing the environmental flow requirements of riverine ecosystems. It is based on the natural hydrological regime of the river and the specific ecological features that should be retained, protected, or perhaps modified, and which therefore require water allocation. The paper then briefly outlines the first attempt to apply the holistic approach in a subtropical stream, Barker-Barambah Creek, southeastern Queensland. The paper concludes with several observations on the need for new directions in the overall field of water allocation for the environment, and the development of sustainable and environmentally-sound management of riverine ecosystems over the long term.

Introduction

In the past decade water resources management in Australia has undergone a fundamental change in direction from a developmental phase, concentrating on the provision of water for urban, agricultural and industrial development, to a more balanced perspective giving proper consideration to environmental and social issues. The term 'in-stream', meaning the various ecological, recreational, commercial, scientific and cultural uses of water resources in their natural setting (Teoh 1989), has gained currency. At the same time, the demand for water has increased and will continue to increase in many areas of Australia towards the year 2000 and beyond (Brown et al. 1983). These changes in circumstance and attitude have led to a situation where both the scientific community, especially river ecologists, and the agencies responsible for water resources management, are under increasing pressure to produce workable strategies for environmental water allocation.

There have been several types of response to these new demands. One has been the initiation of national and international conferences and workshops, bringing together experts from across the disciplines to define the issues, identify areas of inadequate understanding and increase the dialogue between the research community and the agencies with environmental responsibilities (e.g. Teoh 1989, Pigram & Hooper 1992). Several new limnological research centres have been established and an unprecedented amount of funding has been directed towards aquatic ecological research and the application of research findings to the practical problems facing water agencies (LWRRDC 1991). Finally, the water agencies themselves have recruited scientists into units with responsibilities for water management, as well as strategic planning and policy development (Paterson 1989).

Whilst these and other initiatives have certainly increased the pool of expertise in relevant fields and heightened awareness of the issues and problems, there is as yet no consensus view on precisely how we should go about allocating water for the environment. Nor do we have, in Australia, an appropriate set of robust methodologies for estimating the water requirements of aquatic ecosystems. The most recent national review of these issues, initiated by the centre for Water Policy Research at the University of New England (Pigram & Hooper 1992), brought this crucial weakness into focus. What precisely, is the problem?

There are several methodologies for assessing the environmental water requirements of rivers in particular, of which the best known and most sophisticated is the Instream Flow Incremental Methodology (IFIM) developed by the United States Fish and Wildlife Service (Bovee 1982, 1986). The physical habitat component of IFIM (PHABSIM in the USA and RHYHABSIM in New Zealand; see Jowett 1982), and other methods involving transect analysis, are based on the simulation and evaluation of habitat availability ('weighted usable area') for particular aquatic species at different levels of stream discharge. While such methods may be useful in relatively stable, homogeneous rivers for assessing the requirements of economically important fish species, such as salmonids, they are seldom useful for assessing the water needs of entire fish communities, and are far from adequate when the protection of functional aquatic ecosystems is required. Thus in many areas of Australia, where there are few economically-important fish species, the assessment of habitat requirements, whilst important, is only one aspect of environmental water allocations (see papers in Teoh 1989).

In addition, semi-arid rivers typical of Australia, and also South Africa, are generally extremely heterogeneous

0538-4680/94/0024-0165 $ 3.25

geomorphologically, and highly variable and unpredictable hydrologically (e.g. McMahon 1986, 1989, Davies & Day 1989, Bunn & Boughton 1991). They cannot be characterised realistically by transect-based models applied at a few points along river channels. Moreover, there are practical problems inherent in the application of PHABSIM, and IFIM in its entirety (e.g. Gan & McMahon 1990). Most importantly, however, there are many theoretical objections to the ecological assumptions underpinning the Instream Flow Incremental Methodology, reviewed amongst others by Mathur et al. (1985), Scott & Shirvell (1987), Bain & Boltz (1989) and Arthington et al. (1992a).

Such objections have led to the recognition that the utility of IFIM requires further investigation in Australian environments (Richardson 1989, Walker 1989), and that it is probably best regarded as only one component of a suite of methods to be applied cautiously, in appropriate circumstances, and monitored rigorously after application (Arthington et al. 1992a). Meanwhile, there is a view that Australia needs to take a different approach to water allocation for rivers, one that places much greater emphasis on the maintenance of the entire 'riverine ecosystem'. This type of approach could be applied to the conservation and management of rivers outside Australia.

In this context, the term 'riverine ecosystem' is intended to encapsulate a holistic view of rivers, including such components as the source area, river channel, riparian zone, floodplain, groundwater, wetlands and estuary, as well as any particularly important features such as rare and endangered species. Management strategies for rivers must be holistic, because any, or all, components of a river ecosystem may be affected by water resource developments, and the objective should be to maintain, or rehabilitate, as much as is considered to be essential of the original, functional ecosystem in its entirety.

Accordingly, a holistic approach to water allocation for rivers has been proposed (Arthington et al. 1992b). It is considered to be necessary, and long overdue, because:

i) Exisiting methodologies (such as IFIM) for assessing the water requirements of rivers cannot be adopted simplistically in the highly variable and hydrologically unpredictable environments of most Australian rivers;
ii) We lack detailed biological information on many endemic species and generally have a very limited understanding of the ecological functioning of Australian rivers and the influence of flow regulation on riverine ecosystems;
iii) The planning and development of our remaining water resources and the development of water-allocation strategies cannot be postponed until the relevant ecological research has been completed and more appropriate methodologies are available.

This paper presents the key features of the holistic approach for assessing the environmental flow requirements of riverine ecosystems, and outlines the first attempt to apply the approach in a subtropical stream, Barker-Barambah Creek, southeastern Queensland. The paper concludes with several observations on the need for new directions in the overall field of water allocation for the environment, and the environmental management of water resources in general.

The holistic approach to environmental flows

The proposed holistic approach has been elaborated elsewhere (Arthington et al. 1992b), and is presently under development in both Australia and South Africa. In broad outline, it incorporates sound scientific and ecological principles, the best available biological information, and expert opinion on the water requirements of particular systems, but also takes a realistic view of what is possible in given circumstances. The objective of the approach is initially to state the water needs of the riverine ecosystem, and then to negotiate with water-resource planners and managers as to what can practicably be achieved in terms of cost, design constraints and competing water demands.

The first step in the holistic approach is to understand the natural hydrological regime of the river, which is described and then used as a fundamental guide to the environmental conditions that have maintained the river in its characteristic form. With these conditions defined, specific ecological features that should be retained, protected or perhaps modified, are identified. These ecological features are then used to guide the development of a water-allocation strategy that should, to the best available knowledge, maintain the desired natural values of the riverine ecosystem.

Three assumptions are implicit in such an approach. A key assumption, which embodies a substantial change in attitude, at least in Australia, is that water belongs to the environment and that other users of the resource should be accommodated, where practicable, from any 'excess' production of this resource. The second is that there is more water in the system than is needed for maintenance of the riverine ecosystem in its natural state. Finally, if the essential features of the natural (i.e. unregulated) flow regime can be identified and adequately incorporated into the modified or regulated flow regime then, all other things being equal, the extant biota and functional integrity of the ecosystem should be maintained. The term 'functional integrity' incorporates such concepts as genetic and biological diversity, essential ecological processes (e.g. nutrient dynamics, energy flow, reproduction, recruitment and dispersal of biota), and the capacity for adaptive responses to change.

The primary feature of the holistic approach is the hydrological analysis of historical unregulated flow records for the river. This analysis should be based on daily flows in order to use the available data at its finest resolution and to obtain an appreciation of the range of flows and flow patterns likely to occur. Analysis should cover the longest period of records available, using data only from gauging weirs which register natural flows. In those locations where daily flow data are not available, it would be necessary to rely on simulations of daily flows or on approximations derived from an understanding of regional patterns of river flow and rainfall. These fundamental approaches have been documented in Australia (Milner & Knights 1989, McMahon 1989), New Zealand, the USA (Poff & Ward 1989) and South Africa (King & O'Keeffe 1989, O'Keeffe et al. 1989, O'Keeffe & Davies 1991).

At the present stage of development of this approach, it is recommended that water-allocation strategies based on hydrological analyses should present flow recommendations on a monthly basis, or at least seasonally, and should incorporate criteria for defining various attributes of daily flows, such as their variability within and between months. However, it must be recognised that monthly allocations are merely a convenience and may have little biological relevance; other time frames may be more appropriate and this will depend on the system under investigation and the objectives of the water-allocation strategy.

The features of the hydrologic regime which are perceived to be important for maintenance of natural river functioning include the following: seasonal patterns of flow; variability and predictability of flow within seasons and from year to year; low flows; flood flows of different magnitudes and recurrence intervals; flushing flows; the perenniality or non-perenniality of flow; and, periods of natural cessation of flow. Several basic features of the natural hydrological regime in this list have been identified by Arthington et al. (1992b), and each of them is believed to require an allocation of water. The importance to the riverine ecosystem of each of these features has been defined or suggested, but considerably more ecological research is required before the precise ecological flow requirements of many rivers can be stated.

In summary, the holistic approach presently focuses on:

i) Low flows, in order to retain the fundamental lotic characteristics and seasonality of a river ecosystem;
ii) Wet-season flows, including the first major flood of the wet season, medium-sized floods and very large floods;
iii) Flushing flows to achive additional ecological objectives.

The annual water needs of a riverine ecosystem are estimated by summing the low flow requirements throughout the year and the additional wet-season flows and floods. To this sum may be added the requirements for flushing flows to achieve particular objectives which are not likely to be achieved by the main seasonal provisions. The total water requirements of the riverine ecosystem would be defined generally in terms of monthly flow allocations, and monthly maximum and minimum flows, desirable levels of flow variability, and the magnitude, timing and duration of floods and flushing flows.

An important aspect of this approach is the recognition that detailed knowledge of ecological requirements and responses to the hydrological regime will usually not be available for most Australian rivers. Thus the initial water allocation for the river should be regarded as a first estimate of the water to be provided annually and manipulated monthly (or within some more appropriate time frame) within certain defined limits. It is essential that this approach be regarded as iterative, implying that refinement of the first estimate of water requirements would be made over time as the effects of the initial recommendations are monitored and/or special issues are researched in each river system.

The Barker-Barambah environmental flow study

Background and objectives of the study

The Queensland Government has recently completed the construction of the Barker-Barambah Irrigation Project, where impounded water is being used to irrigate alluvial flats along Barambah Creek in the South Burnett region of south-eastern Queensland (Fig. 1). Essentially, the impounded water replaces an inadequate groundwater supply which has been temporally and spatially of poor quality, especially with respect to salinity. The impoundment, Lake Barambah, formed be-

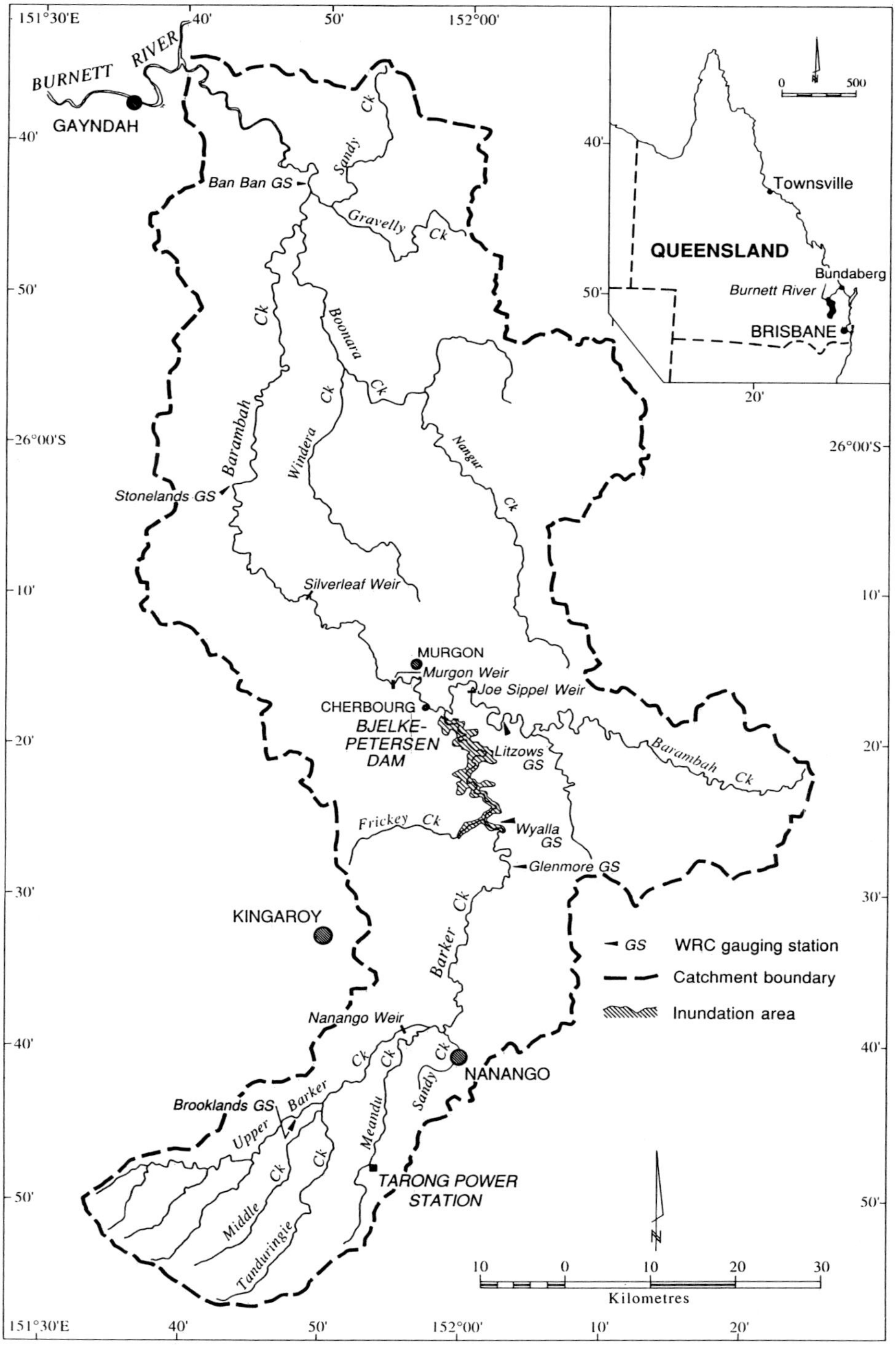

Fig. 1. Map showing location of Barker-Barambah Creek, the Bjelke-Petersen Dam, Tarong Power Station, Silverleaf Weir, Stonelands Gauging Station, and the sampling sites for water quality and ecological studies which support the water-allocation strategy.

hind the Bjelke-Petersen Dam on Barker Creek, intercepts down-valley flow of ground and surface water, as well as water discharged from the Tarong Power Station.

Responsibility for management of the irrigation scheme and Lake Barambah lies with the state's Water Resources Commission. The Commission has recognised that the impounding of Barker Creek, coupled with development of the irrigation system and consequent changes in agricultural practices in the catchment, as well as new patterns of recreational activity, may have adverse impacts on aquatic and riparian environments. There has been little investigation in Queensland of the environmental impacts of river regulation or of methods for determining water allocation for the conservation of aquatic ecosystems (Arthington et al. 1992a). As a result, the Commission has provided funding to the Centre for Catchment and In-stream Research at Griffith University to undertake a long-term environmental study of Barker-Barambah Creek. The background to that investigation has been published (Arthington & Pullar 1991), and the full report (Arthington et al. 1992a) is available from the senior author. The study was designed to develop a water-allocation strategy that would integrate irrigation and other off-stream water demands with the requirements for conservation of the stream ecosystem. The broader objective of the study has been to assist in developing operational and management strategies for this and other irrigation schemes so as to minimise the adverse environmental effects which usually result from river regulation by dams.

It is beyond the scope of this paper to give an account of the details which underpin the water-allocation strategy for Barker-Barambah Creek. Instead, the environmental objectives of the strategy are presented, and the recommendations for their achievement are discussed briefly in terms that illustrate this first application of the holistic approach to environmental flow studies in Queensland.

The water-allocation strategy for Barker-Barambah Creek has been considered in relation to five key environmental objectives:

i) Maintenance of water quality for environmental, irrigation and other purposes;
ii) Maintenance of channel morphology, substrate characteristics and stream habitats;
iii) Maintenance of benthic invertebrate communities and essential stream ecosystem processes (e.g. nutrient dynamics, energy flow);
iv) Maintenance of fish habitat (for shelter, resting, feeding and spawning), and fish reproduction, recruitment and dispersal;
v) Maintenance and management of aquatic plant communities including pest species.

Maintenance of water quality

Various water-quality characteristics were investigated during the study but the most important in terms of in-stream uses were considered to be temperature, dissolved oxygen and nutrients, whereas the major water-quality issue affecting irrigation is salinity. Guidelines have been presented (Arthington et al. 1992a) on the management of water releases from the impoundment so as to avoid problems due to thermal and chemical stratification of the impoundment and any downstream environmental effects. Issues of nutrient enrichment are also incorporated into the overall management strategy for the catchment. The water-allocation strategy as presented here concentrates on the management of salinity problems.

The study confirmed that elevated salinity levels occur throughout much of the Barker-Barambah catchment, bearing out the findings of an historic analysis of salinity trends over the past 50 years (Poplawski 1989). A steep increase in salinity levels in the small section of Barambah Creek passing through the major irrigation area (Fig. 1) is of particular significance. It has been predicted that water quality in this region of Barambah Creek will deteriorate owing to a combination of deep drainage under irrigation and reduced reliance on groundwater resources (Bevin & Shaw 1980).

Management options for reducing stream salinity developed by the Murray-Darling Ministerial Council (1987) for the River Murray are relevant to this study. They involve interception of saline inflows to the stream, reduction of groundwater throughflow, and an increase in freshwater (surface) flow.

The most attractive short-term strategy for reducing stream salinity in Barambah Creek would be to use water releases from the impoundment to increase river discharge. That is, in addition to releases to satisfy irrigation demand, further supplementary water releases to prevent stream salinity increases have been recommended. A first approximation of the necessary quantitative guidelines was derived from the relationship between electrical conductivity and discharge. The specific management goal was that the median stream salinity at Stonelands (Fig. 1) be kept at 1000 μS/cm, with a 90th percentile value of 1500 μS/cm (after Reid et al. 1979). The relationship between electrical conductivity and stream discharge at Stonelands, resulted in the following line of best fit:

$$EC = 2323.0 * Q^{-0.22969} \quad (r^2 = 0.616)$$

Thus, to achieve a conductivity of 1000 μS/cm at Stonelands, the appropriate discharge estimate would be about 40 million l/day (0.46 m^3/s). The provision of these flows would not be required on a twelve-month basis, but only on occasions when irrigation water demand is high and water quality is poor. Based on the historical rainfall and discharge records for the area, these conditions would probably occur in September–October and around March. The water-allocation strategy provides guidance on the management of such flushing flows so that ecological objectives are not compromised.

Maintenance of channel morphology, substrate characteristics and stream habitats

Features of the natural discharge regime of streams and rivers, such as floods, droughts and periods of low flow, have long-term effects on channel morphology, sediment movements, substrate compositions, organic detritus transport and the development of riparian and aquatic vegetation (Anderson & Morison 1988a). Collectively, these characteristics define the physical nature and diversity of stream habitats, which in turn influence the diversity and composition of stream biotic communities. In a broader sense, floods have been regarded as reset mechanisms which are important in maintaining normal community structure (Cummins & Spengler 1978) and ecological processes in river systems.

The environmental study of Barker-Barambah Creek lacked the resources to include specific investigations concerning the magnitude and timing of flows for channel maintenance and broad issues of stream habitat, relying instead on a key assumption of the holistic approach to in-stream flows. It was assumed that if seasonal features of the natural flow regime could be incorporated into the regulated flow regime, then some of the original characteristics of stream channels and habitats should be maintained, albeit with changes resulting from quantitative reductions in stream discharge, decreased sediment deposition and other physical changes introduced by impounding Barker Creek. The water-allocation strategy makes provision for the seasonal flows required to maintain channel morphology, substrate characteristics and stream habitats in Barambah Creek.

Maintenance of invertebrate and fish communities

Most riverine species have morphological, physiological, behavioural and life history adaptations that are related to the physicochemical environment of running water. For instance, many Australian freshwater fish demonstrate reproductive strategies that are responsive to day-length, water temperature and discharge regime (Milton & Arthington 1983, 1984, 1985), whereas the life-history strategies of Australian stream invertebrates are thought to be influenced more by patterns of discharge than by factors such as the seasonality of energy inputs and temperature regime (Lake & Barmuta 1986, Bunn 1988). Two features of the discharge regime appear to be particularly important to riverine biota: the degree of seasonality, and the predictability of the discharge regime (Bunn & Boughton 1991).

The precise seasonal flows required by stream invertebrates, and those that will ensure the migration, successful reproduction and recruitment of Australian fishes, are generally very poorly known. However, a first approximation was achieved for Barambah Creek by analysing the historic hydrological regime of the system and then considering when particular flows appear to be important for the stimulation or completion of essential biological functions. Analysis of fish reproductive strategies and the seasonal timing of reproduction in Barambah Creek indicated the need for a water-release strategy which would mimic several essential features of the seasonal pattern and variability of the historic, unregulated flow regime. This recommendation implied the maintenance of the low and predictable flow conditions which govern the spring reproductive peak of several fish species of significance for recreational fishing, as well as many of the smaller forage species. In addition, it was recommended that the water release strategy should maintain some periods of high wet-season discharge to provide essential biological cues for fish during migration, spawning and dispersal.

When there is insufficient understanding of the precise volumes of discharge required for ecological purposes, one common practice is to recommend a fixed percentile for each month based on the analysis of historical discharge records. The mean monthly 50th percentile exceedance flow has been recommended to maintain optimum fish habitat in Victorian streams, whereas the mean monthly 80th percentile exceedance flow is regarded as an acceptable low flow during periods of drought (Hall 1989, 1991).

The Victorian approach provided a precedent for the Barker-Barambah study and was adopted as the basis for the interim water-allocation strategy for this system. Percentile values (20th, 50th and 80th) expressed in terms of the daily discharge recorded each month at Stonelands Gauging Station (Fig. 1) were calculated, and three levels of discharge were selected from these values to describe the boundary conditions of a desirable water-allocation strategy. The three recommended discharge levels were as follows:

i) The daily 50th percentile flow for each month was recommended for optimum in-stream protection, representing the flow which may be assumed to govern structural and functional features of the stream ecosystem. Provision of this monthly flow pattern should ensure that habitat diversity and seasonal biological cues are maintained, that the life cycles of many species are completed, and that biological recruitment remains at normal levels. This represents the ideal water-allocation strategy for any system (see King & O'Keeffe 1989, Hall 1991, Arthington et al. 1992b).

ii) The daily 20th percentile flow for each month was recommended as the lowest flow permissible for stream ecosystem maintenance in drought years (i.e. years when water for all beneficial uses is in short supply; Hall 1991). In such years, all in-flows to the impoundment less than or equal to the 20th percentile flows should be released downstream to maintain a seasonal pattern of minimum flows. This strategy would provide water to the downstream area only in months and years when water is available naturally. It would not be asking for environmental water when other water users would be under stress.

iii) The daily 80th percentile discharge for each month was selected as a guide to the provision of more extreme monthly flows in some years, to achieve such function as the flushing of pools, channel maintenance, removal of encroaching aquatic vegetation and fish migration. It was recommended that flows of this magnitude should be released from the impoundment only in months when they normally occur, thus ensuring that seasonal biological cues are maintained. An alternative and more scientific approach would be to determine the quantity and duration of flows required to achieve specific ecological and water-quality objectives, which may well require that more water is released than the 80th percentile flows in some years.

The strategy recommends that at each of these flows, water should be released so as to maintain the natural range of daily discharge variability for any given discharge, to ensure that biological systems are not disturbed by unnaturally variable flows or adversely affected by unnaturally dampened flow variability. Under this strategy, a quantity of water would be allocated to in-stream needs each year and distributed seasonally so that monthly flows vary between the 20th and 50th percentile flows. In unusually wet years, it would be expected that monthly flows would vary between the 50th and 80th percentile flows, as a trade-off against acceptance of very low or no flows in some months of dry years.

In practical terms, this approach would amount to making a 'block booking' for an annual environmental water allocation which would be manipulated seasonally within defined limits. The annual allocation would be calculated along with other water allocations in terms of the probability of supply, and of failure to achieve supply, in any given year. This strategy would place environmental water needs on the same footing as off-stream needs, whilst recognising the need to accept some years of low water allocation in the assurance of there being other 'good' years with an allocation closer to the optimum (which is essentially the attitude taken by irrigators). Such a strategy would also ensure that inter-annual patterns of discharge variability are likely to be maintained.

Management of aquatic plants

The study presented general management guidelines with respect to issues of nutrient enrichment and the management of aquatic plants in both Barker-Barambah Creek and the new impoundment. Here, problems concerning the introduced water hyacinth (*Eichhornia crassipes*) are emphasized. Growths of water hyacinth in Barambah Creek develop periodically to the stage where the implementation of chemical and biological controls has been necessary. An alternative or additional approach to continuing problems with the build up of nuisance aquatic plants could be the use of intermittent flushing flows. Since detailed studies could not be conducted on this topic in Barambah Creek, the approach taken was to consider how natural floods have effected Water hyacinth in the past. For example, Table 1 records stream discharge levels during a flood in December 1987 which completely cleared extensive growths of Water hyacinth from Silverleaf Weir (Fig. 1).

The historic discharge record for Stonelands Gauging Station was examined to determine how frequently natural floods of the same magnitude as the December 1987 flood have occurred. It was assumed, conservatively, that flows of 1600 million l/day are required for seven days in sequence (see Table 1) to clear Silverleaf Weir of equivalent massive growths of water hyacinth. This analysis indicated that daily flows suitable for flushing water hyacinth are not uncommon in December, January and February, and in some years even in March. A large flood in April 1988/89 and floods in May 1982/83 could also have achieved successful removal of this plant.

To summarize lengthy analyses of the flow record, natural floods of the size and duration required to flush water hyacinth down Barambah Creek have occurred at least five times since 1964/65. Whether such floods are required with this frequency will depend upon the rate of build up of water hyacinth under the regulated discharge regime imposed by the irrigation system. An important point to consider is that the deposition of the dislodged plants farther downstream may cause local deoxygenation and detract from the amenity value of the creek.

Table 1. Discharge records (from Stonelands Gauging Weir; Fig. 1) for the 7-day flood in December 1987 which cleared Silverleaf Weir of massive growths of Water hyacinth.

Date in December	Discharge (millions l/day)
1	4.0
2	1,628.3
3	9,525.8
4	7,858.9
5	5,153.7
6	3,947.5
7	2.458.4
8	1,327.5

The recommended water-allocation strategy

Quantitative and management guidelines

The recommended water-allocation strategy is summarised in Table 2 in terms of the boundary conditions for monthly stream discharge (the 20th, 50th and 80th percentile daily flows for each month), and flushing flows for special purposes. In this strategy, the fundamental seasonality of the flow regime is achieved by providing the 50th percentile daily flow based on the long-term flow record.

Provision of the 50th percentile flows in each month would require a total volume of 17,443 million l/year. This amounts to about 14% of the full supply volume of Lake Barambah and about 64% of the flow provisionally allocated to licensed irrigators (see discussion of the licensing strategy in ARTHINGTON et al. 1992a, Chapter 2). However, much of the necessary flow will be available in the channel during irrigation releases and as a consequene of natural flows down Barambah Creek. Much less water would be required to maintain the stream ecosystem in drought or dry years, when the 20th percentile flow, or some higher value between the 20th and 50th percentile flows, would be acceptable, following the approach taken in Victoria (HALL 1989, 1991).

Table 2 also lists *ad hoc* flushing flows for specific purposes (water-quality management and removal of water hyacinth) and the special conditions which must be met during such water releases. For instance, when water is released during September–November for irrigation purposes or for salinity management, it should be delivered so as to ensure limited variation in surface water levels and minimal disturbance of fish spawning. This issue is discussed in more detail below.

Any water releases to control stream salinity that are made in April would not appear to pose severe problems for resident fish species since most breeding has ceased by then (ARTHINGTON et al. 1992a). However, flushing flows to remove water hyacinth should be made during periods of normally high flows (January–February) when other in-stream needs would also be served by high flows (e.g. channel maintenance and the removal of fine sediments).

Table 2. Recommended water allocation strategy for Barker-Barambah Creek, showing special conditions to be met during periods of water releases. All discharges are in millions l/day.

Month	Seasonal flows in percentiles			Flushing flows to manage:		Special conditions
	20 th[a]	50 th[b]	80 th[c]	Salinity	Aquatic plants	
January	10.1	100.0	496.0	–	1,600[e]	for 7 days in Jan. or Feb.
February	15.5	108.6	509.7	–	–	
March	5.2	54.8	290.5	40[d]	–	for several days in March
April	3.0	36.5	160.2	–	–	or April
May	5.4	23.7	83.2	–	–	
June	5.4	25.1	105.2	–	–	
July	6.2	29.1	124.6	–	–	
August	3.3	32.4	100.9	–	–	
September	1.0	24.1	122.8	40[d]	–	for several days in Sept.
October	1.0	18.6	112.5	–	–	or Oct.
November	2.3	32.8	285.6	–	–	maintain stable water
December	10.7	91.3	411.8	–	–	levels

[a] Minimum flows permissible only during drought conditions
[b] Optimum flows to maintain fish habitat and essential stream ecosystem functions
[c] Extreme seasonal flows required in some years for pool flushing and channel maintenance
[d] Flushing flows as needed to maintain stream salinity
[e] Flushing flows as needed to remove excessive plant biomass

The role of irrigation releases

Water released for irrigation purposes, if of suitable temperature and water quality, will contribute to ecological needs during its passage through Barambah creek. However, there are two critical issues to be considered in assessing the significance of this water for ecological purposes. The first is: how much water will be available in the stream channel at each point along the length of the irrigation area down to Stonelands when there is a high demand for off-stream uses? Some estimates suggest that only 5 million l/day will be available at Stonelands after withdrawal off-stream. This amount of water will certainly not be adequate to protect the stream ecosystem since it is generally less than the 20th percentile flows (i.e. the level set for drought conditions) for each month.

The second issue is the compatibility of the probable timing of irrigation and in-stream water needs throughout the annual cycle. Irrigation water is required most often during the late dry season (i.e. September–October) when natural stream flows are low and relatively predictable based on historic flow records. Under normal discharge regimes, this is the season when fish and invertebrates with vulnerable life-history stages can avoid the damaging effects of spates and unstable water levels. Large releases of water at this time or fluctuating water levels could compromise fish breeding and the survival of eggs deposited in bottom substrates and attached to aquatic plants (Milton & Arthington 1983, 1984, 1985). The water-allocation strategy therefore requires that daily water level variations during critical spawning periods should not be allowed to exceed the natural changes that occur over the historic range of flow conditions in each month at particular sites.

At the other extreme, the release of irrigation water during periods of high irrigation demand could result in sustained high water levels, such as have already occurred in 1991 during irrigation releases to Gayndah (Fig. 1). This type of water release may affect both water quality and stream biota. For instance, aquatic plants with rapid growth rates could encroach into the stream channel, reducing the amount of open-water habitat for certain fish species, and possibly, their access to food supplies.

The contribution of natural flows

The previous sections have discussed recommendations for seasonal flows and flushing flows to meet in-stream needs and to maintain high-quality water in Barambah Creek. Here, the probability of achieving various stream discharges as a result of rainfall and natural stream flows is discussed.

High stream discharges caused by rainfall will still occur in Barambah Creek after impoundment, providing unregulated flooding, although in some years these events are infrequent. Historical records indicate that flood peaks are more common and greater in Barambah Creek than in Barker Creek (QDPI & QWRC 1979). Freshets originating from the Bunya Mountains and the Nanango region via Barker Creek will influence the area downstream from the impoundment, particularly when it is at full supply level and water is released via the spillway. However, in the two-and-a-half years since completion of the dam this has yet to occur. Other impoundments in southern Queensland have been slower to fill, taking several years before spilling over.

The impoundment is unlikely to mitigate significantly large flood events arising in the Barker-Barambah catchment that typically occur in summer, since it is estimated that the dam would have reduced past floods at Stonelands Weir by only 10–20% (QDPI & QWRC 1979). Hence it is expected that the more extreme seasonal in-stream flow requirements recommended (i.e. the 80th percentile flows) will be met in some months and years almost entirely by natural flows from Barambah Creek coupled with irrigation releases and, in some years, from natural spills from the impoundment. When these requirements are not met, consideration should be given to the release of special seasonal and *ad hoc* flushing flows for environmental purposes.

Future water-allocation studies

The adoption of the 20th, 50th and 80th percentile monthly flows as the desirable boundary conditions of the water-allocation strategy, the guidelines on flushing flows, plus the incorporation of appropriate measures of the variability of flows, should be regarded as providing only the first approximation of a water-allocation strategy for Barker-Barambah Creek. It is a fundamental premise of the holistic approach that targeted research and monitoring of the system will be possible after the first recommendations on water requirements have been put into practice, in order to incorporate increasingly refined recommendations based on knowledge of the needs of the stream ecosystem. A second stage of the Barker-Barambah study is in progress and will report on the ecological impacts of the initial water-allocation strategy in due course.

The Barker-Barambah study has recommended that, in future flow studies, the environmental water requirements of streams and rivers should be defined early in the planning stages of a water development, rather than after the essential design features of the scheme have been finalised. Water managers would then be in possession of estimates of the amount of water available for harvesting rather than estimates of how much water may have to be given back to satisfy environmental goals.

At the very least, environmental in-stream considerations in Australia, as in other countries, need to be placed on an equal footing with off-stream considerations. An ideal starting point for negotiations in water developments would be to assess whether or not the goal of 'no net loss' of productive stream habitat can be achieved within the confines of the development. If this goal cannot be met, then the impact of loss of habitat must be assessed in terms of the conservation significance of the riverine ecosystem and its component species. Habitat restoration and rehabilitation downstream from impoundments offer the possibility of maintaining a viable aquatic ecosystem in the impacted part of a regulated stream or river. This option appears to have been neglected in Australian river management and would be a fruitful area for cooperative research among ecologists, water managers and bodies such as the River Improvement Trusts and Land Care Groups established in Queensland.

The Barker-Barambah environmental study has recommended an approach to the development of water-allocation strategies which is based on sound ecological principles, but with the practical constraints of costs, design constraints and competing water demands borne in mind. The strategy assumes that there will be opportunities for negotiation of an annual water allocation which may vary in any given year between minimum (i.e. drought) and optimum flow conditions, with additional water releases for special purposes. It assumes that all interested parties will recognise compatible and incompatible water requirements, and work towards a reasonable solution suited to particular circumstances. This will require acceptance of two principles.

Firstly, it must be recognized that the provision of water to meet in-stream flow requirements in Australian streams and rivers will be difficult in years of drought. Any water-allocation strategy must take a long-term view of the maintenance of aquatic ecosystems, which have persisted under unusually variable rainfall and discharge regimes by world standards. Secondly, water managers must recognise that discharge variability governs important ecological processes and life cycle patterns in Australian running waters. Thus to protect the natural characteristics of rivers and biodiversity, management strategies must aim to maintain the key features of natural flow variability (daily, seasonal and from year to year).

The fundamental premise of the holistic approach is that water belongs to the environment and that other users should be accommodated, where practicable, from the 'excess' production of this resource. It is only by adopting this perspective that management authorities can hope to achieve sustainable and environmentally-sound management of riverine ecosystems over the long term. This paper and ARTHINGTON et al. (1992b) are intended to serve as a stimulus to further investigation and debate on the environmental flow requirements of riverine ecosystems in Australia and other countries facing major challenges in water-resources management.

Acknowledgements

This paper has benefited from a collaborative workshop, involving South African and Australian scientists, held at the Centre for Catchment and In-stream Research (CCISR), Griffith University, in November 1991 and from various presentations to the Workshop on Water Allocation for the Environment, held at the Centre for Water Policy Research at the University of New England, also in November 1991. The Water Resources Commission (Queensland) is thanked particularly for funding CCISR's research on Barker-Barambah Creek and for the opportunity to apply the holistic approach to water allocation for the environement.

References

ANDERSON, J. R. & MORISON, A. K., 1988: Environmental Flow Studies for the Wimmera River, Victoria – Part C: Water Quality and the Effects of an Experimental Release of Water. Arthur Rylah Institute for Environmental Research, Technical Report Series No. 75. – 100 pp. Dept. Conservation, Forests and Lands, Victoria.

ARTHINGTON, A. H., CONRICK, D. L. & BYCROFT, B. M., 1992a: Environmental Study of Barker-Barambah Creek. Volume 2 Scientific Report: Water Quality, Ecology and Water Allocation Strategy. – 242 pp. Centre for Catchment and In-stream Research (Griffith University) and Water Resources Commission (Department of Primary Industries), Brisbane.

ARTHINGTON, A. H., KING, J. M., O'KEEFFE, J. H., BUNN, S. E., DAY, J. A., PUSEY, B. J., BLUHDORN, D. R. & THARME, R., 1992b: Development of an holistic approach for assessing environmental flow requirements of riverine ecosystems. – In: PIGRAM, J. J. & HOOPER, C. (eds.): *Proceedings of Seminar and Workshop on Water Allocation for the Environment:* 69–76. – Centre for Water Policy Research, University of New England, Armidale.

ARTHINGTON, A. H. & PULLAR, I. S., 1991: A case study in integrated management of a catchment/aquatic ecosystem. Barker-Barambah Irrigation Project, Queensland, Australia. – 781–803. Commission Internationale Des Grands Barrage, Vienna.

BAIN, M. B. & BOLTZ, J. M., 1989: Regulated streamflow and warmwater stream fish: a general hypothesis and research agenda. Biological Report 89 (18). – 28 pp. US Department of the Interior, Fish and Wildlife Service, Washington, D.C.

BEVIN, P. & SHAW, R., 1980: Queensland. Salinity problems in irrigation areas. Special Issue. – Bulletin of Australian National Committee, International Commission of Irrigation and Drainage: 16–19.

BOVEE, K. D., 1982: A guide to stream habitat analysis using the instream flow incremental methodology. Instream Flow Information Paper No. 12. FWS/OBS – 82/86. – 248 pp. U.S. Fish and Wildlife Service, Washington, D.C.

– 1986: Development and evaluation of habitat suitability criteria for use in the Instream Flow Incremental Methodology. Instream Flow Information Paper No. 21. – 235 pp. U.S. Fish and Wildlife Service Biological Report 86.

BROWN, J. A. H., HARRISON, R. D. & JACOBSON, G., 1983: Water demand and availability with reference to particular regions. Water 2000: Consultants Report No. 12. – 321 pp. Australian Government Publishing Service, Canberra.

BUNN, S. E., 1988: Life histories of some benthic invertebrates from streams of the northern Jarrah forest, Western Australia. – *Aust. J. Mar. Freshwat. Res.* **39:** 785–804.

BUNN, S. E. & BOUGHTON, W., 1991: Ecological significance of streamflow patterns in some Australian rivers. – *Unpublished Manuscript.*

CUMMINS, K. W. & SPENGLER, G. L., 1978: Stream ecosystems. – *Water Spectrum* **10:** 1–9.

DAVIES, B. R. & Day, J. A., 1989: Physical and chemical attributes important in the biological functioning of river ecosystems. – In: FERRAR, A. A. (ed.): Ecological Flow Requirements for South African Rivers: 17–40. – South African National Scientific Programmes Report Number 162. Council for Scientific and Industrial Research, Pretoria.

FERRAR, A. A., 1989: Ecological Flow Requirements for South African Rivers. South African National Scientific Programmes Report Number 162: 118 pp.

– Council for Scientific and Industrial Research, Pretoria.

Gan, K. & McMahon, T., 1990: Variability of results from use of PHABSIM in estimating habitat area. – Regulated Rivers: *Research and Management* **5:**233–239.

Hall, D. N., 1989: Preliminary assessment of daily flow required to maintain habitat for fish assemblages in the LaTrobe, Thomson, Mitchell and Snowy Rivers, Gippsland. Arthur Rylah Institute for Environmental Research, Technical Report Series No. 85: 111 pp. – Dept. Conservation, Forests and Lands, Victoria.

– 1991: Management plan for freshwater Fishes in major Gippsland rivers: Water resource requirements. Arthur Rylah Institute for Environmental Research, Technical Report Series No. 107: 61 pp. – Dept. Conservation, Forests and Lands, Victoria.

Jowett, I. G., 1982: The increment approach to instream flow needs. New Zealand case studies. – In: McColl, R. S. (ed.): River Low Flows: Conflicts of Water Use. – *Water and Soil Misc. PLubl.* **47:** 9–15.

King, J. H. & O'Keeffe, J. H., 1989: Looking to the future – South African requirements. – In: Ferrar, A. A. (ed.): Ecological Flow Requirements for South African Rivers: 110–116. – South African National Scientific Programmes Report Number 162. Council for Scientific and Industrial Research, Pretoria.

Lake, P. S. & Barmuta, L. A., 1986: Stream benthic communities: persistent presumptions and current speculations. – In: De Deckker, P. & Williams, W. D. (eds.): Limnology in Australia: 263–276. – CSIRO and Dr W. Junk Publishers, Melbourne and Dordrecht.

LWRRDC, 1991: Land and Water Resources Research and Development Corporation and Annual Report 1991–1992: 48 pp. – LWRRDC, Canberra.

McMahon, T. A., 1986: Hydrology and management of Australian streams. – In: Campbell, I. C. (ed.): Stream Protection: The Management of Streams for Instream Uses: 23–44. – Water Studies Centre, Chisholm Institute of Technology, Melbourne.

– 1989: Understanding Australian streamflow – Implications for instream ecology. – In: Teoh, C. (ed.): Proceedings of the Specialist Workshop on Instream Needs and Water Uses: 33-1–33-11. – Australian Water Resources Council, Canberra.

Mathur, D., Bason, W. H., Purdy, E. J. & Silver, C. D., 1985: A critique of the instream flow incremental methodology. – *Can. J. Fish. Aquatic Sci.* **42:**825–831.

Milner, H. & Knights, P., 1989: Hydrologic analysis – a *de facto* means for evaluating instream needs. – In: Teoh, C. (ed.): Proceedings of the Specialist Workshop on Instream Needs and Water Uses: 35-1–35-2. – Australian Water Resources Council, Canberra.

Milton, D. A. & Arthington, A. H., 1983: Reproduction and growth of *Craterocephalus marjoriae* and *C. stercusmuscarum* (Pisces: Atherinidae) in south-east Queensland, Australia. – *Freshwat. Biol.* **13:**589–597.

– – 1984: Reproductive strategy and growth of the Crimson-spotted Rainbow Fish, *Melanotaenia splendida fluviatilis* (Castelnau) (Pisces: Melanotaeniidae), in south-eastern Queensland. – *Aust. J. Mar. Freshwat. Res.* **35:**75–83.

– – 1985: Reproductive strategy and growth of the Australian Smelt, *Retropinna semoni* (Weber) (Pisces: Retropinnidae), and the Olive Perchlet, *Ambassis nigrippinis* (De Vris) (Pisces: Ambassidae), in Brisbane, south-east Queensland. – *Aust. J. Mar. Freshwat. Res.* **36:**329–341.

Murray-Darling Basin Ministerial Council, 1987: Salinity and Drainage Strategy. Background Paper No. 87/1. – Murray-Darling Basin Ministerial Council, Canberra.

O'Keeffe, J. H. & Davies, B., 1991: Conservation and management of the rivers of the Kruger National Park: suggested methods for calculating instream flow needs. – *Aquatic Conservation Marine and Freshwater Ecosystems* **1:**55–71.

O'Keeffe, J. H., King, J. M., Day, J., A., Rossouw, O., van der Zel, D. W. & Skorowszewski, R., 1989: General concepts and approaches to instream flow assessment. – In: Ferrar, A. A. (ed.): Ecological Flow Requirements for South African Rivers: 41–56. – South African National Scientific Programmes Report Number 162. Council for Scientific and Industrial Research, Pretoria.

Paterson, J., 1989: Since 'Water 2000'. – Law, politics and water uses. – In: Teoh, C. (ed.): Proceedings of the Specialist Workshop on Instream Needs and Water Uses: 1-1–1-3. – Australian Water Resources Council, Canberra.

Pigram, J. J. & Hooper, B., 1992: Water Allocation of the Environment. Proceedings of an International Seminar and Workshop. November 1991. – 282 pp. Centre for Water Policy Research, University of New England, Armidale.

Poff, N. L. & Ward, J. V., 1989: Implications of streamflow variability and predictability for lotic community structure: A regional analysis of streamflow patterns. – *Can. J. Fish. Aquatic Sci.* **46:**1805–1818.

Poplawski, W. A., 1989: Report on Basin 1362: Barker-Barambah catchment statistical analysis of water quality data collected by the Water Resources Commission. Volume 1: Main report: 15 pp. – Water Resources Commission, Brisbane.

Queensland Department of Primary Industries and Queensland Water Resources Commission, 1979: Barker-Barambah Irrigation Project: 120 pp. – QWRC, Brisbane.

Reid, R. E., Shaw, R. J. & Baker, D. E., 1979: Soils and irrigation potential of the alluvial flats of the

Byee area, Barambah Creek, Murgon, Queensland. Agricultural Chemistry Branch Technical Report No. 14: 8 pp. – Queensland Department of Primary Industrie, Brisbane.

RICHARDSON, B. A., 1989: Modelling flow requirements for instream habitats. – In: TEOH, C. (ed.): Proceedings of the Specialist Workshop on Instream Needs and Water Uses: 32-1–32-4. – Australian Water Resources Council, Canberra.

TEOH, C., 1989: Proceedings of the Specialist Workshop on Instream Needs and Water Uses: 100 pp. – Australian Water Resources Council, Canberra.

WALKER, K. F., 1989: Meeting the instream needs of aquatic fauna. – In: TEOH, C. (ed.): Proceedings of the Specialist Workshop on Instream Needs and Water Uses: 31-1–31-5. – Australian Water Resources Council, Canberra.

Author's address:

Centre for Catchment and In-stream Research, Griffith University, Nathan Qld 4111, Australia.

Mitt. Internat. Verein. Limnol.	24	179–186	Stuttgart, Februar 1994

Input, transport and storage of organic matter in two south Indian rivers

M. Arunachalam and L. K. Arun

Abstract

The Achankovil and Pachayar Rivers in south India, the former in the Kerala State and the latter in Tamil Nadu, were studied with the aim of examining downstream patterns in organic matter dynamics and relating them to the predictions of the River Continuum Concept (RCC). Wet- and dry-season estimates of input, movement and storage of organic matter were made at sites on 1st-, 2nd-, 3rd- and 4th-order reaches in each river using comparable methods. Coarse benthic organic matter (CBOM) did not increase regularly from 1st- to 4th-order reaches in Achankovil River but there was evidence for such a downstream trend in Pachayar River. There was a general trend towards less CBOM and more fine benthic organic matter in 4th-order reaches during the dry season. Transported organic matter in the two rivers was dominated by coarse particulate material. The ratio of fine to coarse transported organic matter increased with stream order in both rivers except in 3rd-order reaches. Analysis of the interactions between benthic and transported organic matter indicated that the headwaters of the Achankovil and Pachayar Rivers were more retentive than downstream reaches. While there was concordance between the predictions of the RCC and some of the results of this study, not all of the data followed the expected patterns. Studies of larger Indian rivers and investigation of a wider range of stream types is needed before the RCC can be used as a basis for conservation and management decisions concerning Indian running waters.

Introduction

The importance of organic matter in running waters has been well documented (Hynes 1970, Whitton 1975, Cummins 1974, Cummins et al. 1983). Headwater streams rely heavily on the input of organic matter from the terrestrial environment. This land-water linkage is important both in headwaters and further downstream, and has implications for the River Continuum Concept (RCC) of Vannote et al. (1980) and nutrient spiralling (O'Neill et al. 1975, Webster et al. 1975, Newbold et al. 1982), among other processes (Wetzel 1975, Naiman et al. 1988). The factors which determine how much detritus is entrained, transported and deposited in streams are complex and poorly understood. Most of the present information is from temperate latitudes (Fisher & Likens 1972, Fisher 1977, Naiman & Sedell 1979, Minshall et al. 1982, 1983, Cummins et al. 1983), although some tropical data are available (Bishop 1973, Dudgeon 1982, Pearson et al. 1989, Pearson 1994).

In the present investigation, all organic inputs (detritus and photosynthesis), outputs (transport and respiration) and changes in storage have been measured in two south Indian rivers (Achankovil and Pachayar). A knowledge of these parameters is important because the close links between rivers and their drainage basins (Hynes 1975) have important conservation and management implications. Organic matter dynamics are disturbed by anthropogenic activites such as dam-building or diversion of water from the catchment. Both activities are planned for the rivers selected for the present study. A survey completed in Achankovil River by the Central Water Commission, Government of India, dealt with possible diversion of the river to the neighbouring state of Tamil Nadu. There is also a proposal to dam the upper reaches of the Pachayar River. The results of the present investigation will therefore allow an assessment of the organic-matter dynamics of these rivers in their pre-impacted state.

The study sites

Several small streams originating from Pasukida Mettu, Ramakkal Teri and Rishi Malai, at altitudes ranging from 160–700 m, join to form the Achankovil River in Kerala State (lat. 9°05′–9°15′, long. 76°45′–77°0′; Fig. 1). The Pachayar River originates from Kuvapatti Forest in the Western Ghats. Several streams arising from Kulirattu and a portion of the Kalakkadu Estates join to form the Pachayar River in Tamil Nadu State (lat. 8°20′–8°35′, long. 77°25′–77°35′; Fig. 2). The climate is typically sub-equatorial with three main seasons: the pre-monsoon (February to May), the southwest monsoon (June to September), and the post-monsoon or northeast monsoon (October to January). The pre-monsoon period and the later part of the post-monsoon periods are usually dry. Most precipitation occurs in the southwest monsoon period in the Achankovil River basin (121 mm/month; data from the Department of Irrigation, Government of Kerala), while the post-monsoon period is the wettest for the Pachayar River (113 mm/month; data from the Department of Irrigation, Govern-

0538-4680/94/0024-0179 $ 2.00

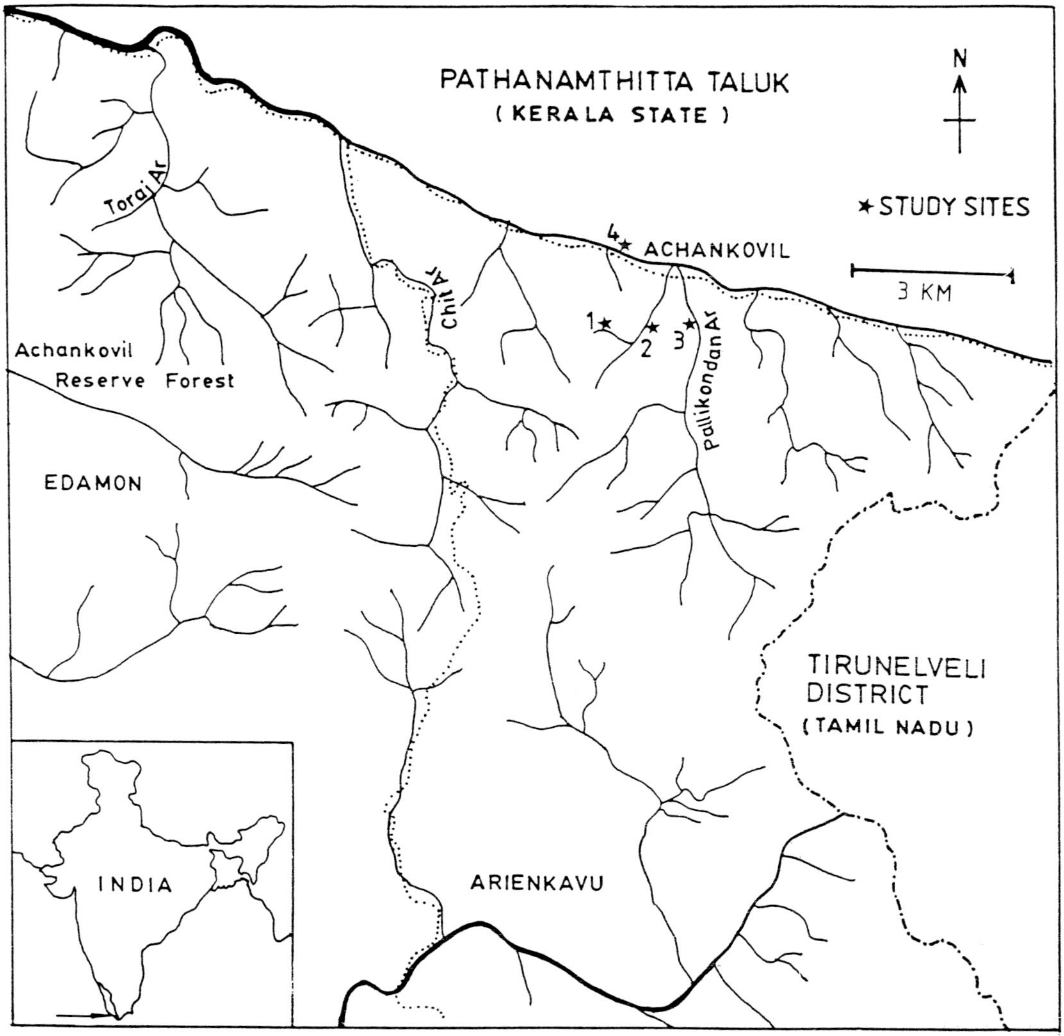

Fig. 1. Map of the study sites along Achankovil River, Kerala, south India.

ment of Tamil Nadu). Temperatures during study period ranged from 29°–33 °C (Achankovil River) and 27°–32 °C (Pachayar River).

Materials and methods

Samples were collected from 1st-, 2nd-, 3rd- and 4th-order sites along the Achankovil ($A_1 - A_4$) and Pachayar ($P_1 - P_4$) Rivers once during the wet season and once during the dry season of 1989–1990. However, samples were obtained from 4th-order reaches only during the dry period, as there was no flowing water at 1st- to 3rd-order sites. Two replicate samples were taken in 1st- and 2nd-order reaches, and three replicates in 3rd- and 4th-order reaches. Benthic organic matter was collected using a 25 × 25 cm quadrat attached to a net (mesh size 80 μm). Subsequently, the material was passed through perspex sieves to separate the size fractions: coarse particulate benthic organic matter (CBOM) ≥ 1 mm; fine particulate benthic organic matter (FBOM), ≥ 52 μm – < 1 mm. Transported coarse (CTOM) and fine (FTOM) organic matter was collected at each site by nets (1 mm and 52 μm mesh, respectively) suspended in the water column for 20–30 minutes. In order to estimate allochthonous inputs of leaves, sticks (including branches

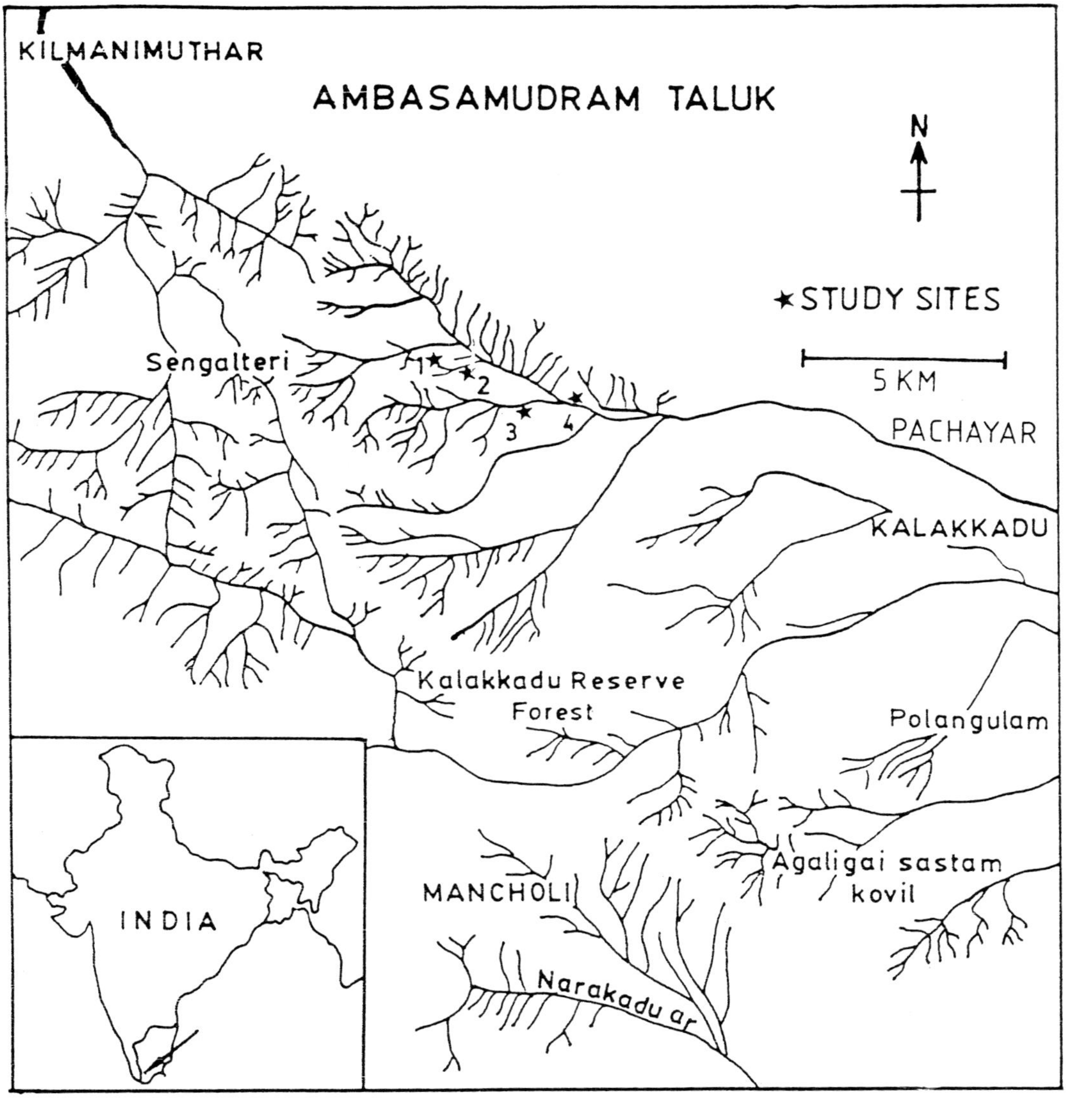

Fig. 2. Map of the study sites along Pachayar River, Tamil Nadu, south India.

< 10 cm diameter), bark and other detrital particles (together designated leaf litter, LL), samples were collected using a 25 × 25 cm quadrat. Dissolved organic matter (DOM) was sampled by passing 1000 ml of stream water through a pre-ashed GF-C glass fibre filter of 0.2 μm pore size (MOELLER et al. 1979, CUMMINS et al. 1983). Organic matter determinations were made following methods described by MINSHALL et al. (1983) and BRUNS et al. (1984). The samples were dried at 50 °C, combusted at 550 °C, rehydrated, redried and weighed to calculate the ash-free dry weight (AFDW). The relationship between detritus in storage and transport was estimated by using the relative measure of reach retention (MINSHALL et al. 1983).

Gross primary productivity and community respiration were estimated by measuring the changes in dissolved oxygen concentrations over one hour in sealed 1000-ml glass jars containing samples of leaves, wood, stream sediments and roots at each site. Respiration measurements involved the use of glass jars covered with black cloth. Two subsamples were siphoned from each jar and oxygen concentration were determined by a modified Winkler method (Strickland & Parsons 1972). Each sample of material from the jar was then dried, weighed, ashed and reweighed to determine AFDW. Changes in oxygen concentration were converted from mg O_2 to mg C by assuming a respiratory quotient of 0.8 (Macfadyen 1963).

Information on water chemistry was obtained by laboratory analysis of water samples which had been filtered in the field. Parameters were measured according to standard methods (APHA 1976); total dissolved solids were estimated from conductance values by multiplying by a factor of 0.65 (APHA 1976).

Results

Physicochemical data for the different stream orders presented in Table 1 show that, in general features, the study rivers were quite similar. Data on organic-matter dynamics are given in Table 2; significant intersite differences within each stream were noted for all of these parameters (Tables 3, 4), with the exception of DOM in Achankovil River (Table 3). CBOM exhibited no regular trend towards an increase from 1st- to 4th-order sites along Achankovil River, however there was such an increase from P_1 to P_4 in Pachayar River (Table 2). During the dry season, both leaf litter and CBOM matter increased at A_4 but not at P_4 (Table 2). The FBOM/CBOM ratio increased from A_1 to A_4 during the wet season except for a low value at A_3 (Table 5); this ratio was much lower at A_4 during the dry season. A similar general trend was seen from P_1 to P_4 (including a decline at P_3), but the ratios in all sites in Pachayar River during the wet season were much lower than along Achankovil River (Table 5). During the dry season, however, the FBOM/CBOM at P_4 was exceptionally high. The amounts of leaf litter increased downstream from P_1 to P_4, but there was no such pattern along the Achankovil River (Table 2).

Transported organic matter at all sites along both rivers comprised mainly coarse material. Dry-season loads of CTOM at A_4 and P_4 were lower than those recorded in the wet season (Table 2), and CTOM loads at P_1 and P_2 were much less than at A_1 and A_2. The FTOM loads were low at P_1 and P_3, but relatively high at A_3. In contrast to the pattern for CTOM, FTOM loads at A_4 and P_4 sites were relatively high during the dry season. FTOM/CTOM ratios (Table 5) did not increase generally with stream size, and wet-season values were highest at 3rd-order sites in both rivers. The dry-season ratio (4th-order sites only) was lower in Achankovil River than in Pachayar River, but both were considerably greater than the wet-season values (Table 5).

Gross primary productivity showed no trends with increasing stream size (Table 2), but was slightly higher at 4th-order sites in both rivers during the dry season. High rates of community respiration were measured in 1st- and 4th-order reaches of Achankovil River, but there was a clear downstream increase in this parameter in Pachayar River (Table 2). Dry-season increases in community respiration were noted in both rivers, most notably in Pachayar River where an elevation of almost ten times was recorded.

Table 1. Physicochemical characteristics of different orders of two south Indian rivers draining tropical rain forest.

Parameter	Season	Achankovil				Pachayar			
		1	2	3	4	1	2	3	4
Discharge	wet	1.23	1.55	5.83	8.75	1.17	1.77	1.45	11.71
(m^3/s)	dry	–	–	–	2.12	–	–	–	1.63
Temperature	wet	24.8	24.5	26.1	26.2	25.7	25.4	24.3	21.8
(°C)	dry	–	–	–	29.3	–	–	–	25.6
Total Alkalinity	wet	163.3	147.0	117.6	141.1	112.7	129.4	117.6	98.0
(mg/l)	dry	–	–	–	130.7	–	–	–	113.6
Hardness	wet	16.5	14.4	12.0	16.0	8.4	14.0	7.2	6.8
(mg/l ($CaCo_3$)	dry	–	–	–	15.0	–	–	–	8.4
Conductivity	wet	751	698	646	728	684	658	583	373
(μs/cm)	dry	–	–	–	706	–	–	–	425
TDS	wet	488.2	453.7	419.9	473.2	444.6	427.7	379.0	244.4
(mg/l)	dry	–	–	–	458.9	–	–	–	276.3

Table 2. Organic matter (expressed as AFDW) in different orders of two south Indian rivers: LL = leaf litter (includes sticks, bark and wood > 10 cm diameter); CBOM = coarse benthic organic matter (g/m²); FBOM = fine benthic organic matter (g/m²) DOM = dissolved organic matter (g/m²); GPP = Gross primary production (mg C/m²/day); CTOM = coarse transported organic matter (g/m²); FTOM = fine transported organic matter (g/m²); CR = community respiration (mg C/m²/day).

Parameter	Season	Achankovil				Pachayar			
		1	2	3	4	1	2	3	4
LL	wet	502.08	422.3	583.8	498.0	423.4	791.1	826.3	1,158.8
	dry	–	–	–	560.7	–	–	–	688.5
CBOM	wet	7.0	15.1	13.9	7.0	2.1	5.3	8.5	24.2
	dry	–	–	–	72.34	–	–	–	19.00
FBOM	wet	23.5	78.2	39.6	35.8	1.3	3.7	3.8	23.1
	dry	–	–	–	61.5	–	–	–	75.7
DOM	wet	0.13	0.14	0.09	0.12	0.09	0.11	0.17	0.16
	dry	–	–	–	0.17	–	–	–	0.17
GPP	wet	189.9	173.1	175.9	192.7	170.3	167.5	138.8	189.9
	dry	–	–	–	217.78	–	–	–	223.4
CTOM	wet	10.6	18.0	81.4	446.3	1.2	1.8	80.2	2,340.3
	dry	–	–	–	152.3	–	–	–	274.1
FTOM	wet	6.09	4.52	52.62	28.36	0.08	0.03	5.99	50.44
	dry	–	–	–	54.24	–	–	–	128.46
CR	wet	41.9	16.8	25.1	58.6	75.4	83.8	16.8	8.4
	dry	–	–	–	67.0	–	–	–	83.8

Table 3. Intersite differences (one-way ANOVA) in organic matter parameters in Achankovil River. Abbreviations as in Table 2; * $P < 0.05$.

Parameters	Source of variation	Sum of squares	d.f.	*F*-ratio
LL	between samples	32,861.9	3	75.82*
	within samples	866.8	6	
CBOM	between samples	138.7	3	12.46*
	within samples	22.3	6	
FBOM	between samples	3,442.7	3	142.3*
	within samples	48.4	6	
DOM	between samples	<0.1	3	2.0
	within samples	<0.1	6	
GPP	between samples	724.2	3	6.3*
	within samples	228.7	6	
CTOM	between samples	55,651.6	3	11,122.1*
	within samples	64.0	6	
FTOM	between samples	3,980.5	3	104.7*
	within samples	76.0	6	
CR	between samples	2,708.0	3	443.2*
	within samples	12.2	6	

Table 4. Intersite differences (one-way ANOVA) in organic matter parameters in Pachayar River. Abbreviations as in Table 2; * $P < 0.05$.

Parameters	Source of variation	Sum of squares	d.f.	*F*-ratio
LL	between samples	>90,000	3	5,122.9*
	within samples	262.4	6	
CBOM	between samples	779.1	3	164.4*
	within samples	9.5	6	
FBOM	between samples	859.5	3	264.1*
	within samples	6.5	6	
DOM	between samples	0.011	3	6.7*
	within samples	0.003	6	
GPP	between samples	3,969.2	3	276.2*
	within samples	28.7	6	
CTOM	between samples	>90,000	3	30,943.3*
	within samples	731.3	6	
FTOM	between samples	4,945.8	3	59.2*
	within samples	167.6		
CR	between samples	11,399.5	3	3,098.8*
	within samples	7.4	6	

Table 5. Ratios of fine particulate organic matter to coarse particulate organic matter in benthic samples (=FBOM/CBOM) and water samples (FTOM/CTOM) from two south Indian rivers. Values are mean ±SE.

	Stream order			
	1	2	3	4
FBOM/CBOM Achankovil River				
wet season	3.39±0.06	5.33±0.69	2.91±0.27	5.24±0.45
dry season	–	–	–	0.85±0.04
FBOM/CBOM Pachayar River				
wet season	0.62±0.01	0.73±0.14	0.45±0.01	0.96±0.03
dry season	–	–	–	4.22±0.61
FTOM/CTOM Achankovil River				
wet season	0.61±0.12	0.65±0.03	0.65±0.3	0.06±0.01
dry season	–	–	–	0.36±0.01
FTOM/CTOM Pachayar River				
wet season	0.07±0.01	0.02±0.01	0.07±0.01	0.02±0.01
dry season	–	–	–	0.47±0.01

Table 6. The ratio of storage to transport of organic matter as a measure of reach retention in different orders of two south Indian rivers. Values are mean ± SE.

	Stream order			
	1	2	3	4
Achankovil River				
wet season	18.5 ± 0.7	37.7±1.5	3.6±0.1	0.13±0.01
dry season	–	–	–	0.79±0.01
Pachayar River				
wet season	33.6±0.5	32.8±0.8	0.3±0.01	0.02±0.01
dry season	–	–	–	0.43±0.02

The ratio of storage to transport of organic material can be used as a measure of reach retention (Minshall et al. 1983). In both river systems, highest reach retention was recorded at the two lowest order sites (Table 6), and values recorded further downstream were considerably lower with 4th-order sites being least retentive. Dry-season retention at the 4th-order sites was slightly greater than wet-season values (Table 6).

Discussion

Research carried out in temperate rivers (Vannote et al. 1980, Minshall et al. 1983) indicates that there is a decrease in the retention capacity from headwaters to downstream reaches, and greater retention was noted at headwater sites during the present investigation. Naiman (1982) noted that rapid loading of carbon occurs in 1st- and 2nd-order reaches of boreal streams, with processing in high order reaches. The data recorded herein accord with this general pattern, despite the fact that the geomorphology of the 1st- and 2nd-order sites of Achankovil River were rather different from those of Pachayar River. The terrestrial setting and biological features were, however, similar in the 3rd-order sites of both rivers. Though reach retention follows the general pattern of the RCC, the rivers studied were small. In addition, the relationship between stream geomorphology (e.g. channel roughness, discharge, depth and width), riparian vegetation and retention capacity of these and other, larger Indian rivers needs to be investigated further before the RCC can be applied widely and used as a management tool in this region.

A general prediction of the RCC is that with increasing stream size a decrease in coarse detritus is accompanied by a relative increase in fine organic particles. However, the ratios of FBOM/CBOM were not consistent with this prediction. Benthic organic matter at the 4th-order site increased dramatically in the Achankovil River during the dry season, but this did not occur in Pachayar River. The amount of benthic detritus and its distribution is a function of input and processing rates, retention structures, stream power and channel morphometry (NAIMANN & SEDELL 1979). It is most likely that low discharge accounted for the dry season increase in detritus in Achankovil River, and a similar connection of detrital standing stocks to discharge has been observed in the temperate zone (NAIMAN & SEDELL 1979); however, it is curious that the increase did not occur in Pachayar River. Investigation of a larger range of stream orders is needed before concordance with predictions of the RCC can be confirmed or ruled out.

There was no clear regular pattern in the CTOM/FTOM ratios in the two rivers, but wet-season CTOM transport was higher in the higher-order sites of both rivers (especially Pachayar River) as reflected in the lower reach retention of these downstream sites. However, the high CTOM levels at the 4th-order site on Pachayar River may have been a result of rainfall (27 mm) during the two days prior to sampling.

References

American Public Health Association, 1976: Standard Methods for the Examination of Water and Waste Water, 14th Edition: 1193 pp. – APHA, Washington D.C.

BISHOP, J. E., 1973: Limnology of a small Malayan river Sunguai Gombak: 485 pp. – Dr W. Junk Publishers, The Hague.

BRUNS, D. A., MINSHALL, G. W., CUSHING, C. E., CUMMINS, K. W., BROCK, J. T. & VANNOTE, R. L., 1984: Tributaries as modifiers of the river continuum concept: analysis by polar ordination and regression models. – *Arch. Hydrobiol.* **99:**208–220.

CUMMINS, K. W., 1974: Stream ecosystem structure and function. – *BioScience* **24:**631–641.

CUMMINS, K. W., SEDELL, J. R., SWANSON, F. J., MINSHALL, G. W., FISHER, S. G., CUSHING, C. E., PETERSEN, R. C. & VANNOTE, R. L., 1983: Organic matter budgets for stream ecosystems: Problems in their evaluation. – In: BARNES, J. R. & MINSHALL, G. W. (eds.): Stream Ecology: Application and Testing of General Ecological Theory: 299–353. – Plenum Press, New York.

DUDGEON, D., 1982: Spatial and seasonal variations in the standing crop of periphyton and allochthonous detritus in a forest stream in Hong Kong, with notes on the magnitude and fate of riparian leaf fall. – *Arch. Hydrobiol. Suppl.* **64** (Mon. Beitr.):189–220.

FISHER, S. G., 1977: Organic matter processing by a stream segment ecosystem: Fort River, Massachusetts, U.S.A. – *Int. Rev. ges. Hydrobiol.,* **62:**701–727.

FISHER, S. G. & LIKENS, G. E., 1972: Stream ecosystem: Organic energy budget. – *BioScience* **22:**33–35.

HYNES, H. B. N., 1970: The Ecology of Running Waters: 555 pp. – University of Toronto Press, Ontario.

– 1975: The stream and its valley. – *Verh. Internat. Verein. Limnol.* **19:**1–15.

MACFADYEN, A., 1963: *Animal Ecology:* Aims and Methods. 2nd Edition: 344 pp. – Pitman, London.

MINSHALL, G. W., PETERSEN, R. C., CUMMINS, K. W., BOTT, T. L., SEDELL, J. R., CUSHING, C. E. & VANNOTE, R. L., 1983: Interbiome comparison of stream ecosystem dynamics. – *Ecol. Monogr.* **53:** 1–25.

MOELLER, J. R., MINSHALL, G. W., CUMMINS, K. W., PETERSEN, R. C., CUSHING, C. E., SEDELL, J. R., LARSON, R. A. & VANNOTE, R. L., 1979: Transport of dissolved organic carbon in streams of differing physiographic characteristics. – *Org. Geochem.* **1:**139–150.

NAIMAN, R. J., 1982: Characteristics of sediment and organic carbon export for pristine boreal forest watersheds. – *Can. J. Fish. Aquat. Sci.* **39:**1699–1718.

NAIMAN, R. J., DECAMPS, H., PASTOR, J. & JOHNSON, C. A., 1988: The potential importance of boundaries. – *J. N. Amer. Benthol. Soc.* **7:**289–306.

NAIMAN, R. J. & SEDELL, J. R., 1979: Benthic Organic matter as a function of stream order in Oregon. – *Arch. Hydrobiol.* **87:**404–422.

NEWBOLD, J. D., O'NEILL, R. V., ELWOOD, J. W. & VAN WINKLE, W., 1982: Organic carbon spiralling in stream ecosystems. – *Oikos* **38:**266–272.

O'NEILL, R. V., HARRIS, W. F., AUSMUS, B. S. & REICHLE, D. E., 1975. – A theoretical basis for ecosystem analysis with particular reference to element cycling. – In: HOWELL, F. G., GENTRY, H. B. & SMITH, M. H. (eds.): Mineral Cycling in Southwestern Ecosystems. – *E.R.D.A. Symposium series, Washington D.C.:* 28–40.

PEARSON, R. G., 1993: Limnology in the northeast tropics of Australia, the wettest part of the driest continent. – *Mitt. Internat. Verein. Limnol.* **24:** 155–163.

PEARSON, R. G., BENSON, L. J. & SMITH, R. E. W., 1989: Standing crop and processing of rainforest litter in a tropical Australian stream. – *Arch. Hydrobiol.* **115:**481–498.

STRICKLAND, J. D. H. & PARSONS, T. R., 1972: A Practical Handbook of Seawater Analysis, 2nd Edition. – *Bull. Fish. Res. Bd. Can.* **167,** 310 pp.

Vannote, R. L., Minshall, G. W., Cummins, K. W., Sedell, J. R. & Cushing, C. E., 1980: The river continuum concept. – *Can. J. Fish. Aquat. Sci.* **37:** 130–137.

Webster, J. R., Waide, J. B. & Patten, B. C., 1975: Nutrient recycling and the stability of ecosystems. – In: Howell, F. G., Gentry, J. B. & Smith, M. H. (eds.): Mineral Cycling in Southern Ecosystems. – *E.R.D.A. Symposium series, Washington D.C.:* 1–27.

Wetzel, R. G., 1975: Limnology: 743 pp. – Saunders, Philadelphia.

Whitton, B. A., 1975: River ecology: 694 pp. – Blackwell Scientific Publications, Oxford.

Authors' addresses:

M. Arunachalam, Department of Aquatic Biology & Fisheries, University of Kerala, Beach P.O., Trivandrum-695 007, India, and Centre for System Conservation and Analysis, D-122, 23 Cross Street, Maharaja Nagar, Tirunelveli – 627 011, India.

L. K. Arun, Department of Aquatic Biology & Fisheries, University of Kerala, Beach P.O., Trivandrum-695 007, India.

Mitt. Internat. Verein. Limnol.	24	187–196	Stuttgart, Februar 1994

Utilization of floodplain water bodies by the fishes of the Fly River, Papua New Guinea

R. E. W. Smith and K. A. Bakowa

Abstract

The Fly River, southern Papua New Guinea, is bordered by extensive floodplains in the lowland reaches. There are four main habitat types within these floodplains: blocked-valley lakes created by flooding of broad, shallow valleys; oxbow lakes formed from old river channels; grassed floodplains, and forested floodplains. This study examined the abundances of fish species in the first three habitat types over a two year period.

The three habitat types all supported large populations of fish, which is in marked contrast to the Sepik River in northern Papua New Guinea where few native fish utilise the grassed floodplain. A significantly greater mean number of species were caught in the blocked-valley lakes (17.4; two sites) than in oxbows (13.2; five sites) or grassed floodplain (14.7; 2 sites), but there were no significant differences in the number of fish, the biomass of fish, or evenness between the habitats. Multivariate analyses showed that the composition of the fish assemblages was significantly different in each habitat type, and that there was a significant difference in the composition at the two grassed floodplain sites. As the total area of the blocked-valley lakes (245 km^2) and grassed floodplain (2473 km^2) greatly exceeded that of the oxbow lakes (122 km^2) those habitats would support a greater stock of fish. However, the much deeper oxbow lakes could serve as refuges during very dry conditions. Furthermore, as most species were found in more than one habitat type, the assemblage in any one habitat should be able to recover from temporary impacts through re-colonisation from other habitats.

Introduction

The Fly River system is one of the world's largest, with a mean discharge of 6000 m^3/s (Ok Tedi Mining Limited 1988), making it comparable to the Niger and Zambesi in Africa, and the Danube in Europe (Welcomme 1985). However, with a catchment are a of only 76,000 km^2, the Fly outranks all the world's major rivers in terms of the runoff per unit catchment area (cf. Holeman 1968, Welcomme 1985). This is due to the very high rainfall in the region, ranging from 10,000 mm per annum in the upper catchment to around 3000 mm per annum near the coast. Although the upper catchment extends to altitudes greater than 4000 m, the majority of the drainage basin is flat, to the extent that the river port of Kiunga, which is 800 river km from the coast, is only 20 m above sea level. The combination of flat land and high rainfall has resulted in an extensive wetland system.

The Ok Tedi copper mine is located on Mount Fubilan in the headwaters of the Ok Tedi, a major tributary of the Fly River ('ok' means river in the Yonggom language). Construction for the project began in 1981 and the mine commenced operation in 1984, initially as a gold mine. Copper production started in 1987 and gold production ceased in 1988. Because of the high rainfall and geological instability of the region, construction of a tailings dam was not feasible, and the mine has operated without waste retention. Extensive environmental studies began in 1981, with permanent monitoring programs established in 1983. An overview of these programs is given by Eagle & Higgins (1991) while details of the biological sampling programs are presented by Smith (1991). The results of these programs have shown that, since gold production ceased, copper is the major metal of environmental concern in the river system (Smith & Morris 1992). The majority of the copper is associated with suspended solids, some of which may be transported onto the floodplain of the Fly River during rising river levels (Higgins 1990).

The study reported here was concerned mostly with the section known as the middle Fly, between the Ok Tedi/Fly River and the Strickland River/Fly River junctions. There are four major habitat types in the middle Fly floodplain: blocked-valley lakes (total area 245 km^2), created where the Fly River acts as an hydraulic dam to flood broad, shallow valleys; oxbow lakes (122 km^2) formed from cutoff meander bends of the river; grassed floodplain, and forested floodplain (2473 km^2 combined). There is little rainfall seasonality in the upper catchment, with the average monthly rainfall at the mine township of Tabubil (see Fig. 1) ranging from 525 mm in November to 754 mm in March. There is more marked seasonality in the middle Fly where rainfall is related to the north-west monsoon (December to April) and the south-east trades (May to November). Because of the difference in rainfall patterns, the water on the floodplain may be derived either from the Fly River, or

0538-4680/94/0024-0187 $ 2.50

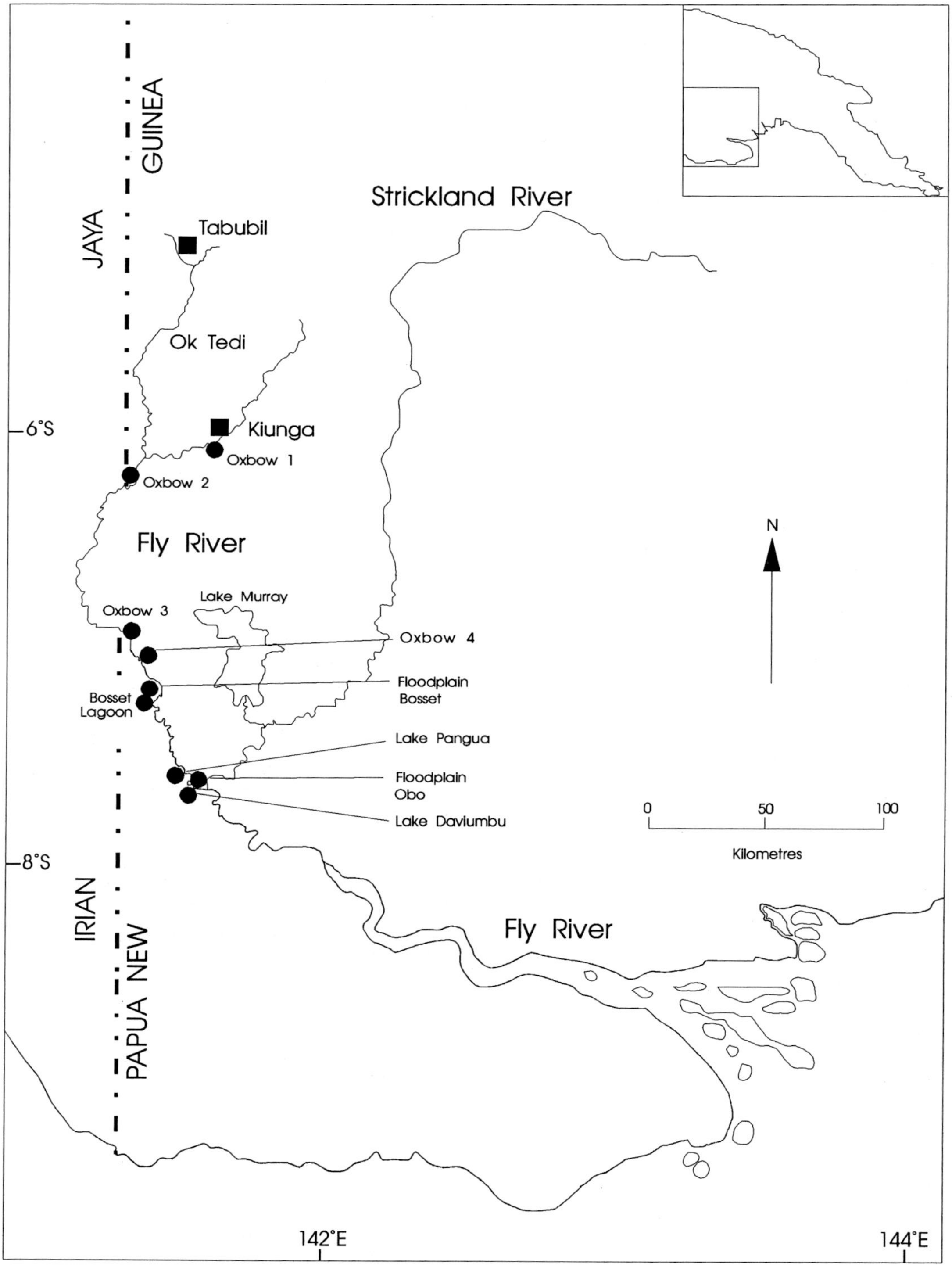

Fig. 1. Map of the sampling locations. Sampling sites indicated by circles, townships indicated by squares.

from local rainfall. In the latter case, the isotopic composition of floodplain water may differ considerably from that in the river channel (Ok Tedi Mining Limited 1988). Furthermore, as the river catchment is quite small, the cycle of flooding and drying of the more shallow areas of the floodplain is erratic, with the time between periods of drying varying from weeks to more than a year.

The freshwater fish fauna of the Fly River is the most diverse in the Australasian region, with a total of 103 species recorded from fresh water by Roberts (1978). Roberts also noted that the Australasian fauna is distinguished by the presence of and, particularly in the cases of the Ariidae and Plotosidae, the dominance of groups not common in fresh waters in other parts of the world. The fauna of the Sepik River, the river closest to the size of the Fly on the island of New Guinea, has a relatively low overall diversity with a total of 57 fish species in fresh water (Allen & Coates 1990). The unusual composition and diversity of the ichthyofauna of the Fly makes the findings of studies of habitat use from other rivers of limited relevance for the developement of management and conservation strategies.

The aims of this study were to investigate the extent to which the various floodplain habitat types were utilised by the fishes of the Fly, and to determine whether there were differences in the fish assemblages among habitat types. A fuller understanding of the importance of the different habitat types to the fish will provide insight into the likely consequences of copper intrusion into those habitats.

Methods

Sampling sites

Bosset Lagoon, which had been sampled since 1983, and Lake Daviumbu, which had been sampled since 1987, were typical of blocked-valley lakes. In 1989, sampling in oxbow lakes and grassed floodplain sites commenced, but no reliable method for sampling of the forested floodplain was found. In the following report, the term lake is used to describe Lake Daviumbu and Bosset Lagoon, lacustrine refers to both the lake and oxbow sites, and floodplain refers to the grassed floodplain.

Logistical constraints played a large part in the selection of sampling sites within habitat types. As the sampling methods (gill nets and rotenone fish poison; see below) required the use of bulky equipment, and the water depths in many of the water bodies dictated the use of a boat, only those sites which could be accessed by boat were sampled. As boat access usually implied free flow of river waters, the sites sampled may have overrepresented habitats well-connected to the river, and therefore more prone to any impacts from mining. All sampling took place after mining had commenced in the upper Ok Tedi catchment. Accordingly, an oxbow located downstream of Kiunga in the upper Fly, which would not have been affected by mining effluents, was selected as a 'control' unimpacted site. Four other oxbow lakes were chosen for sampling in the middle Fly. In addition, two grassed floodplain sites were sampled (Fig. 1). The individual sites are described below.

Oxbow 1 was the first oxbow downstream of Kiunga and was selected as a control site, despite being downstream of the town, as the oxbow lakes further upstream were affected by human habitation. It had background copper concentrations in the bottom sediments (Ok Tedi Mining Limited 1991), indicating negligible contamination from the wharf and copper concentrate drying plant operations at Kiunga. However, it was heavily fished by the local people. In common with the other oxbow lake sites, the gill net station was near the middle of the lake. At this site it was on the outer bank. Rotenoning was done in a small backwater in the middle of the gill net station.

Oxbow 2 was accessed by a long, forested channel which could be blocked by debris and thus was not always navigable at low river levels even when the lake still contained water. The gill net station was on the outer bend, while rotenoning was undertaken in the flooded forest on the opposite bank, near the middle of the gill net station.

The gill net station at Oxbow 3 was on the inner bank, while rotenoning was undertaken in a small subsidiary oxbow on the outer bank on the downstream side of the lake.

Oxbow 4 was probably much older than the nearby Oxbow 3, as the upstream arm had been filled in partially. Gill netting was carried out on the inner bank, with rotenoning in grassy bays on the opposite bank.

Oxbow 5 – or Lake Pangua – was a complex double oxbow/blocked-valley lake system. The gill netting station overlapped the area where the two oxbows joined, with nets set predominantly on the outer bank of the main oxbow. Some nets, particularly the smaller ones, were set on the inner bank on occasions. Rotenoning was done amongst floating grass islands on the inner bank on the upstream side of the gill net station.

The floodplain at Obo was densely vegetated although free of the larger grass species found elsewhere on the floodplain. It was often necessary to compact the vegetation by walking ahead of the net being set, in order to get the lead line to the bottom. The placement of the gill nets was dictated by the available space. Rotenoning was carried out in a small, relatively open area away from the gill nets, or in the gill net area after the nets had been removed. On occasions, when the water level was too low for netting, only rotenone was used at this site.

The floodplain site at Bosset was a small, shallow, open-water area upstream of the entrance to Bosset Lagoon. The nets were set in lake order, almost the full circumference of the open water, but with the channel to the river between the two ends of the net set. Rotenoning was undertaken in a small grassy bay in the lee of the prevailing winds.

Lake Daviumbu was densely vegetated by a rich variety of aquatic macrophytes. The gill net station was in two parts, near two islands in front of Kavananga village. The larger nets were usually set in the more distant section, near a secondary entrance channel where the water was less densely vegetated. Rotenone sampling was carried out on the village side of the area where the smaller nets were set.

At Lake Bosset, the gill net station was along a steep bank near the entrance channel. Rotenone sampling was undertaken near an island on the other side of the channel. These locations were selected in the deeper parts of the lake, and could be fished at low water levels.

Gill netting

The net set used at all the off-river sampling sites has been described elsewhere (Ok Tedi Mining Limited 1986) and is summarised in Table 1. In lacustrine sites, the nets were tied perpendicular to the bank in a series, each net separated from the next by a large enough distance to facilitate fish movements between the nets (usually > 50 m). The order was from larger nets at each end of the series to smaller nets in the middle. The floodplain site at Bosset was fished similarly to the lacustrine sites. The floodplain site at Obo was densely vegetated, and setting of nets usually involved wading ahead of the net setting, to make a path for the net to be dropped into. The nets were spaced as widely as possible, but the order was dictated by available space. Generally, this meant that the larger nets were set closer to the river.

Rotenone

Rotenone was used at all sites in a qualitative fashion only, as the water depth and dense vegetation of the sites precluded the containment of a known area. For each sample, 500 g of powdered derris root, mixed in a polythene bag with water and a small quantity of detergent, was applied to a small bay, with affected fish collected for one hour after application by means of dip nets used from a small boat.

Table 1. Gill nets used in fish sampling. Mono indicates net constructed from nylon monofilament.

Mesh size (mm)	Type	Length (m)	Depth (m)	Area (m^2)	Number used
25	mono	40	2.3	92	1
38	mono	40	1.7	68	1
50	mono	45	2.1	95	1
63	mono	40	2.8	112	1
75	mono	45	3.2	144	1
88	mono	45	3.5	158	1
100	mono	45	4.2	189	1
125	mono	45	4.9	221	1
150	mono	50	6.0	300	1
150	multi	25	2.8	70	2
175	multi	25	3.1	78	2

Sample processing

Fish collected from the nets were identified, measured (fork length to the nearest 1 mm) and weighed (to the nearest 1 g up to 6 kg and to the nearest 100 g over 6 kg) on site, and then given away to nearby villagers. The rotenone samples contained small specimens which were difficult to identify in the field, and which were preserved and brought to the laboratory for processing. These specimens were identified, weighed to the nearest 0.1 g and fork length measured to the nearest 1 mm. When large numbers of a single species were caught in one net, approximately 100 specimens were measured individually, and the remainder were counted and their total weight determined. The subsample of 100 individuals was selected randomly following the method of Gerking (1962).

Statistical analyses

Analyses of variance of the summary catch statistics were undertaken using the GLM procedure of the SAS statistical package (SAS Institute 1985). One-way ANOVAs were used to test for differences between sites, but nested ANOVAs were used to test for habitat type effects, with site nested within habitat. Tukey studentised multiple-range tests were used to locate differences between means for each site and habitat. Before ANOVAs were performed, each parameter was tested for normality using the univariate procedure from the SAS statistical package. Non-normal dependant variables were $\log(x+1)$ transformed; the transformed variables were normal in all cases. Evenness values were arcsine transformed. In the habitat-type analyses, site was nested within habitat.

Tests of catch composition differences were done using the L (permute) statistic of Good (1982) as modified by Smith & Morris (1992). This statistic allows a simple bootstrap test of the significance of separateness of groups of samples, based on the values of a similarity or dissimilarity index. The dissimilarity index used was the symmetric form of the Kulczynski coefficient calculated by the PATN analysis package (Belbin 1988). Hybridised multidimensional scaling (HMDS; Faith et al. 1987) was used to illustrate graphically the similarities between samples and sites, with a cutoff level between parametric and non-parametric multidimensional scaling of 0.8 for the symmetric Kulczynski coefficient. Four dimensions were used in each case, as this was the smallest number of dimensions which gave a stress level of less than 0.15. The HMDS was calculated by the PATN package using ten random starting configurations. Faith et al. (1987) showed that HMDS was an ordination technique that was able to take advantage of the robust nature of the Kulczynski coefficient over a range of ecological distances to produce a plot with a close linear relationship between ordination distances and ecological distances.

Results

Gill net catches

The occurrence of species in gill nets and/or rotenone samples at the study sites is shown in Appendix 1. A feature of the samples at the lacustrine sites was the large catches of Herrings, *Nematalosa* spp., and to a lesser extent, the Groove-snouted catfish, *Arius berneyi.* Herrings are schooling species, and thus catches were quite variable between samples. There were no species found exclusively on the floodplain (Appendix 1). Four species, *Arius acrocephalus, Cinetodus carinatus, Cochlefelis danielsi* and *Melanotaenia sexlineatus,* were collected from oxbows only during this study, but the first three are more typically of river channel sites (Ok Tedi Mining Limited 1986). Roberts (1978) collected *M. sexlineatus* from a river site and Lake Bosset. Similarly, seven species were only collected from blocked-valley lakes during this study – *Aseroggodes klunzingeri, Glossogobius giurus, Pingalla lorentzi, Pristis microdon, Pseudomugil gertrudae, Oxyeleotris nulipora,* and *Zenarchopterus novaeguineae* – but all have been found at river sites (Roberts 1978, Ok Tedi Mining Limited 1986).

A total of 47 species of fish were caught in gill net samples at the off-river sampling sites. Of these, 20 species were caught at each of the two floodplain sites. Herrings were not abundant in the dense vegetation found at the Obo floodplain site, but were numerous in the more open waters of the floodplain at Bosset. The catch from the floodplain at Obo was dominated by *Lates calcarifer* (27% of total biomass caught), *Sclerophages jardini* (18%) and *Neosilurus ater* (18%), while the catches from the floodplain at Bosset were dominated by Herrings (38%), *Arius leptaspis* (16%) and *N. ater* (11%). Herrings accounted for 14–72% of the biomass caught at the lacustrine sites, and were the dominant fish at all sites except oxbow 4 where *L. calcarifer* made up 27% of the catch. The second most dominant species by weight was *A. berneyi* at oxbows 2 and 4 (22% and 23%), *A. leptaspis* at Bosset Lagoon (11%), *L. calcarifer* at oxbow 1 (22%), *Megalops cyprinoides* at oxbows 3 and 5 (21% and 20%), and *N. ater* at Lake Daviumbu (12%). The total number of species caught at the oxbow sites ranged from 20 at oxbow 4 to 31 at oxbow 5. Thirty species were collected from Lake Daviumbu and 27 from Lake Bosset between January 1989 and the end of the study in 1991.

Table 2 shows the results of analyses of variance to test for inter-habitat differences in the number and biomass of fish captured, the number of species caught, and the evenness of the catch. Only samples collected from January 1989 onwards were included in the analysis. The only significant difference among habitats was in the number of species caught, which was higher at the lake sites

Table 2. Analyses of variance for site and habitat type effects on the number, biomass, number of species and evenness of fish caught in the offriver water bodies. Sites and habitat types which were not significantly different at the 5% level are connected by lines. The mean values for each parameter are shown beneath each site code. Site abbreviations are Oxb = Oxbow, Bos = Bosset Lagoon, Dav = Lake Daviumbu, Fld B = floodplain at Bosset and Fld O = floodplain at Obo.

Parameter	Site									Habitat		
Number	Fld O	Oxb 1	Oxb 4	Oxb 2	Oxb 3	Fld B	Dav	Bos	Oxb 5	Floodplain	Oxbow	Lake
	186	455	625	661	670	696	708	1,226	1,339	469	750	987
Biomass	Oxb 1	Fld O	Dav	Oxb 2	Fld B	Oxb 3	Bos	Oxb 4	Oxb 5	Floodplain	Lake	Oxbow
(kg)	58	73	114	108	144	169	194	201	372	112	157	182
ln (x + 1)	3.8	3.8	4.5	4.6	5.0	5.0	5.1	5.2	5.8			
No. spp.	Oxb 1	Fld O	Oxb 4	Fld B	Oxb 2	Oxb 3	Bos	Dav	Oxb 5	Floodplain	Oxbow	Lake
	12.0	13.0	13.0	13.4	14.2	14.8	16.6	18.3	19.6	13.2	14.7	17.4
Evenness	Bos	Oxb 1	Fld B	Oxb 2	Oxb 4	Oxb 3	Oxb 5	Dav	Fld O	Lake	Oxbow	Floodplain
	0.26	0.32	0.37	0.42	0.45	0.46	0.52	0.61	0.76	0.42	0.43	0.54

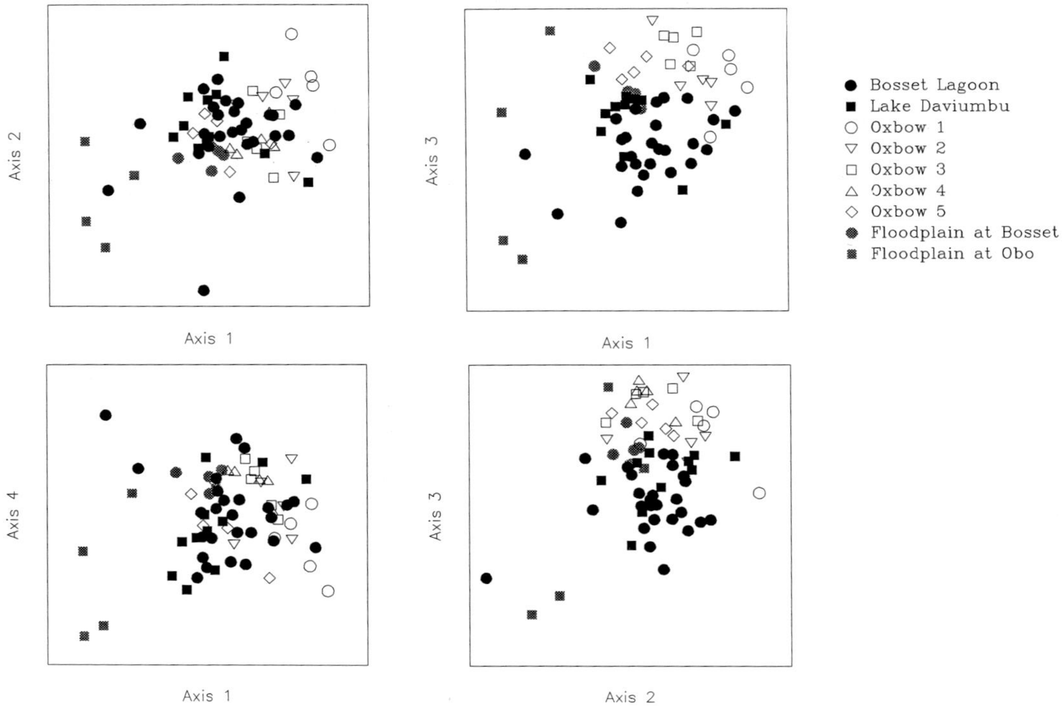

Fig. 2. Hybridised multidimensional scaling ordination of the composition of the catches at each site by the numbers of each species caught. The symbols used for each site are indicated.

than in the oxbow or floodplain sites. In general, any differences in catches among sites were rather inconsistent, depending upon the parameters (numbers, biomass, etc.) used in the comparison. However, the largest catches by numbers and biomass were from Lake Pangua, while the floodplain at Obo and Oxbow 1 had the smallest catches; they were significantly lower than the number, biomass and number of species of fish caught in Lake Pangua. The floodplain at Obo had the greatest evenness, due to the relatively low catches of Herrings at this site. Lake Daviumbu, with the second highest mean evenness yielded relatively few herrings also.

When the composition of the catch, in terms of the number of each species caught, was compared via the L (permute) statistic; there was no significant difference between the oxbow sites or between the two lake sites, but there was a significant difference between the floodplain sites. Fig. 2 shows that in the multidimensional scaling ordination in four dimensions, the samples from the floodplain at Bosset were more similar to the those from the lacustrine sites than were the samples from the floodplain at Obo. The latter were well separated from the majority of the samples. The lake and oxbow groups each differed significantly from the other samples (Fig. 2; Axis 1 by Axis 3), but because of the similarity of the floodplain at Bosset samples to both the oxbow and lake samples, the floodplain group was not significantly different from the other samples.

The results of the comparisons of fish assemblages based on the biomass of each species caught matched those obtained from ordination analyses based on the abundance of each species. There were no significant differences between any of the oxbow sites or between the two lake sites, but there was a difference between the two floodplain sites. The oxbow and lake groupings were both different from the other samples, but the floodplain group was not (Fig. 3).

Rotenone catches

Due to the qualitative nature of the sampling, it is not appropriate to compare the numbers or biomass of fish caught among sites or dates. How-

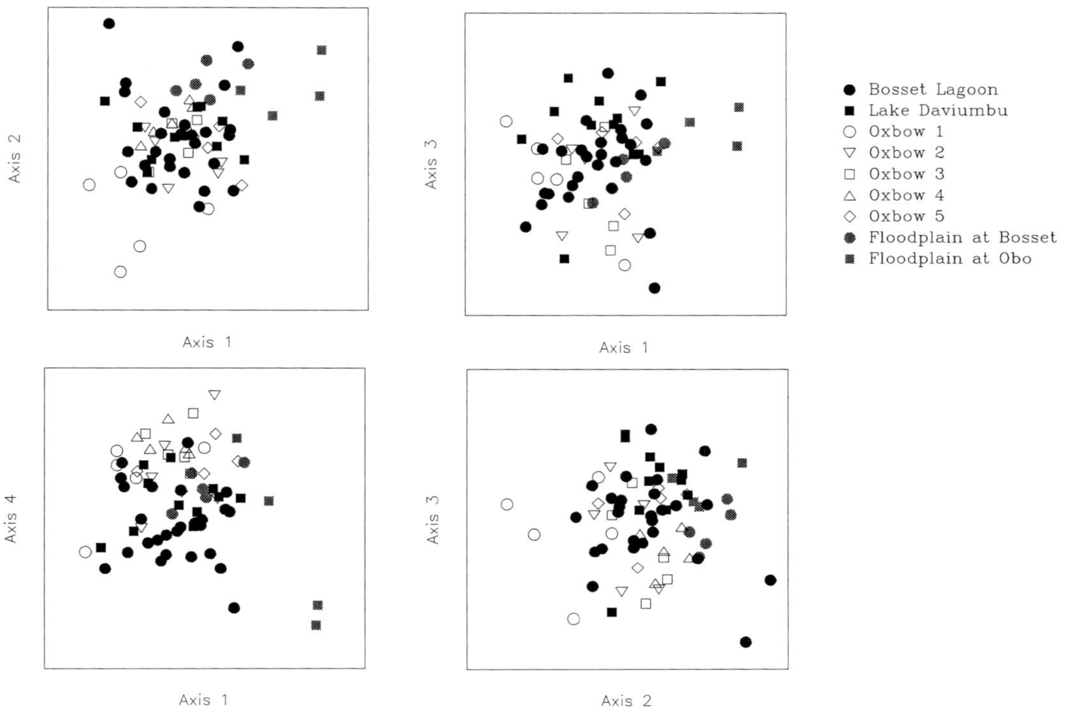

Fig. 3. Hybridised multidimensional scaling ordination of the composition of the catches at each site by the biomass of each species caught. The symbols used for each site are indicated.

Table 3. Total number of species caught at each site by rotenone and the number of species caught by that technique alone.

Site	Total no. species	Rotenone only
Oxbow 1	12	3
Oxbow 2	11	3
Oxbow 3	16	6
Oxbow 4	13	7
Oxbow 5	20	7
Floodplain at Bosset	19	9
Floodplain at Obo	18	4
Bosset Lagoon	16	6
Lake Daviumbu	15	3

ever, a comparison of species composition is possible.

Rotenone sampling alone yielded only a small proportion (maximum 31%) of the total species present at a site (Table 3). In addition, the size of the fish caught by rotenone tended to be relatively small (average weight of individual fish per site ranged from 1.4 to 25.7 g), and a large proportion of the specimens caught by rotenone were young of the species caught by gill netting. This reflected partly the localised effects of the rotenone itself, which required that the fish spend a length of time within the affected area, thus making small fish more susceptible, but the effect was magnified because larger fish were better able to avoid the dip nets used to retrieve specimens. However, the rotenone catches did indicate that many of the gill netted species were reproducing within the off-river water bodies.

Discussion

The results of the sampling in off-river water bodies has shown that the three habitat types sampled all supported large populations of fish, and that there were some differences in the composition of the fish assemblages among habitats. It is important to note that the grassed floodplains of the Fly River were well utilised by the native fish species, which is in stark contrast to the situation along the Sepik River where only three native species of fish show any affinity for the floodplain (ALLEN & COATES 1990). The main inhabitant of the Sepik floodplain is the introduced Tilapia, *Oreochromis mossambicus* (COATES 1985). Interestingly, the exotic Climbing perch, *Anabas testudineus*, was abundant on the floodplain at Obo on the Fly River.

Although the sampling methods employed did not give estimates of fish densities, and despite the fact that the floodplain sites sampled were in close proximity to the river channel, the vast area of grassed floodplain in the middle Fly appears to support a greater stock of fish than the oxbows and blocked-valley lakes. The latter two habitat types had similar overall catches per standard sample, but the blocked-valley lakes – which have approximately twice the total area of the oxbows – would support about twice the fish stocks of the oxbows.

HIGGINS (1990) calculated that three percent of the copper carried by the Fly River could enter the floodplain water bodies, of which 0.2% might be released into the water column. Although elevated copper concentrations have been found in sediments in some oxbows and blocked-valley lakes (Ok Tedi Mining Limited 1989; HIGGINS 1990), there is as yet no indication of any adverse consequences other than slight increases in the liver and kidney copper concentrations of *Arius berneyi* in oxbow 2 (Ok Tedi Mining Limited 1991). Moreover, the presence of juvenile fish in the rotenone catches indicated that recruitment was occurring in those habitats. Most of the copper reaching the floodplain is expected to remain in particulate form (HIGGINS 1990) which has low toxicity (SMITH et al. 1990).

The majority of the floodplain and blocked-valley lake habitats, which represent a much greater total area than the oxbow lakes, are unlikely to experience significant sediment intrusion because of attenuation by the dense vegetation. However, the oxbow lakes are generally deeper than the other floodplain habitats and, at low river levels when they may comprise the only standing water left on the floodplain, they may be an important fish refuge. Their importance needs to be clarified in the light of observations that considerable standing water remained on the floodplain during an 'El Nino' influenced extreme low rainfall event in early 1992 when river levels were at their lowest in ten years.

Although significant inter-habitat differences were found between the fish assemblages, most species occurred in more than one habitat type. Those few species which were found only in a single floodplain habitat have been recorded also in the river channel sites (ROBERTS 1978, Ok Tedi Mining Limited 1986). If a particular habitat suffers from an extreme impact, such as drying out during a drought, the species normally found in that habitat should be able to recolonise from elsewhere. In conservation terms, severe but temporary stresses to one habitat type need not lead to long-term impacts provided other habitats remain as refuges. Presumably in the worst of droughts, only the deepest of oxbows and the river itself would retain fish populations. Additional adverse impacts upon refuges at such times could greatly reduce the potential for recolonizing other habitats when the water levels rise.

An interesting result arising from sampling off-river water bodies was the generally high abundance of Herrings. These short-lived, detritivorous/herbivorous species spawn several times each year, if not continuously (Ok Tedi Mining Limited 1986), and have the potential for a much greater sustainable yield than the Barramundi, *Lates calcarifer*, which is a long-lived, annually-spawning, migratory predator (MOORE 1980). Currently, Barramundi is the only species caught commercially in the Fly River system.

In summary, the oxbows, blocked-valley lakes and grassed floodplain habitats supported a diverse and abundant fish fauna. The fish assemblages differed between habitats, and therefore to maintain the full diversity of the fish fauna of the Fly River wetlands the long-term integrity of each habitat should be maintained. However, as all species occur in more than one habitat type (or one habitat type in addition to the river channel), recolonization can occur following temporary impacts (such as drought or man-made stresses) upon single habitats.

Acknowledgements

The authors wish to thank the staff of the Biology Section of Ok Tedi Mining Limited. Without their efforts this study would not have been possible. The continued support of the management of Ok Tedi Mining Limited is also gratefully acknowledged. An anonymous referee made valuable comments on an earlier draft.

Appendix

Distribution of fish species in the sampled sites. O1 = Oxbow 1, O2 = Oxbow 2, O3 = Oxbow 3, O4 = Oxbow 4, O5 = Oxbow 5, FO = Floodplain at Obo, FB = Floodplain at Bosset, BL = Bosset Lagoon and LD = Lake Daviumbu, *Nematalosa* spp. included *N. flyensis* and *N. papuensis* which are difficult to distinguish in the field.

Family	Species	Sites Present								
		O1	O2	O3	O4	O5	FO	FB	BL	LD
Ambassidae	*Ambassis agrammus*			+	+	+		+	+	
	A. macleayi	+	+	+	+	+	+	+	+	+
	Denariusa bandata					+	+	+	+	+
	Parambassis gulliveri	+	+	+		+			+	
Anabantidae	*Anabas testudineus*				+	+	+	+	+	+
Apogonidae	*Glossamia aprion*	+	+	+	+	+	+	+	+	+
	G. trifasciata	+	+	+		+	+	+	+	+
Ariidae	*Arius acrocephalus*	+	+							
	A. augustus	+				+			+	
	A. berneyi	+	+	+	+	+	+	+	+	+
	A. leptaspis	+	+	+	+	+	+	+	+	+
	A. macrorhynchus	+								
	Cinetodus carinatus		+							
	C. froggatti					+			+	+
	Cochlefelis danielsi					+				
	C. spatula				+	+		+	+	
Atherinidae	*Craterocephalus randi*	+	+	+	+	+	+	+	+	+
Belonidae	*Strongylura kreffti*	+	+	+	+	+	+	+	+	+
Centropomidae	*Lates calcarifer*	+	+	+	+	+	+	+	+	+
Clupeidae	*Clupeoides papuensis*	+	+	+					+	
	Nematalosa spp.	+	+	+	+	+	+	+	+	+
Eleotridae	*Mogurnda mogurnda*					+	+	+	+	+
	Ophieleotris aporos						+	+		+
	Oxyeleotris fimbriata	+	+	+	+	+	+	+	+	+
	O. lineolatus		+	+	+	+	+	+	+	+
	O. nullipora									+
Engraulidae	*Thryssa rastrosa*	+	+	+	+	+			+	+
	T. scratchleyi	+	+	+	+	+	+		+	+
Gobiidae	*Glossogobius giurus*								+	
Hemiramphidae	*Zenarchopterus novaeguineae*								+	
Kurtidae	*Kurtus gulliveri*	+	+	+					+	
Lobotidae	*Datnoides quadrifasciatus*			+	+	+		+	+	+
Lutjanidae	*Lutjanus argentimaculatus*					+			+	+
	L. goldei	+		+	+	+		+	+	+
Megalopidae	*Megalops cyprinoides*	+	+	+	+	+	+	+	+	+
Melanotaeniidae	*Melanotaenia maccullochi*						+	+	+	
	M. splendida	+	+	+	+	+	+	+	+	+
	M. sexlineatus			+						
	Iriatherina werneri					+	+		+	
	Pseudomugil gertrudae								+	+
Mugilidae	*Liza diadema*	+	+	+	+	+	+	+	+	+
Osteoglossidae	*Scleropages jardini*	+	+	+	+	+	+	+	+	+
Plotosidae	*Neosilurus ater*	+	+	+	+	+	+	+	+	+
	Plotosus papuensis			+	+			+	+	+
	Porochilus obbesi	+	+	+	+	+	+	+	+	+
Pristidae	*Pristis microdon*								+	

Appendix. (Continued).

Family	Species	Sites Present								
		O1	O2	O3	O4	O5	FO	FB	BL	LD
Sciaenidae	*Nibea semifasciata*	+								
Soleidae	*Aseroggodes klunzingeri*								+	
Sparidae	*Acanthopagrus berda*				+	+				+
Theraponidae	*Amniataba percoides*	+	+	+		+			+	+
	Hephaestes roemeri	+	+							
	H. trimaculatus		+							
	Pingalla lorentzi									+
	Terapon jamoerensis		+	+	+	+	+	+	+	+
Toxotidae	*Toxotes chatareus*	+	+	+	+	+	+	+	+	+
	T. lorentzi					+	+	+	+	+

References

Allen, G. R. & Coates, D., 1990: An ichthyological survey of the Sepik River, Papua New Guinea. – *Rec. West. Aust. Mus. Suppl.* **34:** 31–116.

Belbin, L., 1988: PATN Analysis Package Reference Manual: 302 pp. – CSIRO, Canberra.

Coates, D., 1985: Fish yield estimates for the Sepik River, Papua New Guinea, a large floodplain system east of Wallace's Line. – *J. Fish. Biol.* **27:** 431–443.

Eagle, A. M. & Higgins, R. J., 1991: Environmental investigations on the effects of the Ok Tedi copper mine in the Fly River. – In: Lawrence, D. & Cansfield-Smith, T. (eds.): Sustainable Development for Traditional Inhabitants of the Torres Strait Region: 97–118. – Great Barrier Reef Marine Park Authority, Townsville.

Faith, D. P., Minchin, P. R. & Belbin, L., 1987: Compositional dissimilarity as a robust measure of ecological distance. – *Vegetatio* **69:** 57–68.

Gerking, S. D., 1962: Production and utilization in a population of blue gill fish. – *Ecol. Monogr.* **32:** 31–78.

Good, I. J., 1982: An index of separateness of clusters and a permutation test for its significance. – *J. Statist. Comput. Simul.* **15:** 81–84.

Higgins, R. J., 1990: Off-river storages as sources and sinks for environmental contaminants. – *Regulated Rivers: Research & Management* **5:** 401–412.

Holeman, J. N., 1968: The sediment yield of major rivers of the world. – *Water Res. Research* **4:** 737–747.

Moore, R., 1980: Migration and reproduction in the Percoid fish *Lates calcarifer* (Bloch): 213 pp. – Unpublished Ph.D. Thesis, University of London, England.

Ok Tedi Mining Limited, 1986: A review of biological sampling of the Ok Tedi and Fly River systems, April 1983 to June 1986: 202 pp. – Ok Tedi Mining Limited, Report ENV 86-9.

– 1988: Sixth Supplemental Agreement environmental study 1986–1988. Final draft report: 702 pp. – Ok Tedi Mining Limited.

– 1989: Supplementary environmental investigations: 163 pp. – Ok Tedi Mining Limited.

– 1991: APL compliance and additional monitoring: Annual report 1991: 100 pp. – Ok Tedi Mining Limited.

Roberts, T. R., 1978: An Ichthyological survey of the Fly River in Papua New Guinea with descriptions of new species. – *Smith. Contrib. Zool.* **281:** 1–72.

SAS Institute, Inc., 1985: SAS User's Guide, Version 5 Edition: 1028 pp. – SAS Institute Inc., Cary, USA.

Smith, R. E. W., 1991: Biological investigations into the impact of the Ok Tedi copper mine. – In: Lawrence, D. & Cansfield-Smith, T. (eds.): Sustainable Development for Traditional Inhabitants of the Torres Strait Region: 216–282. – Great Barrier Reef Marine Park Authority, Townsville.

Smith, R. E. W., Ahsanullah, M. & Batley, G. E., 1990: Investigations of the impact of effluent from the Ok Tedi copper mine on the fisheries resource in the Fly River, Papua New Guinea. – *Environmental Monitoring and Assessment* **14:** 315–331.

Smith, R. E. W. & Morris, T. F., 1992: The impacts of changing geochemistry on the fish assemblages of the lower Ok Tedi and middle Fly River, Papua New Guinea. – *The Science of the Total Environmental.* **125:** 321–344.

Welcomme, R. L. 1985: River Fisheries: 330 pp. – *FAO Fisheries Technical Paper* **262.**

Authors' addresses:

Environment Department, Ok Tedi Mining Limited, P.O. Box 1, Tabubil, W.P., Papua New Guinea.

Present address: R. E. W. Smith, BHP Engineering, P.O. Box 1237, North Sydney, New South Wales, Australia 2059.

Mitt. Internat. Verein. Limnol.	24	197–205	Stuttgart, Februar 1994

The occurrence of natural fish kills, and their causes, in the Darwin-Katherine-Jabiru region of northern Australia

Simon A. Townsend

Abstract

Approximately 50 fish kills have been reported between 1978 and 1990 in the Darwin-Katherine-Jabiru region of the Australian wet/dry tropics. A large number probably go unreported because of the region's sparse population and the absence of any formal reporting scheme. The majority of fish kills occur on the coastal plains, whilst a smaller number have been observed in inland regions. Fish kills occur throughout the year, but are most common during the wet season, particularly from October to January when thunderstorm activity is frequent and watercourses commence wet season flow. In about half reported events between 100 and 1000 fish have died.

The fish kills have been attributed to natural causes unrelated to human activity. In the Jabiru area, fish kills at the start of the wet season have been caused by biotoxic concentrations of aluminium in naturally acidic run-off. Other fish kills have been ascribed to low oxygen concentrations resulting from the entry of high oxygen demand storm run-off into receiving waters, and the oxygen depletion of floodplain waters. These events highlight the significant impact run-off can have on receiving water quality in the wet/dry tropics, and the reduced capacity of warm waters to assimilate organic material with a high oxygen demand. The small proportion of fish kills which occur in the dry season are not associated with run-off events.

Introduction

The term fish kill refers to the catastrophic death of numerous – sometimes thousands – of fish from natural or anthropogenic causes. Fish kills unrelated to human activity are termed 'natural' in this paper. Natural fish kills in the tropics are commonly attributed to low dissolved oxygen concentrations, but the limnological and hydrological factors associated with these events vary. Fish kills in deep African lakes have been attributed to the upwelling of anoxic hypolimnion waters and associated lethal concentrations of hydrogen sulphide (BEADLE 1974, PAYNE 1986). The deoxygenation of shallow Lake Chilwa (Malawi), and consequent deaths of large numbers of *Tilapia*, was caused by the resuspension of lake sediments with a high oxygen demand (MORGAN 1972). In lentic water bodies on river floodplains, oxygen depletion and subsequent fish deaths are associated with the breakdown of stratification by wind and inflow (WELCOMME 1979).

Fish kills commonly occur in the Darwin-Katherine-Jabiru region of northern Australia (Fig. 1). They have been documented by the Alligator Rivers Region Research Institute (ARRRI), Commonwealth Scientific and Industrial Research Organisation (CSIRO), Northern Territory Power and Water Authority (PAWA) and Northern Territory Department of Primary Industry and Fisheries (DPIF). This review is based on fish kill records from those organisations and data from published literature. The occurrence of fish kills in the region is described and their causes are discussed.

Study area

The climate of the Darwin-Katherine-Jabiru region is characterised by two seasons: the 'wet' (November to April) and the 'dry' (May to October), with two transition periods. The wet season is dominated by monsoonal rains, whilst rainfall is negligible in the dry season. During the transition periods convective thunderstorm activity is common. Climatic data for Darwin (Table 1) are indicative of the region's climate, although rainfall is less and temperature ranges are higher inland.

The Darwin-Katherine-Jabiru region is approximately 50,000 km², and comprises the Arnhem Land plateau, hills, lowlands and tidal flats. Wet-season flows inundate the coastal floodplains, and when waters recede numerous billabongs (ox-bow lakes and water holes) remain. Most watercourses cease flowing in the dry season; some contract to a number of isolated pools. The region's total population is approximately 75,000, of which Darwin accounts for 85% and Katherine, Jabiru, Pine Creek, Adelaide River and Batchelor most of the remainder. There are several small open-cut mines in the vicinity of Pine Creek and one at Jabiru. Cattle grazing is generally of low intensity except on parts of the Mary River and Adelaide River floodplains. The catchments of the East and South Alligator Rivers, and a portion of the Katherine River, are contained within national parks. With the exception of areas subject to urban and mining land-use, and the intrusion of various exotic plants and animals, the region's environment is largely undisturbed. There has been no extensive clearing of natural vegetation for agriculture in the region.

0538-4680/94/0024-0197 $ 2.25

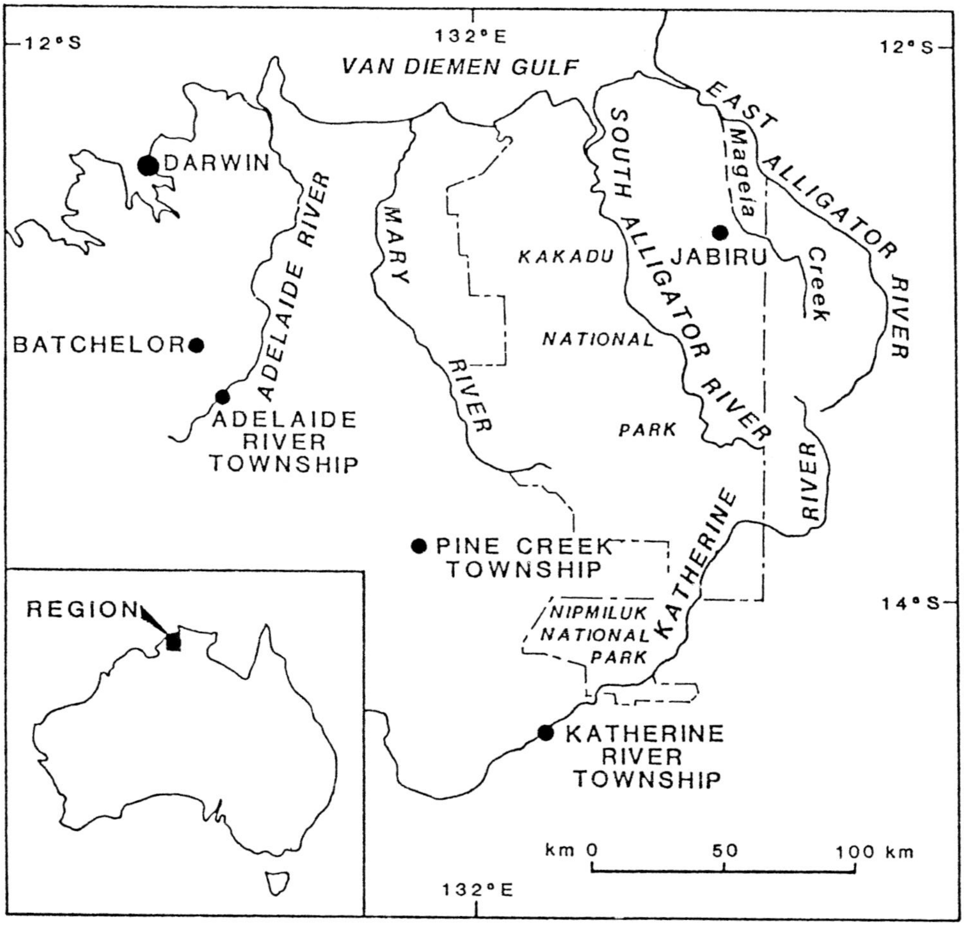

Fig. 1. The Darwin-Katherine-Jabiru region, northern Australia.

Fish kills in the Darwin-Katherine-Jabiru region

Approximately 50 fish kills have been documented in the region between October 1978 and December 1990. This is probably a small proportion of the total number of events because many are liable to be unrecorded because of the region's sparse population and the absence of any formal reporting system. The temporal and spatial unpredictability of fish kills, and their remoteness, have greatly limited detailed investigation of individual events. The location, date, and number of species killed have been recorded for most of the kills (see Appendix 1), but detailed limnological and hydrological data have been collected in only a few cases.

The majority of fish kills reported here occurred on the coastal floodplains, and approximately half of these have been observed by the ARRRI on the Magela Creek floodplain. Fish kills have been recorded throughout the year, but are most frequent during the wet season. The highest incidence of fish kills is between October and January, the period of thunderstorm activity and first wet-season watercourse flow.

The number of fish killed in an event ranges from ten to several thousand. In about half the reported kills, fish mortalities have numbered between 100 and 1000; cases with more than 1000 fish deaths constitute one third of events. The high incidence of large fish kills may result from the greater likelihood of these events being re-

Table 1. Mean monthly climatic data for Darwin, northern Australia.

	Jan	Feb	Mar	Apr	May	Jun	Jul	Aug	Sep	Oct	Nov	Dec	Annual
Rainfall (mm)	404	345	315	100	21	2	1	7	18	72	141	233	1,659
Evaporation (mm)	185	162	172	189	200	189	201	203	232	254	230	205	2,422
Daily temperature (°C)													
Maximum	31.8	31.4	31.8	32.6	31.9	30.5	30.4	31.2	32.4	33.1	33.1	32.5	31.9
Minimum	24.8	24.6	24.4	23.9	22.1	19.9	19.3	20.6	23.1	25.0	25.3	25.2	23.2

Source: Australian Bureau of Statistics.

Table 2. Most abundant species present in six fish kills in the Darwin-Katherine-Jabiru region, northern Australia.

Dec 1978	Leichhardt Billabong (Magela Creek floodplain)	*Ambassis agrammus* (GUNTHER) *Liza diadema* (STEINDACHNER)	BISHOP (1980)
Dec 1979	Ja Ja Billabong (Magela Creek floodplain)	*Hexanematichthys leptaspis* (BLEEKER) *Lates calcarifer* (BLOCH)	BROWN et al. (1983)
Dec 1980	Island Billabong (Magela Creek floodplain)	*Nematalosa erebi* (GUNTHER)	MORELY et al. (1985)
Apr 1982	Cannon Hill Billabong (Magela Creek floodplain)	*Lates calcarifer* (BLOCH)	NOLLER (1983)
Nov 1987	Donkey Camp Pool (Katherine River)	*Arius leptaspis* (BLEEKER) *Nematalosa erebi* (GUNTHER)	TOWNSEND et al. (1992)
Jan 1987	Shady Camp Billabong (Mary River)	*Arius* spp. *Lates calcarifer* (BLOCH) *Nematalosa erebi* (GUNTHER) *Scleropages lardinij* (SAVILLE-KENT)	*DPIF*

DPIF, Department of Primary Industry and Fisheries (Darwin), personal communication.

ported. The maximum number of fish killed in a single event was 10,000 in Ja Ja Extension Billabong on the Magela Creek floodplain in January 1990 (ARRRI, unpubl. data).

The numbers and size distribution of each species killed have been documented by BISHOP (1980) and BROWN et al. (1992). Approximately ten investigations have reported the relative abundance of species killed (MORLEY et al. 1983, NOLLER 1983, TOWNSEND et al. 1992, DPIF, unpubl. data). Between one and four species usually predominate in fish kills (Table 2). The maximum number of species killed in a single event has been eighteen. Other aquatic fauna have died during fish kills: for example, approximately two hundred dead *Macrobrachium rosenbergi* (DE MAN) were reported by TOWNSEND et al. (1992). This palaemonid shrimp and *Cherax* sp. have been observed in Mary River fish kills (unpubl. data, DPIF). NOLLER et al. (1984) reported 60 dead bivalves (*Velesunio* sp.) during a fish kill in Leichhardt Billabong.

Not all the fish exposed to the unfavourable conditions associated with fish kill events die. BISHOP (1980) noted that many small species in Leichhardt Billabong survived, and that a disproportionate number of small *Liza alata* (STEINDACHNER) were not killed. *Ambassis macleayi* (CASTELNAU), *Amniataba percoides* (GUNTHER), *Megalops cyrinoides* (BROUSSONET), *Melanotaenia splendida australis* (CASTELNAU) and *Nematalosa erebi* (GUNTHER) were netted alive from Donkey Camp Pool when dissolved oxygen concentrations were <1.5 mg/l four days after a fish kill (TOWNSEND et al. 1992). BROWN et al. (1983) observed *Megalops cyrinoides* at the surface during the Ja Ja Billabong fish kill, although none were killed. This species has also been observed to survive several Mary River fish kills (DPIF, unpubl. data).

Several fish kills, all during the wet season (DPIF, unpubl. data), have occurred in sections of Shady Camp Billabong which is part of the Mary River system. This water body is about 5 km long, 50–80 m wide and 3–4 m deep in the dry season.

Before the onset of the wet season, oxygen concentrations are typically 4–6 mg/l at the surface and 1–6 mg/l at 4 m depth (unpubl. data, DPIF). Billabong oxygen concentrations are generally lower during the wet season because of the relatively low oxygen content of the Mary River and run-off from the floodplain. In January 1991, for example, surface oxygen concentrations in the Billabong were 1.5–2.4 mg/l (20–32% saturation), whilst the remainder of the water column had values of 0.4–1.6 mg/l (5–20% saturation). It is therefore likely that fish kills in Shady Camp Billabong are caused by low dissolved oxygen concentrations. In January 1987, oxygen concentrations were <0.1 mg/l in the main part of the Billabong two days after the death of 1200 fish (PAWA, unpubl. data).

In November 1987, 5000 fish died in Donkey Camp Pool, a portion of the Katherine River. The Pool is 6 km long, 40–50 m wide and 3–4 m deep in the dry season. In November basal discharge declines to about 0.2 m^3/s. The fish deaths were attributed to low dissolved oxygen concentrations, with possible additional harmful effects from toxic humic compounds (Townsend et al. 1992). Metal and pesticide toxicity were discounted as possible causes. The first wet season run-off from a tributary of the river entered Donkey Camp Pool causing turbidity and colour to increase and, probably, oxygen concentrations to drop. A similar event nine days later caused significant water-quality changes and resultant fish deaths. Pool water was displaced by cool run off which had a substantial organic load and high oxygen demand. Colour, turbidity, iron and manganese were at least an order of magnitude higher – and coliform organisms several orders of magnitude higher – than typical dry season values. In addition, the pool was thermally stratified with low surface dissolved oxygen concentrations (about 1 mg/l) and anoxic conditions in deeper waters. The dead fish were concentrated at the end of the Pool, having been carried by the flood wave or moving ahead of the anoxic water and becoming trapped at the pool's constricted outflow.

Fish kills in floodplain billabongs of Magela Creek during the early wet season have been caused by the inflow of naturally acidic (pH 2–4) water with high aluminium concentrations (Brown et al. 1982, Morley et al. 1983, 1985, Noller & Cusbert 1985). In December 1981, a series of fish kills (total mortality 6000) were observed on the Magela Creek floodplain when the first wet season flow of the creek entered four billabongs (Morley et al. 1983). The billabongs had pH values of 3–4, total aluminium concentrations of 1–7 mg/l and dissolved oxygen concentrations >50% saturation. A fish kill described by Brown et al. (1982) resulted from storm run-off from the immediate catchment of the Ja Ja Billabong on Magela Creek floodplain. The run-off had a pH of 2.7 with high aluminium concentrations, and caused the deaths of 3400 fish over a six day period. Aluminium levels of 425 µg/g and 768 µg/g were measured in the gills of *Lates calcarifer* (Bloch) collected during the event, which contrasts with concentrations of 25 µg/g in the gills of the same species collected several months later. Dissolved oxygen concentrations were >1.5 mg/l and not considered a contributing factor to the fish deaths.

A fish kill reported by Bishop (1980) in Leichhardt Billabong on the Magela Creek floodplain at the beginning of the wet season was attributed to low dissolved oxygen concentrations and possible physiological inhibition of oxygen uptake. However, it is probable that aluminium toxicity caused the fish deaths as the billabong had similar hydrological and chemical characteristics to those recorded during fish kills described by Morley et al. (1983, 1985). Note that the incidence of high aluminium concentrations in the first wet-season flow of Magela Creek was not known to Bishop at the time that the Leichhardt Billabong fish kill was investigated.

Few fish kills have been reported during the dry season. The mortality of 50 *Craterocephalus* sp. in a Magela Creek pool during the dry season was attributed to oxygen depletion resulting from decaying organic matter (Ward & Woodland 1983). A small number of dry-season fish kills, each involving >100 fish deaths, have been observed by CSIRO in the South and West Alligator River catchments.

Discussion

Fish kills attributable to aluminium toxicity have been reported only on the Magela Creek floodplain, and have occurred during the transition period between the dry and wet seasons. They were associated with the first flow (or 'flush') of Magela Creek into the floodplain billabongs. The only exception occurred during a storm run-off event (Brown et al. 1982). Noller & Cusbert (1985) proposed a conceptual model for the Magela Creek fish kills. Aluminium is present in interstitial water in the acid sulphate soils of the floodplain. Before the onset of monsoonal rains, when thunderstorm activity predominates, acidic pools with high aluminium concentrations (maximum 84 mg/l) form on the floodplain from groundwater inflow. This water is transported into the floodplain billabongs by the first flow of Magela Creek, sometimes causing fish kills. NOLLER & CUSBERT (1985) nominate the critical stages of the model – which account for the unpredictable occurrence of the fish kills – to be the formation of acidic pools, and the period between the inflow of water with high aluminium concentrations and subsequent inflow of more dilute water. The dissolved oxygen concentrations of Magela Creek during the first flush are generally in excess of 3 mg/l (BISHOP 1980, MORLEY et al. 1983, 1985, NOLLER 1983); low oxygen concentrations have not been found to be responsible for the fish deaths, nor has low pH *per se* (NOLLER & CUSBERT 1985). Levels of total and labile aluminium in Magela Creek and floodplain decline during the wet season, particularly after major flood events (NOLLER et al. 1984).

The Adelaide River and Mary River floodplains have a similar geomorphological history to the Magela Creek floodplain, as they all originate from estuarine deposition. It is likely fish kills also occur on these floodplains in waters of low pH with high aluminium concentrations, although none have been reported to date. The fish kills documented at Corroboree and Shady Camp Billabongs have been associated with moderate pH (6–7) waters. Fish kills resulting from acid sulphate soils have been documented in other tropical regions (see DENT 1986).

Water-quality changes associated with the entry of storm run-off into receiving waters have caused fish kills, for example the Donkey Camp Pool fish kill (TOWNSEND et al. 1992). These events occur predominately in hilly areas where run-off can attain high velocities. The waters carry a substantial organic load and have a high instantaneous/post-instantaneous oxygen demand. They can significantly deplete the oxygen content of receiving waters, though not always causing fish kills. Density differences between inflow and receiving waters limit mixing, and consequently the assimilation capacity of the receiving waters. Catchment practices which increase soil erosion will also impact on run-off water quality and the frequency of fish kills.

Floodplain fish kills have also been ascribed to low dissolved oxygen concentrations. Vegetation and soils exert a high oxygen demand when initially inundated, and dissolved oxygen concentrations can decrease to < 2 mg/l (DPIF, unpubl. data), and may remain low due to decomposing macrophytes. The slow passage of water over the floodplains also contributes to the low oxygen content of the floodplain waters. Low levels of oxygen on recently-inundated floodplains have been observed in many tropical systems (WELCOMME 1979). Note that fish kills not only occur on the floodplain, but also in watercourses receiving floodplain run-off. The Shady Camp Billabong fish kills in the latter part of the wet season are an example (DPIF, unpubl. data).

Not all fish kills are associated with run-off events. A small number have been reported during the dry season in billabongs and isolated pools, but the limnological conditions associated with these are poorly documented. Evaporative drawdown of the waterbodies, high water temperatures, stratification, an anoxic hypolimnion and marked diurnal fluctuations in dissolved oxygen are probably important causal factors. Overcrowding, reduced food supply and disease may contribute indirectly to the fish kills.

Fish in northern Australia are apparently adapted to low oxygen concentrations. This conclusion is based on observations that not all fish die during fish kill events, and that low oxygen levels do not always cause fish kills. Oxygen concentrations of less than 5% saturation in Kulukuluku Billabong (East Alligator River catchment) have been measured frequently but fish kills did not occur (WALKER & TYLER 1984). There is anecdotal evidence that *Megalops cyrinoides* can survive fish kills. A predominance of large species in fish kills has been reported by BISHOP (1980) and TOWNSEND et al. (1992). MORLEY et al. (1983) has suggested *Nematalosa erebi* is particularly susceptible to the conditions associated with fish kills in Magela Creek billabongs. However, the relationship between water quality and the species-specific survival rates during fish kills is not understood.

Organic compounds have been cited as a possible contributing factor to fish kills in the region (NOLLER 1983, TOWNSEND et al. 1992). Bark compounds from *Owenia vernica* (MUELL.) have been used by Aborigines to induce fish deaths. In laboratory studies, BISHOP et al. (1982) found the susceptibility of fish to freshly cut *Owenia* bark was directly related to fish body length, which contrasts with the survival of a disproportionate number of small *Liza alata* in a fish kill (BISHOP 1980), and the observation that large fishes have high mortality rates during such events (Bishop 1980, Townsend et al. 1992). *Barringtonia* sp. is another potential source of piscicides; this plant contains saprions, which have been detected in the waters of one fish kill which featured neither low dissolved oxygen nor high aluminium concentrations (Noller 1983).

The high incidence of fish kills in the Darwin-Katherine-Jabiru region of northern Australia is related to the tropical climate, in particular the extremes of flow associated with the wet and dry seasons and the year-round warm temperatures. On the Magela Creek floodplain, a combination of aluminium rich acid sulphate soils and the region's climate produce conditions which cause substantial fish kills. The reduced oxygen solubility in warm waters results in a decreased capacity to assimilate material with a high oxygen demand. This phenomenon is compounded by the relatively high respiratory activity of bacteria at elevated temperatures. The occurrence of natural fish kills in the region highlights the significant impact run-off waters can have on receiving waters in tropical regions. Changes in the region's land-use – for example, the establishment of intensive agricultural activities – will affect receiving water quality and probably increase the incidence of fish kills. It is important to understand the causes of natural fish kills in order to assess correctly the anthropogenic contribution to such events in future.

Acknowledgements

Data provided by the Alligator Rivers Region Research Institute, Commonwealth Scientific and Industrial Research Organisation and the Northern Territory Department of Primary Industry and Fisheries are gratefully acknowledged. R. Griffin and G. White (DPIF) are thanked for useful discussion on fish kills.

Appendix

Fish kills reported in the Darwin-Katherine-Jabiru region, northern Australia, between October 1978 and December 1990.

Date	Location	Number of fish	Number of species	Reference
Oct 1978	Mayamarleprard Billabong (Magela Creek floodplain)	10	1	Bishop (1980)
Nov 1978	Jabiluka Billabong (Magela Creek floodplain)	15	2	Bishop (1980)
Dec 1978	Leichhardt Billabong (Magela Creek floodplain)	384	8	Bishop (1980)
Sep 1979	Knotts Crossing (Katherine River)	>100	NR	*DPIF*
Jan 1980	Ja Ja Billabong (Magela Creek floodplain)	3,400	8	Brown et al. (1982)
Dec 1980	Island Billabong (Magela Creek floodplain)	2,640	NR	Morley et al. (1983)
Dec 1981	Hidden Billabong (Magela Creek floodplain)	115	7	Morley et al. (1983)
Dec 1981	Ja Ja Billabong (Magela Creek floodplain)	490	5	Morley et al. (1983)
Dec 1981	Leichhardt Billabong (Magela Creek floodplain)	4,965	16	Morley et al. (1983)
Dec 1981	Jabiluka Billabong (Magela Creek floodplain)	300	6	Morley et al. (1983)
Jan 1982	Coonjimba Billabong (Magela Creek floodplain)	40	1	Morley et al. (1983)
Apr 1982	Cannon Hill (Magela Creek)	167	5	Morley et al. (1983)

Appendix. (Continued).

Date	Location	Number of fish	Number of species	Reference
Apr 1982	Magela Creek outflow	>100	8	Noller (1983)
Jan 1983	Three-croc Billabong (Magela Creek floodplain)	4,755	15	Morley et al. (1983)
Feb 1983	Hidden Billabong (Magela Creek floodplain)	80	NR	Bishop (1991)
May 1985	South Alligator River Crossing	250	NR	*DPIF*
Jul 1985	Red Lily Billabong (West Alligator River catchment)	>100	NR	*CSIRO*
Oct 1985	Adelaide River (near Batchelor)	50	NR	*PAWA*
Oct 1985	Coomalie Creek (near Batchelor)	20	1	*PAWA*
Nov 1985	South Alligator River Crossing	250	NR	*DPIF*
Apr-Aug 1986	Lowland billabongs (Magela Creek floodplain)	1,000	>3	Bishop (1991)
Jun 1986	Rock Hole Billabong (South Alligator River catchment)	>100	NR	*CSIRO*
Jul/Aug 1986	Tim's Hole (West Alligator River catchment)	>1,000	NR	*CSIRO*
Jan 1987	Shady Camp Billabong (Mary River)	800	6	*PAWA*
Mar 1987	Corroboree Billabong (Mary River)	40	NR	*DPIF*
Apr 1987	Corroboree Billabong (Mary River)	400	NR	*DPIF*
Nov 1987	Donkey Camp Pool (Katherine River)	5,000	18	Townsend et al. (1992)
Dec 1987	Leichhardt Billabong (Magela Creek floodplain)	200	3	Bishop (1991)
May 1988	Magela Creek, near Georgetown Billabong	>100	2	Bishop (1991)
May 1988	Island Billabong (Magela Creek floodplain)	>1,000	1	Bishop (1991)
Oct 1988	Edith River (near Katherine)	15	4	*PAWA*
Oct 1988	Tim's Hole (West Alligator floodplain)	>500	NR	*DPIF*
Apr 1989	Magela Creek outflow	>1,000	>2	Bishop (1991)
May 1989	Corndorl Creek (Magela Creek floodplain)	>3,500	>2	Bishop (1991)
May 1989	Magela Creek	>100	>2	Bishop (1991)
May 1989	Coonjimba Billabong (Magela Creek floodplain)	NR	>3	Bishop (1991)
May 1989	Georgetown Billabong (Magela Creek floodplain)	NR	>2	Bishop (1991)
Jul 1989	Rum Jungle Recreation Lake (Batchelor)	20	NR	*PAWA*

Appendix. (Continued).

Date	Location	Number of fish	Number of species	Reference
Dec 1989	Corroboree Billabong (Mary River)	500	NR	*DPIF*
Jan 1990	Kelleys Billabong (Magela Creek floodplain)	2,000	>4	*ARRRI*
Jan 1990	Ja Ja Billabong (Magela Creek floodplain)	6,000	>2	*ARRRI*
Jan 1990	Ja Ja Extension (Magela Creek floodplain)	10,000	>2	*ARRRI*
Feb 1990	Unnamed billabong (Magela Creek floodplain)	>300	>2	*DPIF*
Dec 1990	Corroboree Billabong (Magela Creek floodplain)	200	>4	*DPIF*

NR: not reported.
DPIF: Department of Primary Industry and Fisheries (Darwin), personal communication.
CSIRO: Commonwealth Scientific and Industrial Research Organisation (Darwin), personal communication.
PAWA: Power and Water Authority (Darwin) unpublished data.
ARRRI: Alligator Rivers Region Research Institute (Jabiru), personal communication.

References

BEADLE, L. C., 1974: The Inland Waters of Tropical Africa, an Introduction to Tropical Limnology: 365 pp. – Longman London.

BISHOP, K. A., 1980: Fish kills in relation to physical and chemical changes in Magela Creek (East Alligator River System, Northern Territory) at the beginning of the tropical wet season. – *Aust. Zool.* **20:** 485–500.

– 1991: Biological monitoring using freshwater fishes for the Alligator Rivers Region, internal report 28. – Office of the Supervising Scientist for the Alligator Rivers Region, Alligator Rivers Region Research Institute, unpublished report: 122 pp.

BROWN, T. E., MORLEY, A. W., SANDERSON, N. T. & TAIT, R. D., 1983: Report of a large fish kill resulting from natural acidic water conditions in Australia. – *J. Fish Biol.* **22:** 335–350.

DENT, D., 1986: Acid Sulphate Soils: a Baseline for Research and Development. 204 pp. Institute for Land Reclamation and Improvement (ILRI), The Netherlands.

MORGAN, P. R., 1972: Causes of mortality in the endemic *Tilapia* of Lake Chilwa (Malawi). – *Hydrobiologia* **40:** 101–119.

MORLEY, A. W., BROWN, T. E. & KOONTZ, D. V., 1985: The limnology of a naturally acidic tropical water system in Australia I. General description and wet season characteristics. – *Verh. Internat. Verein. Limnol.* **22:** 2125–2130.

MORLEY, A. W., KOONTZ, D. V., SANDERSON, N. T. & SPRATT, W., 1983: Fish kills in the Magela Creek. – In: Proceedings of the Scientific Workshop on Environmental Protection in the Alligator Rivers Region, Sydney: 62.1–62.8.

NOLLER, B. N., 1983: Physico-chemical aspects of natural fish kills on the Magela Creek system. In: – Proceedings of the Scientific Workshop on Environmental Protection in the Alligator Rivers Region. – Supervising Scientist for the Alligator Rivers Region, Sydney: 61.1–61.15.

NOLLER, B. N., CURREY, N. & CUSBERT, P. J., 1984: Aluminium speciation in Magela Creek waters. – In: Alligator River Region Research Institute Research Report 1983–1984. – Australian Government Publishing Service, Canberra: 26–28.

NOLLER, B. N., CURREY, N., CUSBERT, P. J. & SCHULZ, R., 1984: Natural fish and mussel mortalities. – In: Alligator Rivers Region Research Institute Research Report 1983–1984. Australian Government Publishing Service, Canberra: 28–29.

NOLLER, B. N. & CUSBERT, P. J., 1985: Mobilization of aluminium from a tropical floodplain and its role in natural fish kills: a conceptual model. – Proceedings of the 5th International Conference on Heavy Metals in the Environment, September 1985, Athens: 100–102.

PAYNE, A. I., 1986: The Ecology of Tropical Lakes and Rivers: 301 pp. – John Wiley and Sons, Chichester.

TOWNSEND, S. A., BOLAND, K. T. & WRIGLEY, T. J., 1992: Factors contributing to a fish kill in the Australian wet/dry tropics. – *Water Res.* **2:** 1039–1044.

WALKER, T. D. & TYLER, P. A., 1983: Tropical Australia, a dynamic limnological environment. – *Verh. Internat. Verein. Limnol.* **22:** 1727–1734.

WARD, P. J. & WOODLAND, D. J., 1983: An examination of the causes of mortality in the hardyhead, *Craterocephalus* sp., in pools of Magela Creek during the dry. – In: Proceedings of the Scientific Workshop on Environmental Protection in the Alligator Rivers Region. – Supervising Scientist for the Alligator Rivers Region, Sydney: 39.1–37.7.

WELCOMME, R. L., 1979: Fisheries Ecology of Floodplain Rivers: 252 pp. – Longman, London.

Author's address:

Water Resources Division, Power and Water Authority, P.O. Box 1096, Darwin, N. T., Australia 0801.

Mitt. Internat. Verein. Limnol.	24	207–211	Stuttgart, Februar 1994

An analysis of lake eutrophication in China

Xiang Can Jin

Abstract

An account of the problems of lake eutrophication in China is given, drawing particularly upon recent survey data of 25 lakes and reservoirs scattered across the country. Measurement of physicochemical parameters and samples of lake phytoplankton indicate that the process of eutrophication in China is broadly similar to that occurring in other countries. This has the important implication that methods developed to monitor the onset of eutrophication in other regions can be applied in China. Survey data indicate that the proportion of lakes which can be classified as eutrophic in China has increased dramatically within the past decade (from 5.0 to 55% of lake area surveyed), while the extent of oligotrophic inland waters has decreased (3.2–0.5%). Even lakes in remote areas such as Inner Mongolia and Xinjiang have been affected. Restoration of eutrophic or hypertrophic lakes is difficult because much of China has been densely settled or has been altered profoundly by centuries of human impact with the result that waters flowing into lakes tend to have high sediment and nutrient loads. There is an urgent need for development of management strategies that will reverse the trend towards increased eutrophication of Chinese lakes, and contribute to lake restoration and integrated drainage-basin management.

Introduction

China is a vast country with a large population and many lakes and reservoirs. There are approximately 2300 lakes exceeding 1 km^2 in area. The total extent of lakes amounts to 70,988 km^2, and covers 0.8% of the area of China. The total storage capacity of all the lakes is 707.7 billion m^3, of which 225 billion m^3 is freshwater. There are 86,852 reservoirs with a total storage capacity of 413 billion m^3. Lakes in China support a variety of activities, some of which may lead to eutrophication. According to the National Survey on Lake (Reservoir) Eutrophication of 1987–1990, water in most Chinese lakes is still fit for general use. However, the problem of eutrophication is becoming more and more serious. In many cases, eutrophication has affected the development of industries and agriculture as well as the daily lives of people in the surrounding areas, and is detrimental to economic growth. Therefore, control of the problem of lake eutrophication and improvement of the *status quo* are matterns of great urgency in China.

The effects of lake eutrophication

Eutrophication can have important adverse effects on the biological condition of lakes in general, and fish production in particular. In addition, the quality of drinking water derived from the lakes and the aesthetic value of these water bodies can be reduced significantly as a result of eutrophication. The harmful effects of eutrophication on Chinese lakes are outlined below. A more detailed treatment is presented by Jin et al. (1990).

Most urban lakes in China are shallow, and many are heavily polluted as a result of rapid urbanization (the diaphaneity is 0.10–0.50 m; the water in the lake is black or yellow and green with an offensive smell). The water in these lakes is so polluted that it can no longer be used as a source of drinking water and the lakes have lost their aesthetic attraction.

The water supply to some Chinese cities depends heavily on reservoirs which have been affected by eutrophication and the proliferation of algae. For example, the filter bed of Dahuofang Reservoirs in Fushun City was completely blocked due to algal growths. Similarly, Chaohu Lake in Anhui Province could no longer be used to provide drinking water to the surrounding population as a result of the deteriorating water quality caused by decaying algae and contamination from nearby factories. Eutrophication in reservoirs built in the upper reaches of rivers tends to be less serious. However, the impact from increased human activities such as tourism and net-fishing has also led to a deterioration in water quality in some of these reservoirs (e.g. Miyun Reservoir in Beijing and Gaozhu Reservoir in Guangzhou).

Fish production in many Chinese lakes has been seriously affected by eutrophication and the associated oxygen depletion as a result of the large amount of oxygen consumed by decaying organic matter. In addition, toxins secreted by some algal species pose a threat to the health of people and livestock. For example, in Lake Dalai on Hulunbeier Prairie in Inner Mongolia, domestic animals died after drinking water from the lake when there was a bloom caused by blue-green algae. Eutrophication also limits the utilization of biological resources from the lakes by causing a general reduction in the amount of fish food available such as certain plankton and large hydrophytes. In extreme cases, hydrophytes can be eliminated completely. This results in a decline in the diversity and quality of fish in the lake, although the production of algae-eating fish may rise. Note also that increases in nutrient levels in lakes generally have the overall effect of reducing the aesthetic value of the water

0538-4680/94/0024-0207 $ 1.25

Table 1. Annual means of major water-quality parameters recorded in 25 lakes in China: T-P, total phosphorus; D-P, dissolved phosphorus; DO, dissolved oxygen; Chl-*a*, chlorophyll *a*; SD, water transparency (Secchi disc depth); T-N, total nitrogen.

Lake	T-P (mg/l)	D-P (mg/l)	DO (mg/l)	Chl-*a* (mg/m³)	SD (m)	T-N (mg/l)
Lake Erhai	0.018	0.0055	7.21	1.29	3.30	1.30
Lake Boston	0.018	0.0068	7.47	4.02	1.50	0.92
Yuqiao Reservoir	0.020	0.0010	10.78	6.07	2.60	1.20
Lake Wuliangsuhai	0.067	0.0450	6.43	4.45	0.70	1.87
Gaozhou Reservoir	0.025	0.0046	7.91	0.91	1.90	0.40
Lake Gucheng	0.055	0.0050	9.59	3.32	0.34	1.70
Lake Dianshan	0.088	0.0440	8.97	5.98	0.53	1.90
Lake Cihu	0.090	0.0150	7.33	12.21	0.67	2.20
Lake Dianchi (Waihai)	0.097	0.0077	7.72	23.75	0.68	1.20
Lake Dalai	0.140	0.0560	9.56	5.95	0.46	1.90
Lake Qonghai	0.140	0.026	6.67	0.67	2.10	1.30
The West Lake	0.170	0.070	8.28	56.58	0.55	3.10
Lake Chaohu	0.200	0.034	8.11	15.05	0.28	2.20
Lake Nansi	0.210	0.021	7.37	4.27	0.56	3.40
Lake Luhu	0.220	0.024	9.66	86.41	0.37	3.00
Lake Gantang	0.240	0.130	8.03	43.23	0.55	1.70
Lake Nanhu	0.310	0.049	8.85	1.80	0.36	4.80
Lake Jingpo	0.400	0.130	9.45	3.62	1.80	1.00
Lake Dongshan	0.420	0.051	6.93	132.03	0.29	6.10
Lake Liuhua	0.530	0.037	1.14	239.53	0.19	6.40
Lake Liwan	0.620	0.118	4.75	149.65	0.30	8.30
Lake Mougu	0.60	0.036	7.40	30.21	0.64	2.40
Lake Dianchi (Caohai)	0.83	0.270	4.93	138.64	0.36	8.60
Lake Xuanwu	0.97	0.180	8.31	99.28	0.27	3.90
Lake Moushui	0.74	0.122	4.52	153.59	0.24	20.80

bodies. Jinpo Lake in Heilonjiang Province, Dianchi Lake in Yunnan Province and Donghu Lake in Wuhan city are cases in point.

Indicators of lake eutrophication

Eutrophication of Chinese lakes was investigated by monitoring limnological parameters in 25 lakes and reservoirs (Table 1) between 1987 and 1990 (see also JIN et al. 1990). The annual mean levels of total nitrogen of the study lakes were rather high, and ranged from 0.4 to 20.8 mg/l (Table 1) exceeding the 0.2 mg/l concentration regarded by many limnologists as the critical level for the occurrence of eutrophic conditions (e.g. BEETON & EDMONDSON 1972, OECD 1982). The majority of lakes had total nitrogen levels falling between 1.0 and 5.0 mg/l, and about 20% of them had levels exceeding 5.0 mg/l. In most lakes there were obvious seasonal trends on total nitrogen with higher levels in the spring, especially in urban lakes. The high levels in the water column were maintained by the large amount of nutrients accumulated in the bottom of the lakes.

The annual mean levels of total phosphorus of the study lakes ranged from 0.018 to 0.97 mg/l (Table 1); most (92%) had levels much higher than the 0.02 mg/l concentration that indicates the onset of eutrophication, and nearly half of them had total phosphorus levels of 0.2–1.0 mg/l. Only in Lake Erhai (Yunnan) and Lake Boston (Xinjiang) were the annual average total phosphorus levels below 0.02 mg/l (Table 1). Total phosphorus concentrations were relatively high in urban lakes; for example, in Lake Xuanwu (Nanjing) average concentrations were around 1 mg/l rising to 2.5 mg/l during the spring and summer. Total nitrogen concentrations in most of the lakes were generally 5–12.5 times higher than the critical levels for eutrophication, while total phosphorus levels were 10–50 times greater than the critical level. Clearly, high concentrations of these nutrients are the basic cause of eutrophication in Chinese lakes and reservoirs.

Table 2. Physicochemical parameters of sediments from urban and rural (or suburban) lakes in China: T-P, total phosphorus; TOC, total organic carbon. Sediment pH is shown also.

	pH	T-P (ppm)	TOC (ppm)
Urban Lakes			
Lake Liwan	6.3	1,748.0	3,5581.6
The West Lake	7.0	1,569.0	145,036.0
Lake Xuanwu	7.4	2,160.0	–
Lake Dongshan	5.9	1,255.4	20,741.0
Lake Moushui	6.4	4,504.7	50,921.5
Lake Liuhua	7.1	1,792.9	28,399.3
Lake Luhu	6.5	1,237.6	25,935.9
Rural Lakes			
Lake Mougu	7.7	933.9	33,820.0
Lake Boston	8.4	432.8	48,553.7
Lake Dalai	8.9	405.9	21,680.0
Lake Wuliangsuhai	8.7	382.7	8,150.0
Lake Nansi	8.1	–	–
Lake Qonghai	7.9	–	10,375.0
Lake Cihu	7.5	–	40,357.9
Lake Erhai	7.7	1,005.6	23,522.9
Lake Dianchi	7.3	1,715.9	48,598.9

Table 3. Water transparency (Secchi disc depth, m) of 25 Chinese lakes and reservoirs.

Water transparency	0.19–0.30	0.31–0.60	0.61–1.00	>1.00
Number of lakes	6	9	4	6
Percentage of total	24	36	16	24

Nutrient levels in lake sediments provide a good indication of the eutrophication status of lakes. Concentrations of phosphorus were high in sediments collected from all of the study lakes, especially those in urban areas (Table 2) where levels of total organic carbon were very high also (Table 2). These values could be attributed to direct discharge of industrial waste water and municipal sewage into the lakes. An interesting general feature of sediments in the study lakes was a general decline in sediment pH from lakes in the north to those in the south.

The transparency of the water in the study lakes was generally low in both urban and rural lakes (Table 3). Site-specific seasonal variations in transparency occurred as a result of changes in phytoplankton populations and the amounts of suspended inorganic particles. Transparency is an important indicator of lake eutrophication; in nearly 50% of the study lakes transparency was less than 0.6 m and in 76% it was less than 1.0 m (Table 3). Significantly, the transparency of most urban lakes ranged from 0.2 to 0.4 m, with maximum values at about 0.5–0.6 m. The low water transparency of Chinese lakes in general, and urban lakes in particular, is largely attributable to eutrophication and soil erosion in the drainage basin.

Annual mean levels of chlorophyll *a* in the study lakes were variable among lakes ranging from 0.91 to 239.53 mg/m^3, but were generally high (Table 1). Peak values in most lakes were recorded between March and September, although in a few lakes, chlorophyll *a* levels remained high throughout the year (except in winter). The actual temporal patterns were determined largely by the geographical location of the lakes. Among the study lakes, Yuqiao and Gaozhou Reservoirs are both used as a source of drinking water even though chlorophyll *a* levels in Yuqiao Reservoir can be as high as 6.07 mg/m^3. Despite the remoteness of some of the lakes, chlorophyll *a* levels were nevertheless high. For example, Lake Dalai (Inner Mongolia) is located in sparsely-populated grassland in northeast China, while Lake Boston (Xinjiang) is situated in an arid part of the northwest. Despite these observations, however, it was clear that chlorophyll *a* levels in urban lakes were particularly high and these lakes often had rich growth of hydrophytes. The data on chlorophyll *a* concentrations lend support to the conclusion that most lakes in China are overloaded with nutrients. Dissolved oxygen values were generally above 5 mg/l in most of lakes (Table 1), but dissolved oxygen concentrations in winter tended to be higher in urban lakes where chlorophyll *a* concentrations (and hence photosynthetic activity) were greater.

Blue-green algae dominated the phytoplankton of the study lakes (Table 4), followed by green algae and then diatoms. The dominant species in the algal community is closely related to the trophic status of the lake in China and elsewhere. In China, the typical genera in oligotrophic lakes are *Cyclotella* and the diatom *Tabellaria; Asterionella* and *Fragilaria* in eutrophic lakes; while *Stephanodiscus,* the green algae *Scenedesmus,* and the blue-green algae *Microcystis* characterize hypertrophic lakes (Jin et al. 1990). Significantly, blue-green algae dominated all the study lakes, confirming their eutrophic or hypertrophic condition.

Table 4. Dominant phytoplankton in 20 Chinese lakes and reservoirs.

Lake	Dominant phytoplankton
Lake Erhai	Blue-greens, greens, diatoms, *Cryptomonas*, etc.
Lake Boston	Blue-greens, greens
Yuqiao Reservoir	Blue-greens, diatoms, etc.
Gaozhou Reservoir	Blue-greens, greens, etc.
Lake Gucheng	Blue-greens, greens, diatoms, *Cryptomonas*
Lake Dianshan	Blue-greens, *Cryptomonas*
Lake Cihu	Blue-greens, greens, diatoms, *Cryptomonas*
Lake Qonghai	Blue-greens, greens
The West Lake	Blue-greens, diatoms
Lake Chaohu	Blue-greens, diatoms, *Cryptomonas*
Lake Nansi	Blue-greens, greens, *Cryptomonas*
Lake Luhu	Blue-greens
Lake Gantang	Blue-greens
Lake Nanhu	Blue-greens
Lake Jingpo	Blue-greens, diatoms
Lake Dongshan	Blue-greens, diatoms, *Cryptomonas*
Lake Liuhua	Blue-greens
Lake Liwan	Blue-greens, greens, diatoms, *Cryptomonas*, etc.
Lake Xuanwu	Blue-greens, diatoms, *Cryptomonas*
Lake Moushui	Blue-greens, diatoms

Relationships between factors affecting lake eutrophication

Lake eutrophication is a complex phenomenon involving a large number of interacting factors. However, earlier studies in other parts of the world have revealed some regular patterns, and indicated ways in which eutrophication can be brought under control (e.g. Beeton & Edmondson 1972, OECD 1982, Ryding & Rast 1989). Notwithstanding the diverse lake types, complex interactions of pollution, soil erosion and human influences, as well as the interplay between the high nutrient levels and other environmental factors, it is clear that the basic patterns of eutrophication in Chinese lakes were similar to those in other countries (Jin et al. 1990). The relationships among some of the more important factors affecting lake eutrophication are summarized below; further discussion is presented elsewhere (Jin et al. 1990).

The entry of excessive nutrients into a lake is usually followed by increased chlorophyll *a* concentrations, a classic symptom of lake eutrophication. Data collected from the 25 study lakes in 1987–1989 showed a significant positive correlation between total phosphorus (T-P) level and chlorophyll *a* (Chl *a*) concentration (Chl $a = -0.56 + 171.76$ T-P; $r = 0.72$, $n = 24$; $P < 0.05$). Similar positive correlations were found also between concentrations of total nitrogen and chlorophyll *a*, although the relationship was not as strongly significant as that with total phosphorus.

The transparency of lake water is influenced directly by phytoplankton density. However, the serious problem of soil erosion in China has introduced a confounding variable into this relationship. Nevertheless, data derived from the 25 study lakes show a good correlation between transparency (SD) and chlorophyll *a* measurements (ln chl $a = 1.85 - 1.62$ ln SD; $r = 0.73$, $n = 25$; $P < 0.05$). Other significant relationships obtained during investigation of the study lakes included correlations between total phosphorus and dissolved phosphorus; between total nitrogen and ammonia concentrations; and between total nitrogen and nitrite levels.

Trophic state of major lakes and reservoirs in China

The trophic state of 24 major lakes and reservoirs in China has been determined by the correlation Weighted Eutrophication State Index and the Eutrophication Degree Assessment (Table 5; Jin et al. 1990). A survey conducted in 1982 revealed that 91.8% of the total lake area investigated was mesotrophic, 3.2% oligotrophic, and 5% eutrophic. A more recent survey (1987–1990) indicated that most of the lakes in China were eutrophic or mesotrophic, comprising 55.0% and 44.5% (respectively) of the combined surface area of lakes investigated; only 0.5% of the lake area was oligotrophic (Table 6). This finding underscores the seriousness of the problem of eutrophication in Chinese lakes and the urgent need to take measures to improve the situation.

Difficulties in controlling lake eutrophication

The background nutrient levels in Chinese lakes are generally high. Most river basins in China have been intensively settled and modified for centuries, and human settlement around the lakes results in the discharge of untreated sewage into these water bodies. Furthermore, the removal of vegetation cover has led to soil erosion which

Table 5. Trophic state of urban and rural (or suburban) lakes in China; T-N, total nitrogen loading; T-P, total phosphorus loading.

	T-N (t/yr)	T-P (t/yr)	Trophic state
Urban Lakes			
Lake Liwan	–	–	Eutrophic
Lake Xuanwu	388.6	48.7	Eutrophic
Lake Moushui	1,169.0	45.9	Eutrophic
Lake Cihu	2,622.6	103.5	Eutrophic
Lake Dongshan	–	–	Eutrophic
Lake Liuhua	–	–	Eutrophic
Lake Luhu	–	–	Eutrophic
Lake Gantang	121.7	14.4	Eutrophic
Lake Nanhu	–	–	Eutrophic
Rural Lakes			
Lake Mougu	–	–	Eutrophic
Lake Boston	–	–	Mesotrophic
Lake Dalai	–	–	Eutrophic
Gaozhou Reservoir	–	–	Mesotrophic
Lake Nansi	36,237.5	13,702.6	Mesotrophic
Lake Qonghai	–	–	Oligotrophic
Yuqiao Reservoir	3,699.0	55.5	Mesotrophic
Lake Erhai	988.9	144.7	Mesotrophic
Lake Dianchi	4,906.0	472.0	Eutrophic
Lake Gucheng	–	–	Mesotrophic
Lake Dianshan	–	–	Mesotrophic
Lake Chaohu	22,556.4	777.8	Eutrophic

Table 6. Trophic state of some Chinese lakes investigated between 1987 and 1989.

	Oligo-trophic	Meso-trophic	Eutrophic
Number of lakes	1	7	13
Combined lakes area (km^2)	29.5	2,493.0	3,084.9
% of total area	0.5	44.5	55.0

contributes large quantities of nutrients to inland water bodies. The traditional use of manure as fertilizer also serves as a source of nutrients which may be washed into lakes and reservoirs by torrential rain.

Available data suggest that although there are a limited number of lakes and reservoirs which have not yet become eutrophic, the background nutrient concentrations are dangerously close to the critical levels. Further increases in nutrient levels will lead to eutrophication and, once that state is reached, the situation would be difficult to reverse. This problem is exacerbated by the large numbers of point and non-point pollution sources that exist in densely populated drainage basins, and the difficulties are illustrated by the alarming increase in the area of eutrophic lakes (from 5.0 to 55%; see above) in less than a decade. In extreme cases, extreme measures have been taken to improve lake trophic status: for example Lake Liuhau in Guangzhou was drained and 'cleaned' involving dredging the bottom mud (Jin et al. 1990). However, within months, algae (especially *Microcystis*) started to multiply rapidly and water transparency decreased, and the overall water quality soon returned to its previous hypertrophic state. This example serves to illustrate two of the major problems associated with lake eutrophication in China. Firstly, the large 'nutrient sinks' that exist in most of these lakes and, secondly, the rapid input of nutrients to the lake by waters flowing from densely-settled, man-modified drainage basins. It is clear that rapid, practicable and cost-effective strategies for reversing the trend towards increased eutrophication of Chinese lakes are needed urgently. Their development should be linked to formulation of effective watershed-management strategies, and development of methods to restore degraded, hypertrophic lakes.

References

Beeton, A. M. & Edmondson, W. T., 1972: The eutrophication problem. – *J. Fish. Res. Bd. Can.* **29:**673–892.

Jin, X., Liu, H., Tu, Q., Zhang, Z. & Zhu, X, 1990: Eutrophication of Lakes of China: 652 pp. – Chinese Research Academy of Environmental Sciences, Beijing.

OECD, 1982: Eutrophication of Waters: Monitoring, Assessment and Control: 154 pp. – Final Report OECD Cooperative Programme on Monitoring of Inland Waters (Eutrophication Control), Organization for Economic Cooperation and Development Publication, Paris.

Ryding, S.-O. & Rast, W., 1989: The Control of Eutrophication of Lakes and Reservoirs: 314 pp. – MAB Book Series 1, UNESCO, Paris & Pathenon Publishing, Carnforth.

Author's address:

Chinese Research Academy of Environmental Science, Beiyuan, Anwai, Beijing, China 100012.

Mitt. Internat. Verein. Limnol.	24	213–218	Stuttgart, Februar 1994

Factors limiting algal growth in eutrophic Chaohu Lake, China

Chengqing Yin, Zhiwen Lan and Ming Zhao

Abstract

Enclosure experiments, combined with regular monitoring of limnological parameters, were undertaken to investigate factors limiting algal growth in Chaohu Lake, China, where *Microcystis* was the dominant algal species. Nutrient concentrations in the lake water were high with an annual average total phosphorus concentration of 0.142 mg/l, soluble reactive phosphorus (SRP) concentration of 0.026 mg/l and total nitrogen concentration of 1.63 mg/l. The lake water contained a large quantity of suspended mineral particles and had high turbidity. Light intensity was significantly reduced at 1.0 m below the water surface and net primary productivity was negative at levels deeper than 1.0 m. Algal growth did not increase with elevated phosphorus concentrations above a critical (threshold) level. The threshold concentration of SRP for maximum algal growth in the lake was estimated as 0.019 mg/l, which was lower than the actual SRP concentration commonly recorded in the lake. The data suggested that it was not nutrients but light which limited algal growth in the lake during most of the summer and autumn. A large-scale reduction in the nutrient loads would be required to bring the lake to a phosphorus-limiting state as the first step towards a comprehensive eutrophication control strategy.

Introduction

In many limnetic and marine environments, nutrients are the most important limiting factors (*sensu* ODUM & ODUM 1955) for primary production. The average atomic ratio of carbon, nitrogen and phosphorus in the cellular contents of zoo- and phytoplankton samples is 106C:16N:1P, and this ratio has become a standard reference value for assessing the limiting nutrients in water bodies (RYDING & RAST 1989). The mass ratio (e.g. in units of mg/l) corresponding to the atomic ratio is 41C:7.2N:1P. For most of lacustrine and marine ecosystems, bio-available phosphorus is the limiting factor for algal growth. This is the case for most European and North American lakes where stratification exists and turbidity is low. Minimizing inputs of the 'macro-nutrient' phosphorus therefore represents a primary eutrophication control strategy, and can be highly effective (VOLLENWEIDER & KEREKES 1982).

Recent studies have indicated that the reduction of allochthonous phosphorus load does not always lead to an immediate recovery from eutrophication. This phenomenon can be explained by the high internal nutrient loading from the eutrophic sediment of the lake which maintains dissolved phosphorus concentrations at a level above the threshold for algal growth (SAS 1989). In these lakes, the prevailing phosphorus concentration in water is higher than that required for algal development and hence the growth of algae must be controlled by manipulation of other environmental factors. The present study was designed to address the question of what factors limit algal production in eutrophic Chaohu Lake, China, so as to provide data to permit formulation of management strategies for the lake.

Chaohu Lake (lat. 31 °N, long. 117 °E; surface area, 760 km²) is located on one of the tributaries of the Yangtze (Changjiang) River. It is a shallow (mean depth 2.6 m, maximum depth 4 m) eutrophic lake with an average total phosphorus concentration of 0.142 mg/l and total nitrogen concentration of 1.63 mg/l. It is situated close to the sea and surrounded by a fluvial plain; the mean elevation is 8.3 m + CD. The area is influenced greatly by the southeast monsoon from the Pacific Ocean and the East China Sea: annual precipitation in the catchment is 1100 mm and wind speeds average 4.1 m/sec. There are frequent windy days which cause significant wave movement in the lake and stir up the sediments. Consequently, the lake is well mixed, lacking stable stratification, and the water is usually turbid with an average transparency (Secchi disc depth) of 0.18 m. Water retention time is 3.2 months.

Microcystis dominates the lake algae throughout spring, summer and autumn, and algal blooms – due largely to *Microcystis* – occur in the lake on about 80% of the days from late May to mid-November. The algal blooms create a significant nuisance problem for municipal water supplies. They not only clog filter beds and increase the frequency of backwash, but also reduce the quality of the water supply. In addition, the lake shows other signs of ecological degradation including organic pollution, disappearance of marginal-zone macrophytes, bank erosion, high turbidity and siltation of the lake basin, and reduction of economically valuable fishery products. However, eutrophication is regarded as the key problem influencing the development of the regional economy based on Chaohu Lake.

Materials and methods

Experiments for the determination of limiting factors were carried out using in-lake enclosures. The enclo-

0538-4680/94/0024-0213 $ 1.50

sures were made of composite nylon-polyethylene membrane 0.06 mm thick, and were installed on steel frames supported by foamed plastic. The volume of each enclosure was 2.8 m^3. The enclosures were filled with lake water before the experiment. Prior to the actual experiments, it was determined that the physical and biological parameters inside the enclosures were similar to those prevailing in the lake. The detailed structure and function of the enclosures is given in YIN et al. (1989).

The enclosures were installed in Chaohu Lake near Zhongmiao Village, where there was no interference arising from stream inflows and the water depth was 3.5 m. The experiment was undertaken from September 15 to October 2 1988. The nutrient-rich lake water was first treated with ferric chloride to reduce the phosphorus concentration. Seventy two grams of $FeCl_3 \cdot 6H_2O$ was first dissolved in water and then added to each of the enclosures and mixed well. As a result of flocculation, most of the phosphorus and suspended matter were precipitated to the bottom of the enclosures, and SRP concentrations in the enclosure water samples were reduced to 0.011–0.013 mg/l. After 12 hours, the thick precipitate was pumped out of the enclosures and sodium bicarbonate ($NaHCO_3$) solution was then added to neutralize the acidity caused by the hydrolysis of ferric chloride and to adjust the pH to 7. Since part of the algae was removed in the flocculation process, about 0.1 m^3 of lake water was pumped into each bag to return the algal biomass to near its original level. Controlled amounts of orthophosphate solution were then added to the enclosure to attain a series of soluble reactive phosphorus (SRP) concentrations ranging from 0.014–0.027 mg/l. Water samples were collected for analyses at the beginning of the experiment and every four to five days thereafter. At the time when this study was undertaken, the weather and other environmental conditions in the lake were conducive to algal development.

The sampling points were 0.3 m below the water surface at three different locations within each enclosure. Chlorophyll *a*, SRP concentrations and other parameters were determined using standard methods (APHA 1985). Routine monitoring of the lake and its tributaries was carried out as part of the Cooperative Ecological Research Project (CERP) project (YIN & BERNHARDT 1991) in conjunction with the National Eutrophication Project (TU et al. 1990). Water transparency was measured with a Secchi disc and primary production determined by the oxygen method using light and dark bottles. Algal blooms were monitored in Chaohu Lake by regular observations made along a lane from Shikuo via Zhongmiao to Baishang in 1988 and 1989. The degree of algal blooms was estimated by visual observation using an arbitrary scale of bloom saturation. Data from the lake monitoring programmes, and regular analysis of lake water at the experimental station near Zhongmiao Village, were incorporated in the results of the present experimental study.

Results

Effects of phosphorus concentration on algal growth

After 10 days, the algal biomass differed significantly among the enclosures with different SRP concentrations, suggesting that the phosphorus might be limiting the growth of algae. Chlorophyll *a* concentrations rose rapidly with increasing SRP up to 0.02 mg/l (Fig. 1), beyond which the rise in chlorophyll *a* concentrations was very much slower. The best-fitting straight lines fitted separately to the first three and the last five data points intersected at a concentration of 0.019 mg SRP/l, which was taken as the threshold level of SRP for algal growth in Chaohu Lake. The dominant algal species in the enclosures was *Microcystis,* thus the determined threshold was regarded as applicable to this genus.

Analysis of data from lake monitoring programmes

Chaohu Lake had frequent algal blooms in the summer and autumn. The relative scale of algal bloom occurrence in 1988 and 1989 is shown in Fig. 2. The distribution of algal blooms (expressed as mg chlorophyll a/m^3 in surface waters) as measured by the analysis of a calibrated TM satellite image on August 11 1987 is given in Fig. 3 (CHENG & YIN 1992). Surprisingly, the peaks of the algal bloom were not correlated with the nutri-

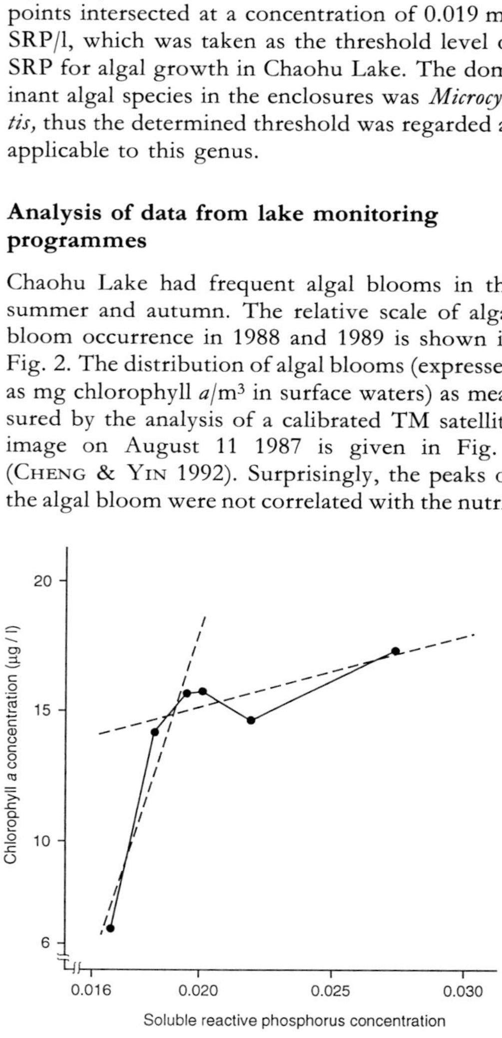

Fig. 1. Relationship between chlorophyll *a* concentrations and soluble reactive phosphate (SRP) levels in the experimental enclosures.

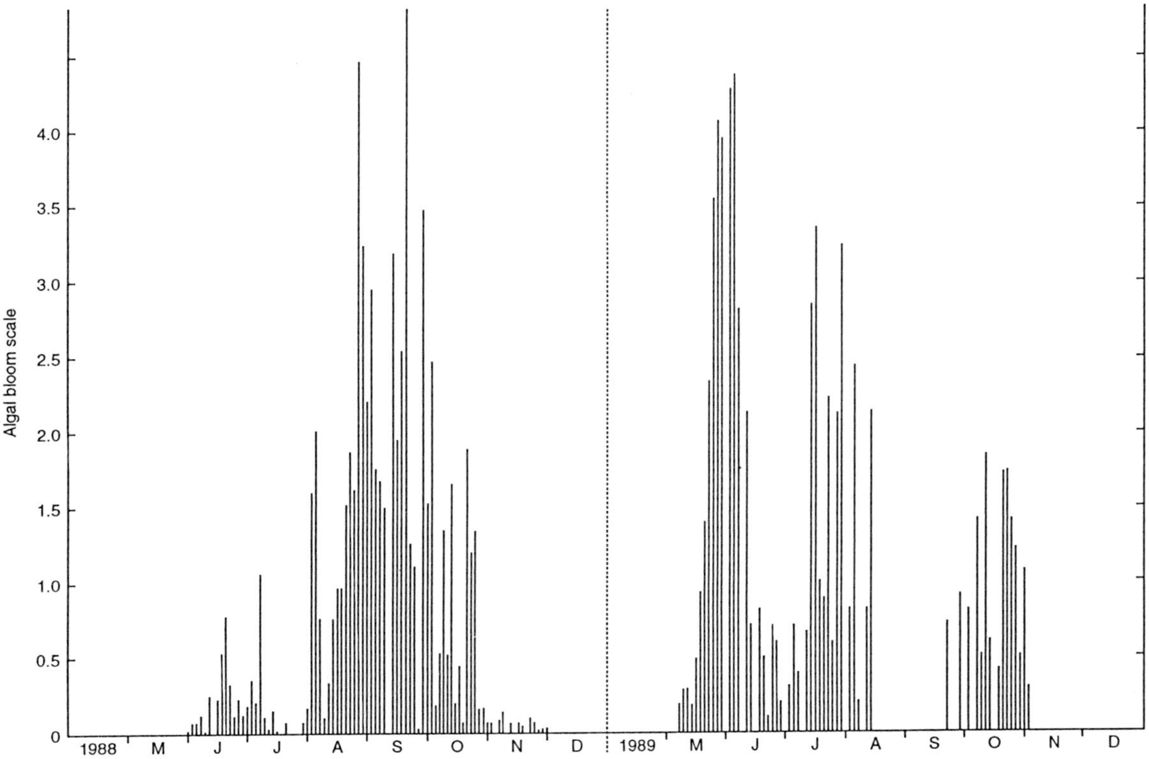

Fig. 2. Daily variations of the extent of algal blooms in Chaohu Lake in 1988 and 1989. There were no observations for a month from mid-August 1989 due to strong winds.

Fig. 3. Distribution of algal blooms expressed as mg chlorophyll a/m^3 in surface waters as measured by the analysis of a calibrated TM satellite image on August 11 1987.

ent concentrations of the lake water, but rather with meterological factors such as relative humidity, precipitation and wind speed (ZHAO, M. & YIN, C. unpubl. observations). The algal blooms were particularly closely related to the mean values of humidity, wind speed, cloudiness and earth temperature. Growth of *Microcystis* is favoured by high temperature, and thus the absence of algal blooms in the winter and spring may be attributable to the low temperatures prevailing at that time. Summer temperatures in Chaohu Lake were around 30 °C, which would have favoured the growth of the blue-green algae.

SUN & LIU (1990) reported that 20.7% of the total phosphorus in the cell contents of algae from Chaohu Lake was present in the form of dissolved inorganic phosphorus in samples taken in September 1987 and 30.9% in October 1988 samples. Previous studies had indicated that if phosphorus was the limiting factor for algal growth, the dissolved inorganic phosphorus absorbed by the phytoplankton would be quickly converted to organic and residue phosphorus in the algal cells, and consequently there would be little or no dissolved inorganic phosphorus (SRP) in fresh algal samples. These findings suggested that algal growth was probably not limited by SRP in Chaohu Lake, but by other environmental factors.

The degree of light penetration measured as irradiance (lux) at different depths in Chaohu Lake is given in Table 1. The readings were taken at 1000 h on two calm days in September 1988 when the Secchi disc depth was approximately 30 cm. On windy days, however, the Secchi disc readings fell to 10–20 cm and the irradiance was less than 70 lux at 1 m depth. Measurements of primary productivity and respiration at six stations in Chaohu Lake from 1987 to 1988 by WANG & JIN (1990) have shown that, during the summer, productivity at depths below one metre is lower than respiration (Fig. 4). It should be noted that these measurements were made on calm days when the water column was sufficiently stable to allow the dominant *Microcystis* to remain at the surface or subsurface layers. It is conceivable that on windy days when the algae were distributed evenly in the four-meter water column, the net productivity should be negative for the whole of the water column (Fig. 5). In situ observations support the above hypothesis, and after nearly one month of continuous strong winds (fromn August 12 1989) *Microcystis* blooms almost disappeared from the lake. Indeed, in late September 1989, the diatoms replaced *Microcystis* to become the dominant algae.

Table 1. Light penetration measured as irradiance (lux) at different depths in Chaohu on two calm days in September 1988.

Depth (m)	Irradiance (lux)	
0.0	40,000	48,000
0.2	8,000	6,000
0.5	4,500	3,200
1.0	750	600
1.5	70	90
2.0	0	0

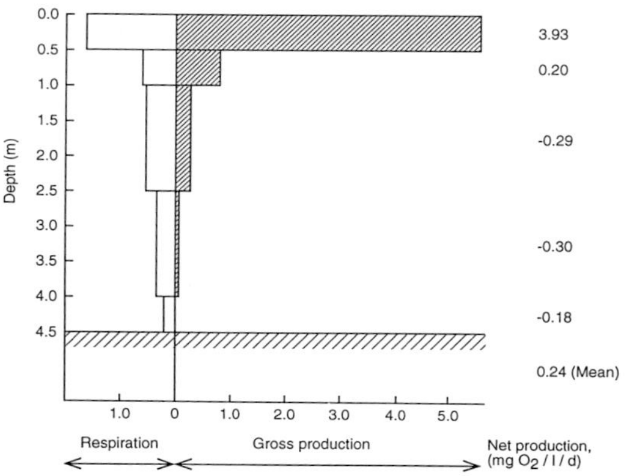

Fig. 4. Gross primary production and respiration in Chaohu Lake measurement on a calm summer day (after WANG & JIN 1990). The net primary production of the water column was 1.09 g O_2/m^2/day.

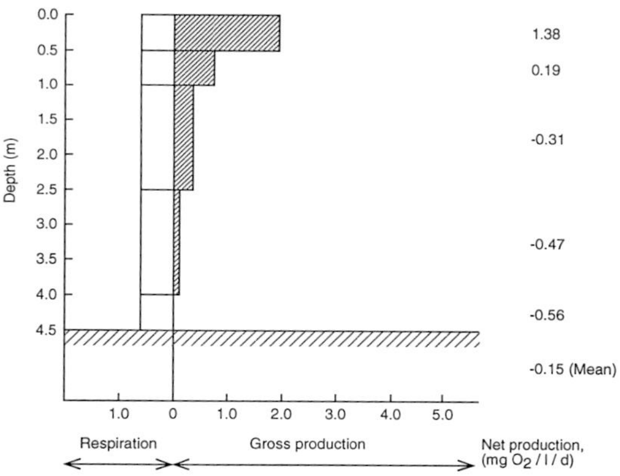

Fig. 5. Gross primary production and respiration in Chaohu Lake calculated for a windy summer day assuming that turbulence mixed the algae evenly in the water column. The net primary production of the water column was −0.67 g O_2/m^2/day.

These observations suggested that light was probably the main factor controlling algal growth in Chaohu Lake during the summer and autumn.

Discussion

Chaohu Lake is a shallow, turbid lake. Wind mixes the water column from the surface to the bottom, and the tropogenic zone is generally less than one metre. As a result, light-limiting conditions develop during the algal growing seasons. *Microcystis* has the ability to control its buoyancy and can to a certain extent adjust its vertical position in response to the low-light intensity, tending to move to the upper layers of the water during the summer. By contrast, chlorophytes and diatoms are usually found throughout the entire water column in the shade of both the mineral particles and the *Microcystis* bloom. The low light penetration therefore restricts the growth of algae in general and non-buoyant ones in particular. Such conditions might also account for the absence of submerged macrophytes in Chaohu Lake.

Light-limiting conditions in lakes have been reported by a number of authors. Kimmel & Groeger (1984) have suggested that light limits primary productivity in the river input end of reservoirs, while nutrient limitation is more common in the lake-like downstream end. Reynolds (1987) considered that a self-shading and resulting light-limited productivity would account for the lack of algal growth in waters where nutrient concentrations exceeded the threshold. However, the present investigation is the first report of a light-limiting condition occurring in a large lake with a surface area of 760 km^2.

The exploitation of light-limiting conditions for lake management is difficult, as the situation actually favours *Microcystis* dominance in the water system on calm days when these algae rise to the water surface. One possible solution is to increase turbulence in the water column thereby forcing *Microcystis* into the dark tropholytic zone, or to cover the water surface with floating macrophytes. An alternative approach would be to reduce the water retention time of the lake so that the blue-green algae, which usually have low reproductive rates, are flushed out of the lake system. Notwithstanding the practical difficulties with these proposals, previous experience in lake management has shown that phosphorus is probably the only essential element that can be manipulated to limit algal growth (Ryding & Rast 1989). Phosphorus concentrations in Chaohu Lake do not limit algal growth for most of the year, and the shallowness of the lake coupled with nutrient release from the bottom sediments presents serious problems for the management of this lake. It is impractical to control environmental factors such as light intensity and temperature on a large scale, but the removal of a sufficient amount of phosphorus from the lake so as to make it a limiting nutrient for primary producers is a possible option (Sas 1989). The important questions here are how much phosphorus needs to be removed and what degree of recovery can be expected. A simplified

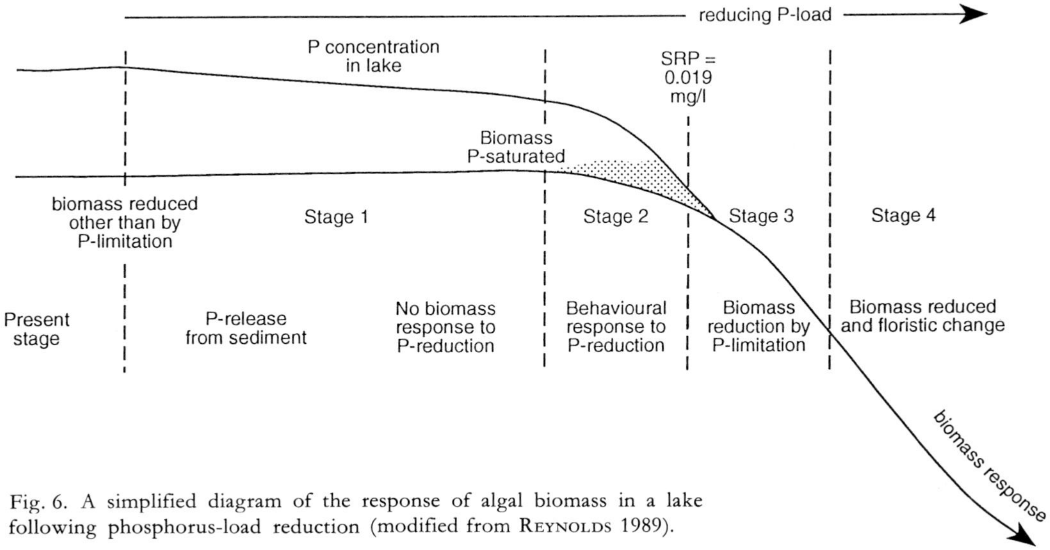

Fig. 6. A simplified diagram of the response of algal biomass in a lake following phosphorus-load reduction (modified from Reynolds 1989).

diagram of possible biomass responses in lakes following a reduction in phosphorus load is given in Fig. 6 (see also REYNOLDS 1989).

The results of the present study indicated that the algal growth was limited by phosphorus only at SRP concentrations below 0.019 mg/l. Above this critical value, the algal growth reached a saturation. Chaohu Lake waters have an annual average SRP concentration of 0.026 mg/l, and it can therefore be predicted that reduction of nutrient inputs would result only in a slight decline in SRP levels, with little reduction in algal biomass initially. Only when phosphorus reserves in the lake sediments are depleted and SRP concentrations in the water column are reduced to a level below 0.019 mg/l, would there be a corresponding appreciable decrease in algal biomass. It is proposed that a management strategy for Lake Chaohu should involve three stages.

i) Stabilization of the lake system by preventing further increases in nutrient levels.
ii) Reduction of allochthonous nutrient inputs so that the SRP concentrations are reduced from 0.026 mg/l to the threshold of 0.019 mg/l.
iii) Further reduction of allochthonous nutrient inputs to reduce SRP levels to below 0.019 mg/l. During the third stage, the lake ecosystem would be in a phosphorus-limiting state, and the algal biomass could then be controlled by the further reductions of allochthonous nutrient input. It is worth noting that during the recovery process, other parameters (especially nutrient concentrations) might change also. Accordingly, the relationship between algal growth and SRP concentrations should be determined periodically using in situ enclosures, and the management modified accordingly.

Acknowledgements

This work was undertaken as part of the Cooperative Ecological Research Project (CERP) sponsored by the Federal Ministry for Research and technology of the Federal Republic of Germany, the Academy of Sciences of the People's Republic of China, and the Man and the Biosphere Programme of UNESCO.

References

AMERICAN PUBLIC HEALTH ASSOCIATION, 1985: Standard Methods for the Examination of Water and Wastewater, 16th edition: 1268 pp. – APHA, Washington, D.C.

CHENG, C. & YIN, C., 1992: Using remote sensing and GIS techniques to estimate surface chlorophyll-*a* of Chaohu Lake. – *J. Environ. Sci. (China)* **4:** 64–72.

KIMMEL, B. L. & GROEGER, A. W., 1984: Factors controlling primary production in lakes and reservoires: a perspective. – In: Lake and Reservoir Management. – Report No. EPA-440/5-84-001: 227–281. – United States Environmental Protection Agency, Washington D.C.

ODUM, H. T. & ODUM, E. P., 1955: Trophic structure and productivity of a windward coral reef community on Eniweetok Atoll. – *Ecol. Monogr.* **25:** 291–320.

REYNOLDS, C. S., 1987: The response of phytoplankton communities to changing lake environment. – *Schweiz. Z. Hydrol.* **49:** 220–236.

– 1989: The relation between in lake-P concentration and algal biomass indicators (subsystem 2). – In: SAS, H. (ed.): Lake Restoration by Reduction of Nutrient Loading: Expectations, Experiences and Extrapolations: 102–147. – Academia-Verlag Richarz, St. Augustin.

RYDING, S. O. & RAST, W., 1989: The control of Eutrophication of Lakes and Reservoirs: 1314 pp. – UNESCO, Paris & Parthenon Publishing Inc., Lancs.

SAS, H., 1989: Lake Restoration by Reduction of Nutrient Loading: Expectations, Experiences and Extrapolations: 497 pp. – Academia-Verlag Richarz, St. Augustin.

SUN, S. & LIU, X., 1990: Speciation of phosphorus and nitrogen in the lake water and algae biomass. – In: TU, Q., GU, D., YIN, C., XU, Z. & HAN, J. (eds.): The Research of Chaohu Lake Eutrophication: 76–77. – University Press of Science and Technology, Hefei, Anhui. (In Chinese).

TU, Q., GU, D., YIN C., XU, Z. & HAN, J., 1990: The Research of Chaohu Lake Eutrophication: 226 pp. – University Press of Science and Technology, Hefei, Anhui. (In Chinese).

VOLLENWEIDER, R. & KEREKES, J., 1982: Eutrophication of Waters: Monitoring, Assessment and Control: 154 pp. – OECD, Paris.

WANG, S. & JIN, C., 1990: The primary productivity of phytoplankton in Chaohu Lake. In: TU, Q., GU, D., YIN, C., XU, Z. & HAN, J. (eds.): The Research of Chaohu Lake Eutrophication: 87–95. – University Press of Science and Technology, Hefei, Anhui. (In Chinese).

YIN, C. & BERNHARDT, H., 1991: Ecological Effects of Pollution in Chaohu Lake: 244 pp. – UNESCO/CERP Technical Report.

YIN, C., LAN, Z. & JIN, W., 1989: Algal bloom control study in enclosure experimental ecosystems. – *Acta Scientiae Circumstantiae* **9:** 95–99. (In Chinese).

Authors' address:

The Research Centre for Eco-environmental Sciences, Academia Sinica, P.O. Box 2871, Beijing, 100085, China.

Mitt. Internat. Verein. Limnol.	24	219–224	Stuttgart, Februar 1994

Management of shallow tropical lakes using integrated lake farming

William Y. B. Chang

Abstract

Integrated lake farming, which has been developed in China, is similar to integrated agriculture and employs a culture system based on fish and aquatic plants to reduce eutrophication. The plants are used as feed for fish and food for humans, while aquatic wastes serve to accelerate plant growth. Such a system can increase food and fish production, and reduce aquatic nutrients, sediment resuspension and the frequency of algal blooms. This paper introduces a successful lake-farming model from China and discusses aquaculture species suitable for use in such systems. Production concerns and conflicts over water use and management, as well as potential research needs, are considered also.

Lake farming

A large class of lakes in the tropics is formed either as a result of fluvial impacts or alterations of coastlines. These lakes are shallow, generally less than 10 m deep, polymictic, and turn over frequently. Wind is one of the primary mechanisms of whole-lake water exchanges. Seasonal temperature changes have less impact on water circulation in these lakes than in temperate lakes. Instead, diurnal temperature changes – which can be more pronounced than seasonal temperature oscillations – often lead to vertical turnover during the night. Many of these shallow inland waters are riverine lakes, which receive large amounts of water and nutrients from upstream and from the surrounding lake basin. Retention time is generally low and water exchange rates are high.

Shallow lakes of this type have been used extensively in recent years to meet the human needs imposed by growing populations in the lowland tropics. Large population movements from inland regions to the coastal cities, where there are better employment opportunities and improved living conditions, have further increased population densities. As a consequence, enhanced food production has become a primary mission of many developing nations. Public waterways, impoundments, and lakes are seen as tools which can be employed to meet food-production targets. Increased use of inland waters for waste disposal has increased the incidence and extent of eutrophication, which can now be observed in most water bodies close to large cities in the tropical lowlands (Chang 1991). Lake farming may provide a means of meeting the two challenges of raising food production and of reducing eutrophication.

Fish productivity in natural lakes is low, rarely exceeding 200 kg/ha, and areal productivity decreases with increasing lake size. Low fish productivity in lakes is attributed to low primary production. Net primary production of lake phytoplankton averages 200 g/m²/yr (Westlake 1963, Le Cren & Lowe-McConnell 1980) which is far lower than the average net production of aquatic macrophytes (Table 1). Raising the levels of harvestable primary production (i.e. that which fish can utilize) is vital if total fish and food production in shallow lakes is to be increased substantially.

The basis of lake farming involves raising primary production levels through the cultivation of aquatic plants that utilize solar energy efficiently. Fish cultured in enclosures are fed with the aquatic vegetation, and rotation between fish enclosures and aquatic plant fields ensures that the plants use excess nutrients accumulated in the sediment during the fish-culture period. The concept of integrated lake farming is similar to integrated cattle farming in which pasture is raised to feed the cattle

Table 1. Annual net primary production estimates (g/m²/yr) for various types of aquatic vegetation (modified from Westlake 1963); * indicates data derived from the lake-farming project in Lake Tai, China.

Vegetation types	Production estimates
Emergent vegetation	
Salt marsh	3,000
Freshwater reedswamp (temperate)	4,300
Freshwater reedswamp (tropical)	7,500
Aquatic plants used in lake farming	
Water spinach (*Ipomoea aquatica*)	3,750 (in 1985)*
Trapa	920 (in 1984)*
Submerged vegetation	
Attached plants (temperate)	600
Attached plants (tropical)	1,700
Phytoplankton	
Freshwater phytoplankton (temperate lake)	200
Freshwater phytoplankton (enriched lake)	600
Marine phytoplankton	200

0538-4680/94/0024-0219 $ 1.50

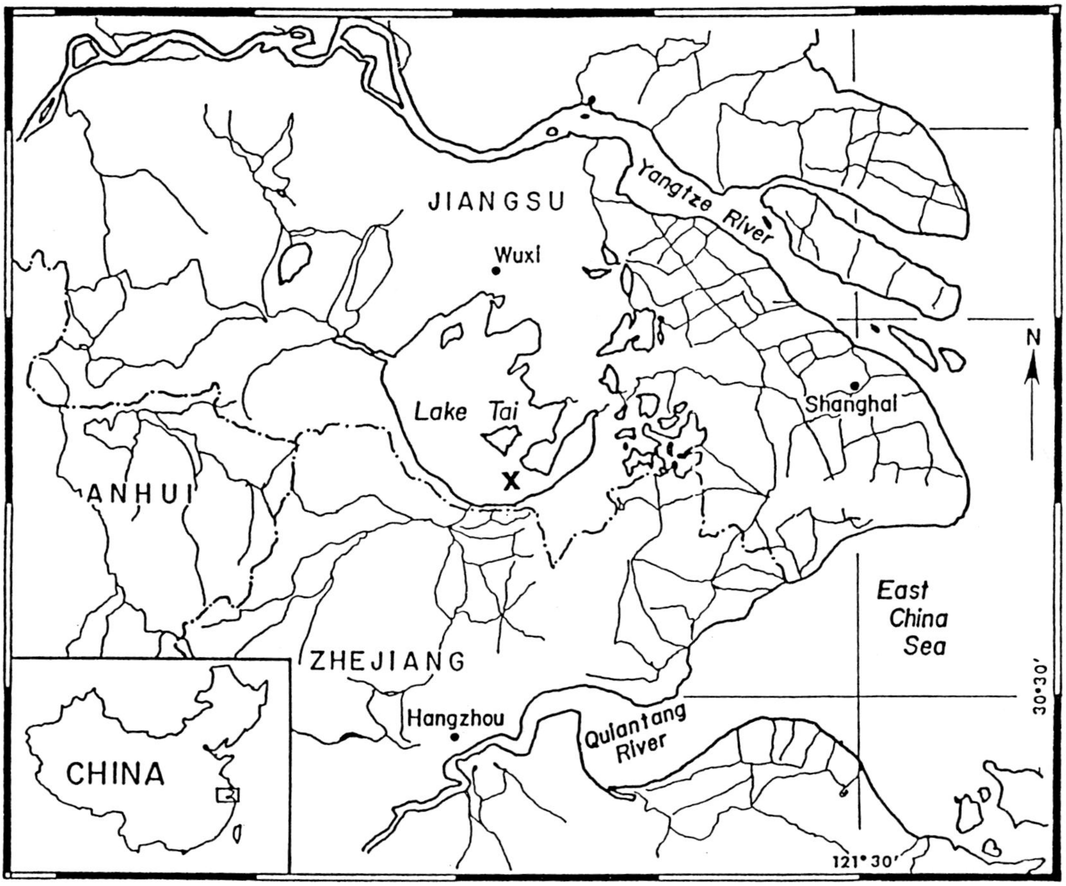

Fig. 1. Taihu Lake and the integrated lake-farming site; X indicates the position of the study site.

and the manure from the animals is, in turn, used to fertilize the pasture. The major difference is that the entire operation for integrated lake farming takes place in natural lakes: aquatic plants replace grass as fodder and fish take over the role of cattle as the harvested animals.

A successful model

Integrated lake farming was first demonstrated in Taihu Lake, China (Ou & Tu 1987) (Fig. 1), the third largest fresh water lake in China (Chang 1987). Taihu Lake – area 2425 km^2 – is shallow, with an average depth of less than 2 m. An integrated lake farm was established on an experimental basis in 1980; currently it occupies an area of about 25 ha and is operated by the Nanjing Institute of Geography and Limnology, Academia Sinica. This integrated production model has substantially increased the rates of food (fish and aquatic plants) production. For example, fish production was 8250 kg/ha in 1984 and reached 15,750 kg/ha in 1985.

In the Taihu Lake experimental system, fish were confined in net enclosures and fed aquatic plants collected from the surrounding area or cultivated in nearby hydro-agriculture production fields. An account of aquaculture methods is given by Zhong (1986). Aquatic plants were also raised at the perimeter of the net enclosures, but served more for reduction of wave impacts than as feed. Water quality in the experimental area of Taihu Lake was generally good: dissolved oxygen concentrations remained high, levels of nitrites and ammonia were low, and reported incidences of fish diseases were lower than those found in ponds and smaller lakes. Problems that frequently caused major die-offs in pond environements, such as early morning dissolved-oxygen deficits and nitrite toxicity (Chang 1986), have not been found in the Taihu Lake culture systems.

The major feed used in integrated lake farming is aquatic vegetation, and thus the types of fish reared differ considerably from those in pond-culture systems (Chang 1985). The total stocking weight for fish is usually 3750 kg/ha. Grass carp (*Ctenopharyngodon idella*) and Wuchang bream (*Megalobrama amblycephala*) were the major species stocked, comprising up to 90% of the individuals in enclosures in 1984 and 1985; the former was more important and invariably made up more than 40% of the fish stock. Black carp (*Mylopharyngodon piceus*) and common carp (*Cyprinus carpio*), which consume molluscs and benthos respectively, made up the remainder of the fish stock but they were not cultured in 1986 because they caused significant losses of sediments from the enclosure area. Silver carp (*Hypophthalamichthys molitrix*) and bighead carp (*Aristichthys nobilis*) did not grow well under the integrated-farming conditions because of the paucity of phyto- and zooplankton inside the Taihu Lake enclosures.

The aquatic plants grown in hydro-agriculture fields included *Trapa natans* (water chestnut), *Euryale ferox* (fox nut) and *Ipomoea aquatica* (water spinach). *Brasenia schreberi, Nelumbo nucifera* (Indian lotus), and rice (*Oryza sativa*) were also raised, but poor results were obtained. In this type of agriculture, plant seedlings are transplanted from the nursery and grown on nets. The growth nets were usually suspended horizontally by bamboo poles to maintain a plane a few centimetres beneath the water surface. All successful culture species were floating aquatic macrophytes (or submerged species with floating leaves) which are usually restricted to sheltered habitats. The production of *Trapa natans* on growth nets was 9225 kg/ha in 1984, and the seed production of *Euryale ferox* was approximately 2300 kg/ha. The annual production of water spinach attained the remarkable value of 37,500 kg/ha in 1985, and this species has great potential for use in the integrated lake-farming system.

The aquatic macrophytes not only provide fish feed, but also food for humans. Water chestnut has long been a major dietary item in China where it is sold in the free markets. Water spinach is an important green vegetable; the green leafy part is consumed by man, and the remaining parts are used as feed for grass carp. Rotation of culture sites between fish enclosures and hydro-agriculture fields reduces the accumulation of detritus and nutrients in lake sediments, because the detritus remaining after macrophyte harvesting is eaten by fish while the macrophytes take up excess nutrients.

Choice of aquatic plants and fish

The selection of suitable aquatic plants and fish species will determine the success of integrated lake-farming systems. Choice of plants is based on a high efficiency in fixing solar energy, and suitability for consumption by humans and fish. High rates of conversion to fish protein are the nutritional criteria for use of macrophytes in aquaculture systems, but fish farmers rarely select plants to use as feed on this basis.

The aquatic macrophytes used in lake farming are mainly submerged species with floating leaves or free-floating species because they use solar energy more efficiently than submerged macrophytes (Chang 1988) or phytoplankton (Edwards 1980). Moreover, areas with dense growths of emergent or floating aquatic plants have lower incidences of algal blooms, while heavy growths of phytoplankton may shade submerged macrophytes and reduce their growth. Further advantages accrue from the efficient digestion by fish of floating macrophytes – which contain only small amounts of lignified tissues – and from the general tendency for floating plants to have higher protein and lipid contents than emergent or submerged macrophytes (Wetzel 1975). Other considerations in the choice of plant species depend upon their palatability or acceptability for human consumption.

Grass carp is the dominant herbivorous fish cultured in lake-farming systems. Because its gut is short for a herbivore – comprising no more than 50% of total body length (Ling 1967, Chang 1989) – the vegetation consumed is only partially digested, and the resulting faeces can be eaten by detritivores or – through the provision of food and nutrients – may enhance the production of phytoplankton, zooplankton, and zoobenthos (Stott & Orr 1970, Chang 1989). Other herbivores, as well as planktivorous and detritivorous fishes, are used in the culture systems, but the stocking levels depend on lake condition and trophic status. Tilapia (*Oreochromis*), Bighead carp and Silver carp are stocked where both phytoplankton and zooplankton are abundant, but planktivores may experience food limitation when confined to enclosures and so these species rarely make up more than 10% of total stocks. Benthos feeders such as Black carp and Common carp are stocked only in lakes which lack strong currents. In the presence of such flows, bottom feeders tend to stir up sediments which are transported away from the enclosure by currents. Furthermore, benthic productivity within the confinement of an enclosure rarely keeps pace with the off-take by bottom feeders, so that growth rates of these fishes are relatively low. However, in small eutrophic lakes, both planktonic and benthic feeders do well, and may make up 60% of the total fish stocked.

Environmental effects of intensive lake farming

Effects on dissolved oxygen concentration

Dense growths of aquatic vegetation can cause diurnal fluctuations in dissolved oxygen and carbon dioxide concentrations (Chang & Ouyang 1988). The nature and extent of these fluctuations differ according to the type and density of aquatic plants cultured. Dissolved oxygen concentrations decline at night within beds of submerged aquatic macrophytes (Edwards 1980) but, during the day, levels are high wherever there is sufficient light for photosynthesis. Carbon dioxide concentrations follow the opposite trend: for example, Krishnamoorthi (1976) reported free CO_2 concentrations of 60–100 mg/l in waters where oxygen was almost zero. Oxygen levels under floating aquatic plants – the predominant aquatic vegetation in Chinese integrated lake-farming sytems – can be quite low whereas free CO_2 may be abnormally high. Schelpe (1961) reported oxygen concentrations under floating *Salvinia* mats of less than 0.7 mg/l, compared to a range of 4.4–6.9 mg/l at open-water sites, while Ashton & Walmsley (1976) found that the water beneath multi-layered mats of floating *Azolla filculoides* was anaerobic. The high CO_2 levels in such conditions are critical because they reduce the affinity of freshwater fish blood for oxygen (Alabaster & Stott 1967, Edwards 1980), and fish can be asphyxiated in the presence of dissolved oxygen if CO_2 levels are elevated.

The extent of oxygen depletion beneath floating macrophytes is related to mat thickness, area of coverage, and the length of time that the mats have been established. Although major current circulation in large lakes can mix the water under floating mats, so reducing the degree of deoxygenation, substantial reductions in natural fish populations due to asphyxiation have been found in waters covered by extensive macrophyte mats.

Effects of species stocked

The major goal of managing Chinese lakes is to increase total food production, and the fish stocked are those that can use all components of the available food resources (Chang 1989). One stocking and management strategy for Chinese Lakes resembles the polyculture approach used in ponds where various carp species are used (see Zhang & Chang 1994). In essence, the carp are stocked at the beginning of the culture cycle and harvested at the end of the culture cycle. However, the policy of stocking large lakes with carp has achieved rather limited success in China. Production usually increases slightly after the initial introduction, but the long-term net gain is small. An aggressive carp-stocking programme can reduce the diversity of indigenous fish species and the genetic diversity of carp species. For example, Liu (1984) reported a reduction of indigenous fish species in Tong Lake, Wuhan, China, as a result of stocking carp fingerlings over several years. By contrast, impacts of integrated lake farming upon indigenous species are much more limited than those arising when fish are stocked in lakes under general management. However, if introduced species are used in lake farming, precautions must be taken to ensure that these species do not establish themselves outside of the enclosures.

Effects of enclosed fish

Loss of aquatic plants due to grazing in natural lakes is usually slight, ranging from 0.5–8% of the total aquatic vegetation (Wetzel 1975). Where there is intensive culture of macrophytes for lake farming, however, grazing by herbivorous fish is significant. The ecological consequence is that remineralization of nutrients from macrophytes does not take place seasonally, following senescence or die-off of the plants, but occurs continuously as the herbivorous fish consume aquatic plants and then release nutrients to the water throughout the culture period (PRFRI 1982). These nutrients can provide a basis for continuous phytoplankton growth in the open-water areas where floating macrophytes are absent. Dissolved organic matter released from fish faeces contributes to the formation of nitrogen-rich detritus, which can be an important food source for lake detritivores.

Reduction in sediment resuspension

Resuspension of sediment is one of the major sources of nutrient input to the water column of many shallow lakes (CHANG 1987). In this situation, control of nutrient inputs may not result in a major improvement in eutrophication conditions. In localities with substantial growths of aquatic macrophytes, wave action is reduced, the sediments are stabilized, and there is a reduction in sediment resuspension and transport. Furthermore, harvesting of macrophytes for consumption by man and his livestock removes nutrients from the lakes. In combination, these processes improve eutrophication conditions and reduce unwanted algal blooms.

Conflicts in the management of inland waters

Increases in human population and in the uses of inland waters have increased the incidence of conflicts over management of lake resources. Tensions are heightened when a water body is administered by more than one political entity, and each group involved has a major stake in a particular lake-management plan. Potential problems that can arise from different management strategies include reductions in productivity of cultured fish and aquatic products, increased pollution and associated adverse health effects, and conversion of the marginal zone to a variety of uses including housing construction and rice fields. The conversion of the marginal zone has been a major cause of the disappearance of many shallow lakes in China's lower Yangtze River basin over the last 30 years (CHANG 1987).

Without proper mediation, conflicts among different interest groups can lead to confrontations, some of which have been violent and resulted in deaths in China. Mismanagement of inland waters – or an absence of management – can result when each group uses lake resources with a consideration only for its own needs. Resolution of conflicts over the use of lakes has received limited attention, even in developed nations. In developing tropical countries, where sound management of inland waters is critical and would be of great benefit to local inhabitants, conflict resolution is often ignored totally. Several approaches can be taken to mediate water use-disputes. Market regulation, administrative direction (hierarchy), and non-intervention are the three major approaches from an institutional perspective. Of these methods, administrative direction and non-intervention are used most frequently, although market regulation may be more common than has been supposed and could assume greater importance in the future.

The nature of water-user groups and their relationships with each other and with the state is an important factor in determining the success of different approaches to conflict mediation. Clearly, this is an important topic which will require more attention. The lack of acceptable social and legal arrangements has retarded progress in development of appropriate management strategies for inland waters, despite the many advances which have been made in our understanding of limnology.

Outlook

Integrated lake-farming systems have many benefits. In addition to providing financial gains, an integrated system can reduce the effects of eutrophication in shallow lakes, and can serve as an efficient approach to whole-lake management. Because shallow (<3 m deep) lakes are easily mixed by winds, sediments are frequently resuspended and nutrients are released into the water column, producing frequent algal blooms. Extensive planting of aquatic macrophytes by lake farmers can decrease wave action, stabilize sediment, reduce nutrient resuspension, and lead to a drop in the frequency of blue-green algal blooms. Lake farming is therefore an efficient way to control algal blooms and to reduce eutrophication. The added benefit of this farming system is that the planting of these macrophytes creates areas of vegetation which serve as spawning grounds for indigenous fishes and refuges for fry.

Lake farming provides additional benefits in that it provides an economically-sustainable method for retrieving nutrients from the aquatic environment. Several projects sponsored by international donor agencies to reduce eutrophication and to improve water quality of tropical lakes have failed after the funding period. Major problems can arise due to the non-sustainability of methods used and the lack of economic incentives for local residents to continue the projects. The economic benefits derived from integrated lake farming provide the incentives needed for farmers to sustain these practices, and thereby reduce levels of unwanted nutrients in aquatic environments.

On the other hand, an increase in management conflicts could result from wider adoption of lake farming, since whole-lake integrated farming can impact those whose use of the lake conflicts with the aims of the lake farmer. Without appropriate mediation, these conflicts can lead to confrontations which hamper management plans. In order for lake farming to be economically sustainable and environmentally acceptable, several areas of research are still needed. The appropriate balance between fish farming and aquatic crop production must be estimated on the basis of several factors: net economic return, environmental gains (e.g. water quality), and risk assessment (e.g. fish diseases and frequency of natural calamities). Research is also needed to determine which aquatic plants will provide the highest rates of primary productivity and permit the maintenance of adequate levels of dissolved oxygen. For successful fish culture, the appropriate level and types of fish stocked must be determined, so as to ensure the high economic returns. Although Grass carp has been the primary fish used for integrated farming, other species (e.g. *Tilapia rendalli, Tilapia zilli* and *Puntius gonionotus*) are worthy of consideration.

Lake farming has great potential for increasing food production from natural water bodies. To date, developing countries have had only limited success in augmenting their aquatic food and fish production. Integrated lake farming extends the lessons of land agriculture to aquatic systems and provides an efficient way of using and managing shallow inland waters. Successful applications of this system – resulting in increased aquatic food and fish production – have been demonstrated in China, where increases in profit of over 100% have been reported by many state fish farms. This farming technique has gained considerable attention in China and southeast Asia and is expected to become more widespread in the region.

References

Alabaster, J. S. & Stott, B., 1967: Grass carp (*Ctenopharyngodon idella*) for aquatic weed control. – Proceedings of the European Weed Research Council, International Symposium on Aquatic Weeds **2:** 123–126.

Ashton, R. J. & Walmsley, R. D., 1976: The aquatic fern *Azolla* and its *Anabaena* symbiont. – *Endeavour* **35:** 39–43.

Chang, W. Y. B., 1985: Pond fish culture in the Pearl River Delta. – *Aquaculture Magazine* **11:** 45–46.

– 1986: Practical methods for treating fish during oxygen stress in ponds. – *Aquaculture Magazine* **12:** 20–21.

– 1987: Large lakes of China. – *J. Great Lakes Res.* **13:** 235–249

– 1989: Integrated lake farming for fish and environmental management in large shallow Chinese Lakes: a review. – *Aquacult. Fish. Manag.* **20:** 441–452.

– 1991: Human population, modernization, and the changing face of China's eastern Pacific lowlands. – *China Exchange News* **18:** 3–8.

Chang, W. Y. B. & Ouyang, H., 1988: Dynamics of dissolved oxygen and vertical circulation in fish ponds. – *Aquaculture* **74:** 263–276.

Edwards, P., 1980: Food potential of aquatic macrophytes. – *ICLARM Studies & Review* **5:** 51 pp.

Krishnamoorthi, K. P., 1976: Aquatic plants in relation to public health aspects in Nagpur District and elsewhere. – In: Varshney, C. K. & Rzoska, J. (eds.): Aquatic Weeds in South East Asia: 162–166. – Dr. W. Junk Publishers, The Hague.

Le Cren, E. D. & Lowe-McConnell, R. H., 1980: The Functioning of Freshwater Ecosystems: 588 pp. – Cambridge University Press, Cambridge.

Ling, S. W., 1967: Feeds and feeding of warm-water fishes in ponds in Asia and the Far East. – *FAO Fish. Rep.* **44:** 291–309.

Liu, A. M., 1984: A brief review of aquaculture in a large lake in Wuxi, China: 3 pp. – National Tai Tung Fish Farm, unpublished manuscript. (In Chinese).

Ou, Y. & Tu, Q., 1987: Brief introduction to a preliminary experiment in water agriculture of East Taihu Lake. 10 pp. – Nanjing Institute of Geography Report, Academia Sinica. (In Chinese).

PRFRI, 1982: Pond Fish Culture in China (A Manual): 190 pp. – Pearl River Fisheries Research Institute, Chinese Academy of Fisheries Science. Guangzhou, China. (In Chinese).

Schelpe, E. A. C. L. E., 1961: The ecology of *Salvinia auriculata* and associated vegetation on Kariba Lake. – *J. S. Afr. Bot.* **27:** 181–187.

Stott, B. & Orr, L. D., 1970: Estimating the amount of aquatic weed consumed by grass carp. – *Progr. Fish. Cult.* **32:** 51-54.

Westlake, D. F., 1963: Comparisons of plant productivity. – *Biological Reviews* **38:** 385–425.

Wetzel, R. G., 1975: Limnology: 743 pp. – Saunders Company, Philadelphia.

Zhang, Hong & Chang, W. Y. B., 1994: Management of inland fisheries in shallow eutrophic, mesotrophic and oligotrophic lakes in China. – *Mitt. Internat. Verein. Limnol.* **24:** 225–229.

Zhong, C. M., 1986: Importance of enclosure aquaculture in the development of lake fishery: 1–7. – Yiyang Region Agriculture, Bureau Report Hunan Province, China. (In Chinese).

Author's address:

Division of International Programs, National Science Foundation, Washington, D.C. 20550, USA, and Centre for Great Lakes and Aquatic Sciences, The University of Michigan, Ann Arbor, Michigan 48109, USA.

Mitt. Internat. Verein. Limnol.	24	225–229	Stuttgart, Februar 1994

Management of inland fisheries in shallow eutrophic, mesotrophic and oligotrophic lakes in China

Hong Zhang and William Y. B. Chang

Abstract

Optimizing fish yields in natural waters has long been the primary goal of lake management in China. Three different approaches that are used to increase fish yields are illustrated with reference to lakes on the Jiang Han Plain. In managing eutrophic lakes, fishes which can exploit the large biomass of phytoplankton, zooplankton, benthos and detritus are stocked. The management of mesotrophic macrophyte-dominated lakes involves stocking primarily herbivorous fish such as grass carp (*Ctenopharyngodon idella*). Stocking densities of these herbivorous fish are estimated from the total biomass of vegetation in each lake. In managing oligotrophic shallow lakes with low primary productivity, the first step is to increase vegetation biomass in the shallower areas. The lakes are then stocked with herbivorous fishes which – through their consumption of macrophytes – increase rates of nutrient remineralization and enhance the growth of plankton and zoobenthos. The overall result has been an increase in total fish production from the three types of lake, and the management approaches applied to Jiang Han Plain Lakes are now being adopted more widely in China.

Introduction

One of the major goals in managing Chinese lakes is to increase food production. All available lake natural resources are used for this purpose. The types and numbers of fish stocked depend on lake trophic level, because each species has a different diet and exploits different resources within the lake (Chang 1987). The ecosystem approach to stocking and management of lake fisheries resembles the polyculture approach used in ponds (FSD 1976, Chang 1989).

Three approaches have been used in lake and fisheries management in Jiang Han (= Jainghan) Plain, Hubei Province, an area known as the 'land of a thousand lakes' (CNG 1985). In each case there was an increase in total fish production from the managed lakes (CFC 1972). These three approaches are described in more detail below.

The study area

Jiang Han Plain (the centre is 30°30′N; 13°30′E) extends over 39,000 km² in the region where the Han River joins the Yangtze River (Fig. 1). More than 7000 years ago, this area was the largest freshwater lake in China (Yunmangze Lake). Sediment brought down by the rivers and changes in climate gradually reduced the size of this lake and it fragmented into numerous small lakes. More than one thousand lakes were present in the Jiang Han Plain during the 1950s. Extensive reclamation of the wetlands and marginal zones of these lakes rapidly reduced their size, and many have since disappeared. There are now only 557 lakes on the Jiang Han Plain. The lakes are interconnected by canals and waterways, forming an extensive water network. The Plain has a subtropical climate with an annual average temperature of 16.4 °C and an annual precipitation of 1200 mm. There are 185 days with a minimum temperature above 15 °C, which is the lower limit for optimal growth of carp species. The suitable climate and extended waterways have made this area one of China's most important fish producing regions (HPCAP 1984).

Past water management

Flood control has been the highest priority in determining habitat management considerations on the Jiang Han Plain, and many dams and weirs have been constructed for this purpose during the last 30 years. Prior to this habitat engineering, the waters of the Jiang Han Plain flowed freely and were regulated only by the natural water levels of the Yangtze and Han Rivers. When the water levels of the Yangtze and Han Rivers were low, the water flowed from the lakes to the rivers; water flowed in the opposite direction when river levels were high. Major construction works carried out between 1950 and 1970 permitted regulation of water flow between the lakes and connecting waterways by means of weirs and dams. The only lakes in the Yangtze River basin free of such regulation are Boyang (= Po Yang) and Tongting (= Dong Ting) Lakes; their size and the large volumes of water flowing through these lakes made regulation by dams impractical (HPGB 1977, Jin 1974).

Water regulation in the lakes of Jiang Han Plain is the responsibility of the Chinese Water Authority and is undertaken primarily for power generation and flood control. The Fisheries Bureau has the responsibility of managing the lakes and their natural resources, and recommends – to the Water Authority – times for opening and closing the weirs to allow recruitment of fishes.

0538-4680/94/0024-0225 $ 1.25

Whether or not the Fisheries Bureau's recommendations are followed is, however, at the discretion of the Water Authority.

Fisheries management

Many of the fish species that spawn in the Yangtze River begin their spawning run from the lakes on the Jiang Han Plain (Yih 1964, STSGDF 1982). The construction of dams and weirs has not only served to regulate lake water levels, but has also seriously affected the migration of fishes into and out of these lakes (Liu 1987). Any saleable fishes yielded by the lakes provide a source of income for those groups managing them. Wherever possible, large nets are positioned at lake outlets to capture any fish that are undertaking breeding migration. Few fishes can complete migration to their spawning grounds and, when combined with the blockage of migration routes by dams and weirs, the result is that only a small fraction of the adult fish are able to spawn each year. Institutional control of hydrological operations in the past 30 years has greatly reduced the indigenous species of fish; more than half of the species have disappeared and once abundant riverine species have become rare (Yi 1982, Zhang 1983). Fish populations in the lakes and impoundments of the Jiang Han Plain now depend on direct stocking, mainly of carp species, and these fishes can significantly affect ecological processes in the lakes (MIFP 1988). For example, if plankton feeders are stocked in a lake containing macrophytes, the plant biomass is under-utilized and secondary production is low; one consequence is that macrophytes can dominate and even choke the entire lake.

Lake management for fisheries

In order to utilize nutrients more efficiently for aquatic food production, studies have been conducted since the 1960s aimed at improving lake productivity and enhancing fish production. Three management approaches are utilized, depending upon lake trophic conditions. To illustrate these approaches, three lakes on the Jiang Han Plain will be considered: Paizhong Lake (oligotrophic), Biandan Lake (mesotrophic) and Chidong Lake (eutrophic) (Allen & Kramer 1972, He 1982). The trophic classification of these lakes is based on indices presented by Wetzel (1975) and Rodhe (1969). Data on the nutrient status and phytoplankton communities of each lake are given in Table 1.

Oligotrophic Paizhong Lake

This shallow, dish-shaped lake has an average depth of 1.2 m and an area of 800 ha. No major sources of nutrient inputs are present in the drainage basin. Before 1975, this lake had a dense growth of macrophytes, but overstocking of grass carp (*Ctenopharyngodon idella*) – which began in 1975 – had almost completely eliminated the macrophytes by 1979. Grass carp production in this lake declined dramatically in subsequent years.

Primary productivity was low in this lake (Table 1). In order to increase fish production during the 1980s, a decision was made to first substantially increase primary production in the lake, then to stock herbivorous fishes. The method used was to plant vegetation in the littoral zone during a spring (March) drawdown period when the water level was low (Chen 1981). Seeds of *Echinochloa crus-galli* and *Zizania latifolia* were sown on 213 ha and 5.5 ha (respectively) of the marginal zone area, where they could draw nutri-

Table 1. Total phosphorus, total nitrogen, primary productivity, and phytoplankton biomass and major species in three Chinese lakes of different trophic status.

	Oligotrophic Paizhong Lake	Mesotrophic Biandan Lake	Eutrophic Chidong Lake
Total P (mg/l)	0.01	0.014 (0.009–0.019)	0.019 (0.010–0.028)
Total N (mg/l)	0.21	0.66 (0.54–0.77)	1.45 (0.40–2.56)
Net primary productivity (g O_2/m^2/day)	0	0.62	5.10
Algal biomass (mg/l)	0.59	1.96	6.67
Dominant species	diatom	diatom, green algae	green algae, bluegreen algae

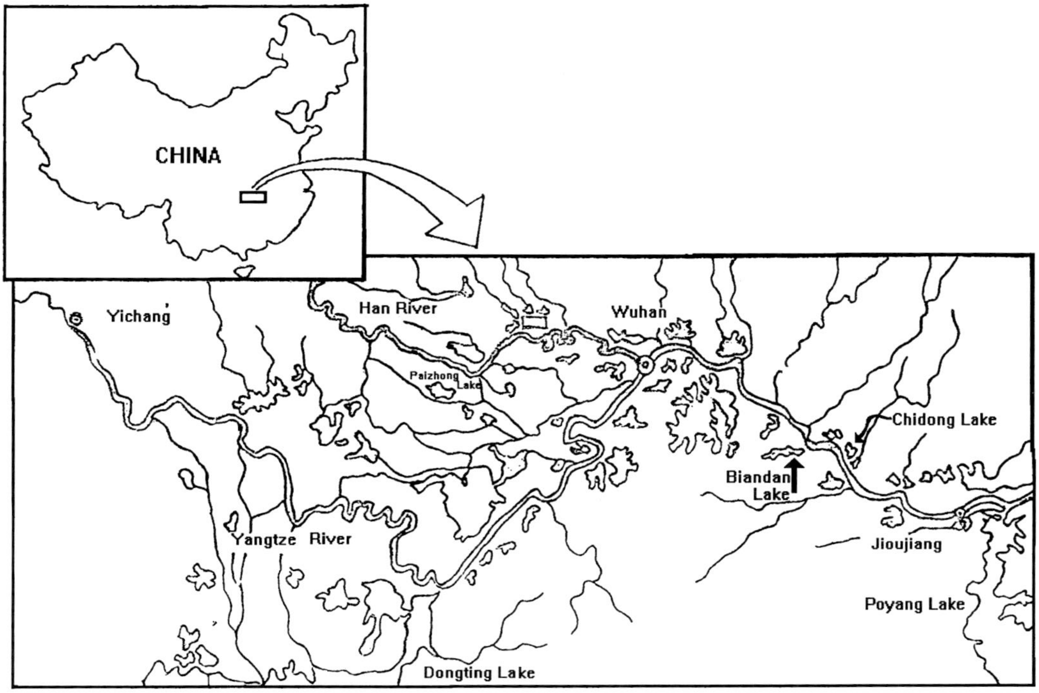

Fig. 1. Lakes of the Jiang Han Plain, China.

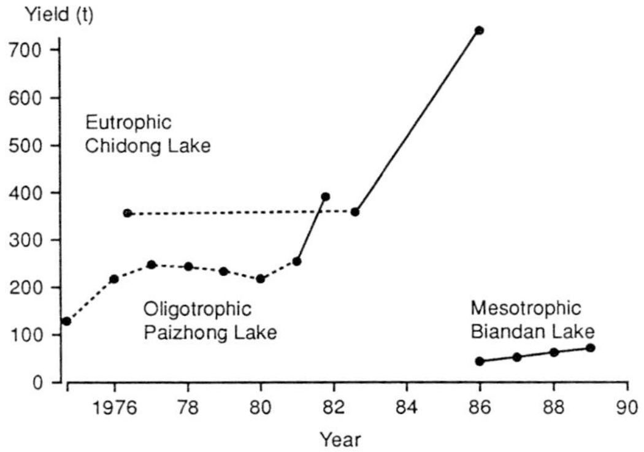

Fig. 2. Annual fish production in three Chinese lakes of different trophic status lakes: ···· before the initiation of the lake fisheries management approach; —— after the initiation of the lake fisheries management approach.

ents from the sediment. The vegation biomass reached 10,000 kg/ha in two months. The plants were inundated by an increase in water levels, and subsequently various species of fishes were stocked, including herbivorous grass carp, together with bottom-feeding and planktivorous species. Herbivorous fish were stocked first, to utilize the aquatic plants and to remineralize the nutrients from the aquatic plants so releasing them into the water column. Bottom-feeding fish were stocked to feed on detritus derived from the plants and, finally, planktivores were added to utilize the growths of phytoplankton and zooplankton which had been stimulated by the nutrients released by remineralization.

Under this system, the total annual fish production reached 370 t (0.46 t/ha), a 62% increase in production on years when there was no vegetation planted in the marginal zone (Fig. 2). Of the fish harvested, herbivorous species exhibited the largest increase of approximately 150%; production of planktivores increased by 60% (ZHANG 1983). The aquaculture approach applied in Paizhong Lake is a traditional method employed in pond culture, and as more Chinese lakes come under management, this approach is being adopted widely.

Mesotrophic Biandan Lake

Biandan Lake has an area of 200 ha and an average depth of 1.5 m (Fig. 1). This dish-shaped lake (which is separated from a much larger neighbouring lake by a large dyke) has a thick layer of organic sediment, and 80% of its area supports dense growths of aquatic macrophytes (*Myriophyllum spicatum, Vallisneria spiralis* and *Nelumbo nucifera*). The total macrophyte biomass has been estimated at about 28,000 kg/ha (Hu 1991). The projected level of herbivorous fish production for the 200 ha lake was estimated by application of formulae devised by Chen (1975) at about 40 tons. The number of grass carp fingerlings stocked in the lake was based on this projection (Opuszynski 1972). Small river crabs were also stocked to utilize the detritus arising from fish faeces and macrophytes. Total food production (all fishes plus crabs) reached 63 t (Fig. 2). River crab production has been growing at a rate of about 40% annually (Hu 1991).

Eutrophic Chidong Lake

Chidong Lake is a 1113 ha eutrophic lake with an average depth of 4 m. It is surrounded by farmland and villages, and receives large quantities of agricultural and household effluents. Algal biomass was higher than in the two lakes described above, and blue green algae were important (Table 1). Zooplankton and benthic populations were also sizable, but aquatic macrophytes were scarce. Fisheries management for this lake involved stocking species which could utilize the sizable phytoplankton and zooplankton populations. Silver carp (*Hypophthalmichthys molitrix*) was stocked to feed on phytoplankton and bighead carp (*Aristichthys nobilis*) were added to exploit zooplankton. The number of fingerlings of each of the species that were stocked, and resulting fish production, were calculated from formulae derived by Wang (1981). At a stocking density of 5000 fingerlings/ha and an appropriate mixture of the two fishes (63% Bighead carp) annual fish yield reached 700 t, compared to a yield of 360 t prior to employment of the lake fisheries management approach (Jin 1974).

Discussion

Attempts to 'turn wastes to resources' have been made increasingly in many countries to mitigate environmental problems. China has a growing population and faces increasing eutrophication of inland waters. Production of sufficient food to feed a population of more than one billion has been the top priority of lake-management strategies. The basic approach has therefore been to use all sources of lake primary and secondary production to increase fish yields (Chang 1987).

Increased human populations have greatly accelerated the extent and incidence of cultural eutrophication of Chinese lakes. While reduction in nutrient loadings is an important means of mitigating eutrophication, channelling the unwanted nutrients into food and fish production is another way to manage this problem (Chang 1994). This practice has been followed in China for many years. The case studies reported here indicate that there are economically-sustainable methods by which eutrophication can be controlled at the same time as food production is increased. Adoption of Chinese lake-farming techniques in developing countries with similar needs could increase income from cash crops, such as fish, and make management of lake environments more efficient.

References

Allen, H. & Kramer, J. R., 1972: Nutrients in Natural Waters: 100 pp. – Wiley, New York.

CFC, 1972: Chinese Fish Culture. – Editorial Committee of Chinese Fish Culture, Science Press, Beijing. (In Chinese).

Chang, W. Y. B., 1987: Large lakes of China. – *J. Great Lakes Res.* **13:** 225–249.

– 1989: Integrated lake farming for fish and enviromental management in large shallow Chinese lakes: a review. – *Aquacult. Fish. Manag.* **20:** 441–452.

– 1994: Management of shallow tropical lakes using integrated lake farming. – *Mitt. Internat. Verein. Limnol.* **24:** 219–224.

Chen, H. D., 1981: Effectiveness of planting cockspur (*Echinochloa*) in ponds for rearing fish fingerlings. – *J. Fish. China* **5:** 317–327. (In Chinese).

Chen, H. T., 1975: Standing crop of the macrophytes of Lake Tung-Hu, Wuchang with reference to the problem of its rational piscicultural utilization. – *Acta Hydrobiol. Sinica* **5:** 410–420. (In Chinese).

CNG, 1985: Chinese Natural Geography. – Chinese Natural Geographic Editorial Committee, Science Press, Beijing. (In Chinese).

FDS, 1976: Fishes of the Yangtze River. – Fish Species Division, Institute of Hydrobiology, Hubei Province, Science Press, Beijing. (In Chinese).

He, Z. H., 1982: Classification of lakes based on eutrophication. – *Reservoir Fishery* **4:** 46–51. (In Chinese).

HPCAP, 1984: Management and Development Strategy of Aquatic Resources in the Jianghan Plain. – Hubei Provincial Committee of Agricultural Planning, Internal Publication. (In Chinese).

HPGC, 1977: Report of Regional Hydrology and Geology. – Hubei Provincial Geological Bureau, Internal Publication. (In Chinese).

HU, C. L., 1991: Fisheries Ecology and Methods for Resource Development in Baoan Lake: 31–48. – In: Collected Papers of C. L. HU, Science Press, Beijing. (In Chinese).

JIN, B. I., 1974: Jianghan Lake District. – Hubei People's Press, Hubei. (In Chinese).

LIU, H. Q., 1987: Primary productivity and fish production in Chidong Lake. – *Freshwat. Fish. China* **4:** 24–29. (In Chinese).

MIFP, 1988: Methods for Increasing Fish Production: – Chinese Institute of Hydrobiology, Jiangxi Provincial Science and Technology Press. (In Chinese).

OPUSZYNSKI, K., 1972: Use of phytophagous fish to control aquatic plants. – *Aquaculture* **1:** 61–74.

RODHE, W., 1969: Crystallization of eutrophication concepts in Northern Europe. In: Eutrophication, Causes, Consequences, Correctives: 50–64. – National Academy of Sciences.

STSGDF, Survey Team of Spawning Grounds of Domestic Fishes in Yangtze River, 1982: An investigation of spawning grounds of Chinese carp after the construction of the Gezhouba Dam on the Yangtze River. – *J. Fish. China* **6:** 287–303. (In Chinese).

WANG, J., 1981: An estimation of the potential productivity and stocking rate of fingerling of silver and black carp in Dong Hu by means of phytoplankton production. – *J. Fish. China* **5:** 343–350. (In Chinese).

WETZEL, R. G., 1975: Limnology: 743 pp. – Saunders Company, Philadelphia.

YI, B. L., 1982: Fish Ecology. – Huazhong Agricultural College. (In Chinese).

YIH, P. L., 1964: Ecological conditions for natural spawning of carp in the Yangtze River. – *Acta Hydrobiol. Sinica* **5:** 1–15. (In Chinese).

ZHANG, H., 1983: A plan for increasing fisheries production in Hubei Province. – Internal Publication, Hubei Provincial Fisheries Institute, Wuhan. (In Chinese).

ZHANG, Z. X., 1983: Effects for increasing fish production by planting vegetation in Paizhong Lake. – *Hubei Fishery* **3:** 32–36. (In Chinese).

Authors' addresses:

HONG ZHANG, Division of Ecology and Fisheries, Hubei Provincial Fisheries Institute, Wuhan, P.R. China.

WILLIAM Y. B. CHANG, Division of International Programs, National Science Foundation, Washington D.C. 20550, USA.
and Centre for Great Lakes and Aquatic Sciences, University of Michigan, Ann Arbor, Michigan 48109, USA.

Mitt. Internat. Verein. Limnol.	24	231–235	Stuttgart, Februar 1994

An assessment of the impact of fish stocking on lake eutrophication in China

Jiankang Liu and Shaolian Chen

Abstract

Fish stocking refers to the release of fish fingerlings into lakes or reservoirs and the harvesting of the resulting fish crop from these waters as a routine practice. Plankton-feeding fish species such as Silver carp (*Hypophthalmichthys molitrix*) and Bighead carp (*Aristichthys nobilis*) are stocked commonly in Chinese lakes, and the juvenile fish subsist on natural food organisms present in the water column without artificial supplementary feeding. The nitrogen and phosphorus budgets of densely-stocked East Lake in Wuhan were determined using data from a routine sampling programme and experimental investigations. This permitted quantification of the nitrogen and phosphorus dynamics of various compartments of the lake ecosystem: the filtered lake water; phytoplankton; zooplankton; organic detritus including bacteria; material ingested by fishes; fish urine and egesta; harvested fish crop; post-harvest fish biomass, and so on. In 1983, it was estimated that the fish population discharged 204.45 t of N and 7.52 t of P into the lake water in the form of nitrogenous wastes and egesta, amounting to 11.8% of the total N (1736.35 t) and 3.5% of the total P (215.00 t) in all of the lake seston. Compared to the total quantities of N (2272.65 t) and P (302.80 t) in circulation in the lake each year, the contribution made by fish excreta is rather minor (9.0% N and 2.5% P). During the same year, 830 t of fish were harvested from the lake; they contained 21.85 t of N and 4.75 t of P.

Introduction

Fish stocking – as undertaken in Chinese lakes – refers to the release of fish fingerlings into lakes or reservoirs, and the harvesting of fish crop from these waters as a routine yearly operation. It can be seen as a form of large-scale, extensive fish farming making use of natural waters (or reservoirs) rather than fish ponds (see also Zhang & Chang 1994). Plankton-feeding fish species such as Silver carp, *Hypophthalmichthys molitrix* (Cuvier & Valenciennes), and Bighead carp, *Aristichthys nobilis* (Richardson), have been used commonly for such stocking. One feature of fish stocking in Chinese lakes is that the fingerlings must feed on organisms already present in the water without any supplementary feeding, although in eutrophic lakes – which are widespread in China (see Jin 1994) – densities of plankton may be extremely high.

The effects of large-scale lake farming practices on eutrophication of Chinese lakes has been the subject of debate for some years (Liu 1984, see also Chang, 1994). It has been suggested that the dense populations of stocked fish would discharge large amounts of faeces and excreta into the water. This, and indeed all types of aquaculture, would accelerate the process of lake eutrophication and hence should be restricted or banned from certain water bodies. Others have argued that eutrophication can be attributed to excess nutrients which enter lakes in the form of waste water, resulting in elevated nitrogen (N) and phosphorus (P) levels and frequent algal blooms (see Jin 1994). Stocking the lake with plankton-feeding fishes might hold algal populations in check and, through harvesting of the fish crop, some of the excess N and P could be removed from the lake (see Zhang & Chang 1994). According to this view, large-scale aquaculture would retard or lessen the degree of eutrophication, and should therefore be encouraged. However, there are insufficient quantitative data to permit assessment of the influence (positive or negative) of aquaculture on lake eutrophication. This paper reports upon a new approach to assess the impact of fish stocking by taking the biological productivity of the seston into consideration; it may thus aid in clarifying the relationship between aquaculture and lake eutrophication.

The study lake

The East Lake (Dong-hu) in Wuhan (Hubei Province) has a surface area of 27.9 km^2, a volume of 62 million m^3, and a mean depth of 2.2 m increasing to 4.8 m in the deepest part (Fig. 1). Residence time of the lake water is 0.44 years. The lake is used for a number of purposes, including commercial fishery, and is now highly eutrophic. Large amounts of industrial and domestic waste water enter the lake reflecting rapid urbanization in the watershed due to an ever-increasing population and pressure for economic development. According to a survey carried out in 1979–1980, annual nutrient inflow into the lake was estimated at 536.3 t of N and 87.8 t of P, while only 213.1 t of N and 20.1 t of P were removed from the lake in that year through water extraction and harvest of fish. Clearly, the primary cause of lake eu-

0538-4680/94/0024-0231 $ 1.25

trophication was the 323.2 t of N and 67.7 t of P that remained in the lake during the year (ZHANG et al. 1984).

The annual harvest of fish from East Lake was generally low in the 1950s and 1960s, but began to rise steadily in the 1970s reaching a peak of 844.0 kg/ha/year in a 1470-ha sector of the lake (Fig. 2). During the past decade, the Institute of Hydrobiology, Chinese Academy of Sciences, has published a series of papers on the biology of East Lake dealing with the biomass and production of phytoplankton (WANG & SHEN 1981, JAO & ZHANG 1980), zooplankton (HUANG & HU 1984, 1989, CHEN 1985), and the trophic structure of the seston (LIN & LIU 1990). In addition, the feeding habits (CHEN 1982, CHEN et al. 1986, 1989), digestion (CHEN et al. 1985, 1990, CHEN & LIU 1989), defecation (CHEN et al. 1990), excretion (CHEN et al. 1991), muscle analysis (CHEN et al. 1983), and the role in the cycling of N and P of Silver carp and Bighead carp (CHEN et al. 1991) have been investigated, along with other aspects of the fish population of the lake (TATSUKAWA et al. 1986). Data from these studies have been used to estimate the amounts of N and P contained or produced in the various compartments (except the bottom deposits) of the East Lake ecosystem (Fig. 3).

Fig. 1. Sketch map of East Lake (Dong-hu), Wuhan: the major sampling sites in the lake (I, II) are shown also.

Calculation of N and P budgets for East Lake

The calculation of the N and P values for the three groups of seston requires some explanation. They were based on the average biomass of the gross seston in stations I and II of the East Lake (Fig. 1) during 1983; i.e. 663.5 mg/m³ for N and 82.0 mg/m³ for P (LIN & LIU [1990] give details). The allocation among the three groups of seston was 221 mg/m³ of N and 26.5 mg/m³ of P for phyto-

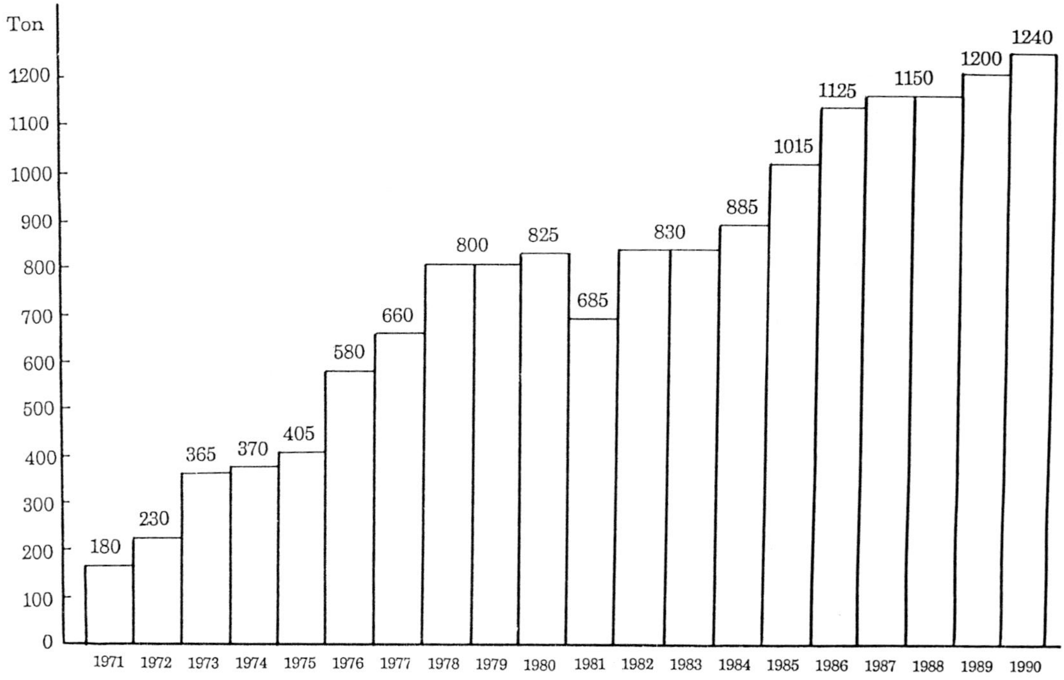

Fig. 2. Fish yields of the East Lake (Dong-hu) of Wuhan from 1971 to 1990.

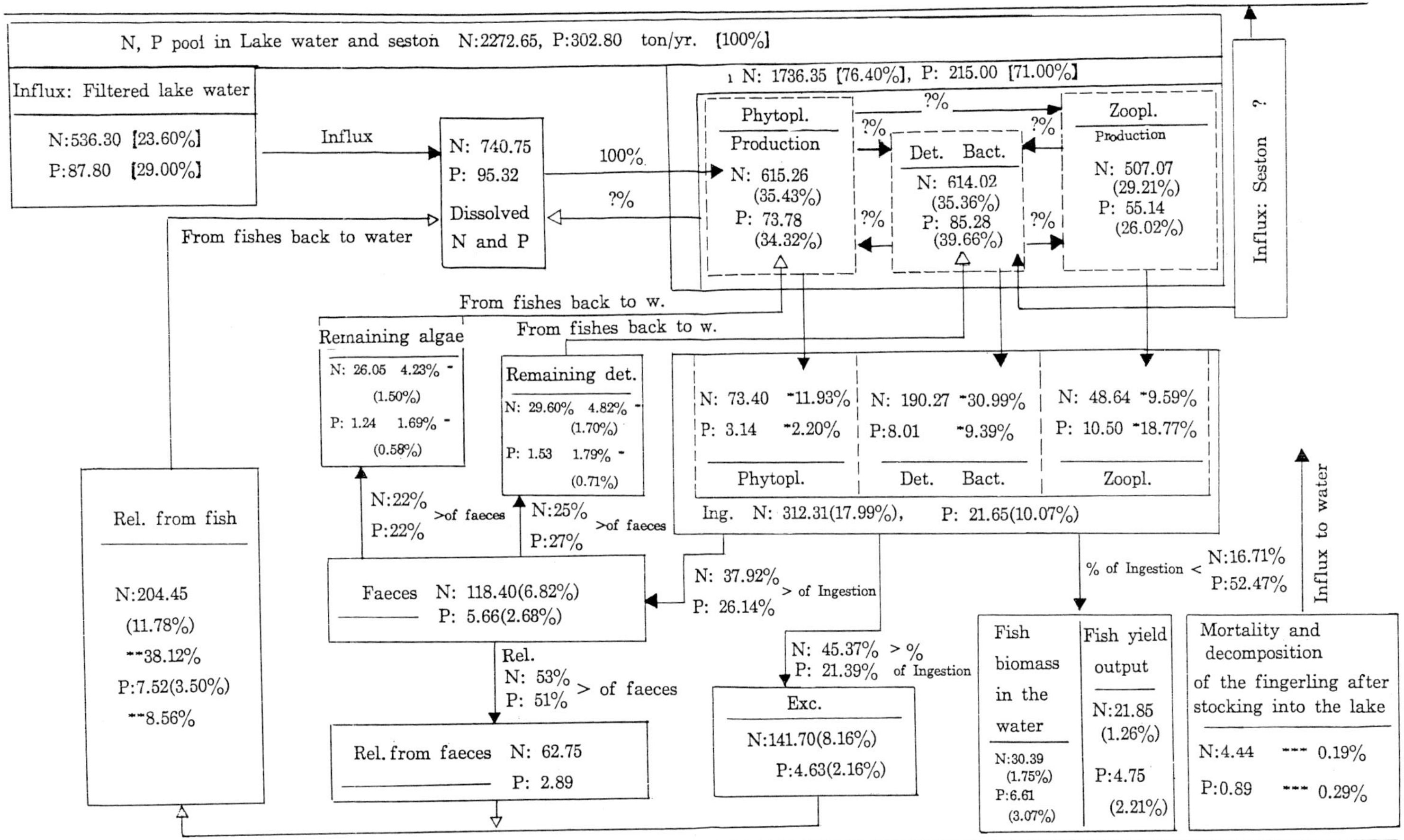

? unknown quantity; * % of N, P in each kind seston, ** % of N, P of filtered lake water *** % of N, P pool; ( ) % of N, P in seston

Fig. 3. The role of fishes in nitrogen and phosphorus cycling in the East Lake (Dong-hu) ecosystem.

plankton, 208.5 mg/m³ of N and 23.0 mg/m³ of P for zooplankton, and 234.0 mg/m³ of N and 32.5 mg/m³ of P for the particulate organic detritus (LIN & LIU, unpubl. data). The quantities of N and P were then converted to production per cubic metre per year by multiplying by the annual production/biomass coefficients of each group. For phytoplankton, a coefficient of 87 (JIAN WANG, unpubl. data) was used, which is much lower than the maximum value of 347 given by WANG & SHEN (1981). For zooplankton, a value of 76 (X. F. HUANG, unpubl. data) was adopted, and for particulate organic detritus – which is usually associated with bacteria – the mean of the phytoplankton and zooplankton coefficients (i.e. 82) was used. Each estimate was multiplied by the total volume of water in the lake (62 million m³ in 1983) to obtain the N and P production values of the lake seston in that year.

The dissolved N and P in the lake water, together with the N and P contained in the biological production of the three groups of seston, amounted to 2272.65 t/year and 302.80 t/year respectively (Fig. 3). N ingested by the fish population constituted 17.99% of the total seston N (1736.35 t) and 10.07% of the total P (215.00 t). Fish faeces and excretion released 204.45 t of N and 7.52 t of P into the lake, comprising 11.78% of N and 3.50% of P in the seston. It should be pointed out here that this component of N and P corresponded to the metabolic products of the ingested seston which were originally present in the lake ecosystem, and not an additional enrichment of an extraneous nature. Finally, knowledge of the total fish harvest of the lake (830 t in 1983), permitted estimation of the removal of N and P from the lake: 21.85 t of N and 4.75 t of P, constituting 1.26% of seston N and 2.21% of seston P respectively.

It is evident from Fig. 3 that the three groups of seston constituted the largest pools of N and P in East Lake. In the absence of data of sedimentary N and P, it is apparent that a reduction of the N and P loading of the lake water should be achieved most effectively by controlling the seston biomass rather than restricting fish stocking or extensive fish farming. However, the large-scale feeding and manuring practices that are associated with intensive aquaculture which use fish 'cages' or 'pens' would accelerate the process of eutrophication and water-quality deterioration in East Lake. Accordingly, limits to such fish-culture practises in the lake should be instituted.

It is important to emphasize that the conclusions about the effects of fish stocking in East Lake were derived mainly from experiments on Silver carp and Bighead carp, which might not be applicable to other species of fish. Indeed, experience with Grass carp has shown us that the 'free-ranching' of Grass carp (*Ctenopharyngodon idella* [CUVIER & VALENCIENNES]) had disastrous consequences for aquatic vascular plants in the lake, and led to an enormous development of phytoplankton. Clearly, the impact of stocking Grass carp upon lake eutrophication would be entirely different from that of plankton feeders (see also ZHANG & CHANG 1994).

References

CHANG, W. Y. B., 1994: Management of shallow tropical lakes using integrated lake farming. – Mitt. Internat. Verein. Limnol. **24:**219–224.

CHEN, S. L., 1982: Feeding habit analysis for the fingerlings of Silver carp and Bighead stocked in the Dong-hu lake. – *Reservoir Fisheries* **3:**21–26. (In Chinese).

CHEN, S. L., HU, C. L. & HUA, Y. Y., 1983: Analysis of biochemical composition of muscle in *Hypophthalmichthys molitrix* and *Aristichthys nobilis*. – *Acta Hydrobiol. Sinica* **8:**125–132. (In Chinese, abstract in English).

CHEN, S. L., HU, C. L., TIAN, L. & SUN, X. W., 1985: Study on the digestion and utilization of *Daphnia hyalina* by fingerlings of Silver carp and Bighead. – *Transactions of the Chinese Icthyological Society* **4:**163–170. (In Chinese, abstract in English).

CHEN, S. L., HU, C. L. & ZHANG, S. Y., 1986: Feeding intensity of Silver carp and Bighead under natural condition. I. Feeding intensity of fingerlings of Silver carp and Bighead in summer. – *Acta Hydrobiol. Sinica* **10:**277–285. (In Chinese, abstract in English).

CHEN, S. L., HUA, Y. Y., ZHU, Z. R. & TIAN, L., 1989: Feeding intensity of Silver carp and Bighead under natural condition. II. Annual feeding intensity of Silver carp and Bighead in Donghu Lake, Wuhan. – *Acta Hydrobiol. Sinica* **13:**114–123. (In Chinese, abstract in English).

CHEN, S. L. & LIU, X. F., 1989: Study on the digestion and utilization of fish faeces by Silver carp and Bighead fingerlings. – *Acta Hydrobiol. Sinica* **13:**250–258. (In Chinese, abstract in English).

CHEN, S. L., HU, C. L., LIU, X. F. & TIAN, L., 1990: On the digestion and utilization of *Microcystis aeruginosa* by fingerlings of Silver carp and Bighead. – *Acta Hydrobiol. Sinica* **14:**49–59. (In Chinese, abstract in English).

CHEN, S. L., LIU, X. F. & HUA, L., 1991: The role of Silver carp and Bighead in the cycling of nitrogen and phosphorus in the East lake ecosystem. – *Acta Hydrobiol. Sinica* **15:** 8–26. (In Chinese, abstract in English).

CHEN, X. M., 1985: A preliminary study on biomass and production of Copepoda in Lake Donghu, Wuhan. – *Acta Hydrobiol. Sinica* **9:** 144–158. (In Chinese, abstract in English).

HUANG, X. F. & HU, C. Y., 1984: Population dynamics and production of *Daphnia hyalina* and *Daphnia carinata* in Donghu Lake, Wuhan. – *Acta Hydrobiol. Sinica* **8:** 405–417. (In Chinese, abstract in English).

– – 1989: Population dynamics and production of *Polyarthra trigla* in Donghu Lake, Wuhan. – *Acta Hydrobiol. Sinica* **13:** 15–23. (In Chinese, abstract in English).

JAO, C. C. & ZHANG, Z. S., 1980: Ecological changes of phytoplankton in Lake Donghu, Wuhan, during 1956–1975 and the eutrophication problem. – *Acta Hydrobiol. Sinica* **7:** 1–8. (In Chinese, abstract in English).

JIN, X., 1994: An analysis of lake eutrophication in China. – *Mitt. Internat. Verein. Limnol.* **24:** 207–211.

LIN, W. L. & LIU, X. Z., 1990: Trophic structure of the seston in Donghu lake ecosystem, Wuhan. – *Oceanol. Limnol. Sinica* **21:** 411–417. (In Chinese, abstract in English).

LIU, J. K., 1984: Lakes of the middle and lower basins of the Chang Jiang (China). – In: TAUB, F. B. (ed.): Lakes and Reservoirs: 331–355. – Elsevier Science Publishers, The Netherlands.

TATSUKAWA, K., ZHU, Z. R. & MIURA, T., 1986: Studies on acoustic estimation of fish populations in Lake Dong-hu. – *Acta Hydrobiol. Sinica* **10:** 311–326. (In Chinese, abstract in English).

WANG, J. & SHEN, G. H., 1981: The primary production of the phytoplankton of Lake Donghu and its correlation with various ecological factors. – *Acta Hydrobiol. Sinica* **7:** 295–311. (In Chinese, abstract in English).

ZHANG, H. & CHANG, W. Y. B., 1994: Management of inland fisheries in shallow eutrophic, mesotrophic and oligotrophic lakes in China. – *Mitt. Internat. Verein. Limnol.* **24:** 225–229.

ZHANG, S. Y., LIU Q. X. & HUANG, Y. T., 1984: The main sources of nitrogen and phosphorus in Lake Donghu, Wuhan. – *Oceanol. Limnol. Sinica* **15:** 203–213. (In Chinese, abstract in English).

Authors' address:

Institute of Hydrobiology, The Chinese Academy of Sciences, Wuhan, Hubei Province, 430072, P.R. China.

Mitt. Internat. Verein. Limnol.	24	237–242	Stuttgart, Februar 1994

Management of Jiangxi Poyang Lake National Nature Reserve, China

David S. Melville

Abstract

Poyang Lake is the largest freshwater lake in the People's Republic of China. It receives water from five main rivers flowing directly to the lake, as well as back-flooding from the Chang Jiang (Yangtze) River. In summer, when water levels are some 11 m higher than in winter, the lake floods much of the surrounding area. In autumn, when water levels drop, small shallow lakes and grassy wetlands emerge. The lake is an internationally-important site for waterfowl as well as being of national importance for two mammal species. The Jiangxi Poyang Lake National Nature Reserve in the northwest of the lake supports over one hundred thousand waterfowl in winter, including some 95% of the world population of Siberian cranes, *Grus leucogeranus*. The grasslands and shallow lakes within the Reserve are heavily utilized by local residents for fishing, grass cutting and livestock grazing. The impacts of these activities on wildlife are discussed, together with possible impacts of major watershed-management projects.

Characteristics of Poyang Lake and surroundings

Poyang Lake is situated on the south bank of the Chang Jiang (Yangtze) River, in northern Jiangxi Province, People's Republic of China, at about 28°22'–29°50'N, 115°47'–116°45'E. Poyang Lake is the largest freshwater lake in China today, although Dong Ting Lake in Hunan Province held that title until extensive reclamation reduced its size. Poyang Lake is 170 km from north to south, with an average width of some 17 km, and a shoreline of 1,200 km. As a result of seasonal drawdown some 330,000 ha of 'littoral' wetlands are formed (Anon 1988, Melville et al. 1992).

Poyang Lake has a subtropical wet monsoon climate, with warm wet summers and cool dry winters. Frosts seldom occur in winter. The minimum temperature recorded in the period 1983–1985 was −4.9 °C, with a summer maximum of approximately 30 °C. Average total annual rainfall is about 1,700 mm, most falling between April and September. Snow fall in winter is rare, and only 3–7 mm are recorded. Winds are predominantly from the north in winter and south in summer. They are often strong, especially in the northern area of the lake where wind is funnelled through the channel leading south from the Chang Jiang.

Poyang Lake basin was formed about 3 million years ago when three large fault groups gave rise to a depression. During the last glaciation some 18,000 years BP the estimated sea level was about 120–130 m below the present level. At that time the bed of the Chang Jiang was much steeper than today and a trough 40 m deep formed at Jiujiang through which the present 'Poyang Lake' drained. Run off to the Chang Jiang was rapid and no lake could form in the Poyang depression. Following warming during the interglacial, the sea level gradually rose to its present level, erosion of the Chang Jiang bed stopped and deposition started. Differences in the level between the Chang Jiang and Poyang Lake were reduced and – starting in the 15th century – the present Poyang Lake was formed gradually. By the 18th century, the lake had reached its present form.

The hydrology of Poyang Lake is complex. The catchment of the lake covers 162,200 km², or some 97.2% of the total area of Jiangxi Province. From February to June inflow exceeds outflow, and between July and January outflow exceeds inflow. The rate of outflow is determined by the water level in the 'Five Rivers' flowing into the Lake (Gan Jiang, Xiu Shui, Xin Jiang, Fu He and Rao He) and that in the Chang Jiang. The maximum outflow is 28,800 m³/s, whilst the minimum is negative due to back-flow from the Chang Jiang – up to 9,450 m³/s. The annual discharge to the Chang Jiang is 134,700 million m³. At a water level of 21.690 m (summer flood) the surface of the lake covers 3,210.22 km² with a capacity of 25,170 million m³, whilst at the winter low of some 9 m it covers only 216.62 km² with a capacity of 460 million m³. On average there is a 10-day turnover period for the lake (Anon 1988).

Silt input to Poyang Lake is largely from the 'Five Rivers'. Each year 21,040,000 t of silt are brought to the lake but half of this is transferred to the Chang Jiang, the rest settling out in Poyang Lake to give an annual average rate of silt build up of 1.7 mm over the lake bed.

Water quality in the lake is generally considered to be quite good, with only local problems of organic pollution, heavy metals (Copper, zinc, lead) and phenols (although the situation deteriorates in the low-water season). The most heavily polluted area is in the southern part of the lake which receives domestic sewage from the provincial capital Nanchang, and the Rao He which

0538-4680/94/0024-0237 $ 1.50

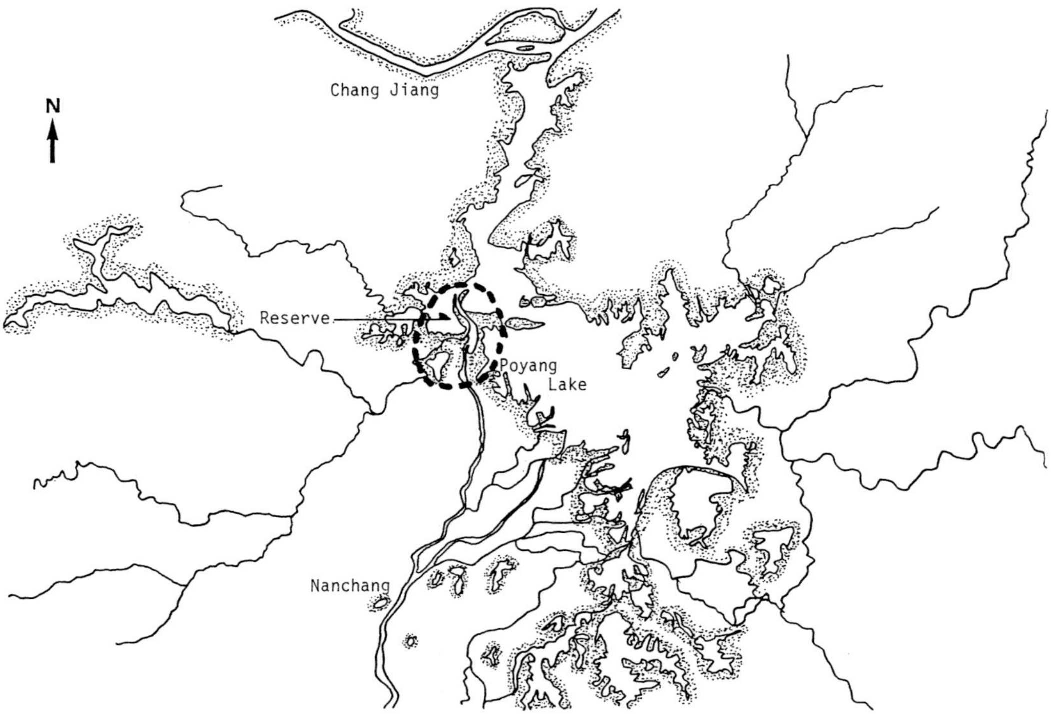

Fig. 1. Location of Poyang Lake National Nature Reserve.

carries waste from the largest copper mine in China, which is situated on the upper reaches. The least-polluted area of the lake is in the northwest (ANON 1988).

Poyang Reserve

Jiangxi Poyang Lake National Nature Reserve (herafter referred to as Poyang Reserve) is located in the northwest corner of Poyang Lake, near the town of Wucheng, at the confluence of the Gan Jiang and Xiu Shui Rivers (Fig. 1). The Reserve, which covers 22,400 ha, was first declared as a provincial-level reserve in 1983, and was upgraded to a national-level reserve in 1988.

The Reserve is essentially flat, being some 11–12 m a.s.l. Water regimes follow those in the main lake. The entire area is under water during the summer except for a few small hills and man-made islands. Once water levels fall below about 17 m a.s.l. in the autumn, land starts to appear and smaller lakes form (Fig. 2).

Vegetation

The vegetation within the Reserve is strongly influenced by water-level fluctuations during the course of the year. The result is a series of communities ringing the lakes at slightly different elevations. A brief survey of the Reserve's flora has been undertaken by WU et al. (1987), who recognised 16 communities. The aquatic zones are characterized by species such as *Vallisneria spiralis, Hydrilla verticillata, Najas* spp., *Potamogeton crispus* and *Potamogeton malaianus, Polygonum hydropiper* and *Ceratophyllum demersum*. Emergent vegetation around the lake margins includes *Eleocharis yokoscensis, Miscanthus sacchariflorus, Scirpus* spp., *Carex* spp., *Astragalus sinica, Artemisia selenegensis,* and *Potentilla kleiiana*. In a few areas there are stands of *Phragmites communis*. Since 1985 there has been extensive planting of the exotic tree *Populus italica* on land above 17 m above sea level around some of the lakes.

Human habitation and land use

The Reserve is surrounded by 40 villages with a total population of some 13,000. The town of Wucheng has a further 3,800 residents. The majority of these people depend upon the Reserve for their livelihood to a greater or lesser extent.

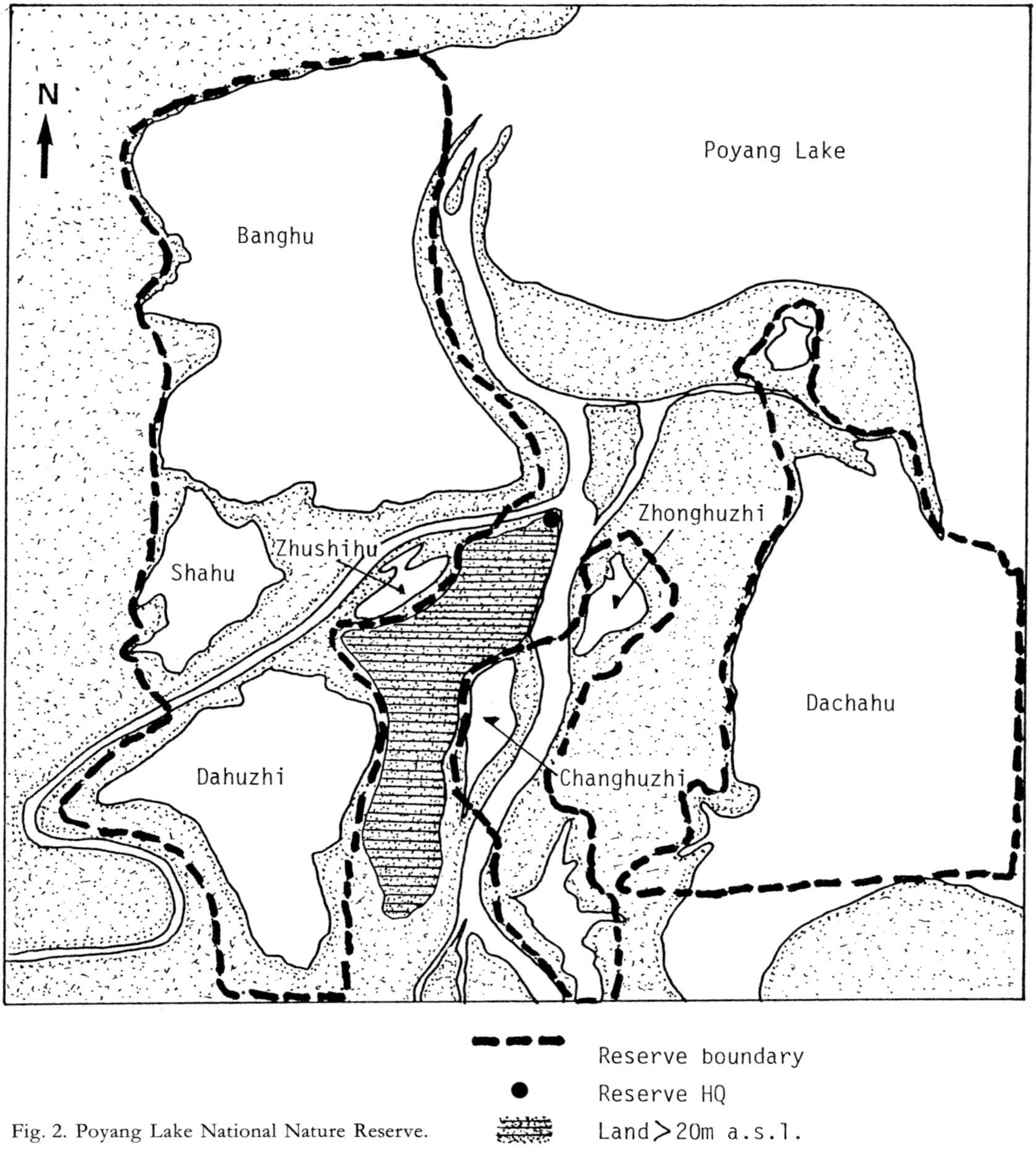

Fig. 2. Poyang Lake National Nature Reserve.

Grassland areas are divided between villages and families. As water levels fall in the autumn and land becomes exposed, people soon move out to the grasslands and start cutting the vegetation. Grass cutting is rapid but, due to the large areas involved, lasts several months (October through December), during which time temporary shelters are established in which grass-cutters live. The cut material, which is removed by boat, is used principally as a cooking fuel and, to a lesser extent, for paper making. *Phragmites,* in particular, is used for this purpose. Total annual harvests are estimated to be 2.23–3.00 t/ha.

Once grass cutting has started, Water buffalo (*Bubalus bubalis*) are brought into the cleared areas to graze. Villages around the Reserve currently have some 2,500 buffalo, most of which graze on the Reserve during the winter. Herds of 100–200 are not uncommon. There is limited grass growth during the winter, but in spring (March) a second cut is made for green fertilizer which is applied to vegetable fields on higher ground.

Fishes

A total of 122 species of fish have been recorded from Poyang Lake of which 11 are of major economic importance; two of these, *Cyprinus carpio* and *Carassius auratus,* account for 40–50% of the total catch. Fishing takes place throughout the Reserve. In summer, due to the deep water, fishing is done with nets, traps and, to a lesser extent, with trained Cormorants *Phalacrocorax carbo*. In autumn, as water levels drop below the levels of the dykes, nine lakes appear within the Reserve. Fish in these lakes are harvested by draining the lakes and capturing the fishes with nets at sluices and weirs. In winter, the lakes are very shallow and fish stocks have been depleted; accordingly, fishing activities are confined largely to the rivers. In addition to fish, shrimps and freshwater mussels are harvested also.

Total annual fish catches throughout Poyang Lake declined considerably from the 1960s to the 1970s (Hou 1989), from a high of 22,670 t (in the early 1960s) to 15,400 t (late 1960s) and 12,720 t (late 1970s). Catches have increased recently, totalling 25,000 t in 1988 (Hou 1989). Reduced catches resulted from mismanagement, overfishing, and wide-scale poisoning to control the snail *Oncomelania hupensis,* which is an intermediate host for the blood fluke *Schistosoma japonica*. Catches within the Reserve also declined, the proportion of 'large' fish in the harvest dropping from 80–90% in 1977 to 25–50% in 1983. Legislation now restricts fishing in the Reserve and there is a closed season between 20 March and 20 June in Banghu and Shahu.

Birds

Poyang Lake supports large populations of waterfowl in winter (Anon 1988, Melville et al. 1992), including significant populations of globally rare species, and thus is of major importance for conservation of biodiversity. The Reserve was initially established following the discovery of large numbers of Siberian cranes (*Grus leucogeranus*); some 95% of the world population winters at the Reserve. Other species of global importance are White-naped crane (*Grus vipio*) and Eastern white stork (*Ciconia* [*Ciconia*] *boyciana*). The Reserve supports the largest known concentration of Swan geese (*Anser cygnoides*) in the world, and over 40,000 individuals were recorded by Kennerley (1987). The wintering population of Japanese marsh warblers (*Megalurus pryeri*) is of national importance, as are the numbers of Tundra's swan (*Cygnus columbarius*), Hooded crane (*Grus monacha*) and Great bustard (*Otis tarda*). Numbers of wintering ducks and geese regularly exceed 100,000. Formerly, these were subject to extensive harvesting by punt gunning and netting. Since the establishment of the Reserve, however, wildfowling has been prohibited but netting and poisoning still continue. In 1986 the People's Daily and China Daily newspapers reported that over 200,000 ducks were poisoned in Poyang County alone during the winter of 1985/86. In winter 1990/91, too, there was extensive poisoning of waterfowl on the Reserve. Waterfowl killed in this way are usually safe for human consumption if gutted carefully, but human fatalities do occur.

Chemical control programmes to reduce populations of *Oncomelania hupensis* (and hence to reduce the incidence of schistosomiasis) which resulted in incidental fish mortality, led to reductions in waterfowl populations reflecting both reduced prey densities and direct poisoning of birds.

Grass cutting in the Poyang Reserve benefits various waterfowl, notably the White-fronted goose (*Anser albifrons*). The removal of tall vegetation results in a short grass sward which is favoured for grazing by this goose. In spring, White-fronted geese at Poyang Reserve feed selectively on freshly-cut areas of grass where there is new growth; these sites are likely to be an important source of material for building up body reserves of the geese before they migrate northwards. Another species which may benefit from removal of tall vegetation is the Great bustard which feeds largely on the short herb *Potentilla kleiniana* (Ding 1988).

Extensive cutting of vegetation is probably a long-established activity around Poyang Lake, and thus those species which are sensitive to such disturbance would have been eliminated. For example, the little-known Chinese parrotbill (*Paradoxornis heudei*), which formerly occurred in reed beds lower down the Chang Jiang (La Touche 1906), has now disappeared. Poyang Reserve still provides wintering grounds for another poorly-known species, the Japanese marsh warbler (*Megalurus pryeri*), which may have been more numerous in the past.

Mammals

The avifauna is the best studied component of the Poyang Reserve fauna. Inventories of many other groups are incomplete or totally lacking. However, there are at least two mammals of conservation importance: the Chinese water deer (*Hydropotes inermis*) and the Black finless porpoise (*Neophocaena phocaenoides*). Nothing is known of the habits of the latter within the Poyang Reserve, but the former has been the subject of some studies at Poyang (Sun & Sheng 1990, Xiao & Sheng 1990). The porpoise may suffer from boat traffic on the rivers, as does the Baiji or Whitefin dolphin (*Lipotes vexillifer*) along the Chang Jiang. The Chinese water deer is still hunted, and Sun & Sheng (1990) note that numbers have been reduced due to a lack of safe refuges during the flood season. Widespread cutting of tall vegetation in the autumn may also affect the animals adversely.

Management of the Poyang Reserve

Proposals for management-related research at the Reserve include the establishment of exclosures and manipulation of vegetation to allow a better understanding of the inter-relationships between vegetation cutting and grazing by buffalo and geese, as well as assessing the potential value of retaining uncut vegetation.

The current fishing practice, whereby lakes are totally drained in the early winter period, appears to be generally deleterious for fish populations, and the impact on wintering waterfowl is often severe. Thus abundant fish are available for only a limited period, restricting the food available for birds such as Dalmatian pelicans (*Pelecanus crispus*) and Eastern white storks and forcing them to leave the Reserve as fish are depleted. The consequent drying of mud on the lake bottoms results in birds having increasing difficulty in digging up the roots, rhizomes and tubers of plants such as *Potamogeton malaianus* and *Vallisneria spiralis,* which account for up to 90% of the winter food of Siberian canes (Liu & Chen 1991) and are important for other species such as Swan geese. These birds are forced to seek food outside the Reserve boundaries where they are more likely to fall victim to hunters.

As is usual with nature reserves in China, the Poyang Reserve Management Office currently has no control over any land use activities within the Reserve boundaries. Control is restricted to enforcing a no-hunting policy. The Jiangxi Nature Reserve Management Office, however, is now in the final stages of negotiations for the take-over of two lakes within the Reserve. This is a most important action as it will allow the Reserve to manage these areas in future, including controlling drawdown to ensure that conditions for waterfowl are optimal.

The long-term future of the Reserve is uncertain in the face of various water-management projects currently under consideration. In March 1992 the 5th Session of the 7th Chinese National People's Congress agreed, despite unprecedented opposition, that China should build the Three Gorges Dam on the Chang Jiang at Sandouping. This project will have downstream impacts which, on currently available information, can (at best) only be guessed at. The 1989 Canadian-funded feasibility study (Anon 1989) failed to address many important issues (Larson 1989). The complex hydrological relationships which characterise Poyang Lake are likely to be affected by changes in flow patterns in the Chang Jiang, and preliminary Chinese studies suggest that suitable feeding habitats for waterfowl at Poyang Reserve may be reduced by one third to one half unless water levels can be controlled within the reserve (Zhu et al. 1987, Melville et al. 1992).

Three additional water-control projects have been proposed for Poyang Lake. These include a dam across the narrow channel, which connects the Lake to the Chang Jiang, for purposes of power generation. This option would result in the total loss of the reserve due to permanent flooding, unless dykes were constructed and pumps installed to allow lowering of water levels in autumn and winter. A barrage to enclose the southern two-thirds of the lake for power generation has been proposed also; it would permanently flood the eastern part of the reserve, and probably reduce water flow in the Gan Jiang in winter. An additional proposal to construct two storage reservoirs to be filled at times of high flood risk so as to reduce the water level in the main lake, would result in the loss of only Dacha Hu in the east of the reserve. Until a decision on the implementation of these projects is undertaken, the fate and long-term viability of the Poyang Reserve remains in jeopardy.

Acknowledgements

The information contained in this paper has been obtained during a series of visits to Poyang Lake National Nature Reserve between 1987 and 1991 as part of

WWF's on-going support to the Reserve. Of particular importance was the October 1989 workshop which resulted in the drafting of a management plan for the Reserve. I wish to thank the many people who have worked with me at Poyang over the years, particularly Wang Baojin, Song Xiangjin and the late Ding Teiming.

References

ANON, 1988: Studies on Poyang Lake: 573 pp. – Shanghai Scientific and Technical Publishers, Shanghai. (In Chinese).

– 1989: The Three Gorges Water Control Project Feasibility Study. Volume 1. Feasibility Report. – Canadian International Development Agency, Ottawa. (No pagination).

DING, T., 1988: Wintering ecology of the Great bustard *Otis tarda*. – *Chinese Wildlife* 1988 (4):9–10. (In Chinese).

KENNERLEY, P. R., 1987: A survey of the birds of the Poyang Lake Nature Reserve, Jiangxi Province, China, 29 December 1985 – 4 January 1986. – *Hong Kong Bird Report* 1984/1985:97–111.

LARSON, J. S., 1989: Downstream environmental impacts. In: RYDER, G. (ed.): Damming the Three Gorges – What the Dam-builders Don't Want You to Know: 67–78. – Probe International, Toronto.

LA TOUCHE, J. J. D., 1906: Field-notes on the birds of Chinkiang, Lower Yangtse basin. Part 1. – *Ibis* 1906:427–450.

LIU, U. & CHEN, B., 1991: The wintering ecology of the Siberian Crane. – In: HARRIS, J. (ed.): Proceedings 1987 International Crane Workshop: 109–111. – International Crane Foundation, Baraboo.

MELVILLE, D. S., MACKINNON, J. R., WANG, B., WANG, H. & SONG, X., 1992: Management Plan for Jiangxi Poyang Lake National Nature Reserve. – Ministry of Forestry People's Republic of China/ WWF: 130 pp. – World Wide Fund for Nature, Hong Kong.

SUN, L. & SHENG, H., 1990: Chinese water deer at the areas of Poyang Lake. – *J. East China Normal Univ. (Mammalian Ecology Suppl.)* 21–26. (In Chinese).

XIAO, B. & SHENG, H., 1990: Home range and activity patterns of Chinese Water Deer (*Hydropotes inermis*) in Poyang Lake region. – *J. East China Normal Univ. (Mammalian Ecology Suppl.)* 27–36. (In Chinese).

ZHU, H., SHEN, G., YU, Y., ZHANG, L. & WANG, Y., 1987: Prediction of impacts of the Three Gorges Project on the ecological function and environment of Poyang Lake. Essays on the impacts and strategies of the Three Gorges Project to the environment and ecology: 319–332. – Science Press, Beijing. (In Chinese).

Author's address:

WWF – World Wide Fund for Nature Hong Kong, GPO Box 12721, Hong Kong.

Mitt. Internat. Verein. Limnol.	**24**	243–249	Stuttgart, Februar 1994

Long-term phytoplankton changes in a tropical reservoir

A. Anton

Abstract

An understanding of the processes controlling primary production is necessary for effective conservation and management of lakes and reservoirs. Phytoplankton populations, limnological parameters and nutrient status have been monitored in the Pansoon Reservoir, Hulu Langat (Malaysia) – which has a mean depth of 30 m and a surface area of 130 km^2 – over a ten-year period. Recent data indicate a deterioration in water quality, with a dominance of chlorophytes and frequent occurrence of dinoflagellate blooms. Results from 1987–1990 are compared with data obtained during the initial stages of impoundment in order to determine the causal factors which triggered a rise in primary productivity. Nitrate-nitrogen and phosphate levels have increased ten- and four-fold, respectively, during the past ten years. The phytoplankton composition has shifted from an equal dominance of chlorophytes and cryptophytes in 1981 to a dominance by chlorophytes only. An increase in the supply of allochthonous nutrients to the lake is the probable explanation for the progressive rise in phytoplankton densities during recent years.

Two rivers draining into the reservoir are responsible for a large input of nutrients during the rainy season. Seasonal changes in phytoplankton populations result from competitive interactions as reflected in the dominance of dinoflagellates during the dry season when nutrient levels are low. The results of this study will contribute towards formulation of management strategies for Malaysian reservoirs.

Introduction

A deterioration in lake water quality and trophic status is often reflected by changes in phytoplankton communities. Consequently, phytoplankton are the most commonly-used indicator of pollution and eutrophication in lakes. Regular monitoring of these communities, combined with a good understanding of the factors underlying the rise and decline of individual phytoplankton taxa, can provide an important basis for management and conservation of lakes and man-made impoundments.

Limnological studies at the Pansoon Dam began in 1981, a year after impoundment. Subsequent studies in the reservoir were carried out in 1987 and 1990 and have continued since, with the purpose of understanding the interactions between water quality and biological processes in tropical reservoirs. This paper describes phytoplankton changes in Pansoon Reservoir over a ten-year period, and attempts to determine the factors causing such changes. Long-term studies such as these generate information which is useful for the development of predictive models which can assist in forecasting effects of different reservoir-management strategies.

Study area

Pansoon Reservoir (3°12′N, 112°26′E) is situated approximately 25 km south east of Kuala Lumpur, in the Hulu Langat district, Malaysia (Fig. 1). It has a holding capacity of approximately 23 million m^3, a surface area of 130 km^2, and mean and maximum depths of 30 m and 50 m, respectively. Mean annual precipitation in the Hulu Langat area is 2500 mm; April–July are the driest months and October–January are the wettest.

The Pansoon Reservoir was constructed in 1980 by the damming of the Langat River which has a catchment area of 1,238 km^2. Approximately 45% of the catchment area is steep hill country (maximum altitude 1, 524 m). Most of the upper reaches of the river is covered with forest which was logged in the late 1970s and early 1980s. Effects of the logging are evident from a comparison of the sediment loads of the river in 1979 and 1984. For example, total suspended solids loads in the impoundment ranged from 11–184 mg/l in 1979/80 to 10–80 mg/l in 1984 (Sarmani & Hamzah 1989).

Limnological investigations of Pansoon Reservoir began in 1980; phytoplankton and nutrients were monitored from June to December 1980, while water temperatures and dissolved oxygen were monitored from September 1980 to December 1981. Sampling phytoplankton was resumed from August 1990 through August 1991; data on nutrients (June–December) and dissolved oxygen and temperature (August 1990–May 1991) are available for part of that period.

Methods

Water samples for phytoplankton and chemical analyses were taken monthly at 2 m depth from two stations (Fig. 1) in the reservoir using a 5-litre horizontal van Dorn sampler. Temperature and dissolved oxygen profiles of the water column were determined using a YSI

0538-4680/94/0024-0243 $ 1.75

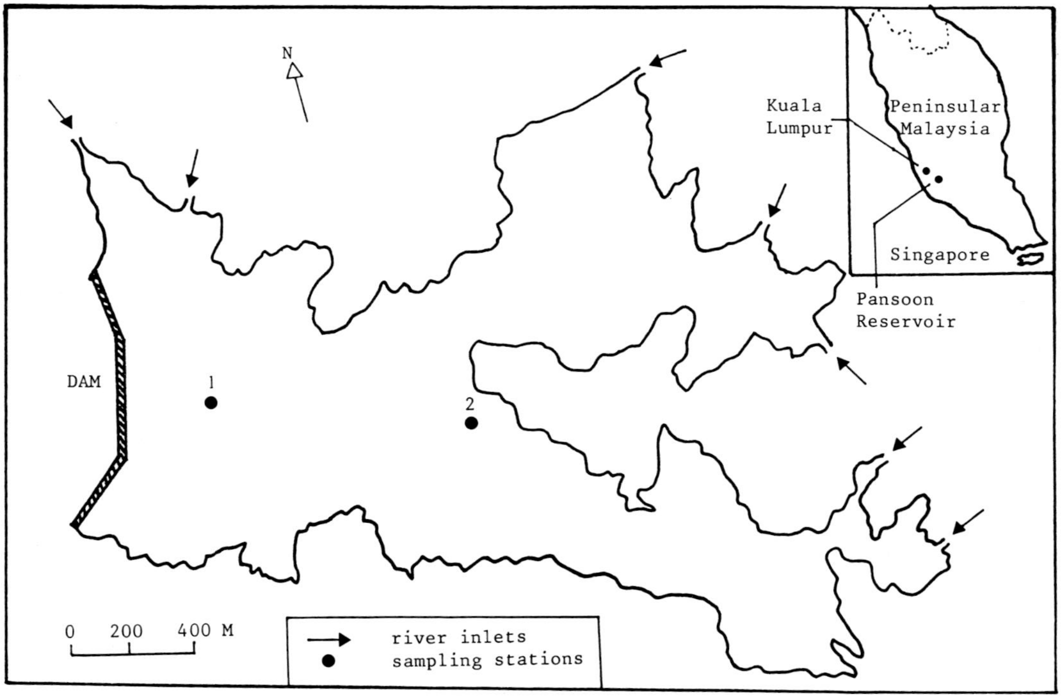

Fig. 1. Pansoon Reservoir, Hulu Langat, Malaysia, showing the sampling stations and river inlets.

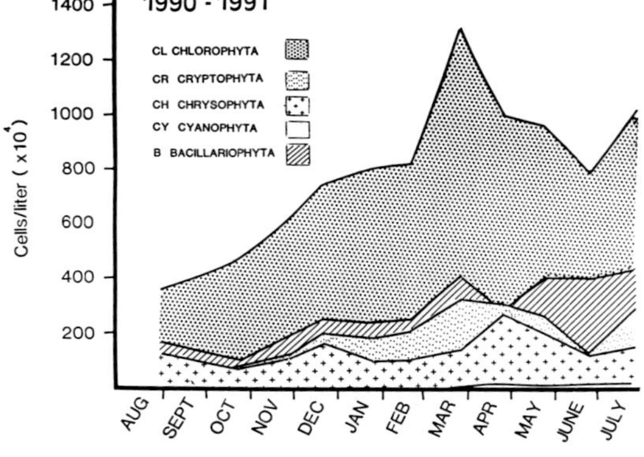

Fig. 2. Phytoplankton densities in the euphotic zone of Pansoon Reservoir, showing species composition in 1981 and 1991.

dissolved-oxygen meter. Specific conductance, pH, and turbidity of surface water were measured using a YSI conductivity-salinity-temperature meter, an ORION pH meter and a secchi disc, respectively. Samples for nitrogen and phosphorus determinations were preserved in the field by acidifying with hydrochloric acid to approximately pH 2. Phosphate-phosphorus concentrations were determined calorimetrically using the molybdenum-blue method and nitrate-nitrogen using phenoldisulphonic acid (APHA 1985). Phytoplankton samples were preserved with Lugol's iodine and sedimented to concentrate the samples. Cells were identified and counted, after further sedimentation in 10-ml Utermohl chambers, using a Nikon (Diaphot) inverted microscope.

Results

Phytoplankton densities in the euphotic zone of Pansoon reservoir increased three fold over ten years from a maximum density of 4,840,000 cells/l in 1981 to 13,100,000 cells/l in 1991. Percent dominance of Chlorophyceae, the most abundant class of phytoplankton, increased from 48.2–53.0% in 1981 to 55.5–62.6% in 1991 (Fig. 2). Cryptophyceae, which was the second most abundant class with percentage dominance of 20.0–42.3% in 1981, was replaced by Bacillariophyceae in 1990–1991 which made up 13.8–18.3% of total phytoplankton density. The diatoms made up <1% of the phytoplankton during the initial stages of impoundment. The desmid, *Euastrum turgidum,* was the most abundant phytoplankton species comprising 9.1% of the total in 1991, but was ranked third in 1981 (Tables 1 and 2). At that time, *Cryptomonas erosa* was the most abundant species (15.2%) followed by *Staurastrum chaetoceros* (12.3%). In 1990–1991, desmids made up most of the Chlorophyceae, while the dinoflagellates constituted more than 78% of the Chrysophyceae and – on occasions – formed dense red scum on the water surface. Dinoflagellate populations peaked in April–May 1991. The dominant taxa in the reservoir changed from a initial composition of cryptophytes, chrysophytes and desmids in 1981 to a flora made up mostly by desmids and diatoms in 1991.

Temperature and oxygen profiles indicate that lake-mixing patterns after impoundment and in 1990–1991 were similar (Fig. 3). The lake was stratified for most of the year and oxygen concentrations fell dramatically below 5 m forming a permanently anoxic layer at the bottom of the reservoir. Oxygen was present in the bottom layers during the wettest periods of the year (December–January and March–April) although the reservoir waters remained stratified. This suggests that the two rivers which drain into the reservoir create turbulence in the deeper water.

Dissolved-oxygen concentrations ranged between 5.4–8.8 mg/l in the upper 3 m of water during 1981 but were lower (0.9–11.2 mg/l) in 1990–1991 (Fig. 3). Surface temperatures showed slight variations of ≤1.5 °C over the same ten-year period. In 1981, however, there was a slightly larger difference (Fig. 4) between surface and bottom temperatures (24–29 °C) compared to the later study (24–27.5 °C). Nevertheless, the isotherms indicate that any mixing which occurred was not sufficient to overturn the whole lake. The depth of the euphotic zone (where the lower limit was taken as 1% of total surface radiation) did not vary over the ten-year study and was limited to the top 3–4 m of the water column. Transparency of the water remained between 1.8 and 2.0 m.

By contrast, there was a great change in the level of nutrients in the water. Nitrate concentrations increased ten fold from 0.012–0.029 mg/l in 1981 to 0.14–0.52 mg/l in 1990–1991 (Table 3 and 4). Phosphates increased four fold from 0.002–0.008 mg/l in 1980 to 0.012–0.038 mg/l during 1990–1991.

Table 1. The dominant phytoplankton species in Pansoon Reservoir during 1981 based upon mean cell counts from two stations.

Rank	Taxon	% Dominance (±SEM)
1	*Cryptomonas erosa*	15.2±1.2
2	*Staurastrum chaetoceros*	12.3±0.9
3	*Euastrum turgidum*	9.3±1.7
4	*Rhodomonas minuta*	6.3±0.6
5	*Cryptomonas caudata*	4.3±0.8
6	*Mallomonas spherica*	1.9±0.5
7	*Ochromonas* sp.	1.3±0.4
8	*Dinobryon divergens*	1.0±0.2

Table 2. The dominant phytoplankton species in Pansoon Reservoir during 1981 based upon mean cell counts from two stations.

Rank	Taxon	% Dominance (±SEM)
1	*Euastrum turgidum*	9.1±0.9
2	*Cryptomonas erosa*	9.0±0.3
3	*Cyclotella striata*	7.2±0.8
4	*Navicula rhyncocephala*	6.6±0.3
5	*Chlorococcum* sp.	6.1±1.0
6	*Staurastrum chaetoceros*	5.3±0.2
7	*Arthrodesmus fuellebornei*	4.9±0.5
8	*Cosmarium constrictum*	3.5±0.3
9	*Gonyaulax apiculata*	1.6±0.7

Discussion

The change in dominant species in the Pansoon Reservoir from a largely cryptophyte-chrysophyte composition in 1981 to dominance by desmids and cryptophytes ten years later can be attributed to increased nutrient availability. This increase, reflected in the substantial rise in nitrate and phosphate concentrations over the study period, resembles the processes that occur during changes in lake trophy which have been documented extensively in temperate latitudes (e.g. HUTCHINSON 1967, LIKENS 1972, SCHINDLER 1978). The source of the nutrients is allochthonous, since the stability of oxygen and temperature profiles (and hence the degree of stratification and lack of mixing) rule out the sediments as a source of nutrients in the

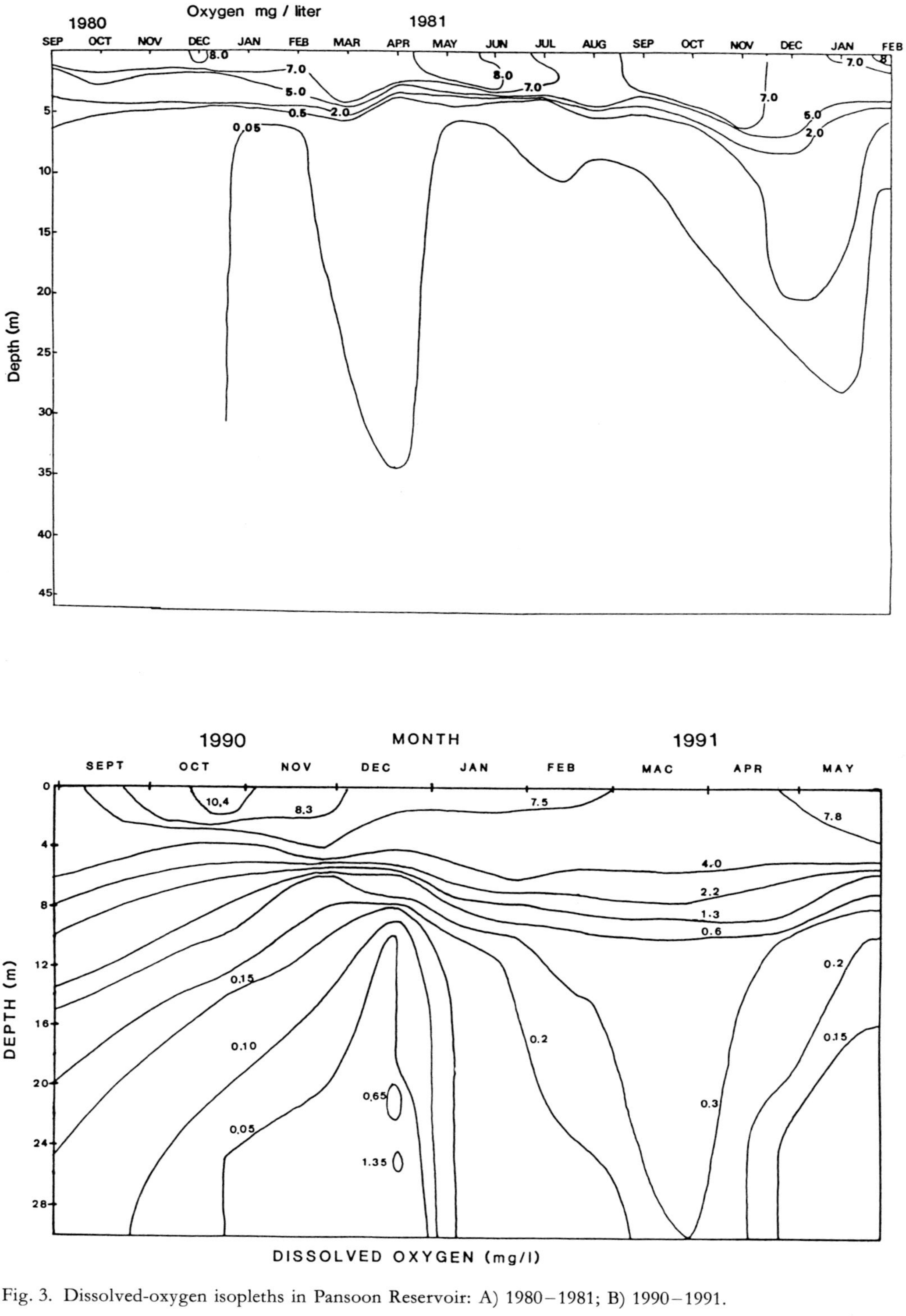

Fig. 3. Dissolved-oxygen isopleths in Pansoon Reservoir: A) 1980–1981; B) 1990–1991.

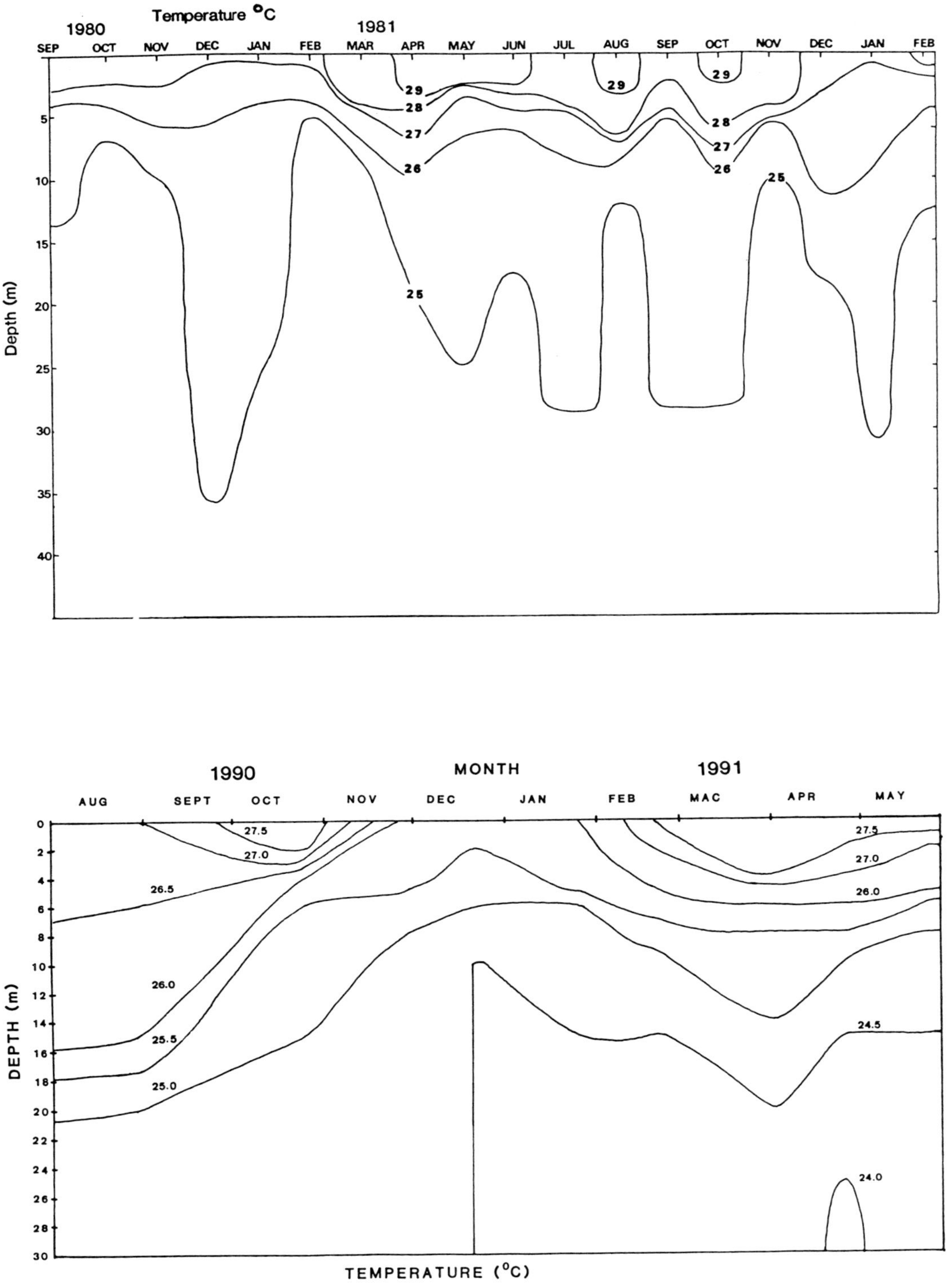

Fig. 4. Water temperature isotherms in Pansoon Reservoir: A) 1980–1981; B) 1990–1991.

Table 3. Seasonal variations in the physicochemical conditions in the euphotic zone of Pansoon Reservoir in 1981. Only mean values are presented.

September	NO_3-N (mg/l)	PO_4-P (mg/l)	Oxygen (mg/l)	Secchi disc at 0–3 m depth (m)
June	0.015	0.006	7.8–8.0	1.9
July	0.018	0.005	6.7–7.2	1.8
August	0.012	0.003	5.4	1.9
September	0.019	0.008	8.1–8.4	1.8
October	0.017	0.002	8.2–8.4	1.8
November	0.029	0.002	8.2–8.8	1.8
Devember	0.023	0.005	5.6–6.1	1.8

Table 4. Seasonal variations in the physicochemical conditions in the euphotic zone of Pansoon Reservoir during 1990. Mean values are presented only.

September	NO_3-N (mg/l)	PO_4-P (mg/l)	Oxygen (mg/l)	Secchi disc at 0–3 m depth (m)
June	0.14	0.031	0.9–7.5	2.1
July	0.15	0.028	7.5–8.2	2.0
August	0.20	0.012	6.9	1.8
September	0.18	0.038	8.1–8.6	1.8
October	0.19	0.034	7.3–11.2	1.8
November	0.52	0.033	7.9–8.4	1.8
Devember	0.45	0.028	6.8–7.7	1.8

water column. Pansoon Reservoir receives considerable inputs of nitrates during the rainy season, as demonstrated by increased nitrate concentrations during the November–December monsoon season. In addition, the study site is located in a forested area in which logging activities occur, and this could contribute to high nutrient loads in run-off entering the lake.

Variations in mixing depths are evident in 1981 and 1990–1991. These differences in depths to which oxygen penetrates can be attributed to the strength and direction of localized winds; interannual variations in this factor are critical in maintaining primary productivity levels in large lakes (Goldman & Jassby 1990). In addition, the Pansoon Reservoir experiences large variations in water levels between the dry and wet seasons. Such variations can hasten the return of nutrients from sediments in areas that are exposed to the air during drawdown and inundated subsequently by rising waters (Baxter 1977).

Seasonal fluctuations in nutrient levels appeared to influence dinoflagellate populations in 1990–1991. Dinoflagellate abundance peaked during the dry months of April to May, when nutrient levels were lowest. Because of their motility and their relatively high cellular phosphorus content (Wynne et al. 1982), the dinoflagellates have a competitive advantage over other phytoplankton (Pollingher et al. 1988) and many therefore become dominant when nutrients are limiting.

Long-term changes in phytoplankton populations such as documented here for the Pansoon Reservoir allow deterministic studies to be carried out with the purpose of developing models to predict the onset of eutrophication. A number of investigations designed to determine the factors limiting phytoplankton growth and production, which will lead eventually to formulation of a nutrient budget for Pansoon Reservoir, are being undertaken currently. Results from these studies will be used to develope predictive models which will be used to formulate recommendations for the management and conservation of lentic habitats in Malaysia.

References

AMERICAN PUBLIC HEALTH ASSOCIATION, 1985: Standard Methods for the Examination of Water and Wastewater, 16th Edition: 1134 pp. – APHA, Washington D.C.

BAXTER, R. M., 1977: Environmental effects of dams and impoundments. – *Ann. Rev. Ecol. Syst.* **8:** 255–283.

GOLDMAN C.-R. & JASSBY, A., 1990: Spring mixing depth as a determinant of annual primary production in lakes. – In: TILZER, M. M. & SERRUYA, C. (eds.): Lakes: Ecological Structure and Function: 691 pp. – Springer-Verlag Publications, Berlin.

HUTCHINSON, G. E., 1967: A Treatise on Limnology. Vol. 2: Introduction to Lake Biology and Limnoplankton: 1115 pp. – Wiley, New York.

LIKENS, G. E., 1972: Nutrients and Eutrophication. – American Society for Limnology and Oceanography Special Symposium **1:** 328 pp.

POLLINGHER, U., BERMAN, T., KAPLAN, B. & SCHARF, D., 1988: Lake Kinneret: response to N and P enrichments in experiments and in nature. – *Hydrobiologia* **166:** 67–75.

SARMANI, S. & HAMZAH, 1989: A review of water quality of the Langat River Basin, Selangor. – In: HADI, A. S. & OTHMAN, M. (eds.): An Urban Ecosystem Study of the Kajang-Bangi Corridor. Vol. 6: Tropical Urban Ecosystems Series: 323 pp. – Technical Report of the Working Group on Urban Ecosystems, Malaysian National MAB Committee.

SCHINDLER, D. W., 1978: Factors regulating phytoplankton production and standing crop in the world's freshwaters. – *Limnol. Oceanogr.* **23:** 478–486.

THORNTON, K. W., KIMMEL, B. L. & PAYNE, F. E., 1990: Reservoir Limnology: 256 pp. – Wiley, New York.

WYNNE, D., PATNI, N. J., AARONSON, S. & BERMAN, T., 1982: The relationship between nutrient status and chemical composition of *Peridinium cinctum* during the bloom in Lake Kinneret. – *J. Plankton Res.* **4:** 125–136.

Author's address:

Biology Department, Faculty of Science and Environmental Studies, Universiti Pertanian Malaysia, 43400 Serdang, Selangor, Malaysia.

Mitt. Internat. Verein. Limnol.	24	251–257	Stuttgart, Februar 1994

A comparative study of phytoplankton populations in two Malaysian lakes

F. M. Yusoff and I. Patimah

Abstract

Phytoplankton composition and production in two Malaysian lakes were studied between February and December 1988. Lake Aman is a shallow (mean depth 0.3 m) nutrient-rich water body, whilst Lake Titiwangsa is comparatively deep (mean depth 3.4 m) and poor in nutrients. Phytoplankton taxa in Lake Aman consisted of four phyla with 19 genera, and Lake Titiwangsa had five phyla with 33 genera. The euglenoids were the most abundant group in Lake Aman throughout the study period, comprising 85.4% of the total phytoplankton population. The second largest group of phytoplankton in this lake was chlorophytes (13.8%), followed by cyanobacteria (0.6%) and diatoms (0.2%). The order of phytoplankton abundance in Lake Titiwangsa was cyanobacteria (45.7%), followed by chlorophytes (28.4%), dinoflagellates (11%), chrysophytes (10%), diatoms (4.3%), and euglenoids (0.6%). Chlorophyll *a* concentrations in Lake Aman ranged from 60.0 µg/l to 969.4 µg/l. Chlorophyll *a* concentrations in Lake Titiwangsa were comparatively low, ranging from 0.5 µg/l to 6.3 µg/l. The composition and biomass of phytoplankton populations in the two lakes indicated that the study lakes were of different trophic status: i.e. Lake Aman was hypertrophic and Lake Titiwangsa was mesotrophic. The physicochemical characteristics of the lake water supported this hypothesis.

Introduction

The structure of phytoplankton communities is determined by a composite of climatic, geographical, physical, chemical and biological factors. Changes in one or more of these factors may result in shifts in phytoplankton production and community composition. Nutrient concentration is widely recognized as a major factor regulating phytoplankton succession in lakes (Zohary & Robarts 1989). For example, nutrient-rich aquatic ecosystems are usually dominated by blue-green and green algae (Leonardson & Ripl 1980). Significant shifts in phytoplankton community structure, following changes in nutrient loading, have been reported from many temperate lakes (Edmondson & Lehman 1981, Cronberg 1982, Daley & Pick 1990, Willen 1990). Several empirical models predict that blue-green algal biomass rises with increasing nutrient concentrations (Zevenboom & Mur 1980, Smith 1985, Trimbee & Prepas 1987), and the trophic state of an ecosystem is a major factor in determining the dominant phytoplankton species (Zevenboom & Mur 1980).

Lake Aman and Lake Titiwangsa are located at 3°06′N, 101°38′E and 3°10′N, 101°43′E respectively in Selangor State, Peninsula Malaysia. Lake Aman is a shallow lake of 2.24 ha surface area with a mean depth of 0.3 m (maximum depth 0.8 m). It receives nutrient-rich water from the surrounding residential areas which enriches the lake sediment. Occasionally, the total heterotrophic bacterial count of Lake Aman reaches 10^6 CFU/ml, a concentration which is usually associated with eutrophic lakes (Shamsuddin et al. in press). Only two species of fish were found in Lake Aman: *Oreochromis mossambicus* (Peters) (99%) and *Channa striatus* Bloch (1%). By contrast, Lake Titiwangsa is relatively large and deep, with a mean depth of 3.4 m (maximum depth 13.0 m) and a surface area of 46.40 ha. It has a relatively low nutrient content and a low total heterotrophic bacterial load (Shamsuddin et al. in press). The fish fauna of Lake Titiwangsa was made up by *O. mossambicus* (43%), *Notopterus notopterus* (Pallas) (28%), *Ctenopharyngodon idella* (Cuvier & Valenciennes) (13%), *Cyprinus carpio* (Linnaeus) (4%), *Oxyleotris marmoratus* (Bleeker) (3%), *Leptobarbus hoevenii* (Bleeker) (2.5%), *Acrossocheilus deauratus* (Cuvier & Valenciennes) (2.5%), *Anabas testudineus* (Bloch) (1%), *Osteochilus hasselti* (Cuvier & Valenciennes) (1%), *Puntius gonionotus* (Bleeker) (1%), and *Tor tambroides* (Bleeker) (1%) (Mustafa Kamal et al. 1989).

These two Malaysian lakes have been studied with the objective of understanding the differences in biomass and composition of the phytoplankton with reference to lake nutrient status. Attempts were also made to correlate the trends in phytoplankton community structure and their biomass with changes in the trophic status of the study lakes.

Materials and methods

The study was carried out between February and December 1988. Monthly water samples from Lake Aman were collected from three depths (surface, 0.4 and 0.8 m) at three sampling stations. Lake Titiwangsa was sampled monthly from six depths (surface, 3, 5, 7, 9 and 11 m depths) at one limnetic station and from three depths

0538-4680/94/0024-0251 $ 1.25

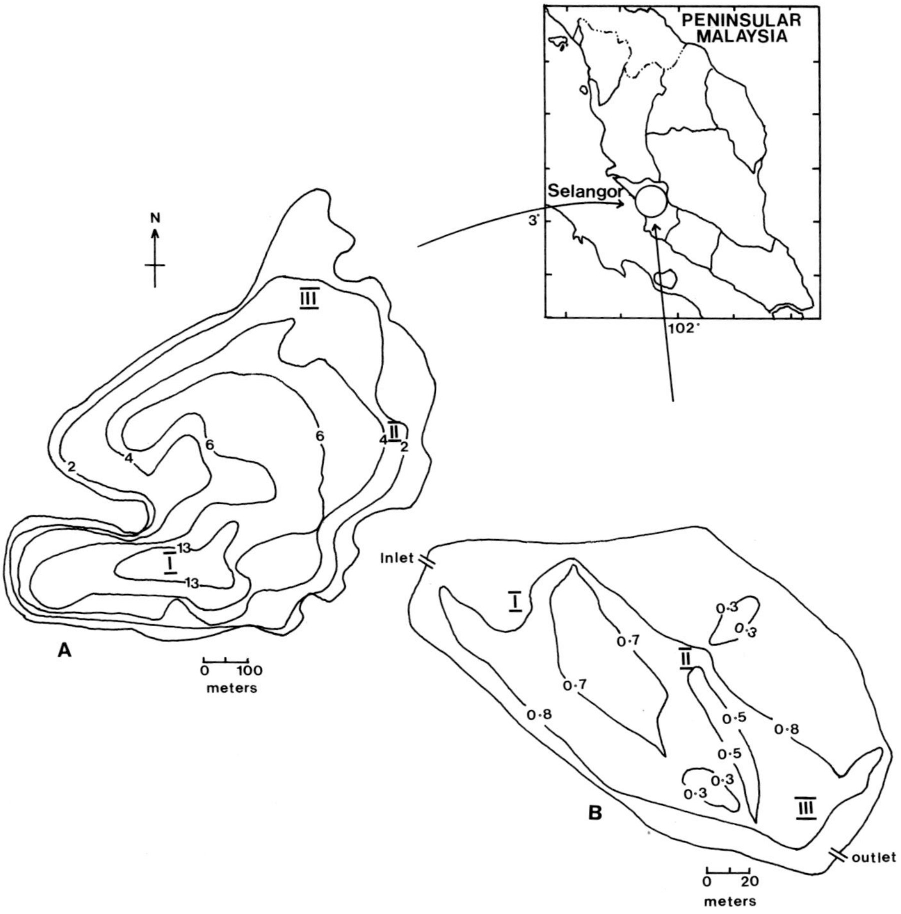

Fig. 1. Bathymetry and sampling stations: Lake Titiwangsa (A) and Lake Aman (B). Depth contours in meters.

(surface, 2 and 3 m depths) at two littoral stations near to the lake margins (Fig. 1).

Water samples were analyzed for a range of physico-chemical and biological parameters. Temperature and dissolved oxygen were measured in situ using a YSI model 57 dissolved oxygen meter fitted with a thermistor. Conductivity was measured using a YSI salinity-conductivity-temperature meter. Determination of pH was done electrometrically with a Metrohms Herisau E 603 pH meter. Alkalinity was measured by titration (see Wetzel & Likens 1979). Soluble reactive phosphorus was determined by ammonium molybdate-ascorbic acid method and nitrate-nitrogen analysis was undertaken using cadmium reduction. The phenate method was used to measure ammonia-nitrogen. For the determination of total phytoplankton chlorophyll *a* concentrations, 300–500 ml water samples were filtered through 0.8 μm membrane filters and measured according to American Public Health Association (1985) procedures. The phytoplankton composition was determined by preserving 500 ml water samples in Lugol's solution and allowing the particles to settle. Samples were concentrated, subsampled and counted using an inverted microscope. Identification was based on Prescott (1984).

Since the objective of the study was to compare and contrast the trophic status of the two lakes using the phytoplankton composition and biomass, data collected from different depths were pooled and mean values were calculated for comparative purposes.

Results

There were noticeable differences in the physico-chemical qualities of the two lakes measured during the study period (Table 1). Mean dissolved oxygen concentrations in Lake Aman were lower than in Lake Titiwangsa. However, nutrient levels

Table 1. Water-quality characteristics in Lake Aman and Lake Titiwangsa during 1988. Values represent spatial and temporal mean ± SE calculated using pooled data. Number of samples is given in parentheses.

Parameter	Lake Aman	Lake Titiwangsa
Temperature (°C)	28.40 ± 0.10 (54)	29.70 ± 0.10 (108)
Secchi Depth (m)	0.3 ± 0.04 (33)	2.40 ± 0.60 (24)
Oxygen (mg/l)	5.15 ± 0.22 (54)	6.38 ± 0.19 (108)
Conductivity (µm hos/cm)	295.35 ± 8.93 (54)	168.85 ± 1.05 108)
Alkalinity (mg · l^{-1} $CaCO_3$)	15.10 ± 1.41 (18)	68.28 ± 0.21 (84)
pH	6.77 – 7.93	6.99 – 8.68
Ammonia-N (mg/l)	5.26 ± 0.21 (54)	0.05 ± 0.01 (108)
Nitrate + nitrite-N (mg/l)	0.02 ± 0.01 (54)	0.03 ± 0.01 (73)
Soluble reactive-P (mg/l)	0.33 ± 0.02 (53)	0.01 ± 0.01 (78)

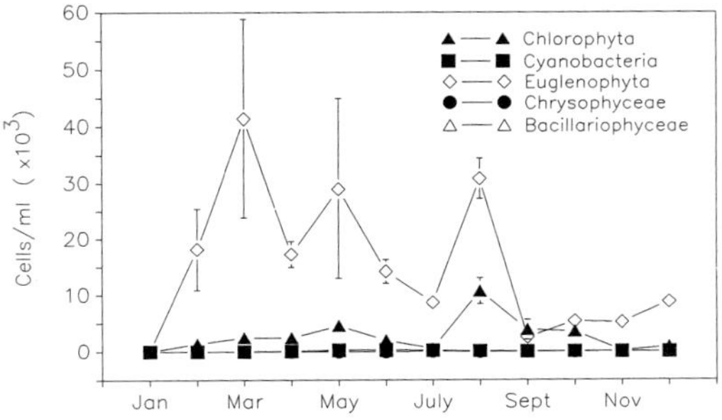

Fig. 2. Fluctuations in phytoplankton populations (spatial mean ± SE) in Lake Aman during 1988.

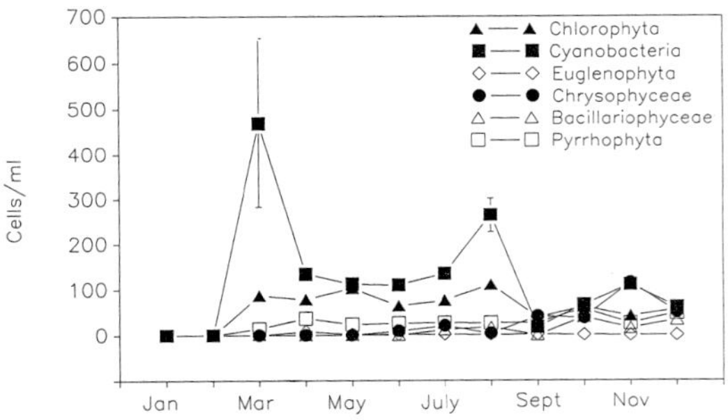

Fig. 3. Fluctuations in phytoplankton populations (spatial mean ± SE) in Lake Titiwangsa during 1988.

(soluble reactive phosphorus, ammonia-nitrogen and nitrate plus nitrite-nitrogen) were notably higher in Lake Aman. Mean Secchi disk transparency in Lake Aman was 0.3 m compared to 2.4 m in Lake Titiwangsa. Lake Aman was less alkaline than Lake Titiwangsa with a mean alkalinity of 15.10 mg/l $CaCO_3$. Mean alkalinity in Lake Titiwangsa was 68.28 mg/l $CaCO_3$ (Table 1).

The phytoplankton of Lake Aman comprised four phyla and 19 genera, whilst those of Lake Titiwangsa consisted of five phyla and 33 genera (Table 2). Euglenoids dominated the phytoplankton of Lake Aman throughout the study period, making up 85.4% of the total population. The second largest group of phytoplankton in this lake was chlorophytes (13.8%), followed by cyanobacteria (0.6%) and diatoms (0.2%) (Table 2 & Fig. 2). The order of phytoplankton abundance in Lake Titiwangsa was cyanobacteria (45.7%), chlorophytes (28.4%), dinoflagellates (11%), chrysophytes (10%), diatoms (4.3%), and euglenoids (0.6%) (Table 2, Fig. 3).

The Lake Aman euglenoids comprised mainly *Euglena* (mean density 12,277.0 cells/ml), followed by *Trachelomonas* (mean density 4,158,0 cells/ml). Densities of *Euglena* peaked at 22,410.0 cells/ml in March 1988 (Fig. 2). *Ankistrodesmus* was the dominant genus (mean density 841.0 cells/ml) among the Lake Aman chlorophytes, followed by *Crucigenia* (769.8 cells/ml), *Chlorella* (557.3 cells/ml), *Scenedesmus* (433.5 cells/ml) and *Oocystis* (38.2 cells/ml). Desmids were present at densities <10.0 cells/ml (Table 2). Cyanobacteria were only a minor group in Lake Aman, consisting primarily of *Microcystis* (mean density 96.2 cells/ml). *Anabaena* and *Oscillatoria* were found only in small quantities at mean densities of 4.8 and 3.8 cells/ml respectively. Diatoms and chrysophytes were rare in Lake Aman except for *Navicula* (mean density 45.2 cells/ml; Table 2).

Merismopedia was the most abundant cyanobacteria (mean density, 87.0 cells/ml) in Lake Titiwangsa, followed by *Microcystis* (18.7 colonies/ml), *Chroococcus* (15.1 cells/ml) and *Aphanothece* (3.8 cells/ml). *Anabaena, Oscillaria* and *Aphanocapsa* were found rarely. There were 16 genera of chlorophytes in Lake Titiwangsa. However, the

Table 2. Densities (cells/ml) of phytoplankton genera in Lake Aman and Lake Titiwangsa from February to December 1988. Values represent spatial and temporal mean ± SE calculated using pooled data. Number of samples is given in parentheses. R = rare (found in not more than five samples); NF = not found.

Phytoplankton taxon	Lake Aman	Lake Titiwangsa
Phylum: Chlorophyta (Green Algae)		
Order Volvocales		
Family Volvocaceae		
Eudorina	NF	14.7 ± 1.6 (118)
Pandorina	NF	5.2 ± 1.0 (119)
Volvox	NF	2.4 ± 0.4 (118)
Order Chlorococcales		
Family Chlorococcaceae		
Tetraedron	NF	R
Family Oocystaceae		
Ankistrodesmus	841.0 ± 165.6 (66)	7.2 ± 1.5 (118)
Chlorella	557.3 ± 320.9 (66)	0.4 ± 0.2 (118)
Oocystis	38.2 ± 17.3 (66)	NF
Family Dictyosphaeriaceae		
Botryococcus	NF	8.9 ± 2.6 (118)
Family Scenedesmacaea		
Coelastrum	NF	4.4 ± 1.5 (119)
Crucigenia	769.8 ± 206.9 (66)	8.0 ± 1.2 (119)
Scenedesmus	433.5 ± 38.4 (66)	7.6 ± 0.9 (119)
Family Hydrodictyaceae		
Pediastrum	3.8 ± 2.3	R
Order Zygnematales		
Family Zygnemataceae		
Spirogyra	NF	R
Zygnema	NF	1.4 ± 0.4 (119)
Family Desmidiaceae		
Cosmarium	2.0 ± 1.4 (66)	0.5 ± 0.2 (118)
Closterium	8.9 ± 3.0 (66)	1.8 ± 0.5 (118)
Staurastum	NF	15.0 ± 8.1 (119)
Phylum: Euglenophyta (Euglenoids)		
Order Euglenales		
Family Euglenaceae		
Euglena	12,277.0 ± 2,401.6 (66)	1.2 ± 0.3 (118)
Phacus	R	R
Trachelomonas	4,158.0 ± 664.7 (66)	0.4 ± 0.1 (118)
Phylum: Chrysophyta		
Subphylum: Chrysophyceae (Yellow-green Algae)		
Order Ochromomadales		
Family Ochromonaceae		
Uroglenopis	R	3.5 ± 0.7 (119)
Family Dinobryadaceae		
Dinobryon	NF	24.0 ± 4.0 (119)
Family Synuraceae		
Mallomonas	R	NF
Subphylum: Bacillariophyceae (Diatoms)		
Order Pennales		
Family Fragilariaceae		
Asterionella	R	R
Family Naviculaceae		
Navicula	45.2 ± 15.6 (66)	11.6 ± 1.6 (118)

Table 2. (Continued).

Phytoplankton taxon	Lake Aman	Lake Titiwangsa
Phylum: Cyanophyta (Blue-green Algae)		
Order Chroococcales		
Family chroococcaceae		
Aphanocapsa	NF	R
Aphanothece	NF	3.8±0.8 (118)
Chroococcus	R	15.1±4.4 (118)
Microcystis	96.2±21.8 (66)	18.7±3.6 (118)
Merismopedia	NF	87.0±7.1 (118)
Order Oscillatoriales		
Family Oscillatoriaceae		
Oscillatoria	3.8±2.2 (66)	R
Order Nostocales		
Family Nostocaceae		
Anabaena	4.8±2.0 (66)	R
Phylum: Pyrrhophyta (Dinoflagellates)		
Order Dinokontae		
Family Ceratiaceae		
Ceratium	NF	1.2±0.5 (118)
Family Peridiniaceae		
Peridinium	NF	28.7±2.0 (118)
Family Glenodiniaceae		
Glenodinium	NF	R

Table 3. Chlorophyll *a* concentrations (µg/l) in Lake Aman and Lake Titiwangsa during 1988. Values represent spatial mean ± SE calculated using pooled data. Number of samples is given in parentheses.

Month	Lake Aman	Lake Titiwangsa
February	211.7± 65.5 (6)	–
March	61.0± 25.9 (6)	1.3±0.7 (12)
April	985.0±169.2 (6)	3.2±0.7 (12)
May	604.0±161.2 (6)	1.7±0.4 (12)
June	617.3±198.3 (6)	1.4±0.4 (12)
July	196.0± 31.2 (6)	0.5±0.3 (12)
August	969.4±164.7 (6)	–
September	164.2± 16.4 (6)	4.5±0.6 (12)
October	771.2±165.6 (6)	4.2±0.6 (12)
November	332.2± 35.7 (6)	6.3±1.2 (12)
December	732.0± 48.1 (6)	–

density of each type was low, with a maximum of 15.0 cells/ml for the desmid genus *Staurastrum*. Besides *Eudorina* (14.7 cells/ml), the density of other genera were <10.0 cells/ml (Table 2). Dinoflagellates, dominated by *Peridinium* (mean density 28.7 cells/ml) were found only in Lake Titiwangsa. Chrysophytes, comprising *Dinobryon* (24.0 cells/ml) and *Uroglenopsis* (3.5 cells/ml), were more abundant in Lake Titiwangsa than Lake Aman (Table 2).

The mean chlorophyll *a* concentrations in Lake Aman ranged from 61.0 in March to 969.4 µg/l in August 1988. Lake Titiwangsa showed relatively low chlorophyll *a* concentrations, ranging low, ranging from 0.5 µg/l in July to 6.3 mg/l in November (Table 3).

Discussion

Lake Aman differed from Lake Titiwangsa in terms of morphometry, physicochemical and biological characteristics. Lake Aman was nutrient-rich with higher phytoplankton densities and biomass than Lake Titiwangsa. According to Forsberg & Ryding's (1980) lake classification scheme, which is based on physicochemical and biological characteristics, Lake Aman can be categorised as hypertrophic (or hypereutrophic) while Lake Titiwangsa matches the characteristics of a mesotrophic environment. This categorization parallels the work of Watanabe (1990) who classified the Japanese Lakes Suwa and Okutama (which have similar limnological characteristics to

Lakes Aman and Titiwangsa) as hypertrophic and mesotrophic respectively.

Differences in chlorophyll *a* concentrations indicated the trophic status of the study lakes. ZOHARY & ROBARTS (1989) used chlorophyll *a* concentration (926.0 mg/m^2) to categorise Hartbeesport Dam as hypertrophic, while SZILAGYI et al. (1990) concluded that the Keszthely basin in Hungary was hypertrophic on the basis that it had a chlorophyll *a* concentration of 250 mg/m^3. Chlorophyll *a* concentrations in Lake Aman exceeded 200 mg/m^3 for most of the year, with peak levels over 900 mg/m^3, and thus categorization of this lake as hypertrophic seems appropriate. Note that chlorophyll *a* concentrations in Lake Aman were similar to those of Laguna de Bay in the Philippines, a highly productive lake (JORGENSEN & VOLLENWEIDER 1989). Shallow lakes are more susceptible to eutrophication than deep lakes (JORGENSEN & VOLLENWEIDER 1989), and these characteristics, along with the high nutrient loads, could account for the relatively high chlorophyll *a* concentrations in Lake Aman. Moreover, the shallow nature of Lake Aman would have provided a constant nutrient supply from its enriched sediments (KAMP-NEILSEN 1980).

The number of phytoplankton genera found in Lake Titiwangsa was 3.8 times higher than that in Lake Aman. Approximately 85% of Lake Aman's phytoplankton community consisted of euglenoids. The dominance of euglenoids in Lake Aman indicated the effects of organic pollution (WETZEL 1983). In contrast, low euglenoid densities (0.6% of total) in Lake Titiwangsa suggested that this was an unpolluted lake. The present study showed clearly that hypertrophication resulted in low biodiversity and changed phytoplankton community structure. This trend is in accordance with the findings of WILLEN (1990), who reported that eutrophication results in an impoverished phytoplankton flora.

Blue-green algae dominated the phytoplankton community of Lake Titiwangsa and blue-greens, especially *Microcystis* and *Anabaena,* are abound in eutrophic waters (CRONBERG 1982, WETZEL 1983, WILLEN 1990). Both of these genera were found in higher densities in Lake Aman than in Lake Titiwangsa. Significantly, ZOHARY & ROBERTS (1989) recorded that *Microcystis aeruginosa* dominated phytoplankton populations of a hypereutrophic (=hypertrophic) lake in subtropical South Africa, and JENSEN & ANDERSEN (1990) found concordance of high phosphorus loading, dominance of *Microcystis,* and depletion of nitrogen in lake water. By contrast, the blue-green algae in mesotrophic Lake Titiwangsa were dominated by *Merismopedia,* and it is notable that low phosphorus concentrations can be related to *Merismopedia warmingiana* dominance in lakes elsewhere (ILMAVIRTA 1990).

Chlorophytes were the second most abundant group of phytoplankton in both study lakes and their population densities were higher in Lake Aman (Table 2, Fig. 2 & 3). DALEY & PICK (1990) and ILMAVIRTA (1990) reported that *Ankistrodesmus* and *Scenedesmus* dominate chlorophyte populations under nutrient-rich conditions, and the dominance of Lake Aman by *Ankistrodesmus, Crucigenia, Chlorella* and *Scenedesmus* supports the categorisation of this lake as hypertrophic. The desmid genus *Staurastrum* – which is generally found in oligotrophic waters (WETZEL 1983) – was the most abundant chlorophyte in Lake Titiwangsa, highlighting the relative scarcity of nutrients in this lake.

The chrysophyte *Dinobryon* and the dinoflagellates *Peridinium* and *Ceratium,* which are found commonly in oligotrophic lakes (WETZEL 1983), were confined to Lake Titiwangsa in the present study. Indeed, *Dinobryon* populations tend to increase following declines in nutrient loading in temperate eutrophic lakes (CRONBERG 1982, DALEY & PICK 1990). According to HUNTER et al. (1990), the presence of chrysophytes in combination with one or two other algal groups, generally cryptophytes, diatoms and/or dinoflagellates, indicates oligotrophic or mesotrophic conditions in lakes, as exemplified by Lake Titiwangsa in the present study. The absence of *Dinobryon, Peridinium* and *Ceratium* in Lake Aman provide support for the view that it was hypertrophic. In this context, it is significant that the presence/absence and relative abundance of phytoplankton genera (e.g. WETZEL 1983, HUNTER et al. 1990) can be used to indicate trophic conditions in tropical Malaysian lakes as well as in temperate and subtropical lakes.

Although Lake Aman is a shallow lake which is inhabited by only two species of fish, its large surface area has made it attractive to the public for recreational fishing. However, recreational activities would be enhanced if the lake's hypertrophic status could be improved and the lake ecology restored to 'more natural' conditions. This could be achieved by controlling the drainage of nutrient-rich water from surrounding residential areas, and by dredging the lake bottom. Since this study was undertaken, there has been rapid development around the mesotrophic Lake Titiwangsa. A canal has been constructed that connects it to an adjacent highly-eutrophic lake. Although Lake Titiwangsa is still mesotrophic, without appropriate management measures to control the nutrient input, it will become eutrophic within a few years with concomitant changes in community structure of the aquatic biota.

Acknowledgements

This study was funded by the Malaysian Government through the Intensified Research Priority Areas programme, grant no. 50258. The authors thank Mr. ABDUL AZIZ KAMARUZAMAN, Ms. NAHARIAH MAT LIA, Mr. PERUMAL KUPPAN and Mr. SABRI OMAR for their technical assistance and Dr. ROHANA SUBASINGHE for his critical review of the manuscript.

References

AMERICAN PUBLIC HEALTH ASSOCIATION, 1985: Standard Methods for the Examination of Water and Wastewater. 16th edition: 1134 pp. – APHA, Washington D.C.

CRONBERG, G., 1982: Changes in the phytoplankton of Lake Trummen induced by restoration. – *Hydrobiologia* **86:**185–193.

DALEY, R. D. & PICK, F. R., 1990: Phytoplankton biomass and composition of Kootenay Lake, British Columbia, following reductions in phosphorus loading. – *Verh. Internat. Verein. Limnol.* **24:**314–318.

EDMONDSON, W. T. & LEHMAN, J. T., 1981: The effect of changes in the nutrient income on the condition of Lake Washington. – *Limnol. Oceanogr.* **26:**1–29.

FORSBERG, C. & RYDING, S. O., 1980: Eutrophication parameters and trophic states indices in 30 Swedish waste-receiving lakes. – *Arch. Hydrobiol.* **89:**189–207.

HUNTER, D. A., GOLDMAN, C. R. & BYRON, E. R., 1990: Changes in the phytoplankton community structure in Lake Tahoe, California-Nevada. – *Verh. Internat. Verein. Limnol.* **24:**505–508.

ILMAVIRTA, V., 1990: Occurrence of phytoplankton species along nutrient, pH, and colour gradients in eastern Finnish lakes. – *Verh. Internat. Verein. Limnol.* **24:**702–706.

JENSEN, H. S. & ANDERSEN, F. O., 1990: Impact of nitrate and blue-green algae abundance on phosphorus cycling between sediment and water in two shallow, eutrophic lakes. – *Verh. Internat. Verein. Limnol.* **24:**224–230.

JORGENSEN, S. E. & VOLLENWEIDER, R. A., 1989: Guidelines of Lake Management. Vol. 1: Principles of lake Management: 199 pp. – ILEC, UNEP, Japan.

KAMP-NEILSEN, L., 1980: The influence of sediments on changed phosphorus loading to hypertrophic L. Glumso. – In: BARICA, J. & MUR, L. R. (eds.): Hypertrophic Ecosystems. Developments in Hydrobiology 2: 29–36. – Dr. W. Junk Publishers, The Hague.

LEONARDSON, L. & RIPL, W., 1980: Control of undesirable algae and induction of algal succession in hypertrophic lake ecosystems. — In: BARICA, J. & MUR, L. R. (eds.): Hypertrophic Ecosystems. Developments in Hydrobiology 2: 57–65. – Dr. W. Junk Publishers, The Hague.

MUSTAFA KAMAL, A. S., DAUD, S. K., AZIZ, A., PATIMAH, I. & SHAMSUDDIN, M. N., 1989: Recreational Fisheries. – Annual Research Report, Faculty of Fisheries and Marine Science, Universiti Pertanian Malaysia, Serdang, Selangor.

PRESCOTT, G. W., 1984: How to Know Freshwater Algae: 293 pp. – Wm. C. C. Brown Company Publishers, Iowa.

SHAMSUDDIN, M. N., Aziz, A., YUSOFF, F. M. & PATIMAH, I., in press: Water quality of two recreational lakes of Malaysia: Lake Aman and Lake Titiwangsa. – Paper presented at the First Malaysian Applied Biology Symposium, Serdang, Selangor. February 1990.

SMITH, V. H., 1985: Predictive models for the biomass of blue-green algae in lakes. *Water Res. Bull.* **21:**433–439.

TRIMBEE, A. M. & PREPAS, E. E., 1987: Evaluation of total phosphorus as a predictor of relative biomass of blue-green algae with emphasis on Alberta lakes. – *Can. J. Fish. Aquatic Sci.* **44:**1337–1342.

WATANABE, Y., 1990: C:N:P ratios of size fractionated seston and planktonic organisms in various trophic levels. – *Verh. Internat. Verein. Limnol.* **24:**195–199.

WETZEL, R. G., 1983: Limnology: 767 pp. – Saunders College Publishing, New York.

WETZEL, R. G. & LIKENS, G. E., 1979: Limnological Analyses: 357 pp. – W. B. Saunders Company, Philadelphia.

WILLEN, T., 1990: Phytoplankton and ecoregions in Sweden. 1. Distribution of species and life forms. – *Verh. Internat. Verein. Limnol.* **24:**655.

ZEVENBOOM, W. & MUR, L. R., 1980: N_2-fixing cyanobacteria: why they do not become dominant in Dutch hypertrophic lakes. – In: BARICA, J. & MUR, L. R. (eds.): Hypertrophic Ecosystems. Developments in Hydrobiology: 123–130. – Dr. W. Junk Publishers, The Hague.

ZOHARY, T. & ROBARTS, R. D., 1989: Diurnal mixed layers and the long-term dominance of *Microcystis aeruginosa*. – *Water Res.* **11:**25–48.

Authors' address:

Faculty of Fisheries and Marine Science, Universiti Pertanian Malaysia, 43400 Serdang, Selangor D. E. Malaysia.

Mitt. Internat. Verein. Limnol.	24	259–264	Stuttgart, Februar 1994

Agroecosystem analysis of Laguna Lake in the Philippines

Enrique P. Pacardo

Abstract

The development and management of Laguna Lake as a fishery resource at a sustainable level has been unsuccessful, and fish production has declined in quantity and quality. This problem stems from the conflicts which arise from the multiple use of the lake. The usual uni-disciplinary approach to solving the problem was inadequate, and the need for an interdisciplinary and holistic approach that would consider not only the lake but the drainage basin and their interactions became imperative. The agroecosystem analysis technique was applied in Laguna Lake through a multidisciplinary and multisectoral workshop in early 1991. The results of the analysis showed that the decline in fish productivity of the lake was a result of the interplay of biophysical, socioeconomic and political factors prevailing within and outside the lake basin. Discussion of these findings by those with a vested interest in the lake was a first step towards mitigating the social conflicts which had arisen. In turn, this facilitated identification of priority areas for research and development programmes aimed at maintaining a sustainable ecosystem centred on Laguna Lake.

Introduction

Laguna Lake (known previously as Laguna de Bay) is the largest natural lake in the Philippines and probably in Southeast Asia (Fig. 1). It is bounded by Metro Manila in the west, provinces of Rizal in the north, and Laguna in the south and east. The lake, with an area of 90,000 ha, is located at the centre of its 280,000 ha drainage basin. As the human population of the drainage basin has increased in recent years, so too has the demand for services from the lake. The lake has developed from a fishing ground in the early 1950s into a multi-purpose resource providing water for irrigation, navigation, power generation, tourism and domestic use by Metro Manila residents.

As occurs with other common resources, the multiple use of the lake has spawned complex problems and issues. These included conflicts with respect to quality and quantity of space allocation, and dissension related to the environmental impacts of development projects in the lake and its drainage basin. Solutions to these problems were difficult to find due to a lack of common understanding of the problems themselves among those parties with vested interests. Over and above that, the Laguna Lake Development Authority (LLDA), a government agency mandated by law to manage the lake basin, did not have a full grasp of the complexitiy of the problems.

Recently an interdisciplinary team in the Institute of Environmental Science and Management (IESAM; University of the Philippines at Los Banos College) initiated an agroecosystem analysis study of Laguna Lake using an approach developed by Conway & Sajise (1986). The objectives of the analysis were to gain some understanding of the biophysical and socioeconomic conditions of the lake basin, as well as the institutional and organizational arrangements related to lake management. In addition, the study was aimed at formulating mutually-agreed programmes for research and development in order to enhance lake productivity. The present paper reports the results of this study with a particular focus on the lake ecosystem.

Agroecosystem framework of analysis

The agroecosystem analysis of the whole Laguna Lake basin followed the procedure described by Conway &

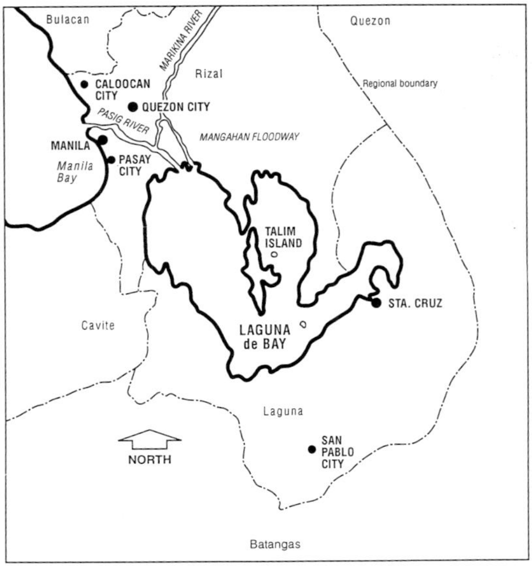

Fig. 1. Map of the Laguna Lake region.

0538-4680/94/0024-0259 $ 1.50

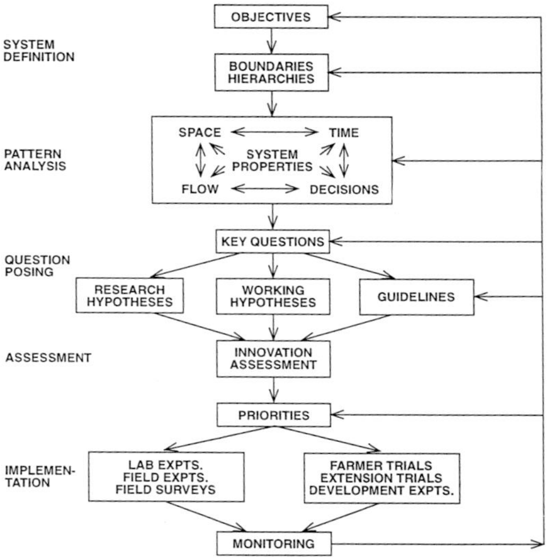

Fig. 2. Procedure of agroecosystem analysis for research and development.

SAJISE (1986). The procedure outlined in Fig. 2 was adopted at a multidisciplinary and multisectoral workshop held recently in Los Banos. Data used in the analysis included both primary and secondary information obtained from a range of sources (e.g. PACARDO et al. 1988, FELLIZAR et al. 1989).

Prior to the workshop, preparatory activities such as data gathering and analysis, preparation of audiovisual materials, and so on were initiated by various interdisciplinary teams. One team was assigned to each of the three major agroecosystems in the basin: the drainage basin (termed watershed herein), the lake itself, and the Pasig-Marikina-Mangahan system. Interactions were an important and necessary feature of the interdisciplinary teams, and they occurred at four levels: interaction within the team, among the teams, and within small groups, and at the workshop plenary sessions.

Environmental profile of Laguna Lake drainage basin

The watershed

The Laguna Lake watershed encompasses all lands surrounding the lake whose slopes and stream channels drain towards the lake. It lies within the provinces of Rizal, Cavite, Laguna, Batangas and Quezon, and covers 52 municipalities and one city. The approximate area of the watershed is 381,000 ha of which 279,663 ha (78%) is land, and 98,076 ha (22%) is the lake proper. Of the total land area, 200,274 h ha are given over to agriculture while 181,826 ha is described as forest. The Laguna Lake watershed surrounds the lake, and contains many urban settlements. Thus, management of the lake drainage basin is much more complicated than watersheds encompassing rural or undeveloped areas.

Rainfall, topography and land use

The annual average rainfall in the drainage basin is 2,490 mm. June to November is the wet season (average monthly rainfall >200 mm), but there are peaks in rainfall (to almost 400 mm) in July and October. Monthly average rainfall is <75 mm from January to April (inclusive). Thirty-five percent of the watershed can be described as gently sloping, 45% rolling, 15% steep, and 5% very steep. Land use in the basin is as follows: urban, 24,830 ha (6.5%); rice paddy, 54,642 ha (14.4%); diverse cropland, 42,620 ha (11.2%); fruit trees and coconut palms, 101,203 ha (26.7%); forest 90,862 ha (23.9%); grasslands 61,703 ha (16.3%); and marshland, 3811 ha (1.0%).

Socioeconomic conditions

Population growth in the Laguna Lake drainage basin was estimated to be 5.2%, a rate which reflects immigration from other parts of the Philippines in addition to local population increase. The present population is not known exactly, but may have reached 3.5 million, thereby placing significant environmental pressure on the lake. The total number of households in the drainage basin in 1980 was 472,684 (63.4% urban and 36.6% rural). The majority of households (60.1%) depended on wages and salaries for their livelihood, 24.9% on agriculture and 2.6% on fishery. The number of fishermen operating in Laguna Lake was 13,000 in 1963, but had fallen to 8620 in 1983 reflecting a decline in fish production (see below).

The industrial sector contributed 68% of Gross Domestic Productivity in the drainage basin, and this is expected to increase to 78% by the year 2000. The industrial sector provided employment for 33% of the population. Manufacturing and – to a lesser extent – construction dominated the industrial output, accounting for 89% and 9% respectively. This pattern is likely to remain unchanged in the year 2000 in view of the extensive preparatory programmes for the implementation of a regional industrial strategy. The industrial sector is important to the regional economy not only in terms of the income it brings to the region but also in terms of the employment opportunities it offers to the labour market.

The lake

Laguna Lake has a shoreline of 220 km, a mean depth of 2.8 m, and a volume of 3 billion m^3. Twenty-one rivers (excluding small creeks and streams) drain into the lake. Prior to the mid-1970s, the lake contained 23 species of fish, some of which were migratory. In 1991, however, it was

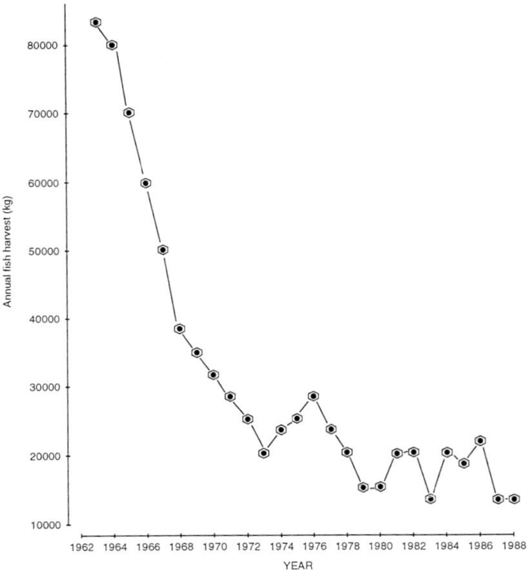

Fig. 3. Annual fish harvest by open fishing in Laguna Lake.

estimated that there were no more than 10 species remaining. The species loss reflects a range of factors, including pollution and the environmental effects of a barrage erected on the Pasig River to prevent saline intrusions from Manila Bay.

Fish productivity

Fish yields from the lake were relatively high during the early 1960s (Fig. 3), when an annual catch of about 80 t (predominantly milkfish and catfish) was supplied to Metro Manila. The annual fish catch had declined steeply to approximately 15 tons in 1988 – the last period of monitoring by LLDA. Circumstantial evidence suggests that the declining fish yields reflect a combination of factors, including over-fishing, increased levels of pollution and the Pasig River salinity barrier.

Phytoplankton

A 14-year monitoring programme for phytoplankton has revealed that blue-green algae were most

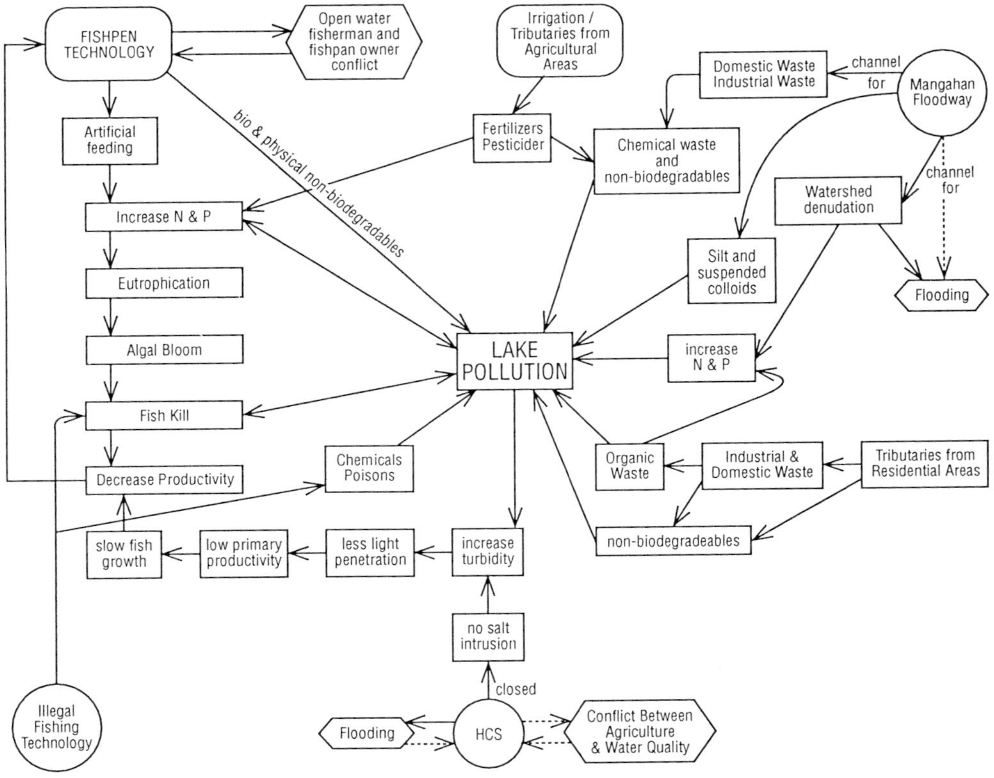

Fig. 4. Flow diagram of pollution sources and their consequences in Laguna Lake.

Table 1. Manganese levels in surface waters in some selected areas in Laguna Lake tributaries. Figures in parentheses are ranges.

	Manganese concentrations (μg/l)			
	1973	1974	1975	1976
San Pedro River upstream	601 (500–660)	925	147	290 (55–210)
San Pedro River downstream	325 (2–630)	675	857	1000 (470–1425)
San Cristobal River	568 (298–816)	900	647	740 (218–1415)
San Juan River upstream	151 (123–172)	1000	169	50 (20–552)
San Juan River downstream	195 (18–348)	1175	105	70 (54–222)
Santa Cruz River	118 (80–150)	100	59	70 (25–114)
Pagsanjan River upstream	173 (100–268)	180	59	65 (30–62)
Pagsanjan River downstream	– –	1425	124	25 (38–275)
Bay River	– –	–	225	60 (100–350)

abundant when the diatoms were most scarce and vice versa, although the diatoms are the dominant group. There were also temporal variations between the dry seasons and wet seasons, with blue-green algal biomass increasing (and sometimes exceeding) diatom biomass. The net primary productivity of the lake was rather high, and a value of about 1.3 g C/m^2/day was recorded by LLDA in 1984. However, net primary productivity appears to be decreasing with time, with an average of approximately 0.6 g C/m^2/day in 1988.

Lake turbidity and pollution

Turbidity of the lake water is caused by colloidal silicate clays entering the lake as a result of soil erosion in the drainage basin, and Secchi disc readings are typically 30–50 m. Limnological data collected between 1981 and 1988 indicate an inverse relationship between turbidity and chloride concentration, which may be due to the flocculating effects of chlorides leading to precipitation of the suspended clays.

The sources and consequences of pollution in Laguna Lake are summarized in Fig. 4. There are more than 1000 firms or factories around the lake; most do not have waste treatment facilities and are potential point sources of pollution. Indeed, concentrations of manganese and mercury in rivers draining into the lake are high (Tables 1 & 2), and close to unacceptable limits. In addition, total phosphorus concentrations in the waters of East Bay and West Bay are far in excess of 0.1 mg/l (Table 3) and average levels of ammonia-nitrogen have exceeded 0.025 mg/l each year between 1980 and 1988. It is worth mentioning that although the phosphorus and nitrogen in Laguna Lake are high, there were no visible signs of eutrophication (e.g. algal blooms) even in the dry season. The high turbidity combined with frequent wind-induced mixing of the water column may reduce light penetration to such an extent that algal growth is inhibited.

Multisectoral and multidisciplinary agroecosystem workshop

The entrustment of the management of the lake to the LLDA combined with subsequent development activities in the Laguna Lake gave rise to complex problems and issues which could not be resolved at the management level. It became ap-

Table 2. Mercury levels in surface waters in some selected areas in Laguna Lake tributaries in 1976. Figures in parentheses are ranges.

	Mercury concentration (µg/l)
San Pedro River upstream	0.36 (0.25–0.44)
San Pedro River downstream	0.50 (0.45–0.56)
San Cristobal River	0.34 (0.05–0.58)
San Juan River upstream	0.58 (0.05–1.00)
San Juan River downstream	0.20 (0.05–0.40)
Santa Cruz River	1.06 (0.02–3.36)
Pagsanjan River upstream	0.38 (0.33–0.44)
Pagsanjan River downstream	0.76 (0.15–1.60)
Bay River	0.46 (0.02–0.92)

Table 3. Annual mean concentration (mg/l) of total phosphorus in Lake Laguna. Figures in parentheses are ranges; ND = not detected.

		East Bay	West Bay
1986	Surface	0.14 (0.10–0.19)	0.26 (0.057–0.55)
	Bottom	0.17 (0.12–0.28)	0.29 (0.17 –0.58)
1987	Surface	0.099 (0.064–0.13)	0.092 (ND–0.19)
	Bottom	0.11 (0.071–0.14)	0.11 (ND–0.22)
1988	Surface	0.16 (0.11–0.22)	0.11 (0.09–0.36)
	Bottom	0.18 (0.14–0.24)	0.25 (0.13–0.40)
Surface (mean)		0.15	0.21
Bottom (mean)		0.16	0.26

parent that a larger forum with participation of the various users of the lake was necessary. A workshop was organized in February 1991 during which views on the perceptions and understanding about the lake and its watershed were exchanged. Some participants proposed the introduction of innovative changes in the lake, and priority research agenda and development projects were identified. Most important of all, the workshop provided an opportunity for various parties with a vested interest in the lake to meet each other for the first time. A series of recommendations were made, and are listed in approximate priority order below.

i) Form a multisectoral, multidisciplinary research group to study the lake's ecology and productivity, including a review of existing data to assess their reliability and identify information gaps.
ii) Develop charges and compensation mechanisms at the basin level to cost pressures on the lake.
iii) Review laws and regulations on the lake for possible realignment.
iv) Develop institutional mechanisms for promoting equity.
v) Formulate a community-generated charter on Laguna Lake stating different users' and stakeholders' claims and interests in the lake.
vi) Adopt procedures for working with non-government organizations (NGOs) and local social organization to enforce regulations on the lake.
vii) Establish a Laguna Lake Research Centre.
viii) Adopt procedures/guidelines for optimizing the multiple use of lake resources.

Research needs

There is an overall requirement to describe and understand the social, economic and environmental impacts of development programmes on the Laguna Lake. Specifically, there is a need to identify the causes of the decline in fish productivity and diversity, and to evaluate policies on fish harvest and production technologies in the lake (including an assessment of the environmental effects and usefulness of fish pens). An investigation of the effects of salinity fluctuations and saline water intrusion on lake ecology should be undertaken, along with a comparison of rates of primary production in the East, West, Central and South Bays of the lake. These studies need to be carried out in association with investigations of lake pollution and trophic status, with the ultimate goal of identifying viable measures for preventing degradation of the lake.

References

CONWAY, G. R. & SAJISE, O. E., 1986: The Agroecosystems of Buhi: Problems and Opportunities. – Proceedings of the Buhi Agroecosystems Analysis Workshop, November 1985, Institute of Environmental Science and Management, University of the Philippines at Los Banos College, Laguna.

FELLIZAR, F. P., PACARDO, E. P., FRANCISCO, F. R., ESPALDON, M. V. O., NEPOMUCENO, D. N. & ESPALDON, C. F., 1989: Policy Responses to Fishery Conflict in Laguna Lake: A Case Study. – Unpublished monograph, Institute of Environmental Science and Management University of the Philippines at Los Banos College, Laguna.

PACARDO, E. P., BARTOLOME, B. J., FRANCISCO, F. R., ESPALDON, M. V. O. & PATINDOL, S. L., 1988: Basic Approach to Laguna Lake Water Resource Management. – Unpublished monograph, Institute of Environmental Science and Management University of the Philippines at Los Banos College, Laguna.

Author's address:

Institute of Environmental Science and Management (IESAM), University of the Philippines at Los Banos College, Laguna, Philippines.

Mitt. Internat. Verein. Limnol.	24	265–272	Stuttgart, Februar 1994

Present utilization and recommendations for management of tin-mine lakes in Malaysia

Phillip T. Arumugam

Abstract

Tin-mine lakes are a consequence of abandoned tin-mine pits, slime-retention pools and mining excavations becoming filled with water. There are approximately 4300 tin-mine lakes in Peninsular Malaysia, with a combined area of 16,440 ha. They are used for aquaculture, as water sources and for recreation, as well as for waste disposal and dumping. The physicochemical characteristics of the water in 41 such tin-mine lakes were highly variable with wide ranges. Indeed, most other inland waters in Malaysia have values that fall within the ranges recorded for the study lakes. The tin-mine lakes supported a diverse array of organisms including 55 aquatic macrophytes and 42 fish taxa. By drawing together information on the uses, biota (plants and fishes), and physicochemical features of tin-mine lakes, it is possible to classify them into five main groups: new lakes, acidic lakes, buffered lakes, aquaculture lakes, and post-aquaculture lakes. The main characteristics that differentiate lake categories are pH and the composition of floral communities.

Tin-mine lakes are generally isolated from one another, but several lakes with different physicochemical characteristics can occur in one locality. Because of the proximity of lakes of different types, tin-mine lakes and their surroundings have potential conservation or heritage value. This value includes their use as a sanctuary for aquatic wildlife (birds, fishes, reptiles, mammals); an arboretum of native aquatic plants; a gene pool for aquatic resources; and a resource for teaching and research.

Introduction

Tin mining is the largest and most important sector of the mining industry of Malaysia. The country is the world's largest tin producer, accounting for about one-third of total tin production (Chan 1991). The long history of tin mining in Peninsular Malaysia has resulted in extensive tracts of wasteland, including sand or slime tailings and pits, slime-retention pools and excavations. Tin-mine lakes are a consequence of the latter becoming filled with water. There are about 4300 such lakes in Peninsular Malaysia covering approximately, 16,440 ha. They represent 18.9% of the total area used for freshwater fish pond culture.

Tin-mine lakes occur mainly in Perak (2873 lakes), Selangor (542), Johore (280) and Pahang (229) in Peninsular Malaysia. The largest lake is about 99 ha, and only 26% of these lakes are less than 1 ha in extent. The lakes may be fan-shaped, more-or-less circular or irregular in shape, with depths which can exceed 60 m. Fan-shaped lakes are formed mainly from the gravel-pumping method of tin extraction, while the circular and irregular lakes are mainly a consequence of bucket dredging and open-cast mining. These three main mining methods also lead to the formation of slime-retention lakes.

Tin-mine lakes and their surrounding wastelands have been classified as 'disused mining land' by planners mainly because of the poor soil. However, abandoned mining lands have been utilised for agriculture and other purposes (Ding et al. 1981, Lim et al. 1981). Jothy (1968) was the first to undertake limnological studies on tin-mine lakes. Subsequent investigators have compared their limnology with that of natural water bodies in Malaysia (Mizuno & Mori 1970, Richardson & Lim 1975, Palmieri et al. 1980). More recently, Saravanamuthu & Lim (1982) and Yusuff & Patimah (this volume) studied tin-mine lakes landscaped as recreational parks. Biological data on tin-mine lakes includes research by Palaniappan (1972) and Kiew (1975) on aquatic macrophytes, and Mohsin & Ambak (1983) on fish. Elsewhere, Djajadiredja & Hardjamulia (1976) have provided information on some Indonesian tin-mine lakes, while Alverson (1973) and Canton & Ward (1981) have reported upon lakes formed by ore mining in temperate regions.

This paper describes the characteristics, biology, utilization and classification of Malaysian tin-mine lakes, and makes recommendations concerning their role in conservation. The latter point is important because of proposals that abandoned tin mines and their tailings could be included in plans for Malaysian national parks (Ding 1976, Gunasillan 1976).

Survey methods

Forty-one lakes, mainly in Selangor and Perak, were sampled during 1980–1982. General observations of aquatic macrophytes, fishes, aquaculture, lakes and tailings utilisation at these lakes were made between 1976–

0538-4680/94/0024-0265 $ 2.00

1982 and 1986–1990. The selection of study sites included both new and old (20–40 years old) lakes, lakes used for aquaculture and those in which aquaculture had been abandoned, and sites where pH of the waters ranged from acid to alkaline. Some of the lakes studied have since been filled in to provide land for housing development.

Water temperature, specific conductance and dissolved oxygen were measured with YSI meters, and pH with a Lamotte Comparator. Data on transparency and light transmission were obtained using a Secchi disc and a Tsurimi-Seiki light meter respectively. Chemical composition of lake waters was determined using standard procedures (Mackereth 1963, Golterman 1971, APHA 1975). The following parameters were measured: total alkalinity, free carbon dioxide, chloride, calcium, magnesium, nitrate-nitrogen, ammonia-nitrogen, orthophosphate-phosphorus and sulphate. The development of aquatic macrophyte communities was assessed by visual comparisons – which sometimes involved SCUBA diving – and collection of samples for species determination. Fish were obtained by the use of a variety of nets. Only a portion of the results – those relevant to management of tin-mine lakes and tailings – are presented here; further details of the survey methods and findings are available from the author.

Physicochemical parameters

The range of values for various physicochemical parameters measured in the study lakes are given in Table 1. Wide ranges were observed for most parameters especially pH, light transmission, Secchi disc transparency, specific conductance, free carbon dioxide, total alkalinity, chloride, sulphate, calcium and magnesium. The study lakes seemed to embrace almost the entire range of physicochemical conditions recorded as a result of investigations of other lentic waters in Peninsular Malaysia, such as reservoirs and impoundments (Ho 1976, Lai & Chua 1976, Arumugam & Furtado 1980, Khan et al. 1990), lakes in recreational parks (Saravanamuthu & Lim 1982, Fatimah & Sharr 1987, Yusoff & Patimah 1994), natural swamp lakes (Furtado & Mori 1982) and a variety of other habitats (Johnson 1967, Mizuno & Mori 1970, Palmieri et al. 1980) including some additional tin-mine lakes (Anonymous 1968, Jothy 1968). Malaysian water bodies which fall outside this range of conditions include Tasek Dayang Bunting (north Malaysia) which has a high sodium chloride content (Yadav & Ratnasabapathy 1974), and coastal ricefields which are influenced by saline influxes and/or treated with high fertiliser dosage and thus have high specific conductances (Ali 1987).

Table 1. The range of physiocochemical parameters prevailing 35 Malaysian tin-mine lakes.

Parameters	Range
Surface area, ha.	0.5–51
Max. depth, m	1.5– >60.0
pH	2.7–9.2
Temperature °C	27–35
% Light Transmission @ 1 m depth	0–91
Secchi disc transparency (cm)	20– >960
Specific conductance, µmhos/cm	18–620
Free CO_2, mg/l $CaCO_3$	0–143.8
Dissolved O_2, mg/l O_2	0.7–13.7
Total alkalinity, mg/l $CaCO_3$	0–269
Chloride, mg/l Cl	0–23.3
Sulphate, mg/l SO_4-S	0–99.1
Orthophosphate, µg/l PO_4-P	0–500
Nitrate, mg/l NO_3-N	0–4.4
Ammonia, mg/l NH_4-N	0–1.00
Calcium, mg/l Ca	0–84
Magnesium, mg/l Mg	0–112

In essence, one aspect of the conservation value of tin-mining lakes is that they can be considered to represent the full extent of physicochemical conditions in Malaysian lentic waters. Added to this is the fact that lakes with markedly dissimilar water chemistries occur close together in a single locality, offering the potential for conservation of a series of water bodies of differing character.

Aquatic macrophytes

Fifty-five species of aquatic macrophytes were recorded in the 41 study lakes (Table 2). Some of them are emergent hydrophytes which can tolerate temporary submergence in water. Based on visual assessment of macrophyte communities (especially the identity of dominant species), a general trend in plant community development or 'succession' can be proposed. Colonization of slime-retention lakes is rapid because of the presence of silty soil and the generally shallow condition (depth usually less than 2 m). Benthic algae are initial colonizers and blanket the bottom sediments; within a few months a diversity of aquatic macrophytes can be recorded, comprising a majority of emergent species that can tolerate temporary submergence. In later stages of community development, these water bodies become marshlands. Precise species composition seems to depend on chance, dispersal mechanisms, and the presence of a source of colonists nearby. Some species, such as *Nelumbium*

Table 2. A checklist of aquatic macrophytes from tin-mine lakes in Peninsular Malaysia.

Blyxa auberti RICH. (= *B. malayana* RIDL.)
Brachiara mutica (FORSSK) STAPF.
Chara spp.
Colocasia esculenta (L.) SCHOTT
Cyperus elatus L.
C. halpan L.
C. iria L.
C. pilosus VAHL
C. polystachyus ROTTB.
C. rotundus L.
Eichhornia crassipes (MART.) SOLMS
Eleocharis dulcis (BURM.F) TRIN. ex HENSCHEL
E. geniculata (L.) ROEM. & SCHULT
E. ochrostachys STEUD.
Eragrostis atrovirens (DESF.) TRIN. ex STEUD.
E. unioloides (RETZ.) NEES ex STEUD.
Eriocaulon sexangulare L.
Fimbristylis acuminata VAHL.
F. dichotoma (L.) VAHL.
F. ferruginea (L.) VAHL.
F. globulosa (RETZ.) KUNTH.
F. milliacea (L.) [? = *F. littoralis* GAUDICH.]
Fuirena umbellata ROTTB.
Hydrilla verticillata (L.F.) ROYLE
Hymenachne acutigluma (STEUD.) GILLILAND
Ipomoea aquatica FORSSK.
Isachne globosa (Thumb.) O. KTZE
Ischaemum muticum L.
I. indicum (HOUTT.) MERR.
Leersia hexandra SW.
Lemna perpusilla TORR.
Limnocharis flava (L.) BUCH.
Lipocarpha chinensis (Osb.) KERN
Ludwigia octovalvis (JACQ.) RAVEN
L. hyssopifolia (G. DON) EXELL
L. adscendens (L.) HARA
Mikania cordata (BURM.F.) B.L. ROBINSON
Monochoria vaginalis (BURM.F.) PRESL.
Nelumbium nelumbo (L.) DRUCE
Nitella spp.
Nymphaea lotus L. ?
Nymphoides indica O. KUNTZE
Paspalum longifolium ROXB.
P. conjugatum BERG.
Phragmites karka (RETZ.) TRIN. ex STEUD.
P. australis (CAV.) TRIN. ex STEUD.
Pistia stratiotes L.
Polygonum barbatum L.
Rhynchospora corymbosa (L.) BRITT.
Sacciolepis indica (L.) A. CHASE
Salvinia molesta D. S. MITCHELL
Scirpus mucronatus L.
S. grossus L.F,
Scleria spp.
Typha angustifolia L. [? = *T. domingensis* PERS.]
Utricularia flexuosa VAHL.
Xyris pauciflora WILD.

nelumbo, may be deliberately introduced. Communities in slime lakes can change quickly; PALANIAPPAN (1972) observed that a community of *Cyperus iria* and *Nelumbium nelumbo* was replaced by *Typha angustifolia* and *Scirpus mucronatus* within six months.

In lakes formed as a result of gravel-pump mining, *Leersia hexandra, Nelumbium nelumbo* and *Typha angustifolia* are abundant, together with *Ludwigia hyssopifolia, Cyperus polystachyus, Phragmites* spp., *Mikania cordata* and *Scirpus mucronatus* in shallow areas. Generally, slime-retention lakes and gently-shelving marginal zones of deep lakes support similar communities that are dominated by emergent macrophytes. Moreover, many lakes have steep shores and lack marginal-zone communities. In the initial stages of colonization, such lakes support some benthic algae (although growth is limited by the depth of the euphotic zone); subsequently, macrophytes including *Chara* spp., *Nitella* spp., *Utricularia flexuosa, Fimbristylis* spp. and *Eleocharis* spp. become abundant. *Fimbristylis* and *Eleocharis* dominate acidic lakes while the three former taxa are more important in buffered lakes. In most cases, phytoplankton is generally sparse. Once colonization is complete, community structure remains unchanged for many years if the lake is left undisturbed. This reflects, in part, the small amounts of allochthonous inputs derived from the sparse vegetation that develops on the nutrient-poor mine tailings.

Despite the range of aquatic macrophytes encountered, in terms of the conservation importance of tin-mine lakes it should be noted that two species are not recorded in these habitats: the emergent sedge *Lepironia articulata,* and *Pandanus helicopus* which is a woody pandan. The latter is a significant component of southeast Asian swamp forests. The former occurs in older reservoirs, Subang Lake (ARUMUGAM 1976) and Tasek Bera swamp (FURTADO & MORI 1982) where *Pandanus helicopus* is found also.

In situations where tin-mine lakes receive significant nutrient inputs or are otherwise modified by anthropogenic activities, drastic changes in macrophyte communities take place. Phytoplankton increases in abundance in lakes used for fish culture and *Hydrilla verticillata, Salvinia molesta* and *Lemna perpusilla* dominate macrophyte communities. Feeding by grass carp (*Ctenopharyngodon idellus*), when present, tends to eliminate these macrophytes. Once fish culture has been abandoned, tin-mine lakes tend to support a mixed community of floating macrophytes. In those lakes which are used as dumping sites for organic wastes, *Eichhornia crassipes* may cover up to 90% of the surface area; *Ipomoea aquatica* and *Ludwigia adscendens* are common also in such lakes.

Fishes

Forty-two fish taxa have been identified from tin-mine lakes (Table 3), including species taken in the present survey and earlier records by JOTHY (1968) and MOHSIN & AMBAK (1983). Streams are the source of some of these species, including *Aplocheilus panchax, Puntius tetrazona pentipentazona, Chela* sp., *Rasbora* spp., *Cyclocheilichthys apogon* and *Channa* spp., but additional species were introduced for aquaculture. Acidic tin-mine lakes contain relatively sparse fish populations, including air-breathers such as *Channa striatus* and *Trichogaster trichopterus*. Buffered lakes support a greater abundance of fishes including *Aplocheilus panchax, Puntius tetrazona pentipentazona* and *Stigmatogobius isognathus*. Aquaculture lakes contain a variety of Chinese carps (*Aristichthys nobilis, Cyprinus carpio, Ctenopharyngodon idellus* and *Hypophthalmichthys molitrix*), as well as *Trichogaster pectoralis,* catfish (*Clarias* spp.), *Puntius gonionotus* and Tilapia (*Oreochromis* spp. and hybrids). The Malaysian government Fisheries Department have also stocked some of the buffered lakes (and those in urban areas) with Chinese carps, Tilapia and *Puntius gonionotus*.

Lakes in which aquaculture has been abandoned, and especially those with a dense surface cover of *Eichhornia crassipes,* contain mainly air-breathing fishes (*Channa* spp., *Trichogaster pectoralis*) which tolerate the low levels of dissolved oxygen under the mat of floating vegetation. Lakes lacking the dense cover of floating macrophytes support indigenous fishes and Tilapia. Urban lakes such as Aman Lake and Taman Jaya Lake contain the exotic *Poecilia reticulata* which have colonized the lakes from the polluted drains. In Titiwangsa Lake, hobbyists have introduced ornamental Cichlidae which seem to have established self-sustaining populations.

Table 3. A checklist of fishes from Tin-mine Lakes in Malaysia. Data derived from the present study, JOTHY (1968) and MOHSIN & AMBAK (1983).

Indigenous fishes
Anabas testudineus (BLOCH)
Aplocheilus panchax (HAMILTON)
Channa lucius (CUVIER & VALENCIENNIES)
C. striata (BLOCH)
Chanda siamensis FOWLER
Chela sp.
Clarias batrachus (L.)
C. macrocephalus (GÜNTHER)
Cyclocheilichthys apogon (VALENCIENNES)
Dangila sp.
Hampala macrolepidota (KUHL & VAN HASSELT)
Mastacembelus maculatus (CUVIER & VALENCIENNES)
Mystus sp.
Notopterus notopterus (PALLAS)
Ompok sp.
Osphromenus goramy (LACEPEDE)
Osteochilus hasseltii (CUVIER & VALENCIENNES)
Oxyleotris marmoratus (BLEEKER)
Paralaubuca sp.
Pristolepis fasciatus (BLEEKER)
Puntius binotatus (VALENCIENNES)
P. lateristriga (VALENCIENNES)
P. pentazona hexazona WEBER & BEAUFORT
P. schwanefeldii (BLEEKER)
P. tetrazona pentipentazona FOWLER
Rasbora einthovenii (BLEEKER)
R. heteromorpha (DUNCKER)
R. trilineata STEINDACHNER
Stigmatogobius isognathus (BLEEKER)
Trichogaster trichopterus (PALLAS)
Exotic fishes
Aristichthys nobilis (RICHARDSON)
Catla catla (HAMILTON)
Ctenopharyngodon idellus (CUVIER & VALENCIENNES)
Cyprinus carpio (L.)
Hypophthalmichthys molitrix (VALENCIENNES)
Labeo rohita GÜNTHER
Poecilia reticulata (PETERS)
Puntius gonionotus (BLEEKER)
Oreochromis mossambicus (PETERS)
O. niloticus (L.)
Tilapia (*Oreochromis*) hybrids
Trichogaster pectoralis (REGAN)

Utilisation of tin-mine lakes

Aquaculture

Small, shallow lakes are used as fish ponds, but cage culture is undertaken in larger lakes. Some lakes are used as a source of water for fish culture and flow-through aquaculture systems. Fish culture of this type is frequently integrated with animal husbandry (ducks or pigs) and small orchards. *Nelumbium nelumbo* is grown as a cash crop in shallow slime-retention lakes.

Water source

Tin-mine lakes are used as a source of potable water as well as water for light industry, irrigation, and washing pens and enclosures used for rearing livestock (pigs, cattle, goats, chickens and ducks). Squatters and farmers in the vicinity of tin-mine lakes use the water for various household activities. In certain localities, latrines have been sited over the lake waters. Such 'enrichment' of the waters is often associated with fish culture, but the practice of building latrines along margins is being discouraged near urban areas.

Recreation and tourism

A few tin-mine lakes – especially those in urban parks – have been developed for recreational fisheries. Some of the larger lakes are used for water sports including water skiing, SCUBA diving, sailing, boating and swimming. Others have been landscaped by local authorities to enhance the aesthetics of urban areas by development of parks, 'lake-view' housing estates, and aquatic 'green belts'. Some of these lakes serve also as oxidation ponds. The potential of abandoned tin-mining lakes has not been lost on developers who have begun to make significant investments in landscaping and designing multi-million dollar tourism and recreational amenities incorporating aspects of modified Malaysian ecosystems. One successful venture of this type is Lake Titiwangsa which includes prime residential properties, a park and playground, a floating restaurant, and a lake with watersports and other recreational facilities. A more grandiose development, Taman Sungai Besi Indah in Selangor, will – upon completion – include a golf course, condominiums, woodlands, and facilities for recreational fisheries.

Threats

Many lakes are lost as a consequence of filling for development and building, but the most pervasive problem for existing lakes is that of waste disposal and dumping. These wastes which include household refuse and litter, as well as industrial and agricultural effluents, threaten to reduce the potential conservation value that appropriately-managed tin-mine lakes could have.

Classification of tin-mine lakes

By drawing together the information presented above on the uses, biota (plants and fishes) and physicochemical features of tin-mine lakes, it is possible to classify them. The main characteristics that differentiate lake categories are pH and floral communities. Five lake types can be identified (Table 4): new lakes, acidic lakes, buffered lakes, aquaculture lakes, and post-aquaculture lakes.

New lakes generally have high loads of suspended solids which reduce Secchi disc transparency. During rainy periods, some settled particles are resuspended by inflowing waters and sub-surface flow. The nutrient status of these lakes depends on the balance of inputs and loss through outflow, as well as the extent and frequency of resuspension of particulates and the presence of continued mining activity in the vicinity. Members of the acidic and buffered lakes category have not been influenced by mining works for at least one year. They have plant communities dominated by submerged or emergent macrophytes. The water chemistry of these lakes depends upon the nature of the soil making up the mine tailings. Acid lakes result from lateritic, pyritic and sandstone-derived soils but, in limestone areas, buffered lakes prevail. The natural inland waters of Peninsular Malaysia are predominantly acidic and sometimes darkly stained by humic leachates (Johnson 1967, Furtado & Mori 1982), but tin-mine lakes lack the humic and fluvic acids which impart this acidity. Instead, they are clear, with colour ranging from green to greenish-blue depending on water depth.

Tin-mine lakes used for aquaculture are eutrophic as a consequence of fertiliser loadings which are mainly animal or household wastes. Macrophytes are relatively sparse but phytoplankton are abundant. The water is generally brown except during surface algal blooms when the water may appear green (due to chlorophytes and cyanophytes) or rust-coloured (due to *Euglena* spp.). Rehabilitated tin-mine lakes that receive effluents from residential areas have similar characteristics to aquaculture lakes and are included within the same category. Such lakes are stocked for recreational fishing. In lakes where aquaculture has been abandoned – post-aquaculture lakes – or lakes used as a dumping site for organic effluents, the water is brown and discoloured due mainly to the presence of humic substances. The plant community is dominated by floating macrophytes.

Table 4. General limnological characteristics used in the classification of Tin-mine Lakes in Peninsular Malaysia. Ap = *Apocheilus panchax*; Ch = Chlorophytes; Cs = *Chara* spp.; Cy = Cyanophytes; Ec = *Eichhornia crassipes*; Eo = *Eleocharis ochrostachys*; Eu = *Euglena* spp.; Fa = *Fimbristylis acuminata*; Hv = *Hydrilla verticillata*; Lh = *Leersia hexandra* sp.; Nn = *Nelumbium nelumbo*; n.d. = no data; Pk = *Phragmites karka*; Pp = *Puntus tetrazona partipentazona*; Sm = *Salvinia molesta*; Sm = *Scirpus mucronatus*.

	New lakes	Acidic lakes	Buffered lakes	Aquaculture lakes	Post-aquaculture lakes
pH	2.7–8.1	2.7–5.5	5.6–8.1	6.3–9.2	6.2–7.0
Cations	variable	poor	Ca-rich	moderate	poor
Anions	variable	high	variable	variable	poor
Benthic algae	high	poor	poor	poor	poor
Periphyton on macrophytes	poor	high	high	poor	high
Macrophytes	poor	high Eo; Fa	high Cs; Lh; Pk; Nn; Su	poor	high Ec; Hv; Sm
Phytoplankton	poor	poor	poor	high Cy; Ch; Eu	poor
Fishes	n.d.	Few air-breathers	Indigenous Pp; Ap	Tilapia; Chinese carps	variable

Conservation

NORAMLY (1986) recorded that waterfowl, including migratory species, use marshy tin-mine lakes as feeding sites, and suggested that such habitats should be conserved. Indeed, there have been attempts to include tin-mine lakes and mine tailings in two conservation plans for National Parks in Perak (DING 1976, GUNASILLAN 1976). Unfortunately, neither proposal was accepted by the relevant authorities. The degradation and loss of some potentially-valuable water bodies is exemplified by a suggestion made during the early stages of this study (1980) that (what was then) the Fisheries Unit of Universiti Pertanian Malaysia (UPM) acquire some abandoned mining land adjacent to their grounds to be used for conservation education, and research and training. The area contained about 20 tin-mine lakes of various ages including some given over to acquaculture, as well as abandoned aquaculture lakes and marshland lakes. In addition to these, four tin-mine lakes were present within the UPM grounds. Over the last 10 years, however, all of the lakes have been filled and used as sites for housing development, additional UPM buildings and, in one case, for a waste-dumping site.

The Malaysian government (Public Works Department and State Development Corporation) do practise applied conservation in the urban areas. A few tin-mine lakes have been landscaped to serve as 'urban lungs' and recreation areas in parks. The private sector has also realised the recreation and tourism potential of such habitats (see above). The conservation value of these developments can be enhanced with appropriate management strategies. For example, the current practise of cutting or removing reeds and emergent plants to make the lake margins look neat and tidy has the effect of removing a potential habitat for indigenous and migratory birds and destroying the breeding sites of some fishes.

When combined with appropriate management practices, tin-mine lakes and their surroundings can be used as a sanctuary for aquatic widlife (native and migratory birds, fishes, reptiles and mammals) and an arboretum of native aquatic plants. The area can serve as a gene pool for aquatic flora and fauna; i.e. a source of wild types for commercial stock improvement. Such habitats can be studied to provide insight into lake processes and applied rehabilitation approaches, and this applied research can be combined with the use of tin-mine lakes for research and training in conservation and management.

Clearly, there are conflicting views as to what is the best use for tin-mine lakes, but these need not be irreconcilable. For example, the Taman Sungai Besi Indah development project (see above) could be combined with appropriate management practices to conserve wildlife. Indeed, where a developer can be convinced to landscape a lake or part of a lake as a bird sanctuary, the abundance of wildlife may be generally enhanced, thereby increasing the amenity value of the whole development. Appropriate conservation and management practices are not always expensive, and – where the infrastructure associated with a major recreational development already exists – the managed habitat and its wildlife may become a tourist attraction. Given vision and a spirit of cooperation, tin-mine lakes in Malaysia could provide an ideal opportunity for the integrated development of strategies for recreation, habitat rehabilitation and conservation.

Acknowledgements

The author wishes to thank the Faculty of Fisheries & Marine Sciences, Universiti Pertanian Malaysia for use of facilities and a research grant, and UNESCO for a travel grant. Special thanks are due to Mr. Kuppan for laboratory assistance, and Prof. Enoch for identification of aquatic macrophytes.

References

Ali, A. B., 1987: The ecology of fish culture in ricefields: some biological aspects of fish culture system of North Krian, Perak, Malaysia. – In: Agriculture and Biological Priorities in Asia. – Proc. IFS Symp. Science, Asia '87, Kuala Lumpur, Malaysia: 17–20.

Alverson, K., 1973: Cattle and catfish on surface-mined land. – *Soil Conserv.* **39:**4–6.

AMERICAN PUBLIC HEALTH ASSOCIATION (APHA), 1975: Standard Methods for the Examination of Water and Wastewater, 14th Edition: 1193 pp. – American Public Health Association, Washington, D.C.

Anonymous 1968: A general ecological survey on the Timor Pond, Petaling Jaya, Selangor. – *Malay. Nat. J.* **21:**106–124.

Arumugam, P. T., 1976: Recovery of an Eutrophicated Reservoir, Subang Lake, Malaysia: 111 pp. – Unpublished M. Sc. Thesis, University of Malaysia, Kuala Lumpur.

Arumugam, P. T. & Furtado, J. I., 1980: Physico-chemistry, destratification and nutrient budget of a lowland eutrophicated Malaysian reservoir and its limnological implications. – *Hydrobiologia* **70:**11–24.

Canton, S. P. & Ward, J. V., 1981: Benthos and zooplankton of coal strip mine ponds in the mountains of northwestern Colorado, U.S.A. – *Hydrobiologia* **85:**23–31.

Chan, Y. K., 1991: Tin mining land – an overview of the current situation in Peninsular Malaysia. – In: Ex-mining Land and Bris Soil Prospects and Profit: 17 pp. – Kejora Management Services Sdn Bhd. 15–16 October 1990, Paper No. 1.

Ding C. H., 1976: Proposal for an integrated plan of a National Park in Perak. – *Malay. Nat. J.* **29:**282–306.

Ding, T. H., Vimala, P. & Yusof, S., 1981: An Agroeconomic Survey of Vegetable Farming in Peninsular Malaysia: 139 pp. – MARDI.

Djajadiredja, R. R. & Hardhamulia, A., 1976: Development of abandoned tin mining pools in Indonesia. – *Symp. Indo-Pacific Fish. Counc.* **17:**1–21.

Fatimah, M. Y. & Sharr, H. A., 1987: Physico-chemical limnology of Zoo Negara Lake, Malaysia. – *Arch. Hydrobiol. Beih. Ergebn. Limnol.* **28:**435–446.

Furtado, J. I. & Mori, S., 1982: The Ecology of a Tropical Freshwater Swamp, Tasek Bera: 484 pp. – Dr. Junk Publishers, The Hague, Netherlands.

Golterman, H. L., 1971: Methods for Chemical Analysis of Fresh Waters: 166 pp. – Blackwell Scientific Publications, Oxford.

Gunasillan, G., 1976: Potential sites for National Parks. – *Malay. Nat. J.* **29:**262–264.

Ho, S. C., 1976: The physico-chemical limnology of the Ampang Impounding Reservoir, Kuala Lumpur. – *Malay. Agri. J.* **50:**527–544.

Johnson, D. S., 1967: On the chemistry of freshwaters in Southern Malaysia and Singapore. – *Arch. Hydrobiol.* **63:**477–496.

Jothy, A. A., 1968: Preliminary observations of disused tin-mining pools in Malaysia and their potentials for fish production: 21 pp. – Paper presented at IPFC/C68/Tech 25, 13th Session, Brisbane, Australia. Oct. 1968.

Khan, M. S., Ambak, M. A., Ang, K. J. & Mohsin, A. K. M., 1990: Physical, chemical and plankton studies of a lowland tropical hydroelectric reservoir, Tasek Chenderoh, Malaysia. – *Malay. Appl. Biol.* **19:**109–112.

Kiew, R., 1975: The reproductive biology of some tin tailing weeds. – *Malay. Nat. J.* **29:**52–57.

Lai, H. C. & Chua, T. E., 1976: Limnological features of Muda and Pedu Reservoirs with an observation on their suitability for fish culture. – *Malay. Agric. J.* **50:**480–501.

Lim, K. H., Maene, L. M., Maesschalck, G. G. & Wan Sulaiman, W. H., 1981: Reclamation of tin tailings for agriculture in Malaysia: 61 pp. – *Tech. Bull., Soil Sci. Dept, Universiti Pertanian Malaysia.*

Mackereth, F. J. H., 1963: Some methods of Water Analysis for limnologists. – *Freshwat. Biol. Assoc. Scientific Publication* No. **21:**68 pp.

MIZUNO, T. & MORI, S., 1970: Preliminary hydrobiological survey of some Southeast Asian inland waters. – *Biol. J. Linn. Soc.* **2:** 77–117.

MOHSIN, A. K. M. & AMBAK, M. A., 1983: Freshwater Fishes of Peninsular Malaysia: 284 pp. – Penerbit Universiti Pertanian Malaysia.

NORAMLY, G., 1986: Wasteland – or wonderland? – *Malay. Nat.* **40:** 24–27.

PALANIAPPAN, V. M., 1972: History, flora and edaphology of tin tailings areas around Kuala Lumpur. – *Trop. Ecol.* **13:** 202–225.

PALMIERI, M. D., PALMIERI, J. R. & SULLIVAN, J. T., 1980: A chemical analysis of the habitat of nine commonly occurring Malaysian freshwater snails. – *Malay. Nat. J.* **34:** 39–45.

RICHARDSON, J. L. & LIM, T. J., 1975: Algal productivity of natural and artificially enriched freshwaters in Malaysia. – *Verh. Internat. Verein. Limnol.* **19:** 1383–1389.

SARAVANAMUTHU, J. & LIM, R. P., 1982: A preliminary limnological survey of an eutrophic pond, Taman Jaya Pond, Petaling Jaya. – *Malay. Nat.* **35:** 83–97.

YADAV, M. & RATNASABAPATHY, M., 1974: Some biological observations on Tasek Dayang Bunting, Langkawi. – *Malay. Nat. J.* **27:** 50–55.

YUSOFF, F. M. & PATIMAH, I., 1994: A comparative study of phytoplankton populations in two Malaysian lakes. – *Mitt. Internat. Verein. Limnol.* **24:** 251–257.

Author's addresses:

Centre of Applied Sciences, Universiti Pertanian Malaysia Kampus Bintulu, P.S. 396, 97008 Bintulu, Sarawak, Malaysia.
Present address: Faculty of Fisheries and Marine Science, Universiti Pertanian Malaysia, 43400 UPM Serdang, Selangor, Malaysia.

Mitt. Internat. Verein. Limnol.	24	273–278	Stuttgart, Februar 1994

Ecology of a tropical man-made lake in Brunei Darussalam with proposals for its development and management

Webber E. Booth, Satish C. Choy and Kamariah A. Salim

Abstract

The Benutan Reservoir began to fill following impoundment in 1989, and had filled completely by 1991. Physicochemical and biological data obtained on a monthly basis since February 1990 indicate that this is a stratified, dystrophic black-water lake with low levels of inorganic nutrients, high organic loads, and high productivity. Currently (1991), semi-commercial fishing is being undertaken, based on seven or eight local riverine fish species which have become established in the lake. The catchment area, covered with mixed dipterocarp forest and containing abundant wildlife, is spectacular and of great biological interest. In addition to its role in the country's freshwater supply strategy, the reservoir and catchment could also be used for a variety of recreational and pollution-free economic activities which are relevant to current government policies of economic diversification and enhancement of eco-tourism and recreation. Well laid out trails, together with support facilities, could be established in the catchment forest with lake views and lake access points. The lake could be stocked with sport fish to encourage recreational angling. Non-motorized boating and water sports would be feasible on a limited scale. If well managed, such developments would optimize lake utilization and generate revenue without adverse ecological effects.

Introduction

Brunei Darussalam is situated on the northwest coast of Borneo (lat. 4°4′–5°5′N, long. 114°24′–115°23′E). It shares a common border with the Malaysian state of Sarawak, which divides the country into two (Figs. 1 a & B). Brunei Darussalam has an equatorial climate of high temperature (mean $= 28 \pm 10\,^{\circ}C$), high rainfall (2300–4500 mm/yr) and high relative humidity ($>85\%$). The rainfall pattern is a reflection of two monsoons, the wetter northeast monsoon (November–January) and the southwest monsoon (May–October). Between these monsoons, occasional droughts may occur.

There are four main river systems in Brunei Darussalam: the Belait, Tutong, Brunei and Temburong (Fig. 1 b). The Benutan Reservoir is situated in the Ladan foothills, formed by the impoundment of the Sungai Benutan, a tributary of the Tutong River (Fig. 1 c), by an earth dam. Impoundment was completed on 24 March 1989 and by the beginning of February 1990, when the current survey was begun, the water level was at a maximum depth of 12.5 m; by the end of May 1991 the water had risen a further 4.5 m to the spillway level, 35 m + CD. When full, the reservoir has a volume of 44.7×10^6 m^3 and covers a surface area of 4.972 km^2. Controlled release of water from this reservoir (from a depth of 9 m) will prevent saline intrusion into the Sungai Tutong, the major source of fresh water for Bandar Seri Begawan.

Although there is a growing literature on the limnology of tropical lakes (see Payne 1986, Lewis 1987, 1990 and references therein), there is no such information on the lakes (natural or man-made) of Borneo. The formation of the Benutan Reservoir provided an excellent opportunity to study the limnology of a newly-impounded lake, particularly in light of the fact that many smaller lakes and ponds in Brunei Darussalam have become progressively oligotrophic, highly acidic and turquoise in colour. It was considered important, therefore, to establish baseline data and monitor changes which occur during the filling and subsequent ageing of the reservoir, and to provide information on water quality, productivity and fish harvest to permit rational management of the lake.

Materials and methods

This study was carried out between February 1990 and August 1991. Rainfall data, collected at the dam site, was supplied by Watson Hawksley Asia with the permission of the Public Works Department (JKR), Ministry of Development, Negara Brunei Darussalam. Physicochemical and biotic parameters of the reservoir were measured between 1000 and 1300 h during each site visit. Water depths were determined by taking soundings with a weighted rope. Water temperature and conductivity profiles were obtained with a YSI Model 33 SCT meter (equipped with a 15 m cable), while measurement of oxygen profiles was made with a YSI Model 57 dissolved-oxygen meter (with a 30 m cable). Light penetration was monitored by means of an underwater Licor Model LI-193SB quantum sensor attached to a LI-1000 data logger. Water samples were taken with a vertically closing two-litre perspex van Dorn bottle at depth intervals of 1 m; subsequently, pH was determined with a portable Hanna Piccolo temperature-compensated pH

0538-4680/94/0024-0273 $ 1.50

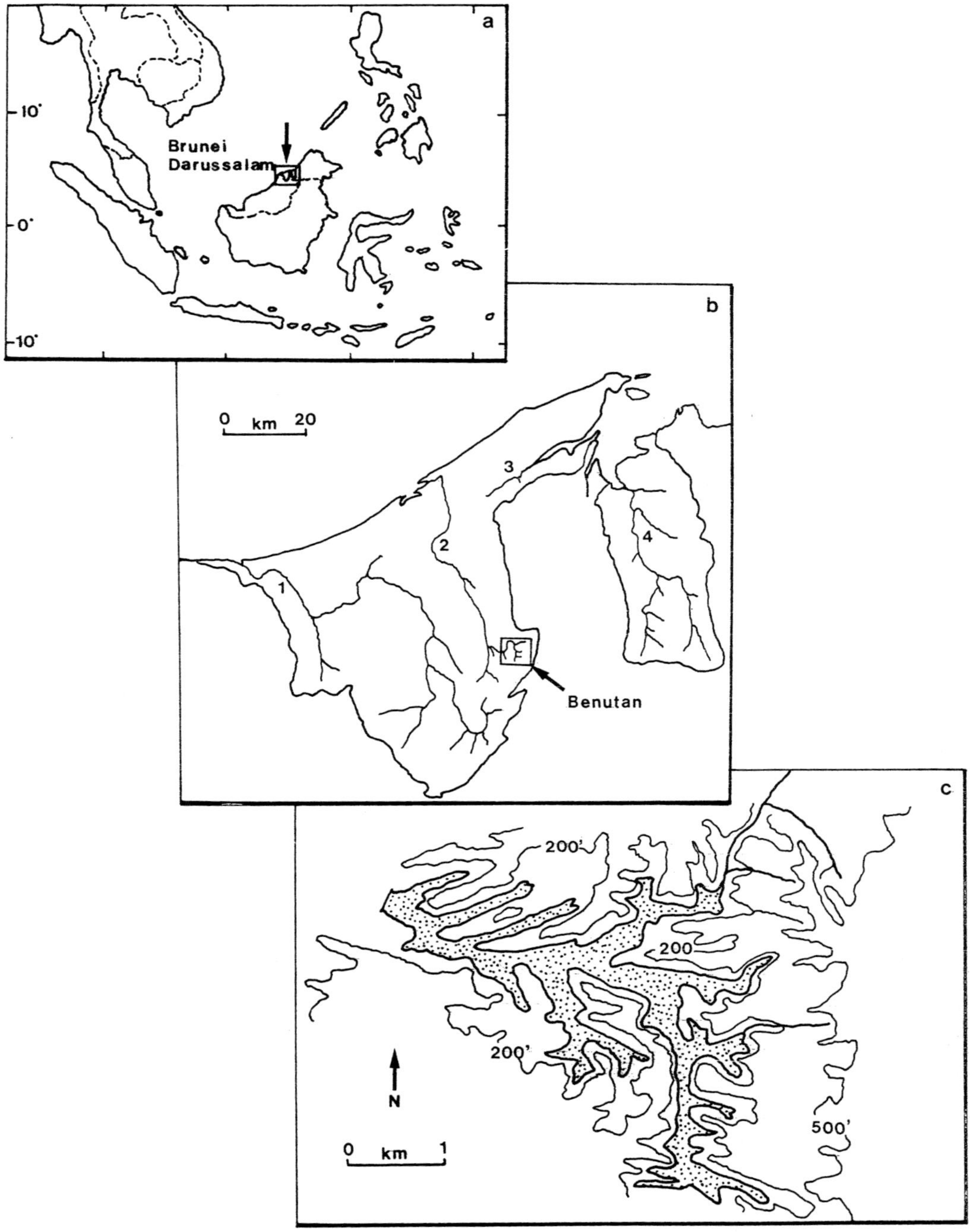

Fig. 1. Location map of Brunei Darussalam (a); Benutan Reservoir (b); and, a contour map of Benutan Reservoir (c). The stippled area indicates the water level of the Reservoir. Also shown are the main river systems: 1) Belait River; 2) Tutong River; 3) Brunei River; 4) Temburong River.

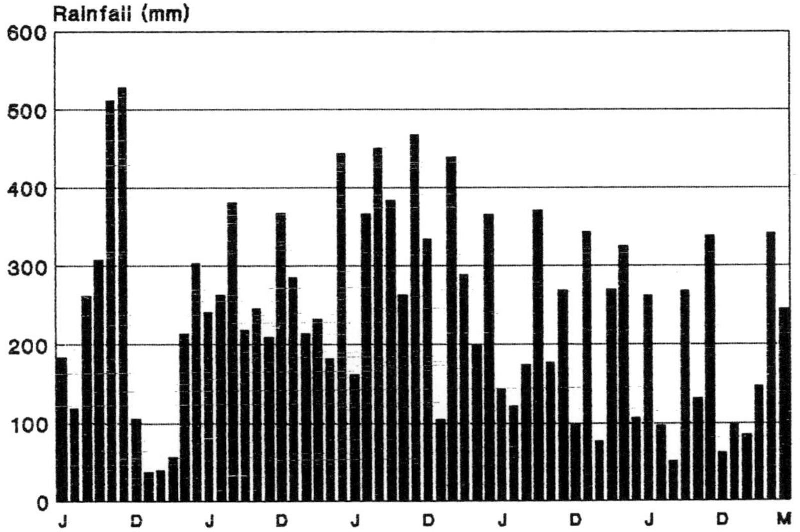

Fig. 2. Monthly rainfall distribution at the dam site of the Benutan Reservoir from June 1986 to May 1991 (J = June; D = December).

meter. Other water-chemistry parameters were determined using ion chromatography or standard methods (Anonymous 1985).

Total chlorophyll *a* profiles were determined from 300–500 ml water samples collected at the surface or at depth by the van Dorn sampler. The water was transported to the laboratory where 10 ml subsamples were filtered through 0.2 μm Nucleopore membrane filters (25 mm diameter) to separate out the photosynthetic organisms (high loads of particulate organic matter precluded filtration of greater volumes). Chlorophyll *a* in the filtrate was extracted in 90% ethanol (Jespersen & Christoffersen 1987), then determined quantitatively using a calibrated Turner-Sequoia digital filter fluorometer equipped with a blue excitation filter (Corning 5-60) and a red emission filter (Corning 2-64). The fluorometer calibration was based on the spectrophotometric determination of chlorophyll *a* from actual lake water samples, corrected for phaeophytin using absorbances at 664 nm and 665 nm before and after acidification (Anonymous 1985). Size fractionation of the phytoplankton was achieved by using a series of filters (20 μm, 2 μm and 0.2 μm) which allowed the chlorophyll *a* content of size fractions >20 μm (netphytoplankton), 20 to 2 μm (nanophytoplankton) and 2–0.2 μm (picophytoplankton) to be determined.

Zooplankton was sampled using either a 60 μm or 125 μm plankton net which was swept or towed over a distance of approximately 10 m; the samples were transported to the laboratory and then preserved in 5% buffered formalin until analysis. The littoral benthic fauna was collected with a hand net, and fish were obtained from the gill nets (100 m length, 5 mm stretched mesh) of fishermen. These data were supplemented by collection and identification of aquatic macrophytes, and assessment of the presence of vertebrates around the Reservoir based on visual and auditory evidence gathered during day and night visits. The quality of the riparian forest in terms of its scientific and aesthetic values was assessed subjectively.

Results

Rainfall data from the dam site (Fig. 2) indicate some seasonality, with the September–January period being more rainy than the February-August period. However, there are considerable seasonal and interannual variations. Daytime water temperature profiles (Table 1) indicate that the reservoir is stratified with a thermocline existing between 3 and 6 m. Similar stratification was observed for conductivity, dissolved oxygen and chlorophyll *a* (Table 1). The immediate surface layer was strongly influenced by the ambient air temperature, and standard deviations associated with the mean temperature values for each depth over the period February 1990 to June 1991 indicate greater stability below the thermocline than above. Conductivity increased sharply between 3–5 m depth and then increased steadily with increasing depth. High levels of dissolved oxygen were confined to depths <4 m, which was not surprising considering the limited light penetration (Table 1). Mean Secchi depth was 1.2 m.

Table 1. Physicochemical and biological characteristics of Benutan Reservoir; mean daytime values ± SD (*n* = 15–18).

Depth (m)	Temperature (°C)	Conductivity (μmhos/cm)	Dissolved Oxygen (mg/l)	pH	Chlorophyll a (μg/l)	Light (%)	Secchi (m)
0	31.3 ± 0.8	67 ± 4	5.8 ± 1.1	6.7 ± 0.5	9.8 ± 3.6	100 ± 0	–
1	30.7 ± 0.7	68 ± 3	5.3 ± 1.1	6.6 ± 0.6	13.1 ± 7.7	26 ± 7	–
2	30.2 ± 0.5	67 ± 4	4.7 ± 1.0	6.5 ± 0.6	12.8 ± 4.7	6.7 ± 3	–
3	29.9 ± 0.5	77 ± 18	3.4 ± 1.6	6.4 ± 0.6	16.7 ± 6.5	1.6 ± 1	–
4	29.3 ± 0.6	110 ± 27	1.3 ± 0.8	6.1 ± 0.5	39.0 ± 21.0	0.4 ± 0.7	–
5	28.8 ± 0.4	140 ± 18	0.9 ± 0.4	5.9 ± 0.5	35.9 ± 14.0	0.07 ± 0.1	–
6	28.6 ± 0.4	158 ± 15	0.8 ± 0.4	5.8 ± 0.5	23.8 ± 8.7	0.02 ± 0.01	–
7	28.3 ± 0.3	170 ± 22	0.8 ± 0.4	5.8 ± 0.5	19.6 ± 8.6	0.01 ± 0	–
8	28.2 ± 0.2	178 ± 31	0.8 ± 0.4	5.8 ± 0.5	12.2 ± 3.9	0	–
9	28.0 ± 0.3	183 ± 37	0.8 ± 0.4	5.9 ± 0.6	7.7 ± 2.9	–	–
10	28.0 ± 0.2	195 ± 34	0.8 ± 0.4	5.9 ± 0.5	5.9 ± 1.5	–	–
11	28.0 ± 0.2	208 ± 35	0.8 ± 0.4	5.9 ± 0.5	5.9 ± 1.5	–	–
12	27.9 ± 0.2	230 ± 37	0.9 ± 0.2	5.9 ± 0.6	4.7 ± 0.5	–	–
13	28.0 ± 0.2	267 ± 44	0.9 ± 0.2	5.9 ± 0.6	4.1 ± 0.5	–	–
14	28.0 ± 0.1	286 ± 51	0.9 ± 0.2	5.8 ± 0.5	3.8 ± 0.1	–	–
15	28.0 ± 0.1	310 ± 10	–	5.7 ± 0.1	–	–	–
–	–	–	–	–	–	–	1.2 ± 0.2

Table 2. Chlorophyll *a* concentration and the size distribution of phytoplankton contributing to the chlorophyll concentration (μg/l and % of chlorophyll *a* distribution) at different depths in Benutan Reservoir on 26 March 1991.

Depth (m)	Chlorophyll *a* conc (μg/l)	Phytoplankton size categories		
		>20 μm	2–20 μm	0.2–2 μm
0	14.83	1.33 (9%)	8.75 (59%)	4.75 (32%)
1	24.83	–	–	–
2	25.63	5.38 (21%)	12.82 (50%)	7.43 (29%)
3	22.70	–	–	–
4	19.88	2.78 (14%)	9.94 (50%)	7.16 (36%)
5	81.40	2.12 (3%)	17.10 (21%)	61.86 (76%)
6	46.83	0.46 (1%)	5.57 (12%)	40.39 (87%)
7	54.50	–	–	–
8	22.94	0.46 (2%)	4.36 (19%)	18.12 (79%)
9	8.88	–	–	–
10	7.63	0.31 (4%)	2.29 (30%)	5.04 (66%)

Chlorophyll *a* distribution (Table 1) showed an interesting pattern with moderate concentrations in the range 10–25 μg/l in the upper 3–4 m then a peak between 4 and 6 m. The majority of this deeper chlorophyll *a* was associated with picophytoplankton while surface chlorophyll *a* was primarily associated with the nanophytoplankton fraction (Table 2). pH values were close to 7 in the upper layers of the reservoir (Table 1), and fell to pH 6 at depths of 4–5 m, below which little change occurred. Levels of inorganic nutrients in the water were low (Table 3), but the high organic load, black colouration, and the distinct hydrogen sulphide smell – especially in the subsurface waters – were indicative of a dystrophic, blackwater system.

Zooplankton density in the limnetic zone decreased with increasing depth, but biomass was greatest at depths between 3 and 6 m (Table 4) due to the presence of relatively large *Chaoborus* larvae (Diptera) at these levels. The marginal zone and beds of submerged *Utricularia* (Lentibulariaceae) supported large numbers of benthic and epiphytic insect larvae. The fish fauna of the reservoir was diverse (Table 5), yielding a mean catch by fishermen of approximately 200 kg per night. The

Table 3. Chemical constituents (mg/l) of Benutan Reservoir water in July, 1991 (nd, not detectable).

Depth (m)	NO_3-N	PO_4-P	NH_3-N	SO_4	Cl^-	Fe^{3+}	Al^{3+}	Si^{4+}
0	nd	0.79	112.9	62.82	nd	0.01	nd	46.52
4	nd	nd	263.0	4.69	nd	0.02	0.09	47.30
9	5.27	34.93	1638.0	5.09	nd	0.11	0.67	55.55

Table 4. Zooplankton and benthos in Benutan Reservoir (mean ± SD).

Zone	Density (no./l)	Biomass (g. 1000/l)	Dominant taxa
Surface (<2 m)	16 ± 12	0.65 ± 0.8	Copepoda & Cladocera
Subsurface (3–6 m)	11 ± 9	1.23 ± 0.9	Copepoda & *Chaoborus*
Epibenthic (>9 m)	4 ± 2	0.48 ± 0.4	*Chaoborus*
Utricularia & Littoral zooplankton	8 ± 6	0.41 ± 0.3	Ostracoda & Cladocera
Ultricularia & Littoral benthos	43 ± 21	5.32 ± 1.6	Insecta

Table 5. Checklist of fish caught in Benutan Reservoir.

Cyprinidae
- *Nematabramis alestes borneensis* INGER & CHIN
- *N. everetti* BOULENGER
- *Rasbora eithoveni* (BLEEKER)
- *R. sumatrana* (BLEEKER)
- *Rasbora* spp.
- *Cyclocheilichthys repasson* (BLEEKER)
- *Chela oxygastroides* (BLEEKER)
- *Otseochilus spilurus* (BLEEKER)

Channidae
- *Channa melanosoma* BLEEKER
- *C. striata* BLOCH

Bagridae
- *Mystus baramensis* (REGAN)

Claridae
- *Clarias teijsmanni* BLEEKER

Anabantidae
- *Anabas testudineus* (BLOCH)

catchment supported lowland tropical rainforest and was rich in spectacular dipterocarps including a large number of *Shorea* spp. Epiphytes, including the giant *Grammatophylum* orchid, were common, as were a variety of lianas including strangling figs and the primitive gymnosperm *Gnetum*. Clumps of a range of palms were clustered on the lower slopes of the Ladan Hills which rise over 300 m above the dam and are clad in dense forest that changes in composition with altitude. The catchment provides a habitat for a wide range of reptiles, amphibians, birds (hornbills, eagles, kingfishers, the Oriental darter, etc.) and mammals (gibbons, monkeys, civets, lemurs, squirrels, shrews, bats, porcupines, deer, etc.).

Discussion

As the short-term Benutan Reservoir records show, seasonality in rainfall is not well-defined. This is in agreement with data from long term records for other parts of Brunei Darussalam which show wide variations in monthly and annual means (SIRINANDA 1990). Most authors describing the rainfall pattern of Brunei Darussalam suggest that there is seasonality, which is a reflection of the northeast and southwest monsoons. (CHUA et al. 1987, SCOTT 1989, SIRINANDA 1990). There is also evidence of occurrence of drought (BECKER in press). Such events are most frequent between February and April and during July and August. Droughts may be severe enough to lower the flow of the Sungai Tutong to such an extent that salt water intrudes up the river to the intake pipes of Bandar Seri Begawan's freshwater supply. It was for this reason that the Benutan Reservoir was constructed, thus providing a source from which water could be released into the Sungai Tutong to push back the sea water. Because the water of the reservoir is not destined for human consumption, and in view of the aesthetic value and great natural interest of the surrounding catchment, the reservoir can be put to some form of secondary use without adversely affecting its primary role. However, the current biological and physical characteristics have a bearing on potential uses.

Physicochemical and biological data indicated that the Benutan Reservoir was a stratified dystrophic black water lake with low levels of nutrients, high organic loads and high productivity. A strong discontinuity between 3 and 6 m separated the water column into two distinct layers. The upper layer was oxygenated, of moderately high pH and low solute content, and supported moderately dense phytoplankton populations. The lower layer was nearly anoxic with high levels of solutes, including sulphides and particulate organic matter. At or just below the discontinuity, high picophytoplankton-associated chlorophyll *a* was present, suggesting the presence of photosynthetic organisms which were able to exist in a low-oxygen, low-light, high-sulphide regime. These organisms are the subject of an on-going study.

The high productivity of the Reservoir is indicated by the overall chlorophyll *a* levels, zooplankton biomass, and the magnitude of fish landed by the semi-commercial fishery on the lake. The terrestrial flora and fauna is diverse, abundant, and of great interest to amateur and professional naturalists. The extensive and much indented form of the lake with its topographically-varied surroundings is aesthetically attractive.

In view of the above and guided by the Government's policy to promote economic diversification, recreational facilities for the public and ecotourism, the following development plan is suggested. A portion of the catchment should be developed as a recreational park with a few well laid out trails, picnic and barbecue facilities and an information centre; easy access adjacent to the picnic facilities should be provided. The objective is to provide an opportunity for the public to appreciate the flora and fauna of the lake and its surrounds by offering a range of activities in a limited area where a combination of careful planning of access and usage and strict conservation rules will result in a minimum of disturbance. Water sport, including non-motorized boating can be permitted, but fuel and noise pollution associated with motorized vessels will be avoided. Regular monitoring would be needed to ensure that the environmental impacts of recreational activities are minimal, and such monitoring would provide useful data on changes that take place as the reservoir ages. The idea of pluralistic utilization is not new. If well managed, resource utilization can be optimized, so increasing ecosystem value and promoting public awareness of the environment.

The high productivity of the reservoir may be exploited through recreational fishing in areas close to picnic and trail facilities. Further research will have to be undertaken to determine sustainable fishing activity. Controlled aquaculture ventures could be undertaken in areas of the lake away from the recreational development centre. Stocking the lake with 'non-breeding' fish for aquaculture and recreational fishing could be considered. However, the introduction of exotic species could have unforeseen consequences and should be opposed vigorously.

Acknowledgements

We are grateful to Dr. D. S. Edwards, Head of Biology, Universiti Brunei Darussalam and the staff of Jabatan Kerja Raya (JKR) and Watson Hawksley Asia (WHA) for providing assistance throughout this study. We would like to thank in particular Hj. Samat bin Hj. Abbas (Assistant Director, JKR), Awg. Mohammed Matali bin Lassim (Chief Technical Assistant, JKR Layong), Mr. R. Hamilton, Mr. C. Arunachalam and Mr. Gene Japlit (staff of WHA).

References

Anonymous, 1985: Standard Methods for the Examination of Water and Wastewater, 16th Edition; 1120 pp. – American Public Health Association, American Water Works Association and Water Pollution Control Federation, New York.

Becker, P., in press: Seasonality of rainfall and drought in Brunei Darussalam. – *Asian Geographer.*

Chua, T. E., Chou, L. M. & Sadorra, M. S. M., 1987: The coastal environment profile of Brunei Darussalam: resource assessment and management issues. – *ICLARM Technical Report* No. **18:** 193 pp.

Jespersen, A. M. & Christoffersen, K., 1987: Measurements of chlorophyll *a* from phytoplankton using ethanol as extraction solvent. – *Arch. Hydrobiol.* **109:** 445–454.

Lewis, W. M., 1987: Tropical Limnology. – *Ann. Rev. Ecol. Syst.* **18:** 159–184.

– 1990: Comparisons of phytoplankton biomass in temperate and tropical lakes. – *Limnol. Oceanogr.* **35:** 1838–1845.

Payne, A. I., 1986: The Ecology of Tropical Lakes and Rivers: 301 pp. – Wiley Publishers, New York.

Scott, D. A., 1989: *A Directory of Asian Wetlands:* XIV + 1181 pp. – IUCN, Gland, Switzerland.

Sirinanda, K. U., 1990: Rainfall seasonality in Negara Brunei Darussalam. – *Asian Geographer* **9:** 39–52.

Authors' address:

Biology Department, Universiti Brunei Darussalam, Gadong 3186, BSB, Brunei Darussalam.

Mitt. Internat. Verein. Limnol.	24	279–283	Stuttgart, Februar 1994

Conservation and management of Lake Manapao (Philippines), a 'Sinarapan' (*Mistichthys luzonensis*) sanctuary: Status, problems and solutions

Victor S. Soliman

Abstract

Lake Manapao – a mountain lake in San Ramon, Buhi, Camarines Sur Province, Philippines – is the only natural habitat which supports a viable population of 'Sinarapan', *Mistichthys luzonensis* SMITH (Gobiidae). This species is only 1.2 cm when adult and is considered the world's smallest commercial fish. The Lake Manapao population is especially important because of the near-total collapse of stocks of Sinarapan in Lakes Buhi and Bato, both in Camarines Sur, where the goby once formed the basis of commercial fishing. The reason for this decline is not known, but a brief history of Sinarapan fishery in Camarines Sur is presented and present concerns relating to the Lake Manapao sanctuary are highlighted.

In view of the urgent need to manage Lake Manapao and conserve this endangered goby, the paper focuses on three aspects of its biology: population dynamics (growth, mortality, exploitation rate, yield-per-recruit and virtual population analyses); the continuing threat posed by degradation of the lake's drainage basin due to logging, increasing human settlements near the lake, and illegal fishing; and the need to foster international linkages leading to collaborative researches on strategies for rational management of the sanctuary.

Aside from a fishing ban on Sinarapan in Lake Manapao, this paper advocates the immediate implementation of specific activities such as reduction through fishing of Sinarapan predators (*Oreochromis, Ophicephalus* and *Clarias*), prohibition of further fish introductions, and assignment of personnel to conduct studies and manage the sanctuary.

Introduction

Lake Manapao is a freshwater, mountain lake 122 m above sea level in San Ramon, Buhi, Camarines Sur Province, Philippines (13°26′N, 123°29′E). It is 3.75 ha in area, with a mean depth of 7.6 m. It was declared a sanctuary for Sinarapan or Tabios (*Mistichthys luzonensis* SMITH) in 1982 by virtue of a Buhi municipal ordinance. This fish is endemic to the Philippines, where it is fished commercially, and is found only in a few lakes and along the Bicol River system (GINDELBERGER 1981 a, 1981 b). *Mistichthys luzonensis* mature at a length of 1.2 cm (SMITH 1902) and thus this species is the world's smallest commercial fish. On the evidence of its teeth and exceptionally short digestive tract, it is a predator (TE WINKEL 1935), although TRAICHAIYAPORN (1985) reported that 53 phytoplankton species constituted 30 to 50% of the stomach contents of Sinarapan in Lake Katugday. Other data on the biology of *M. luzonensis* are given by PAULY (1982) and LIU & WALFORD (1970); SOLIMAN (1989, 1991) has studied the population dynamics of Sinarapan in Lake Manapao.

Lake Manapao is significant as a sanctuary in view of the near-total collapse of Sinarapan stocks in Lakes Buhi and Bato (Camarines Sur), the only Philippines lakes where this goby was fished commercially. Sinarapan was very abundant in both lakes between the 1930s and 1960s, but it had almost disappeared by 1979 and numbers remain low. The reasons for the decline of Sinarapan are unclear but, in 1976, collapsible push-nets known as *sakag* – which were operated by fitting them to the bow of a motorized pumpboat – came into use and led to overfishing in both lakes (GINDELBERGER 1981 a) with destruction of the breeding, feeding and refuge areas of the goby. Predation by tilapias (*Oreochromis niloticus* and *O. mossambicus*), Snakeheads (*Ophicephalus striatus*) and the Catfish, *Clarias macrocephalus,* might also have contributed to this disappearance. The collapse of the commercial Sinarapan fishery in Lake Buhi in 1979 led to displacement of some 200 subsistence fishermen (GINDELBERGER 1982).

Today, Lake Manapao is the only natural habitat where Sinarapan are abundant, but both the lake and its fishes are virtually unstudied. Because mature Sinarapan are no larger than the larvae and post-larvae of many fishes, studies on their population dynamics and exploitation would be of interest in representing extreme values in fishery biology. As a source of Sinarapan stock, Manapao will play an important role in future plans to repopulate Lakes Buhi and Bato with the goby, and will also provide insights into the ecology of this diminutive species. Moreover, Lake Manapao also faces threats posed by natural and man-induced factors such as sulphur upwelling, illegal fishing, and disturbance in the drainage basin including increasing human settlement. There is thus an urgent need to conserve and manage Lake Manapao and protect the Sinarapan stock.

0538-4680/94/0024-0279 $ 1.25

Fish stocks and current fishing activities

Seven fish species (*Oreochromis niloticus, O. mossambicus, Cyprinus carpio, Ophicephalus striatus, Clarias macrocephalus, Glossogobius guirus* and *Therapon* sp.), a palaemonid shrimp (*Macrobrachium* sp.) and an ampullariid snail (*Pomacea canaliculata*) have been introduced into Lake Manapao by nearby residents. In addition to Sinarapan, several other indigenous species of small goby occur which have yet to be identified. How Sinarapan spread among Lakes Manapao, Buhi and Bato is not known. There are no connections between Lakes Buhi and Manapao, and both were probably formed during the last eruption of Mount Iriga in 1641.

A ban on capture of Sinarapan, except for strictly educational or scientific purposes, is being enforced in Lakes Buhi, Bato and Manapao. In Lake Manapao, fishing of other species is regulated by a single overseer who is employed by the Buhi municipal government on a casual basis. Fishing gears commonly used are gill nets, hook and line, fish traps and bamboo enclosures. The fishermen are Filipino natives ('Aetas') who live on the mountain slopes bordering the lake. The scientific input for management of Lake Manapao has been provided by the Inland Fisheries Section of Bicol University College of Fisheries (BUCF). As there is reason to believe that fishing in the lake will intensify, the possible effect on its ecology (including the Sinarapan population) requires close investigation.

A kilometre northwest of Lake Manapao is the 2.66-ha Lake Katugday. Along with Lake Manapao, it was declared a Sinarapan sanctuary in 1982 by virtue of a Buhi municipal ordinance. Six years later it was disastrously depleted of its Sinarapan stock as a result of a chemical pesticide applied by a villager who intended to capture Tilapias and other introduced fishes. Repeated sampling in May 1988 by a team of BUCF researchers confirmed the virtual absence of Sinarapan in Lake Katugday; only two individuals were caught after almost 3 hours of push-net operation.

Population parameters and their management implications

SOLIMAN (1989, 1991) has researched the population dynamics of Sinarapan in Lake Manapao; the results of this work – and their management implications – are summarized below. The parameters of growth and mortality, indices of yield-per-recruit, and virtual population have been estimated, based on 11 months (April 1988–May 1989) of size-frequency and catch data, by using the routines of Compleat ELEFAN (see PAULY 1986, GAYANILO et al. 1989). The reliability and assumptions of length-based stock assessment methodologies, which mainly were used to generate the quantitative information presented here, are well documented in various works (BEVERTON & HOLT 1957, RICKER 1975, GULLAND 1983, PAULY 1984, PAULY & MORGAN 1987, SPARRE 1989). Fish samples were collected using a push-net.

Investigation of the von Bertalanffy parameters for Sinarapan (see SOLIMAN 1989) yielded an estimated asymptotic total length of 24.6 mm and a growth constant (annual *K*) of 2.25/yr. The high growth constant is typical of most short-lived tropical fish (PAULY 1978). The asymptotic length (L_∞) matched closely the greatest total length (24.5 mm) achieved by Sinarapan in Lake Manapao. Total length (TL) and standard length (SL, mm) were related as follows: $TL = 1.125 + 1.0011*SL$ ($n = 252$, $r^2 = 0.98$); the relationship between TL and live weight (LW, g) was described by: $TL = 1.947 \times 10^{-6}*LW^{3.499}$ ($n = 151$, $r^2 = 0.98$).

The greatest standard length attained in the field (23.5 mm) was longer than that recorded for Sinarapan by HERRE (1927; 14.0 mm) or TE WINKEL (1935; 14.5 mm). By contrast, the maximum standard length recorded by GINDELBERGER (1981 b; 24 mm) was close to that in Lake Manapao, but greater than that in earlier studies on Sinarapan from Lake Buhi. This could reflect the fact that GINDELBERGER's samples were taken during a period when Sinarapan stocks had diminished greatly, which may have led to concomitant increases in food availability and hence increases in size attained.

Following methods given in JONES (1976) and SINODA et al. (1979) – and equations in PAULY's (1983) monograph – the foregoing parameters, complemented by other vital metric characteristics of Sinarapan, were used to estimate an optimum mesh size of push-net for sustainable harvest of Sinarapan. A mesh size of 4.1 mm appears necessary for the protection of the Sinarapan stock. This is considerably greater than the very fine-meshed nets used by indigenous fisherman in the past. Unfortunately, there are – as yet – no data available to demonstrate the actual benefits to fish stock of using this mesh size.

Fig. 1 shows the length-converted catch curve which was used to calculate the total instantaneous mortality (*Z*) of 9.234 per year. Substituting the

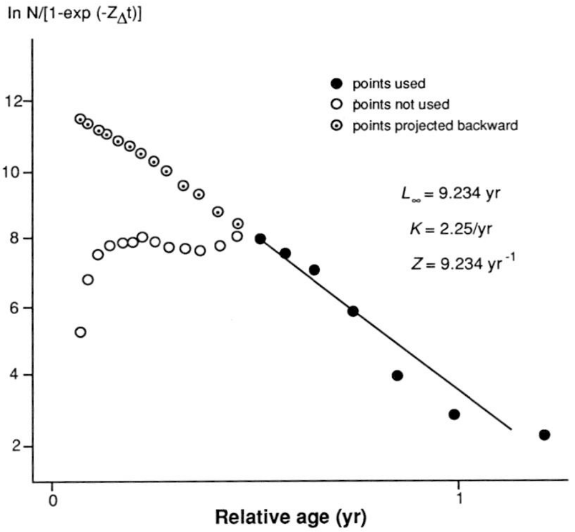

Fig. 1. Length-converted catch curve for *Mistichthys luzonensis* from Lake Manapao.

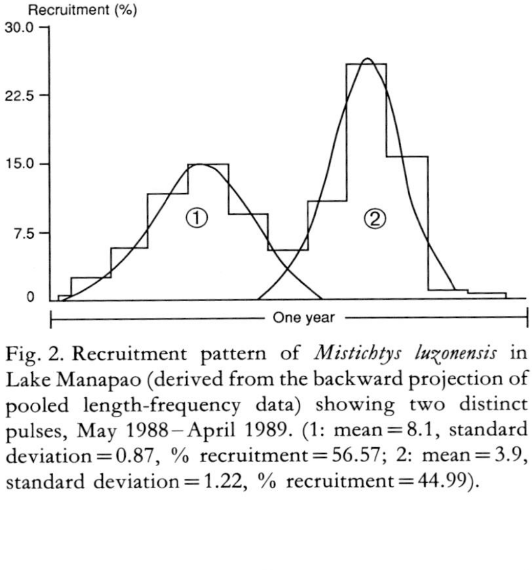

Fig. 2. Recruitment pattern of *Mistichtys luzonensis* in Lake Manapao (derived from the backward projection of pooled length-frequency data) showing two distinct pulses, May 1988–April 1989. (1: mean = 8.1, standard deviation = 0.87, % recruitment = 56.57; 2: mean = 3.9, standard deviation = 1.22, % recruitment = 44.99).

von Bertalanffy growth parameters presented above into equations given by PAULY (1980), the natural instantaneous mortality (M) of Sinarapan was estimated to be 6.201 per year at a mean annual water temperature of 29°. Fishing mortality ($F = Z - M$) was thus determined to be 3.033 per year. Using those mortality estimates for Sinarapan, a stock exploitation rate ($E = F/Z = F/[F + M]$) of 0.328 was calculated. The low E reflects the viability of the Lake Manapao stock which, together with possible growth compensation due to high M, may have contributed to the high value of K and relatively great body size of Lake Manapao Sinarapan. The data indicate also a fast turnover rate of Sinarapan which could sustain higher F levels. However, in view of Lake Manapao's importance to Sinarapan, an increase in fishing pressure upon this endangered goby should be discouraged. The fishing mortality of 3.033 per year is equivalent to an annual catch of 1180 kg.

On the basis of these projections, the Sinarapan stock may be considered to be moderately underexploited ($E = 0.328$; i.e. $0.20 \leq E \leq 0.40$); this rests upon the assumption that optimum exploitation (E_{opt}) is obtained when mortality due to fishing is equivalent to mortality resulting from natural causes ($F = M$; i.e. $E = 0.5$). This further assumes that a stock-recruitment relationship does not exist (GULLAND 1971). However, more data are needed urgently because the assumption of $E_{opt} = 0.5$ may be a significant overestimate for small, short-lived tropical fishes (see BEDDINGTON & COOKE 1983); under such circumstances, the annual harvest of 1180 kg may not be sustainable.

Projections of the outcome of increasing E (hence F) from the present level are given elsewhere (SOLIMAN 1989, 1991). It is worth noting here that the bulk of the catch is composed of small individuals (4–7 mm) as it is these which make up a major portion of the population. Overharvesting of these small, pre-reproductive individuals could have grave consequences for the Lake Manapao population. Note that the use of empirical data – which are presently scarce – in analyses of possible outcomes of different levels of harvesting, is to be preferred over projections based on assumptions and limited data. The Sinarapan is virtually unstudied and relevant information on stocks of this goby in other areas is scarce. Data on biological interactions (predation on Sinarapan by other fishes) is needed before appropriate levels of harvest by fishermen can be set.

The recruitment pattern of Sinarapan (Fig. 2), as suggested by the backward projection of pooled length-frequency data, appears bimodal with possible peaks during the months of July and November (when rainfall peaks). This is consistent with the observations of fishermen in Lake Buhi on the abundance of Sinarapan during the rainy months of July to December (GINDELBERGER 1981 b). Most (70%) of female Sinarapan in Lake Manapao which gather underneath Water hyacinth (*Eichhornia crassipes*) at this time are gravid; those collected during the same period in areas lacking vegetation comprise approximately 20% gravid females. An interim management scheme to protect Sinarapan in the sanctuary has been implemented recently, whereby collection of Sinarapan is prohibited from June to August and in October and November. Even when allowed during other months, collection of fish from underneath floating macrophytes and other vegetation is prohibited.

Problems and solutions

The problems faced by the Lake Manapao sanctuary have biological as well as human dimensions. The depletion of fish stocks in Lake Katugday as a result of deliberate use of poisons exemplifies the importance of the social components of management problems. While the immediate relocation of the residents along the shores of Lake Manapao (20 households) may not be necessary, there should be measures to limit access to, and use of, the sanctuary's resources in order to preserve the integrity and biodiversity of the ecosystem. These should include the regulation of non-fishery uses of the lake; for example, as a source of potable water, for bathing, washing clothes, and a host of other household purposes.

Some specific management strategies, which have been implemented recently, need to be assessed in terms of their actual benefits to the sanctuary as a whole, and to Sinarapan in particular. Such assessment should take the form of continuous collection/monitoring of biological and environmental data in the lake. Such data can serve also as biological inputs to inform rational management strategies. Moreover, there are basic research concerns which must be addressed if the goal of Sinarapan conservation is to be achieved. For example, the feeding and food habits, reproductive cycle, and ecology of Sinarapan are poorly known. It will be particularly important to survey other lakes in the mountains of Camarines Sur and Albay Provinces to elucidate the distributional status of Sinarapan.

Lake Manapao is surrounded by mountain slopes which are the site of privately-owned agricultural lands. In view of the possible adverse affects of further vegetation clearance in the drainage basin of the Sanctuary there is a need to establish some mechanism whereby concerned government and private entities can jointly protect the areas surrounding the Sanctuary. Moreover, further introductions of fish, molluscs, and other organisms must be prohibited in the absence of conclusive studies that such transfer will be beneficial to both Sinarapan and the lake ecosystem. Lake Buhi and Lake Manapao have received introductions of a variety of fishes (see **Introduction**), but there have been no studies on the potential long-term benefits (or otherwise) of these introductions.

Links with national and international agencies for financial and technical assistance will be necessary to conserve the Sinarapan of Lake Manapao and ultimately to repopulate Lakes Buhi, Bato and Katugday so that the commercial fishery can be revived. Such linkages would complement the present level of protection provided by BUCF and Buhi municipal government which jointly manage the sanctuary.

References

Beddington, J. R. & Cooke, J. G., 1983: The potential yield of fish stocks. – *FAO Fish. Tech. Pap.* **242:** 47 pp.

Beverton, J. R. & Holt, S. J., 1957: On the dynamics of exploited fish populations. – *Fish. Invest. Sec. II,* Vol. **19:** 1–532.

Gayanilo Jr., F. C., Soriano, M. & Pauly, D., 1989: A draft guide to the Compleat ELEFAN: 60 pp. – ICLARM Software 2, ICLARM, Makati, Metro Manila, Philippines.

Gindelberger, B., 1981 a: Fishery management in Camarines Sur, Philippines: why Sinarapan almost disappeared from Lake Buhi. – *ICLARM Newsletter* **4:** 3–5.

– 1981 b: A brief history of the ecological changes in Lake Buhi and associated research into their causes – Unpublished manuscript: 14 pp.

– 1982: After Sinarapan: the planned small-scale fish cage industry of Lake Buhi. – *ICLARM Newsletter* **5:** 6–7.

Gulland, J. A., 1971: The Fish Resources of the Oceans: 425 pp. – FAO & Fishing News Books Ltd., Surrey, England.

Herre, A. W. (1927): Gobies of the Philippines and the China Sea. – *Bur. Sci. Monogr. Publ. Fishes,* No. **23,** Bureau of Printing, Manila.

Jones, R., 1976: Mesh regulation in the demersal fisheries of the South China Sea area. – South China Sea Development Programme, Manila, SCS/76/wp/35: 75 pp.

Liu, R. K. & Walford, R. L., 1970: Observations on the lifespan of several species of annual fishes and of the world's smallest fishes. – *Exp. Geront.* **5:** 241–246.

Pauly, D., 1978: A preliminary compilation of fish length growth parameters. – *Ber. Inst. Meersk. Univ. Kiel.* **55:** 200 pp.

– 1980: On the interrelationships between natural mortality, growth parameters and mean environ-

mental temperature in 175 fish stocks. – *J. Cons. Inst. Explor. Mer.* **39:**175–192.
– 1982: Further evidence for a limiting effect of gill size on the growth of fish: the case of the Philippine goby (*Mistichthys luzonensis*). – *Philipp. J. Biol.* **11:**379–383.
– 1983: Some simple methods for the assessment of tropical fish stocks. – *FAO Fish. Tech. Pap. No.* **234:**52 pp.
– 1984: Fish population dynamics in tropical waters: a manual for use with programmable calculators: 325 pp. – ICLARM Studies and Reviews 8, ICLARM, Manila.
– 1986: On improving the operation and use of ELEFAN programs. Part II. Improving the estimation of L_∞. – *Fishbyte* **4:**18–20.

PAULY, D. & MORGAN, G. R., 1987: Length-based methods in fisheries research. – *ICLARM Conference Proceedings* **13:** 468 pp. – ICLARM, Makati, Metro Manila & Kuwait Institute for Scientific Research, Safat, Kuwait.

RICKER, W. E., 1975: Computation and interpretation of biological statistics of fish populations. – *Bull. Fish. Res. Bd. Can.* **191:**1–382.

SINODA, M., TAN, S. M., WATANABE, Y. & MEEMESKUL, Y., 1979: A method for estimating the best codend mesh size in the South China Sea area. – *Bull. Choshi Mar. Lab. Chiba Univ.* **11:**65–80.

SOLIMAN, V. S., 1989: Population dynamics of 'Sinarapan' (*Mistichthys luzonensis Smith*) in Lake Manapao, Buhi, Camarines Sur, Philippines: 65 pp. – Unpublished M. Sc. thesis, Central Luzon State University, Munoz, Nueva Ecija, Philippines.
– 1991: Exploitation rate, yield-per-recruit and virtual population of Sinarapan (*Mistichthys luzonensis*) in Lake Manapao, Buhi, Camarines Sur. – Paper presented at the 13th Annual Scientific Meeting of the National Academy of Science and Technology, Philippine International Convention Centre, Manila, 9–11 July 1991.

SPARRE, P., 1989: Introduction to tropical fish stock assessment. – Rep. Mar. Rev. Denmark Funds-in-Trust, Fl: GCP/392/DEN Manual **1:**388 pp.

TE WINKEL, L. E., 1935: A study of *Mistichthys luzonensis* with special reference to conditions correlated with reduced size. – *J. Morphol.* **58:**463–535.

TRAYCHAIYAPORN, S., 1985: Selected physico-chemical and biological characteristics of Lake Katugday, Buhi, Camarines Sur, Philippines: 187 pp. – Unpublished Ph.D. dissertation, University of the Philippines, Los Banos, Laguna.

Author's address:

Bicol University, College of Fisheries, Tayhi, Tabaco, Albay 4511, Philippines.

Mitt. Internat. Verein. Limnol.	24	285–292	Stuttgart, Februar 1994

Pest control in tropical aquaculture: An ecological hazard assessment of natural and synthetic control agents

Donald J. Baird

Abstract

As in terrestrial farming, fish farmers suffer yield losses due to the actions of pests, which in tropical ponds can include fish, Amphibia, snakes and a variety of insect species. The resulting use of aquaculture pest-control agents in tropical inland waters involves the unregulated application of a wide variety of potentially hazardous chemicals, ranging from synthetic compounds such as organochlorines, diesel oils and phosphine to natural, plant-derived toxins such as rotenone and croton oil. In contrasting the use of natural and synthetic agents, the potential impact of their associated use patterns on non-target species, health of operators, and long-term sustainability of tropical aquaculture systems is discussed in relation to the need for pest control.

Introduction

Aquaculture necessarily involves the control or manipulation of natural aquatic systems, and therefore carries with it a risk of causing damage, particularly if the functional aspects of the system are poorly understood. Although our understanding of the environmental impact of aquaculture developments on temperate freshwater aquatic habitats is advancing (e.g. Phillips et al. 1991), impacts on tropical systems are currently more difficult to predict (Beveridge & Phillips 1993). The reason for this is probably a combination of the lack of information available on basic functional processes within tropical aquatic ecosystems, coupled with the increasing awareness that conceptual models formulated from observations on temperate systems do not transfer easily to tropical systems (Dudgeon 1994). As a result, the increasing promotion and development of aquaculture in tropical areas is leading to growing problems of environmental degradation, such as the impact of prawn farming on mangroves (Phillips et al. 1991), and increasing conflicts with other resource users, such as fishermen (Pacardo 1994). Aquaculture systems can be classified along a continuum of 'management intensity' ranging from minimal input extensive systems such as managed lagoon fisheries, through low-input semi-intensive rural pond culture to intensively managed cage and raceway systems. Unlike extensive systems, intensive systems can be considered to exist in a state far from equilibrium with the environment in which they are embedded, and as a result rely increasingly on chemicals to maintain this non-equilibrium state. Obviously, where increased use of chemicals is accompanied by poorly defined, or badly enforced legislation, this is likely to pose particularly serious problems.

Chemicals are used for a variety of purposes in aquaculture, but those which are used as biocides, i.e. specifically to poison biological systems, obviously present the most significant hazard both to users and natural habitats. The potential impact of chemical disease treatments, particularly antibiotics and parasiticides, is currently the focus of much research (e.g. Samuelsen 1989) reflecting the fact that they are generally associated with high economic value, intensive systems situated in developed countries. In contrast, the potential impact of pest control chemicals has received less attention, since they are generally associated with small-scale semi-intensive fish culture in rural areas in third world countries. Rural fishpond aquaculture is widespread, however, particularly in Asia, and is currently being promoted on a massive scale by government and aid agencies as a solution to the acute shortage of dietary protein in many third world countries.

Why are pest control agents used?

In rural fishpond aquaculture, pest control agents are used primarily, although by no means exclusively, in fish fry 'nursery ponds'. They are employed to combat two classes of pest: those which feed directly on the young fish fry stocked in the pond (predators), thus causing mortality, and those which compete with the fry for food, thus causing poor growth. Indeed, the presence of competitors may also indirectly affect survivorship, through increasing the period of vulnerability to size-selective predation. These pests are primarily other fish species including predatory species such as catfish (e.g. *Wallago, Clarias* and *Heteropneustes*), snakeheads (*Channa*), eels (*Anguilla, Macrognathus*), and climbing perch (*Anabas*), and also competitor or 'weed' fish such as cyprinids (e.g. *Puntius, Chela*) and garfish (*Xenentodon*). In addition, aquatic insects and larger zooplankton

0538-4680/94/0024-0285 $ 2.00

may compete with fry, particularly during the early developmental stages, and insects such as beetles, water scorpions and backswimmers may also prey directly upon fry (see JHINGRAN 1991 for a more detailed list of species). This wide range of taxa, which also includes freshwater crabs, snakes and predatory birds, emphasises the wide range of animals that are considered as 'pests'. This poses a major problem in that the so-called 'target species' are broadly defined, including species which occupy a wide variety of ecological niches, possessing a wide range of tolerances to chemical stress (see below). As a result, chemical control is a rather crude procedure, in many cases involving complete eradication of free-living animals within the pond system, including both target and non-target species (e.g. JANA et al. 1987).

What types of compound are used?

The range of chemicals used for pest control in tropical aquaculture systems is vast, reflecting both the ingenuity of indigenous people to adapt tribal knowledge of toxic plant extracts, and their equal readiness to use any available commercially-produced chemical biocide (assuming it is cost-effective). For this reason, this review seeks to contrast the use of natural, plant-derived toxins as pest control agents with the use of synthetic industrially-produced chemicals, bearing in mind that the latter are generally assumed to be potentially more harmful to the natural environment (e.g. Guerrero 1989).

Natural pest control agents used in fishponds

The use of toxins extracted from plants to kill and catch fish is practised by tribal people throughout the world: e.g. in North America (SWANTON 1946; reference cited by MORRISON 1986), South America (MORS et al. 1973, TEIXEIRA et al. 1984), and Asia (BHUYAN 1967). As would be expected from the origins of such methods, numerous varieties of plants are used, and the toxic modes of action of the extracts are generally unknown, and in many cases are probably due to more than one active ingredient. In addition, it is worth emphasising that many of these plant-derived toxins are produced for the purpose of self- and resource defence, and are hence extremely toxic to a wide spectrum of organisms, including micro-organisms, invertebrate and vertebrate animals, and indeed other plant species (so-called allelochemicals).

Perhaps the best known of all the plant-derived compounds currently in use is rotenone, which can be obtained by crushing the roots of tropical plants of the Leguminosae family, such as *Derris* (=*Lonchocarpus, sensu* NASCIMENTO et al. 1976). The widespread use of rotenone outside the tropics (see above) has ensured that, unlike many other plant toxins employed to control pests, its mode of action, fate (HORGAN et al. 1968, GINGERICH & RACH 1985), persistence in the environment (ENGSTROM-HEG & COLESANTE 1979), and impact upon non-target species (CHANDLER & MARKING 1982) are comparatively well-studied.

In contrast to the genus *Derris,* which is used to produce commercial rotenone, a bewildering variety of other plant species from tropical regions of the world are used to extract fish and invertebrate poisons. The species included in Table 1 do not constitute an exhaustive listing, but serve to illustrate the complexity of the problem facing ecotoxicologists concerned with the potential environmental problems associated with their use.

It is a commonly-held belief that so-called 'natural' fish poisons are more 'environmentally benign' than synthetic chemicals. This view is based on a number of assumptions: that they are less toxic to operators and non-target species, do not lead to resistance problems, are less persistent than synthetics, and do not cause significant environmental side-effects. However, the available evidence does not always support these assumptions. If targeting specificity is considered, it is apparent that with the notable exception of rotenone (e.g. CHANDLER & MARKING 1982; but see also HARBORNE 1979 for an alternative viewpoint), the few studies which have been carried out on plant-derived pest-control agents suggest that the more commonly used compounds are relatively non-specific. Indeed, one of the major problems of toxic seed lipids extracted from mahua or croton is that the primary target species – predatory, air-breathing fish such as catfish – are more tolerant to the application of such water-borne toxins than are fish breathing dissolved oxygen (HOMECHAUDHURI et al. 1986, KULAKKATTOLICKAL & KRAMER 1988), with the result that there will be a tendency to overdose so as to make sure that all the target species are killed. Frequent reports that air-breathing fish are more difficult to eradicate (e.g. JHINGRAN 1991) may reflect a lower rate of uptake of toxins resulting from surface breathing, and this has been demonstrated in laboratory experiments

Table 1. Some tropical plants from which extracted toxins have been used, or suggested for use as fish or invertebrate poisons.

Plant taxon	Common name	Source of toxin(s)	Region used	Reference
Aegiceras corniculatum	mangrove	seeds, leaves	Pacific	GOMEZ et al. (1986)
Albizzia spp.	–	bark	Asia	JHINGRAN (1991)
Artemesia vulgaris	–	?	Asia	JHINGRAN (1991)
Barringtonia acutangulata	–	seeds	Asia	JHINGRAN (1991)
Balanites roxhburghii	–	roots	Asia	JHINGRAN (1991)
Bassia latifolia[1]	mahua tree	seeds	Asia	MISRA et al. (1986)
Berberis aristata	berberry	?	Asia	JHINGRAN (1991)
Callopyllum inophyllum	laurel	sap (?)	Asia	JHINGRAN (1991)
Camellia sp.	tea	seeds	Asia	MINSALAN & CHIU (1986)
Croton tiglium	–	seeds	Asia	GUERRERO (1989)
Dahlstedtia spp.	–	whole plant (?)	Amazonia	GARCEZ et al. (1988)
Derris spp.[2]	–	root	Asia, Amazonia	MORS et al. (1973)
Dioscorea sp.	yam	?	Asia	JHINGRAN (1991)
Exoecaria agallocha	mangrove	sap, roots	Pacific	GOMEZ et al. (1986)
Heriteria littoralis	mangrove	sap, roots	Pacific	GOMEZ et al. (1986)
Hydnocarpus sp.	–	?	Asia	JHINGRAN (1991)
Ichthyothere terminalis	–	foliage, bark	Amazonia	CASCON et al. (1965)
Juglans sp.	walnut	?	Asia	JHINGRAN (1991)
Millettia spp.	millet	roots	Asia	JHINGRAN (1991)
Mundulea sp.	–	whole plant	Amazonia	MORS et al. (1973)
Pachyrrhizus sp.	–	whole plant	Amazonia	MORS et al. (1973)
Phyllanthus urinaria	–	?	Asia	JHINGRAN (1991)
Piscidia sp.	–	whole plant	Amazonia	MORS et al. (1973)
Randia dimetorum	–	seeds	Asia	JHINGRAN (1991)
Rhododendron spp.	–	leaves, flowers	Asia	JHINGRAN (1991)
Saccharinum officinaris	sugarcane	stems	Asia	JHINGRAN (1991)
Serjania sp.	–	stems	Amazonia	TEIXEIRA et al. (1984)
Strychnos nuxvomica	'vomit-nut'	seeds	Asia	JHINGRAN (1991)
Tephrosia spp.	hoard pea	?	America, Asia	TEIXEIRA et al. (1984)
Tagetes spp.	marigold	whole plant (?)	–	KAGAN et al. (1986)
Tamarindus indica	tamarind	seeds	Asia	MISRA et al. (1986)
Verbascum thapsus	–	?	Asia	JHINGRAN (1991)
Walsura piscidia	–	bark	Asia	JHINGRAN (1991)

[1] Genus often erroneously cited as *Brassica* (e.g. JANA et al. 1987).
[2] *Derris* = *Lonchocarpus* (proposed synonymy of NASCIMENTO et al. (1975).

(KULAKKATTOLICKAL & KRAMER 1988). The same factor is presumably important in responses to synthetic pest-control agents (see below). Studies on effects of plant-derived pest-control agents on pond planktonic and benthic invertebrate species are almost non-existent. The experimental study of JANA et al. (1987) suggests that applications of the extract of mahua seeds (one of the more commonly used pest-control agents in India) cause an initial depression followed by rapid recovery of phyto- and zooplankton populations, but that benthic invertebrates are more seriously affected. Unfortunately, the low level of replication in their study makes the determination of significant trends almost impossible. Clearly this is an area which requires more detailed study in future.

The ultimate non-target organisms of concern are human beings, and there is some cause for concern over worker exposure to plant-derived compounds. One seed extract which is currently being advocated as a 'safe' pest control agent is obtained from *Croton* seeds (GUERRERO 1989). Far from being safe to humans, *Croton* oil is one of the most potent naturally-occurring co-carcinogens known to science. In addition, it is a powerful contact poison which causes ulceration of the skin, dermatitis and other potentially serious side-effects (SEIGLER 1979). It has been pointed out also that *Derris*-extracted toxins can be harmful to groups other than fish and insects: Harborne (1979), for example, notes that 'rotenone-containing roots have been employed for committing suicide by New Guinea natives, and as a basis for arrow poisons in Sumatra'. In addition, milling of *Derris* root in Bangladesh has been reported to cause acute lung damage in workers exposed to dust (C. Price, pers. comm.).

With the exception of rotenone, which appears to break down rapidly at higher temperatures and UV-light levels (see above), the fate of plant toxins in the aquatic environment has received little or no attention from applied scientists working on pond management. The few studies which have been carried out in the tropics on the extract obtained from *Derris* root and the seeds of the mahua tree (Jana et al. 1987), respectively, indicate that the 'residual toxicity to fish' (measured in the former by bioassay in aquaria) within ponds can last for up to 30 days. Such measures are of course indirect, and the fate, possibility of uptake, and food-chain accumulation of these compounds are at present unknown.

A related issue is that exposure of pest species to plant-derived control agents may lead to resistance in exactly the same manner as is found in the development of synthetic pesticide resistance, as has been demonstrated by Orciari (1979) for Golden shiner (*Notropis*) populations exposed repeatedly to rotenone. In an earlier study, Fabacher & Chambers (1972) reported that mosquitofish (*Gambusia*) populations which had not been exposed to rotenone previously were more tolerant than a control population, and postulated that this was a result of cross-resistance due to pre-induction of mixed function oxidase (MFO) enzymes (which are known to be involved in rotenone detoxification) probably through prior exposure to synthetic pesticide residues such as organochlorines (also potent MFO inducers), of which traces were present in tissues of fish from the resistant population.

Clearly the use of plant-derived pest control agents carries with it a certain amount of hazard, both to the environment (in terms of effects on non-target species) and to users. Presently, the degree of hazard cannot be quantified, due to an acute lack of information on compounds used, their active ingredients, their persistence, specificity and associated health risks. Furthermore, researchers working in this area seem almost completely unaware that the 'active toxic components' within plant extracts include a numerous and diverse range of organic substances. Although the toxicity of many plant extracts is often attributed to the presence of 'saponins', and these are indeed toxic to fish, there is some evidence that saponins themselves may facilitate (through solubilization) the availability of a range of other, potentially even more toxic substances, including phytochaemagglutinins, glycosides, terpenoids, alkaloids and flavonoids (for an excellent review of this area, see Rosenthal & Janzen 1979).

In addition to these unpredictable hazards, there are a number of practical problems associated with the use of plant-derived pest control agents, such as cost and availability (e.g. Hussain 1990), and also in the determination of the potency of the substances used. This latter problem, highlighted by Ameen et al. (1987), will certainly reduce the efficiency with which compounds such as rotenone are used, but moreover will lead inevitably to overuse, as pond managers will over-apply pest control agents in order to ensure their effectiveness. Again, what little evidence is available in the literature suggests that amounts required will vary considerably according to temperature and water chemistry (e.g. Chakraborty et al. 1987), and for most compounds, even rough guidelines do not exist.

Synthetic pest control agents used in fishponds

The range of synthetic compounds used to control fishpond pests is again large, and examples of such compounds currently used or proposed for use in Asia are given in Table 2. The variety of synthetic agents reflects the fact that in many poorer areas of the world rural fish-farmers will use whatever is available to control pests, regardless of hazard to themselves or the local environment (largely due to ignorance of the risks involved), as long as the compound is locally cost-effective.

Inorganic compounds such as cyanides, potassium permanganate and quicklime are used (for references see Table 2), but preferences vary from country to country: in Thailand, cyanides are seen as a cheaper alternative to commercial rotenone – although obviously dangerous to handle (Gribgratok 1981). Phosphine pellets, normally used for the fumigation of grain stores, are popular in India and Bangladesh, despite the fact that their use in fishponds can release clouds of poisonous phosphine gas, with consequences for the user

Table 2. Some inorganic and organic chemicals currently used or proposed for use as pest control agents in fish ponds in Asia.

Compound	Name/Class	Source
i) Inorganics		
aluminium phosphide	fumigant	PERSBACHER & SARKAR (1989 b)
potassium permanganate	–	JHINGRAN (1991)
sodium chloride	salt	JHINGRAN (1991)
sodium hypochlorite	bleaching powder	JHINGRAN (1991)
sodium cyanide	–	GRIBGRATOK (1981)
calcium oxide	quicklime	S. S. SHEA (pers. comm.)
ii) Pesticide organics		
aldrin	organochlorine	JHINGRAN (1991)
endrin	organochlorine	JHINGRAN (1991)
DDT	organochlorine	ANON. (1989)
dieldrin	organochlorine	JHINGRAN (1991)
endosulfan	organophosphate	KENNEDY (1990)
DDVP	organophosphate	KONAR (1969)
fenitriothion	organophosphate	PERSBACHER & SARKAR (1989 a)
methyl parathion	organophosphate	CHAKRABORTY & BANERJEE (1988)
malathion	organophosphate	PERSBACHER & SARKAR (1989 a)
phosphamidon	organophosphate	KONAR (1969)
thiometon	organophosphate	JHINGRAN (1991)
trichlorphon	organophosphate	HAQUE & BARHUA (1988)
iii) Non-pesticide organics		
benzene hexachloride	–	KHANNA (1957)
detergents	domestic soap	JHINGRAN (1991)
mixture	diesel oil	JHINGRAN (1991)
Teepol B-300	dispersant	JHINGRAN (1991)

which will depend upon wind direction (R. JENSEN, pers. comm.).

The use of commercial pesticide formulations for the control of pest fish and insects is well-documented in Asia (e.g. JHINGRAN 1991), and is almost certainly widespread throughout the tropics. Despite the obvious problems of hazard to the user, unpredictable biodegradability, persistence, and lack of specificity, their extreme potency, particularly as fish poisons, has made them a popular choice where they are available and cost-effective (JHINGRAN 1991; but see also PERSBACHER & SARKAR 1989 b). Organochlorines are effective fish poisons at relatively low application rates, and unlike organophosphates, are more toxic to fish than to most invertebrates (CHAUDHURI 1960, cited in JHINGRAN 1991). Although ponds can be detoxified after pesticide treatment, for example by the application of charcoal, the long-term use of these types of compound must give cause for concern: in the case of organochlorines, because of their well-documented persistence in the aquatic environment and in the case of organophosphates because of the extremely high application rates often employed (e.g. >200 mg/l trichlorphon used in Bangladesh, personal observation).

A number of other organic compounds are employed in fishpond pest control: a common method aquatic-insect control is to cover the water surface with a layer of oil (e.g. diesel oil; JHINGRAN 1991) or detergent (e.g. domestic soap or Teepol) in order to prevent air-breathing aquatic insects from replenishing their oxygen supply. This practice again may result in the accumulation of toxic materials (e.g. toxic oil fractions) within the pond sediments, with unknown long-term effects, but no studies have been carried out on this to date.

Non-chemical methods of fishpond pest control

It is clear from an examination of the literature that this area has received little study. Many workers make the obvious statement that the simplest and most effective method to remove predatory fish and invertebrates from drainable ponds is to drain them. What is less obvious is that the practice of netting-out of non-drainable nursery ponds may also be effective in some circumstances, if a fine-mesh net is employed. However, comparative studies to test this possibility have yet to be undertaken. In addition, the prevention of pest infiltration, while practically impossible in the case of flying insects, could be accomplished easily in many circumstances by the construction of dikes to prevent the ingress of larger predatory fish species (e.g. catfish, snakeheads or climbing perch), although this may be of limited utility in floodplain areas, where fishponds are periodically inundated by rising waters. In addition, a recent aid project in Thailand has demonstrated that a new practise of stocking ponds with larger 'predator-resistant' fry may indeed remove the need for predator control altogether (LITTLE et al. 1991), and this approach should be actively studied and encouraged in the future.

Conclusions and recommendations

The purpose of this short review has been to highlight a potentially serious environmental problem, which has received almost no attention, even from workers concerned with problems in tropical freshwater environments. Here, only the use of pest control chemicals in tropical freshwater aquaculture is dealt with; similar problems exist, and are probably even more widespread, in the use of such chemicals in tropical riverine and lake fisheries. Indeed, in the latter case, the potential impacts are likely to be more widespread, since they occur in natural water bodies, as opposed to the (mainly) managed water bodies used in semi-intensive aquaculture, and for this reason alone require urgently to be addressed.

In summary, chemical agents used in aquaculture pest control generally suffer from the following problems:

i) *Lack of specificity*. These chemicals are used to kill fish. In many cases, the target species are among the most tolerant to the compounds used: for example, in a study carried out on the effects of croton seed extract on 41 common species of Indian freshwater fish, target species such as catfish and snakeheads were among the most tolerant (DIVAKARAN & BALAKRISHNAN 1983). Thus to be effective, they must be used at extremely high concentrations, with potentially devastating consequences for non-target species.

ii) *Unknown long-term effects*. The problem of bioconcentration of organochlorines is well-known, but the possibility of residual accumulation of toxic components from the other compounds used has for most received little or no attention.

iii) *The development of resistance*. The continual, heavy application of individual compounds may also result in the development of resistance among the target species. This has been demonstrated for both synthetic compounds such as organochlorines, and 'natural' compounds such as rotenone, leading to even higher application rates.

iv) *Unforeseen acute and chronic human health problems*. In addition to the obvious problems of safe handling, a further cause for concern from the safety point-of-view is that the fish killed by pest control agents such as organochlorines are often eaten immediately afterwards (e.g. KENNEDY 1990).

v) *An increasing phenomenon*. The use of chemical control agents is strongly advocated by both government and aid agencies involved in promoting aquaculture in third world countries. In Bangladesh, for example, two recent reports commissioned by aid agencies and government in Bangladesh both identified the 'lack of available piscicides' as a major constraint on the continuing development of aquaculture in that country (AMEEN 1987, HUSSAIN 1990).

A considerable amount of information is available on the natural and synthetic chemicals used in tropical aquaculture, but researchers have concentrated on the ability of compounds to eradicate the target species, giving little or no concern to non-target species, although it has been generally accepted that the use of organochlorines should not be encouraged. What is lacking at present is an integrated evaluation of the compounds currently in use to determine the most suitable, in terms of their potential impact on the aquatic environment. Furthermore, little effort has been devoted towards the evaluation of non-chemical methods such as drag-netting or the prevention of pest infiltration. Future research efforts in these areas are urgently required, and should be carried out in the wider context of a sustainable aquatic resource management strategy.

Acknowledgements

I would like to thank all of the people, too numerous to mention, who have provided information and access to unpublished data and manuscripts during the preparation of this paper and in particular, Dr. WALTER MORS for his generous information and advice. I also thank the Royal Society of London for the provision of a travel grant to attend the meeting in Hong Kong.

References

AMEEN, M., 1987: Resources and Opportunities in Freshwater Fish Culture in Bangladesh: 244 pp. – DANIDA NRD-II Project Publications, Noakhali, Bangladesh.

AMEEN, M., AHMED, M., SHIREEN, K. F., MUSTAFA A., ROY, T. K. & RAHMAN, P. M. M., 1987: Persistence of piscicidal effect of ethanol extract of rotenoids from *Derris* roots stored in commonly available containers. – *Bangladesh J. Fish.* **10:** 23–30.

Anonymous, 1989: A baseline survey on the pesticides and used in Bangladesh with particular reference to their toxic effects on Indian major carps: 125 pp. – Unpublished report to the Faculty of Fisheries, Bangladesh Agricultural University, Mymensingh, Bangladesh.

BEVERIDGE, M. C. M. & PHILLIPS, M. J., 1993: Environmental impact of tropical inland aquaculture. – In: PULLIN, R. S. V., ROSENTHAL, H. & MACLEAN, J. L. (eds.): Environment and Aquaculture in Developing Countries: 213–216. – *ILLARM* Conference Proceedings **31.** *Bellagio Conference on environment and Third World Aquaculture Development.*

BHUYAN, B. R., 1967: Eradication of unwanted fish from ponds by using indigenous plant fish poisons. – *Science and Culture* **33:** 82–83.

CASCON, S. C., MORS, W. B., TURSCH, B. M., APLIN, R. T. & DURHAM, L. J., 1965: Ichthyothereol and its acetate, the active polyacetylene constituents of *Ichthyothere terminalis (Spreng.) Malme,* a fish poison from the lower Amazon. – J. Amer. Chem. Soc. **87:** 5237.

CHAKRABORTY, P. S. & BANERJEE, S., 1988: Methyl parathion as a fish toxicant for eradication of trash fishes from a freshwater pond. – *Environment & Ecology* **6:** 148–151.

CHAKRABORTY, P. S., DAS, A. & BANERJEE, S., 1987: Evaluation of efficiency of mahua oil cake as fish poison in relation to hardness of water. – *Environment & Ecology* **5:** 165–167.

CHANDLER, J. H. & MARKING, L. L., 1982: Toxicity of rotenone to selected aquatic invertebrates and frog larvae. – *Progressive Fish-Culturist* **44:** 78–80.

DIVAKARAN, O. & BALAKRISHNAN, N. M., 1983: *Croton tiglium (Linn)* as an ideal eradicant of pests and predators in fish farms. – *Fishery Technology* **20:** 101–104.

DUDGEON, D., 1994: The need for multiscale approaches to the conservation and management of tropical inland waters. – *Mitt. Internat. Verein. Limnol.* **24:** 11–16.

ENGSTROM-HEG, R. & COLESANTE, R. T., 1979: Predicting rotenone degradation in lakes and ponds. – *New York Fish Game J.* **26:** 22–36.

FABACHER, D. L. & CHAMBERS, H., 1972: Rotenone tolerance in mosquitofish. – *Environmental Pollution* **3:** 139–141.

GARCEZ, F. R., SCRAMIN, S. & MORS, W. B., 1988: Prenylated flavonoids as evolutionary indicators in the genus *Dahlstedtia.* – *Phytochemistry* **27:** 1079.

GINGERICH, W. H. & RACH, J. J., 1985: Uptake, biotransformation, and elimination of rotenone by bluegills (*Lepomis macrochirus*). – *Aquatic Toxicology* **6:** 179–196.

GOMEZ, E. D., DE LA CRUZ, A., CHAVEZ, V., MILES, D. H. & CAJIPE, G., 1986: Toxicants from mangrove plants: II. Toxicity of aqueous extracts to fish. – *Philippines J. Science* **115:** 81–89.

GRIBGRATOK, S., 1981: The role of cyanide in the fisheries. – *Thai Fisheries Gazette* **34:** 499–506.

GUERRERO, R., 1989: Fish toxicants from local ponds for better pond management. – GREENFIELDS, September Issue: 29.

HAQUE, M. Z. & BARHUA, G., 1988: Toxic and sublethal effect of the Dipterex on *Oreochromis niloticus (Linn.).* – *Bangladesh J. Fish.* **11:** 75–79.

HARBORNE, J. B., 1979: Flavonoid pigments. – In: ROSENTHAL, G. A. & JANZEN, D. H. (eds.): Herbivores: Their interaction with secondary plant metabolites: 619–655. – Academic Press, New York.

HOMECHAUDHURI, S., PANDIT, T., PODDAR, S. & BANERJEE, S., 1986: Effect of mahua oil cake on the blood cells and blood values of an air-breathing catfisch, *Heteropneustes fossilis* and a carp *Cyprinus carpio.* – *Proceedings of the Indian Academy of Sciences (Animal Science)* **95:** 617–622.

HORGAN, D. J., SINGER, T. P. & CASIDA, J. E., 1968: Studies on the respiratory chain-linked reduced nicotinamide adenine dinucleotide dehydrogenase. XIII. Binding sites of rotenone, piericidin A and amytal in the respiratory chain. – *J. Biol. Chem.* **243:** 834–843.

HUSSAIN, M. R., 1990: Aquaculture in Bangladesh. – In: MOHAN, J. M. (eds.): Aquaculture in Asia: 105–139. – Asian Fisheries Society, Indian Branch, Mangalore.

JANA, B. B., MANNA, A. K. & KUNDU, G., 1987: Effect of an oil-cake (*Brassica latifolia*) piscicide on the physico-chemical and biological spectrum of waterbodies. – *Limnologica* **18:** 431–439.

JHINGRAN, V. G., 1991: *Fish and Fisheries of India.* 3rd Edition: 727 pp. – Hindustan Publishing Corporation, Delhi.

KAGAN, J., KAGAN, E. & SEIGNEURIE, E., 1986: Alphaterthienyl, a powerful fish poison with light-dependent activity. – *Chemosphere* **16:** 49–57.

KENNEDY, R., 1990: An initial resource survey of Southern Bhola Island to assess the factors limiting the development of aquaculture. – Unpublished report produced for Action Aid Bangladesh by the Intermediate Technology Development Group.

KHANNA, D. V., 1957: How to get rid of aquatic insects from fish nurseries. – *Indian Farming* **7:**12–14.

KONAR, S. K., 1969: Laboratory studies on two organophosphorus insecticides, DDVP and phosphamidon as selective toxicants. – Trans. Amer. Fish Soc. **98:**403–437.

KULAKKATTOLICKAL, A. T. & KRAMER, D. L., 1988: The role of air breathing in the resistance of bimodally respiring fish to waterborne toxins. – J. Fish Biol. **32:**119–127.

LITTLE, D. C., INNES-TAYLOR, N. L., TURONGRUANG, D. & KOMOLMARL, S., 1991: Large-scale fish seed for small-scale aquaculture. – *Aquabyte* **4:**2–3.

MINSALAN, C. L. O. & CHIU, Y. N., 1986: Effects of teaseed cake on selective elimination of finfish in shrimp ponds. – In: MACLEAN, J. L., DIXON, I. B. & HOSILLOS, L. V. (eds.): The First Asian Fisheries Forum: 79–82. Asian Fisheries Society, Manila, Philippines.

MISRA, S., HOMECHAUDHURI, S. & BANERJEE, S., 1986: Evaluation of mahua oil cake and tamarind seed husk as fish toxicants. – *Environment & Ecology* **4:**388–390.

MORRISON, B. R. S., 1986: Use and effects of piscicides. – In: MAITLAND, P. S., TURNER, A. K. (eds.): Angling and Wildlife in Fresh Waters. – *Institute of Terrestrial Ecology, Natural Environmental Research Council* (*NERC, London*) *Publication* No. **19:**47–52.

MORS, W. B., NASCIMENTO, M. C., VALLE, J. R. & ARAGAO, J. A., 1973: Icthyotoxic activity of plants of the genus *Derris* and compounds isolated therefrom. – *Ciencia e Culture* **25:**647–648.

NASCIMENTO, M. C., DE VASCONCELOS, DIAS, R. L. & MORS, W. B., 1976: Flavonoids of *Derris obtusa:* aurones and auronols. – *Phytochemistry* **15:**1553.

ORCIARI, R. D., 1979: Rotenone resistance of Golden shiner (*Notemigonus crystoleucas*) from a periodically reclaimed pond. – *Trans. Amer. Fish. Soc.* **108:**641–645.

PACARDO, E. P., 1994: Agroecosystem analysis of Laguna Lake Basin, the Philippines. – Mitt. Internat. Verein. Limnol. **24:**259–264.

PERSBACHER, P. W. & SARKAR J., 1989a: Toxicity of selected organophosphorus insecticides to the backswimmer, *Notonecta* sp. – *Asian Fisheries Science* **2:**265–268.

– – 1989b: Toxicity of selected pesticides to the snakehead, *Channa punctatus*. – *Asian Fisheries Science* **2:**249–254.

PHILLIPS, M. J., BEVERIDGE, M. C. M. & CLARKE, R. M., 1991: Impact of aquaculture on water resources. – *Advances in World Aquaculture* **3:**568–591.

PHILLIPS, M. J., KWAI LIN, C. & BEVERIDGE, M. C. M., 1993. – Shrimp culture and the environment: lessons from the world's most rapidly expanding warmwater aquaculture sector. – PULLIN, R. S. V., ROSENTHAL, H. & MACLEAN, J. L. (eds.): Environment and Aquaculture in Developing Countries. *ILLARM* Conference Proceedings **31.** *Bellagio Conference on Environment and Third World Aquaculture Development.*

ROSENTHAL, G. A. & JANZEN, D. H. (eds.): Herbivores: Their interaction with secondary plant metabolites. – Academic Press, New York.

SAMUELSEN, O. B., 1989: Degradation of oxytetracycline in seawater at two different temperatures and light intensities, and the persistence of oxytetracycline in sediment from a fish farm. – *Aquaculture* **83:** 7–16.

SEIGLER, D. S., 1979: Toxic seed lipids. – In: ROSENTHAL, G. A. & JANZEN, D. H. (eds.): Herbivores: Their interaction with secondary plant metabolites: 449–470. – Academic Press, New York.

TEIXEIRA, J. R. M., LAPA, A. J., SOUCCAR, C. & VALLE, J. R., 1984: Timbós: ichthyotoxic plants used by Brazilian Indians. – *J. Ethnopharmacology* **10:**311–318.

Author's address:

Environment Group, Institute of Aquaculture, University of Stirling, Stirling, Scotland FK9 4LA.

Mitt. Internat. Verein. Limnol.	**24**	293–314	Stuttgart, Februar 1994

Development of biological monitoring programs to detect mining-waste impacts upon aquatic ecosystems of the Alligator Rivers Region, Northern Territory, Australia

Christopher L. Humphrey and Peter L. Dostine

Abstract

The Alligator Rivers Region (ARR) lies in the wet-dry tropics of northern Australia where highly seasonal, summer rains fall between November and April. The Region encloses Kakadu National Park, renowned for its rich and diverse, cultural and natural heritage and also as the location of significant mineral deposits including uranium, gold, platinum and palladium. Research programs considered necessary for the protection of the environment from the effects of mining in the Region have been underway since 1978 and have included extensive studies of physicochemical limnology and of the biota of aquatic and terrestrial ecosystems. These early baseline and ongoing studies are reviewed in relation to the development and refinement of techniques and procedures to monitor and assess effects of mining activities on aquatic ecosystems of the Region.

Benthic macroinvertebrate and fish communities (or representative populations or assemblages within these communities) have been selected as the most practical and useful groups of organisms for use in the current programs of biological monitoring in the ARR. Adequate monitoring of macroinvertebrate community structure requires identification to species level; deficiencies in taxonomic information have been redressed in recent studies.

Present studies are confined to a seasonal tributary (Magela Creek) of the East Alligator River near the Ranger Uranium Mine and, until recently, in the upper South Alligator River near the Coronation Hill gold, platinum and palladium prospect. A variety of monitoring methods is presently under development. These range from the detection of short-term effects of releases of waste-water from mine sites during the wet season to the detection of longer-term effects of mining generally. Included in the program are experimental field manipulations aimed at improving the design and sensitivity of community-based techniques for biological monitoring.

Introduction

The most intensive limnological research in tropical Australia has been conducted by two research bodies: the Alligator Rivers Region Research Institute (ARRRI) located at Jabiru in the 'Top End' of the Northern Territory, and the Australian Centre for Tropical Freshwater Research located at James Cook University of North Queensland in Townsville, Queensland. The research of the latter Centre is carried out in tropical Queensland and has been reviewed elsewhere (see Pearson 1994). The research of the ARRRI is confined to the Alligator Rivers Region (ARR) – an area renowned for its rich cultural and natural heritage (the Region incorporates Kakadu National Park) and large, economically important, mineral reserves including uranium, gold and platinum-group metals (see Braithwaite & Werner 1987).

The ARRRI is the research arm of the Office of the Supervising Scientist (OSS), and was established by the Commonwealth Government to conduct appropriate research that would ensure a high level of environmental protection from the effects of mining and processing operations in the Region. The research program of the Institute is multidisciplinary and includes sub-programs in aquatic biology (toxicity testing and biological monitoring), environmental radioactivity, environmental chemistry and rehabilitation (geomorphology and revegetation).

From 1978 to 1987, the responsibilities of the OSS were specific to the effects of uranium mining and processing operations on the environment. Two mines commenced construction within the Region in 1979 and are located within catchments of seasonal tributaries of the East Alligator River, Ranger on Magela Creek and Nabarlek on Cooper Creek. In 1987, the functions of the OSS were extended to general mining operations in a so-called 'Conservation Zone' following the discovery of significant concentrations of gold and platinum-group metals at Coronation Hill in the upper South Alligator River catchment. In June 1991, the Government decided not to allow mining at Coronation Hill and to incorporate the Conservation Zone into Kakadu National Park.

A research program on biological monitoring has been established by the ARRRI to develop procedures for monitoring and assessing effects of mining operations on the freshwater ecosystems of the ARR. A full description of the program up to 1988 has been presented elsewhere (Humphrey et al. 1990). The focus of the present paper is to provide and review additional

0538-4680/94/0024-0293 $ 5.50

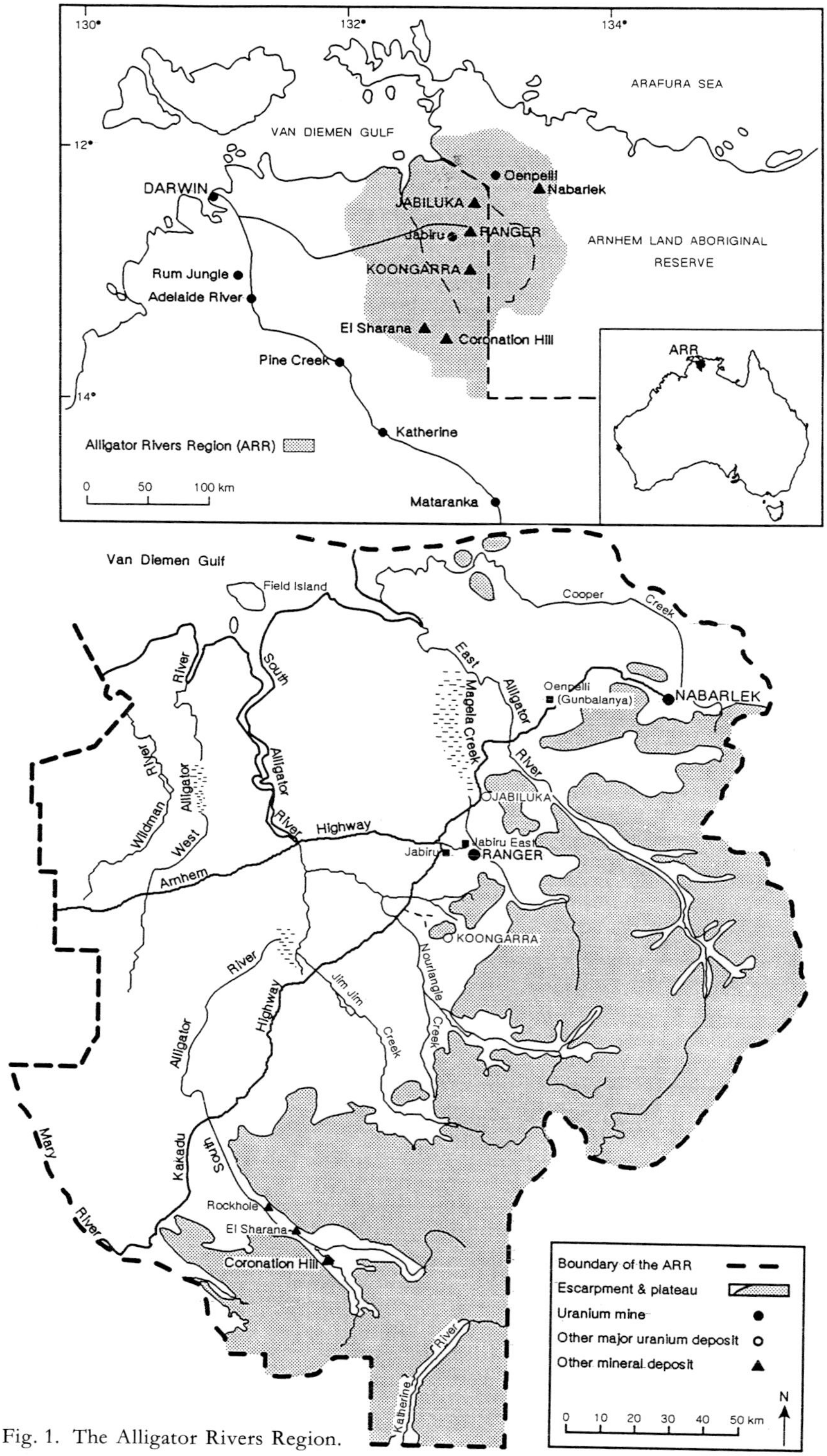

Fig. 1. The Alligator Rivers Region.

information and findings relevant to this program, including those listed below.

i) An overview of biological monitoring procedures in the context of the broader issue of mine waste-water management and environmental controls, including recent (post-1988) developments.
ii) A review of the groups of organisms that have been investigated in baseline and other studies by the ARRRI, its consultants or other workers in the ARR; and of the suitability or otherwise of these groups for biological monitoring in the Region.
iii) A description and review of recent developments since 1988 in the program on benthic macroinvertebrate communities from streams of the ARR.

Description of the study area

A detailed description of the geography, climate and major characteristics of the aquatic ecosystems of the ARR was given by HUMPHREY et al. (1990). A brief summary is provided here. The Alligator Rivers Region is situated east of Darwin in the Northern Territory (Australia) (Fig. 1). Major streams of the Region arise to the south and east in the Arnhem Land sandstone plateau which rises some 200–300 m above sea level. After leaving the plateau, often through deep gorges, the major streams occupy sandy, braided channels and flow through extensive and flat lowlands, to enter broad, seasonally-inundated floodplains. The extensive floodplains eventually merge into the estuaries.

The Region has a monsoonal climate, the wet season occurring generally between November–March and the dry season between May–September; April and October are usually transitional months. Annual rainfall at Jabiru over the 18-year period 1971–1989 has averaged 1500 mm (SD = 300 mm). Further inland, however, rainfall decreases, averaging, for example, about 1200 mm per year at El Sharana in the upper South Alligator River. The distinct seasonality of the rainfall results in flow along the entire length of most streams of the Region occurring only from about January to May. In Magela Creek, total annual flow past Ranger over the 18-year period 1971–1989 has averaged 349 Mm^3 (SD = 186). Total annual flow in the upper South Alligator River near Coronation Hill is estimated to average about 107 Mm^3.

Flow ceases over much of the length of the streams during the dry season, continuing only in short upstream sections fed by escarpment springs and seepage. Thus Magela Creek downstream of Ranger flows only during each wet season, while the South Alligator River near Coronation Hill flows throughout the year. The temporary sections of streams, channels and floodplains dry out, and the remaining surface waters of each stream consist of strings of waterbodies (billabongs) in which aquatic organisms of the lowlands become confined. During the dry season, water quality in the remaining surface waters of the streams vary widely, as described by HUMPHREY et al. (1990). Only in permanent sections of the streams and in some billabongs lying within the main stream-channels, does water tend to retain qualities of the wet season throughout the year.

During the wet season proper, however (i.e. once continuous flow has been established), water quality is generally uniform within and amongst streams of the Region. In Magela Creek, for which considerable information is available, wet-season water is acidic (arithmetic mean *p*H 5.2). This is the result of the natural acidic quality of the rain and the low ability of the catchment rocks and soils to buffer the acidity of the runoff. Conductivity of the water is very low (5–17 µS/cm), as are concentrations of suspended materials (suspended solids, 4–59 mg/l), major ions, nutrients and trace metals, including radionuclides. Wet-season waters are extremely soft with low buffering capacity, and have relatively high temperatures (mean ~28 °C).

Waste-water management and environmental controls

The most important environmental concern associated with the operational phase of mining in the ARR has been the management of excess water that accumulates each year within mine sites as a consequence of the summer, monsoonal rainfall. These waste-waters are complex and contain enhanced (relative to adjacent natural surface waters) concentrations of naturally-occurring substances (heavy metals, radionuclides, suspended solids) and exotic chemicals (hydrocarbons, process chemicals) that would pose an environmental risk if they were allowed to drain uncontrolled from a mine site. Much of the research at the ARRRI has focused on the issue of disposal of aqueous wastes with considerable resources being directed at the study of aquatic ecosystems of the Region. Aquatic organisms are continuously exposed to substances present in water and uptake, and therefore potential risks, are greatest for these organisms. The objective of all environmental protection is to maintain the biotic integrity of ecosystems and only studies conducted on aquatic organisms can define or be used to assess the overall effect of waste-waters on the organisms. The ARRRI has developed a two-fold approach to the biological assessment of effects that could result from releases of mine waste-waters on the environment, which will be outlined below.

Pre-release, laboratory determination of the toxicity of waste-waters

Controlled release of excess mine waste-water during the wet season has been recommended by ARRRI as a solution to management of these waters in the ARR, with minimum dilution requirements being determined from pre-release biological testing of the waters. The rationale for the approach has been discussed by BROWN (1986): in short, because the impact of complex and varying wastes on aquatic environments cannot be predicted from their individual constituents (cf. water-quality standards regulated by chemical analysis), testing the toxicity of mine waste-water on living aquatic organisms is essential. A comprehensive description of the developments that have led to the present control regime based on toxicity testing is provided in a recent review by JOHNSTON (1991). The principal features of the approach are listed below.

i) The direct measurement of the change in toxicological responses (lethal and sublethal) of local organisms selected from widely different taxa and trophic levels, to the actual waste-water as it is diluted with receiving water.
ii) The dilution of the whole waste required to render it harmless can be used as a control parameter to regulate its discharge. However, this must follow the application of a safety factor to account for possible occurrence of large undetected risks, additivity of undetected effects and protection of species other than those tested.

The ARRRI has assessed the suitability of 19 species of local tropical freshwater organisms as toxicity test animals; three of these, a vertebrate (fish) and two invertebrates (cnidarian and crustacean), are employed now in pre-release toxicity tests for routine use. The three species and end-points used are listed below.

i) Purple-spotted gudgeon (*Mogurnda mogurnda*): embryo survival and hatchability.
ii) Hydra (*Hydra viridissima*): population growth rate.
iii) Cladocera (*Moinodaphnia macleayi*): survival and reproduction.

Biological monitoring of aquatic environments

When mine waste-waters are released into surface waters, it is essential that a program is implemented to identify, quantify and assess effects on organisms in the natural surface waters resulting from the release. Such a program is required in order to achieve the overall environmental protection objective: i.e. no observable effects upon these organisms in a comprehensive and sensitive biological monitoring program. Developments and procedures of this program have been described by HUMPHREY et al. (1990) and are the focus of the rest of this paper.

Almost all of the research developed to assess the effect of mine waste-waters on aquatic systems has focused on Magela Creek near the Ranger project area. This has arisen mainly because the method of water disposal at Nabarlek has, to date, relied solely upon land application (irrigation) over the dry season (i.e. no direct release to surface water systems). Constituents which are present in the Ranger mine waste-waters, at concentrations well above those at which they occur in Magela Creek, include a variety of metals (especially uranium, manganese, magnesium and radionuclides) and sulphate. In addition, ratios of biologically-essential 'bulk' elements (e.g. calcium, magnesium) present in some of the waste-waters differ substantially from those found in the local natural surface waters. The principal hazard arising from the presence of radionuclides is radiation exposure of humans. A review of published data on acute and chronic radiation-induced effects on aquatic animals showed that radiological effects on non-human organisms would not be expected when water release standards required to safeguard human health are applied (JOHNSTON 1989).

The more hazardous heavy metals associated with mining (e.g. copper, cadmium, mercury, lead) are not at sufficiently high concentrations in the Ranger mine waters to pose a significant risk to the environment. HOLDWAY (1988), nevertheless, identified three potentially important abiotic factors that are characteristic of the surface waters of freshwater ecosystems of the ARR during the wet season that could lead to enhanced toxicity of any of a number of constituents, including the other less-hazardous metals, present in mine waste-waters. These factors are: continuously high water temperatures (28 °C or greater); extremely soft water with low buffering capacity and low pH; and, intermittent or greatly-reduced flow.

The last factor (creek flow) is pertinent to the method of waste-water disposal currently being used by Ranger mine, namely discharge through a 'Wetland Filtration' system. The complex hydrology of this system is such that released waste-waters enter Magela Creek on a falling hydrograph, that is during periods of low flow that can arise at any time during the wet season and, in particular, during the 'tapering flow' period of the late wet-early dry season. Thus, while the use of wetland filtration has the potential for partial removal of some constituents by absorption processes, control of dilution is lost and it is essential that an adequate biological monitoring system is in place to verify the adequacy of environmental protection.

Potential of the ARR biota for monitoring

Based on the conclusions of workshops held in 1978 and 1979, the OSS established a baseline research program to provide the information required to assess any future impact of mining on the ARR ecosystems. It was recognised that the major environmental impact of the proposed mining operations would be from the release of contaminated mine waste-waters to the natural surface waters of the Region. Aquatic organisms would be at most risk from dispersion of such wastes and therefore the studies formulated by the workshops focused mainly on aquatic ecosystems. Prior to these baseline studies, virtually nothing was known about the biota of aquatic ecosystems of the ARR. Thus, in order to provide a base of knowledge against which to assess the effects of mining, three specific study aims were established.

i) To obtain information on the identity (including necessary taxonomic study), distribution, abundances and seasonality of organisms making up communities.
ii) To describe the biology and ecology (autecology) of the biota (or at least 'key' organisms) of aquatic ecosystems.
iii) To obtain sufficient information to enable suitable choices to be made of organisms for use in biological monitoring (and biological toxicity testing) programs.

The baseline studies conducted by the ARRRI (some of which are continuing) are briefly reviewed below. In particular, major ecological findings and, where information is available, biogeographical relationships of the group are presented, while the potential of the group for monitoring in the ARR is assessed.

Algae

Surveys of the freshwater algae of the ARR have revealed a rich and diverse flora (Thomas 1983, Ling & Tyler 1986). The diatom flora comprises more than 160 taxa from 32 genera and includes representatives of both tropical and cosmopolitan taxa (Thomas 1983). The non-diatom algal flora includes more than 530 taxa, and shows affinities with that of tropical Southeast Asia and the Indian subcontinent (Ling & Tyler 1986). The community dynamics of phytoplankton (Kessell & Tyler 1983) and epiphytic diatoms (Mc Bride 1983) have been investigated in billabongs of Magela Creek.

Apart from their obvious value in eutrophication studies, Hellawell (1986) believed that algae were not particularly useful indicators of other types of pollution, including that associated with the majority of heavy metals (copper is an exception). Moreover, studies on the algae of Magela Creek (epiphytic diatoms (McBride 1983, pers. comm.) and phytoplankton (Kessell & Tyler 1983)) have documented spatial and temporal variations in these communities that are considered too large for the groups to be of practical use for biological monitoring of mine waste-water releases (viz. changes in community structure).

Macrophytes

The aquatic macrophyte flora of Magela Creek includes 75 species from 29 families (Finlayson et al. 1990). The dominant families by species richness are Cyperaceae (10 species), Poaceae (8 species) and Hydrocharitaceae (7 species). There have been several attempts to categorise and map the aquatic vegetation of the Magela floodplain e.g. Morley (1981), Sanderson et al. (1983), Finlayson et al. (1989). Finlayson et al. (1989) recognised ten macrophyte community types on the basis of 'indicator species' prominent at the time of maximum plant biomass and diversity. *Melaleuca* open forest and woodland community covered 34% of the floodplain, whilst *Pseudoraphis* and *Oryza* grassland covered 14% and 12% respectively. The floodplain vegetation exhibits marked seasonality in species composition and standing crop (Finlayson 1988).

Like the algae, macrophytes are regarded as potentially useful indicators of nutrient enrichment. Toxicity data for macrophytes are few but indicate, nevertheless, that only a small number of forms is particularly sensitive to metals; protocols for toxicity testing have been established for duckweeds (*Lemna*) which have been shown to be relatively sensitive to some metals (Wang 1990, Outridge & Noller 1991). Rather, submerged and emergent plants in general can accumulate high concentrations of metals without apparent toxicity (Crowder 1991), and for this reason Hellawell (1986) believed the group held much promise as bioaccumulating monitors of these substances. In this role, however, Outridge & Noller (1991) concluded that rooted macrophytes were of little use for biomonitoring of sedimentary metals but that free-floating species could be potentially useful for biomonitoring metals in water. Most workers agree that macrophytes serve useful roles in 'on-site' wetland filtration systems, designed to scavenge metals from industrial effluent.

Zooplankton

The zooplankton communities of 8 lowland billabongs of Magela Creek were studied by Tait et al. (1984). Rotifers comprised over 80% (227 species) of all species listed, with 14 Copepoda, 35 Cladocera and 5 Ostracoda. A large proportion of species were littoral or epiphytic. Most rotifer species were rare in samples, being represented by few specimens. Koste (1981) noted the Indo-Malayan affinities of the fauna, and the virtual absence of species common elsewhere in the tropics (e.g. brachionids). Tait et al. (1984) reported considerable spatial variations and extremely rapid changes in species composition and abundance of zooplankton over time. Species diversity increased in the wet season and then declined throughout the dry season, a pattern similar to that exhibited by littoral macroinvertebrates (Marchant 1982).

Zooplankton are very sensitive to a wide range of pollutants, including metals (Pickering et al. 1989, Wren & Stephenson 1991, Spry & Wiener 1991). This sensitivity has led to the use of microcrustacea as standard test organisms in toxicity testing programs worldwide (including the ARRRI program). As with algae, however, the overriding consideration precluding the use of community structure (at least) for use in biological monitoring programs in the ARR is the excessive heterogeneity of zooplankton. A further disadvantage of this group alluded to by Tait and co-workers (op. cit.) is that while communities may be diverse in the wet season, actual densities may either be greatly reduced as the result of dilution, or animals may be absent in sites where flow velocities are too high for populations to establish. Hence, the group would serve no useful role in monitoring short-term effects of mine waste-water releases. (These comments apply equally to planktonic algal forms.)

Macroinvertebrates

Documentation of the composition of the aquatic macroinvertebrate fauna has been progressing since the 'ARR Environmental Fact-finding Study' conducted between 1972 and 1973. Surveys undertaken during this study produced a large collection of principally adult aquatic and non-aquatic material for examination whenever taxonomic expertise became available. More recently, research consultancies have been initiated by ARRRI to elucidate the composition of the major aquatic insect orders. Table 1 summarizes the composition of some major aquatic taxa in the ARR, and is based on information from Wells (1991), Suter (1992), Watson & Abbey (1990) and Cranston (1991).

Table 1. Number of genera within families of major aquatic macroinvertebrate taxa in the ARR.

Order	Number of genera
Odonata	
Coenagrionidae	9
Isostictidae	3
Protoneuridae	1
Lestidae	3
Gomphidae	4
Aeschnidae	4
Corduliidae	4
Libellulidae	21
Trichoptera	
Leptoceridae	5
Ecnomidae	2
Hydropsychidae	2
Calamoceratidae	1
Hydroptilidae	7
Psychomyiidae	1
Helicopsyche	1
Polycentropodidae	2
Philopotamidae	1
Ephemeroptera	
Leptophlebiidae	5
Baetidae	6
Caenidae	2

The ARR Environmental Fact-finding Study provided the basis for the description of the odonate fauna (Watson 1973, Watson & Abbey 1980), its comprehensiveness being the exception amongst the aquatic taxa. Seventy-seven odonate species were recorded in the ARR; this comprises a large proportion of the number known from the northern section of the Northern Territory (Watson 1974). The fauna contains eight families and is dominated by the northern elements Coenagrionidae (19 species) and Libellulidae (38 species). Notable species include the Gondwanan elements *Aus-*

trocordulia territoria (Corduliidae) and *Hemigomphus magela* (Gomphidae).

The trichopteran fauna of the ARR contains at least 105 species in nine families. The familial composition of the fauna is as defined previously by Neboiss (1981), with the addition of the recently recognised Psychomyiidae (Neboiss 1990). All nine families are well represented in the Oriental region and New Guinea (Wells 1991, D. Dudgeon pers. comm.). A notable feature of the fauna is the high representation of three genera: *Oecetis* (Leptoceridae) 20 species, *Orthotrichia* (Hydroptilidae) 17 species, and *Ecnomus* (Ecnomidae) 16 species. Although there has been no detailed analysis of the habitat relationships of the trichopteran fauna, there appear to be marked differences between the fauna inhabiting sections of streams in or near the escarpment and that of sections of the streams in the lowlands. Hydropsychid species exhibit longitudinal zonation: *Asmicridea* is confined to plateau streams and the upstream reaches of lowland streams; *Cheumatopsyche* sp. 11 and 12 occur sympatrically in the upper and middle reaches of larger lowland streams, whilst *Cheumatopsyche* sp. 10 is confined to smaller shaded streams and spring-fed creeks.

The known ephemeropteran fauna of the ARR includes twenty five species, most of which are unnamed. The family Caenidae is well represented with 9 species, primarily in the genus *Tasmanocaenis*. An undescribed baetid species recorded from the upper South Alligator River resembles *Platybaetis*, known from a few localities in South-east Asia (P. Suter pers. comm.). Two undescribed leptophlebiid species belonging to the genus *Bibulmena* are found characteristically in temporary streams in the ARR. *Bibulmena* sp. 1 is known from rocky escarpment streams, whilst *Bibulmena* sp. 2 is known from sandy streams and is abundant in the lowland portion of Magela Creek during the early phase of the wet season.

Studies on the composition of the chironomid (Diptera) fauna of the ARR have revealed at least 116 species in the subfamilies Tanypodinae (11 genera), Orthocladiinae (seven genera), Chironominae (24 genera) and Aphroteniinae (one genus). The chironomine genera *Tanytarsus, Polypedilum* and *Dicrotendipes* are relatively speciose. The richness within the typically cold-stenothermic Orthocladiinae is of some interest, as is the presence of the Gondwanan element *Aphroteniella filicornis* (Aphroteniinae) (P. Cranston pers. comm.). A group of taxa including *Conochironomus* and *Skusella* is also of biogeographic interest. These genera are distributed across central Africa, India and northern Australia (P. Cranston pers. comm.). The composition of the remaining aquatic dipteran families (e.g. Empididae, Tipulidae, Tabanidae and Ceratopogonidae) is not well known. Similarly, knowledge of aquatic coleopteran and hemipteran faunas is insufficient to permit much comment. A notable element of the hemipteran fauna is the riffle-dwelling, brachypterous naucorid *Aphelocheirus australicus,* known from a single locality in the ARR and few localities in northern Queensland.

The molluscan fauna includes two bivalve and at least eleven gastropod species. The freshwater mussel *Velesunio angasi* is present in most parts of all catchments in the ARR. The biology and ecology of *V. angasi* in Magela Creek have been described by Humphrey & Simpson (1985). The genus *Corbiculina* is known presently in the ARR only from riffle sections of the upper South Alligator River. Common gastropod genera include *Glyptophysa, Gyraulus, Lymnaea, Amerianna, Notopala* and *Gabbia*. Most are widespread in lentic parts of the systems.

Caridean decapods are represented by at least three *Macrobrachium* species (*M. rosenbergii, M. bullatum* and *M. handschini*), two undescribed palaemonid genera and several atyid types. *Macrobrachium handschini* is common in cobble sections of riffles in the upper South Alligator River, but has not been recorded from other streams in the ARR. The undescribed palaemonid species are known from few localities in escarpment plateau streams.

Seven poriferan species are known from the ARR, belonging to the genera *Radiospongilla, Eunapius, Spongilla* and *Metania* (J. Stanisic pers. comm.), but the composition of the remaining invertebrate fauna has only been documented partially. Outridge (1987) recorded 101 macroinvertebrate species in Magela Creek, and noted the high species diversity compared to other Australian or tropical lentic systems. However, these conclusions (high diversity) were recently criticised by Shiel & Williams (1990) because of the invalid comparative base used by Outridge.

The dynamics of benthic macroinvertebrate communities in three lowland billabongs and an escarpment riffle and billabong of Magela Creek were described by Outridge (1988). Species diversity, abundance and biomass declined over the dry season to minima in December. These patterns were ascribed to seasonal variation in the inputs of allochthonous detritus. Marchant (1982) described similar patterns for the littoral macroinvertebrate fauna of billabongs in Magela Creek. There has been no detailed analysis of the dynamics of benthic communities in lotic systems of the ARR. Preliminary results reveal a marked reduction in the abundance of benthic organisms during the wet season as the result of scouring by the annual summer flooding (ARRRI 1988). Predicted changes in the functional organisation of benthic communities due to the seasonal availability of allochthonous detritus are yet to be confirmed. The role of macroinvertebrates in the process of litter breakdown in ARR streams has not been described. 'Shredder' species (e.g. the leaf and wood-mining chironomine *Stenochironomus*) appear to be few in number. A notable feature of macroinvertebrate communities in streams is the diversity of predatory organisms. Amongst the Chironomidae for example, the Tanypodinae (11 genera) and chironomine genera including *Cryptochironomus, Robackia, Parachironomus* and *Cladopelma* are common and well represented in streams of the Region (Cranston 1991; pers. comm.). Predatory groups from amongst the Trichopteran families Ecnomidae and Leptoceridae are particularly numerous (Wells 1991). Thus, ten species of *Ecnomus* (Ecnomidae) were recorded from a single site on Kambolgie Creek, a tributary of the SAR. Similarly, ten species of *Oecetis* (Leptoceridae) were recorded from a Magela Creek site. Given the high species richness and abundance of fish in streams of the ARR (see paragraph Fish below), fish predation could be an important factor in determining macroinvertebrate community structure. Such interactions have yet to be studied in the ARR.

Among aquatic organisms, macroinvertebrate communities are used most extensively in biological monitoring programs. The advantages that they offer are listed below.

i) A diversity of forms and accordingly, a wide range of sensitivities to many kinds of stresses (including metals).
ii) Relatively limited mobility.
iii) Relatively long life cycles which overcome, to some extent, the extreme variations in community dynamics evident, for example, in communities of micro-organisms. In addition, certain groups are sufficiently long-lived for use in bioaccumulation studies.
iv) Sampling techniques and methods of data analysis that are well established (Hellawell 1986, Abel 1989).
v) High diversity and abundance of benthic macroinvertebrates – some of which are rather well known taxonomically (see paragraph Taxonomy below) – in streams of the ARR.

Fish

Freshwater fish have been the most intensively studied group of aquatic organisms in the ARR (Taylor 1964, Midgley 1973, Pollard 1974, Bishop et al. 1986, 1990, in press). The composition, ecology and biogeographic relationships of the fauna are reasonably well known and were described and reviewed recently by Bishop & Forbes (1991). The following account is mainly a brief summary of that review. About 50 fish species have been collected in the fresh waters of the Region. The greatest proportion of species (62%) can be termed principal freshwater species, a small proportion (15%) are diadromous and the remainder (23%) are marine vagrants. The fauna includes representatives from twenty eight families (Bishop et al. 1986). The small-bodied fish fauna of the Region is dominated in overall abundance by centropomids (Perchlets), melanotaeniids (Rainbow fish) and atherinids; the larger bodied fish fauna is dominated by ariids and plotosids (Fork- and Eel-tailed catfish), clupeids (Boney bream and Tarpon) and, to a lesser extent, teraponids. The diversity of fish communities in the Region varies between seasons and habitat types. Characteristic species of the stream headwaters include Black-striped rainbow fish (*Melanotaenia nigrans*), Gertrude's blue eye (*Pseudomugil gertrudae*) and a number of teraponid species (*Syncomistes butleri, Pingalla midgleyi* and *Hephaestus fuliginosus*).

A characteristic feature of the ecology of the fish communities is the movement of fish between habitats with the re-linking of dry-season refuge areas of the escarpment, corridor and floodplain zone once wet season flows commence. Fish movement can be regarded as a response to the patchiness of resources. Feeding, breeding and recruitment of juveniles mostly occurs during the wet season months in the lowland billabongs and floodplain areas. In some seasonal tributaries of the larger Alligator Rivers, including Magela Creek and Nourlangie Creek (Fig. 1), there are massive migrations in the late wet season of mainly small-bodied fishes from floodplain nursery areas to dry season refuges upstream.

The seasonal patterns of abundance of small carnivorous fish reflect the same pattern of abundance described by Marchant (1982) for macroinvertebrates of the billabong littoral. The trophic organisation of fish communities varies between habitats. Upstream escarpment habitats are nutrient poor and are dominated by herbivore/detritivores and omnivores. Archerfish (*Toxotes chatareus*) have a unique method of capturing terrestrial prey animals. A range of trophic categories is represented amongst the fish communities of lowland waterbodies. There are no strongly herbivorous species present. Fish in the ARR exhibit a number of breeding strategies. A high proportion of the species in the Region exhibit some form of parental care, e.g. live bearing, buccal incubation, guarding of nests.

Bishop & Forbes (1991) showed that diversities (species richness) of freshwater fish communities in Australia's northern tropical coastlands, relative to drainage basin areas, were higher than in temperate Australian counterparts. Extending the analysis (diversities versus drainage basin areas), they also noted that diversities in the northern tropical coastlands (including the ARR) were higher than those in overseas floodplain rivers. However, small catchments only of tropical northern Australia were included in the analysis; the suggestion that diversities in Australia's northern tropical coastlands are higher than in overseas counterparts will probably not hold when data from large catchments are scrutinised.

Fish have many advantages for use in biological monitoring programs, including those given below.

i) Sensitivity to changes in water quality, including elevated concentrations of many of the heavy metals.
ii) Their position at the top of many aquatic food webs, such that they reflect effects of pollutants on other organisms as well as direct effects on themselves.
iii) Relatively long life cycles (see comments above on macroinvertebrates).
iv) High public profile and utilisation by man (Hellawell 1986, Karr et al. 1986, Spry & Wiener 1991).

Hellawell (1986) listed a number of disadvantages in the use of fish for monitoring, including their mobility, sampling demands and costs and difficulties in sampling in deep, swift-flowing rivers. All but the first of these factors may be countered for freshwater fishes of the ARR: the high clarity of many of the surface waters of the Region and the relative ease of identification of the fauna mean that much of the data can be collected by direct observation, relatively easily, quickly and at low cost (Humphrey et al. 1990). Lake (1986) listed other disadvantages in the use of fish communities in Australia for monitoring, including the modification of communities by presence of introduced species and low species richness for streams over much of the continent. In the ARR, however, there are no introduced fish species; moreover, the fish fauna is conspicuous, diverse and abundant, and species richness is high by Australian standards at least (Humphrey et al. 1990).

Frogs

The composition and ecology of the frog fauna of the ARR has been extensively studied (Tyler & Cappo 1983, Tyler et al. 1983, Braithwaite 1985, Tyler & Crook 1987, Woinarski et al. 1989). Twenty five species within eight genera are known from the ARR. Of this number, four species are characteristic of escarpment habitats: *Litoria coplandi, L. personata, L. meiriana* and *Megistolotis lignarius*. The majority of frog species occur in wet, low-lying forest margins between open forest and seasonally-flooded wetlands during the wet season (Haynes et al. 1991).

The fully-aquatic larval stages of amphibians are sensitive to the presence of a variety of pollutants, including metals (Freda 1991). Further, the semi-permeable nature of the skin of amphibians places all life-stages at risk from uptake of contaminants present in the ambient environment (Tyler & Crook 1987). Nevertheless, amphibians have received little attention concerning their possible role for biological monitoring of freshwater pollution. This is despite increasing concern and attention in the past decade in particular, to the toxicological and ecological effects on amphibians of a variety of water-borne contaminants (Freda 1991). Presumably the semi-aquatic nature of the life cycle of frogs explains, to some extent, why the group has not been considered for assessment of water quality in standard references on the subject; the fully aquatic (larval) phase of the life cycle is more often highly seasonal and transient, and opportunistic in so far as the selection of breeding sites by adults is concerned.

Freda (1991) listed a number of problems in the interpretation of data derived from 'biological surveys' used to determine the distribution and abundance of amphibians. These included the mobility of adults, high inter-annual variability of breeding adults, spawn and recruitment and the wide range of physicochemical and habitat structural variables that control distribution. Other than the problem of mobility, however, the remaining factors would appear to be no less a problem for most other groups of organisms used for monitoring.

Of the 24 species of frog known to occur in the Magela Creek system, only one, the floodplain frog *Litoria dahlii,* is fully aquatic during the wet season. Moreover, breeding of most species occurs in the early wet season in temporary pools and other habitats away from the main watercourses (TYLER & CROOK 1987). Thus eggs are laid in sites that would probably not receive mine waste-waters or otherwise be directly affected by mining activity. While community study therefore is not warranted, autecological and metal-content data gathered on one or two species could provide suitable information for monitoring mine wastewater releases. *Litoria dahlii* is one possible candidate for monitoring. This species (and possibly others) apparently aestivates in, or in crevices within, the acid floodplain soils during the dry season – known sites of deposition of particulate material transported in the streams of the ARR, which would include mine waste substances. According to FREDA (1991), such species inhabiting acidic soils may be at risk from mobilisation of any metals present in the soils, including those deposited from anthropogenic sources.

An additional role for biological monitoring using frogs in the ARR was proposed by TYLER et al. (1981). Baseline studies by these authors documented the incidence of skeletal deformities of adults, the rationale being that these incidences might provide an index of deleterious environmental change – in particular, exposure to radiation arising from mining and milling of uranium. However, although relatively high incidences (~7%) of such deformities were reported at sites near Ranger at 'natural' (pre-mining) radiation levels, subsequent laboratory experiments could find radiation-induced effects only at exposures well above those that could arise from naturally occurring radioactive materials in the field (OSS 1983).

Aquatic and semi-aquatic reptiles and waterbirds

Aquatic and semi-aquatic reptiles are well represented in the ARR; the fauna includes two varanid lizards, an acrochordid snake, two crocodile species and six turtle species. The biology of the semi-aquatic varanids, *Varanus mertensi* and *V. mitchelli,* and the fully-aquatic acrochordid, *Acrochordus arafurae,* were described by SHINE (1986a, 1986b). Approximately 40% of the biomass of prey ingested by the semi-aquatic varanids is derived from aquatic sources. *Varanus mertensi* feeds primarily on freshwater crabs; the diet of *V. mitchelli* varies with habitat, but includes fish and terrestrial insects (SHINE 1986a). *Acrochordua arafurae* occurs in high densities in Magela floodplain billabongs (SHINE 1986b) and is harvested for food by Aboriginal people (SHINE 1986c). The sexes are dimorphic in body length and head size, and exhibit differences in diet and habitat preference (SHINE 1986d). Both sexes are piscivorous.

LEGLER (1980) provided data on the diet and habitat preferences of freshwater turtles in the ARR. The Pig-nosed turtle, *Carettochelys insculpta,* is a geographic and taxonomic relic species (GEORGES & KENNETT 1989); it is present in the upper reaches of the South Alligator River catchment. The ecology of this and other turtle species in the ARR are not well known.

Two species of crocodile occur across northern Australia – both are found in the ARR. The species tend to be allopatric in their distribution (WEBB 1991) – the estuarine crocodile, *Crocodylus porosus,* inhabits tidal rivers, floodplain creeks, billabongs and swamps; the freshwater crocodile, *C. johnstoni,* occupies the upstream reaches of waterways. Surveys of Magela Creek revealed a high density of large *C. porosus* (MESSEL et al. 1979).

The wetlands of the ARR provide the primary habitat for 68 bird species, or nearly a quarter of the species occurring in the 'Top End' of the Northern Territory (MORTON & BRENNAN 1991). Numerically dominant species include the Magpie goose (*Anseranas semipalmata*), Wandering whistle-duck (*Dendrocygna arcuata*), Intermediate egret (*Egretta intermedia*) and Glossy ibis (*Plegadis falcinellus*). Species richness is enhanced by the arrival of migratory waders from the Northern Hemisphere (such as Little curlew, *Numenius minutus*) and by nomadic waterbirds including Grey teal (*Anas gibberifrons*) from southern Australia. Many species utilise a range of wetland types according to the seasonal availability of resources (BAYLISS & YEOMANS 1990, MORTON et al. 1990). Wetland bird communities are dominated in richness by species consuming aquatic invertebrates and in biomass by herbivores (MORTON & BRENNAN 1991). The composition of the diet of species within trophic groups can differ markedly; differences may be evident between congeners (DOSTINE & MORTON 1988) and sexes of the same species (DOSTINE & MORTON 1989). Herbivorous species depend on relatively few plant species for food. For example, the bulbs of spike-rush (*Eleocharis dulcis*) are important dry season food items for Magpie geese, while the seeds of Wild rice (*Oryza meridionalis*), which are produced in the mid- to late wet season but may persist over the dry season, are utilised by a range of granivorous species (e.g. Little corella *Cacatua sanguinea*).

In general, air-breathing animals linked to aquatic food chains are at no risk from water-borne metal contaminants, including increases in metals arising in the diet (Luoma 1983, Scheuhammer 1991). The exceptions here are certain organic forms of metals such as methyl mercury; these substances, as well as certain other non-metallic organic compounds (e.g. some pesticides), can biomagnify through food chains to levels of high toxicity. For non-alkylated metals, however, gastrointestinal absorption and retention from dietary sources is typically a very low percentage of the ingested dose (Scheuhammer 1991). The efficiency of the vertebrate gastrointestinal tract to discriminate against and excrete dietary metals contrasts to the generally poor discrimination possible at the more permeable, respiratory membranes (V. M. Brown, pers. comm.). Hence, gill-breathing, aquatic organisms are at most risk from water-borne contaminants.

The inorganic compounds that make up the bulk of the waste substances in mine waters of the ARR are not those that pose a risk to air-breathing vertebrate organisms. Thus, food-chain transfer of these substances (either bioaccumulation or biomagnification) is unlikely in these animals. A possible (but remote) concern for such vertebrate organisms in the ARR might arise indirectly in the possible mine-related extinction of aquatic organisms from their diet. Scheuhammer (1991) for example, thought that a drastic decrease in the availability of dietary calcium, due to the loss of such aquatic invertebrate taxa as molluscs and crustaceans, could lead to adverse effects on egg laying and eggshell integrity in waterbirds. However, with proper waste-water management at mine sites, such events would be unlikely, and in a comprehensive and sensitive monitoring program there would be warning of such impacts well in advance of any manifestation in higher organisms. In any event, the study of waterbirds at least, is fraught with problems of interpretation given that these animals can readily move amongst wetlands.

The above discussion does not mean to imply that air-breathing animals linked to aquatic food chains are not susceptible to metal poisoning. In some wetlands of the Northern Territory's 'Top End' for example, there is a considerable hazard to waterbirds arising from ingestion of lead pellets. Indeed considerable amounts of lead shot accumulate in the sediment of many wetlands both in Australia and worldwide as the result of hunting activities. Many waterfowl species, including Magpie geese (*Anseranas semipalmata*), actively turn over the soil/sediment to obtain plant material for food. Lead shot may be ingested either deliberately or incidentally (this is unclear) with this food and associated sediment. Where natural grit is limited, active retention and grinding of lead shot in the gizzard as a grit supplement (where it aids breakdown and digestion of food) increases the chances of poisoning (Harper & Hindmarsh 1990). Despite the generally low gastrointestinal absorption of metals, including lead, in birds and mammals (Scheuhammer 1991), it is clear that very high source concentrations associated with the diet of waterbirds will result – at some level of intake – in lead poisoning (Koh & Harper 1988, Harper & Hindmarsh 1990). In the Northern Territory, lead poisoning of *A. semipalmata* has been documented for some wetlands in the Darwin district (Whitehead & Tschirner 1991).

Choice of organisms for monitoring

Biological monitoring can be expensive in time and resources; for this reason it is never possible to include all groups of organisms in monitoring programs. Rather, it is important to select those organisms most useful for the particular problem in question (Hellawell 1986). In practice, the foremost consideration here is identifying, in advance, possible hazards arising from new projects and selecting groups potentially at risk from these hazards. A thorough literature search should suffice in addressing this step. In the ARR for example, the above discussion of the various groups of biota confirms the assumption made early by the OSS, that fully aquatic organisms (or life stages of organisms) are those most at risk from the release of mine waste-waters to the environment.

Other important attributes in the selection of monitoring organisms, including sound taxonomic base, adequate autecological information where necessary and low variability in community dynamics, may be provided in, or assessed from, baseline study. Specific problems may require additional and particular attributes of the monitoring organisms. Long-lived organisms for example,

PROGRAMS	CONCERN AND RATIONALE FOR STUDY		METHOD EMPLOYED
DETECTION OF SHORT-TERM EFFECTS (occurring within the Wet season) exposure to substances in water column	• **Arising during release** (provides early warning of unexpected effects, enabling prompt adjustment or termination of release when necessary)	**Early detection**	**FIELD TOXICITY TESTS**
	• **Arising during or shortly after release** (provides verification of the adequacy of the measures adopted in the control of water release)		
	• **Arising during the Wet season of concern** (consequential or delayed effects)	**Delayed detection** (at end of Wet season)	**STUDIES OF NATURAL POPULATIONS AND COMMUNITIES; STUDIES OF BIOACCUMULATION IN LONGER-LIVED ORGANISMS**
DETECTION OF LONGER-TERM EFFECTS	• **Arising from consequential or delayed effects** (exposure to short-term increases of substances in water column)		
	• **Arising from cumulative effects** (exposure to substances deposited in sediments)		

Fig. 2. Structure or programs for biological monitoring in the ARR.

are desirable in bioaccumulation studies, while organisms readily visible to the unaided eye assist in timely detection of responses in field toxicity tests (Humphrey et al. 1990).

The requirements and attributes described above were considered in the selection of organisms for monitoring of aquatic ecosystems of the ARR. Because of their diversity and abundance in streams of the Region, and inherent and traditional virtues of the groups, benthic macroinvertebrate and fish communities (or representative populations or assemblages within these communities) were regarded by Humphrey et al. (1990) as the most practical and useful choices for monitoring. Macroinvertebrates reflect conditions at the site of sampling, whereas fish, being mobile, more readily reflect overall water quality throughout the extent of the stream in which they move.

Programs for biological monitoring in the ARR

A comprehensive and sensitive biological monitoring program should be able to provide 'early-warning' of short-term (acute) effects of waste-water releases and detection of longer-term effects (delayed in expression or chronic) of mining generally. With these and other geographical factors considered, the latter reflecting the dispersive characteristics of released waste-waters, a variety of methods is being developed for monitoring in the ARR. The development of monitoring programs is most advanced in Magela Creek; elements of these programs, however, would be readily adapted to other catchments of the Region.

A schematic representation of the comprehensive approach taken to monitor aquatic ecosystems of the ARR is shown in Fig. 2. The outline shown in this figure is a generalised and modified summary of a more detailed schema presented in Humphrey et al. (1990). There are two major groups of studies, one designed to detect short-term effects (i.e. effects occurring within, and detected prior to the end of, the wet season), the other focusing on longer-term effects. Detection of short-term effects may be early (i.e. during or shortly after release) or delayed. Studies addressing short-term, delayed effects also contribute data that will be useful for detecting longer-term effects.

Early detection of short-term effects

The biological 'early detection systems' used in this type of monitoring provide early warning of any unexpected, harmful responses occurring during releases. Thus if necessary, releases can be quickly adjusted or terminated, so reducing the risk of any adverse effects occurring in the receiving waters. 'Creekside' and in situ monitoring methods that examine the 'whole-body' responses of captive organisms have been developed to provide such prompt detection. These responses combine possible acute and chronic, and lethal and sub-lethal effects of sensitive organisms and/or life stages. As such, the monitoring techniques provide, apart from early warning of unexpected effects, verification of the adequacy of release standards based on laboratory toxicity tests, employing equally sensitive end-points. Development of these methods has been confined to Magela Creek near the Ranger mine.

In creekside monitoring systems, organisms in containers located on the creek bank are exposed to a flow of appropriately diluted waste-water pumped from the creek. These systems, unlike in situ techniques, have the important advantage of providing continuous monitoring during release and have been the main focus of study to date. The goal in the refinement of the creekside monitoring program has been to parallel the approach used in the ARRRI Aquatic Toxicology program, where three standard test organisms are employed in pre-release testing of mine waters (described previously). This does not mean that both field and laboratory programs should be identical in terms of the species of organisms tested. It is more desirable to maximise the responses examined across both programs, although overlap of one test species might be regarded as optimal. In any case, organisms successfully reared and tested in the laboratory may not necessarily be appropriate organisms for field monitoring (and vice versa) (Humphrey et al. 1990).

For creekside monitoring, a number of essential or desirable attributes should govern the selection of test organisms, as indicated below.

i) A sensitivity to mine waste-waters comparable to organisms and/or life stages employed in the laboratory toxicity testing program (essential requirement).
ii) Low (natural) mortality when exposed to creek waters (essential) (see Humphrey et al. 1990).
iii) At least one of the test organisms must provide early feed-back of adverse effects (essential). The response (e.g. mortality) should be readily detected and identified, or should be a rapid precursor of longer-term detrimental effects;
iv) Responses must be varied and include sub-lethal, chronic end-points as well as acute effects.
v) Organisms from different phyla and/or trophic levels should be represented.
vi) The test organisms must be cultured readily.
vii) The biology of the test organisms should be well understood.

So far, viable creekside tests have been developed for two species of freshwater snails, *Amerianna cumingii* and *A. carinata* (reproduction, early development and juvenile mortality), and two species of fish, *Mogurnda mogurnda* and *Melanotaenia nigrans* (larval mortality and growth). These tests combine to a large extent, all of the seven attributes listed above except for the important items (i) and (iii); i.e. sensitivity and ability to provide early warning of unexpected adverse effects. Larval fishes are not always sensitive to Ranger mine waters, while the snail tests, being of the subchronic type, are lengthy (c. 15 days).

Other rapid response tests are presently under development at ARRRI. None, however, has yet been applied to creekside monitoring. One such promising 'whole-body' response used in the Aquatic Toxicology program, namely tentacle retraction and mortality of *Hydra,* has the advantage that the method is specific to enhanced concentrations of uranium (Hyne et al. 1993) and therefore effects can be attributed directly to waste-water discharge from Ranger. Biochemical and histopathological techniques are also under development at ARRRI. These rapid-screening methods are regarded as particularly sensitive indicators of early pathological changes which, under conditions of extended exposure, can be correlated with longer-term detrimental effects at the 'whole-body' level (e.g. survival, growth or reproduction).

The responses of a number of test organisms have so far (from 1985) been successfully used for the early detection of short-term effects arising from Ranger mine waste-water releases. These include creekside tests using freshwater snails (*Amerianna cumingii,* juvenile mortality) and larval fish

(*Mogurnda mogurnda,* larval mortality), and in situ study of freshwater mussels (*Velesunio angasi,* reproduction) (Humphrey et al. 1990, ARRRI 1991). Adverse effects detected were of short duration and localised, being confined to a 'mixing zone'. Measurement of reproductive responses of freshwater mussels (*V. angasi*) held in mesh-covered containers buried along the creek edges (Humphrey et al. 1990) has been the most successful in situ technique used to date.

Delayed detection of short-term effects and detection of longer-term effects

These effects are either delayed in expression or chronic. Breeding failures or effects on recruits may only be evident at later dates by poor year-class abundances. Other effects, such as bioaccumulation, may be gradual over time. Using the schema of Humphrey et al. (1990), effects occurring during the wet season of concern (i.e. short-term effects) may be detected by the end of the particular wet season (delayed); otherwise, these or other delayed or cumulative effects might only be detected at later dates (i.e. longer-term effects). Studies at ARRRI are of two main types: investigation of natural communities and populations, and chemical monitoring of biota (bioaccumulation).

Natural communities and populations

Evidence of any detrimental mining-related effects upon natural populations and communities will rely mainly on statistical comparisons of post-release (or post-mining) biological data and those of historical baselines. Studies have been continuing for a number of years now in order to describe and account fully for fluctuations and temporal trends.

The main strategy adopted in these studies is to make observations at the end of the wet season. Monitoring at this time offers information about the summation of organismic responses (to waste-water releases for example) and also provides information which can serve as an integrated index of wet-season breeding success of many aquatic organisms; i.e. it indicates overall seasonal effects. Additional advantages of monitoring at the end of the wet season are listed in Humphrey et al. (1990, Table V).

Investigation of benthic macroinvertebrate communities and populations have been ongoing since 1987 in both Magela Creek and the upper South Alligator River. Brief descriptions of the studies are contained in Humphrey et al. (1990). Considerations and requirements for community-based monitoring using benthic macroinvertebrates are discussed below. Apart from community studies, biological attributes of freshwater mussels (*Velesunio angasi*) in Magela Creek (Humphrey & Simpson 1985), will also have considerable potential for monitoring and assessment of both short-term and longer-term mining impact.

Daily counts of fish migrating upstream in Magela Creek past Ranger have been made for seven consecutive wet seasons to date. Such movement to upstream, dry season refuges follows wet-season spawning and feeding in downstream billabong and floodplain habitats. This migration is an essential survival strategy and released waste-waters should not impair recruitment and subsequent movement of fish. The total counts made by the end of each wet season represent some index of recruitment success of fish during the wet season in breeding habitats downstream of Ranger. Interannual patterns in these counts in relation to hydrological variables are being investigated currently.

Fish communities have been surveyed in billabongs of Magela Creek (Gulungul and Mudginberri) and in pools of the upper South Alligator River since 1988. The high clarity of most of these surface waters at the wet-dry season transition, has enabled non-destructive visual methods to be used for sampling. The main technique used is the direct counts of fish from a glass-fronted canoe. Data from extensive baseline studies collected between 1978 and 1986 on eight of the 'backflow' billabongs of Magela Creek near Ranger are not now considered valuable for monitoring purposes because of non-mining related, environmental changes to the billabongs. These changes, involving increases in macrophyte growth in the billabongs, resulted from removal of Asian water buffalo from the Magela Creek catchment (and elsewhere in the Northern Territory) and are described in Humphrey et al. (1990). Data collection in Magela Creek is continuing.

Chemical monitoring of biota

The surface waters of the floodplains of streams in the Region lie in a zone of major deposition of water-borne materials (Johnston et al. 1988) and, as such, could well constitute sites of enrichment of metals discharged from mining operations over prolonged periods of time. These substances may become available to the biota through subsequent remobilisation (chemical or biological) and any resulting bioaccumulation therefore, presents the largest potential 'far-field' hazard to organisms of aquatic ecosystems.

Baseline ('equilibrium') concentrations of chemical elements in body organs of fish and soft-parts of freshwater mussels from these (and other) sites are being or have been determined so that future concentrations might be compared. Should increases have occurred, potential risks can then be assessed by appropriate laboratory experiments. Long-lived fish, being at the top of the truly aquatic food web can reflect long-term accumulation via food and ambient water. Freshwater mussels, being similarly long-lived, can also reflect long-term water quality but also short-term increases of substances in the ambient water and, unlike fish, information is generally specific to the particular part of the stream in which they occur. Studies completed in Magela Creek are cited in Humphrey et al. (1990).

OBJECTIVE:

To develop the capability to detect and assess the significance of change in macroinvertebrate community structure due to mining.

SOME CONSIDERATIONS AND REQUIREMENTS OF THE STUDY IN MEETING THE OBJECTIVE:

- application of rigorous statistical design; and
- sensitivity to (= power to detect) an impact
  - taxonomic resolution
  - best community 'summary' (e.g. functional descriptors, total abundance vs presence/absence) and dissimilarity measure
  - adequate replication (at various levels)
  - accepting a larger probability of Type I error

Fig. 3. Objectives, considerations and requirements for community-based monitoring in the ARR using benthic macroinvertebrates.

Considerations and requirements for community-based monitoring using benthic macroinvertebrates

The objective of any community-based monitoring program in the ARR is to develop techniques capable of detecting and assessing the significance of short-term and longer-term change in community structure due to mining. Implicit in this objective is the need for rigorous experimental designs, combined with the development of techniques for statistical analysis that have high power or high probability of detecting an effect (Fig. 3). While these should be goals of all experiments or field monitoring data-sets (Peterman 1990), they are crucial ones in sensitive environments such as the ARR where the cost of failing to detect impacts (i.e. occurrence of a Type II error) is potentially high. The requirements of the study design that will improve the power (sensitivity) of monitoring techniques, and so minimise the amount of community change that remains undetected, are listed in Fig. 3 and include: an adequate taxonomic base for the monitoring group in question; information on the best (most powerful) community descriptors; provision of sufficient, statistically independent replicates; and, accepting a more liberal level of α (the probability of committing a Type I error). These considerations and requirements for community-based monitoring in the ARR are discussed below.

The issues raised in the following sections are described in a manner that is specific to benthic macroinvertebrates. They are nevertheless relevant to any other group of monitoring organisms, including fish, of the ARR.

Taxonomy

The emphasis in the protection of aquatic ecosystems of the ARR has been in the development of a capacity to detect subtle rather than gross mining-related changes in communities of aquatic organisms. This is a necessary goal in highly-valued environments such as the ARR, where high standards of environmental protection are required. Apart from employing an analytical design that minimises the amount of community change that remains undetected (see sections below), biological monitoring techniques using macroinvertebrate communities will be more sensitive to such changes when detailed taxonomic 'penetration' of samples to the level of species is possible. Such taxonomic discrimination is also critical to any assessment of the conservation status of the biota in a particular environment – an issue raised during the recent debate over future mining in the ARR (Resource Assessment Commission 1991).

In particular cases, species level identifications may not always be essential for water quality assessment and monitoring (references cited in Ferraro & Cole 1990). Some pollution gradients in marine benthos, for example, were maintained by higher taxa with little loss of information (Warwick 1988a, 1988b). Grouping of the dipteran family Chironomidae as a single taxon had little effect on the discrimination between sites in a Welsh river (Morris & Brooker 1979). But where, as in the ARR, emphasis is on the detection of subtle effects, such aggregation may not be appropriate (Kingston & Riddle 1989). Congeners may have different tolerances to pollutants (Resh & Unzicker 1975), a result, it has been suggested, of the particular mode of speciation (Cranston 1990). The consequences of disturbance on stream benthic communities in the ARR are not predictable at this stage, nor are the pollution tolerances of any species known in detail. Hence there is no a priori basis for either selecting indicator species or ignoring redundant elements (sensu Gray et al. 1988 quoted in Warwick 1988a). Moreover, detailed life-histories of particular populations may be required to interpret and assess environmental impacts properly; this information is dependent also upon species-level identifications (Rosenberg et al. 1986). A final caveat on the need for species-level determinations was illustrated by the findings of Faith & Norris (1989): the inclusion of rare freshwater macroinvertebrate taxa in their ordination analyses revealed additional significant correlations between the ordination space and physicochemical variables.

The ARRRI has initiated a number of research consultancies on the taxonomy of aquatic macroinvertebrate fauna of the Region. These projects have provided both identification keys accompanied by illustrations of distinctive and diagnostic featurs and sets of voucher specimens for reference by ARRRI biologists. Most of the aquatic immature stages of species belonging to the dominant macroinvertebrate orders (i.e. Ephemeroptera, Trichoptera, Odonata and chironomid Diptera) have been associated with the adult stage and can be identified. The constituents of several minor taxa remain unknown and cannot be named.

Statistical design and analysis

Much of the following discussion summarises and reviews recent work conducted in the ARR by Faith et al. (1990, 1991). Statistical design is a crucial consideration for any effective biological monitoring procedure used to assess potential mining impacts on freshwater ecosystems of the ARR, because practical tests to detect possible mining-related changes will be required. Development of such tests is limited not only by natural variability but by basic requirements of proper control and independent replication – requirements which are particularly difficult to establish in lotic systems. The typical form of experimental design used in a stream, i.e. comparing samples taken from upstream control sites and sites downstream of a point of disturbance, both before and after an impact (e.g. Green 1979), has been criticised because replicates are not statistically independent (Hurlbert 1984). The treatment effect cannot be interspersed or randomly assigned to upstream (control) and downstream (disturbed) sampling sites, and as a result of segregated sites ('treatments'), replicates at a site may be linked (through hydrology, biological processes) or may share properties not found at the other site. Moreover, any natural differences occurring between upstream and downstream sites will not necessarily remain constant over time. Without statistical independence, the treatment effect cannot be implicated statistically; i.e. it is possible to test for differences between locations, but not for significant effects of the impact (Hurlbert 1984).

While there are situations and methods for which statistical analysis can be informative even when treatments cannot be replicated and properly randomised (Carpenter 1990 and ensuing articles of the same volume), such replicated and randomised designs should nevertheless be used whenever possible. An alternative, so-called 'BACI' design has been proposed as a way of overcoming the 'pseudoreplication' problem discussed above (Stewart-Oaten et al. 1986). This strategy utilises a form of temporal replication. A control and impact site are sampled simultaneously at a number of times, both before and after the disturbance. Each time of sampling is characterised by some measure of the difference between the control and impact sites, rather than by the data for the individual samples at the two sites. The BACI design provides a basis for a statistical test for impact by comparing, with a *t*-test or the equivalent, the set of differences before and after the disturbance. Note that because measurements are based on differences – and providing there are sufficient temporal replicates – the natural differences between the sites are dampened and are less critical; hence statistical independence of the temporal replicates is more likely to be demonstrated. Nevertheless, such independence needs to be verified.

While STEWART-OATEN et al. (1986) provided an example of an application of the BACI design to population data, there is no information available on the application of the design beyond the univariate level to community or multivariate data. The potential of the BACI design for community-level monitoring in the ARR is currently being investigated at two stages. The first stage is experimental while the second is the possible implementation of the design to the larger streams of the Region (where practical monitoring programs are required), using some of the experimental findings.

In the first, experimental approach, the BACI design is being applied in the vicinity of an existing disturbance due to previous mining at Rockhole Mine Creek (RMC), in the southern portion of the ARR (Fig. 1); the creek is polluted for much of its length from acid mine drainage from an old uranium mine adit. The experiment consists of a simple BACI exercise carried out in two consecutive (early dry) seasons. Weekly benthic macroinvertebrate samples are collected in both years from two sites upstream of the point-source of disturbance. The first year (1991, already completed) acts as the baseline, pre-disturbance period, while in the second year (1992), polluted adit water will be diverted and introduced between the two upstream sites. Differences between the sites in community structure can then be compared between the baseline and disturbance years. The experiment aims to provide information on the application of the BACI design to community or multivariate data, and ultimately on the implementation of the approach in the larger streams of the ARR.

In application of the BACI design to community-level data, the choice of the measure of difference between the sites at each time of sampling is important. Multivariate dissimilarities appear to be the best option here; these measures reduce the differences between the two communities over many different species to a single value. A pair of samples with similar species composition and abundances, for example, will have a relatively low dissimilarity value. An important research issue has concerned the choice of the dissimilarity measure with most statistical power (i.e. one most sensitive to any impact arising from the disturbance), and therefore the measure that has the most potential for use in the BACI design. FAITH et al. (1991) found from baseline work in RMC in which upstream and 'currently-disturbed' sites were sampled, that the alternative dissimilarity measures varied by an order of magnitude in their statistical power, with the Bray-Curtis measure providing consistently high power.

Other than the choice of the best community dissimilarity measure, the RMC studies will also provide important data for evaluating alternative community 'summaries', e.g. differences based on abundance vs presence/absence, different taxonomic levels and functional descriptors. The effect of different data standardisations and transformations on the community dissimilarity measures and summaries can be investigated also.

Apart from choices of the most powerful and robust community dissimilarity and community summary measures, improvements to the sensitivity of the BACI design will depend on adequate replication at a number of levels. Data from replicate samples taken from within a site on a particular sampling occasion will contribute to the calculation of a single dissimilarity measure. These measures take account of the abundance of different taxa and so require relative abundance information for their calculation. Such information is provided by 'semi-quantitative' sampling (sensu HELLAWELL 1986); most sampling methods will yield some information on the relative abundance of the taxa recovered (ABEL 1989).

UNDERWOOD (1989, 1991) criticised the BACI design in which only single control and disturbed sites were compared, arguing that there was no valid reason to suppose that any pattern of difference between two populations evident before the disturbance would continue unchanged over time if the disturbance had no effect. The only solution here, according to UNDERWOOD, is to incorporate several replicate control and disturbed sites, or at worst, to have several control sites even if there is only one disturbed site. In streams of the ARR, two or more control sites and several disturbed sites are incorporated in monitoring designs, leaving some options open for assessing the similarity of community information between or amongst particular sites, selecting 'suitable' sites and combining (averaging in some way) the information from these sites.

The most critical form of replication to be considered in the implementation of BACI designs for biological monitoring is temporal replication because, to be valid, a long time-series of data is required at least prior to the impact. FAITH et al. (1990) argued that in sensitive environments such as in the ARR, monitoring programs should be designed to establish with some high level of probability that there is no detectable impact on the ecosystem – as opposed to simply allowing development (such as mining) to continue as long as 'proof' of impact is missing (i.e. 'shifting the burden of proof', PETERMAN 1990). This would require application of statistical tests with adequate power to guarantee that an impact no greater than a prescribed amount would go undetected. A minimum number of baseline years, prior to disturbance, would therefore be required using a BACI design in order to achieve some desired level of statistical power.

Information that would allow policy-makers to address the trade-off between the number of baseline years required and the level of disturbance that could ultimately be detected is provided in power curves. Such curves are shown in Fig. 4 (hypothetical example) and are derived from information on the natural variability of community structure in the baseline period. While no such information is yet available for aquatic ecosystems of the ARR upon which to construct such curves, this work is continuing. Another area of research being actively pursued in this regard, is the frequency at which temporal replicates might be incorporated in the BACI design. Sampling at intervals more frequently than on an annual basis for example, would reduce the duration of the baseline period and this would make the BACI design a viable and practical one for many applications in biological monitoring. A constraining factor with this approach, however, may be in ensuring that samples are not taken at regular, as opposed to randomly chosen, intervals. Thus, STEWART-OATEN et al. (1986) and UNDERWOOD (1991) warned that temporal variance would not be accurately estimated and that the magnitude of a disturbance could be under- or overestimated when samples were taken from some fixed, regular schedule.

Higher power can be obtained in statistical tests by adopting more liberal levels of α; i.e. accepting a larger probability of Type I error. This procedure has been recommended in situations where the costs of committing a Type II error are much greater than the cost of Type I error (HAYES 1987, PETERMAN 1990). In particular, increasing α to 0.1 or some other value rather than the traditional setting of $\alpha = 0.05$ can enable small and subtle, but often biologically significant, effects to be detected.

In the ARRRI Aquatic Toxicology program, higher protection from statistical Type II error is

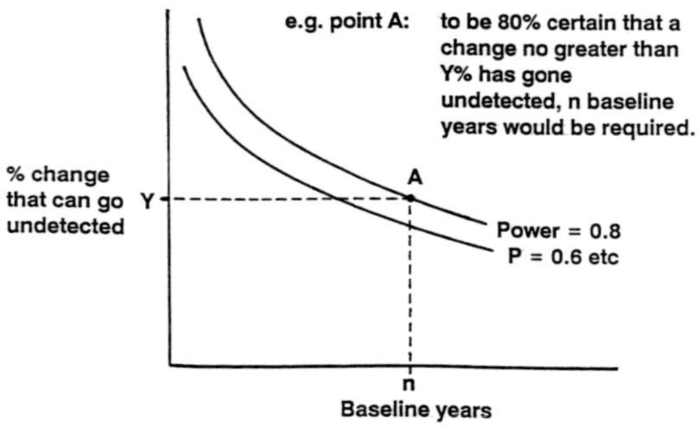

Fig. 4. Isopleths of power, or probability of detecting a statistically-significant change in community response to disturbance, in relation to number of baseline years of data available. High power (close to 1) corresponds to a low risk of the impact going undetected (i.e. a Type II error), and low power (close to 0) corresponds to a high risk.

afforded by assessing the statistical significance of results at the 0.1 (instead of the usual 0.05) probability level (HOLDWAY 1988). It is logical to extend this practice to statistical tests employed in all ARRRI Biological Monitoring programs, from these programs designed to detect short-term effects to those designed to detect longer-term effects (including effects upon benthic macroinvertebrate communities).

Acknowledgements

We are grateful for the assistance of all permanent, temporary and voluntary staff of the ARRRI Biological Monitoring Section. We thank in particular, A. JOHNSTON, R. PIDGEON and R. FRY for critical comments on the manuscript. JACQUI HARBORT completed the typing in a timely and cheerful manner.

References

ABEL, P. D., 1989: *Water Pollution Biology:* 231 pp. – Ellis Horwood Limited, Chichester, England.

ARRRI, 1988: Alligator Rivers Region Research Institute Annual Research Summary 1987–1988. Supervising Scientist for the Alligator Rivers Region: 160 pp. – AGPS, Canberra.

– 1991: Alligator Rivers Region Research Institute Annual Research Summary 1988–1989. Supervising Scientist for the Alligator Rivers Region: 156 pp. – AGPS, Canberra.

BAYLISS, P. & YEOMANS, K. M., 1990: Seasonal distribution and abundance of magpie geese, *Anseranas semipalmata* LATHAM, in the Northern Territory, and their relationship to habitat, 1983–1986. – *Aust. Wildl. Res.* **17:**15–38.

BISHOP, K. A., ALLEN, S. A., POLLARD, D. A. & COOK, M. G., 1986: Ecological studies on the freshwater fishes of the Alligator Rivers Region, Northern Territory. Vol. I. Outline of the study, summary, conclusions and recommendations. Research Report 4(1), Supervising Scientist for the Alligator Rivers Region: 55 pp. – AGPS, Canberra.

– – – – 1990: Ecological studies on the freshwater fishes of the Alligator Rivers Region, Northern Territory. Vol. II. Synecology. Research Report 4(2), Supervising Scientist for the Alligator Rivers Region: 142 pp. – AGPS, Canberra.

– – – – in press: Ecological studies on the freshwater fishes of the Alligator Rivers Region, Northern Territory. Vol. III. Autecology. Research Report 4(3), Supervising Scientist for the Alligator Rivers Region. – AGPS, Canberra.

BISHOP, K. A. & FORBES, M. A., 1991: The freshwater fishes of northern Australia. – In: HAYNES, C. D., RIDPATH, M. G. & WILLIAMS, M. A. J., (eds.): Monsoonal Australia: Landscape, Ecology and Man in the Northern Lowlands: 79–107. – A. A. Balkema, Rotterdam, Brookfield.

BRAITHWAITE, R. W., 1985: The Kakadu Fauna Survey: an Ecological Survey of Kakadu National Park: 391 pp. – Report to Australian National Parks and Wildlife Service from CSIRO Wildlife and Ecology, Darwin.

BRAITHWAITE, R. W. & WERNER, P. A. (1987): The biological value of Kakadu National Park. – *Search* **18:**296–301.

BROWN, V. M., 1986: Development of water quality criteria from ecotoxicological data. – In: HART, B. T. (ed.): Water Quality Management: Freshwater Ecotoxicology in Australia: 107–117. – Water Studies Centre, Chisholm Institute of Technology, Melbourne.

CARPENTER, S. R., 1990: Large-scale perturbations: opportunities for innovation. – *Ecology* **71:** 2038–2043.

CRANSTON, P. S., 1990: Biomonitoring and invertebrate taxonomy. – *Environmental Monitoring and Assessment* **14:**265–273.

– 1991: Immature Chironomidae of the Alligator Rivers Region: 263 pp. – Open File Record 82, Supervising Scientist for the Alligator Rivers Region.

CROWDER, A., 1991: Acidification, metals and macrophytes. – *Environ. Poll.* **71:**329–375.

DOSTINE, P. L. & MORTON, S. R., 1988: Notes on the food and feeding habits of cormorants on a tropical floodplain. – *Emu* **88:**263–266.

– – 1989: Feeding ecology of the whiskered tern, *Chilodonias hybrida* in the Alligator Rivers Region, Northern Territory. – *Aust. Wildl. Res.* **16:** 549–562.

FAITH, D. P., HUMPHREY, C. L. & DOSTINE, P. L., 1990: Requirements for effective biological monitoring of aquatic ecosystems in the area of the Kakadu Conservation Zone: Submission to the Resource Assessment Commission Kakadu Inquiry No. KA90/047: 9 pp. – AGPS, Canberra.

– – – 1991: Statistical power and BACI designs in biological monitoring: comparative evaluation of measures of community dissimilarity based on benthic macroinvertebrate communities in Rockhole Mine Creek, Northern Territory, Australia. – *Aus. J. Mar. Freshw. Res.* **42:**589–602.

FAITH, D. P. & NORRIS, R. H., 1989: Correlation of environmental variables with patterns of distribution and abundance of common and rare freshwater macroinvertebrates. – *Biol. Conservation* **50:** 77–98.

FERRARO, S. P. & COLE, F. A., 1990: Taxonomic level and sample size sufficient for assessing pollution impacts on the Southern California Bight macrobenthos. – *Mar. Ecol. Prog. Ser.* **67:**251–262.

FINLAYSON, C. M., 1988: Productivity and nutrient dynamics of seasonally inundated floodplains in the Northern Territory. – In: WADE-MARSHALL, D. & LOVEDAY, P. (eds.): North Australia: Progress and Prospects. *Vol.* **2.** Floodplain Research: 58–83. – ANU Press, Darwin, Australia.

FINLAYSON, C. M., BAILEY, B. J. & COWIE, I. D., 1989: Macrophyte vegetation of the Magela Creek floodplain Alligator Rivers Region, Northern Territory. Research Report 5, Supervising Scientist for the Alligator Rivers Region: 38 pp. – AGPS, Canberra.

FINLAYSON, C. M., COWIE, I. D. & BAILEY, B. J., 1990: Characteristics of a seasonally flooded freshwater system in monsoonal Australia. – In: WHIGHAM, D. F., GOOD, R. E. & KVĚT, J. (eds.): Wetland Ecology and Management: Case Studies: 141–162. – Kluwer Academic Publishers, Dordrecht.

FINLAYSON, C. M., FREELAND, W. J., BAILEY, B. & FLEMING, R., 1988: Wetlands of the Northern Territory. – In: MCCOMB, A. J. & LAKE, P. S. (eds.): The Australian Wetlands: 103–126. – Chipping North, Surrey-Beatty & Sons Pty Limited, Australia.

FREDA, J., 1991: The effects of aluminium and other metals on amphibians. – *Environ. Poll.* **71:**305–328.

GEORGES, A. & KENNETT, R., 1989: Dry-season distribution and ecology of *Carettochelys insculpta* (Chelonia: Carettochelydidae) in Kakadu National Park, Northern Australia. – *Aust. Wildl. Res.* **16:**323–335.

GRAY, J. S., ASCHAN, M., CARR, M. R., CLARKE, K. R., GREEN, R. H., PEARSON, T. H., ROSENBERG, R. & WARWICK, R. M., 1989: Analysis of community attributes of the benthic macrofauna of Frierfjord/Langesundfjord and in a mesocosm experiment. – *Mar. Ecol. Prog. Ser.* **46:**151–165.

GREEN, R. H., 1979: Sampling Design and Statistical Methods for Environmental Biologists: 257 pp. – Wiley, New York.

HARPER, M. J. & HINDMARSH, M., 1990: Lead poisoning in magpie geese *Anseranas semipalmata* from ingested lead pellet at Bool Lagoon Game Reserve (South Australia). – *Aust. Wildl. Res.* **17:**141–145.

HAYES, J. P., 1987: The positive approach to negative results in toxicology studies. – *Ecotoxicology and Environmental Safety* **14:**73–77.

HAYNES, C. D., RIDPATH, M. G. & WILLIAMS, M. A. J., 1991: Part 3: The vertebrate animals. Introduction. – In: HAYNES, C. D., RIDPATH, M. G. & WILLIAMS, M. A. J. (eds.): Monsoonal Australia: Landscape, Ecology and Man in the Northern Lowlands: 75–77. – A. A. Balkema, Rotterdam, Brookfield.

HELLAWELL, J. M., 1986: Biological Indicators of Freshwater Pollution and Environmental Management: 546 pp. – Elsevier Applied Science Publishers, London and New York.

HOLDWAY, D. A., 1988: Mining and tropical freshwater environments: laboratory studies: 11 pp. – Australian and New Zealand Association for the Advancement of Science Centenary Congress/Australian Institute of Biology Symposium on Aquatic Toxicology, Sydney, 19 May.

HUMPHREY, C. L., BISHOP, K. A. BROWN, V. M., 1990: Use of biological monitoring in the assessment of effects of mining wastes on aquatic ecosystems of the Alligator Rivers Region, tropical northern Australia. – *Environmental Monitoring and Assessment* **14:**139–181.

HUMPHREY, C. L. & SIMPSON, R. D., 1985: The biology and ecology of *Velesunio angasi* (Bivalvia: Hyriidae) in Magela Creek, Northern Territory: 476 pp. – Open File Record 38, Supervising Scientist for the Alligator Rivers Region.

HURLBERT, S. H., 1984: Pseudoreplication and the design of ecological field experiments. – *Ecol. Monogr.* **54:**187–211.

HYNE, R. V., RIPPON, G. D. & ELLENDER, G., 1993: Investigation of uranium-induced toxicity in freshwater hydra. – In: DALLINGER, R. & RAINBOW, P. S. (eds.): Ecotoxicology of Metals in Invertebrates: 149–173. – Lewis Publisher, Chelsea. USA.

JOHNSTON, A., 1989: An assessment of the potential for radiation induced biological effects on aquatic animals in the Alligator Rivers Region: 16 pp. – Internal Report 15, Supervising Scientist for the Alligator Rivers Region.

– 1991: Water management in Alligator Rivers Region: A research view. – In: Proceedings of the 29th Congress of the Australian Society of Limnology. Jabiru, NT, 1990: 10–34. – AGPS, Canberra.

JOHNSTON, A., MURRAY, A. S., MARTEN, R. & MARTIN, P., 1988: The transport and deposition of radionuclides discharged into creek waters from the Ranger Uranium Mine. – In: Proceedings of Seventh International Congress of the International Radiation Protection Association: 652–655. – Pergamon Press, Sydney.

KARR, J. R., FAUSCH, K. D., ANGERMEIER, P. L., YANT, P. R. & SCHLOSSER, I. J., 1986: Assessing biological integrity in running waters: A method and its rationale. – *Illinois Natural History Survey, Special Publication* **5:**1–28.

KESSELL, J. A. & TYLER, P. A., 1983: Phytoplankton populations of the Magela Creek system, Alligator Rivers Region, Northern Territory: 21 pp. – Open File Record 18, Supervising Scientist for the Alligator Rivers Region.

KINGSTON, P. F. & RIDDLE, M. J., 1989: Cost effectiveness of benthic faunal monitoring. – *Mar. Poll. Bull.* **20:**490–496.

KOH, T.-S. & HARPER, M. J., 1988: Lead-poisoning in black swans, *Cygnus atratus,* exposed to spent lead shot at Bool Lagoon Game Reserve. South Australia. – *Aust. Wildl. Res.* **15:**395–403.

KOSTE, W., 1981: Morphology, systematics and ecology of new monogonont Rotifera from the floodplain of Magela Creek in the Alligator Rivers Region of Australia, NT. – *Osnabrücker naturw. Mitt.* **8:**97–126. (In German.)

LAKE, P. S., 1986: Stream communities and the management of streams. – In: CAMPBELL, I. C. (ed.): Stream Protection: The Management of Rivers for Instream Uses: Water Studies Centre: 3–22. – Chisholm Institute of Technology, Melbourne.

LEGLER, J. M., 1980: Taxonomy, distribution and ecology of freshwater turtles in the Alligator Rivers Region, Northern Territory: 22 pp. – Open File Record 2, Supervising Scientist for the Alligator Rivers Region.

LING, H. U. & TYLER, P. A., 1986: A limnological survey of the Alligator Rivers Region II: Freshwater algae exclusive of diatoms. Research Report 3, Supervising Scientist for the Alligator Rivers Region: 176 pp. – AGPS, Canberra.

LUOMA, S. N., 1983: Bioavailability of trace metals to aquatic organisms – a review. – *The Science of the Total Environment* **28:**1–22.

MARCHANT, R., 1982: Seasonal variation in the macroinvertebrate fauna of billabongs along Magela Creek, Northern Territory. – *Aust. J. Mar. Freshw. Res.* **33:**329–342.

MCBRIDE, T. P., 1983: Diatom Communities of the Muginberri Corridor, Northern Territory, Australia: 194 pp. – Unpublished Ph.D. thesis, Macquarie University, Sydney, Australia.

MESSEL, H., WELLS, A. G. & GREEN, W. V., 1979: Surveys of tidal river systems in the Northern Territory of Australia and their crocodile populations. Monograph 4, the Alligator Rivers Region System: 70 pp. – Pergamon Press, Sydney.

MIDGLEY, S. H., 1973: Freshwater fish inventory and associated habitat information: 30 pp. – Alligator Rivers Region Environmental Fact Finding Study. Department of the Northern Territory, Canberra.

MORTON, S. R. & BRENNAN, K. G., 1991: Birds. – In: HAYNES, C. D., RIDPATH, M. G. & WILLIAMS, M. A. J. (eds.): Monsoonal Australia: Landscape, Ecology and Man in the Northern Lowlands: 133–149. – A. A. Balkema, Rotterdam, Brookfield.

MORTON, S. R. & BRENNAN, K. G. & ARMSTRONG, M. D., 1990: Distribution and abundance of magpie geese, *Anseranas semipalmata,* in the Alligator Rivers Region, Northern Territory. – *Aust. J. Ecol.* **15:** 307–320.

MORRIS, D. L. & BROOKER, M. P., 1982: An assessment of the importance of the Chironomidae (Diptera) in biological surveillance. – In: MURRAY, D. A. (ed.): Chironomidae. Ecology, Systematics, Cytology and Physiology: 195–202. – Pergamon Press, Oxford.

NEBOISS, A., 1981: Distribution of Trichoptera families in Australia with comments on the composition of fauna in the south-west. – In: MORETTI, G. P. (ed.): Proc. 3rd. Int. Symp. on Trichoptera: 265–271. – Dr. W. Junk Publishers, The Hague.

– 1990: The family Psychomyiidae (Trichoptera) re-established in Australia. – *Memoirs of the Museum of Victoria* **51:** 83–86.

OUTRIDGE, P. M., 1987: Possible causes of high species diversity in tropical Australian freshwater macrobenthic communities. – *Hydrobiologia* **150:** 95–107.

– 1988: Seasonal and spatial variations in benthic macroinvertebrate communities of Magela Creek, Northern Territory. – *Aust. J. Mar. Freshw. Res.* **39:** 211–223.

OUTRIDGE, P. M. & NOLLER, B. N., 1991: Accumulation of toxic trace elements by freshwater vascular plants. – *Reviews of Environmental Contamination and Toxicology* **121:** 1–63.

OSS, 1983: *Office of the Supervising Scientist for the Alligator Rivers Region, Annual Report 1982–1983:* 73–74. – AGPS, Canberra.

PEARSON, R. G., 1994: Limnology of the northeastern tropics of Australia, the wettest part of the driest continent. – *Mitt. Internat. Verein. Limnol.* **24:** 155–163.

PETERMAN, R. M., 1990: Statistical power analysis can improve fisheries research management. – *Can. J. Fish. Aquat. Sci.* **47:** 2–15.

PICKERING, Q., CARLE, D. O., PILLI, A., WILLINGHAM, T. & LAZORCHAK, J. M., 1989: Effects of pollution on freshwater organisms. – *J. Wat. Poll. Cont. Fed.* **61:** 998–1042.

POLLARD, D. A., 1974: The freshwater fishes of the Alligator Rivers 'Uranium Province' area (Top End, Northern Territory) with particular reference to the Magela Creek catchment (East Alligator River System). Report. I. – In: NEWTON, P. J. F. (ed.): Alligator Rivers Area Fact Finding Study, Four AAEC Reports: 1–71 pp. – Report E305, Australian Atomic Energy Commission, AAEC, Sydney.

RESH, V. H. & UNZICKER, J. D., 1975: Water quality monitoring and aquatic organisms: the importance of species identification. – *J. Wat. Poll. Cont. Fed.* **47:** 9–18.

Resource Assessment Commission, 1991: Kakadu Conservation Zone Inquiry: Final Report Vols 1 and 2: 251 + 302 pp. – AGPS, Canberra.

ROSENBERG, D. M., DANKS, H. V. & LEHMKUHL, D. M., 1986: Importance of insects in environmental impact assessment. – *Environmental Management* **10:** 773–783.

SANDERSON, N. T., KOONTZ, D. V. & MORLEY, A. W., 1983: The ecology of the vegetation of the Magela Creek floodplain: Upper section from Oenpelli road crossing to Nankeen Billabong: 9 pp. – Unpublished report in Scientific Workshop, Environmental Protection in the Alligator Rivers Region, Jabiru, 17–20 May 1983, Australia.

SCHEUHAMMER, A. M., 1991: Effects of acidification on the availability of toxic metals and calcium to wild birds and mammals. – *Environ. Poll.* **71:** 329–375.

SHIEL, R. J. & WILLIAMS, W. D., 1990: Species richness in tropical fresh waters of Australia. – *Hydrobiologia* **202:** 175–183.

SHINE, R., 1986 a: Food habits, habitats and reproductive biology of four sympatric species of varanid lizards in tropical Australia. – *Herpetologica* **42:** 346–360.

– 1986 b: Ecology of a low-energy specialist: food habits and reproductive biology of the Arafura filesnake (Acrochordidae). – *Copeia* **1986:** 424–437.

– 1986 c: Predation upon filesnakes (*Acrochordus arafurae*) by Aboriginal hunters: selectivity with respect to body size, sex and reproductive condition. – *Copeia* **1986:** 238–239.

– 1986 d: Sexual differences in morphology and niche utilization in an aquatic snake, *Acrochordus arafurae.* – *Oecologia* **69:** 260–267.

SPRY, D. J. & WIENER, J. G., 1991: Metal bioavailability and toxicity to fish in low-alkalinity lakes: a critical review. – *Environ. Poll.* **71:** 243–304.

STEWART-OATEN, A., MURDOCH, W. & PARKER, K., 1986: Environmental impact assessment: 'Pseudoreplication' in time? – *Ecology* **67:** 929–940.

SUTER, P., 1992.: Taxonomic key to the Ephemeroptera (Mayflies) of the Alligator Rivers Region, Northern Territory: 112 pp. – Open File Record (96), Supervising Scientist for the Alligator Rivers Region.

TAIT, R. D., SHIEL, R. J. & KOSTE, W., 1984: Structure and dynamics of zooplankton communities, Alligator Rivers Region, Northern Territory, Australia. – *Hydrobiologia* **113:** 1–13.

TAYLOR, W. R., 1964: Fisheries of Arnhem Land. – In: Records of the American-Australian Scientific Expedition to Arnhem Land, Vol. **IV:** Zoology 45–307. – Melbourne University Press, Melbourne.

TYLER, M. J. & CAPPO, M., 1983: Diet and feeding habits of frogs of the Magela Creek system: 124 pp. – Open File Record 10, Supervising Scientist for the Alligator Rivers Region.

TYLER, M. J. & CROOK, G. A., 1987: Frogs of the Magela Creek system. Technical Memorandum 19, Supervising Scientist for the Alligator Rivers Region: 41 pp. – AGPS, Canberra.

TYLER, M. J., CROOK, G. A. & DAVIES, M., 1983: Reproductive biology of the frogs of the Magela Creek system, Northern Territory. – *Records of the South Australian Museum* **18:**415–440.

TYLER, M. J., WATSON, G. F., DAVIES, M. & CROOK, G. A., 1981: Frogs as environmental monitoring organisms. Program A: abnormalities in frogs: 9 pp. – Open File Record 24, Supervising Scientist for the Alligator Rivers Region.

UNDERWOOD, A. J., 1989: The analysis of stress in natural populations. – *Biol. J. Linn. Soc.* **37:**51–78.

– 1991: Beyond BACI: experimental designs for detecting human environmental impacts on temporal variations in natural populations. – *Aust. J. Mar. Freshw. Res.* **42:**569–587.

WANG, W., 1990: Literature review on duckweed toxicity testing. – *Environmental Research* **52:**7–22.

WARWICK, R. M., 1988a: Analysis of community attributes of the macrobenthos of Frierfjord/Langesundfjord at taxonomic levels higher than species. – *Mar. Ecol. Prog. Ser.* **46:**167–170.

– 1988b: The level of taxonomic discrimination required to detect pollution effects on marine benthic communities. – *Mar. Poll. Bull.* **19:**259–268.

WATSON, J. A. L., 1973: Odonata (dragonflies): – In: Alligator Rivers Region: Environmental Factfinding study: Entomology: 21 pp. – CSIRO Div. Ent. Canberra.

– 1974: The distributions of the Australian dragonflies (Odonata). – *J. Aust. Ent. Soc.* **13:**137–149.

WATSON, J. A. L. & ABBEY, H. M., 1980: Dragonflies (Odonata) from the Northern Territory. – *CSIRO Division of Entomology Report No.* **21:**1–44.

WEBB, J. W., 1991: The influence of season on Australian crocodiles. – In: HAYNES, C. D., RIDPATH, M. G. & WILLIAMS, M. A. J. (eds.): Monsoonal Australia: Landscape, Ecology and Man in the Northern Lowlands: 125–131. – A. A. Balkema, Rotterdam, Brookfield.

WELLS, A., 1991: A guide to the caddisflies (Trichoptera) of the Alligator Rivers Region, Northern Territory: 105 pp. – Open File Record 84, Supervising Scientist for the Alligator Rivers Region.

WHITEHEAD, P. J. & TSCHIRNER, K., 1991: Lead shot ingestion and lead poisoning of magpie geese *Anseranas semipalmata* foraging in a northern Australian hunting reserve. – *Biological Conservation* **58:**99–118.

WOINARSKI, J. C. Z., GAMBOLD, N., MENKHORST, K. & BRAITHWAITE, R. W., 1989: Wildlife survey of Kakadu National Park Stage 3: 142 pp. – Final report to Australian National Parks and Wildlife Service from CSIRO Wildlife and Ecology, Darwin.

WREN, C. D. & STEPHENSON, G. L., 1991: The effect of acidification on the accumulation and toxicity of metals to freshwater invertebrates. – *Environ. Poll.* **71:**205–241.

Authors' address:

Alligator Rivers Region Research Institute, Office of the Supervising Scientist, Jabiru, NT 0886, Australia.

Mitt. Internat. Verein. Limnol.	24	315–320	Stuttgart, Februar 1994

Scope for growth in a tropical freshwater snail, *Brotia hainanensis:* Implications for monitoring sublethal toxic stressors

Patrick C. C. Lai and Paul K. S. Lam

Abstract

Scope for growth (SfG), the difference between the energy input to an organism from its food and the output from respiratory metabolism, has been used as a bioassay for environmental stress in the temperate region. Here, the same technique was applied to a tropical freshwater snail, *Brotia hainanensis* (Thiaridae), to investigate whether the technique is applicable to biological systems at lower latitudes. In this study, the effects of copper and low pH on the SfG of the snails were examined. The results show that both copper and low pH can significantly reduce the SfG of individual snails through a decrease in the amount of energy absorbed, while the change in energy expenditure is not apparent. It was also found that the SfG assay is most informative at stress levels too low to be detected by the corresponding acute tests. The potential value of SfG assays in assessing the impact of environmental toxicants at an ecosystem level is discussed.

Introduction

Traditionally, toxicological tests in the freshwater environment often rely on the laboratory determinations of the mortality of test organisms exposed to different concentrations of specific toxicants (Maltby & Calow 1989). Despite the popularity of these acute tests, more attention has recently been paid to investigations concerned with the sublethal effects of pollutants as such effects may have important long-term influences on individual organisms as well as significant ecological impacts on natural populations and communities (Sprague 1976, Anderson & D'Apollonia 1978, McGreer 1979). More importantly, studies involving subtle responses may be of particular value in monitoring important long-term effects of pollutants that occur at relatively low concentrations. Indeed, chronic tests of this type may help to provide an early warning system in the conservation of valuable aquatic resources (Connell & Miller 1984).

Response criteria used in sublethal assays often involve variations in the behaviour (e.g. Phelps et al. 1983, Chapman et al. 1985), key life-history parameters (e.g. growth rates and reproductive effort), and patterns of energy allocation (e.g. scope for growth) of test organisms. Scope for growth (SfG), defined as the difference between energy intake and total metabolic losses (Warren & Davis 1967), was developed for toxicological assessments of a wide range of sublethal stressors in both marine (e.g. Bayne et al. 1979, Widdows et al. 1981) and freshwater environments (e.g. Naylor et al. 1989, Maltby et al. 1990) in the temperate region. In this study, the SfG assay with copper and low pH as the stressors was performed on a tropical freshwater snail, *Brotia hainanensis* (Brot 1872), to investigate whether the technique can be applied to biological systems in the tropics. Snails were also subjected to acute tests involving the same two stressors to provide data for a comparison with the SfG assay.

Materials and methods

Scope for growth test

Scope for growth (SfG) can be calculated from the balanced energy equation of Winberg (1960):

$$C-F=A=R+U+P$$

or

$$P=C-F-R-U$$

where C = energy consumed as food; F = energy lost as faeces; A = energy absorbed; R = energy lost through respiration; U = energy lost as excreta; and P = energy available for somatic and gametic production.

Assuming that energy excreted (U) is negligible in freshwater invertebrates (cf. Naylor et al. 1989), SfG, equivalent to the production term P, can be estimated as follows:

$$SfG=C-F-R$$

SfG can thus be determined experimentally for individual test organisms exposed to varying levels of sublethal stress. SfG, a measure of energy devoted to production, is in theory related to the growth of an individual organism (Naylor et al. 1989). Since growth is a general response which integrates separate physiological processes, the use of SfG in ecotoxicological tests should provide a better understanding of whole-organism responses (Widdows 1978, Donkin & Widdows 1986). On this basis, SfG is considered as a useful and readily quantifiable parameter that can reflect the condition of an organism.

0538-4680/94/0024-0315 $ 1.50

Test species

Brotia hainanensis (Gastropoda: Prosobranchia: Thiaridae) is a freshwater snail generally confined to clear, stony hill streams and the upper coarse of rivers in Hong Kong and tropical Asia (DUDGEON 1982, 1989). Apart from their high abundance, these snails were chosen as the test species because of their potential ecological importance as shredders (sensu CUMMINS 1973) in the processing of allochthonous leaf materials, converting leaf litter to particulate organic matter (DUDGEON 1982). The 'role' of *B. hainanensis* in tropical streams is similar to that of the amphipod *Gammarus pulex* in temperate running waters. Significantly, *Gammarus pulex* had also been used as a test species in ecotoxicological studies carried out in the temperate region (e.g. NAYLOR et al. 1989).

Field collection

Snails were collected from the upper course of Lam Tsuen River, New Territories, Hong Kong. The site was completely shaded by evergreen trees and climbers, and thus allochthonous organic matter was likely to be an important source of energy for the stream community. As the energy-allocation pattern of an aniamal is likely to be affected by its age and reproductive state, and the minimum reproductive size (aperture width) for *B. hainanensis* is 14.5 mm (DUDGEON 1989), only animals with aperture width of 10 (± 1) mm were used in the present study.

Food

In situ observations revealed that leaf litter of *Bauhinia* spp. was included in the natural diet of *B. hainanensis*. As leaf litter at different stages of decomposition might have different nutritive qualities (CUMMINS & KLUG 1979), freshly fallen *Bauhinia* leaves (i.e. leaves of similar colour and texture, and without any signs of decomposition) were collected adjacent to the stream where *B. hainanensis* was taken. The leaves were then washed and carefully brushed to remove the silt on the surface. The washed leaves were cut into 2 cm × 4 cm pieces, oven-dried at 70 °C, and stored for subsequent use. The leaves were rehydrated for two days before being presented to the snails.

Laboratory investigations

All snails were maintained in aerated, artificial pond water (APW; NAYLOR et al. 1989) at 20 (± 1) °C, under a 12 hour light and 12 hour dark cycle, and fed with a *Bauhinia* leaves (see above). Snails were selected randomly from the stock and acclimated to the experimental conditions for at least a week prior to a test. All tests were carried out using APW as the basic testing medium.

Solutions of different levels of copper ions for use in the tests were made up by dissolving copper sulphate ($CuSO_4 \cdot 5H_2O$) in APW to the desired concentration. Various acidity levels were achieved by adding controlled amounts of 0.01 M hydrochloric acid to APW whilst monitoring the solution with a bench pH meter (Orion Model 920A). The acidities of the test solutions were checked, and if necessary, solutions were changed every eight hours throughout the experimental period.

Scope for growth test

The calculation of SfG requires the estimation of two energy terms, namely the amount of energy absorbed ($A = C - F$) and energy respired (R). A single snail was placed in each experimental chamber containing 250 ml of the test solution. The concentrations of the copper solutions were 0, 0.01, 0.02, 0.03, 0.04, 0.05, 0.07 and 0.10 mg/l, while the acidic solutions had pH values of 7.8, 6.0, 5.0 and 4.0. Each treatment group consisted of twelve snails. A known weight of food was supplied *ad libitum* to the snails. A perforated platform was placed at the bottom of each chamber so as to facilitate the collection of faeces. The copper solutions were aerated throughout the whole experimental period which lasted for 7 days, but the acidic solutions were not aerated continuously in order to avoid undesirably large pH fluctuations. These solutions were aerated at eight-hour intervals when the pH of each solution was checked. Five control chambers (no animals) were set up for each toxicant to obtain a correction factor for weight loss in the leaves due to leaching.

At the end of the experiment, unconsumed leaves were collected, oven-dried at 70 °C and weighed. Simiarly, the faeces were filtered, oven-dried and weighed. The energy content per unit dry weight of leaves and faeces was determined by bomb calorimetry (Ballistic bomb calorimeter, Gallenkamp model CB-370) to allow an estimation of the amount of energy consumed (difference between final and initial weights of leaves) and energy egested (details are given by NAYLOR et al. 1989). At the end of the experimental period, individual snails were removed from the chambers and their respiratory rates determined separately.

The technique used to determine oxygen consumption in this study was similar to that described by DAVENPORT (1976). The respiratory chamber was a 200 ml sealed glass vial completely filled with the test solution which was saturated with oxygen. The solution was kept at 20 °C in a temperature-controlled water bath and well mixed by a magnetic stirrer. The concentration of oxygen in the chamber was monitored continuously by an oxygen electrode (Electrode 1302) connected to an oxygen meter (Strathkelvin Instrument Model 781b). A snail was placed in the chamber and allowed to acclimate for one hour. The oxygen content of the medium was then monitored every five minutes for one hour. The average rate of change of oxygen content was taken as the rate of oxygen consumption by the snail. There were no obvious changes in the locomotory behaviour of the animals except at very high stress levels, and respiratory data were collected on actively-moving snails only. All measurements were taken between 0900 and 1200. The oxygen consumed by a given snail was subsequently converted to energy utilization by the following energy equivalent equation: 1 mg oxygen consumed = 14.14 J (ELLIOTT & DAVISON 1975).

The somatic (flesh) weights of individual snails were determined by dissolving the snail shells in 10% nitric acid and then oven drying to constant weight at 70 °C (cf. DUDGEON 1986). The amount of energy consumed, egested and respired can thus be expressed in terms of Joules per unit dry weight of snail, and SfG in terms of Joules per day of experimental period per mg of snail dry weight. Analysis of variance (ANOVA) was used to test the null hypothesis that the different levels of copper and acidic stress do not affect the SfG of *B. hainanensis*. Multiple comparisons of SfG data were carried out using Tukey tests (ZAR 1984).

Acute toxicity tests

Acute tests involving copper and low pH were performed on *B. hainanensis*. The concentrations of the copper solutions used were 0, 0.05, 0.10, 0.15, 0.20, 0.25, 0.30, 0.35, 0.40 and 0.50 mg/l, while the acidic solutions had pH values of 4.0, 3.5, 3.0 and 2.5. Three replicates performed for each treatment. For each replicate, 10 snails were placed in a 1000 ml beaker filled with a test solution of a specific copper concentration or a particular pH. The experimental conditions were the same as those for the SfG assays. Ten snails were kept in APW as a control. The snails were checked every day and dead animals removed. Mortality was checked by keeping the 'dead' animals in normal APW for 24 hours, and those that did not show any sign of movement were assumed to be dead. The percentage of snails surviving after 96 hours was determined for each treatment. The 96-h LC_{50} was then calculated for both the copper and pH variables by probit analysis following FINNEY (1980).

Results

Scope for growth assay

The effect of sublethal concentrations of copper on energy absorbed (A), energy respired (R), energy consumed (C) and absorption efficiency (A/C) of *Brotia hainanensis* are shown in Table 1. There was a significant decrease in the amount of energy absorbed with increasing copper concentrations (ANOVA): $F_{7,88} = 30.15$, $P < 0.001$) but no significant change in the amount of energy lost in respiration ($F_{5,66} =$ 0.55, $P > 0.05$). Respiration rates obtained at 0.07 and 0.10 mg/l of copper were

Table 1. Effect of copper on enery adsorption (A), energy loss via respiratory (R), energy consumption (C) and absorption efficiency (A/C) of *Brotia hainanensis*. Values are means ± 1 SEM.

Concentration of copper (mg/l)	A (J/mg/day)	R (J/mg/day)	C (J/mg/day)	A/C (%)
0	1.50 ± 0.13	0.51 ± 0.03	2.40 ± 0.23	62.96 ± 2.28
0.01	1.29 ± 0.10	0.57 ± 0.05	2.21 ± 0.11	57.67 ± 2.84
0.02	1.19 ± 0.13	0.52 ± 0.04	2.13 ± 0.11	55.06 ± 5.52
0.03	1.04 ± 0.09 *	0.50 ± 0.03	2.00 ± 0.08	54.15 ± 6.19
0.04	0.52 ± 0.06 *	0.48 ± 0.04	1.31 ± 0.11 *	39.79 ± 2.90
0.05	0.44 ± 0.05 *	0.52 ± 0.43	1.00 ± 0.08 *	44.00 ± 3.46
0.07	0.35 ± 0.07 *	0.36 ± 0.02	0.72 ± 0.09 *	28.61 ± 19.84
0.10	0.12 ± 0.08 *	0.32 ± 0.05 *	0.45 ± 0.12 *	12.84 ± 14.81 *

* = significantly different from 'control' (i.e. 0 mg/l) at $P < 0.05$.

Table 2. Effect of pH on enery adsorption (A), energy loss via respiratory (R), energy consumption (C) and absorption efficiency (A/C) of *Brotia hainanensis*. Values are means ± 1 SEM.

pH	A (J/mg/day)	R (J/mg/day)	C (J/mg/day)	A/C (%)
7.8	1.25 ± 0.10	0.47 ± 0.03	1.46 ± 0.10	85.07 ± 2.43
6.0	0.85 ± 0.10 *	0.57 ± 0.05	1.30 ± 0.16	65.87 ± 2.09
5.0	0.65 ± 0.05 *	0.60 ± 0.03	0.89 ± 0.06 *	73.39 ± 2.67
4.0	0.11 ± 0.06 *	0.50 ± 0.07	0.21 ± 0.06 *	42.45 ± 11.37 *

* = significantly different from 'control' (i.e. pH = 7.8) at $P < 0.05$.

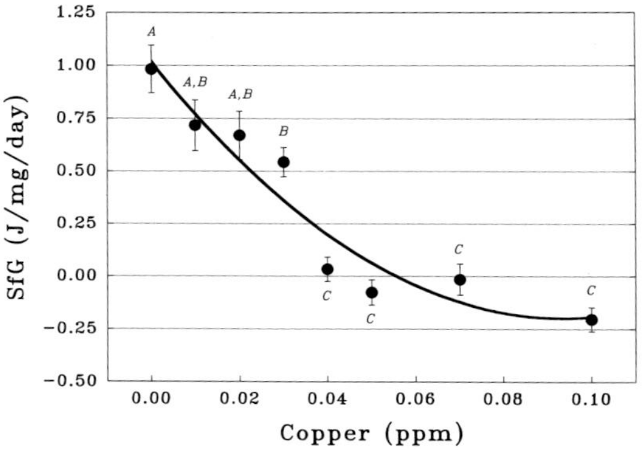

Fig. 1. Effect of various concentrations of copper on the scope for growth in *Brotia hainanensis*. Different letters indicate groups that are statistically different at $P<0.05$.

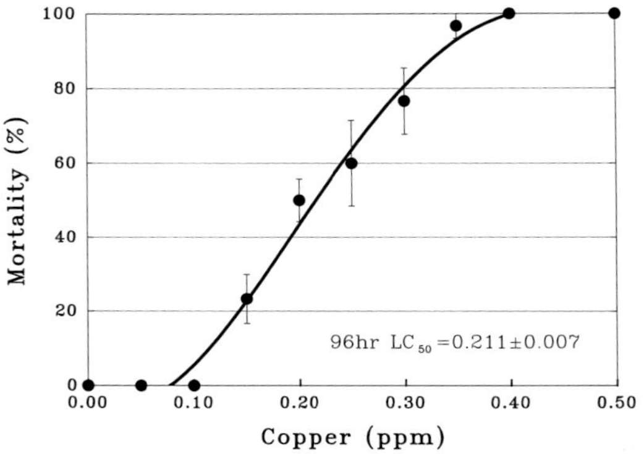

Fig. 3. Percentage mortality of *Brotia hainanensis* snails exposed to various concentrations of copper for 96 hours.

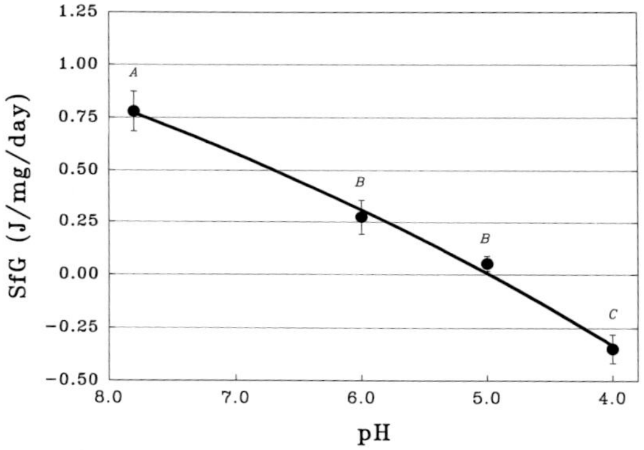

Fig. 2. Effect of reducing pH on the scope for growth in *Brotia hainanensis*. Different letters indicate groups that are statistically different at $P<0.05$.

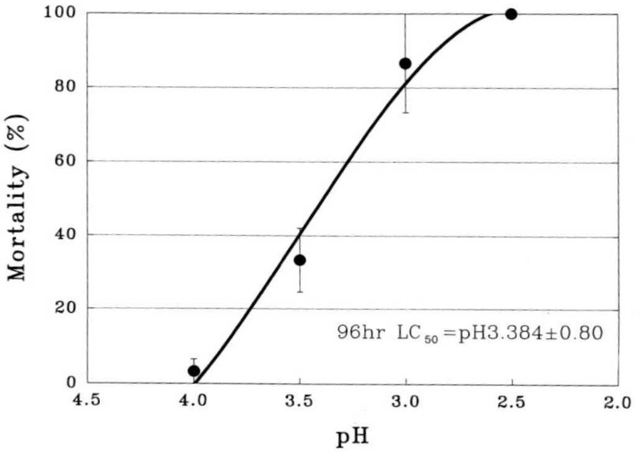

Fig. 4. Percentage mortality of *Brotia hainanensis* snails exposed to different levels of acidity for 96 hours.

excluded from the above analysis as some of the snails had retracted into their shells and closed their opercula, probably as a result of the high levels of stress. The reduction in energy absorption was attributed to a decline in energy consumption ($F_{7,88}=35.95$, $P<0.001$) with increasing copper concentrations. A decrease in absorption efficiency ($F_{7,88}=8.85$, $P<0.001$) with increasing copper concentration was also observed. Overall, an increase in the copper concentration caused a significant decrease in the SfG of *B. hainanensis* ($F_{7,88}=26.12$, $P<0.001$). SfG decreased rapidly when the copper concentration was increased from 0.03 to 0.04 mg/l, above which SfG tended to level off (Fig. 1).

Changes in the SfG of *B. hainanensis* exposed to different pH shows a similar pattern to copper (Table 2). At low pH, there were significant reductions in SfG ($F_{3,44}=41.07$, $P<0.001$; Fig. 2). Again, this was attributed to a decline in the amount of energy absorbed ($F_{3,44}=33.56$, $P<0.001$) through a decrease in the amount of energy consumed ($F_{3,44}=29.21$, $P<0.001$), with no apparent variations in respiratory energy loss ($F_{3,44}=2.55$, $P>0.05$). There was a decrease in absorption efficiency ($F_{3,44}=19.63$, $P<0.001$) at low pH.

Acute toxicity tests

The 96-h LC_{50} for copper and low pH were 0.21 ± 0.007 mg/l and pH 3.38 ± 0.8 respectively (Figs. 3 & 4).

Discussion

Our data indicate that SfG of *Brotia hainanensis* is sensitive to varying copper levels and acidity. The assay lasted for seven days which is significantly shorter than chronic tests involving measurements of life-history parameters such as growth rates and fecundity. Importantly, SfG assays are able to detect sublethal stresses, which cannot be revealed by acute LC_{50} tests. The 96-h LC_{50} of copper was 0.21 ± 0.007 mg/l while the SfG assay was effective in detecting copper concentrations from 0.03 to 0.10 mg/l. For the low-pH stress, 96-h LC_{50} value was pH 3.38 ± 0.8, but the SfG assay was sensitive enough to detect a change in acidity between pH 7.8 and pH 6.0. Hence, in response to the presence of copper and at low pH levels, SfG assays were more sensitive than their corresponding acute tests, particularly at low stress levels.

Another advantage of the SfG assay is that it provides information on which particular components of the energy budget are affected by a specific toxicant. Such information might provide useful insights into the possible mechanisms of toxicological responses. In the case of *B. hainanensis,* the most sensitive component of the energy budget appears to be the amount of energy absorbed while the energy lost through respiration remains more or less unchanged. The effects of low pH and zinc on the energy budget of the temperate amphipod *Gammarus pulex* also exhibits a similar pattern (Naylor et al. 1989). It is possible that such patterns might be characteristic of macroinvertebrates inhabiting the upper courses of streams in general. Respiration rates might have been evolutionarily-fixed at near maximum levels in these animals as a result of high feeding and metabolic activities to obtain sufficient energy and essential minerals from the generally nutrient-poor stream waters. Interestingly, other studies reveal that the oxygen consumption of the intertidal snail *Littorina littorea* is affected by Buler C oil and dispersant Corexit 8666 (Hargrave & Newcombe 1973). Similarly, oxygen consumption of the mud snail *Nassarius obsoletus* is altered upon exposure to heavy metal (MacInnes & Thurberg 1973). The apparent constancy of respiratory energy loss in some freshwater shredders exposed to different levels of stress points to the possibility of a simpler assay which requires no measurements of respiratory rates. However, it is conceivable that individual species might adopt contrasting strategies in dealing with environmental stresses, and more investigations involving other freshwater macroinvertebrates exposed to a wider range of stressors is required to establish the generality of the present observations. Other studies have demonstrated that the avoidance behaviour of the amphipoid *Gammarus pulex* (cf. Costa 1966) is even more sensitive than the corresponding SfG assay for zinc (Maltby et al. 1990). It would be instructive to perform similar tests on *B. hainanensis* in future investigations.

Although the results suggest that scope for growth can be used in a bioassay for monitoring sublethal stresses, the present methodology has some limitations. Firstly, the range of copper concentrations that can be detected by the SfG assay is relatively narrow (0.03–0.10 mg/l). Copper concentrations above 0.10 mg/l result in high snail mortality, and approach the type of conditions for acute toxicity tests. The same pattern was observed for the low-pH stress. Secondly, the amount of energy loss via respiration was calculated from oxygen consumption data collected at one particular time of the day, and thus might not be truly representative of respiration rates over the seven-day experimental period.

It is hoped that the SfG assay, since it measures variations in energy allocation within an organism, would eventually provide an insight into the long-term impact of environmental toxicants on aquatic macroinvertebrates which are important in the functioning of the ecosystem (Calow & Sibly 1990). This type of information cannot be retrieved from the traditional acute toxicity tests. Moreover, it would be instructive to relate the results of the SfG assay to changes in the growth rates and fecundity of the stressed organisms (e.g. Maltby & Naylor 1990) to separate the real physiological stress response from the initial shock reactions of the organism to which it can quickly acclimate.

Although our ultimate concern is the effect of toxicants on the ecosystem, it is argued that tests which concentrate on sub-organismic responses such as the physiology-based SfG assay should be employed in addition to those that deal directly with the actual ecosystem because the former has a higher repeatability and a faster response time (cf. Maltby & Calow 1989). Of course, those studies that concentrate on sub-organismic responses will be disadvantaged by a lack of realism and the difficulty of interpreting the ecological relevance of the responses observed. It is important, therefore, that ecotoxicological tests should study parameters which are directly related to the fitness (e.g. growth and reproduction) of the organisms. Test species should be both widely distributed and important in ecosystem functioning.

Acknowledgements

We thank Dr. Steven Bigger for providing helpful comments on an earlier draft of the manuscript.

References

Anderson, P. D. & D'Apollonia, S., 1978: Aquatic Animals. – In: Butler, G. C. (ed.): Principles of Ecotoxicology. – Scientific Committee on Problems of the Environment (SCOPE) report No. **12:**187–221. – John Wiley & Sons.

Bayne, B. L., Moore, M. N., Widdows, J., Livingstone, D. R. & Salkfeld, P., 1979: Measurement of the responses of individuals to environmental stress and pollution: studies with bivalve molluscs. – *Phil. Trans. Roy. Soc. London. B.* **286:**563–581.

Calow, P. & Sibly, R. M., 1990: A physiological basis of population processes: ecotoxicological implications. – *Functional Ecology* **4:**283–288.

Chapman, H. F., Hughes, J. M. & Kitching, R. L., 1985: Burying response of an intertidal gastropod to freshwater and copper contamination. – *Mar. Poll. Bull.* **16:**442–445.

Connell, D. W. & Miller, G. J., 1978: Chemistry and Ecotoxicology of Pollution. – Wiley, New York.

Costa, H. H., 1966: Responses of *Gammarus pulex (L.)* to modified environment. I. Reaction to toxic substances. – *Crustaceana* **11:**245–256.

Cummins, K. W., 1973: Trophic relations of aquatic insects. – *Ann. Rev. Entomol.* **18:**183–206.

Cummins, K. W. & Klug, M. J., 1979: Feeding ecology of stream invertebrates. – *Ann. Rev. Ecol. Syst.* **10:**147–172.

Davenport, J., 1978: A technique for the measurement of oxygen consumption in small aquatic organisms. – *Laboratory Practice* **25:**693–695.

Donkin, P. & Widdows, J., 1986: Scope for growth as a measurement of environmental pollution and its interpretation using structure-activity relationships. – *Chemistry and Industry,* November 1986: 732–737.

Dudgeon, D., 1982: The life history of *Brotia hainanensis* (Brot 1872) (Gastropoda: Prosobranchia: Thiaridae) in a tropical forest stream. – *Zool. J. Linnean Soc.* **76:**141–1514.

– 1986: The life cycle, population dynamics and productivity of *Melanoides tuberculata* (Müller 1774) (Gastropoda: Prosobranchia: Thiaridae) in Hong Kong. – *J. Zool., Lond.* **208:**37–53.

– 1989: Ecological strategies of Hong Kong Thiaridae (Gastropoda: Prosobranchia). – *Malacol. Rev.* **22:** 39–53.

Elliott, J. M. & Davison, W., 1975: Energy equivalents of oxygen consumption in animal energetics. – *Oecologia* **19:**195–201.

Finney, D. J., 1989: *Probit analysis.* 3rd edition: 333 pp. – Cambridge University Press, Cambridge.

Hargrave, B. T. & Newcombe, C. P., 1973: Crawling and respiration as indices of sublethal effects of oil and a dispersant on an intertidal snail *Littorina littorea.* – *J. Fish. Res. Bd Can.* **30:**1789–1792.

McGreer, E. R., 1979: Sublethal effects of heavy metal contaminated sediments on the bivalve, *Macoma balthica (L.).* – *Mar. Poll. Bull.* **10:**259–262.

MacInnes, J. & Thurberg, F. P., 1973: Effects of metal on the behaviour and oxygen consumption of the mud snail. – *Mar. Poll. Bull.* **4:**185–186.

Maltby, L. & Calow, P., 1989: The application of bioassays in the resolution of environmental problems; past, present and future. – *Hydrobiologia* **188/189:**65–76.

Maltby, L. & Naylor, C., 1990: Preliminary observations on the ecological relevance of the *Gammarus* 'scope for growth' assay: effect of zinc on reproduction. – *Functional Ecology* **4:**393–397.

Maltby, L., Naylor, C. & Calow, P., 1990: Effect of stress on a freshwater benthic detritivore: Scope for growth in *Gammarus pulex.* – *Ecotoxicology and Environmental Safety* **19:**285–291.

Naylor, C., Maltby, L. & Calow, P., 1989: Scope for growth in *Gammarus pulex,* a freshwater benthic detritivore. – *Hydrobiology* **188/189:**517–523.

Phelps, H. L., Hardy, J. T., Pearson, W. H. & Apts, C. W., 1983: Clam burrowing behaviour: inhibition by copper-enriched sediment. – *Mar. Poll. Bull.* **14:**452–455.

Sprague, J. B., 1976: Current status of sublethal tests of pollutants on aquatic organisms. – *J. Fish. Res. Bd Can.* **33:**1988–1992.

Warren, C. E. & Davis, G. L., 1967: Laboratory studies on the feeding of fishes. – In: Gerking, S. D. (ed.): The Biological Basis of Freshwater Fish Production: 175–214. – Blackwell Scientific Publications, Oxford.

Widdows, J., 1978: Physiological indices of stress in *Mytilus edulis.* – *J. Mar. Biol. Assoc. U.K.* **58:**125–142.

Widdows, J., Phelps, D. K. & Galloway, W., 1981: Measurement of physiological condition of mussels *Mytilus edulis* transplanted along a pollution gradient in Narragansett Bay, Rhode Island, USA. – *Marine Environmental Research* **4:**181–194.

Winberg, G. G., 1960: Rate of metabolism and food requirements of fishes. – *Fisheries Research Board of Canada, Translation Series* **194:**1–253.

Zar, J. H., 1984: *Biostatistical analysis.* 2nd edition: 718 pp. – Prentice-Hall International, New Jersey.

Authors' address:

Department of Environmental Management, Victoria University of Technology, St. Albans Campus, Victoria 3021, Australia.

Mitt. Internat. Verein. Limnol.	24	321–326	Stuttgart, Februar 1994

Microbiological indicators of freshwater pollution in Hong Kong

I. J. Hodgkiss

Abstract

Freshwater quality has been assessed using a number of lines of investigation, namely chemical, biological and micro-biological. Each approach has its uses and yields different information; each also has limitations. Microbiological indicators are particularly useful in that they respond directly and rapidly to environmental changes and, bacteria in particular, offer an immediate bioindicator system for both sewage (and animal manure) and chemical pollutants.

Organic pollution of Hong Kong streams has been assessed using a number of techniques and this paper reviews the results obtained using these different methods. Thus, the results provided by the enumeration of bacterial indicator species are compared with the results provided by various methods of algal (particularly diatom) community structure analysis. The results from these microbiological indexes of pollution are then compared with the results obtained from two extensively used chemical indexes of pollution, namely Biochemical Oxygen Demand (BOD_5) and ammoniacal nitrogen (NH_3-N) content, which are the methods currently used by the Hong Kong Government Environmental Protection Department to prepare a water quality index for Hong Kong streams.

Of the four algal indexes of pollution used, only the algal genus pollution index (AGPI) showed significant correlation with both chemical and bacteriological indicators. Faecal coliform counts showed significant correlations both with BOD_5 and NH_3-N content (as did total coliform counts with the latter). Although both the AGPI and bacterial count methods of biological assessment showed correlation with chemical methods of assessment, the relative ease of use, simplicity and speed of results of the bacterial indicator enumeration technique compared with the algal community structure analysis required in the AGPI, makes the former method particularly useful where fast results are essential or where non-ecologists are involved in environmental studies. Furthermore, and of great advantage, using bacterial counts, the faecal coliform to faecal streptococcal ratio indicates the origin of the pollution and its significance (human or animal wastes and possible disease potential).

Introduction

Stream pollution in Hong Kong became of serious concern in the 1970s and 1980s; by then the majority of streams passing through the lowland areas were grossly polluted with agricultural wastes and excreta. Untreated human wastes also contributed a substantial pollution load (equivalent to 10–20% of the agricultural load), whereas industrial wastes were in general of less significance (Hodgkiss 1981). This pollution problem is exacerbated at certain times of the year because highly seasonal rainfall (85% of Hong Kong's 2320 mm of rainfall falls between May and October) means that during the drier months, stream flow becomes negligible and stagnant pools and banks of putrescent organic matter develop. With the advent of the first monsoon rains, this organic load is poured into the sea within a short period (Hodgkiss 1981).

An awareness of stream contamination as a serious cause of marine pollution over a decade ago (Hodgkiss 1979), led to a series of investigations aimed at assessing the land-generated, stream-carried, pollution load of mainly animal and human wastes in the aquatic environment. Various lines of investigation were employed, namely chemical, biological and mirobiological, but here, mainly the latter approach is discussed. In this microbiological approach, two types of communities have been studied, the bacterial community using indicator species and the diatom community using diversity indexes.

The use of bacteria as water quality indicators rests on the fact that the greater the level of faecal contamination in the water, the higher the indicator bacterial level. A variety of bacterial groups or individual species have been used as indicators; the advantages and disadvantages of each 'type' of indicator have been reviewed by James & Evison (1979) and Pipes (1982) and will not be elaborated upon here. Various studies of Hong Kong streams (e.g. Hodgkiss & Chan 1983, 1986) involved investigation of three of the most widely used of these indicators, namely the Total Coliform (TC) group, the Faecal Coliform (FC) group and the Faecal Streptococcal (FC) group, and all of these pointed to serious pollution, particularly of the lowland watercourses, by agricultural and human wastes.

Diatoms have also been used widely as indicators of water quality, particularly organic pollution (e.g. Round 1991) and the various diversity indexes employed have been reviewed by Washington (1984). Only two studies have been carried out in Hong Kong to link diatom diversity with stream pollution (Hodgkiss & Kan 1978; Hodgkiss & Law 1985). The first of these involved

0538-4680/94/0024-0321 $ 1.50

three of the most widely used indexes of algal (diatom) community diversity and, in addition, a new index devised by the authors (Hodgkiss & Kan 1978) – the tolerant species abundance index – was used.

Study sites

A large number of streams were studied (Hodgkiss & Kan 1978, Hodgkiss 1981, Hodgkiss & Chan 1983, Hodgkiss & Law 1985, Hodgkiss & Chan 1986). This paper will discuss results from only two of these streams – the Lam Tsuen River and the Shing Mun Stream – since, not only are these streams typical of the other streams studied, but they also drain into Tolo Harbour to the North East of Hong Kong, one of Hong Kong's most polluted marine areas. A number of stations were investigated on each stream, three in the Lam Tsuen River, representing near the source (L1), mid length (L2) and near the mouth (L3) and two in the shorter Shing Mun Stream representing near the source (S1) and near the mouth (S2).

Methods

Algal survey

At monthly intervals from December 1978 to January 1980, Hodgkiss & Law (1985) scraped three replicate samples of epilithic algae from 100 mm² areas of underwater rock surface at each of the five stations. These samples were centrifuged at 2500 rpm for 15 min and the resulting algal pellet digested with 5 ml concentrated nitric acid at 100 °C for 30 min. They were then recentrifuged and the residue washed with distilled water three times. The final residue was resuspended in 5 ml of distilled water and 0.1 ml aliquots used for microscopic analysis. Naphrax (refractive index, 1.74) was used as the mountant. Further details of mounting, identification and counting are given in Hodgkiss & Law (1985). Four biological indexes of pollution were applied to the results of this study as listed below.

(i) Shannon's H' diversity index (DI):

$$DI = -\sum_{i=1}^{s} \frac{N_i}{N} \ln \frac{N_i}{N}$$

where DI = diversity index
N = total number of individuals in the community
N_i = number of individuals belonging to the ith species
S = total number of species in the community

This mathematical expression of community structure has been used widely in aquatic pollution studies (e.g. Wilhm & Dorris 1968), since it reflects not only the distribution of species but also includes the relative abundance of each species in the community. The higher the DI value, the less polluted is the system.

(ii) Algal genus pollution index (AGPI) (Palmer 1969).

(iii) Algal species pollution index (ASPI) (Palmer 1969): for both AGPI and ASPI, a pollution index factor is assigned to selected genera or species based on their tolerance to organic pollution as rated by the number of authors who considered them to be pollution tolerant. Palmer (1969) gives methods for calculation. The lower the index value, the lower the pollution level.

(iv) Tolerant species abundance index (TSAI; Hodgkiss & Kan 1978). This index is calculated from information on the pollution tolerance of each species (using a grading system) together with the relative abundance of the species, using the formula:

$$TSAI = \sum_{i=1}^{S} GA$$

where TSAI = the index
G = the tolerance grading of a species
A = the % abundance of that species
S = the number of tolerant species in the community.

The higher the index which results, the higher the pollution load.

The monthly average value of each of these four indexes for each site was correlated with the monthly average values of BOD_5 and ammoniacal nitrogen for each of the stations. These were chosen for comparison because they are the major variables used locally by the Hong Kong Government Environmental Protection Department to obtain a stream water quality index (EPD 1989). BOD was determined by collecting three replicate water samples in pre-sterilized amber glass bottles using standard sampling techniques, and keeping them in the dark at 4 °C prior to analysis. This involved the use of a BOD probe and a magnetic stirrer at a temperature of 20 °C. The samples were diluted where necessary and then kept at 20 °C in the dark for five days before the second BOD measurement was made. The ammoniacal nitrogen determination followed the procedures of Solorzano (1969).

Bacterial survey

Duplicate water samples were collected by Hodgkiss & Chan (1986) twice monthly over a fourteen-month period between January 1978 and February 1979 at 15 stream stations including the same five stations used in the algal survey. Only the data from these five stations are used in this paper. Various bacterial indicators were examined, including TC, FC and FS; in addition, the FC:FS ratios were subsequently calculated from these data. The sampling and analytical procedures used were standard bacteriological methods as used by the American Public Health Association (1976). The FC:FS ratios were assigned to various graded categories of pollution based on the method of Geldreich & Kenner (1969). Again, the monthly averages of the TC and FC values

Table 1. Mean values of the pollution indexes monitored.

Pollution index	Lam Tsuen River			Sha Tin Stream	
	L1 Upstream	L2	L3 Downstream	S1 Upstream	S2 Downstream
Diversity Index (DI)[a]	3.75	4.39	4.35	3.24	3.79
Algal Genus Pollution Index (AGPI)	15	22	25	14	20
Algal Species Pollution Index (ASPI)	11	17	18	9	12
Tolerant Species Abundance Index (TSAI)	0.91	1.47	1.19	0.64	0.60
BOD_5 (mg/dm^3)[b]	4.07	21.39***	47.15***	3.02	5.39*
NH_3-N (mg/dm^3)[c]	0.73	1.82**	6.03**	0.02	2.97**
Total Coliform Count (TC/100 cm^3)[d]	85,114***	100,000***	186,209***	1,950**	131,826***
Faecal Coliform Count (FC/100 cm^3)[e]	37,674***	40,738***	97,724***	174**	56,234***

[a] Lower values indicate more polluted water in this index whereas, in the other 3 algal indexes, lower values indicate less pollution.
[b] <2: clean; 2–5: fairly clean; 5–10: doubtful quality; 10–12: polluted; >12: grossly polluted (Department of the Environment 1970)
[c] <1: clean; 1–10: polluted; >12: grossly polluted (Government of Hong Kong 1974).
[d] >1000 per 100 cm^3: unacceptable (WHO 1967).
[e] >1000 per 100 cm^3: unacceptable (EEC 1975).
* Doubtful quality, ** polluted, *** grossly polluted.

were correlated with the monthly averages for BOD_5 and ammoniacal nitrogen at the five stations.

Correlation

Since these two sets of data come from the same sites and overlap in timing (i.e. December 1978 – January 1980 for the algal data and January 1978 – February 1979 for the bacterial data), the average BOD_5 and ammoniacal nitrogen values used in the correlation analysis are the average values of the two surveys.

Results

Algal survey

A summary of the results obtained using the four types of diversity indexes is given in Table 1 together with the means for BOD_5, ammonium N, TC and FC levels, and the correlation coefficients derived between these values are shown in Table 2. Three of the four indexes (the DI being the exception) showed increased pollution from the upper to lower course of the Lam Tsuen River, being highest in the case of the TSAI, however, in the mid reaches (Table 1). In the case of the AGPI and ASPI, this was also true of the Shing Mun Stream in that the lower course values were higher than the upper course values. However, in the case of the DI and the tolerant species abundance index, pollution was highest in the upper reaches of the stream. A consideration of the chemical and bacteriological data reveals that in fact, organic pollution increases downstream from L1 to L3 and from S1 to S2.

There was significant correlation amongst the indexes, except between the TSAI and AGPI values (Table 2). Similarly, there was significant correlation amongst the chemical and bacteriological data, except in the case of BOD_5 and TC. There was significant correlation between the AGPI/ASPI and BOD_5 and between the AGPI and NH_3-N, TC and FC (Table 2).

Table 2. Pearson Product Moment Correlation Coefficients between various indexes of pollution.

	DI+	AGPI	ASPI	TSAI	BOD_5	NH_3-N	TC	FC
DI	–							
AGPI	0.894*	–						
ASPI	0.970**	0.941**	–					
TSAI	0.865*	0.631	0.851*	–				
BOD_5	0.782	0.868*	0.892*	0.662	–			
NH_3-N	0.690	0.894*	0.767	0.338	0.870*	–		
TC	0.791	0.878*	0.795	0.405	0.745	0.923**	–	
FC	0.758	0.862*	0.773	0.395	0.815*	0.961**	0.986**	–

+ See Table 1 for key to indexes.
* Significant where $P<0.05$ ($r>0.811$).
** Significant where $P<0.01$ ($r>0.917$).

Table 3. The monthly incidences and (in brackets) % occurrence of the various FC:FS ratios.

FC:FS ratio category	L1	L2	L3	Total	S1	S2	Total
>4[a]	6 (43)	7 (50)	6 (43)	19 (45)	6 (43)	2 (14)	8 (29)
2–4[b]	3 (21)	1 (7)	2 (14)	6 (14)	2 (14)	2 (14)	4 (14)
1–2[c]	2 (14)	6 (43)	5 (36)	13 (31)	5 (36)	8 (57)	13 (46)
0.7–1[d]	1 (7)	0 (0)	0 (0)	1 (2)	1 (7)	1 (7)	2 (7)
<0.7[e]	2 (14)	0 (0)	1 (7)	3 (7)	0 (0)	1 (7)	1 (4)

[a] Pollution from human wastes (N.B. danger of disease transmission).
[b] Predominance of human wastes in mixed pollution.
[c] Uncertain.
[d] Predominance of livestock and poultry wastes in mixed pollution.
[e] Pollution from livestock/poultry wastes (N.B. danger of transmission of animal diseases to man).

Bacterial survey

Table 1 shows the mean values for TC and FC levels in relation to stream sites and Table 2 the correlation coefficients derived between these counts and the other pollution indicators. TC and FC levels were alarmingly high at most stations (Table 1) (the exception being the upper Shing Mun Stream) and they both showed significant correlation with NH_3-N, although only FC showed correlation with BOD_5; they also showed good correlation with each other (Table 2). BOD_5 was significantly correlated also with NH_3-N. The lack of correlation between BOD_5 and TC is not surprising since BOD_5 reflects increased organic load whereas TC does not (unlike FC) necessarily do so. Unlike the pollution gradients determined by the algal indexes, those determined by TC, FC and chemical values were the same in the two streams, that is values were highest (indicating most pollution) in the lower reaches of both. The monthly distribution of the different FC:FS ratio categories is given in Table 3.

Discussion

There does not appear to be any other study referred to in the literature which has compared bacterial and algal indicators of stream pollution, and thus, the results obtained in the present study cannot be looked at in relation to results from elsewhere in this respect.

The concept underlying the use of the diversity indices in pollution studies is that diversity decreases with increasing degree of pollution. This was not the case in the present study, since the DI showed an increasing trend downstream, that is, against the pollution gradient. Hence, the index did not reveal the degree of pollution at stations L2, L3 and S2 as determined by chemical and bacterial measures in these and other studies, and there was no significant correlation between the index and either BOD_5, NH_3-N, TC or FC levels. Neither did PALMER's (1969) ASPI give a truly representative picture of the water quality, since, although it indicated increasing pollution downstream, it only showed positive correlation with BOD_5 and not the other factors. His AGPI index was, however, better and showed both increasing pollution downstream and good positive correlation with BOD_5, NH_3-N, TC and FC.

The algal methods failed to varying extents because PALMER's AGPI does not take abundance of the different genera into account while the DI neglects to consider the kinds of organisms present. The TSAI (proposed by HODGKISS & KAN 1978) includes both types of information, and it was hoped that it would thus help to alleviate the weakness in PALMER's AGPI by taking into account the percentage abundance of those species making up the community and help to overcome the problems of the DI by taking account of the range of tolerant species found in different communities. However, this index again did not show any agreement with the chemical or bacterial data and no significant correlation was shown. Indeed, the TSAI (Table 1) was actually *worse* than either of PALMER's indexes, since, in common with the DI, in the Lam Tsuen River at L3 it indicated (falsely) *cleaner* water than the other diatom indexes where both chemical and bacteriological indexes indicated the most polluted conditions.

Both BOD_5 and NH_3-N levels indicated increasingly polluted conditions in the Lam Tsuen River from source to mouth and, to a lesser extent, in the Shing Mun Stream. The same patterns were shown by the TC and FC levels and so all chemical and bacterial indicators (with the exception of BOD and TC) showed significant correlation with each other.

The higher level of correlation between the bacterial indicator enumeration technique and the chemical methods compared with the results obtained for the algal community structure analysis (with the exception perhaps of the AGPI) indicates that bacterial counts are reasonable pollution indicators when compared with the classical BOD_5 and NH_3-N tests. Their relative ease of use, simplicity, and speed of results make the bacterial analysis particularly useful where fast results are essential or where non-ecologists are involved in environmental studies, and here, bacterial analysis scores over the AGPI.

Other than the fact that the presence of coliform bacteria indicates most directly recent faecal contamination, the other great advantage that bacterial analyses have over purely chemical techniques such as the BOD_5 and NH_3-N analyses (as used currently in Hong Kong by the Environmental Protection Department to prepare a stream water quality index) is that, by using FS as well as FC analyses, FC:FS ratios can be calculated and the incidence of various categories of this ratio can be used to indicate the nature of the pollution and its significance in terms of potential health risks. From Table 3 it can be seen that in the Lam Tsuen River, category 1 (human wastes) was the most frequent (45% overall) whereas in the Shing Mun Stream, category 3 (uncertain) was the largest and category 1 (human wastes) second largest at 29% overall. Thus, using bacterial analysis, the danger of human disease transmission is shown to be high in both water courses, a situation not revealed by either chemical or algal data.

References

American Public Health Association, 1976: Standard Methods for the Examination of Water and Wastewater. 14th Edition. – American Public Health Association Washington, D.C.: 1193 pp.

Department of the Environment, 1970: River Quality. – In: Report of a River Pollution Survey of England Wales. Vol. **1**:8–13. – H.M.S.O. London, U.K.

Environmental Protection Department, 1989: River Water Quality in Hong Kong, 1988: 61 pp. – Government Printer, Hong Kong.

European Economic Community Council, 1975: Council directive concerning the quality of bathing water (76/160/EEC). – *Official Journal of the European Community* **L31/**1:5:2:76, 1–7.

GELDREICH, E. E. & KENNER, B. A., 1969: Concepts of faecal streptococci in stream pollution. – *J. Water Poll. Contr. Fed.* **41**:336–352.

Government of Hong Kong, 1974: New Territories Stream Pollution Study: 26 pp, 13 appendices, 10 figures. – Government Printer, Hong Kong.

HODGKISS, I. J., 1979: The pollution of Hong Kong's coastal waters and seashore. – In: MORTON, B. S. (ed.): The Future of the Hong Kong Seashore: 151–173. – Oxford University Press.

– 1981: Stream pollution in Hong Kong – an appraisal. – *Environmental Conservation* **8**:119–124.

Hodgkiss, I. J. & Chan, B. S. S., 1983: Pollution studies on Tolo Harbour, Hong Kong. – *Marine Environmental Research* **10:** 1–44.

– – 1986: Studies on four streams entering Tolo Harbour, Hong Kong in relation to their impact on Marine water quality. – *Arch. Hydrobiol.* **108:** 185–212.

Hodgkiss, I. J. & Kan, H. W. P., 1978: A comparison of four biological indexes of pollution based on studies of streams in the New Territories, Hong Kong. – *Water Pollution Control* **77:** 532–538.

Hodgkiss, I. J. & Law, C. Y., 1985: Relating diatom community structure and stream water quality using species diversity indices. – *Water Pollution Control* **84:** 134–139.

James, A. & Evison, L., 1979: Biological Indicators of Water Quality: 626 pp. – Wiley Press Inc., New York.

Palmer, C. M., 1969: A composite rating of algae tolerating organic pollution. – *J. Phycology* **5:** 78–82.

Pipes, W. O., 1982: Bacterial Indicators of Pollution: 174 pp. – CRC Press Inc., Florida.

Round, F. E., 1991: Diatoms in river water: Monitoring studies. – *Appl. Phycol.* **3:** 129–145.

Solorzano, L., 1969: Determination of ammonia in natural waters by the phenol-hypochlorite method. – *Limnol. Oceanogr.* **14:** 799–801.

Washington, H. G., 1984: Diversity, biotic and similarity indices. A review with special relevance to aquatic ecosystems. – *Water Research* **18:** 653–944.

Wilhm, J. L. & Dorris, T. C., 1968: Biological parameters for water quality criteria. – *Bioscience* **18:** 477–481.

World Health Organization, 1967: Control of Water Pollution: 210 pp. – WHO, Geneva.

Author's address:

Department of Botany, The University of Hong Kong, Hong Kong.

Mitt. Internat. Verein. Limnol.	24	327–336	Stuttgart, Februar 1994

The effects of water quality, epilithic algae and organic matter on communities of stone-dwelling invertebrates in a Hong Kong river

She Sang Shea

Abstract

Samples of water, periphyton and benthic animals were collected over a 9-month period from two sites on the Lam Tsuen River, New Territories, Hong Kong, to assess the effects of water quality, epilithic algae and organic matter on the structure of stone-dwelling invertebrate communities. The study sites were approximately 2.5 km apart; the lower one received domestic and agricultural wastes while the upstream site was relatively unaffected by such wastes.

Temperature, pH, electrical conductivity and dissolved oxygen were similar at the two study sites. However, Biological Oxygen Demand (BOD_5), dissolved phosphates, epilithic organic matter and epilithic algal biomass were higher at the lower site. The quantities of epilithic organic matter and epilithic algal biomass at the lower site varied seasonally in relation to the monsoonal rains; values were low and constant in the wet season but increased up to 5-fold in the dry season. The abundance of stone-dwelling animals at the lower site was correlated positively with algae and organic matter, and peaked during the dry season. The species richness and diversity during the study period were lower at the downstream site compared with the upper stream site, although population densities at the downstream were five times higher on average than the upper stream site. This difference was especially obvious during the dry season. Faunal community structure (i.e. relative abundance of major taxonomic groups) also differed between the two sites, and Ephemeroptera and Trichoptera were relatively abundant upstream, whereas Chironomidae dominated the downstream site. This study demonstrates that the influence of organic enrichment on the stone-surface invertebrate community of a stream in the seasonal tropics parallels such effects in temperate regions.

Introduction

Hong Kong (22°7′N, 113°5′E) is situated some 320 kilometres south of the Tropic of Cancer on the southern coast of China and is one of the most densely-populated places in the world, with over 5.8 million people dwelling in an area of less than 1100 km^2. Inevitably such high population densities have had serious environmental effects. For example, a comprehensive survey in the early 1970s and another investigation conducted by the Environment Protection Department (Hong Kong Government) in the early 1980s revealed that about two-thirds of the 500 km of streams and rivers surveyed were grossly contaminated by livestock wastes, domestic sewage and industrial effluents (Ho 1991).

All of the larger rivers in Hong Kong are affected by the activities of man to a greater or lesser degree. Among the Territory's rivers, however, the Lam Tsuen River shows some of the original pattern of longitudinal zonation of fauna, albeit altered by the effects of organic wastes (Dudgeon 1983, 1984a, 1984b, 1990). Since Dudgeon's earlier studies on the benthic community of the river were completed, Hong Kong Government legislation has been introduced to control dumping of certain agricultural wastes into the river (1987). It was therefore of interest to determine, within the limited nature of the present study, whether this had led to an alteration of the longitudinal patterns of benthic community dynamics as described by Dudgeon (1984b). In that study, seasonal changes in community structure were noted at polluted sites, with species richness declining and standing stocks increasing as river discharge declined during the dry season.

The objective of this study was to evaluate the effects of water quality, epilithic algae and organic matter on the structure of the stone-dwelling invertebrate communities. Benthic invertebrates are used commonly in water-quality assessment programs; the distinct virtues that they offer in this role were outlined in Welch (1980). Here, epilithic invertebrates were the focus of attention because sampling benthic communities on individual rocks is regarded as an accurate and efficient method for descriptive and experimental research in stream ecology. Since epilithic data are less confounded by substrate heterogeneity or interstitial detritus, comparisons between habitats may be more easily interpreted (Clements 1987). In addition, epilithic communities are relatively easy to sample and usually include a large number of species thereby offering, potentially, a wide range of responses to pollution.

Study sites

The Lam Tsuen River, running from southwest to north east across the New Territories, Hong Kong, is a perma-

0538-4680/94/0024-0327 $ 2.50

nently-flowing river about 9 km in length, draining an area of approximately 20 km^2. The river arises to the southwest of Tai Po, on the slopes of Tai Mo Shan and flows through relatively undisturbed shrubland with a few hill farms. Intensive agriculture, including market gardening and chicken rearing, is undertaken in the valley.

The climate in Hong Kong is tropical with an obvious wet and dry season. Here the wet season refers to the months from April to September, while the dry season extends from October to March; approximately 80% of the annual rainfall in 1990 fell between May and September (ROHK 1989–1991).

Two study stations were chosen, designated the upper and lower sites. Sampling took place between April and December 1990 and encompassed the main periods of fluctuating discharge in Lam Tsuen River, as shown by seasonal changes in rainfall (Fig. 1). The lower site was between sites 3 and 4 of Dudgeon (1984a, 1984b), and the upper site was above site 3. Characteristics of the sample reaches measured in accordance with the definitions of Newbury (1984) are described in Table 1. The average current velocities and the substrate size distribution were similar at the two sampling sites although the average gradient of the upper site (including a small water fall) was greater than at the lower site. The lower site had a higher discharge due to water received from tributaries joining the river between two sites. Both sites were open riffles, and were not shaded by riparian vegetation.

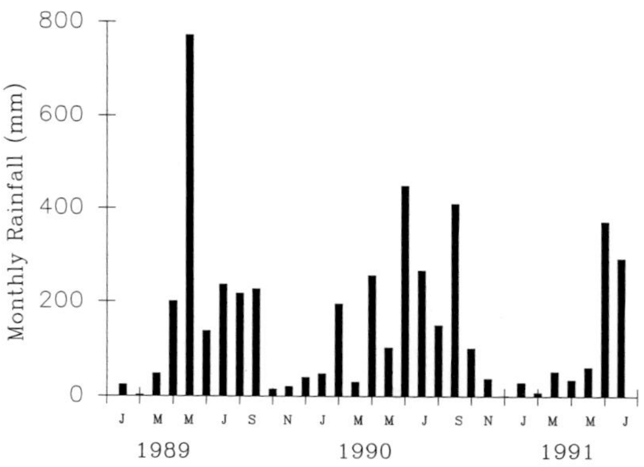

Fig. 1. Monthly rainfall (mm) in Hong Kong from January 1989 to July 1991. The data are derived from Royal Observatory reports (Hong Kong Government) (Rohk 1989, 1990, 1991).

The upper site was located at Pak Ngau Shek, about 7 km from the mouth of the river. The riparian vegetation comprised mainly grasses, herbs and creepers. *Microstegium ciliatum, Coix lachryma-jobi* (Poaceae) and *Boehmeria nivea* (Urticaceae) were abundant. The stream was 7 m in bankfull width, and the average water depth on 24 April 1991 was 3.6 cm (range 0.5–9.0 cm). The substrate comprised pebbles, cobbles and boulders ranging from 2.0–48.0 cm in diameter.

The lower site, located at San Uk Tsai, was 2.5 km downstream of the upper site and 4.5 km upstream of the river mouth. Again, the site was a shallow riffle (average depth 4.1 cm, range 0.5–14.0 cm) which was 13 m wide under bankfull conditions. The substrate was made up of pebbles, cobbles and boulders (3.0–35.0 cm diameter). When the discharge was low during the dry season, the stones were covered with a thick layer of organic debris, sewage 'fungus' (*Sphaerotilus*) and filamentous algae. The western bank was covered with secondary woodland, while the eastern side was farmland (market gardening). Aquatic hydrophytes were abundant along the river margins, especially *Commelina nudiflora* (Commelinaceae) and *Ludwigia adscendens* (Onagraceae). The tall grass *Coix lachryma-jobi* and the broad-leaved herb *Colocasia esculenta* (Araceae) were also common.

Materials and methods

Water analyses

Water samples were collected from both study sites at monthly intervals from April–December 1990. Dissolved oxygen was measured in the field using an oxygen

Table 1. Descriptions of the sample sites along Lam Tsuen River, Hong Kong. Measurements were made on 24 April 1991, and presented as mean value with the range in parentheses if more than one measurement (*n*) was taken.

Factor	Upper site	*n*	Lower site	*n*
Velocity (m/s)	0.46 (0.17–0.18)	13	0.35 (0.07–0.84)	13
Substrate (diameter in cm)	14.61 (2.0–48.0)	62	12.60 (3.0–35.0)	62
Gradient (m)	4.80%	1	3.60%	1
Discharge (m/s)	0.01	1	0.03	1
Water Depth (cm)	3.6 (0–9.0)	16	4.1 (0–14.0)	16

meter (YSI model 51B); 5-day biological oxygen demand (BOD_5) was from the difference between initial dissolved oxygen concentrations and those measured after five days incubation. Nitrate and phosphate were estimated by the nitrate electrode screening method (a pH meter PHM 62 Radiometer Copenhagen, combined with a NO_3 electrode probe) and stannous chloride method respectively (APHA 1985). A pH meter (PHM 83 Radiometer Copenhagen) was used for measuring pH values in the laboratory; conductivity was measured using a Schott Gerate Konduktometer CG 858 or a HI 8333 conductivity meter.

Sample collection and treatment

Epilithic invertebrate samples were collected by sampling individual stones using the method described by Macan (1958). Fifteen stones with the longest dimension (axial diameter) ranging from 7 to 20 cm were taken randomly without obvious preselection at both riffle sites each month from April to December 1990. A hand net (mesh size 150 µm) was held on the substrate immediately downstream of the rock. The rock was then lifted off the substrate and the net brought forward to enclose the rock. The net and rock were removed from the stream and taken to the bank. The rock, detached animals and debris were transferred to a polythene bag and preserved in 8 % neutral formalin. The algae and surface matter of the stones from riffle habitats were tightly attached to the stone, and there was no obvious loss of material during transportation from stream to laboratory. In the laboratory, the stone was put into a basin holding 1–2 l water; the epilithic animals were brushed off the stone and the stone was also washed carefully within the basin to make sure all animals were detached. The water containing animals and debris was strained through a 150 µm mesh sieve and preserved in 80 % ethanol. All invertebrates (and two benthic fishes which were closely associated with stream rocks) were sorted, counted and identified to the lowest practicable taxonomic unit (taxon). Letters and numbers were used to designate morphotypes within taxonomic units. Diptera larvae were identified to family or subfamily in most cases and to genus in a few instances. Nematoda, Oligochaeta and Hydracarina were not identified.

The biomass of epilithic algae was estimated by measuring the chlorophyll *a* content of samples. Before the stones were brushed to remove the fauna, five stones were taken out randomly from each site in order to collect subsamples of algae and organic matter. The upper surface of stone was identified by algal colour in the laboratory, as it was greener or darker then lower surface. An area of 4 × 4 cm was marked on the upper surface of the stone using a ruler and forceps. Then, with a small stiff brush, the epilithic algae and other organic matter were brushed off vigorously from this defined area to a petri dish using approx. 10 ml water. Animals in the dish were picked out under a dissecting microscope, then the algae and other adhering matter were filtered through a Whatman GF/F glass-fibre filter. Pigments of some algae are particularly resistant to extraction and, accordingly, the hot methanol method recommended by SCA (1986) for determining the chlorophyll *a* content of samples was followed. A phaeophytin correction was also made (SCA 1986). Assuming that chlorophyll *a* constitutes, on average, 1.5 % of the dry weight of organic matter of algae, the algal biomass on upper stone surface was estimated by multiplying the chlorophyll *a* content by a factor of 67 (APHA 1985).

In a similar manner to that employed for collecting algal samples, the organic matter (including algae) on the same stone surfaces was estimated by brushing off attached material from a known area of the upper surface and filtering the resulting material through a pre-ashed and weighed Whatman GF/F filter. A varied area of 2–16 cm² was defined according to amount of epilithic materials. The dry weight was obtained after drying the filter disk at 103–105 °C to constant weight, and the ash-free dry weight was determined after igniting the filter in a muffle furnace at 500–550 °C for 20 minutes (APHA 1985).

The linear regression equation of GRAHAM et al. (1988) was followed for estimating stone surface area.

$$\text{Surface Area} = K(xy + yz + zx)$$

where K is a coefficient constant and x, y, and z are the axial perimeters of stones. Considering that the shapes or the degree of erosion of stones in Hong Kong streams may differ from those studied by GRAHAM et al. (1988), a new coefficient (0.114) of the equation was obtained by regression analysis between known surface area and the axial perimeters from a representative sample of 20 stones. In the regression analysis, the dependent variable, the surface area of the stones, was derived from the conversion of the weight of aluminum foil used to wrap the stone. The independent variable was defined as the sum of products xy, yz and zx. The mean percentage error or areal estimation was 4.7 %. Epilithic invertebrate densities on each stone were expressed as the number of individuals per 100 cm².

Statistical procedures

MINITAB (1989) statistical software was employed for simple and multiple regression analysis, principal components analysis and calculation of confidence limits. The data for statistical analysis were log-transformed to meet the requirements of normality (ZAR 1984). Computation of Shannon-Wiener diversity indices and cluster and discriminate analysis of community data were undertaken using the software of LUDWIG & REYNOLDS (1988).

Cluster analysis is a technique that sorts sampling units (SUs) into groups or clusters based on their overall resemblance to one another. Similar SUs will form clusters distinct from other clusters of SUs. The results of cluster analysis can be conveniently summarized in a dendrogram, which displays the similarity of the samples in a tree-like structure. In this study, quantitative data from the monthly epilithic-faunal samples were treated as SUs. The same SUs were subjected to principal components analysis (PCA). PCA is a multivariate eigenanalysis method that produces an SU ordination by extracting axes of maximum variation from a species or SU resemblance matrix. The results of PCA applied to the sample units of the current study were illustrated, as in most ordination procedures, by way of reduced dimensional, two-axis ordinations, to expose community patterns. Finally, discriminant analysis was used in order to search for and describe important underlying environmental factors that might be responsible for determining the structure of observed community patterns at the two study sites. This method is a powerful procedure for examining many factors simultaneously in order to define community differences (LUDWIG & REYNOLDS 1988).

Results

Temperature, pH, conductivity and dissolved oxygen showed only minor differences between the two sites, while BOD_5 and phosphate loads were (respectively) approximately two and three times greater downstream (Table 2). Nitrate concentrations were higher at the upstream site, but allowing for utilization by algae downstream, and the fact that ammonia and nitrites were not measured, total nitrogen loads may have been greater at the downstream site. The mean value of phosphate (0.17 mg/l) in 1990 was eight to nine times lower than those of adjacent station 3 (1.35 mg/l) and 4 (1.50 mg/l) in 1978 (DUDGEON 1984a, 1984b) and three times lower than that in 1976 at station 3 (0.50 mg/l).

The monthly averages (mean ± 95% confidence limits) of epilithic algal biomass and the epilithic organic matter were similar at both sites in the wet season, but were greater during the dry season at the lower site (Fig. 2). The epilithic invertebrate community at the two sites differed with respect to species richness, diversity and overall density (Fig. 3). Mean species richness and the Shannon-Wiener diversity index were higher at the upstream site than at the downstream site. By contrast, the lower site supported higher faunal densities. The epilithic community structure at the two study sites in the Lam Tsuen River is presented according to species and major taxa in Tables 3 and 4: a total of 72 taxa were recorded; 61 at the upstream site and 38 at the downstream site. Both sites were dominated numerically by Diptera and Ephemeroptera, but were obviously different in terms of species composition. The upper site had more aquatic insect species (52 taxa) than the lower site (23 taxa). Among Plecoptera, Coleoptera, Hemiptera and Trichoptera, 41 morphospecies occurred at the upper site, but only 12 at the lower site. However Chironomidae larvae were eight times more abundant downstream than at the upper site.

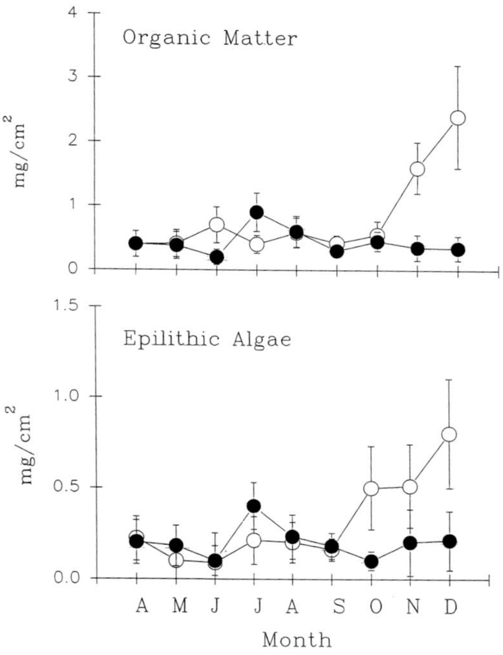

Fig. 2. A comparison of organic matter on stone-surfaces and epilithic algae (mean ± 95% confidence limits, mg/cm²) at two study sites on the Lam Tsuen River. Monthly samples were taken from April to December 1990. (Filled circle: upstream site; empty circle: downstream site).

Table 2. Mean values (with range in parentheses) of environmental variables measured along two study sites in the Lam Tsuen River. Monthly samples were taken from April to December 1990 ($n=9$). Temp., temperature (°C); Cond., conductivity (µmh/cm); DO, dissolved oxygen (mg/l); BOD_5, 5-day biological oxygen demand; NO_3, nitrate (mg/l); PO_4, dissolved phosphate (mg/l).

	Upstream Site		Downstream Site	
Temp.	22.9	(13.0–28.0)	21.0	(10.6–29.0)
pH	6.89	(6.4–7.4)	6.72	(6.02–7.40)
Cond.	70.6	(53.0–80.0)	76.3	(50.0–109.0)
DO	8.0	(7.4–9.5)	7.3	(5.0–9.2)
BOD_5	1.1	(0.3–2.6)	2.3	(0.8–5.7)
NO_3	0.44	(0.16–1.86)	0.13	(0.02–0.34)
PO_4	0.051	(0.003–0.07)	0.166	(0.004–0.65)

Table 3. Community composition and abundance of epilithic macrobenthos (mean count with 95% confidence limits in parentheses) at two sites along the Lam Tsuen River, Hong Kong. Monthly samples ($n = 15 \times 19$ months) were taken from upper (right column) and lower (left column) sites from April to December 1990. (Absence of 95% C.L.s indicates the values were <0.22).

TURBELLARIA		
Dugesia	0.1	1.0 (0, 1.8)
NEMATODA	0.4 (0, 1)	4.7 (0, 4.3)
GASTROPODA		
Brotia hainanensis	88.5 (54.5, 132.8)	0.1
Melanoides tuberculata	0	0.2 (0, 0.8)
Sinotaia quadrata	0	6.4 (3.7, 8.0)
Pomacea lineata	0	0.3 (0, 1.0)
Hippeutis cantonensis	0	0.1
Radix sp.	0	6.4 (0, 8.2)
Corbicula fluminea	0.1	0.1
Ferrissia sp.	0	27.5 (1.9, 47.2)
OLIGOCHAETA	0.3 (0, 0.8)	48 (0, 33.1)
HIRUDINEA		
Helobdella stagnalis	0	5.2 (0, 9.2)
Glossiphonia weberi	0	3.4 (0, 3.8)
Barbronia weberi	0	0.2
HYDRACARINA	3.3 (0, 8.5)	1.6 (0, 2.8)
CRUSTACEA		
Cryptopotamon anacoluthon	0.2 (0, 0.8)	0
EPHEMEROPTERA		
Ephemera sp.	0.2	0
Paegniodes cupulatus	0.1	0
Cinygmina sp.	1.2 (0, 2.5)	0
Electrogena	7.1 (1.7, 13.1)	0
Epeorus T1	2 (0, 5.3)	0
Epeorus T2	9.77 (2.5, 21)	0
Pseudocloeon TD	26.3 (23.5, 40.7)	0
Pseudocloeon L3	55.8 (2.8, 127.4)	268.0 (21.0, 637)
Baetis spp.	93.4 (56.9, 143.8)	848.0 (44.0, 1463.0)
Chopralla sp.	0.3 (0, 0.8)	1.9
Indobaetis sp.	1.9 (0, 3)	0
Baetiella sp.	0.1	0
Choroterpes spp.	13.3 (0.2, 22.4)	0.1
Habrophlebiodes gilliesi	0.2	0
Isca purpurea	14.7 (5.6, 21.3)	0.1
Serratella T2	3.7 (1, 7)	0
Caenis spp.	2.9 (0, 3.8)	3.2 (0, 6.5)
ODONATA		
Euphaea decorata	0.8 (0, 2)	0
Zygonyx iris	2.9 (0, 5)	2 (0, 2.8)

PLECOPTERA		
Perlidae indet.	0.7 (0, 1.8)	0
HEMIPTERA		
Heterotrephes sp.	0.1	0
MEGALOPTERA		
Neochauliodes sp.	0.7 (0, 1)	0.1
LEPIDOPTERA		
Aulocodes sp.	38.7 (26.7, 52.2)	8.1 (0, 17.4)
TRICHOPTERA		
Rhyancophila sp.	0.22 (0, 0.8)	0
Ecnomus sp.	0.1	0
Hydroptila triangularis	0.1	6.2 (0.2, 13)
Macrostemum spp.	1.1 (0, 1.8)	0.1
Chimarra T1	1.7 (0, 3.5)	0
Agapetus spp.	4.3 (1.3, 7.5)	0.1
Hydropsyche Tz	0.8 (0, 2.5)	0
Hydropsyche Ly	0.2	0
Hydropsyche Tv	0.3 (0, 0.8)	0
Cheumatopsyche spp.	18.3 (8, 29.3)	0
Pseudoneureclipsis spp.	1.1 (0, 2.5)	0
Psychomyia sp.	32.3 (0.5, 60.0)	0
Melanotrichia serica	5.4 (0.5, 8.6)	0.1
DIPTERA		
Empididae	4.1 (1.0, 7.0)	0.9 (0, 1.8)
Orthocladiinae	187.0 (125.9, 238.0)	1181.0 (759.0, 1547.0)
Chironominae	261.0 (221.0, 332.0)	2880.0 (1033.0, 4213.0)
Corynoneura spp.	7.8 (1.2, 11.0)	19.0 (3.0, 46.3)
Tanypodinae	25.0 (2.2, 42.6)	66.2 (31.0, 121.5)
Simulium spp.	6.7 (1.0, 11.5)	11.7 (0, 19.5)
Tipulidae	3.9 (0, 6.0)	0
Ceratopogonidae #1	0	0.7 (0, 1.5)
Ceratopogonidae #2	0	0.2
COLEOPTERA		
Psephenoides sp.	34.3 (19, 58.3)	0.9 (0, 2)
Mateopsephus sp.	3.1 (1.0, 5.0)	0
Elmidae larva #3	22.1 (0.7, 21.4)	0
Elmidae larva #6	0.3 (0, 1.0)	0.1
Elmidae larva #4	0.4 (0, 1.5)	0
Elmidae adult s1	0.4 (0, 1.0)	0
Hydrophilidae #1	0.3 (0, 0.8)	0
Hydrophilidae #2	0.4 (0, 1.0)	0
Eulichas sp.	0.1	0
PISCES		
Pseudogastromyzon myersi		0.3 (0, 1.0)0
Ctenogobius duospilus	0.22 (0, 0.8)	0

Gastropoda and Hirudinea were more species-rich at the lower site where oligochaetes were also relatively more abundant. The gastropods at the upper site were dominated by a single species, *Brotia hainanensis*, which is widely distributed in unpolluted stony streams and the upper courses of rivers in Hong Kong (DUDGEON 1989). Other gastropod species, i.e. *Sinotaia quadrata, Radix* sp. and *Ferrissia* sp. were abundant at the downstream site where *Brotia hainanensis* was very scarce.

The results presented above show that the community structure of invertebrates at the two study sites were different. To what extent were these faunal differences related to the different environ-

Table 4. Relative abundance of the major taxa of epilithic fauna in the Lam Tsuen River.

	Upstream Site			Downstream Site	
	n	%		*n*	%
Diptera	4,461	49.8	Diptera	37,463	77.0
Ephemeroptera	2,099	23.4	Ephemeroptera	10,106	20.8
Gastropoda	798	8.9	Oligochaeta	430	0.9
Trichoptera	595	6.7	Gastropoda	372	0.8
Coleoptera	555	6.2	Hirudinea	80	0.2
Lepidoptera	349	3.9	Other taxa combined	–	0.3
Trichoptera	59	0.1			
Other taxa combined	–	1.0			
Total	8,948	100		48,678	100

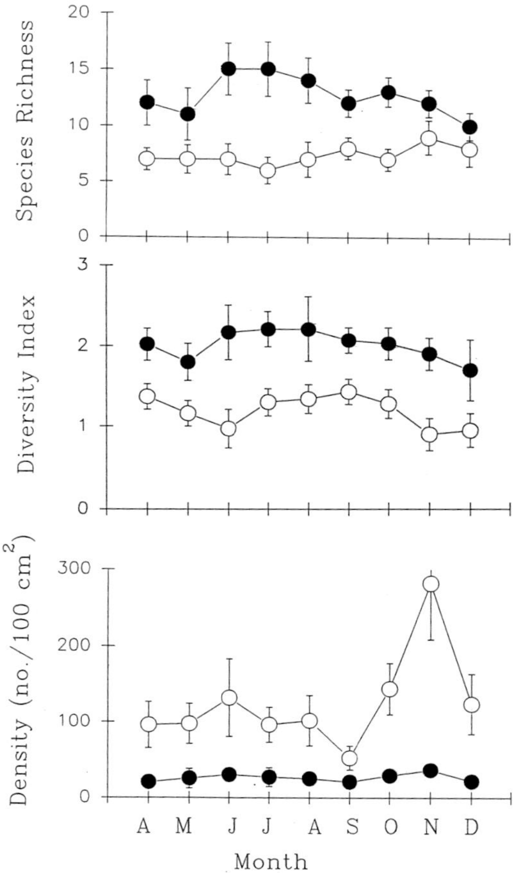

Fig. 3. A comparison of epilithic faunal communities between two study sites on the Lam Tsuen River, Hong Kong. Fifteen samples were taken from each site at each month from April to December 1990. The error bars are 95% confidence limits. (Filled circle: upstream site; empty circle: downstream site).

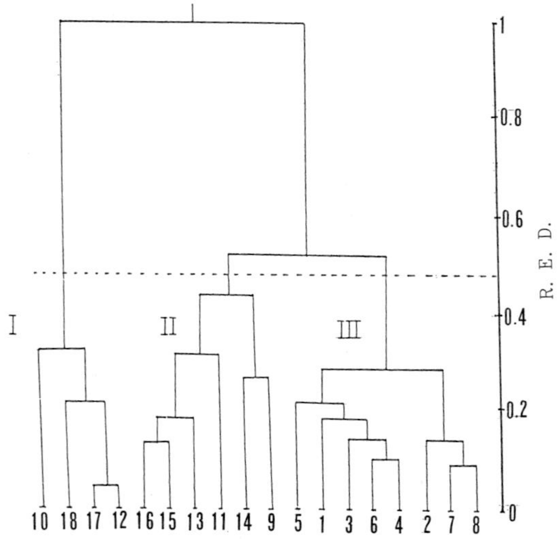

Fig. 4. Dendrogram for cluster analysis of 18 sample units (monthly samples) from two study sites along Lam Tsuen River, Hong Kong, using RED (Relative Euclidian Distance). The horizontal line shows the arbitrary division line for defining clusters I, II and III. SUs 1–9 were assigned to the nine individual months of samples from the upstream site (April to December 1990), SUs 10–18 to the samples from the downstream site over the same period.

mental factors? Cluster analysis (Fig. 4) shows that the samples taken on each month from the two sites can be divided into three clusters: sample units 10, 12, 17 and 18 from the lower site were grouped in cluster I; sample units 11, 13, 14, 15, 16 from the lower site and sample 9 from upstream belong to cluster II; and sample units 1 to 8 from the upper site belong to cluster III. This indicates clearly that the monthly samples from upstream

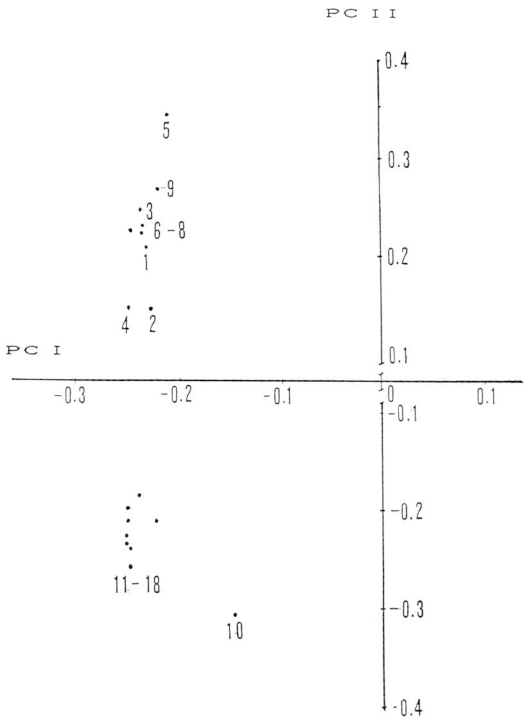

Fig. 5. Principal components ordination of 18 sampling units from two sites along Lam Tsuen River, Hong Kong. SUs 1–9 were assigned to the 9 individual months of samples from the upstream site (April to December 1990), SUs 10–18 to the samples from the downstream site over the same period.

Table 5. Discriminant analysis of epilithic faunal communities based on environmental factors. The percentage values for each environmental factor were the relative contribution made to the total multivariate distances between clusters. Three clusters were coded with I, II and III. Cluster I included four sampling units (SU): 10, 12, 17, 18; Cluster II included six SU: 9, 11, 13–16; Cluster III included eight SU: 1–8. Note that SU 1–9 were assigned to the 9 individual months of samples from the upstream site (April to December 1990), SU 10–18 to the samples from the downstream site over the same period.

Environmental Factor	Percentage Contribution		
	I & II	I & III	II & III
Phosphate	7.7	17.5	95.1
Organic Matter	98.9	106.4	2.5
Epilithic Algae	−6.6	−23.9	2.4
Total	100.0	100.0	100.0

were more similar to each other than they were to those from the lower site and vice versa. PCA showed that the sample units from upper and lower sites were well separated (Fig. 5). Discriminant analysis was carried out by relating the three clusters of the sample units to three environmental factors: phosphate, epilithic organic matter and epilithic algae. The analysis demonstrated that organic matter was the most important factor distinguishing cluster I from II, as well as I from III, while phosphate was more important for distinguishing cluster II from III (Table 5).

Discussion

Sampling individual stones with a hand net as used in this study appears to be one of the most appropriate methods for the quantitative collection of rock fauna. Surber, kick, suction and grab samples all severely disturb a wide area of substrate, leading to the collection of animals not associated with the rock community (Doeg & Lake 1981). Although improved sampling methodologies (e.g. Doeg & Lake 1981) may collect the epilithic fauna more efficiently than the method used herein, contamination from surrounding substrates within the sampler is hard to quantify and control. The technique of lifting stones upstream of a hand net is simple and convenient to use, and may be suitable for stream riffle habitats in all latitudes.

The greater amounts of phosphates and organic matter at the lower site in Lam Tsuen River were probably due to pollution arising from farmland runoff and unsewered residential discharge in the middle course of the river. High nutrient levels would have favoured the growth of algae, hence the relatively higher algal biomass at the lower site. The lower nitrate levels downstream could have been due to utilization by algae. The higher algal biomass during the dry season reflected phosphate enrichment and the reduced flooding disturbance. Phosphate levels are naturally low in unpolluted streams in Hong Kong, such as the upper Lam Tsuen River and Tai Po Kau Forest Stream, where the concentrations are generally less than 0.03 mg/l (Dudgeon 1990); at these low concentrations epilithic algal growth may be limited (see also Caqblancq 1990). Significantly, nutrient experiments conducted on freshwater benthic algae using in situ substrata, revealed that phosphorus-releasing substrata increased the chlorophyll content and biovolume of standing stocks of the attached algal microflora (Carrick & Lowe 1989).

Table 6. Comparison of invertebrate community composition in Lam Tsuen River between the present study and that in 1978 at the downstream study site. The data from 1978 were derived from collections at sampling stations 3 and 4 of Dudgeon (1981, 1984). (+: present; —: absent; R: rare; C: common; nematodes, oligochaetes and Hydracarina were not included.)

	1978	1990
TURBELLARIA		
Dugesia	—	R
GASTROPODA		
Brotia hainanensis	—	R
Melanoides tuberculata	+	R
Sinotaia quadrata	+	C
Pomacea lineata	—	C
Hippeutis cantonensis	+	R
Radix sp.	+	C
Corbicula fluminea	+	C
Ferrissia sp.	—	C
Physella acuta	+	—
HIRUDINEA		
Helobdella stagnalis	—	C
Glossiphonia weberi	+	C
Barbronia weberi	+	C
CRUSTACEA		
Cypridae	+	C
Potamidae	+	—
EPHEMEROPTERA		
Cinygmina sp.	+	—
Pseudocloeon L3	+	C
Baetis spp.	+	C
Chopralla sp.	—	R
Choroterpes sp.	+	R
Isca purpurea	+	R
Caenis spp.	+	C
ODONATA		
Zygonyx iris	+	C
Onychogomphus sp.	+	—
NEUROPTERA		
Neochauliodes sp.	+	R
LEPIDOPTERA		
Aulocodes sp.	—	C
TRICHOPTERA		
Hydroptila triangularis	—	C
Macrostemum spp.	—	R
Agapetus spp.	—	R
Hydropsyche spp.	+	—
Cheumatopsyche sp.	+	—
Melanotrichia sp.	—	R

Table 6. (Continued).

	1978	1990
DIPTERA		
Empididae	—	C
Orthocladiinae	+	C
Chironomidae	+	C
Tanypodinae	+	C
Simulium spp.	+	C
Ceratopogonidae #1	—	R
Ceratopogonidae #2	—	R
COLEOPTERA		
Psephenoides sp.	—	R
Elmidae genus indet.	+	—
Elmidae larva #6	—	R

Organic enrichment in streams generally results in a reduction in the number of aquatic insect species (Hynes 1960). However, since some species benefit from the increased supply of food and reduced competition, the total number of animals may increase. This pattern was apparent at the lower site in Lam Tsuen River where the organic enrichment resulted in fewer insect species but a higher density of organisms. The highest recorded density on an individual stone sample was 2188/100 cm^2 at the lower site in January 1991 and occurred at a time when filamentous algae flourished on the stony substrate. The highest density of organisms recorded at the upper site was 382/100 cm^2, nearly six times less than at the organically enriched lower site. As a result of the rich supply of food, gastropods, including *Sinotaia quadrata* (Viviparidae) and the exotic prosobranch *Pomacea lineata* (Ampullariidae), were abundant at the lower site. Because of their large size, both species made up a high proportion of the benthic standing stock, although *P. lineata* did not appear frequently on stones in fast currents.

The Shannon-Wiener index is one of the most widely used diversity indices for pollution surveillance (Abel 1989). Application of this index to pollution assessment (e.g. Cook 1976, Bryce et al. 1978, Pinder & Farr 1987, Metcalfe 1989) is based on the well-documented observation that unpolluted waters generally support a diverse fauna, compared with, at the other extreme, grossly-polluted waters which tend to support a species-restricted community of abundant individuals. In the present study, the mean diversity value of the organically enriched site (1.18) was lower than that of the upstream unpolluted site (2.01).

This is in general agreement with the results of other investigations of organic pollution (e.g. COOK, 1976, BRYCE et al. 1978, WELCH 1980, WIEDERHOLM 1984).

During the dry season, thick organic material deposition, and sewage 'fungus' indicated serious pollution of the lower site despite the controls on animal wastes discharge imposed by the Hong Kong Government. In this situation, only a few taxa – such as chironomids, oligochaetes and leeches – were abundant, while other intolerant species such as *Electrogena, Epeorus* (Heptageniidae) and *Choroterpes* (Leptophlebiidae) were absent at the downstream site. Table 6 showed the comparison of invertebrate community composition between the present study and those of 1978 at the downstream site in Lam Tsuen River. Most of the common species (70 %) recorded at the downstream site in 1990 occurred at the adjacent sampling sites (station 3 and 4) in 1978. However, a more detailed comparison is precluded because of the different sampling methods used in the two studies.

In essence, this study showed that the seasonal and longitudinal patterns of benthic community dynamics were similar to that described by DUDGEON (1984 a, 1984 b), notwithstanding control of some livestock waste discharge. Although some phosphate concentrations in the river were reduced somewhat, it is likely that the situation as it now stands will persist until complete control of livestock – especially fowl – wastes are imposed.

There are some drawbacks which need to be mentioned with regard to this study. One of the difficulties was establishment of adequate control sites. The ideal control sites should be selected from similar habitats along different streams with similar gradients, hydrological characteristics, riparian vegetation and so on. However, there are no unpolluted rivers similar to the Lam Tsuen River in Hong Kong. The most practical way to choose a comparable site in this case is to use an unimpacted upstream site as a control site for an organically enriched downstream site. But this design is pseudoreplicated (HURLBERT 1984), and thus inferential statistics cannot be applied in data analysis. Another problem is that there was no temporal control, i.e. pre-disturbance data. This problem is commonly encountered in environmental impact assessments, but is rarely addressed specifically. The matter is discussed in greater depth by HUMPHREY & DOSTINE (1994).

Multivariate analyses techniques were used in this study to determine and assess whether or not the communities of the two sites differ and possible causes of these differences. As descriptive tools, cluster analysis and PCA certainly showed that the two sites differed (Figs. 4 and 5). Recent studies (e.g. FAITH et al. 1987, LUDWIG & REYNOLDS 1988) pointed to the weaknesses of ordination techniques, such as PCA, that utilize a Euclidean model as the dissimilarity measure. Such a model assumes a linear relationship with ecological distance, while FAITH et al. (1987) have shown relatively low linear correlations of Euclidean distance with the ecological distance. In the present study, discriminate analysis indicated that organic enrichment was the possible cause of differences in faunal community structure at the two study sites. While it is not possible to infer too much from this result given the weaknesses of the study design, the chemical data and the early studies of DUDGEON (1981, 1984 b) give credence to this conclusion.

Acknowledgements

I would like to thank Dr. DAVID DUDGEON for assistance with faunal identification, manuscript correction and support in various ways. Thanks are also extended to Kadoorie Agricultural Research Centre, the University of Hong Kong, for providing facilities for water analysis. Dr. CHRISTOPHER HUMPHREY is thanked specially for his valuable suggestions and comments on this paper.

References

ABEL, P. D., 1989: Water Pollution Biology: 231 pp. – Ellis Horwood Limited, England.

American Public Health Association (1985) Standard Methods for the Examination of Water and Wastewater. 16th Edition: pp. 1134. – APHA, Washington D.C.

BRYCE, D., CAFFOOR, I. M., DALE, C. R. & JARRETT, A. F., 1978: Macro-invertebrate and the bioassay of water quality: a report based on a survey of the River Lee: 44 pp. – Nelpress, North East London Polytechnic.

CAQBLANCQ, J., 1990: Nutrient dynamics and pelagic food web interactions in oligotrophic and eutrophic environments: and overview. – *Hydrobiologia* **207**: 1–14.

CARRICK, H. J. & LOWE, R. L., 1989: Benthic algal response to N and P enrichment along a pH gradient. – *Hydrobiologia* **179**: 119–127.

CLEMENTS, W. H., 1987: The effect of rock surface area on distribution and abundance of stream insects. – *J. Freshwat. Ecol.* **4**: 83–91.

COOK, S. E. K., 1976: Quest for an index of community structure sensitive to water pollution. – *Environ. Pollution* **11**: 269–288.

Doeg, T. & Lake, P. S., 1981: A technique for assessing the composition and density of the macroinvertebrate fauna of large stones in streams. – *Hydrobiologia* **80**: 3–6.

Dudgeon, D., 1981: Aspects of the ecology of the macrobenthos of three freshwater habitats in Hong Kong: 1617 pp. – Unpublished Ph.D. Thesis, The University of Hong Kong.

– Spatial and temporal changes in the distribution of gastropods in the Lam Tsuen River, New Territories, Hong Kong, with notes on the occurrence of the exotic snail, *Biomphalaria straminea*. – *Malacol. Rev.* **16**: 91–92.

– 1984 a: Seasonal and long-term changes in the hydrobiology of the Lam Tsuen River, New Territories, Hong Kong, with special reference to benthic macroinvertebrate distribution and abundance. – *Arch. Hydrobiol., Suppl.* **69** (*Mon. Beitr.*) 55–129.

– 1984 b: Longitudinal and temporal changes in functional organization of macroinvertebrate communities in the Lam Tsuen River, Hong Kong. – *Hydrobiologia* **111:** 207–217.

– 1989: Ecological strategies of Hong Kong Thiaridae (Gastropoda: Prosobranchia). – *Malacol. Rev.* **22**: 39–53.

– 1990: Determinants of the distribution and abundance of larval Ephemeroptera (Insecta) in Hong Kong running waters. – In: Campbell, I. C. (ed): Mayflies and Stonesflies: 221–232. – Kluwer Academic Publishers, Dordrecht.

Faith, D. P., Minchin, P. R. & Belbin, L., 1987: Compositional dissimilarity as a robust measure of ecological distance. – *Vegetatio* **69**: 57–68.

Graham, A. A., McCaughan, D. J. & McKee, F. S., 1988: Measurement of surface area of stones. – *Hydrobiologia* **157**: 85–87.

Ho, K. C., 1991: Water quality in the priority watercourses of Hong Kong in respect of various environmental control measures. – *Water Sci. Tech.* **23**: 85–91.

Humphrey, C. L. & Dostine, P. L., 1994: Development of biological monitoring programs to detect mining-waste impacts upon aquatic ecosystems in the Alligator Rivers Region, Northern Territory, Australia. – *Mitt. Internat. Verein. Limnol.* **24**: 293–314.

Hurlbert, S. H., 1984: Pseudoreplication and the design of ecological field experiments. – *Ecol. Monogr.* **54**: 187–211.

Hynes, H. B. N., 1960: *The Biology of Polluted Waters*. 202 pp. – Liverpool University Press, Liverpool University Press, Liverpool.

Ludwig J. A. & Reynolds, J. F., 1988: Statistic Ecology: A Primer on Methods and Computing: 337 pp. – Wiley, New York.

Macan, T. T., 1958: Methods of sampling the bottom fauna in stony streams. – *Mitt. Internat. Verein. Limnol.* **8**: 1–21.

Metcalfe, J. L., 1989: Biological water quality assessment of running waters based on macroinvertebrate communities: History and present status in Europe. – *Environmental Pollution* **60**: 101–139.

Minitab, 1989: Minitab Statistical Software Release 7. – Minitab Inc., USA.

Newbury, R. W., 1984: Hydrological determinants of aquatic insect habitats. – In: Resh, V. H. & Rosenberg, D. M. (eds.): The Ecology of Aquatic Insects: 323–357. – Praeger Publishers, New York.

Pinder, L. C. V. & Farr, I. S., 1987: Biological surveillance of water quality – 3. The influence of organic enrichment on the macroinvertebrate fauna of small chalk streams. – *Arch. Hydrobiol.* **109**: 619–637.

ROHK (1989–1991): Monthly Weather Summary. – Royal Observatory of Hong Kong, Hong Kong.

SCA (Standing Committee or Analysts), 1986: The determination of chlorophyll *a* in aquatic environments. In: Methods for the Examination of Water and Associated Materials, Vol. 4: Section 2 – 5–25 – HMSO, London.

Welch, E. B., 1980: Ecological Effects of Waste Water: 337 pp. – Cambridge University Press, Cambridge.

Wiederholm, T., 1984: Responses of aquatic insects to environmental pollution. – In: Resh, V. H. & Rosenberg, D. M. (eds.): The Ecology of Aquatic Insects: 508–557. – Praeger Publishers, New York.

Zar, J. H., 1984: *Biostatistical Analysis*. 2nd Edition: 718 pp. – Prentice-Hall International, Inc., New Jersey.

Author's address:

Department of Zoology, Hui Oi Chow Science Building, The University of Hong Kong, Pokfulam Road, Hong Kong.

Mitt. Internat. Verein. Limnol.	24	337–344	Stuttgart, Februar 1994

An analysis of dynamic stability in two inland lakes of northern Australia

Kevin Boland and Jorg Imberger

Abstract

Lake Number, a recent innovation in the assessment of vertical turbulence transport in lakes, is introduced and described. Application of Lake Number in Lake Moondarra and Lake Julius, two shallow, arid-zone tropical impoundments of north Australia, showed that there was a direct relationship between Lake Number and dissolved oxygen levels in the surface regions of the reservoirs. The relationship was inverse in deep regions of the lake. Mechanisms governing dissolved oxygen levels in the lakes have been clarified, in particular the role of turbidity in the oxygen dynamics of each system. The large volume of deeper anoxic water in both lakes was shown to cause depletion of oxygen in the surface waters as Lake Number decreased. However, dissolved oxygen levels in deeper waters rose as turbulence transport increased.

Introduction

The vast majority of limnological research has been conducted in northern, temperate and sub-temperate climes. While this work has been productive and forms the corner-stone of modern limnology, some authors, notably WILLIAMS (1988), question the relevance of much of this work to tropical and sub-tropical regions. One objective of a considerable amount of limnological research has been the examination of mixing regimes in order to classify lakes into particular categories such as those defined by HUTCHINSON & LOFFLER (1956). However, these categories are inappropriate for some tropical systems (TOWNSEND & BOLAND 1987). The basis of traditional classification has been the specification of various types of mixing regimes used to describe the physical changes in the water profile. For example, FINLAYSON et al. (1980) uses the term 'warm polymictic' to characterize one tropical Australian lake. This classification is derived by examination of temperature isopleths and several water column stability statistics calculated according to RUTTNER (1963). However, destabilizing factors are not quantified, and therefore the relevance of particular stability values cannot be established.

Stability calculations and mixing classifications in lakes have frequently been used in conjunction with discussion on associated water-quality effects of stratification, often with particular reference to variations in dissolved oxygen levels through the water column. The stability values calculated represent the work required to mix the water column to a uniform density and are based on the work of various authors (e.g. SCHMIDT 1928, HUTCHINSON 1957, RUTTNER 1963, IDSO 1973). While these calculations may be of some value, none of them take account of destabilizing factors which may be acting simultaneously to mix the lake under scrutiny. Thus while a tropical lake may (due to high summer radiation levels) exhibit a significant level of stability at a particular time, this may be less relevant than (for example) the fact that the elevated temperatures are associated with storm activity. Storms may generate winds which exert significant shear force on the surface of the lake. Conversely, even with quite low stability values, a lake may undergo little mixing if wind velocities and other destabilizing factors are low.

A recent innovation in the assessment of lake stability is Lake Number, a dimensionless index which takes account of the driving forces acting to counter stability. Developed and discussed by IMBERGER & PATTERSON (1990), Lake Number may be defind as the ratio, about a lake's centre of volume, of the moment of the stabilizing force due to gravity to the moment of the destabilizing forces due to wind. Lake Number $\ll 1$ implies that stratification is weak in relation to wind stress and that there is a high potential for vertical turbulence transport. Lake Number $\gg 1$ indicates that a lake is not susceptible to vertical mixis. This could be a result of strong thermal (hence density) stratification and relatively low wind energy, but may also be due to relatively minor stratification combined with a virtual absence of wind. Thus, Lake Number is a measure of a lake's susceptibility to mixing rather than simply a measure of its internal gravimetric stability. Regular measurement of Lake Number will give an indication of the dynamic stability of a water body.

ROBERTSON et al. (1990) examined two North Australian monsoonal region reservoirs to demonstrate the relationship between changes in Lake Number and fluctuations in water quality parameters. In this paper, Lake Number in Lake Moondarra and Lake Julius, two shallow, arid zone reservoirs in North-western Queensland, is examined over the period October 1989 to December 1990. The relationship between Lake Number, dissolved oxygen levels at the water supply offtake point in each lake, and the role of turbidity in the oxygen dynamics of each system is described.

0538-4680/94/0024-0337 $ 2.00

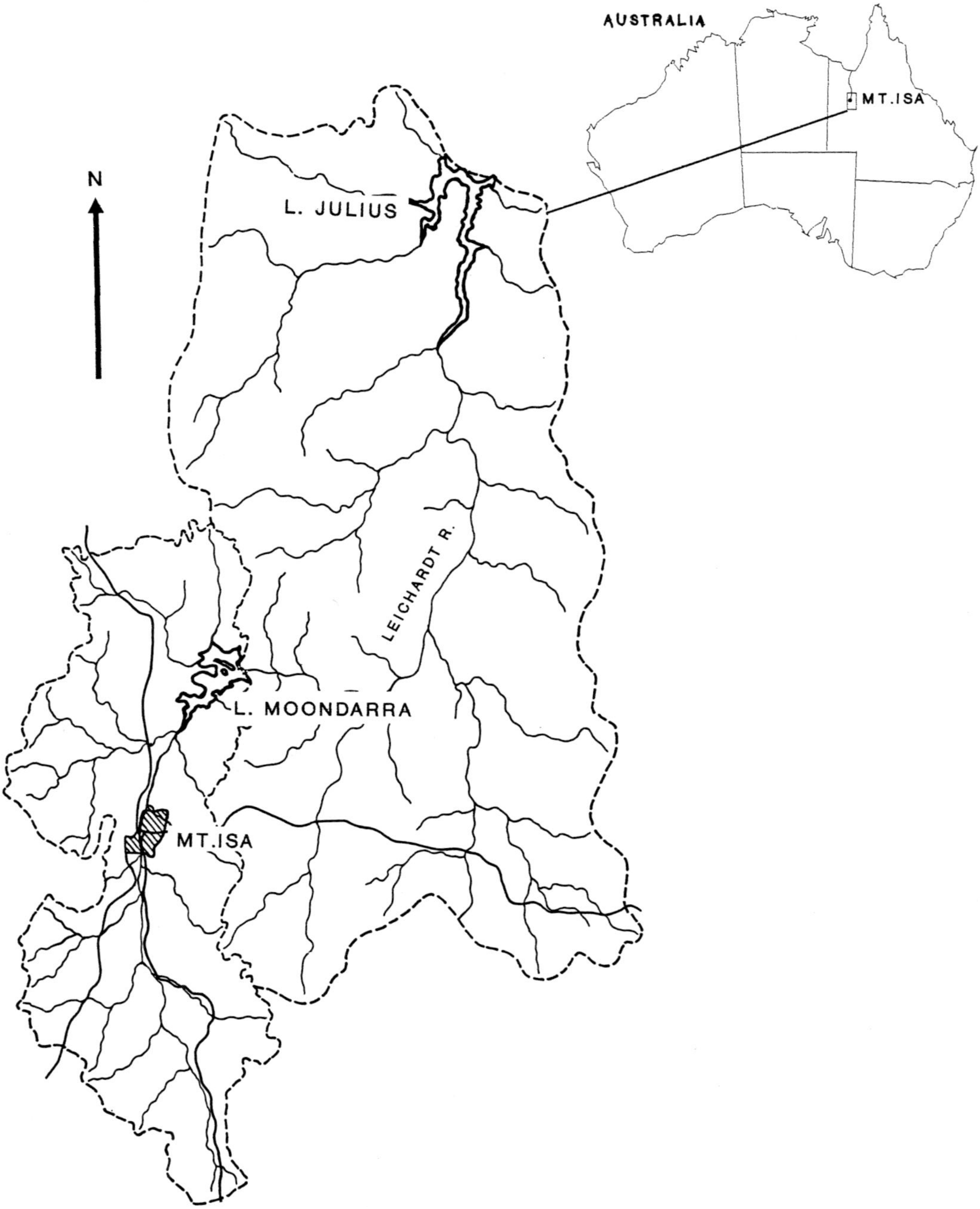

Fig. 1. Location map: Lakes Moondarra and Julius (dotted line indicates the catchment of each reservoir).

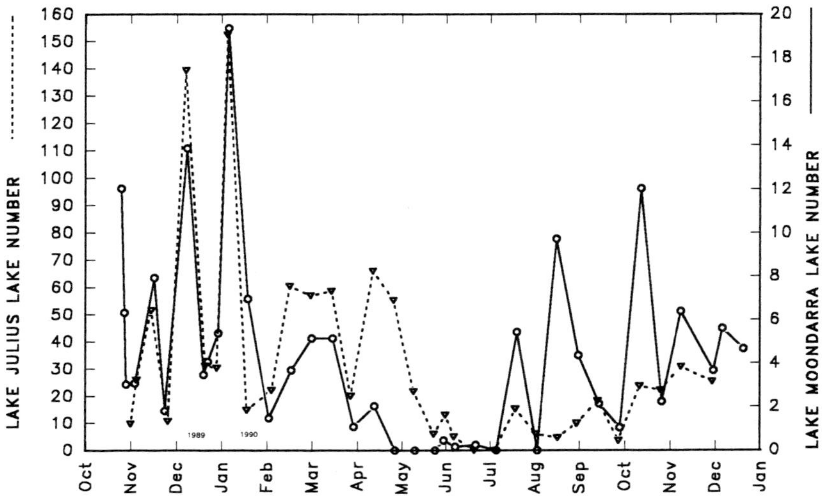

Fig. 2. Lake Moondarra and Lake Julius: Lake Numbers.

Study sites

Lake Moondarra and Lake Julius are man-made impoundments located in North-west Queensland in Australia's arid tropics. Lake Moondarra (20°35′S, 139°34′E) lies 19 kilometres north of the mining town of Mt. Isa (population 25,000), while Lake Julius (20°08′S, 139°43.5′E) lies a further 60 kilometres north. Both reservoirs are located on the Leichardt River (Fig. 1), which passes through Mt. Isa (located upstream of the reservoirs), and provide domestic and industrial water supply sources to the town. Lake Moondarra is essentially a eutrophic water body as a result of enrichment associated with urban run-off from Mt. Isa. This results in periodic infestations of various macrophytic plants (Finlayson et al. 1984). Lake Julius, which lies further downstream, is largely protected from enrichment because Lake Moondarra acts as a sink for incoming nutrients associated with seasonal runoff. Indeed, at the time of this study Lake Moondarra had not overtopped its spillway for 12 years. As a result, Lake Julius can be described as a mesotrophic to eutrophic water body. Because it experiences less supply drawdown than Lake Moondarra, and has a larger catchment area, Lake Julius overtops each year.

Methods

Both lakes were sampled on a fortnightly basis from October 1989 to December 1990. Profiles for temperature, dissolved oxygen and conductivity, were constructed at 1 metre intervals close to the dam wall at the deepest point in each lake. Similar measurements were made at the water supply offtake point in each reservoir. In almost all cases, the analysis was conducted between 1000 and 1200 h. Temperature, dissolved oxygen and conductivity results were obtained using a 'HydroLab, Surveyor 2' submersible multiparameter water-quality analyser, while turbidity was measured in situ with a 'Hach' portable turbidimeter. Average daily wind speeds were calculated from five-minute readings taken at the Mt. Isa Mines Ltd. weather station located in Mt. Isa. Lake numbers were calculated using the temperature profile data and daily wind speeds averaged over the three days preceding thermocline measurement (for further details, see Imberger & Patterson 1990).

Results

Lake Numbers for Lake Moondarra and Lake Julius were computed using the algorithm of Robertson et al. (1990), and are plotted in Fig. 2. Lake Numbers in Lake Moondarra ranged from a minimum of zero to a maximum of 19, contrasting with Lake Julius where the range was from zero to 150. Low Lake Numbers occurred in both lakes in winter (May to July), although in 1990 Lake Moondarra Lake Numbers stayed at or near zero from the end of April until early July. In contrast, Lake Numbers in Lake Julius remained near zero for a much shorter period (mid-June to early July). Outside the winter mixing period, both lakes showed dynamic mixing regimes similar to those recorded by Boland (1990) for two reservoirs in Australia's monsoonal region.

Dissolved oxygen levels were measured at two metres depth at the offtake point of each lake, as well as in the deepest region (10 m depth in Lake

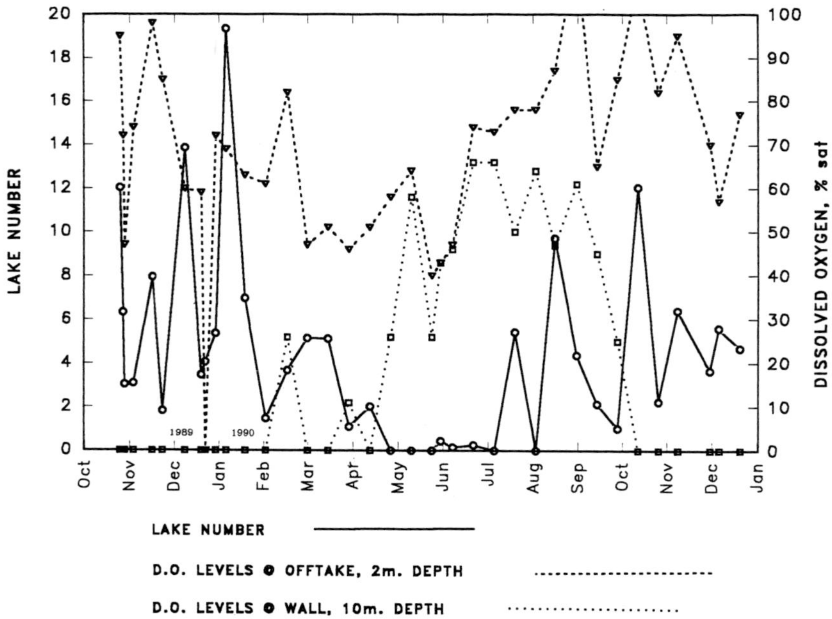

Fig. 3. Lake Moondarra: Lake Number and dissolved oxygen levels at the offtake and dam wall sites.

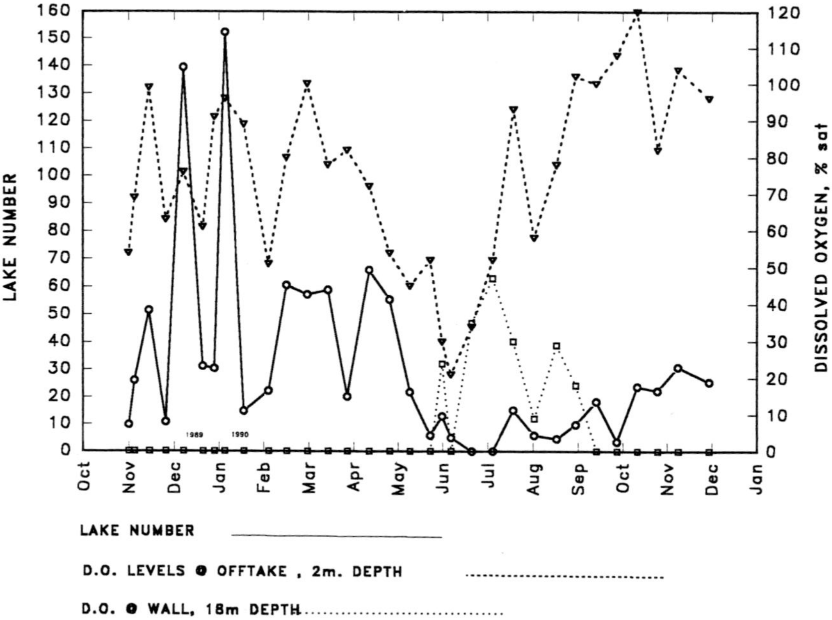

Fig. 4. Lake Julius: Lake Number and dissolved oxygen levels at the offtake and dam wall sites.

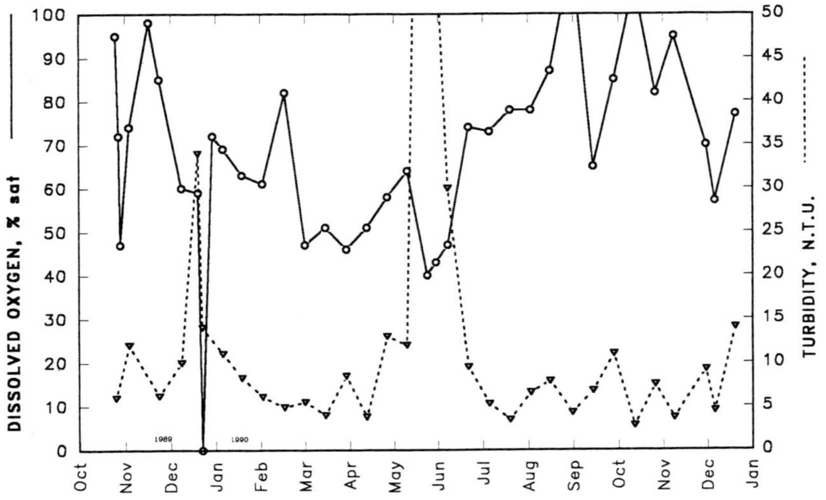

Fig. 5. Lake Moondarra: surface water turbidity and dissolved oxygen.

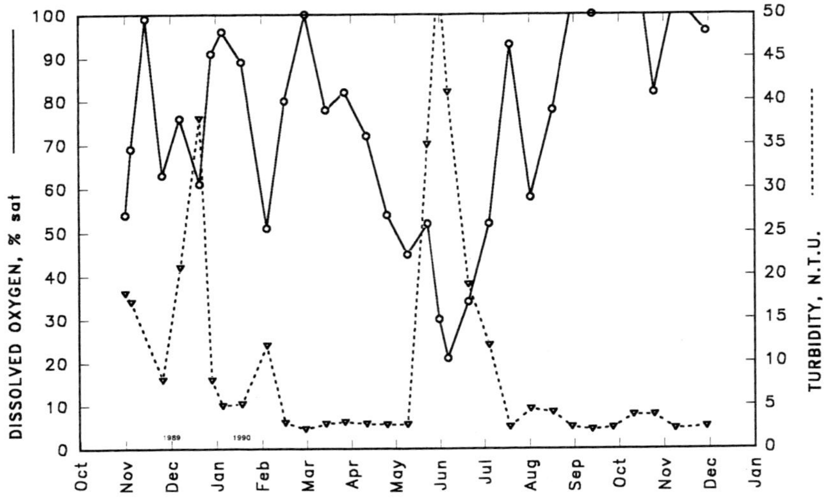

Fig. 6. Lake Julius: surface water turbidity and dissolved oxygen.

Moondarra, 18 m depth in Lake Julius) close to the dam wall. The results are shown, with Lake Numbers for each lake, in Figs. 3 and 4. General trends in both lakes were similar, and suggest that there is a high response in dissolved oxygen to driving forces and other factors influencing the water columns. Turbidity of the surface waters was measured at the offtake site in each lake and these data are shown, with dissolved oxygen, in Figs. 5 and 6. There were peaks in turbidity in both lakes during late 1989 and again in mid-1990 corresponding to inflow of turbid waters associated with heavy rain in the reservoir catchments.

Discussion

The contrast in the range of Lake Numbers recorded in the study reservoirs resulted from several factors. Lake Moondarra is a relatively shallow lake with a large surface area compared to Lake Julius. The ratios of surface area to depth in Lakes Moondarra and Julius (at the time of the study) were 217 and 163 respectively. Therefore, a given wind velocity at Lake Julius would have less effect on the water column than at Lake Moondarra. Furthermore, the predominance of southeast winds would have had less effect at Lake Julius because it is substantially sheltered from winds from this direction by a line of large hills. Lake Moondarra, by contrast, is set in relatively undulating country and is relatively exposed to wind. The most influential wind directions at Lake Julius – that is, those that exert maximum shear force at the air/water interface – would have to come from the direction of significant fetch in the water body. Because of the steep edges and the shape of this reservoir, that direction would have been from approximately 170–190° or from the northerly complement 350–10°. Wind from these sectors accounts for only 18 % of total average yearly wind run in the region. This protection and the lower surface area/depth ratio accounts for the fact that Lake Julius has a higher range of Lake Numbers than Lake Moondarra.

In both study lakes dissolved oxygen levels at the offtake site showed a strong direct relationship with Lake Number (Figs. 3, 4). This was apparent despite the fact that the offtakes for each reservoir were some distance from the location near the dam wall where profiles used to compute Lake Number were measured. In Lake Moondarra the offtake is four kilometres from the dam wall whereas in Lake Julius the distance is five kilometres. IMBERGER (1987) discusses the rapid spread of energy in the surface mixed layer of lakes, and accounts for the relationship between Lake Number, an index of dynamic stability, and other causally related water quality parameters such as dissolved oxygen. ROBERTSON et al. (1990), found a clear, inverse relationship between Lake Number and deep water dissolved oxygen levels in two monsoonal region lakes in the Northern Territory, Australia. In these lakes there is little fluctuation in near-surface dissolved oxygen levels (BOLAND 1990), so that Lake Number only shows a relationship with dissolved oxygen trends near, or below, the summer thermocline. Thus, in these lakes, the only clear relationship between dissolved oxygen and Lake Number is an inverse one, at depth; whereas in Lake Moondarra and Lake Julius there is a direct relationship near the surface and an inverse relationship at depth (Figs. 3, 4).

The difference between the Northern Territory lakes and Lakes Moondarra and Julius relates to the mechanisms which influence dissolved oxygen concentrations in the water columns of each system. During the two year period of BOLAND's (1990) study, both Northern Territory lakes had low to moderate algal loads in their water columns with surface chlorophyll maxima of 6 μg/l. In the present investigation, maximum surface chlorophyll levels in Lake Moondarra and Julius were 12 μg/l and 27 μg/l respectively. These reservoirs had mean annual chlorophyll levels approximately twice as high as their Northern Territory counterparts. Furthermore, Lakes Moondarra and Julius undergo periods of high turbidity caused by colloidal clays in runoff following rain, and this may persist in the water column for extended periods or can be associated with the resuspension of sediments during mixing. This phenomenon is not significant in the two Northern Territory lakes where surface turbidity rarely exceeds 2 N.T.U., even during periods of inflow (BOLAND 1990). The result is that deep-water oxygen levels in the water columns of the clearer, less enriched, Northern Territory lakes, are largely influenced by vertical turbulence and therefore show the expected inverse relationship with Lake Number. In Lakes Moondarra and Julius, Lake Number relates directly to near-surface dissolved oxygen because of the strongly anoxic water present in each lake during stratified conditions. Hence vertical turbulence transport results in a depletion of surface mixed layer oxygen levels as this deeper, anoxic water mixes with the oxygenated upper layer. Similarly deep-water oxygen levels increase as Lake Number falls and result in an inverse relationship similar to the situation in Northern Territory lakes.

The high volumes of anoxic water in Lake Moondarra and Lake Julius are caused by different factors. In Lake Moondarra, turbid surface waters lead to rapid attentuation of incident energy and hence the photic zone is shallow. The lake is highly enriched with the result that the hypolimnion exerts considerable chemical and biochemical oxygen demand and becomes anoxic (FINLAYSON et al. 1984). Lake Julius is less turbid but, because of its bathometry and a depth to volume ratio that is close to linear, there is a relatively small volume of mixed surface water compared to the deeper anoxic layer that is maintained under stratified conditions. The turbidity of both lakes affects light regimes thereby influencing photosynthetic activity of algae and hence the rate of oxygen production. The lakes contain significant populations of the blue green algae *Microcystis aeruginosa* and, especially in their deeper regions, a large number of diatoms. Many diatoms are capable of surviving in a low light environment such as can occur when Lake Number is low (GANF et al. 1982), whereas *Microcystis* is favoured in high light environments (HARRIS 1978, HARRIS & PICCININ 1980) as occurs in Lakes Moondarra and Julius when Lake Number is high. The response of these phytoplankton to fluctuations in turbidity and their consequent photosynthetic rates influence dissolved oxygen levels in the surface waters. For example, super-saturation levels of dissolved oxygen were recorded in Lake Moondarra in August/September and October 1990, and in Lake Julius in September, October and November 1990 (Figs. 5, 6), when turbidity was low and Lake Numbers were >1. Dissolved oxygen levels during such periods were driven predominantly by photosynthesis, whereas during the mid-year mixing period, and again during the December to February storm periods, dissolved oxygen levels were influenced most strongly by vertical turbulence transport and turbid inflow.

The influence of vertical turbulence can be seen clearly in Lake Julius during April and May. A decrease in Lake Number was associated with seasonal cooling of the water column (Fig. 4), accompanied by a fall in dissolved oxygen concentrations while turbidity was low (Fig. 6). In May, turbid inflow assisted the mixing process and dissolved oxygen was depleted to 20 % saturation in early June, which was followed by a period when Lake Numbers were low or zero. During this time, vertical turbulence was the dominating factor in the re-oxygenation of the water column because high turbidity limited photosynthesis until mid-July when oxygen levels began to approach saturation (Fig. 6).

Much research has been conducted on the response of chemical and biological water quality parameters to changes in water column stability (see **Introduction**), but in most cases no account has been taken of destabilizing factors. The use of traditional internal stability results has often disguised critical points because they take no account of coincidental driving forces such as seasonal or short-term changes in wind velocity.

Continuous measurement of Lake Number is relatively simple and provides an assessment of the dynamic stability of a system. Dissolved oxygen levels in the water column show a strong relationship with Lake Number and it may be expected that a similar relationship will be found with other parameters associated with oxygen, for example, chlorophyll *a*, iron, manganese, etc. As a management tool, real time Lake Number provides a justification for proactive decisions on offtake depth and pumpage periods in water-supply reservoirs. Research to relate biological factors to Lake Number may provide an understanding of primary physical driving forces and their effects on species diversity.

Acknowledgements

We thank Mt. Isa Mines Ltd. for their assistance with funding, and field and laboratory support; the Australian Water Resources Advisory Committee for their sponsorship of the project; Dr. JOHN SNELL of the Centre for Water Research; S. TOWNSEND of the Northern Territory Power & Water Authority and Prof. D. J. GRIFFITHS from the Australian Centre for Tropical Fresh Water Research, James Cook University of North Queensland.

References

BOLAND, K. T., 1990: The limnology of Darwin River and Manton River Reservoir. – Northern Territory Power and Water Authority, Report 32/88.

FINLAYSON, C. M., FARREL, T. P. & GRIFFITHS, D. J., 1980: Studies of a tropical lake in north-western Queensland. II. Seasonal changes in thermal and dissolved oxygen characteristics. – *Aust. J. Mar. Freshwater Res.* **31**: 811–827.

– – – 1984: The hydrobiology of five man-made lakes in north-western Queensland. – *Proc. R. Soc. Qld.* **95**: 29–40.

GANF, G. G., OLIVER, R. L. & STONE, S. J. L. 1982: Phytoplankton growth. – In: O'LOUGHLIN, E. M. & CULLEN, P. (eds.): Predition in Water Quality: 201–222. – Australian Academy of Science, Canberra.

HARRIS, G. P., 1978: Photosynthesis, productivity and growth: the physiological ecology of the phytoplankton. – *Arch. Hydrobiol./Beih. Ergeb.* **10**: 1–171.

HARRIS, G. P. & PICCININ, B. B., 1980: Physical variability and phytoplankton communities. IV. Temporal changes in the phytoplankton community of a physically variable lake. – *Arch. Hydrobiol.* **89**: 447–473.

HUTCHINSON, G. E, 1957: A Treatise on Limnology. Vol. 1 Geography, Physics and Chemistry: 1016 pp. – Wiley, New York.

HUTCHINSON, G. E. & LÖFFLER H., 1956: The thermal classification of lakes. – *Proc. Natl. Acad. Sci.* **42**: 84–86.

IDSO, S. B., 1973: On the concept of lake stability: *Limnol. Oceanogr.* **28**: 681–683.

Imberger, J., 1987: Hydrodynamics of Lakes. – *Technical Papers,* Australian Water and Wastewater Association 12th Federal Convention, Adelaide, 1987.

Imberger J. A. & Patterson, J. C., 1990: Physical limnology. – *Advances in Applied Mechanics* **27**: 303–475.

Robertson, D. M., Imberger, J. & Boland, K. T., 1990: Lake Number. An indicator of reservoir mixing: a water quality management tool. – *Water* (Australian Water and Wastewater Association) **17**: 29–33.

Ruttner, F., 1963: Fundamentals of Limnology. 3rd Edition: 307 pp. – University of Toronto Press, Toronto, Canada.

Schmidt, W., 1928: Über Temperatur und Stabilitätsverhältnisse von Seen. – *Geog. Ann.* **10**: 145–177.

Townsend, A. A. & Boland, K. T., 1987: Reservoir stratification and mixing in the monsoonal region of the Northern Territory. – *Technical Papers, Australian Water and Wastewater Association, 12th Federal Convention, Adelaide,* 1987.

Authors' addresses:

Kevin Boland, Centre for Tropical Freshwater Research, James Cook University of North Queensland, Townsville, Queensland 4811, Australia.

Present address: Power and Water Authority, Water Resources Division, P.O. Box 1096, Darwin, NT 0801, Australia.

Jorg Imberger, Centre for Water Research, University of Western Australia, Nedlands, WA, Australia.

Mitt. Internat. Verein. Limnol.	24	345–347	Stuttgart, Februar 1994

Application of satellite remote sensing to estimate lake water quality

Mikiyasu Nakayama

Abstract

Remote sensing enables estimation of water quality of lakes where traditional measuring by sampling during ground surveys is difficult to conduct. It also provides information on the spatial variations of water quality over the entire lake surface, which can not be achieved by traditional methods. Medium- or high-resolution satellites such as LANDSAT and SPOT have been used in previous studies. These satellites are difficult to employ in humid tropical areas where few cloud-free images are obtainable. NOAA/AVHRR takes images of a certain place much more frequently than LANDSAT and SPOT, though its spaital resolution is coarse and the number of sensors in visible and near-infrared region is limited. A case study of Lake Biwa (Japan) has shown that NOAA/AVHRR can be used to estimate water quality of a relatively large lake with an accuracy comparable to LANDSAT.

Introduction

Many lakes in both developed and developing countries are either polluted or on the brink of deterioration, due to increased siltation, eutrophication, industrial and domestic discharges, airborne pollution and other human induced degradation. There is thus an increasing need for establishing sound scientific principles for sustainable development of lake resources. It is now widely accepted that lakes cannot either be understood in their functioning, nor efficiently managed, without due consideration being given to their drainage basins. Collecting information on the whole limnosystem is thus a methodological prerequisite, as well as a sound managerial practice.

In view of the above, the UNEP (United Nations Environment Programme) and ILEC (International Lake Environment Committee) started a joint project in 1987 entitled *Survey of the State of World Lakes* for the purpose of compiling geographical, limnological, socioeconomic and environmental data on the world's important lakes. The aim of the project was essentially to provide a basis for sound lake management consistent with sustainable development policies. Four data books have been published dealing with those water bodies where sufficient data are available.

In the course of data collection, it became apparent that there were few lakes for which sufficient basic limnological information existed to provide a basis for rational lake management. Such data were particularly unevenly distributed in developing countries. It is therefore an urgent priority to establish practical methodologies for rapid collection of data on lakes and their drainage basins.

It is obvious that the processes occurring in large limnosystems have geographical dimensions. Drainage basins often are heterogeneous in terms of climate, soils, slopes, agricultural practices and other human activities. Likewise, physical and biological conditions and thus water quality can vary spatially within the water body. Furthermore, the patterns of spatial variation within the lake or its drainage basin can change over time owing to the sheer size and complexity of many lake basins. Classical data collection methods, based solely on ground surveys, are clearly inadequate to generate a complete, up-to-data and usable data bank, and their short-comings are especially noticeable when dealing with lakes in remote regions.

Methods and study site

Remote-sensing information, essentially from high- and moderate-resolution satellites, has already proven its potential in soil, vegetation and land-use mapping. Recent applications of remote-sensing data, taken by LANDSAT (Lathrop & Lillesand 1986) and SPOT (Lathrop & Lillesand 1989), to water quality surveys have provided encouraging results (see also Lukens). LANDSAT and SPOT provide repeat coverage of only 15–20 days. This can be a significant limitation in the application of the technology in some humid tropical areas such as southern Thailand and Indonesia where cloud covers the land very frequently. The AVHRR (Advanced Very High Resolution Radiometer) on NOAA weather satellites has been employed in the present study, because the repeat cycle is half a day. Furthermore, the cost of AVHRR images is relatively inexpensive when compared with LANDSAT and SPOT.

The AVHRR was designed for weather monitoring, and has the limitation that there are only two sensors in the visible and near infrared region. It therefore has a basic spatial resolution of just over one kilometre at

0538-4680/94/0024-0345 $ 0.75

nadir (Szekielda 1988), while LANDSAT/TM, for example, has four sensors in the same domain with a spatial resolution of 30 metres (Table 1). Nevertheless, NOAA/AVHRR data could be utilised to estimate the water quality of relatively large lakes in tropical regions, where medium- to high-resolution satellite data are difficult to obtain due to the paucity of cloud-free images (but see Lukens 1994). The objective of this study is therefore to examine the feasibility of estimating water quality of lakes with AVHRR, with a view to applying the technology to tropical lakes.

A test study was conducted in Lake Biwa, the largest lake in Japan. Lake Biwa is located in central Honshu Island and measures 63.5 km from north to south. It is strongly constricted at about 16 km from its southern end reaching a minimum width of only 1.35 km. The deep main basin (average depth 44 m) north of the constriction is known as the Northern Lake, while the shallow sub-basin (average depth 3.5 m) to the south is termed the Southern Lake. The catchment area is 4.7 times as wide as the lake itself, and corresponds closely to the administrative limits of Shiga Prefecture. Forest-covered hills and mountains account for nearly 60 % of the land area of the Prefecture, and farmlands (mostly wet paddy fields) make up an additional 25 %. There are several cities of moderate size within the drainage basin; the largest is Otsu with population of 240,000 (ILEC 1987). The water quality of Lake Biwa has been monitored every month at 47 surface stations, where chlorophyll *a*, total suspended solids, Secchi disc depth (m), chemical oxygen demand, total-nitrogen and total-phosphorus were measured. The water-quality data during 1988 and 1989 were provided for this study by the Environmental Division of the Shiga Prefectural Government through ILEC.

Table 1. A comparison between NOAA/AVHRR and LANDSAT/TM.

	NOAA/ AVHRR	LANDSAT/ TM
Coverage per scene	2,700 × 5,000 km	180 × 180 km
Spatial resolution	1.1 × 1.1 km	30 × 30 m
Frequency of monitoring	every 1/2 day	every 15 days
Number of visible and Near-IR sensors	2	4

Three NOAA-10/AVHRR scenes taken on 6 April, 6 July and 25 November 1989, purchased from the Japan Weather Association, were employed for this study. The digital number of the pixel corresponding to each sampling point was converted to spectral radiance using the methods described in the NOAA Polar Orbiter Data User Guide (NOAA 1991). Water-quality parameters monitored in the lake during the same months were used to calculate coefficients of correlation between the remote-sensing data and within-lake measurements. For comparison, a LANDSAT/TM scene of 6 June 1988 was purchased from the Remote Sensing Technology Centre of Japan. A 3 × 3 pixel window centred on the terrestrial sampling point was used to extract the digital number for TM band 1 through 4. The digital number data were converted to radiance using the coefficients in Price (1987). The correlation between the LANDSAT/TM radiance and water quality parameters were then calculated.

Results

Table 2 shows the correlation between measured values of water-quality parameters and radiance of AVHRR bands 1 and 2; similar correlations for LANDSAT/TM bands 1 to 4 are presented in Table 3. NOAA/AVHRR data yielded correlation coefficients which were close to or even higher than those of LANDSAT/TM.

Table 2. Correlation between radiance of NOAA/AVHRR and water quality data on 6 April, 6 July and 25 November 1989.

	Correlation coefficients					
Date	April 6		July 6		November 25	
Band	1	2	1	2	1	2
Chlorophyll *a*	0.83	0.75	0.69	0.65	0.63	0.56
Suspended solids	0.72	0.60	0.67	0.71	0.68	0.62
Secchi disc depth	−0.76	−0.67	−0.64	−0.64	−0.55	−0.57
Total-Nitrogen	0.64	0.59	0.45	0.51	0.60	0.57
Total-Phosphorus	0.76	0.71	0.59	0.71	0.69	0.66
Chemical oxygen demand	0.81	0.73	0.57	0.61	0.48	0.46

Table 3. Correlation between radiance of LANDSAT/TM and water quality data on 6 June 1988.

Band	Correlation coefficients			
	1	2	3	4
Chlorophyll *a*	0.45	0.53	0.58	0.61
Suspended solids	0.49	0.57	0.61	0.72
Secchi disc depth	−0.60	−0.66	−0.70	−0.67
Total-Nitrogen	0.23	0.30	0.33	0.44
Total-Phosphorus	0.36	0.46	0.47	0.52
Chemical oxygen demand	0.38	0.50	0.51	0.53

Discussion

The results suggest that NOAA/AVHRR data can be used to estimate water quality of relatively large lakes. For lakes in areas of frequent cloud cover, NOAA/AVHRR can provide more cloud-free images than other remote-sensing satellites such as LANDSAT and SPOT although these technologies have significant value for investigations of wetlands (Lukens, this volume). NOAA/AVHRR has the additional advantage of a relatively low cost per image. Frequent acquisition of cloud-free images by NOAA/AVHRR may realise quasi-real-time monitoring of lake water quality.

Greater spatial coverage of NOAA/AVHRR may make it a powerful tool to monitor water quality of multiple lakes. Further case studies should be carried out to estimate the feasibility of this application. Case studies should also be conducted for lakes in tropical regions to find out if the methodologies developed for Lake Biwa, which is in the temperature zone, could be applied for lakes in the tropical region, where behaviour of both lakes and lake basin may be expected to differ considerably.

References

ILEC 1987: The Survey of the State of World lakes, Vol. **1**: 1–19. – International Lake Environment Committee, Otsu, Japan.

Lathrop, R. G. & Lillesand, T. M., 1986: Use of thematic mapper data to assess water quality in Green Bay and central Lake Michigan. – *Photogrammetric Engineering and Remote Sensing* **52**: 671–680.

– – 1989: Monitoring water quality and river plume transport in Green Bay, Lake Michigan with SPOT-1 imagery. – *Photogrammetric Engineering and Remote Sensing* **55**: 349–354.

Lukens, J. E., 1994: Mapping southeast Asian wetlands using remote sensing: The training project approach. – *Mitt. Internat. Verein. Limnol.* **24**: 349–355.

NOAA 1991: NOAA Polar Orbiter Data Users Guide: 17–19. – National Oceanic Atmospheric Administration, Washington, D. C.

Price, J. C., 1987: Calibration of satellite radiometers and the comparison of vegetation indices. – *Remote Sensing of the Environment* **22**: 15–27.

Szekielda, K. H. 1988: Satellite Monitoring of the Earth: 326 pp. – Wiley, New York.

Author's address:

Faculty of Agriculture, Utsunomiya University, 350 Mine-machi, Utsunomiya-shi, Tochigi 321, Japan.

Mitt. Internat. Verein. Limnol.	24	349–355	Stuttgart, Februar 1994

Mapping southeast Asian wetlands using remote sensing: The training project approach

John E. Lukens

Abstract

The natural inland wetlands of southeast Asia can be effectively inventoried, assessed and monitored with the aid of remote-sensing technology. Appropriate combinations of satellite imagery and aerial photography at various scales can greatly reduce the amount of field work needed to delineate wetland boundaries and identify wetland types. In some cases, depending upon project requirements (map scale, wetland category detail, whether categories are based upon vegetation structure or species associations, spatial and thematic accuracy specifications, and availability of collateral data), field work may be practically eliminated.

The most accurate and rapid results will be achieved by trained image analysts who are familiar with the wetlands of the region. In most cases, organizations with wetland mapping/management responsibilities do not have this trained and experienced manpower. This paper describes the 'training project' approach, a joint activity between a training institution and the organization which must produce a wetlands map, usually a national government natural resources agency. Agency employees receive training in specific project needs, which may include wetland identification, image processing, airphoto interpretation, field work, and mapping. Concurrent with the classroom training, the employees carry out the project, under supervision, over a period of several months. At the completion of the training project, the organisation receives the needed wetlands inventory and maps, as well as employees who are trained in wetland mapping.

Training needs for wetland mapping

Wetlands must be inventoried and mapped for a variety of reasons. Among these are the preservation of significant wildlife habitats, the protection of areas necessary for food and fibre production, the identification of areas with severe limitations for development, and the understanding of relationships among wetland functions affecting related ground and surface water regimes. Examples from Thailand illustrate these points clearly. There is a need to protect the Rangsit Marshes (near the Asian Institute of Technology [AIT], Bangkok) for waterfowl habitat (Scott 1989). This two to three square kilometre area is perhaps the largest freshwater wetland remaining in the southern Central Plains which, 100 years ago, was a vast area of natural wetlands. However, one of the chief constraints upon the use of the area by the more sensitive, larger waterbirds appears to be the lack of undisturbed wooded nesting sites close to suitable swampy feeding areas. Efforts made to establish and preserve the remaining wetland and its wildlife must identify the major ecosystem components, and should include mapping nearby wooded nesting areas in addition to the marshes.

In Narithiwat Province, southern Thailand, attempts have been made recently by the provincial government to clear sections of the Pa Phru (Phru to Daeng) peat swamp for rice cultivation (Eiumnoh 1990). However, within two to three years after clearing and drainage, water table fluctuations have led to oxidation of the peat which in turn has created acid-sulphate soil conditions severe enough to reduce yields to uneconomic levels. The cleared areas are now largely abandoned. Not only is this destroying the only remaining peat swamp forest in Thailand, a species-rich wildlife habitat, but the ground water moving from the swamp towards the nearby coast has also become acid. This, in turn, is reacting with calcareous coastal sands to produce a shallow iron-aluminum (spodic) hardpan layer which inhibits tree root penetration, thereby damaging coconut groves and fruit orchards in these areas. Maps of the Pa Phru boundaries are needed to help local planners delineate the limits of permissible development.

The mangroves along the coasts of Chantaburi and Trat Provinces, on Thailand's eastern seaboard, adjacent to Kampuchea, are seriously threatened by conversion to aquaculture, especially prawn farming (Neame 1991). Over the past five years, extensive areas in Khung Krabaen and Klung Districts have been almost completely destroyed. Thailand's Royal Forestry Department (RFD) is charged with mangrove protection, and has designated on maps approximate zones within the mangrove as areas for conservation as well as for limited exploitation (primarily for polewood and charcoal). This is under the questionable assumption that the RFD could protect the remaining mangrove areas, but monitoring and enforcement will be extremely difficult unless the designated areas are mapped in such a manner that the boundaries can be established and clearly identified on the ground.

0538-4680/94/0024-0349 $ 1.75

As a final example, the Mekong Secretariat of the Mekong Committee is committed to environmental studies, usually as part of their integrated basin planning activities (Interim Committee for the Coordination of Investigations of the Lower Mekong Basin 1991). These include an inventory of the wetlands along the main areas of the Mekong River in Thailand as the first step in preparing a management plan for the wetlands and related areas.

The types of mapping projects described above for Thailand are typical of those needed for every country in the region. Each of these types of mapping projects requires persons skilled in the recognition of wetlands in the field as well as from aerial photographs and satellite imagery. However, these countries have neither private firms nor government agencies with units dedicated to wetland mapping. Wetland mapping projects tend to be *ad-hoc*, occur infrequently, and have specialized requirements. This situation does not justify the creation of permanent wetland mapping units within national agencies, nor does it encourage the creation of private consulting firms to serve the government agencies responsible for wetland mapping.

Natural wetlands and paddy are shown in a general way (with varying accuracy depending upon the recognition skills of the stereoplotter operator) on the standard product of national mapping agencies, the 1:50,000 topographic map. However, the wetland areas are not delineated, but shown by symbols, and do not show the structure or species composition of natural wetlands. Until the time comes when wetland mapping projects occur frequently enough to lead to the creation of dedicated government or (more likely) private consultants, each wetland mapping project will require the creation of a temporary mapping team and training of the team members in the wetland interpretation and mapping skills necessitated by the requirements of each project.

Remote sensing and wetland mapping

Remote sensing, defined in the broadest sense of the term, includes all modes of measurement of a phenomenon which do not use contact devices. This includes radiation detectors visual observations such as the human eye, photography, line-scan imagery, and radiometry. The information is usually collected from a distant vantage point, such as an aircraft or a satellite, and is processed to produce an image in order to gain a "synoptic" view of the phenomenon.

Wetland definitions abound. At least 22 types of wetlands are recognized in Asia (Scott 1989). They are classified by degree of man's influence (natural or artificial), by degree of salinity (fresh, brackish or salt water) by degree of vegetation cover (open, floating, emergent, or woody), and by degree of permanence (perennial or seasonal). For example, a salt pan is a man-made, saline, open, seasonal wetland; a peat swamp is a natural, fresh, forested, permanent wetland; and a paddy is a man-made, fresh, grass-covered, seasonal wetland.

Information derived by remote sensing can help delineate and characterize all 22 wetland types. Open water types and artificial types are relatively easy to identify and are not considered in this paper. The only imaging systems of common use in Asia are satellite imagery and aerial photography. Therefore, this paper will be restricted to discussing the use of satellite imagery and airphotos to map natural, partially-vegetated or completely-vegetated wetlands. These wetlands include mangrove, riverine marshes, seasonally-flooded grassland, and peat swamps.

Wetland mapping requirements

Wetland mapping projects vary from a regional reconnaissance, to the characterization of functions of wetland types within a watershed, to identification of individual species and species-associations within wetlands. Map scales will range from 1:50,000 to 1:1000, with associated (increasing) locational accuracy requirements. Boundaries of wetlands may be generalized for regional, statistical studies, or must be described to within a few metres (or centimetres) for legal or regulatory purposes. As greater spatial accuracy is needed, greater ground resolution of the remote-sensing data is required. Where detail of vegetation structure is needed, stereoscopic coverage with greater height resolution is necessary. As more detail on species and species associations is needed, greater ground resolution and spectral resolution is required.

Satellite imagery can be used for regional mapping projects which require generalized boundaries and aggregated wetland categories. This may be the first stage of a multi-stage project, designed to identify smaller areas for more detailed study, or to generate statistical data. As the need for detail on vegetation structure and species increases for legal or regulatory purposes, medium- to low-altitude, stereoscopic aerial photography is required.

Data sources: satellite imagery and aerial photography

Most satellite data come as a line-scan image in which the analog electronic data in each scan line is broken (digitized) into discrete picture elements or pixels. The colours and brightness of the light reflected from landscape are captured within each pixel by dividing the spectrum of reflected light into small spectral bands. The level of brightness of each spectral band in the pixels is represented by a digital number. When a regular raster of pixels is displayed on a cathode ray tube or as a photographic print, a two-dimensional digital image results. Three spectral bands are usually displayed or printed together as a composite to produce a colour image.

The area of the earth's surface covered by a pixel is referred to as the ground 'spot size', and varies from about 80 metres for the older United States satellites to between 10 and 30 metres for the newer US and French satellites. The smaller the spot size, the greater the ground resolution and the lesser the spectral resolution. The 10 metre resolution French SPOT satellite image is single-band (panchromatic) only. The SPOT satellite also can be programmed to provide stereoscopic coverage with a height resolution of two to five metres.

These remote-sensing parameters are not sufficient to identify directly wetland species composition, nor wetland structure. However, computer-assisted classification of multi-spectral imagery, combined with a limited amount of field data, can be used by experienced wetland ecologists to infer these characteristics for areas not field-sampled. Depending upon the ground resolution, the minimum size (diameter) of these wetland areas must be on the order of one half to one kilometre if thematic accuracies are to be 80 % or greater. A wetland/upland boundary could be transferred from a geometrically-corrected raster image (or classified image) to a base map with an accuracy of 50 to 100 metres.

The spectral, spatial and height resolution of aerial photography is three to four orders of magnitude greater than satellite imagery, and coverage is nearly always stereoscopic. When thematic and spatial accuracy requirements exceed those described above for satellite imagery, aerial photography flown at appropriate scales is required. Airphoto interpretation carried out by experienced interpreters, combined with limited field work, will usually achieve thematic accuracies of 90–95 % for areas as small as 20 metres. Boundaries can be transferred to (sufficiently accurate) base maps with an accuracy of two to five metres. NOAA/AVHRR remote-sensing technologies (which are generally associated with weather satellites) are not considered here, but their application to monitoring lake water quality are described by Nakayama (1994).

Advantages and disadvantages

The major advantage of satellite imagery over aerial photography is its repetitive coverage, which assures that relatively cloud-free imagery less than one year old can be obtained for most areas of Asia. By contrast, aerial photographic coverage for most of the region is likely to be ten to 20 years old (as also are the base maps compiled from that coverage). Therefore, satellite imagery may be the only source of current synoptic data for wetland mapping projects in areas undergoing rapid development. In areas where the land use and land cover changes are less dynamic, ten to 20-year-old aerial coverage may be sufficient.

In most Asian countries, aerial photography – even outdated coverage – has a security classification which restricts its use. In some countries, all airphoto interpreters must be registered and obtain a security clearance. This means that there is often a lack of trained interpreters, and that training programmes carried out by international or aid agencies are often constrained to use photography from third countries. This situation inhibits the use of aerial photography, and tends to force what would be otherwise inappropriate and inefficient use of satellite imagery. However, mosaics or index sheets prepared at a reduced scale from the original stereoscopic coverage may also be useful. Before aerial photography is dismissed as a data source because of security restrictions, it may pay to determine whether the mosaics are also classified.

Cost is usually cited as a major restriction on the use of satellite imagery. Colour hard copies may cost US$ 200 to $ 1000, while digital tapes can run to US$ 4000 or $ 5000. However, these costs (on a per square kilometre basis) are comparable to the costs of new medium-scale aerial coverage over the same area as covered by a satellite scene (on the order of 10,000 to 40,000 square kilometres). In other words, any type of remote-sensing data is expensive, and should be considered for wetland mapping either when it can lower overall project costs by reducing the amount of field work required, or when necessary to meet schedule deadlines within overall accuracy requirements.

Image-processing equipment is also a major constraint to use of satellite imagery, unless only hard-copy imagery is to be used. The minimal image processing system, using public-domain software and a personal computer with EGA graphics and a colour dot-matrix printer, will cost US$ 10,000 to $ 15,000 to purchase, operate and maintain for a year. This is two hundred times the cost of the equipment used for airphoto analysis: a pocket stereoscope and colour pencils.

If a wetland mapping project has both satellite image and airphoto mapping capabilities, the multi-stage approach may be efficiently employed, initially using satellite imagery for small-scale surveys for large areas in order to identify smaller areas for subsequent larger-scale aerial surveys and mapping.

Matching mapping requirements to data sources

Each wetland mapping project tends to be unique, and calls for a systematic analysis by matching the data collection and reduction systems with the spatial and spectral characteristics of the wetlands (the input), and with the desired map categories (the output). For example, if it is necessary to distinguish floating emergent marsh vegetation, stereoscopic airphoto coverage and interpretation is necessary. As a second example, if it is necessary to distinguish *Nipa* palm from mangrove, stereoscopic aerial coverage could distinguish between the two vegetation types by height differences. Alternatively, black and white monoscopic coverage could be used at a scale large enough to show canopy textural differences, or colour monoscopic coverage could be used at smaller scales which would be sufficient to differentiate the two vegetation types by colour.

As a third example, if it is necessary to distinguish vegetated wetlands from vegetated uplands, false colour aerial photography or satellite imagery taken during the dry season might be the best match. In false colour imagery the green spectral band is displayed as blue, the red band as green, and the near-infrared band as red to give a false colour composite (FCC) image, similar to the camouflage detection films developed during the Second World War. In this presentation, most healthy green vegetation appears as shades of red and magenta, which provides greater visual contrast than the generally more subtle green colour variations in natural colour imagery (and photography). These colour variations (hue and saturation differences) become more pronounced during dry periods as upland vegetation undergoes moisture stress, while wetland species retain their vigour. However, while FCC mapping might distinguish upland from wetland associations, or (at a much larger scale) distinguish among species associations in, for examples, peat swamps, it would be a mistake to assume that FCC imagery or false-colour photography would distinguish well among areas of different species in marshes. Under permanent wetland conditions, marsh vegetation does not undergo moisture stress; natural colour aerial photography may carry more information about species composition and vegetation structure than false colour photography.

The most difficult mapping situations occur with seasonal wetlands which have been cleared of natural vegetation, unless used for a wetland crop such as rice. During dry seasons these areas resemble prairies. The surface and underlying geologic conditions, subtle landscape depressions, soil tones, and relationships to nearby natural and cultural features all converge to indicate probable seasonal wetland conditions. Here is where stereoscopic aerial photography must be used by a skilled interpreter who has considerable experience in the area, and preferably who has been educated in a natural science.

Wetland mapping project procedures

The remarks in this section derive from the author's ten years' experience in designing and undertaking wetlands mapping projects in temperate zones, involving the use of colour or black and white stereoscopic aerial photography in projects which mapped inland and coastal wetlands over approximately 104,000 km^2.

Identifying objectives and scope

One of the more difficult steps in project design is to reach a cost-effective compromise between the amount of map detail which clients would like to have (the ideal) and the budget available (the practical). When wetland regulations and laws are vague on some point, or when the map is attempting to satisfy more than one purpose, maps can be generated which prove to be of little value at a later date. A careful examination of the needs of the actual users, and of the environment in which the map information is used, should always be undertaken.

The following questions must be answered: which categories are necessary? Are categories determined by surface water conditions or ground water conditions, by general species associations or by key species, by hydrologic function or some combination of all of these factors? What is the minimum wetland size to be mapped? What scales, what degree of boundary accuracy, and what thematic accuracy for each category will be used? Can combined categories be used in complex areas? How are gradational boundaries to be shown? How will the spatial and thematic accuracy be measured? How can the map be kept up-to-date (if necessary)? How often will it be necessary to update the map? Most clients do not have definite answers for these questions, unless highly specific criteria have been mandated or legislated. Clients therefore appreciate the assistance of an experienced wetland mapper in the project design. Design criteria should be contained in the project terms of reference (TOR), but the TOR should be flexible and subject to change when necessary, as most projects have unique aspects and often encounter unexpected conditions.

Building the mapping team

Wetland mapping teams, by the nature of the work, are generally composed of individuals who (except for the supervisor) have not mapped wetlands previously, and who probably have not worked together before. Most of the team members will not have been exposed to remote sensing previously, except perhaps for a university course taken after joining a government agency.

In making the selection of team members, a background in a natural science, biology, botany, geology, geography, or even engineering is preferable to previous experience in remote sensing. It is far easier to train a wetland ecologist to interpret aerial photographs or operate an image processing workstation, than to train a remote sensing specialist, often a computer scientist, to understand the complex biophysical and land use relationships required for wetland identification, analysis and mapping.

The size of the team will vary with the time available, scale of the project, and remote sensing system used. In an airphoto interpretation project, production can be estimated in terms of square kilometres per man-hour. One divides the project area by the productivity and trains a staff large enough to finish the project on time. When image processing is involved, production may be constrained by the number of workstations available. More often, the production bottleneck is an output device shared by a number of workstations. Common devices are pen plotters, ink-jet plotters and dot-matrix printers (at the relatively inexpensive end of the price scale), or film-writers and a photographic laboratory at the high end.

Training requirements

In general, a team of reasonably competent airphoto interpreters can be trained within one week to interpret and annotate airphotos for wetland mapping. Within another three weeks, after sufficient feedback from field checking, they are producing at an optimum rate. Because the interpretation requires demanding concentration, an unusual physical position, and the use of the illusion of stereoscopy which may cause eyestrain and fatigue, frequent work breaks for the interpretation team and a relatively short work day will assure uniform quality and sustained production over the life of the project. On the other hand, it will require at least three weeks to train the same types of individuals to operate a computer image processing workstation effectively, and another three weeks with feedback from field checking before they begin to operate at optimum performance.

In both cases, production is increased if the work environment is pleasant, air-conditioned, and carried out in the same open-plan work area to afford both social and professional interaction with other team members. Morale is an important factor in both the quality and quantity of the mapping.

Training approaches for wetland mapping

Three approaches to formal training in wetland mapping are described below: *Standard training*, *Project case work*, and the *Training project*. Each is a useful approach, depending upon the needs and incentives of the individuals and their agencies. In addition, on-the-job training is an effective informal approach when feasible. Only the formal approaches are discussed below.

Standard training

Two types of standard training are usually practised: those which stress technology, and those which stress process transfer. Technology transfer is by far the most common, and has the advantage that in a short period, practical, operational skills are taught which can be directly applied to interpretation, analysis, and mapping.

In process transfer, the same skills are taught, augmented by more in-depth knowledge of the situations in which the range of skills imparted can be applied. This is considered especially desirable when computer image processing skills are being taught, so that the trainee learns which processing functions are appropriate and inappropriate to a given situation; i.e. deliver a useful product under project constraints. The 'why' and 'when' are considered to be as important as 'how' in process transfer training.

Technology – transfer courses

These are one- to three-week intensive courses in which simple skills, such as the detection, identification, and mapping of wetlands by airphoto interpretation, or all of the major pre-processing, enhancement, classification, and output functions of a software package are explained and practised. No theory is involved, and hands-on practical laboratory sessions are stressed. No outputs from the training, other than the maps and images resulting from simple exercises, are expected. This is especially useful for persons with a background and experience in wetland mapping who wish to learn a new technique, and/or who will immediately return to work on the systems covered by the training.

Process – transfer courses

These are six- to 15-week courses in which the skills described above are taught, along with enough theory to enable the individual to apply the knowledge and skills in a range of situations. The conceptual design of mapping projects may also be taught, and the lecture and practical sessions reinforced by a project designed to demonstrate the applications of this knowledge, as well as the drawbacks and advantages of the various tools and procedures involved.

A map or series of map products is expected as an output in this approach. The accuracy of the products is of less importance than evidence that the concepts and procedures have been understood. This approach is especially useful for persons with a background and experience in wetland (or other natural resources) mapping who wish to move into project design and management as well as to learn a new technique, or who (individually or as part of a management team) may be charged with the establishment of a mapping operation, staffing and specification of equipment.

Project case work

Like process-transfer courses, project case work (PCW; THARUN 1986) courses run from six to 15 weeks. However, the PCW approach extends the process-transfer training a step further by fully integrating a project into every phase of the training, module by module, following a modified business school case study approach. The approach is less open-ended than the process-transfer approach in which the understanding of the procedures is of more importance than the accuracy of the final products. In the PCW approach, equal stress is placed on both the process and the product.

The modules follow in logical sequence from project design through project proposal design, data collection, analysis, draft mapping, field checking, final mapping and presentation. The overall goal (and end products) of the PCW training are defined ahead of time, which requires that the objectives of each module also be determined in advance. All trainees must work towards these objectives and goals. Thus flexibility and spontaneity is traded for thoroughness. In working through each module, the trainees (or trainee teams) will select different pathways to reach the same objectives. This brings the realization that at many different turning points, numerous decisions have to be taken by them in order to proceed.

Experience with project modules, together with the varied results of the different working groups, demonstrate the fact that many options exist in planning and management. Thus, through simulated real-world projects, problem analysis and decision-making processes are practised. Political and sociocultural aspects are involved, as are value judgements. This will prepare the trainees for actual development projects better than standard training approaches. Where the traditional courses are usually lecture- or laboratory-centred. Here, the omnipresent and central position of a trainer as teacher-lecturer vanishes and gives way to the position of initiatior, facilitator, and advisor. More is demanded of the trainees during the sessions, and the trainer has to put in much more work and thought beforehand.

Although the emphasis is on practicality, time is allotted for case studies and sessions explaining the theoretical basis for some of the procedures. AIT is currently following the PCW approach for a short course on 'Coastal Zone Environmental Planning', being conducted for twenty trainees supported by Carl Duisberg Gesellschaft.

Training project

The training project approach incorporates all steps of an actual mapping project, including technology transfer training for the mapping team at the front end. The course generally runs for 12 to 15 weeks, long enough to deliver a finished mapping product to the client. The product is stressed, with proof of the effectiveness of the training being demonstrated by the quality and timeliness of the product.

The process is not taught through a series of modules, but in parallel activities which separate the project tasks or assign them so that each trainee works independently (but with consistent standards) towards the same objective. The activities follow a goal-oriented sequence from data collection through analysis, draft mapping, field checking, final mapping and reporting. Problem analysis and decision-making processes and value-judgements are subordinated to project planning and time management decision-making.

A training project also holds potential for cooperation between AIT and sister organizations having parallel interests, such as the Mekong Secretariat. For example, the Secretariat has approved the study: 'Inventory and Management of the Wetlands in the Lower Mekong Basin' (Interim Committee for the Coordination of Investigation of the Lower Mekong Basin 1991). Considering the scope of the project, timetable, and availability of funding, the project's inventory phase is well suited to the training project approach. Such a training project would see AIT fulfilling its regional role in training government agency employees, perhaps two each from the three riparian countries of Thailand, Laos and Vietnam, and would result in the Secretariat receiving a wetland inventory and map product necessary to the completion of the Lower Mekong Basin study. This concept has been approved in principle by the Mekong Secretariat.

Conclusions

In the range of types of formal training courses described above, the technology transfer approach is the most productive in terms of student-teacher ratios and in meeting course assessment objectives. After some experience has developed, the course can often be 'canned' and presented periodically with little preparation required for each offering.

The process transfer approach is perhaps least effective in meeting course assessment objectives. Its success depends to a large degree upon common objectives being understood by trainers and trainees at the beginning, but these objectives may be side-tracked or lost in the open-ended process. Trainees looking for standard (or 'cookbook') process are often disappointed by this approach. It is thus especially important that the client and trainer work closely together in the development of the course and its objectives, and trainees understand these objectives (process rather than product) prior to entering the course.

Because the course objectives usually change from course to course, it is not possible to develop a standard package, and individual lectures and laboratory sessions must be revised from one offering to the next. This is relatively demanding of the instructor's time and energy.

The modules of the project case work approach leave no doubt that both process and project are of equal importance. Because work on one module does not proceed until the previous module has been successfully completed, the final product automatically appears when the last module is completed, and course assessment objectives are thus likely to be met satisfactorily.

However, in terms of manpower devoted to assuring that the modules are designed and executed properly, the approach is relatively inefficient in terms of the student-teacher ratio. Furthermore, the project objectives and area will change from course to course, placing even more demands on the instructor's time and energy than the process-transfer approach. Because much of the material must be prepared beforehand, the PCW approach is relatively inflexible and unable to change direction. The training project approach is the most likely to meet assessment objectives. Depending upon the project management ability as well as the teaching ability of the instructor(s), the course is likely to be fairly efficient in terms of the student-teacher ratio. Although the project objectives and area change from course to course, the process places less demands upon the instructors, as more of the responsibility for task design and (self) instruction falls upon the trainees. The instructors function more as supervisors in a quality-control role, and less as lecturers and laboratory instructors, or as facilitators and advisors.

References

Eiumnoh, A., 1990: A study on the Environmental Impact Assessment of the Phru To Daeng Project. Final Report by the TEAM Project, Asian Institute of Technology, to the Royal Irrigation Department, Bangkok, Thailand: 56 pp. (In Thai).

Interim Committee for the Coordination of Investigations of the Lower Mekong Basin, 1991: Mekong Work Programme, Ongoing Investigations and Proposed Projects: 72 pp. – MKG/R.90036, Mekong Secretariat, Bangkok, Thailand.

Nakayama, M., 1994: Application of satellite remote sensing to estimate lake water quality. – *Mitt. Internat. Verein. Limnol.* **24**: 345–347.

Neame, P. A., 1991: Conceptual Design and Schedule: A Coastal Zone Environmental Management Case Study. 137 pp. – AgroDev Canada, Inc., Bangkok, Thailand.

Scott, D. A., 1989: A Directory of Asian Wetlands. 1157 pp. – IUCN, Gland, Switzerland.

Tharun, G., 1986: Project Casework-Based Training for Better Planning and Management of Water Pollution Control in Developing Countries: 42 pp. – Paper presented at: World Water '86 Conference, London, England, 14–16 July.

Author's address:

Asian Institute of Technology, G.P.O. Box 2754, Bangkok, 10501, Thailand.

Mitt. Internat. Verein. Limnol.	24	357–363	Stuttgart, Februar 1994

Constraints to the conservation and management of tropical inland waters

W. D. Williams

Abstract

The general status of tropical limnology is in a relatively parlous position: less is known about tropical inland waters than is desirable and needed for their proper conservation and management. Limnological knowledge of waters in the nothern temperate zone is much more extensive, reflecting, first, the larger amounts of financial support available there, and, second, better dissemination of knowledge (acceptance of a common scientific language [English], better networks of informal knowledge between limnologists, and effective scientific publication). Tropical limnologists have not adequately recognized the importance of knowledge dissemination. Measures to correct this inadequate recognition are advanced. Amongst general measures, the attention of governments should be drawn more closely to the need to underpin conservation and management of inland waters with greater limnological knowledge. Several specific measures suggested are concerned broadly with improving scientific communication. Finally, the need to inform key members and decision-makers in governments is stressed. They need to be made more aware that tropical inland waters:

i) are a valuable resource;
ii) can be degraded, perhaps irreparably;
iii) that their conservation and management is of national importance; and
iv) that their effective management and conservation can only be based upon thorough limnological knowledge.

Introduction

In this paper, firstly, I discuss the general status of our knowledge of tropical inland waters. My assessment, in accord with that of other contributors to this volume, is that limnologists are a long way from any adequate knowledge upon which to base fully-informed procedures to conserve and manage tropical inland waters. Secondly, I discuss reasons for this state of affairs. Why is it that we know so little about waters in some of the most populous parts of the planet? And thirdly, I discuss measures to support and encourage efforts to provide a better basis for research on tropical inland waters, and thereby their more effective conservation and management. Mostly, the measures discussed involve suggestions as to how information can be better disseminated: in particular, how the results of scientific research on tropical inland waters can be more widely and effectively disseminated.

I have little doubt that much of this will be somewhat stale bread to many readers. Nevertheless, by highlighting and juxtaposing these points, I hope this paper will form a useful contribution to our proceedings.

The general status of tropical limnology

An important point perhaps obvious to most readers, but an important one to make for the written record given the emphasis that most papers in this volume have had, is that tropical inland waters are not just permanent freshwater lakes, streams and rivers in warm, humid and well-watered parts of the planet. That may well be the common perception held by Europeans and North Americans (and perhaps even by many limnologists including some who have actually written about tropical waters, cf. Payne 1986, Armentano 1990). But even the most cursory glance at world maps of biome distribution indicates that a variety of biomes occurs within the tropics, and in some of these, waters are often ephemeral and saline and found in semi-arid or arid environments. Many such environments extend well-beyond the tropics (as, for example, deserts in the Middle East and Central Asia). Indeed, no tropical biome is restricted to the tropics; even the most characteristic one, the tropical evergreen rainforest, extends north of the tropic of Cancer in Asia. The only vegetational zone confined to the tropics is the equatorial rainforest zone.

The relative importance of wetlands (i.e. shallow, standing bodies of water) in humid and semi-arid/arid regions of the tropics is indicated in Table 1. It can be seen that although both the absolute and relative area and production of wetlands in humid tropical regions are greater than in semi-arid and arid tropical regions, the areas and production of wetlands in the latter are by no means insignificant. It is worth noting here that the temperate deciduous forest biome, which nowhere extends into the tropics, is of relatively small extent: leaving Antarctica out of account, it comprises much less than 20 % of global land area. It is important to recognize this because it is upon waters in this biome that most limnological knowledge is based. Moreover, to a considerable degree, it is upon extrapolations of knowledge

0538-4680/94/0024-0357 $ 1.75

Table 1. Areas and production of wetlands in humid and semi-arid/arid tropical regions. Extracted from table 1.2 of M. Williams (1990) but actual data from various other sources.

Region	Area		Production	
	(km² × 10³)	% total of tropical zone	(t/ha)	(× 10⁶t)
Humid	2,317	8.7	255	24,273
Semi-arid/arid	321	2.2	40–60	1,726

about waters in Europe and North America that the conservation and management of tropical waters is predicated. Of course, there are many basic limnological phenomena which show no latitudinal variation and for which tropical extrapolation is quite valid; but there are certainly many phenomena to which this statement does not apply.

Attention has been drawn to this limnological imbalance elsewhere (Fernando 1980, Williams 1988) where it has also been argued as a corollary that many conceptions widely held by limnologists about waters outside the northern temperature zone appear not to accord with reality. Three (mis)conceptions of particular interest here are that:

i) biodiversity and latitude correlate such that biodiversity is highest in the tropics (and thus in tropical inland waters) and decreases polewards;
ii) temporary bodies of water are generally small, do not have high biodiversity, and contain widespread or cosmopolitan species with good dispersal mechanisms; and
iii) saline water-bodies are uncommon and unusual habitats, of restricted distributed, and of rather little scientific interest.

All three conceptions appear to be in error. Thus, without providing details, it seems that:

i) tropical inland water-bodies are not notably more biologically diverse than waters elsewhere (e.g. Lewis 1987, Shiel & Williams 1990);
ii) temporary bodies of water are often large, have a high biodiversity, and many species in them are regionally restricted in distribution; and
iii) saline lakes are numerous, geographically widespread, and of considerable scientific interest (e.g. Hammer 1986, Williams 1986).

The purpose of the above discussion is to emphasize three points for the conservation and management of tropical inland waters. First, tropical inland waters are a good deal more diverse in character than waters typical of the northern temperate zone. Large, seasonally flooding rivers, saline lakes, and large bodies of temporary fresh water are three sorts of geographically widespread water-body of global importance and typically found in many tropical regions but which do not occur in the temperate zone. Our knowledge of these sorts of water-body remains poor. Second, most limnological knowledge is based upon the study of waters in the northern temperate zone: that is to say of hydrologically stable, permanent, fresh waters. Third, it is unwise to extrapolate ideas based upon research on temperate waters for conservation and management of tropical inland waters without considerable caution and critical examination.

The overall conclusion to be drawn is that the general status of tropical limnology is in a relatively parlous position. We know less about the limnology of tropical inland waters than is desirable and needed for their proper conservation and management. This comment receives added emphasis when it is recalled that over half of the world's population (i.e. presently ca. 2.5 billion people) lives in the tropics and subtropics and it is here that our population is growing fastest and is poorest.

The imbalance explained

It takes no great insight to recognize how the situation described above arose. Limnologists have been more active in Europe and North America because that is where money has been made available to support them. It is not because waters of the northern temperate zone are more important than waters elsewhere, or because mankind is more populous there. It is simply because more money has been and is available there for scientific research of a sort which need not necessarily return an immediate economic benefit. In short, Europe and North America could and can afford more basic limnological research than tropical countries. There are many who claim that monies spent on limnology in temperate countries remains inadequate (e.g. Jumars 1990), but this does not contradict the gross differences between the support of limnology in North America and Europe and its support elsewhere.

Most tropical countries would have no immediate capacity to amend the limnological imbalance were comparative wealth the only direct explanation for it. However, comparative wealth is only part of the explanation, albeit an important direct one. Also involved is the fact that limnologists of the northern temperate zone have accepted a common scientific language (English), have carefully constructed and nurtured networks enabling the informal and rapid transfer of information (computer networks, scientific societies and associations, international symposia), and have developed a means whereby scientific results can be made formally available to colleagues in a manner both credible and accessible (refereed scientific papers in internationally reputable journals, books and conference proceedings). To a considerable degree, these activities too reflect wealth, but do so at least less directly.

The importance of activities like this should not be underestimated. Indeed, neglect of them can largely negate research results whatever the significance and cost of these. I think they are being neglected by tropical limnologists. In my view, limnological research supporting the conservation and management of inland tropical waters is bedevilled not only by a paucity of direct support for it (salaries, institutions, infrastructure), but also to a significant degree by the relative inability of tropical limnologists to recognise the importance of communication or implement recognition. There are some exceptions to this statement, of course, and I do not wish to underestimate the difficulties that tropical limnologists in this area face: but, unless limnologists in tropical countries bring about better communication between themselves and between themselves and limnologists elsewhere, the limnological imbalance alluded to previously will obviously worsen, and the gap between the extent of knowledge concerning non-tropical and tropical waters will widen.

It is salutary to recall at this point the general comments recently made by Toffler (1990) on global wealth (power). Toffler emphasised that increasingly the world will be divided into wealthy nations which are 'information-rich' and where information is easily accessed and transferred, and poorer nations which are 'information-poor' and where information is not easily accessed and transferred. He added that the gap between these two sorts of nation is expanding rapidly. His comments have particular point in the present context since well-managed, carefully conserved inland waters are clearly likely to result from adequate limnological information (as in northern temperate regions), whereas inadequate information will result in badly-managed and poorly conserved water resources that may be irreparably damaged or lost forever (as in tropical regions). In short, lack of information will further impoverish those who lack it.

Measures

It is easy to suggest general measures to correct the limnological imbalance and improve the status of tropical limnology; it is much less easy to suggest practicable, effective and particular measures to do so. The most obvious general measure, of course, is for governments to provide better financial support for limnology. For them to be persuaded thus, I can suggest only that their closer attention be directed to the fact that effective conservation and management of inland waters as an essential basic resource can only come from a thorough understanding of how not only water quantity but also water quality is determined.

Logically, those governments who want the inland waters of their country to remain a viable resource should need little persuasion. That water can provide a sustainable resource of significant economic, cultural, aesthetic and scientific value, and, in tropical countries to a degree unequalled in temperate ones, can be medically hazardous, should speak for itself. But, as I need hardly say, not all governments are logical animals, even those of countries, such as my own, where water is far from abundant [my arrangement of words here is deliberately obtuse]; usually, the strident, more immediate but less important imperatives are met first, and quietly argued demands of greater importance in the long-term national interest run second-best. Certainly, most if not all of the general and eminently sensible provisions of the 1980 'resolution on the promotion of limnology in developing countries (especially those in tropical and arid [*sic*] zones)' put forward by the International Association for Limnology (Mori & Ikusima 1980) – well-meaning and high-sounding that they were – seem not to have been implemented seriously anywhere.

As for particular measures, whatever the difficulty of suggesting them, a first step is recognition of the sorts of specific problems facing tropical limnologists. They are many and varied. Some particular problems that I focus on, and that I believe are tractable largely within the present financial framework, are those concerned broadly with communication: that is to say, those problems I alluded to above which bedevil limnological research on tropical waters in addition to the paucity of direct support for it. Major problems of this sort relate to the relatively restricted use of English as the medium of communication, the need fully to recognize the integral value of tropical limnology both in its own right and as a contribution to global knowledge, the difficulties of publishing tropical research, poorly-developed informal communication networks, and poor access to the scientific literature.

Nobody can deny that during the past half century English has increasingly become the language most used to communicate at international conferences and in which a good deal of the scientific literature appears. It is the first language of some 350 million people and the second language of another 400 million. It dominates the knowledge distribution network (Altbach 1987). It is perhaps not the easiest language to learn (it has, for example, a huge lexicon), and it is perhaps not an immediately attractive language to those tropical limnologists domiciled in countries formerly part of the colonial empire of the United Kingdom or those who prefer to view American culture at a distance; but it has become the language of science, for good or ill. If tropical limnologists want both better access to the broader limnological literature, and wish to improve communication between themselves, then more complete acceptance of this fact is needed. Tropical limnologists need to develop greater facility with speaking, reading and writing English than many of them presently have. This is not to denigrate the role of national languages in science, but rather to stress that the acceptance of a common scientific language by European and North American limnologists (and other scientists) has been a key element in the ease with which they now communicate. I need scarcely add that it makes no sense to decide at this stage that some language other than English should be the medium of communication for tropical limnologists! All of this may seem old hat to many, but I assure you as the editor of several books and scientific journals that there is room for improvement in this area, at least so far as written English is concerned.

As for the integral value of tropical limnology in its own right, one of the many hurdles that tropical limnologists face in this matter – indeed, a hurdle faced by all limnologists working outside the northern temperate zone – is that studies by them seem generally to be perceived in the international literature as interesting regional studies first and contributions to mainstream limnology second, whereas studies of northern temperate waters are contributions to mainstream limnology first and regional studies second. Judging from the way in which the significance of many limnological studies of non-temperate water-bodies is often introduced, this perception of studies outside Europe and North America seems also to have been accepted even by those limnologists who undertook the studies in question. This is perhaps understandable when the limnologists concerned are scientific 'itinerants', that is, limnologists ordinarily domiciled in Europe and North America who have gathered information whilst on 'expeditions' to countries other than their own. It is not understandable when the limnologists involved are local residents. This is not, of course, to belittle the importance of early contributions to tropical limnology made for example, by RUTTNER, THIENEMANN, WORTHINGTON and others [RUTTNER 1931, THIENEMANN 1931, WORTHINGTON & WORTHINGTON 1933; general accounts of the Deutsche Limnologische Sunda-Expedition (1928–1929) and of the Cambridge Expedition to the East African lakes (1930–1931) are given by THIENEMANN [1959] and WORTHINGTON (1983)]. But, tropical limnology will never develop a satisfying cohesive and conceptual framework until the intellectual hegemony of temperate limnology is clearly seen as the conceptual constraint it is. It is not surprising that tropical limnology in particular, but all limnological studies beyond the northern temperate zone in general, present constitute an ad hoc, conceptually derivative, and fragmented area of limnology (WILLIAMS 1988). This situation is not likely to change until tropical limnologists (and other 'non-temperate' limnologists) themselves recognize the full significance of their work, relate it to the wider limnological perspective, and draw attention to it in their own published papers.

The difficulties of publishing the results of research on tropical waters are manifold. Assuming that publication in a journal of some international repute is desired, there is first the physical difficulty of acutally producing acceptable typescript and publication-quality artwork. Then there is the difficulty of providing a text in acceptable English. Not least, there is the difficulty of selecting an appropriate journal in which to publish. Difficulties like these are usually greater for tropical limnologists (many of whom lack word-processors, access to artists, and fluency in English), but they are not insuperable.

At least one way to minimize their impact is to decrease the rate of publication (i.e. the annual number of papers submitted for publication), and thus provide for an increase in the amount of time that can be devoted to individual papers so that the overall quality of manuscripts submitted is raised. The elimination of all non-essential figures and the submission of draft manuscripts for comment to several colleagues fluent in English (especially, if possible, to those for whom English is the first language) will also help. Overlong, pretentious, badly-presented manuscripts in poor English invariably attract immediate rejection by referees whatever the fundamental value of the limnology reported. Journal referees are usually busy people unwilling if not unable to give much time to improving the manuscripts of limnologists they may not know and who cannot even directly acknowledge their help since most referees are anonymous. Faced by manuscripts requiring the input of significant amounts of time, most referees opt to return the manuscript to the editor with the suggestion that 'revision' is needed.

Often, unfortunately, rejection results in either no further attempt by the author to publish, or submission of the unrevised manuscript to another journal, usually of more restricted, local circulation and perhaps in a language other than English. In either case, the results of the original research are effectively lost to the wider limnological community. Many local journals are not subscribed to by libraries in the north temperate zone (where, in any case, there has been a recent trend to decrease the number of journal subscriptions), especially when their contents are not of immediate interest to users, and scientific papers in journals which are difficult to obtain are often ignored even if their titles do appear in the abstracting literature and are relevant. Such biasses, it might be added, operate even within the north temperate zone: for example, North American limnologists tend to cite papers in North American journals more frequently than papers in European journals, and vice versa.

The initial selection of the journal to which the manuscript was originally submitted also provides difficulties. Submission to any of the many journals which now impose page charges is generally out of the question. But submission to others that do not may subsequently be preempted because they impose charges for 'difficult' typesetting: e.g. *Limnology and Oceanography* charges for typesetting mathematical formulae. The new journal *Tropical Freshwater Biology* has the potential to be an appropriate means of publishing results of limnological studies in the tropics, but whether it actually achieves its potential remains to be seen because shortly before I wrote this paper I received a status report from its Editor-in-Chief. This informed me that *Tropical Freshwater Biology* (TFB) has achieved only mild acceptance so far from the scientific community. The main difficulties are apparently threefold. Quote:

"1) *Lack of papers.* This is not necessarily the reflection of the paucity of work done in tropical freshwaters, but rather the preference of authors to seek more established western journals. The authors are not to be blamed because the circumstances under which they work demand supporting the myopic view that journals published in the tropics are substandard.

2) *The quality of articles.* Unfortunately, the establishment of local journals in the past for various lofty as well as nefarious reasons has led to the belief that quality is a bargainable commodity with the newly created tropical journals. Most of the articles received by *TFB* have either been rejected by the 'reputed' journals or not publishable elsewhere. We tried to keep up the standards of *TFB* by favouring a stringent review system and a strong editorial hand. The obvious result was the high rejection rate (85–90 %) of manuscripts submitted. To encourage many authors who submitted potentially good papers, but very weak on presentation due to various reasons including the use of the English language, we went out of our way to help by offering editorial, graphic and other technical help free of charge. We just have to wait and hope that the quality of articles submitted will improve in the future.

3) *Financial constraints.* This is a normal but a major problem for many tropical journals and is in no way unique to *TFB*. The cost of materials tends to fluctuate unpredictably; unavailability of materials and inflation are other reasons. To keep up a regular publishing schedule we need international subscribers. *TFB* has not fared well in this respect. We now feel that it may be realistic to publish only one issue a year. Even then, we have to be frugal by using lesser quality material when compared to other western journals. Unless the circulation of *TFB* increases and subscriptions soar, we are likely to follow the present trend."

These comments will be published in the third volume of *Tropical Freshwater Biology* but are given fully here because most provide specific examples of the many general problems under discussion concerning the publication of research on tropical inland waters. The experience of *Tropical Freshwater Biology* provides lessons for both tropical limnologists and those who wish to publish their results. Its future lies largely in your hands.

Whatever its future, the past history of this journal underscores many of the inequalities referred to by ALTBACH (1987) with regard to the international system of disseminating knowledge: a system "dominated and controlled by the large, wealthy and prestigious academic systems, publishers, and research enterprises in the major industrialized nations . . . the central intellectual powers of the world." Journals outside this privileged circle, however, can succeed, as ALTBACH (1987) also noted, providing their publishers plan carefully, cultivate specific markets, and develop close relations between authors, readers and institutions.

As for the need to improve the relatively poor state of the informal networks along which knowledge passes in tropical countries, significant improvement can be effected without much expenditure providing clear recognition of goals, problems and resources occurs. All that is required is a little confidence and energy! This is not a counsel of perfection for I speak from some recent experience.

My own special interest is in the limnology of salt lakes. The vast majority of these occur beyond the northern temperate zone and often in countries which are not wealthy and/or which have non-convertible currencies. These financial restraints notwithstanding, most limnologists interested in salt lakes in these countries now participate in an informal grouping (the International Consortium for Salt Lake Research) which is advised by a prestigious panel of Co-directors and which publishes a biennial newsletter (*Salinet*) containing news, notices of meetings (together with abstracts of papers where appropriate), notes on recent or forthcoming books of interest, a directory of members (areas of interest and addresses), and an ongoing and comprehensive bibliography of recent scientific papers concerned with salt lakes. *Salinet* is distributed freely to all members of the Consortium and is supported only by donations from those of its members who can afford to donate. Initially, the Consortium comprised some 100 members; its membership, rapidly growing, is now several times that number. A recent development has been the decision to launch a journal (the *International Journal of Salt Lake Research*) to support the activities of Consortium members further.

Salt lakes are important elements of the limnological environment, but I do not believe that tropical inland waters are significantly less important. If an informal network to aid communication between limnologists interested in salt lakes proved possible to develop, I see no reason why a similar network to aid informal communication between tropical limnologists should also not be developed. That tropical limnologists cannot meet as frequently as do limnologists from North American and Europe, or even salt lake limnologists (who now meet regularly every three years), is all the more reason why alternative methods of informal communication should be developed. Perhaps this matter can be raised in the final session of this symposium?

Finally, a few comments on the problem of poor access to the limnological literature. The causes of the problem are obvious: many libraries in tropical countries subscribe to a restricted number of journals and have small holdings of books; books themselves are costly and becoming increasingly more so; and it is expensive to participate even in systems which provide an indication of what literature is available let alone give access to the actual literature. Resolutions to these problems must be found if tropical limnologists are to be kept fully informed and thus contribute effectively to the management and conservation of water resources.

At least some of the resolutions need not necessarily involve the expenditure of much money. Better cooperation between libraries and individual scientists in the purchase of books and journals could help. More importantly, tropical limnologists could publish their own books locally (and in English to promote wider comprehension). At present there are few if any texts of this sort on tropical limnology, and most books about tropical waters have been published by European and North American publishers (and are therefore expensive) and written by authors who may well have paid extended visits to the tropics but who were essentially domiciled elsewhere (e.g. Serruya & Pollingher 1983, Payne 1986). The book by Beadle (1981) provides a notable exception so far as its authorship is concerned, but it too was published in Europe.

With regard to participation in systems which provide information on the recently published literature, again, better cooperation between libraries and individuals can provide some resolution. One system that I have used for most of my professional life that is relatively cheap yet extremely comprehensive is the *Current Awareness Service* of the Freshwater Biological Association, U.K. (FBA Library and Information Service, The Ferry House, Far Sawrey, Ambleside, Cumbria, U.K. LA22 OLP). This provides a monthly listing of all papers and books accessed to the very comprehensive library of the Freshwater Biological Association. Recently, it has become possible to obtain a copy by return post of any item listed on payment of a small fee (*FBA Document Delivery Service*).

Final comment

This paper is an attempt to provide constructive advice to tropical limnologists. It has attempted to illuminate the significance of tropical inland waters both in a global scientific sense and as a natural resource, and to suggest a few practical measures which may improve the degree to which knowledge about tropical waters is disseminated and can be obtained. Whilst the emphasis has been upon scientific knowledge and communication between limnologists, the opportunity is taken here to stress the utmost importance of making available more general knowledge and engaging in wider communication. This is particularly important in so far as it informs decision-makers and other key members in governments. It is critically important to ensure that such people are made aware that:

i) tropical inland waters constitute a valuable natural resource of considerable economic, cultural, aesthetic, scientific, educational and ecological value;
ii) water resources can be significantly degraded in value, sometimes irreparably so;
iii) the conservation and management of water resources both for present and future generations is in the interests of the State; and
iv) effective conservation and management of inland waters can only be based upon a thorough scientific knowledge of them.

References

ALTBACH, P. G., 1987: The Knowledge Context. Comparative Perspectives on the Distribution of Knowledge: 203 pp. – State University of New York Press, Albany.

ARMENTANO, T. V. (1990): Soils and ecology: tropical wetlands. – In: WILLIAMS, M. (ed.): Wetlands. A Threatened Landscape: 115–144. – Blackwell Scientific Publications, Oxford.

BEADLE, L. C., 1981: The Inland Waters of Tropical Africa. An Introduction to Tropical Limnology 2nd. ed.: 475 pp. – Longman, New York.

FERNANDO, C. H., 1980: Some important implications for tropical limnology. – In: MORI, S. & IKUSIMA, I. (eds.): Proceedings of the First Workshop on the Promotion of Limnology in the Developing Countries: 103–107. – Societas Internationalis Limnologiae, Kyoto.

HAMMER, U. T., 1986: Saline Lake Ecosystems of the World: 616 pp. – Dr. W. Junk Publishers, Dordrecht.

JUMARS, P. A., 1990: W(h)ither limnology? – *Limnol. Oceanogr.* **35**: 1216–1218.

LEWIS Jr., W. J. (1987): Tropical limnology. – *Ann. Rev. Ecol. Syst.* **18**: 159–184.

MORI, S. & IKUSIMA, I., 1980: Proceedings of the First Workshop on the Promotion of Limnology in the Developing Countries: 172 pp. – Societas Internationalis Limnologiae, Kyoto.

PAYNE, A. I., 1986: The Ecology of Tropical Lakes and Rivers: 301 pp. – John Wiley & Sons, Chichester.

RUTTNER, F., 1931: Hydrographische und hydrochemische Beobachtungen auf Java, Sumatra und Bali. – *Arch. Hydrobiol., Suppl.* **8**, (*Trop. Binnengewässer I*): 197–454.

SERRUYA, C. & POLLINGHER, U., 1983: Lakes of the Warm Belt: 569 pp. – Cambridge University Press, Cambridge.

THIENEMANN, A., 1931: Tropische Seen und Seetypenlehre. – *Arch. Hydrobiol., Suppl.* **9** *(Tropische Binnengewässer II)*: 205–231.

– 1959: Erinnerungen und Tagebuchblätter eines Biologen: 499 pp. – Schweizerbart, Stuttgart.

TOFFLER, A., 1990: Powershift. Knowledge, Wealth and Violence at the Edge of the 21st Centruy: 571 pp. – Bantam, New York.

WILLIAMS, M., 1990: Understanding wetlands. – In: WILLIAMS, M. (ed.): Wetlands. A Threatened Landscape: 1–14. – Blackwell Scientific Publications, Oxford.

WILLIAMS, W. D., 1986: Limnology, the study of inland waters: a comment on perceptions of studies of salt lakes, past and present. – In: DE DECKKER, P. & WILLIAMS, W. D. (eds.): Limnology in Australia: 471–484. – CSIRO, Melbourne and Dr. W. Junk Publishers, Dordrecht.

– 1988: Limnological imbalances: an antipodean viewpoint. – *Freshwat. Biol.* **20**: 407–420.

WORTHINGTON, E. B., 1983: The Ecological Century. A Personal Appraisal: 206 pp. – Clarendon, Oxford.

WORTHINGTON, E. B. & WORTHINGTON, S., 1933: Inland Waters of Africa: 259 pp. – Macmillan, London.

Author's address:

Department of Zoology, University of Adelaide, GPO Box 498, Adelaide, SA 5001, Australia.

Mitt. Internat. Verein. Limnol.	24	365–368	Stuttgart, Februar 1994

Constraints and opportunities for training in wetland management

Patrick J. Dugan

Abstract

Wetlands have been destroyed in the past because their many contributions to human welfare were not recognized. Today, much has changed and there is increasing national and international concern that these natural ecosystems must be managed more effectively. As awareness has grown, so has concern for the need to build institutional capacity to manage wetlands. At present, most institutions concerned with wetlands are organised in a sectoral fashion. Yet the importance of these resources lies in their multiple values, including fisheries, forestry, grazing, agriculture, flood control, water treatment, and many others. Such integrated management of wetlands will require major institutional change in almost all countries, and a substantial investment in staff training. This will, in turn, require us to learn general lessons from specific examples of sustainable wetland use. This paper examines these issues, discusses approaches to cross-sectoral training, and suggests ways in which the lessons of specific case studies in wetland management can be applied more widely.

Introduction

For much of human history, wetlands have been lost worldwide because people did not recognize their many contributions to human welfare. While there remains a major need for continued investment in building awareness of the public value of wetlands, there is now increasing national and international concern that these natural ecosystems must be conserved and managed more effectively. In turn, however, this rising concern for wetland conservation has brought with it a clearer understanding of the limited institutional capacity to manage these ecosystems. Thus while wetland science has advanced substantially in the past 20 years, only in a few countries have those institutional structures with jurisdiction over wetland resources been provided with staff qualified to exercise this mandate. If the current interest in wetland conservation is to lead to a clear reduction in the rate of wetland loss, much more needs to be done now to build institutional capacity to manage these resources. Precise training needs have to be identified as well as the constraints and opportunities for meeting them. The present paper attempts to assist in this process by reviewing the need for greater investment in wetland training, and examining a number of major constraints and opportunities.

Critical issues for training in wetland management

Integrated management

Biologists have long been at the forefront of wetland conservation, a role emphasised by the special focus on waterfowl by the Ramsar Convention in its early days. As a result, investment in wetland training has focused traditionally upon the biological values of wetlands and their management needs. The tendency in the past has been for wildlife biologists to be trained exclusively in the details of wildlife biology, foresters in forest management, and fisheries managers in fish biology. Only rarely have specialists in these varied biological disciplines been brought together with each other and with other disciplines, and provided with a grounding in these related fields. There is now growing recognition that wetland conservation and management are inter-disciplinary issues which require simultaneous approaches to diverse biological and physical issues together with economic, social, cultural, and administrative ones (Dugan 1990). Accordingly, the incidence of interdisciplinary training courses has begun to increase.

Looking to the future, the tentative development of integrated training courses needs to be strengthened and expanded. In particular, the integrated approach must be adopted by institutions of higher learning in order that, from the outset, students can be encouraged to understand and work with other disciplines.

Development of career structures

Training individuals for integrated wetland management will be of little value if the newly-trained

0538-4680/94/0024-0365 $ 1.00

specialists do not receive motivation to apply and develop their skills further. While there are a number of measures which can be taken to address this problem, the critical need is for the development of an appropriate career structure which provides the incentives for staff to seek training, and then pursue a career within those institutions responsible for wetland management. Development of such a career structure requires much greater appreciation by governments of the importance of wetland resources and the need to increase substantially the institutional capacity to manage them. In only a few countries is this political commitment present, with the result that many well-qualified people are unable to pursue careers in wetland conservation.

By recognising the need for an effective career structure, the scale of the investment that is required to provide wetland training becomes clearer. Thus not only must governments examine how best to provide the needed incentives to their wetland managers, but investment in training needs to be made at several levels. These include universities where specialized courses in specific aspects of wetland conservation and management can be pursued, regional institutions where more intensive training in management issues relevant to particular regions should be developed, and within government departments where courses designed to meet the needs of individual departments should be held on (at least) an annual basis.

Follow-up to training

While the development of a career structure in support of wetland management, and training at several levels, are of critical importance for the development of an increased capacity to manage wetland resources sustainably, they will on their own have little long-term impact on wetland conservation. In addition, training must be pursued as a central element of both national and regional strategies designed to address priority wetland conservation problems. Training courses should be seen as a part of a multi-faceted approach to conservation, and be designed to support and draw upon other initiatives such as field projects, research, economic analyses, and policy development.

Constraints to addressing the training challenge

There are many constraints to addressing the training issues identified above. Three are of special importance.

Funding

The comprehensive approach to training advocated here will require a major increase in funding. This, in turn, requires a substantial increase in awareness among the various funding agencies of the importance of wetland conservation and management, and in particular the contribution that wetlands can make to meeting the needs of the rural poor.

Development of integrated courses

Training courses which teach an integrated approach to wetland management will require a major change in the way in which most trainers approach their work. For example, biologists and limnologists will need to set their own expertise within the full biological, physical, social, and institutional context, and give emphasis to the fact that the answers to most problems in wetland management lie in working together with experts in other disciplines. The need for integration will require much greater care in designing training courses, while priority in selecting participants will need to be given to those who can be seen to benefit most from this broadening of horizons. This selection process will be most effective in countries where the various national institutions involved in wetland management have achieved an understanding of their true training needs.

Institutional capacity

Assuming that the previous two constraints can be addressed, it is essential that each institution with the capacity to provide training in wetland conservation and management can design training activities which accord most closely with their capacity. To assist in this planning process, concerned institutions should work together to analyze national and regional requirements for training in wetland management and follow this with an analysis of the potential and capacity of each institution. Such analysis will require difficult decisions to be taken by many individuals and institutions. In some cases, institutions will be able to play a catalytic role by taking the lead in being first to hold training courses in one particular field. These courses could be taken up by other institutions, most appropriately by those which have a wider national or regional mandate and a greater long-term capacity to meet training needs. At the same time, institutions will need to assess whether areas in which they have particular expertise, such as remote sensing, have a central role to play in addressing the priority wetland management issues of their country or region. In the absence of these analyses a great deal of effort – and substantial funding – may be invested in training courses which have only minimal impact upon reducing the rate of wetland loss.

Opportunities for strengthening training in wetland management

Growing awareness

Despite the constraints identified in the preceding paragraphs, there is growing cause for optimism that there can be a major increase in investment in wetland training worldwide, and that this can be more effective in addressing the problems of conservation. Underlying this optimism is the slow but steady increase in awareness of the importance of wetlands, and the social, economic, and environmental consequences of their loss. As a result, governments, together with bilateral and multilateral aid agencies are giving substantially greater attention to wetland conservation, and are looking for ways to invest in developing national capacity to manage wetland resources. Thus, despite the current funding limitations, there is a greater likelihood than ever before that a well-designed programme of training in wetland management – one can be shown to make a significant difference at national, regional or international level – will receive support.

Institutional interest

Coinciding with this growing awareness of the importance of wetland conservation there is a noticeable increase in the number of institutions contributing to wetland conservation and, amongst these, a particularly strong increase in the attention being given to training in wetland management. For example, in South-East Asia, the University of Malaysia, the Asian Institute of Technology (AIT), the International Centre for Living Aquatic Resource Management (ICLARM), the Asian Wetlands Bureau (AWB), and IUCN have all examined recently how they might best contribute to training in wetland management. This process needs to be encouraged and supported with funding from the bilateral and multilateral aid agencies. Of particular importance the growing institutional interest in wetland conservation is spread across a range of disciplines with many foresters, fisheries specialists, hydrologists, social anthropologists and economists now joining with biologists to argue for improved management. This has greatly increased the potential for integrated courses, and several institutions which have a broad disciplinary base (such as AIT) are examining how best to bring together various disciplines and faculties to design and teach courses in coastal-zoneplanning and wetland management.

Support for field programmes

In the past, the ultimate impact of many training courses has been limited because, in the absence of an ongoing programme of wetland conservation action at national level, many such efforts were neither targeted at priority issues, nor designed for those individuals who would benefit most. Today, however, with increased investment in wetland conservation and management on the ground, there is now a much greater opportunity to target training courses at the priority needs of national institutions concerned with wetland management, and to identify individuals for whom a specific type of training course can make a major difference to the work they pursue. A strong field programme also allows training activities to draw upon specific case studies in wetland management and to derive general lessons from these. Perhaps most important, such field programmes provide the trainees with the opportunity to return home at the end of a training course and continue to apply what they have learned.

This is a substantial change from the situation where many training courses had little follow-up, and individuals returned home to a shortage of funds, and to frustration at not being able to apply what they had learned.

Concluding remarks

Training in wetland management has long been a 'privileged solution' to the challenge of wetland conservation; that is, investment in training has presented a relatively easy means of spending funds and 'demonstrating' that action was being taken to address the steady loss of the world's wetland resources. However, while this has done much to build enthusiasm for wetland conservation in many regions, the sporadic nature of much of this training investment and its (often) limited focus on selected biological aspects of wetland management have meant that the training offered was inadequate to meet the need for a substantial and lasting increase in national and international capacity to manage wetland resources. Although there are many reasons for this, and a number of important constraints continue to exist, there is today growing potential for a substantially increased international investment in training in wetland conservation. For this interest to be maintained, however, growing awareness of the importance of wetlands and the need for integrated management needs to be consolidated and expanded, while truly integrated training courses need to be developed. In the face of this challenge, a wide range of institutions – ranging from universities and technical training centres, to national, regional and global conservation organisations – must identify and undertake the specific type of training courses that they can provide most effectively. Moreover, they should endeavour to ensure that this training forms part of a coherent national and/or regional programme which provides appropriate opportunities for trainees to apply what they have learned.

Acknowledgements

I thank Jean-Yves Pirot for comments on a draft of this paper.

References

Dugan, P. J., 1990: Wetland Conservation: A Review of Current Issues and Required Action: 96 pp. – IUCN, Gland, Switzerland.

Author's address:

Wetlands Programme Coordinator, IUCN – The World Conservation Union, Ave du Mont Blanc, CH-1196 Gland, Switzerland.
Present address: Director of Regional Affaires, IUCN, Rue Mauverney, 28, CH-1196 Gland, Switzerland.

Mitt. Internat. Verein. Limnol.	24	369–386	Stuttgart, Februar 1994

Conservation and management of tropical Asian and Australian inland waters: Problems, solutions and prospects

David Dudgeon, Angela H. Arthington, William Y. B. Chang, Jon Davies, Christopher L. Humphrey, R. G. Pearson and P. K. S. Lam

Abstract

This paper summarizes the individual contributions contained in the volume *Inland Waters of Tropical Asia and Australia: Conservation and Management*. It explores the principles and philosophies, as well as the problems and constraints, related to the conservation and management of tropical inland waters in general and Australian and Asian systems in particular. It also addresses a range of issues specific to the conservation of individual habitat types: i.e. rivers and streams, lakes, and wetlands. With regard to the conservation of running waters in the tropics, it is evident that future research should focus on the impact of river regulation and flow control on the aquatic biota. Patterns of energy flow and nutrient cycles, and interactions between lotic systems and their drainage basins or catchments, are in need of investigation also. Eutrophication of standing water bodies is a major concern, especially in China where many of the region's large natural lakes are concentrated. Possible management strategies to reduce nutrient loads include source reduction and 'nutrient-stripping' through fish farming. Here closer examination of the potential negative impacts of prevailing management practices on the overall biodiversity of lentic systems is called for, as protection of the habitats does not automatically translate into preservation of their natural inhabitants. This point is reinforced by the effects of exotic introductions on the native aquatic fauna of tropical Asia and Australia, and a serious lack of information (and predictive ability) regarding this important subject is evident. The complexity of wetland systems poses a real challenge to environmental scientists and managers, and it is clear that successful conservation and management of these endangered habitats can only be accomplished by a multi-scale–multidisciplinary–multi-sectoral approach. It is argued that environmental monitoring and, in particular, biological monitoring should form an integral part of all conservation programmes. The complementary nature of monitoring techniques suitable for investigations at different scales, as well as the importance of proper experimental design and statistical analysis, are discussed. Suggestions are made with the aim of improving the scientific rigour of environmental monitoring, establishing sound and relevant water-quality standards, and providing better training and career prospects for conservation personnel, particularly those in developing countries. The paper concludes with comments on the conflict between the economic development of some tropical countries and the safeguarding of biodiversity, and the role that scientists can play in influencing the outcome of this conflict. Some recommendations are made which could serve to direct the efforts of limnologists towards conservation and management of tropical inland waters.

Introduction

This chapter synthesizes contributions made in the individual papers in this volume, attempts to elucidate trends or generalizations which can be applied usefully to conservation and management efforts, and to indicate where more research and data are needed. To facilitate this, the chapter is subdivided along habitat lines: rivers and streams, lakes, and wetlands. It is recognized that these divisions are not totally satisfactory; for example, there are overlaps between the wetland category and both lentic and lotic habitats, and – in nature – there are drainage connections between them. However, the artificial categorization is retained here because the management strategies for lakes are, for instance, quite different to those applied to streams, and these habitats tend to be studied by different groups of investigators using disparate techniques.

The chapter also takes account of two major areas of concern arising from some of the papers in this volume: introduced species and environmental monitoring. Particular emphasis is placed on the latter topic because appropriate biological monitoring techniques can be used to assess the success of conservation and management strategies, and can provide an early warning of environmental change and degradation.

Rivers and streams

Those concerned with running waters must be prepared to deal with issues of conservation and water-resource management at the species level, as well as with stream communities and ecosystem processes. By natural progression, ecological link-

0538-4680/94/0024-0369 $ 4.50

ages across stream–riparian zone boundaries should be considered also, in addition to the broader question of catchment (or watershed) processes and their impacts on aquatic environments. This synthesis of the volume's papers follows such a trajectory.

The conservation and management of lotic biota

The range of anthropogenic impacts on tropical and subtropical aquatic systems includes deforestation, disturbance of the riparian zone, river diversion, impoundment and flow regulation, establishment of settlements, crop plantations and industries, urbanization, chemical and biological pollution, sand, ore and gem mining, the over-exploitation of endemic species, and the introduction of exotic species. These phenomena have been documented for fishes and atyid shrimps in Sri Lanka (de Silva 1984, de Silva & de Silva 1994), but the problems that these papers highlight are by no means confined to those countries (see Ho 1994, Khondker 1994, Lowe-McConnell 1994, Nontji 1994).

A key issue, which perhaps should be the starting point for research and management agendas, is to ascertain how much is actually known about the taxonomic relationships, diversity and conservation status of endemic aquatic faunas, such as fishes, in particular countries. These data are lacking for most countries in tropical Asia, and only in Sri Lanka can the fauna be described as reasonably well known (see Costa 1994, de Silva 1994, de Silva & de Silva 1994, and references therein). Such an inventory-type project has commenced recently in Malaysia under the direction of the Asian Wetland Bureau, with the support of several national agencies and international sources of funding (see also Davies & Giesen 1994). With the nature and status of endemic biota categorized, the next step towards the development of management plans and rehabilitation strategies would be to accumulate essential biological and ecological information that could be used to establish management plans for the protection of particular species and their habitats.

Knowledge of habitat requirements and environmental tolerances, reproductive biology, patterns of dispersal and interactions amongst species will be critical here, and such information is inadequate for many tropical aquatic systems. For instance, our need for greater knowledge of the biota of many large river systems is exemplified by papers dealing with fish kills in the Darwin-Katherine-Jabiru floodplains of northern Australia (Townsend 1994), and the utilization of floodplain habitats by the fishes of the Fly River, Papua New Guinea (Smith & Bakowa 1994). Even the migration patterns of commercially-important fish species up and down rivers, in response to food supply and to reach breeding grounds, is almost unknown in most tropical Asian countries (Dudgeon 1992a). Smith & Bakowa (1994) highlight several important methodological issues, including the difficulties of quantitative sampling in large river systems and the need for sophisticated multivariate analyses of biological and environmental data sets. Clearly, execution of the types of studies needed in many tropical aquatic systems will challenge our ingenuity and resources in many ways.

One of the surprising gaps in the literature in tropical Asia is the question of the water (or in-stream flow) requirements of aquatic species and river ecosystems. Arthington (1994) has described a case history using the In-stream Flow Incremental Methodology (IFIM) and a range of other approaches to the development of a water allocation strategy for an impounded subtropical system in Australia. The IFIM, developed by the United States Fish and Wildlife Service (Bovee 1982, 1986), is considered by many to be the most sophisticated methodology for assessing the environmental water requirements of rivers. The physical habitat component of IFIM (PHABSIM in the USA and PHYHABSIM in New Zealand; see Jowett 1982) and other methods involving transect analysis are based on the simulation and evaluation of habitat availability (expressed in terms of 'weighted useable area') for particular aquatic species at different levels of stream discharge.

It is possible that with appropriate modifications and care in project execution (e.g. Kwak et al. 1992), IFIM methods will be of value as techniques for fish and habitat management in tropical streams. However, Arthington (1994) concludes that while IFIM and related methods may be useful for assessing the requirements of economically-important fish species (e.g. salmonids) in relatively stable, homogeneous rivers, they are seldom useful for assessing the water needs of entire fish communities, and are far from adequate when the protection of functional aquatic ecosystems is required. Furthermore, the application of transect-based models applied at a few points along river channels cannot realistically characterise the geomorphologically heterogeneous and hydrologically variable and unpredictable river systems that typically occur in most of the arid tropics of Australia (McMahon 1986, 1989), South Africa (Davies & Day 1989) and other subtropical and tropical areas. Even where there is seasonal predictability in flow – in the wet tropics of Australia and much of monsoonal Asia – there is unpredictability at a finer temporal scale, and this may be more the rule than the expection in streams throughout much of the planet. Finally, there are practical problems inherent in the application of PHABSIM, and IFIM in its entirety (e.g. Gan & McMahon 1990) and many theoretical objections have been raised (e.g. Mathur et al. 1985, Scott & Shirvell 1987, Bain & Boltz 1989).

There is growing recognition that the utility of IFIM requires further investigation in – at least – Australian and South African environments, where a different approach to water allocation for rivers must be taken. Much greater emphasis needs to be placed on the maintenance of the entire riverine ecosystem, including such components as the source area, river channel, riparian zone, floodplain, groundwater, wetlands and estuary, as well as any particularly important features such as rare and endangered species. The holistic approach to water allocation for rivers proposed by Arthington et al. (1992), and applied in Queensland (Arthington 1994), is intended to address these deficiencies. The results of the latter paper indicate that much more emphasis should be given to water allocation for the environment in other subtropical and tropical regions, and especially those with markedly-seasonal flow regimes; i.e. much of tropical Asia.

The need for development of ecologically-sound water-allocation strategies is urgent given the extent and magnitude of water transfers and river control projects in tropical Asia, as well as some of their known deleterious effects (Dudgeon 1992a and references therein). The control of the Ganges (and effects on the fisheries) and proposals for large-scale projects on the Mekong and Yangtze (Chang Jiang) Rivers are conspicuous examples but, in densely-populated areas, almost every stream is dammed or impounded, and reduced flows or even dewatering of reaches downstream is a frequent occurrence. There has been alarmingly little research on the ecological effects of river regulation in Asia. On a small scale (Dudgeon 1992b), dry-season dewatering downstream of weirs or dams has short-term effects because drift of animals from upstream leads to rapid recolonization of defaunated reaches. On a larger scale however, loss of organisms from downstream (potamal) sections is not compensated for by drift from upstream (rithral) areas, and river regulation or dewatering changes the flow characteristics of these downstream sections so altering conditions for life there. Human impact on the potamon of major rivers in Europe, North America and Asia is severe (Benke 1990, Zwick 1992, Dudgeon 1992a), perhaps because they are separated by distances beyond the average dispersal capacity of the fauna; i.e. they are widely-separated ecological islands, with known risk of species losses (Zwick 1992). In contrast, faunal exchange between adjacent headwater streams in uplands with intact stream nets is easy, at least for amphibiotic insects. In Europe, modification of potamal reaches has led to the disappearance of specialist stoneflies (Plecoptera) and fishes, and the dominance of potamal rivers by 'ubiquitous' species (Zwick 1992). In Hong Kong, the original fauna of lowland rivers and streams affected by flow regulation has been replaced by exotic fishes (especially Poeciliidae and tilapias) and gastropods (Ampulariidae and Planorbidae) (Yipp 1990, 1991, Dudgeon 1992b). Exotic species and their impacts on endemic species and ecosystems are a significant source of concern in inland waters throughout much of the tropics, and this topic will be considered in greater depth below.

Stream communities and ecosystem processes

The significance of allochthonous energy sources and organic matter in stream energy budgets is now widely recognised from studies in most major continents, although most of the available information has been derived from research in temperate systems (Lake & Barmuta 1986, but see Arunachalam & Arun 1994, Pearson 1994). While there are key processes governing detritus-based systems that are still unknown, forests in general, and tropical forests in particular, are being destroyed at an alarming rate. Limnologists must increase our understanding of the roles of riparian vegetation and energy sources in detritus-based stream systems as a basis for managing these streams and their catchments. One problem is that plantations of exotic species alter the pattern, biomass and palatability of litter entering streams when compared with the native flora, and may influence rates of mobilization of allochthonous energy (M.A.S. Graca, pers. comm.).

Perhaps the key message here is that tropical limnology – and limnologists – must be encouraged to question the axioms and generalizations derived from research in temperate systems where catchments are dominated by deciduous forest species and climatic factors impose fundamentally different regimes on aquatic biota and ecological processes (WILLIAMS 1994). Rigorous testing of the River Continuum Concept (RCC; VANNOTE et al. 1980) – in particular – is needed to determine whether this can be used as a predictive model for tropical Asian and Australian ecosystems. At present, there are no complete studies of any tropical Asian river system of any size which would allow us to test fully the predictions of the RCC, nor has there been any attempt to interpret the RCC in terms of river metabolism and fisheries. In almost no cases do limnologists know what type of organisms occur in each habitat type, nor how much each habitat contributes to the productivity of the river as a whole. The picture is complicated by the fact that certain fish and shrimps use various habitats at different times in their lives, and some of these habitats are inundated for only part of the year. Further complexity is introduced by year-to-year variations in the intensity of monsoonal rains which affect the extent of floodplain inundation, the magnitude of land-water interactions, and the amounts of allochthonous inputs into the river system.

Although more research is needed, consideration of floodplain ecology suggests that, for tropical rivers, the conventional longitudinal continuum of change in geomorphic and biological features from headwaters to mouth, must be augmented by a second axis running perpendicular to the first across the floodplain and encompassing the lateral extent of aquatic, semiaquatic and terrestrial habitats. This river-floodplain ecosystem would include the river channel(s), backwaters, oxbows and relict channels, floodplain pools, and seasonally-inundated areas of the terrestrial environment. The importance of this lateral axis is indicated by the observation that large floodplain-river systems cannot be addressed adequately using the RCC alone (SEDELL et al. 1989). Where the floodplain is well-developed, the primary and secondary production of the floodplain will be essential to fauna in the main channel. The seasonal pulsing of flood flows onto the floodplain provides the driving force for the river-floodplain interaction (WELCOMME 1979, JUNK et al. 1989) and determines the magnitude and extent of land-water interactions and allochthonous inputs. As water inundates the floodplain it produces a 'moving littoral' which prevents permanent stagnation and allows rapid recycling of nutrients and organic matter. This results in higher productivity than in systems which are either permanently wet or dry (JUNK et al. 1989). In addition, most fish production in large rivers is derived from floodplain habitats (WELCOMME 1979, JUNK et al. 1989). This is shown by the development of flood-control measures (canals, levees and dykes) on the Ganges floodplain which have deprived major carp of their extensive breeding sites and caused a significant decline in the fishery (NATARAJAN 1989).

There are two additional concepts of lotic ecology not mentioned in this volume which may have implications for effective conservation and management. Spiralling is used to refer to the process of reuse of allochthonous material in streams (WALLACE et al. 1977) and may contribute significantly to the tightness of nutrient cycles and retentiveness of the lotic community (NEWBOLD et al. 1983a, 1983b). The spiralling concept may have utility in the development of models for understanding the dynamics of nutrients and carbon in stream ecosystems. Secondly, the serial discontinuity concept (WARD & STANFORD 1983) seems to be a useful construct for assessing the impacts of impoundments on rivers in the north-temperate zone, but has yet to be applied to the many regulated rivers of tropical Asia.

Riparian and catchment transition zones (ecotones)

It is axiomatic that catchment (watershed) processes play a significant role in defining the character and functioning of river ecosystems. The role of riparian vegetation as a source of energy is but one of many aspects of the intimate linkages between the catchment and the aquatic ecosystem it supports. The transition zones between terrestrial and aquatic systems vary in size and permanence or stability. They may be extensive spatially and temporally, or of small areal extent and limited persistence. Some transition zones may usefully be termed 'wetlands', but not all all wetlands are transition zones (GOPAL 1994). In this regard, the utility of the concept 'ecotone' may not be of great consequence in terms of illuminating the processes governing transition zones and linking them to adjacent systems, although it is a convenient label. The more important questions are: how do ecological processes in transition zones differ, if at all, from those operating in terrestrial and aquatic environments, and how should we use our knowledge of these processes to assist in efforts to rehabilitate and conserve lotic ecosystems?

Integrated approaches to catchment and stream management

Land and water management in many tropical areas of the world has been focused on a developmental phase where the concern is to provide raw materials, food and fibre, as well as land and water for urban, agricultural and industrial development (CHOOWAEW et al. 1994). Such multiple uses or values seem to be characteristic of all types of wetland (DUDGEON 1994, DUGAN 1994a). However, socioeconomic pressures towards development have resulted in many perturbations to aquatic ecosystems and irreversible degradation in many of them. This volume has inevitably given emphasis to the need for a more balanced perspective, where there is proper consideration of ecological, recreational, scientific and cultural uses of natural resources. It is clear that to achieve this balance, not only a better understanding of the scientific issues is needed, but also improved approaches to the integration of these broader concerns. One example of this type of approach is the Wetlands Management Programme of the Mekong Secretariat for the lower Mekong basin (see CHOMCHAI 1987, PETERSEN & SKOGLUND 1990), which provides a model of the type of structure and organization that is required for a large river.

It is clear that multi-scale (cf. DUDGEON 1994) and multidisciplinary studies – including the application of system analysis techniques – are becoming increasingly important in the planning and decision making processes that accompany and underlie natural resource management. There cannot be but general agreement with this perception, although many limnologists will be reluctant to extend their efforts into such fields when there is an outstanding need for more taxonomic and biological information on tropical biota and a much better understanding of ecological processes in tropical ecosystems. Our need for understanding is confounded because there are probably no large rivers in Asia in pristine condition (HYNES 1989), and it is difficult to know what they were like in their original state. Studies which have been undertaken were often done on an ad hoc basis, with borrowed boats, improvised apparatus, and often with little continuity; the only data that are fairly good (and that is only true for some rivers) are fisheries statistics, but they are at best only a crude estimate of the totality of conditions in a large water body (HYNES 1989). However, pressure upon running-water systems dictates that fundamental inventory work and ecological research must proceed in parallel with studies contributing to better management, strategic planning and policy development in the land and water arena. To achieve this expertise many disciplines will need to be drawn upon as will interdisciplinary skills. Such a goal will not be attained by isolated individuals but by large (sometimes multinational) teams (the cross-sectoral approach of DUGAN [1994a, b]). Furthermore, if limnologists wish to understand the ecology of aquatic environments, we must not focus our efforts on one element of the system at the expense of others, or of the whole system. Long-term studies are needed also, for without a knowledge of the consequences of ecological 'crunch' times – for example, a year when the monosoonal rains are insufficient to inundate the floodplain – we will be in no position to predict the effect of management plans (such as controlling water flow) on river productivity.

Lakes

Remarkable increases in human population during recent decades have resulted in major changes in the ecology of inland waters, and particularly lakes. This reflects the use of these waters as receiving bodies for disposal of an unprecedented amount of human and agricultural effluents. As a result, many lakes have undergone or are undergoing major changes, and becoming eutrophic or hypertrophic. Such changes are most notable in the areas close to large population centres, as exemplified by the summary of extensive data from China presented by JIN (1994, see also JIN et al. 1990). To mitigate the increased nutrient loads, two approaches have been employed, summarized by papers in this volume: either the increased nutrients are used as a basis for food and fish production, or steps are taken to reduce nutrient loads of the water and lake sediments.

CHANG (1994) and ZHANG & CHANG (1994) give an account of the methods used in China to take advantage of increased nutrient loadings for aquatic production of food and fish. CHANG (1994) describes integrated lake-farming systems, which yield aquatic plants that take up the excess nutrients and can, in turn, be consumed by humans and herbivorous fish such as Grass carp (*Ctenopharyngodon idella*). The fish production that is based upon consumption of aquatic plants is harvested to provide income for farmers, and serves as a way of removing nutrients from the aquatic system. Clearly, appropriate stocking densities and species of both aquatic plants and fishes are vital to ensure that integrated lake-farming systems are both economically profitable and ecologically efficient. ZHANG & CHANG (1994) describe fisheries methods for managing lakes of differing trophic status. Aquatic plants and herbivorous fish are used to increase and remineralize the nutrients in oligotrophic lakes and in lakes where macrophytes predominate, while planktivorous fishes such as Silver carp (*Hypophthalmichthys molitrix*) and Bighead carp (*Aristichthys nobilis*) can be used to harvest the large biomass available in eutrophic waters. Complementary research on the use of these two fishes has been undertaken by LIU & CHEN (1994) in East Lake (Wuhan), where the proportion of total nutrient loads in the lake that was removed by fish harvesting has been calculated. The amounts removed (1.3% of seston nitrogen and 2.2% of seston phosphorus) were, however, rather small, and it is evident that an improvement in lake water quality could be achieved most effectively by controlling the seston biomass and hence the nutrient inputs.

Reduction of eutrophication in Chinese lakes will ultimately involve control of inputs, but it is notable that algal growth in lakes does not always increase in proportion to nutrient loads. In Chaohu Lake, Yin et al. (1994) found that high levels of suspended inorganic particles reduced light penetration and restricted algal production; PACARDO (1994) recorded a similar phenomenon in Laguna Lake in the Philippines. In both cases, high suspended-sediment loads were probably related to soil erosion resulting from agricultural practises in the drainage basin of the lake and its inflowing tributaries. These and other problems are by no means confined to lakes in China or the Philippines, as demonstrated by the reviews of NONTJI (1994), GIESEN (1994) and KHONDKER (1994), and research on lake trophic status in Malaysia (ANTON 1994, YUSOFF & PATIMAH 1994).

Overall integrated plans for the control of nutrient loads and management of lakes must include the control of point and non-point source loads, which can be achieved in a variety of ways (e.g. RYDING & RAST 1989). Appropriate legislation and discharge permits can be used to control or reduce the amount of loading from point sources, while improved land-use plans will be needed to reduce non-point source inputs from the drainage basin. The removal of sediment to reduce nutrient availability in shallow lakes is a management alternative, but the efficiency of reducing eutrophication in this way depends upon the extent of sediment storage, and the costs incurred may be high. (There will be additional problems involving the proper disposal of 'contaminated' sediment removed from lakes receiving industrial pollutants). If major reductions in point- and non-point sources of loads can lead to a significant elevation in dissolved oxygen levels in the water column, then the availability of nutrients from the sediment would be reduced and sediment removal might be unnecessary.

While Chinese experiences with lake management are instructive and demonstrate effective management of lakes as giant fish ponds, they do little to further conservation, because diverse communities of indigenous lake fish and other organisms are supplanted by a few species of commercially-important carp, with an overall loss in biodiversity (JIN et al. 1990, MELVILLE 1994). This trend is apparent over much of Asia. Where introductions or translocations of fishes have occurred widely and been accompanied by destructive fisheries practices, a loss of native or endemic lake species has been recorded (e.g. GIESEN 1994, PACARDO 1994, SOLIMAN 1994, see also **Introduced species** below), and this parallels the decline of lotic biodiversity recorded in the some parts of the region (e.g. DE SILVA 1994, DE SILVA & DE SILVA 1994).

Habitat creation or restoration has an important role to play in conservation and management of inland waters, as exemplified by development plans for a man-made impoundment in Brunei Darussalam (BOOTH et al. 1994) and abandoned tin-mine lakes in Malaysia (ARUMUGAM 1994). While these may serve as important habitat for waterfowl and other biota, their use for recreational angling and (perhaps) boating may restrict their value for the conservation of species that are sensitive to human disturbance or are liable to be predated by game fish. The addition of commercially-available or exotic fishes is an easy option for management authorities, and will certainly reduce the conservation value – although not necessarily the recreational or commercial value – of restored or man-made lakes. This situation parallels the conflicts seen in China – in Poyang Lake, for example (MELVILLE 1994) – between lake farming for economic gain and/or food production and the desire to conserve lentic biodiversity. For so long as the pressure of an increasing population drives development plans in tropical Asia, biodiversity will continue to decline until such a time that it can be assigned a significant economic value and its loss factored into the costs of developments. Only when the 'indirect use value' provided by environmental functions can be estimated (see AYLWARD & BARBIER 1992, DUGAN 1994 a), will ecology be considered on a par with economics by those whose decisions are most likely to influence the long-term fate of tropical ecosystems.

Wetlands

Many of the comments made with reference to lakes and lotic habitats can be applied to wetlands. However, the fact that wetlands are disappearing quickly or are being degraded irreparably, yet are a valuable resource used in a variety of ways by man (e.g. CHOOWAEW et al. 1994, MELVILLE 1994), has spurred attempts to assess, inventory, monitor and conserve these habitats (SCOTT & POOLE 1989, DAVIES & GIESEN 1994, DUGAN 1994, LUKENS 1994, MELVILLE 1994). From these and other papers, it is clear that a more multi-disciplinary approach is needed, entailing not only collaboration among limnologists involved with wetland research, conservation and management, but involvement of scientists other than aquatic ecologists: for example, terrestrial ecologists (for studies of the drainage basin and riparian zones), soil scientists, geologists, hydrologists and engineers. Such collaboration could involve scientists within the same disciplines from different types of institutions and different countries. Links between institutions or specialists from developed countries and host scientists or institutions in developing countries would lead to exchanges and flow of information, funds and expertise, and could also provide encouragement and boosts to the morale of scientists working in isolation or in small, under-funded organizations (see also DUGAN 1994 b).

Community-development and organization specialists will also be needed to integrate the needs and aspirations of the local inhabitants into conservation and management plans for wetland areas. Steps need to be taken to ensure that these people are involved in 'participatory research' or in monitoring programs. This could be facilitated by establishing links with local non-government organizations. However, this proposed increased collaboration among scientists and managers will need good coordination, which may involve input from broadly-based international agencies (such as IUCN). Major institutional changes will be needed in almost all countries, as well as substantial investment in training staff (DUGAN 1994 b). Mechanisms to facilitate stronger coordination must be devised, and should incorporate stronger 'networking' among scientists, and efficient division of labour to ensure that individuals are complementing rather than competing with the efforts of others.

It is particularly important for conservationists and managers to bear in mind the dynamic nature of wetlands. Rates of change in wetlands may be rapid; for example, in floodplain lakes where siltation rates are very high. Here changes brought about by natural and anthropogenic processes can be accelerated by human activities (land-use practices) in drainage basins which may lead to even greater rates of siltation. In view of the rapid rate of change due to natural processes, long-term wetland monitoring to trace the ecological history of areas of interest will have great value. Information gained can be used to design management strategies, by using a knowledge of the past to make decisions about what is likely to happen in the future. In this regard, there is a need to establish long-term, multi-dimensional monitoring programmes for selected sites which are representative of particular wetland types, with the goal of applying information obtained on each type to the management of other wetlands in the same category. More studies on the ecological history of representative wetlands are needed to aid in the design of management strategies. In this context, the method for assessing the conservation value and, importantly, the conservation feasibility of wetlands devised by DAVIES & GIESEN (1994) is likely to be especially valuable. It provides a method for rapidly assessing wetlands on the basis of their physical and biological characteristics, and would allow them to be placed into categories thus facilitating the identification of representative habitats for long-term monitoring and experimental studies. Other research priorities for wetland conservation and management are discussed by DUGAN (1994 a).

Experiments on the effects of artificial perturbation or manipulation of wetlands will be of particular value in the development of options for active management of these habitats (DUGAN 1994 a), which might involve trying to maintain a wetland at one particular stage in succession or maintaining habitat heterogeneity. While herbicides and burning (as well as cutting or dredging) are possible active-management options, the use of traditional management practices is more desirable. By this is meant encouragement of the traditional use of wetlands by local people where one spin-off is the appearance of another habitat; for example, the low swards of grass that result from buffalo grazing. This approach has the advantage of involvement of local inhabitants and can engender their support for wetland conservation and management efforts.

Introduced species

Species introductions into aquatic systems have been, and are, commonplace: Welcomme (1988) lists 1,354 international introductions of 237 freshwater species into 140 countries. They are of concern because of the potential effects of the exotics on native species (e.g. Arthington et al. 1990; Ross 1991), and because some aquatic plants have the potential to become nuisance weeds. The preeminent aquatic introduction in tropical Asia and Australia has been the Tilapia, *Oreochromis mossambicus*, although *O. niloticus* and its 'improved' strains have superseded *O. mossambicus* in parts of tropical Asia. The spread of *O. mossambicus* in Australia has been uncommonly well documented (Arthington & Blühdorn 1994), and more such data are needed to allow us to predict patterns and rates of habitat invasion by exotics. Tilapias are by no means the only successful and widespread exotic species in the region. Water hyacinth (*Eichhornia crassipes*) and the floating fern *Salvinia molesta* have also become widely distributed and are nuisance weeds in many areas (e.g. Nontji 1994).

Where introductions are accidental, they seem to have a greater chance of succeeding in disturbed or man-made habitats (Ross 1991), but this is by no means always true for plants (e.g. *Salvinia*; Room 1990) or top predators (the Nile perch, *Lates niloticus*, in Lake Victoria: Witte et al. 1992, see also Lowe-McConnell 1994). Where disturbance is necessary for initial establishment, however, thereafter populations can sometimes spread into undisturbed areas. Generalist species appear to do particularly well as introductions (e.g. Bruton 1989, Arthington et al. 1990, Yipp 1990, Arthington 1991). While it could be argued that colonization and/or range extensions are a natural process this does not make one feel comfortable about exotic introductions if they lead to extinction of indigenous species. Nevertheless, introduced species – such as Chinese major carps and tilapias – have been useful in boosting protein resources for human consumption in many parts of Southeast Asia. Such introductions are probably justifiable if they take place in habitats which lack a diverse or harvestable biota, and they have been of value in raising fish yields in man-made lakes in parts of Asia which lack an indigenous lacustrine fish fauna (e.g. Sri Lanka; Costa 1994). Similarly, the introduction of *Oreochromis niloticus* into Laguna de Bay (Philippines) has been beneficial to small fishing communities because the commercially-important migratory fish fauna has been destroyed by pollution of the main inflowing river (see also Pacardo 1994). An additional example is the Sepik River in Papua New Guinea which lacks the species that support significant inland fisheries in Asia. Fish yields are low with feral *O. mossambicus* comprising the bulk of landings. Introduction of a species which could support a sustainable capture fisheries would provide protein for the growing population of the Sepik drainage basin (Coates 1987). This case raises the dilemma of conflicting philosophies between the 'rich' and the 'poor' nations, which are difficult to resolve. Scientists in the former may be concerned about preservation of pristine natural ecosystems in the tropics, while decision-makers 'on site' are faced with socioeconomic pressures from a growing populace who may lack the necessities of life.

In general terms, it can be difficult to assess whether introductions are undesirable without proper documentation of both accidental and intentional introductions and, where research on the effects of an introduction have been undertaken, pre-introduction data are generally lacking (Ross 1991). This is exemplified by the case of Lake Lanao in Mindanao (the Philippines) where circumstantial evidence indicates that the introduction of the predatory goby, *Glossogobius giurus*, from elsewhere in the Philippines, contributed to the extinction of some members of a species-flock of cyprinids endemic to the lake. Circumstantial evidence also implicates the translocation and introduction of native piscivores as the cause of the extinction of an endemic rainbowfish (*Melanotaenia eachamensis*) in Lake Eacham in northern Queensland (Arthington 1989).

Biologists have a limited ability to predict the outcome of introductions because of an inability to answer some fundamental biological questions. For example, it is not known whether introduced biological control agents are more efficacious than indigenous species, nor if introduced species increase biological production in the long term (but see COATES 1987). Neither can biologists assess whether translocation of species within a country (i.e. enhancing the rate of natural spread among water bodies within a country) is more or less damaging than introduction of a species from another biogeographic region. While papers in this volume suggest that habitat degradation is often seen as the gravest threat to inland waters, it is not known if appropriate drainage-basin and habitat management will lessen the incidence and effects of introductions of exotic species.

It must not be supposed that problems associated with introduced species are confined to developing countries. For instance, the aquarium fish trade in Australia has been quite cavalier in its approach to import of exotic species, and there has been a poor response from governments to appeals from scientists for more stringent control. Indeed, *Lates niloticus* – which has had devastating effects on the fisheries of Lake Victoria following its introduction (WITTE et al. 1992) – was mooted for introduction as a sport fish to Australia to replace its congener, the native *L. calcarifer*, which has to migrate to the sea to breed and is therefore excluded from impounded waters in which *L. niloticus* does very well. Despite protestations about the likely effects of such an introduction, it was only following successful artificial breeding of *L. calcarifer* that interest in *L. niloticus* waned.

Biologists need to know more about the factors determining the success of exotic invaders, so as to improve the ability to predict their effects on indigenous biotas. It is unlikely that introductions can be prevented entirely, and some may be desirable for socioeconomic reasons. Nevertheless, better documentation of introductions, combined with improved communication with relevant authorities and tighter controls over introduced species would at least reduce the incidence of accidental introductions, and lessen the chance of the deliberate release of potentially-damaging species such as *Lates niloticus*. In this regard it would be useful to compile case studies where the introduction of exotic fishes has had a deleterious effect on native, commercially-important species or where there has been a marked decline in income from fishing as a result of such introductions.

Environmental monitoring

Any solutions to the problem of conservation and management of tropical inland waters will need to include and take into account some regular assessment of the environment to determine how effective management was in keeping impacts within acceptable limits, i.e. environmental monitoring. An array of contributions to this volume (BOLAND & IMBERGER 1994, HODGKISS 1994, HUMPHREY & DOSTINE 1994, LAI & LAM 1994, LUKENS 1994, NAKAYAMA 1994, SHEA 1994) had the basic aims of using the biota as tools to sample or monitor the environment in order to be in a position to detect disturbance at an early stage in the future. Nevertheless, a great range of scales was addressed – from the effects of stress on individual organisms (LAI & LAM 1994), to microbial and macroinvertebrate community monitoring (HODGKISS 1994, HUMPHREY & DOSTINE 1994, SHEA 1994), whole-lake assessment (BOLAND & IMBERGER 1994) and remote sensing (LUKENS 1994, NAKAYAMA 1994). This is to be expected in environmental monitoring: the type of approach taken will depend, for example, on the target group being protected, the habitat in question and the timescale; i.e. whether the concern is short- or long-term.

Monitoring techniques: needs and approaches

Of the contributors to this volume who considered large-scale monitoring techniques, NAKAYAMA's (1994) discussion of satellite imagery addressed a developing and innovative technology that has the potential to provide enormous cost-savings in a variety of water-quality measurements of inland lakes. Such techniques will obviously have much wider applications for the monitoring of water quality and habitat structural (including vegetation) changes in wetlands generally. Indeed, the technology must be viewed as more than labour-saving conveniences, but as central to the future monitoring of large- scale perturbations and any field experimentation associated with managing such disturbances. LUKENS (1994) considers in detail how remote sensing can be used as a tool for wetland conservation and management, and makes specific, practical recommendations concerning the development and training of a team of personnel to undertake such work. BOLAND & IMBERGER (1994) discussed new developments in applied physical limnology (involving the calculation of Lake Number) that will also provide relatively inexpensive means of predicting changes in water quality.

Other contributions dealt with monitoring in its more traditional sense, namely biological monitoring. Before referring to these papers and biological monitoring in general, however, it is essential to consider the requirements for environmental protection that will alleviate considerably the burden on environmental monitoring. Thus, it is far easier to keep impacts within acceptable limits by ensuring that criteria for receiving waters are set in place and a regulatory body has the power to ensure that there is compliance with particular standards. BAIRD (1994), for example, demonstrated clearly that use of chemicals of high toxicity to both target and non-target organisms is apparently encouraged in aquaculture settings, with the implication that criteria for disposal of these substances to the environment are either not in place, or not adhered to. ALABASTER's (1986) comprehensive review of the state of water pollution affecting inland fisheries in Southeast Asia confirms the view that, up to 1985 at least, some progress was being made in combating pollution, but there was at that time generally no comprehensive pollution control enactment in place to deal with serious and widespread pollution resulting from, in particular, suspended solids, low dissolved oxygen, heavy metals and pesticides. It is clear, moreover, that receiving water criteria in many developing countries are today still flexible or quite lax (e.g. DUDGEON 1992a; NONTJI 1994). This is probably true in many developed countries too, and if this problem is leading to the degradation of tropical inland waters then action is required. Notwithstanding, environmental protection agencies may have to accept that the level of environmental impact which is considered acceptable is often determined by socioeconomic factors. At least one environmental consultant in the Southeast Asian region considers that the usual 'bogeys' of pollution or mining waste impacts associated with large developments are overshadowed by secondary effects of the settlement resulting from infrastructure provision: for example, catchment clearance, habitat destruction and their effects upon aquatic ecosystems (K. HORTLE, pers. comm.). The challenge here is in providing an incentive for all parties to engage in environmental protection.

To return to monitoring, it is easy to persuade interested parties of the need to carry out environmental monitoring programs on waters when human usage or health, or commercial resource management, are the issue. Yet convincing governments of the need to conduct monitoring programs on aquatic ecosystems with the specific aim of protecting these ecosystems and promoting biodiversity remains a challenge even in some of the most affluent countries of the world. The 1992 Earth Summit in Rio de Janeiro was an object lesson in this regard (cf. ZUCKERMAN 1992).

Advantages of biological monitoring

Even when the need for some form of environmental monitoring is accepted, a further challenge remains in convincing policy makers and managers of the need for biological monitoring of aquatic systems – as opposed to chemical measurements alone. However, only studies on aquatic organisms can define, or be used to assess, the overall effect of contaminants on biota. It was on this basis that the Alligator Rivers Region monitoring programs described by HUMPHREY & DOSTINE (1994) were founded. In this volume, HODGKISS (1994), in particular, clearly showed that measurement of living organisms through microbial monitoring was the best method of assessing the quality of Hong Kong waters for human health.

Managers might accept this argument readily, but scientists can also advise relevant authorities on some possible misconceptions regarding chemical versus biological monitoring methods. It is worth considering the 'myths' that may be barriers to the wider adoption of biomonitoring approaches; some of these were recently and succinctly examined and refuted by CULLEN (1990). Thus there is the perception that biological monitoring is expensive and that living organisms are too variable. In reality, chemical data are also prone to sampling and analytical errors and, when the same standards of variability are required, biological monitoring of aquatic ecosystems has not been shown to be any more expensive than chemical monitoring (NORRIS & GEORGES 1986). Furthermore, the calculations which these latter authors used to compare biological and chemical approaches were based on a particularly expensive biomonitoring method, namely monitoring of benthic invertebrate communities.

Another perception is that biomonitoring takes longer to achieve results than chemical methods. In fact, an array of techniques for rapid biological assessment is available now, including whole-body, biochemical and histopathological bioassays, and toxicity tests. Some say biological monitoring is disadvantaged by the lack of established methods available. On the contrary, many toxicity tests and bioassays are now standardised over wide geographical bases. Where a method needs to be specific to the problem in question – as is often the case – there is a wide variety of methods and organisms which can be called upon to meet different objectives and situations.

Others say the interpretation of biological data is a problem. It should not be if proper experimental and analytical designs are set in place with sufficient temporal and spatial controls to account for natural variability (HUMPHREY & DOSTINE 1994 give further details). Of course, there are some basic prerequisites without which biological monitoring could not be conducted, nor the results interpreted: for example, a sound taxonomic base, an understanding of biological and ecological processes within aquatic systems, and information on natural variability in the absence of disturbance, both spatially and over time.

Because of disillusionment or ignorance at the regulatory level, it may be the case that most biomonitoring-related studies in the tropics are carried out by academics or students who are more concerned with documenting effects of pollution on an aquatic fauna than with developing monitoring methods. This is certainly the history of developments in biological monitoring in developed countries such as Australia (see CAMPBELL 1991). Of course, much of the credit for drawing the attention of society and ultimately policy-makers to the gross and subtle effects of water pollution must be given to these workers; they have taken on this role by default because government instrumentalities have been slow to act on the problems besetting aquatic ecosystems. Nevertheless, the result is that biomonitoring in the tropics (as was and still is the case elsewhere) might be perceived as an esoteric exercise. If this is the case, then how can the image of this scientific discipline be enhanced so that its status is one of an essential and valuable tool in water quality assessment?

Priorities for environmental monitoring

Apart from educating and persuading governments and regulators of the need for water-quality assessment programs in inland waters, such programs will be better focused when they consider and incorporate the following lines of investigation.

Firstly, the most environmentally acceptable method(s) of aqueous waste disposal should be determined from a risk-assessment program. Land application of effluents may be a safer method of disposal than release of waste-waters to aquatic ecosystems. Even if it is concluded that releases to the aquatic environment are environmentally acceptable, significant reductions in the hazards present in waste water might be achieved by passing effluent through a wetland filtration system before release. A number of different methods of waste disposal might be combined or rotated on a seasonal basis to reduce environmental risks. An essential element of any such risk assessment program would be the use of biological criteria to determine the capacity of a system to assimilate wastes.

Secondly, wherever disposal of waste waters to aquatic ecosystems is a feature of a water management scheme, there must be more emphasis on toxicity testing. Toxicity data are essential in the formulation of quality standards for receiving waters; compliance with a toxicity standard should be a legal requirement for effluent to be discharged. Indeed, one of two recommendations arising from ALABASTER's (1986) review of the state of water pollution affecting fisheries in Southeast Asia was a call for workshops to be held amongst ASEAN countries to discuss the methodology of toxicity testing and the approach to developing water quality criteria for Asian species of freshwater fish. Good water-quality assessment programs will include complementary toxicological and biological monitoring programs (HUMPHREY & DOSTINE 1994; see also LAI & LAM 1994).

Thirdly, the fate of hazardous, non-degradable substances that enter systems needs to be determined, and sites of deposition and accumulation of these substances identified. These sites will typically include lakes, floodplains and estuaries. Monitoring programs would then need to be conducted to determine the flux of hazardous substances, and bioaccumulation and toxicity that could result from possible remobilization.

Fourthly, it is essential to keep abreast with new developments in the statistical design of, and analysis of data derived from, water-quality assessment programs. If the most rigorous designs impose unrealistic constraints on monitoring programs, then the limitations of other designs used must be borne in mind. While it may be the case that all parties can agree unequivocally that an impact upon an aquatic system has occurred, attributing cause or fault in other situations where the impacts are subtle will require statistical rigor in design and analysis. There is a tendency for those involved in data analysis to take refuge in various diversity, pollution, biotic and (dis)similarity indices for summarising community responses. These indices, to varying degrees, ignore information on the taxa from which the initial data-set was derived. They may be appropriate (and statistically powerful) when married with a rigorous design and statistical test (FAITH et al. 1991), otherwise they need to be supplemented by other multivariate and graphical methods of description and testing (see CLARKE & GREEN 1988).

Fifthly, there should be more emphasis on field experiments where environmental variables of interest can be manipulated. These experiments will serve the role of calibrating biological monitoring programs and identifying possible indicator species; they will allow greater control over relevant variables and allow prediction of effects; and, they can indicate ecological mechanisms controlling responses of organisms to environmental change.

Another major reason for advocating the experimental approach is that environmental disturbances are going to exist anyway – therefore why not treat all proposed developments that might have environmental impacts as experiments? This approach has been proposed in the literature a number of times – for example, HILBORN & WALTER (1981), WALTERS & HOLLING (1990) and UNDERWOOD (1991). The approach is termed 'experimental management', wherein predictions about a planned disturbance are followed up by monitoring through all phases of the development from pre-construction to post-development. All such disturbances must include replicated control areas and if possible, parallel or similar developments in the same region should be treated as replicates of the experimental treatments. The results of the 'experiment' will enable similar future developments to be better planned in order to minimise environmental impact.

Sixthly, staffing problems are considered by some as significant impediments to successful monitoring and this issue must be addressed. CULLEN (1990) believed that monitoring was not a 'fashionable' area of science and that therefore the inexperienced (or inept) were left to design and operate such programs; many programs with biologically-oriented goals, moreover, were controlled by chemists. The long time-frame necessary for many monitoring programs and associated experimental studies, can lead to other problems. Programs can outlive the working lives of the scientists that initiate them (WALTERS & HOLLING 1990), or lead to either the initiator of a program having no involvement in the analysis, interpretation and write-up of results, or his/her successor having no role in the stimulating task of designing the program (MCCOMB & MAHER 1990). In other cases, a worthwhile program initiated by one authority might be dismissed as irrelevant by another (MCCOMB & MAHER 1990). Various remedies to these problems prescribed by these authors centre around ensuring that monitoring programs are both well funded and intellectually challenging and rewarding. Incentive schemes by way of, for example, 'side investigations' underpinned by the main program, have been suggested as ways to encourage persistent involvement of researchers in the design and conduct of monitoring programs.

The seventh suggestion to be advocated here, is provision of adequate training programs for researchers – in developing countries in particular – to design and conduct well-planned monitoring programs (for example, LUKENS 1994, DUGAN 1994b). As a first step, simple keys have to be developed to allow scientists from developing countries to be able to identify aquatic flora and fauna in general, and macroinvertebrates in particular. Ultimately, it may be possible to select indicator species to provide rapid and simple assessment of deleterious changes in aquatic systems. There is an opportunity here for collaboration in formulating keys and identifying potential indicator species which would involve taxonomists from developed countries and workers in a host institution in a developing country. This could be undertaken hand-in-hand with enhancement of opportunities for tropical scientists (see general remarks in this regard by COSTA 1994, HO 1994, NONTJI 1994), improvement of communication among tropical scientists (COOLEY & GOLLEY 1989), and action on the part of workers in the north-temperate zone to encourage the publication or dissemination of research undertaken in the tropics (WILLIAMS 1994 gives details).

Concluding remarks

In the final analysis, volumes such as this one or that edited by LOWE-MCCONNELL et al. (1992) concerning the resource use and conservation of the African Great Lakes are useful for promulgating methods for investigating – and possible remedies for solving – some of the problems that affect tropical inland waters (see WORTHINGTON et al. 1990 for another example). Sharing knowledge and effective communication among limnologists, conservationists and managers in the tropics is especially important, since the potential solutions for problems are most likely to come from latitudinally comparable areas. However, better communication and a higher publication rate alone can do nothing to preserve habitats (see also DUGAN 1994a). It is vital to communicate the scientific message to decision-makers and planners. Even where this is possible, the environmental equation is complex and problems arising from increasing human populations – and the socioeconomic considerations that must be factored into all political decisions – combine to create a situation where the preservation of biodiversity and conservation of habitats are accorded a low priority. A particular problem relating to inland waters is that development in much of the tropics has to take place under genuine water scarcity (and, in some cases, devastating floods) which necessitates manipulation of river flows, water extraction and so on (FALKENMARK & SUPRAPTO 1992).

The trend towards socioeconomic advancement in tropical developing countries must continue as a way of reducing poverty, disease and deprivation, and the "... fact that the safeguarding of biodiversity is a desirable goal for the whole world is meaningless to the tens of millions who live on the edge of starvation" (ZUCKERMAN 1992) is inescapable. Another fact is that the solutions to most environmental problems lie in the political domain, and not in the hands of scientists (see also DUDGEON 1992a). It may be possible to change the latter circumstance by raising the scientific profile through the formation of strong pressure groups at local, national and international levels, and this could help bring some integrated expertise to bear upon factors leading to the degradation of tropical inland waters. However, as ZUCKERMAN (1992) has pointed out, conservation and environmental management are hindered because national interests differ (a particular problem where rivers and lakes cross national boundaries); because long-term and short-term social and environmental issues do not belong in the same category; and because development in 'poorer' countries almost inevitably brings in its train new environmental problems. The latter problem is exacerbated because, in many countries, the power structure effectively concentrates the vast majority of the resources in the hands of a favoured few, and leads to a desperate struggle among the dispossessed for the remaining resources. A change in the political structure of certain tropical developing countries may be the only way in which valuable natural resources can be safeguarded.

Ultimately, there is no easy answer to the question of what is the best or most effective method to promote the conservation and wise management of tropical inland waters. It is clear, however, that all limnologists must now review their research agendas carefully with a view to undertaking research and related work which has some relevance to the goals of conservation and management. Limnologists must all try to become part of those decision-making processes which have direct effects on the environment, and bring appropriate scientific methods to bear upon assessment of environmental problems so that politicians have access to up-to-date and reliable data (see WILLIAMS 1994). Scientists should also attempt to provide information to lay people about the value of inland waters, and involve the local public directly in decision making and the execution of conservation and management schemes. A failure by scientists to take up these issues will lead to the degradation or disappearance of the habitats and biota which are the subject of our life's work. To conclude in this context, seven recommendations are proposed below to direct the efforts of limnologists.

i) There is a need to identify, assess, and monitor components of biological diversity in and/or associated with inland waters to provide information on the status of species and communities that could inform conservation and management initiatives.
ii) There is a need to establish a system of protected areas; inclusion into the system could take account of data derived from the implementation of Recommendation (i). An additional need is development of rapid methods to assess the conservation value and the feasibility of protecting areas to be included in the system.
iii) There is a need to integrate considerations relating to the conservation and management of inland waters into national and regional decision-making processes. This could be achieved by, for example, highlighting the 'service value' or 'indirect use value' of habitats such as freshwater wetlands, thus providing an incentive for their conservation.
iv) There is a need to develop assessment and monitoring procedures to ensure that impacts on inland waters are detected rapidly, taken into account, and minimized during the design, planning and operation of developments.
v) Greater collaboration among ecologists, hydrologists, engineers and water managers during research is needed. These specialists should also combine their expertise in order to communicate their findings effectively to managers and policy makers. This collaboration must entail innovative strategies to include the full participation of workers in developed and less-developed countries, and should contain a training element wherever relevant.
vi) Limnologists must take full account of new and emerging technologies that are relevant to the conservation and management of inland waters at a variety of scales. This may involve the production of practical manuals and textbooks dealing with the use and integration of new technologies and techniques, and should be complemented by the formulation and dissemination of keys and identification guides to the biota of tropical inland waters.

References

ALABASTER, J. S., 1986: Review of the state of water pollution affecting inland fisheries in Southeast Asia. – *FAO Fisheries Technical Paper* **260**: 25 pp.

ANTON, A., 1994: Long-term phytoplankton changes in a tropical reservoir. – In: DUDGEON, D. & LAM, P. K. S. (eds.): Inland waters of tropical Asia and

Australia: Conservation and Management. – *Mitt. Internat. Verein. Limnol.* **24**: 243–249.

ARTHINGTON, A. H., 1989: Impacts of introduced and translocated freshwater fishes in Australia. – In: DE SILVA, S. S. (ed.): Proceedings of a Workshop on Introduction of Exotic Aquatic Organisms in Asia. – *Asian Fisheries Society Special Publication* **3**, Asian Fisheries Society, Manila: 7–20.

– 1991: The ecological and genetic impacts of introduced freshwater fishes in Australia. – *Can. J. Fish. Aquat. Sci.* **48** *(Suppl. 1)*: 33–43.

– 1994: A holistic approach to water allocation to maintain the environmental values of Australian streams and rivers: A case history. – In: DUDGEON, D. & LAM, P. K. S. (eds.): Inland Waters of Tropical Asia and Australia: Conservation and Management. – *Mitt. Internat. Verein. Limnol.* **24**: 165–177.

ARTHINGTON, A. H. & BLÜHDORN, D. R., 1994: Distribution, genetics, ecology and status of the introduced cichlid, *Oreochromis mossambicus*, in Australia. – In: DUDGEON, D. & LAM, P. K. S. (eds.) Inland Waters of Tropical Asia and Australia Conservation and Management. – *Mitt. Internat. Verein. Limnol.* **24**: 53–62.

ARTHINGTON, A. H., HAMLET, S. & BLÜHDORN, D. R., 1990: The role of habitat disturbance in the establishment of introduced warm-water fishes in Australia. – In: POLLARD, D. A. (ed.): Introduced and Translocated Fishes and Their Ecological Effects. – *Bureau of Rural Resources Proceedings No. 8:* 61–66. Australian Government Publications Service, Canberra

ARTHINGTON, A. H., KING, J. M., O'KEEFE, J. H., BUNN, S. E., DAY, J. A., PUSEY, B. J., BLÜHDORN, D. R. & THARME, R. (1992): Development of an holistic approach for assessing environmental flow requirements of riverine ecosystems. – In: Proceedings of an International Seminar and Workshop on Water Allocation for the Environment. – Centre for Water Policy Research, Armidale: 69–76.

Arumugam, P. T., 1994: Present utilization and recommendations for management of Tin-mine lakes in Malaysia. – In: DUDGEON, D. & LAM, P. K. S. (eds.): Inland Waters of Tropical Asia and Australia: Conservation and Management. – *Mitt. Internat. Verein. Limnol.* **24**: 265–272.

ARUNACHALAM, M. & ARUN, L. K. 1994: Input, transport and storage of organic matter in two South Indian Rivers. – In: DUDGEON, D. & LAM, P. K. S. (eds.): Inland Waters of Tropical Asia and Australia: Conservation and Management. – *Mitt. Internat. Verein. Limnol.* **24**: 179–186.

AYLWARD, B. & BARBIER, E. B., 1992: Valuing environmental functions in developing countries. – *Biodiversity & Conservation* **1**: 34–50.

BAIN, M. B. & BOLTZ, J. M., 1989: Regulated streamflow and warmwater stream fish: a general hypothesis and research agenda. Biological Report 89 (18) 28 pp. – US Department of the Interior, Fish and Wildlife Service, Washington, D. C.

BAIRD, D. A., 1994: Pest control in tropical aquaculture: An ecological hazard assessment of natural and synthetic control agents. – In: DUDGEON, D. & LAM, P. K. S. (eds): Inland Waters of Tropical Asia and Australia: Conservation and Management. – *Mitt. Internat. Verein. Limnol.* **24**: 285–292.

BENKE, A. C., 1990: A perspective on America's vanishing streams. – *J. N. Am. Benthol. Soc.* **9**: 77–88.

BOLAND, K. & IMBERGER, J., 1994: An analysis of dynamic stability in two inland lakes of Northern Australia. – In: DUDGEON, D. & LAM, P. K. S. (eds.): Inland Waters of Tropical Asia and Australia: Conservation and Management. – *Mitt. Internat. Verein. Limnol.* **24**: 337–344.

BOOTH, W. E., CHOY, S. C. & SALIM, K. A., 1994: Ecology of a tropical man-made lake in Brunei Darussalam with proposals for its development and management. – In: DUDGEON, D. & LAM, P. K. S. (eds.): Inland Waters of Tropical Asia and Australia: Conservation and Management. – *Mitt. Internat. Verein. Limnol.* **24**: 273–278.

BOVEE, K. D., 1982: A guide to stream habitat analysis using the instream flow incremental methodology. Instream Flow Information paper No. 12. FWS/OBS – 82/86. – U.S. Fish and Wildlife Service, Washington, D. C.: 248 pp.

– , 1986: Development and evaluation of habitat suitability criteria for use in the Instream Flow Incremental Methodology. Instream Flow Information Paper No. 21: 235 pp. – U.S. Fish and Wildlife Service Biological Report 86.

BRUTON, M. N., 1989: The ecological significance of alternative life-history styles. – In: BRUTON, M. N. (ed.): Alternative Life-history Styles of Animals: 503–553. – Kluwer Academic Publishers, Dordrecht

CAMPBELL, I. C., 1991: Biological monitoring of Australian streams, past, present and future potential. – In: Proceedings of the 29th Congress of the Australian Society of Limnology, Jabiru, NT, 1990: 97–104. – AGPS, Canberra.

CHANG, W. Y. B., 1994: Management of shallow tropical lakes using integrated lake farming. – In: DUDGEON, D. & LAM, P. K. S. (eds.): Inland Waters of Tropical Asia and Australia: Conservation and Management. – *Mitt. Internat. Verein. Limnol.* **24**: 219–224

CHOMCHAI, P., 1987: The Mekong project: an exercise in regional cooperation to develop the lower Mekong basin. – In: ALI, M., RADOSEVICH, G. E. & ALI KHAN, A. (eds.): Water Resources Policy for Asia: 497–508. – A. A. Balkema Publishers, Boston.

CHOOWAEW, S., WANCHAI CHANDRACHAI & PETERSEN, JR., R.C. 1994: The socioeconomic conditions in the vicinity of Huai Nam Un Wetland, Songkhram River, Lower Mekong Basin, Thailand. – In: DUDGEON, D. & LAM, P. K. S. (eds.): Inland Waters of Tropical Asia and Australia: Conservation and Management. – *Mitt. Internat. Verein. Limnol.* **24**: 41–46.

CLARKE, K. R. & GREEN, R. H., 1988: Statistical design and analysis for a 'biological effects' study. – *Mar. Ecol. Prog. Ser.* **46**: 213–226.

COATES, D., 1987: Consideration of fish introductions into the Sepik River, Papua New Guinea. – *Aquacult. Fish. Manag.* **18**: 231–241.

COOLEY, J. H. & GOLLEY, F. B., 1989: Restraints to communication for ecologists in developing countries. – *BioScience* **39**: 805–809.

COSTA, H. H., 1994: The status of limnology in Sri Lanka. – In: DUDGEON, D. & LAM, P. K. S. (eds.): Inland Waters of Tropical Asia and Australia: Conservation and Management. – *Mitt. Internat. Verein. Limnol.* **24**: 73–85.

CULLEN, P., 1990: Biomonitoring and environmental management. – *Environmental Monitoring and Assessment* **14**: 107–114.

DAVIES, B. R. & DAY, J. A., 1989: Physical and chemical attributes important in the biological functioning of river ecosystems. – In: FERRAR, A. A. (ed.), Ecological Flow Requirements for South African River. – *South African National Scientific Programmes Report Number* **162**: 17–40. Council for Scientific and Industrial Research, Pretoria.

DAVIES, J. & GIESEN, W., 1994: Towards a methodology for identifying tropical freshwater wetlands for protection. – In: DUDGEON, D. & LAM, P. K. S. (eds.): Inland Waters of Tropical Asia and Australia: Conservation and Management. – *Mitt. Internat. Verein. Limnol.* **24**: 27–39.

DESILVA, K. H. G. M., 1994: Diversity and endemism of three major freshwater groups in Sri Lanka: Atyidae (Decapoda), Gastropoda and Teleostei. – In: DUDGEON, D. & LAM, P. K. S. (eds.): Inland Waters of Tropical Asia and Australia: Conservation and Management. – *Mitt. Internat. Verein. Limnol.* **24**: 63–71.

DESILVA, K. H. G. M. & DESILVA, P. K., 1994: The effects of human modification of lotic habitats on the freshwater fauna of Sri Lanka. – In: DUDGEON, D. & LAM, P. K. S. (eds.): Inland Waters of Tropical Asia and Australia: Conservation and Management. – *Mitt. Internat. Verein. Limnol.* **24**: 87–94.

DUDGEON, D., 1992a: – Endangered ecosystems: the conservation status of tropical Asian rivers. – *Hydrobiologia* **248:** 167–191.

– 1992b: Effects of water transfer on aquatic insects in a stream in Hong Kong. – *Regulated Rivers: Research & Management* **7:** 369–377.

– 1994: The need for multi-scale approaches to the conservation and management of tropical inland waters. – In: DUDGEON, D. & LAM, P. K. S. (eds.): Inland Waters of Tropical Asia and Australia: Conservation and Management. – *Mitt. Internat. Verein. Limnol.* **24**: 11–16

DUGAN, P. J., 1994a: The role of ecological science in addressing wetland conservation and management in the tropics. – In: DUDGEON, D. & LAM, P. K. S. (eds.): Inland Waters of Tropical Asia and Australia: Conservation and Management. – *Mitt. Internat. Verein. Limnol.* **24**: 5–10.

– 1994b: Constraints and opportunities for training in wetland management. – In: DUDGEON, D. & LAM, P. K. S. (eds.): Inland Waters of Tropical Asia and Australia: Conservation and Management. – *Mitt. Internat. Verein. Limnol.* **24**: 363–366.

FAITH, D. P., HUMPHREY, C. L. & DOSTINE, P. L., 1991: Statistical power and BACI design in biological monitoring: comparative evaluation of community dissimilarity based on benthic macroinvertebrate communities in Rockhole Mine Creek, Northern, Territory, Australia. – *Aust. J. Mar. Freshwat. Res.* **42**: 589–602.

FALKENMARK, M. & SUPRAPTO, R. A., 1992: Population-landscape interactions in development – a water perspective to environmental sustainability. – *Ambio* **21**: 31–36.

GAN, K. & MCMAHON, T., 1990: Variability of results from use of PHABSIM in estimating habitat area. – *Regulated Rivers: Research & Management* **5**: 233–239.

GIESEN, W., 1994: Indonesia's major freshwater lakes: A review of our current knowledge, development processes and threats. – In: DUDGEON, D. & LAM, P. K. S. (eds.): Inland Waters of Tropical Asia and Australia: Conservation and Management. – *Mitt. Internat. Verein. Limnol.* **24**: 115–128.

GOPAL, B., 1994: The role of ecotones (transition zones) in the conservation and management of tropical inland waters. – In: DUDGEON, D. & LAM, P. K. S. (eds.): Inland Waters of Tropical Asia and Australia: Conservation and Management. – *Mitt. Internat. Verein. Limnol.* **24**: 17–25.

HILBORN, R. & WALTERS, C. J., 1981: Pitfalls of environmental baseline and process studies. – *Environmental Impact Assessment Review* **2**: 265–278.

HO, S.-C., 1994: Status of limnological research and training in Malaysia. – In: DUDGEON, D. & LAM, P. K. S. (eds.): Inland Waters of Tropical Asia and Australia: Conservation and Management. – *Mitt. Internat. Verein. Limnol.* **24**: 129–145.

HODGKISS, I. J. 1994: Microbiological indicators of freshwater pollution in Hong Kong. – In: DUDGEON, D. & LAM, P. K. S. (eds.): Inland Waters of Tropical Asia and Australia: Conservation and Management. – *Mitt. Internat. Verein. Limnol.* **24**: 321–326.

HUMPHREY, C. L. & DOSTINE, P. L., 1994: Development of biological monitoring programs to detect mining-waste impacts upon aquatic ecosystems of the Alligator Rivers Region, Northern Territory, Australia. – In: DUDGEON, D. & LAM, P. K. S. (eds.): Inland Waters of Tropical Asia and Australia: Conservation and Management. – *Mitt. Internat. Verein. Limnol.* **24**: 293–314.

HYNES, H. B. N., 1989: Keynote address. – *Can. Spec. Publ. Fish. Aquat. Sci.* **106**: 5–10.

JIN, X., 1994: An analysis of lake eutrophication in China: – In: DUDGEON, D. & LAM, P. K. S. (eds.): Inland Waters of Tropical Asia and Australia: Conservation and Management. – *Mitt. Internat. Verein. Limnol.* **24**: 207–211.

JIN, X., LIU, H., TU, Q., ZHANG, Z & ZHU, X. (1990): *Eutrophication of Lakes in China*: 652 pp. – Chinese Research Academy of Environmental Sciences, Beijing.

JOWETT, I. G., 1982: The incremental approach to instream flow needs. New Zealand case studies. – In: MCCOLL, R. S. (ed.): River Low Flows: Conflicts of Water Use. – *Water and Soil Misc. Pub.* **47**: 9–15.

JUNK, W. J., BAYLEY, P. B. & SPARKS, R. E., 1989: The flood pulse concept in river-floodplain systems. – *Can Spec. Publ. Fish. Aquat. Sci.* **106**: 110–127.

KHONDKER, M., 1994: The status of limnological research in Bangladesh. – In: DUDGEON, D. & LAM, P. K. S. (eds.): Inland Waters of Tropical Asia and Australia: Conservation and Management. – *Mitt. Internat. Verein. Limnol.* **24**: 147–154.

KWAK, T. J., WILEY, M. J., OSBORNE, L. L. & LARIMORE, R. W., 1992: Application of diel feeding chronology to habitat suitability analysis of warmwater stream fishes. – *Can. J. Fish. Aquat. Sci.* **49**: 1417–1430.

LAI, P. C. C. & LAM, P. K. S., 1994: Scope for growth in a tropical freshwater snail, *Brotia hainanensis:* Implications for monitoring sublethal toxic stressors. – In: DUDGEON, D. & LAM, P. K. S. (eds.): Inland Waters of Tropical Asia and Australia: Conservation and Management. – *Mitt. Internat. Verein. Limnol.* **24**: 315–320.

LAKE, P. S. & BARMUTA, L. A., 1986: Stream benthic communities: persistent presumptions and current speculations. – In: DEDECKKER, P. & WILLIAMS, W. D. (eds.): Limnology in Australia: 263–276. – CSIRO, Melbourne & Dr. W. Junk Publishers, Dordrecht.

LIU, J. & CHEN, S., 1994: An assessment of the impact of fish stocking on lake eutrophication in China. – In: DUDGEON, D. & LAM, P. K. S. (eds.): Inland Waters of Tropical Asia and Australia: Conservation and Management. – *Mitt. Internat. Verein. Limnol.* **24**: 231–235.

LOWE-MCCONNELL, R., 1994: Threats to, and conservation of, tropical freshwater fishes. – In: DUDGEON, D. & LAM, P. K. S. (eds.): Inland Waters of Tropical Asia and Australia: Conservation and Management. – *Mitt. Internat. Verein. Limnol.* **24**: 47–52.

LOWE-MCCONNELL, R. H., CRUL, R. C. M. & ROEST, F. C. (1992): Symposium on the resource use and conservation of the African Great Lakes. – *Mitt. Internat. Verein. Limnol.* **23**: 1–128.

LUKENS, J., 1994: Mapping southeast Asian wetlands using remote sensing: the training project approach. – In: DUDGEON, D. & LAM, P. K. S. (eds.): Inland Waters of Tropical Asia and Australia: Conservation and Management. – *Mitt. Internat. Verein. Limnol.* **24**: 349–355.

– 1989: Understanding Australian streamflow – Implications for instream ecology. – In: THEOH, C. (ed.): *Proceedings of the Specialist Workshop on Instream Needs and Water Uses*: 33-1–33-11. – Australian Water Resources Council, Canberra.

MCCOMB, A. & Maher, W., 1990: Symposium review. – *Environmental Monitoring and Assessment* **14**: 395–399.

MCMAHON, T. A., 1986: Hydrology and management of Australian streams. – In: CAMPBELL, I. C. (ed.): Stream Protection: The Management of Streams for Instream Uses: 23–44. – Water Studies Centre, Chisholm Institute of Technology, Melbourne.

MATHUR, D., BASON, W. H., PURDY, E. J. & SILVER, C. D., 1985: A critique of the instream flow incremental methodology. – *Can. J. Fish. Aquatic Sci.* **42**: 825–831.

MELVILLE, D. S., 1994: Management of Jiangxi Poyang Lake National Nature Reserve, China. – In: DUDGEON, D. & LAM, P. K. S. (eds.): Inland Waters of Tropical Asia and Australia: Conservation and Management. – *Mitt. Internat. Verein. Limnol.* **24**: 237–242.

NAKAYAMA, M., 1994: Application of satellite remote sensing to estimate lake water quality. – In: DUDGEON, D. & LAM, P. K. S. (eds.): Inland Waters of Tropical Asia and Australia: Conservation and Management. – *Mitt. Internat. Verein. Limnol.* **24**: 345–347.

NATARAJAN, A. V., 1989: Environmental impact of Ganga Basin development on gene-pool and fisheries of the Ganga River system. – *Can. Spec. Publ. Fish. Aquat. Sci.* **106**: 545–560.

NEWBOLD, J. D., ELWOOD, J. W., O'NEILL, R. V. & SHELDON, A. L., 1983a: Phosphorus dynamics in a woodland stream ecosystem: a study of nutrient spiralling. – *Ecology* **64**: 1249–1265.

NEWBOLD, J. D., ELWOOD, J. W., O'NEILL, R.V. & VAN WINKLE, W., 1983b: Resource spiraling: an operational paradigm for analysing lotic ecosystems. – In: FONTAINE, T. D. & BARTELL, S. M. (eds.): Dynamics of Lotic Ecosystems: 3–27. – Ann Arbour Science Publishers, Michigan.

NONTJI, A., 1994: The status of limnology in Indonesia. – In: DUDGEON, D. & LAM, P. K. S. (eds.): Inland Waters of Tropical Asia and Australia: Conservation and Management. – *Mitt. Internat. Verein. Limnol.* **24**: 95–113.

NORRIS, R. H. & GEORGES, A., 1986: Design and analysis for assessment of water quality. – In: DEDECKKER, P. & WILLIAMS, W. D. (eds.): Limnology in Australia: 555–572. – CSIRO, Melbourne & Dr. W. Junk Publishers, Dordrecht

PACARDO, E. P. (1994): Agroecosystem analysis of Laguna Lake in the Philippines. – In: DUDGEON, D. & LAM, P. K. S. (eds.): Inland Waters of Tropical Asia and Australia: Conservation and Management. – *Mitt. Internat. Verein. Limnol.* **24**: 259–264.

PEARSON, R. G., 1994: Limnology in the northeastern tropics of Australia, the wettest part of the driest continent. – In: DUDGEON, D. & LAM, P. K. S. (eds.): Inland Waters of Tropical Asia and Australia: Conservation and Management. – *Mitt. Internat. Verein. Limnol.* **24**: 155–163.

PETERSEN, R. C. & SKOGLUND, E., 1990: Wetlands Management Programme. Study to Formulate Plans for the Management of the Wetlands in the Lower Mekong Basin (1.3.13/88/SWE): 245 pp. – Published by the Mekong Secretariat, Bangkok, Thailand.

ROOM, P. M., 1990: Ecology of a simple plant-herbivore system: biological control of *Salvinia*. – *Trends in Ecology & Evolution* **5**: 74–79.

ROSS, S. T., 1991: Mechanisms structuring stream fish assemblages: are there lessons from introduced species? – *Environ. Biol. Fish.* **30**: 359–368.

RYDING, S.-O. & RAST, W., 1989: *The Control of Eutrophication in Lakes and Reservoirs:* 314 pp. – Unesco, Paris & Parthenon, Carnforth.

SCOTT, D. A. & POOLE, C. M., 1989: A Status Overview of Asian Wetlands: 140 pp. – Asian Wetland Bureau, Kuala Lumpur.

SEDELL, J. R., RICHEY, J. E. & SWANSON, F. J., 1989: The River Continuum Concept: a basis for the expected ecosystem behavior of very large rivers? – *Can. Spec. Publ. Fish. Aquat. Sci.* **106**: 49–55.

SHEA, S. S., 1994: The effects of water quality, epilithic algae and organic matter on communities of stone-dwelling invertebrates in a Hong Kong river. – In: DUDGEON, D. & LAM, P. K. S. (eds.): Inland Waters of Tropical Asia and Australia: Conservation and Management. – *Mitt. Internat. Verein. Limnol.* **24**: 327–336.

SMITH, R.E.W. & BAKOWA, K., 1994: Utilization of floodplain water bodies by the fishes of the Fly River, Papua New Guinea. – In: DUDGEON, D. & LAM, P. K. S. (eds.): Inland Waters of Tropical Asia and Australia: Conservation and Management. – *Mitt. Internat. Verein. Limnol.* **24**: 187–196.

SOLIMAN, V.S., 1994: Conservation and management of Lake Manapao (Philippines), a 'Sinarapan' (*Mistthys luzonensis*) sanctuary: Status, problems and solutions. – In: DUDGEON, D. & LAM, P. K. S. (eds.): Inland Waters of Tropical Asia and Australia: Conservation and Management. – *Mitt. Internat. Verein. Limnol.* **24**: 279–283.

TOWNSEND, S. A., 1994: The occurrence of natural fish kills, and their causes, in the Darwin-Katherine-Jabiru region of northern Australia. – In: DUDGEON, D. & LAM, P. K. S. (eds.): Inland Waters of Tropical Asia and Australia: Conservation and Management. – *Mitt. Internat. Verein. Limnol.* **24:** 197–205.

UNDERWOOD, A. J., 1991: Biological monitoring for human impact: how little it can achieve. In: *Proceedings of the 29th Congress of the Australian Society of Limnology, Jabiru, NT,* 1990: 105–123. AGPS, Canberra

VANNOTE, R. L., MINSHALL, G. W., CUMMINS, K. W., SEDELL, J. R. & CUSHING, C. E., 1980: The River Continuum Concept. – *Can J. Fish. Aquat. Sci.* **37**: 130–137.

WALLACE, J. B., WEBSTER, J. R. & WOODALL, W. R. 1977: The role of filter-feeders in flowing waters. – *Arch. Hydrobiol* **79**: 506–532.

WALTERS, C. J. & HOLLING, C. S., 1990: Large-scale management experiments and learning by doing. – *Ecology* **71**: 2060–2068.

WARD, J. V. & STANFORD, J. A., 1979: The serial discontinuity concept of lotic ecosystems. – In: FONTAINE, T. D. & BARTELL, S. M. (eds.): Dynamics of Lotic Ecosystems: 29–42. – Ann Arbour Science Publishers, Michigan.

WELCOMME, R. L., 1979: Fisheries Ecology of Floodplain Rivers: 317 pp. – Longman, London.

– 1988: International introductions of inland aquatic species. – *FAO Fisheries Technical Fisheries Paper* **294**: 1–318.

WILLIAMS, W. D., 1994: Constraints to the conservation and management of tropical inland waters. – In: DUDGEON, D. & LAM, P. K. S. (eds.): Inland Waters of Tropical Asia and Australia: Conservation and Management. – *Mitt. Internat. Verein. Limnol.* **24**: 356–362.

WITTE, F., GOLDSCHMIDT, T., WANINK, J., VANOIJEN, M., GOUDSWAARD, K., WITTEMAAS, E. & BOUTON, N. 1992: The destruction of an endemic species flock – quantitative data on the decline of haplochromine cichlids of Lake Victoria. – *Environ. Biol. Fish.* **34**: 1–28.

WORTHINGTON, E. B., WELCOMME, R. L. & POLUNIN, N., 1990: Leading conclusions of the (first) International Conference on River Conservation and Management. – *Environmental Conservation* **17**: 366–367.

YIN, C., LAN, Z. & ZHAO, M., 1994: Factors limiting algal growth in eutrophic Chaohu Lake, China. – In: DUDGEON, D. & LAM, P. K. S. (eds.): Inland Waters of Tropical Asia and Australia: Conservation and Management. – *Mitt. Internat. Verein. Limnol.* **24**: 213–218.

YIPP, M. W., 1990: Distribution of the schistosome vector snail *Biomphalaria straminea* (Pulmonata: Planorbidae) in Hong Kong. – *J. Moll. Stud.* **56**: 47–55.

– 1991: The relationship between hydrological factors and distribution of freshwater gastropods in Hong Kong. – *Verh. Internat. Verein Limnol.* **24**: 2954–2959.

YUSOFF, F. M. & PATIMAH, I., 1994: A comparative study of phytoplankton populations in two Malaysian lakes. – In: DUDGEON, D. & LAM, P. K. S. (eds.): Inland Waters of Tropical Asia and Australia: Conservation and Management. – *Mitt. Internat. Verein. Limnol.* **24**: 251–257.

ZHANG, H. & CHANG, W. Y. B., 1994: Management of inland fisheries in shallow eutrophic, mesotrophic, and oligotrophic lakes in China. – In: DUDGEON, D. & LAM, P. K. S. (eds.): Inland Waters of Tropical Asia and Australia: Conservation and Management. – *Mitt. Internat. Verein. Limnol.* **24**: 225–229.

ZUCKERMAN, LORD, (1992): Between Stockholm and Rio. – *Nature* **358**: 273–276.

ZWICK, P. 1992: Stream habitat fragmentation – a threat to biodiversity. – *Biodiversity & Conservation* **1**: 80–97.

Authors' addresses:

DAVID DUDGEON, Department of Zoology, Hui Oi Chow Science Building, The University of Hong Kong, Pokfulam Road, Hong Kong.

ANGELA H. ARTHINGTON, Centre for Catchment and In-stream Research, Griffith University, Nathan, Queensland 4111, Australia.

WILLIAM Y. B. CHANG, Division of International Programs, National Science Foundation, 1800 G. Street, Washington, D.C. 20550, USA.

JON DAVIES, Asian Wetland Bureau, Institute of Advanced Studies, Universiti Malaya, Lemba Pantai, 59100, Kuala Lumpur, Malaysia.

CHRISTOPHER L. HUMPHREY, Alligator Rivers Region Research Institute, Office of the Supervising Scientist, Jabiru, NT 0886, Australia.

R. G. PEARSON, Australian Centre for Tropical Freshwater Research, James Cook University of North Queensland, Townsville, Queensland 48111, Australia.

P.K.S. LAM, Department of Environmental Management, Victoria University of Technology, St. Albans Campus, Victoria 3021, Australia.